Roots of
Reform

American Politics and Political Economy
A series edited by Benjamin I. Page

Elizabeth Sanders

Roots of
Reform

*Farmers, Workers, and the
American State, 1877–1917*

The University of Chicago Press
Chicago & London

Elizabeth Sanders is professor of government at Cornell University and author of *The Regulation of Natural Gas: Policy and Politics, 1938–1978.*

This book has been published with the generous assistance of the Hull Memorial Publication Fund of Cornell University.

The University of Chicago Press, Chicago 60637
The University of Chicago Press, Ltd., London
© 1999 by The University of Chicago
All rights reserved. Published 1999

08 07 06 05 04 03 02 01 00 99   1   2   3   4   5

ISBN: 0-226-73476-5 (cloth)
ISBN: 0-226-73477-3 (paper)

Library of Congress Cataloging-in-Publication Data

Sanders, Elizabeth.
    Roots of reform : farmers, workers, and the American state,
1877–1917 / Elizabeth Sanders.
        p.   cm. — (American politics and political economy)
    Includes bibliographical references and index.
    ISBN 0-226-73476-5 (cloth : alk. paper). — ISBN
0-226-73477-3 (pbk. : alk. paper)
    1. Trade regulation—United States—History. 2. United
States—Economic Policy—To 1933. 3. United States—
Politics and government—1865–1933. 4. Populism—United
States—History. 5. Progressivism (United States politics)
I. Title. II. Series.
JK1118.U47S25   1999
338.973—dc21   98-50839
                                                         CIP

For my mother, Mildred Atkins Rowe

Contents

Acknowledgments

I am greatly indebted to the scholars who read and criticized drafts of chapters, to a wonderful series of research assistants, and to institutions providing financial support.

For reading and criticism, thanks go to Richard Bensel for reading the manuscript and for years of dinner-table conversations that gave rise to one of our son Seth's sardonic catchphrases: "I'd rather stay home and listen to my parents argue about the gold standard"; and to Kimberly Geiger, Michael Goldfield, Ira Katznelson, Jeffrey Ostler, Nick Salvatore, Joel Silbey, Stephen Skowronek, Mary Summers, Charles Tilly, Richard Valelly, Kim Voss, and several anonymous readers. It makes me profoundly sad that Arthur Link, who read and commented on the entire manuscript and gave me the early encouragement I needed to undertake this work, did not live to see its publication. He was one of the greatest historians of this century and a very fine human being.

In the ten years that I have worked on this project I have been extremely fortunate to have the help of a series of research assistants, many of whom have now begun their own scholarly careers. In rough chronological order, they are: Paul Gebhard, Robert Peterson, Kimberly Geiger, Jytte Klaussen, Andrew Schlewitz, Richard Magoo, Derrick Chollet, Margaret Sena, Jonathan Campos, Sanford Gordon, Scott Kastner, Sudip Bose, Paul Krieger, and James Harney. I owe a particularly large debt to James Harney, who, as the most recent research assistant, bore the burden of final footnote and table checking in a large manuscript undergoing several rounds of serious cutting. Kimberly Geiger has seen me through the entire project, and her extensive and diverse assistance was simply invaluable. Perhaps I could have done it without her . . . in another ten years.

I am grateful to the Woodrow Wilson International Center for Scholars, the American Philosophical Society, the University of Wisconsin Legal History Program, and the National Endowment for the Humanities for their financial support.

Thanks also go to Ben Page, who first encouraged me to break off this early portion of a work I foolishly imagined could, in one volume, cover a century of American political development. I am also indebted to John Tryneski, Betsy Solaro, and Alice Bennett at the University of Chicago Press, to the staff of Olin Library at Cornell, to Amy Bowden for producing the maps in chapter 2, and to the masterful editing of Teddy Diggs. And I thank Michael Miller and Mary Lindemann for a great dinner in London that generated the title.

I have dedicated this book to my mother, who not only has been a loving and supportive parent far beyond the call of duty but also has inspired me in the conduct of her own life. A child of two warm and wonderful farmer-schoolteachers, she took her first job out of college with the Farm Security Administration (where she met my father) helping tenant farmers make the transition to yeomanry. Devotion to helping others has been her life's work. I have been extraordinarily lucky to have her.

1
Introduction

When the American national state began, in the late nineteenth century, to acquire the legal authority and the administrative capability to regulate a mature industrial economy and protect its citizens from the acknowledged pathologies of large-scale capitalism, it did so in response to the demands of politically mobilized farmers. When, by 1917, the state had acquired its embryonic modern form, supervising—via administrative agencies, statutory entitlements, and judicial enforcement—the processes of transportation, banking, storage and trading of commodities, business competitive practices, and labor relations, it was imprinted with the agenda of the agrarian reformers who had instigated its expansion. Although some of the features, particularly the seemingly boundless growth of bureaucratic discretion, were not of the farmers' *design*, they nonetheless represented responses to the agrarians' unremitting pressure for public control of private economic power. In pursuing this reformulation of the state, the agrarians reached out to fellow citizens who shared, they believed, their class position and their enemies. The alliance between farmers and the workers who staffed the nation's industries, mines, and railroads was a difficult one to effect and maintain, and it existed more in the farmers' perception than in the workers'. Nevertheless, its legislative fruits were more abundant than is commonly realized, and the vision of this alliance of "producers against plutocrats" was central to the Populist and Progressive Eras and to subsequent reform efforts as well.

It is the contention of this book that agrarian movements constituted the most important political force driving the development of the American national state in the half century before World War I. And by shaping the form of early regulatory legislation and establishing the centrality of the farmer-labor alliance to progressive reform and the Democratic Party, the agrarian influence was felt for years thereafter. Indeed, its characteristic ideological conceptions and language are with us still.

Historical and sociological scholarship of the past several decades has produced a large body of literature probing the social positions and ideologies of American farmers and industrial workers and the conditions that seem to have produced the failure of dynamic nineteenth- and early-twentieth-century agrarian and labor movements to restructure economic relationships and erect a positive populist or social democratic state.[1] What this rich literature has not provided is an account of the political interaction of these two sectors and the extent to which Progressive Era national state expansion embodied the demands of farmers and workers.[2]

Two scholarly tendencies may account for the divided attention given to farmers and workers and the failure to credit their public-policy achievements. One is the strong urban labor bias of the first wave of the new social history.[3] The other is the revived interest in state theory in the 1980s. In its Marxist-derived variant, state theory treats all state expansion as a response to the expressed needs of individual capitalists, a hegemonic capitalist class, or the structural requirements of the capitalist system.[4] "State managers" are viewed almost exclusively as executive branch officials, and the industrial working class is perceived as the only significant constituency—apart from capitalists—for those state actors.[5] In work stressing state autonomy from capitalist class interests, there has also been a common focus on the executive branch and a small proto-public service intelligentsia.[6] Both schools devote little attention to broad-based farmer or labor movements, and both slight the national legislature in which social forces and "state managers" meet to bargain, demand, threaten, and win or lose heated battles over public law. The lack of attention to the legislative process is particularly unfortunate in the United States, where Congress, particularly in this period, was far from an executive tool and produced a quite explicit statute law that mattered, both substantively and as a constraint on executive discretion.

These contemporary lines of debate have, I believe, missed important aspects of early-twentieth-century state expansion in the United States. With agrarian populism relegated to the dustbin of failed crusades, it has been assumed that labor had no political allies with which to fight state and corporate repression and that the policy choices of the Progressive Era public were limited to the varieties of "corporate liberalism" embodied in the three major presidential candidates of 1912.[7] The most frequently cited explanation of early-twentieth-century state development remains the instrumentalist account of Gabriel Kolko, despite the volumes of prior and subsequent work disputing his argument that Progressive Era state expansion reflected almost exclusively the interests of large capitalists.

This book represents an attempt to set the record straight by examining in close detail the agendas of farmer and worker movements and the legislative histories and support patterns of the major late-nineteenth-century and Progressive Era statutes that forged the design, purposes, and method of the modern American state. Moving beyond the realm of executive and elite politics and working with a database very different from the private correspondence and association archives typically relied on by the "capitalist-dominance" school, this analysis reveals—in a far less selective and ambiguous way—the public positions taken by the political representatives of capital, labor, and farmers on the actual legal formulations of contemporary issues. These patterns of support and opposition present a very different picture of the origins of the twentieth-century state from those offered both by business-dominance accounts and by many writings of intellectual historians. Among the abundant records left behind by capitalists and intellectuals, some evidence of support for—even creative fostering of—programs expanding national state capacities can always be found. But to generalize from such instances to assertions of class responsibility for actual legislation is a great mistake. Business opinion favored a new national bank in the early 1900s but *not* the one produced in 1913. (Business opposition sparked the strong resistance of industrial-area Republicans to the Federal Reserve Act.) Certain northeastern, urban-based intellectuals—a Louis Brandeis or a George Rubley, for example—generated ideas about antitrust policy; but to credit that intelligentsia with the Clayton Antitrust Act is to say that it was the sword that won Jerusalem and not Saladin's Muslim army. The point is that in the territorially based American legislature, ideas had to find geographic vessels. Proposals that might have been generated elsewhere were seized upon by regional politicians. In the case of antitrust policy, ideas that were blunted by capitalist resistance in the core industrial cities became the weapons of agrarian forces who championed new laws in 1914.

The sorting out of direct responsibility for the early interventionist state illuminates the dynamics of social, political, and economic relations in this capitalist democracy and perhaps, by comparison, in others as well. It may be that agrarianism has been too often discounted as a basis for social democracy everywhere in the West;[8] or it may be that the radicalism and the numerical and territorial strength of periphery farmers constitute an underappreciated source of American exceptionalism. Either way, analysis of legislative politics in this critical period provides a key to understanding both what was and what might have been in the gestation of the American interventionist state.

My argument is that the dynamic stimulus for Populist and Progressive Era state expansion was the periphery agrarians' drive to establish public control over a rampaging capitalism. The periphery generated the bulk of the reform agenda and furnished the foot soldiers that saw reform through the legislature. It did so because the political economy of the late-nineteenth- and early-twentieth-century periphery was innately antagonistic to the designs of core industrial and financial capitalism and had no effective means with which to fight it other than the capture and expansion of state power.[9]

The agrarians hoped, through their control of the national state, to restructure the domestic market and to slow or reverse the concentration of wealth and power that was the legacy of nineteenth-century industrialization. Periphery representatives sought neither to impose a general collectivism nor to restore a mythical state of laissez-faire. Rather, they believed that the mass of citizens would benefit if powerful government mechanisms were created to restrain rapacious corporations, prevent excessive concentration of wealth and market power, and publicly provide certain goods and services that either would not be sufficiently furnished by private enterprise or would be supplied only through monopolistic exactions. Within the decentralized market to be fostered and policed by the state, they hoped that a genuinely free commerce would flourish and believed that both individual and collective efforts would yield a more just and broadly prosperous society. The ends, if not the means, were distinctly Jeffersonian and republican.

The capitalist response to this challenge was reactive and largely negative; it did, however, establish the outer limits of reform and succeeded in significantly modifying the agrarian statist agenda. The force of capitalist resistance was all the more powerful because of the failure of the labor movement in the industrial North to meaningfully challenge corporate political hegemony in its local bastions. That failure has been variously attributed to federalism, immigration, judicial intervention, conservative leadership, internal ideological division, and other factors that weakened labor's organizational force. In my view, labor's tentative and ineffective political mobilization must also be viewed in juxtaposition to the greater programmatic cohesion and institutional strength of agrarian interests. The existing two-party system, not rigidly bound by partisan discipline or centralized around a unitary government, was flexible enough to accommodate rising political demands from new quarters. But the Democratic Party of the post-1896 period was an overwhelmingly agrarian vehicle that carried the legacy of populism. The periphery farmers' enthusiasm for politics and the territorial nature of their political demands interacted with the structure of Congress and the electoral system to give them a driving force and an institutional strength that workers could not match.[10] Thus labor was offered a subordinate role in a party coalition, the content of whose program, because of its strong agrarian bias, could be labeled by its opponents as a threat to the health of the northern industrial economy. The pull of region diminished the counterpull of class in the industrial cities.

In the early twentieth century the alliance with the cotton South in the Democratic Party was a problematic one for northern labor, not because (as some scholars have argued) the party served the interests of a Bourbon elite antagonistic to labor by virtue of its class position but because the party embodied the political demands of export-oriented agricultural producers whose position in the national economy differed fundamentally from that of northern industrial workers. Yet less than 40 percent of the national workforce was employed in manufacturing, mining, transportation, and construction in 1910, and fewer than 9 percent of nonagricultural workers were members of trade unions.[11] Clearly, labor needed allies to achieve any success in politics, and the other coalition alternatives—capitalists and the conservative northern agricultural producers tied to them in the Republican tariff coalition, or the small and dependent urban white-collar class—were hostile, indifferent, or of insufficient size to make reliable partners. Organized labor thus eventually allowed itself to be wooed and won by the agrarian periphery, although its heart was not in the marriage. As a result of labor's ambivalence, the threat that might have been posed to northern capital by the coalescence of its two great antagonists was muted. The United States did not, in the pre–World War I decade, establish a rudimentary welfare state on the model of Britain and Germany, nor did its workers secure the fundamental organizational rights that would have enhanced their private economic power. That these things did not happen cannot be attributed entirely to political (electoral) weakness, because elements of constitutional structure (particularly federalism and the role of the courts in determining legal meaning) formed powerful barriers to a victory of the "producer" classes. But it is also clear that the political weakness of the farmer-worker coalition often made it impossible to overcome capitalist resistance in the executive and the legislature and to override the Supreme Court's constricted view of national legislative powers.

Nevertheless, the farmer-labor political alliance did succeed in constructing a rudimentary interventionist state that limited corporate prerogatives in ways that seemed genuinely frightening to capitalists at the time. The survival of capitalism was, of course, never in doubt. That marvelously resilient system adapts so easily to state intervention that it has become fashionable to say that capitalism was "rationalized" by reform and to assume that since capitalists prospered all along, they themselves must have desired, even *led*, the reform efforts. That one finds the political representatives of core capitalists fighting tooth and nail to prevent enactments of most Progressive Era reforms is a problem that the "corporate liberalism" school has generally ignored.

The legislative victories won by the farmers and their labor allies and the limitations imposed on them by both the *external* opposition of capitalists, executive officials, and intelligentsia and the *internal* divisions in the reformers' ranks are the subjects to be explored herein. In addition to tracing the political-economy roots of the modern interventionist state, this book will describe the sources of a major anomaly in American political development: social forces profoundly hostile to bureaucracy nevertheless instigated the creation of a bureaucratic state.

This work takes a consciously *interactive* approach to political development, avoiding the (to my mind) artificial distinctions often made in the "state-centered" versus "society-centered" debate.[12] Democratic states respond to pressures from the larger society because they must; but the institutional positions of state actors, particularly in the executive and judicial branches, allow them to respond in ways that reflect their own institutional power concerns or their ingrained class or cultural (including ideological) predispositions in ways that are difficult to sort out.

State and society are particularly entangled in the legislature, that portion of the state that has been historically most penetrated by social forces and has, thus, been the most sensitive to social movements. Members of the U.S. Congress have always been closely tied to their local electoral constituencies, but the aggregating function of political parties, still strong in Progressive Era legislative organization (although the caucus was rapidly waning at the end of the period), could make members of Congress responsive to distant social movements as well. The theory of representation implicit here thus acknowledges both localistic and broad coalitional forces in legislative action. The approach taken is most appropriately labeled "political economy," since it emphasizes the primacy of economic interest in the generation of political demands yet accepts that the law itself, and its administration by state officials, shape the evolution and expression of economic and other interests.

The following chapter will lay out the book's empirical methodology, describe the position of farmers and workers at the threshold of the age of reform, and differentiate the three broad economic regions (core, diverse, and periphery) into which a newly maturing capitalism had congealed. This regionalization was based on the nature of production, but equally significant for politics was the market destination of goods produced—which distinguished, for example, farm economies that were linked by tariff sensitivity and interdependency with domestic industry from those agricultural regions heavily involved in international trade.

The geographic concentration of the industrial working class parallels the concentration of manufacturing in the national economy. By the early twentieth century, wage-earner and union density, regional competition for industry, and the predominance of extractive economies in the periphery clearly placed the smaller number of industrial workers there in a very different position from that of their counterparts in the core industrial areas. While regional economic specialization made it possible for southern agrarians—even the plantation elite—to back the national political program of northern labor, it also rendered the formation of a national working-class movement extremely problematic.

The next two chapters describe the political-organizational strength of farmers and workers from the agrarian and labor upheavals of the late nineteenth century to the Progressive Era. Chapter 3 describes major features of labor politics, from the Knights of Labor to the Socialist Party and the American Federation of Labor. Chapter 4 traces the agrarian political uprisings of the 1870s, 1880s, and 1890s and the failed electoral coalition of 1896. The political weakness and ambivalence of labor in a territorial legislature and electoral college are contrasted with agrarian political strength.

In an epoch in which European labor movements made their parliamentary breakthroughs, American labor thus played a relatively insignificant role in the agrarian-capitalist duel for control of national politics. Workplace strength was undermined by the political failure to secure organizational rights, and political clout was dissipated by indecision and the inability to deliver a labor vote—a fatal cycle of impotence in which modest policy victories could be won only through the patronage of the agrarians. The last chapter in part 1 describes the regional and class bases of the post-1896 party system, the progressive insurgency in the Republican Party, and farmer and labor political organization on the eve of the national progressive reform era.

Part 2 analyzes, in four chapters, the agrarian statist agenda and its statutory and administrative results from the late 1880s to the eve of World War I. An extensive body of evidence will be presented to support my contention that the main contours of Progressive Era state expansion were direct results of the pressing of agrarian claims in the national legislature: the redefinition of trade policy; the creation of an income tax; a new, publicly controlled banking and currency system; antitrust policy; the regulation of agricultural marketing networks; a nationally financed road system; federal control of railroads, ocean shipping, and early telecommunications; and agricultural and vocational education. These constituted the core of the agrarian political agenda. When regulation appeared insufficient to achieve the aims of the agrarian regions, direct state control of production and transportation was urged, refuting the popular image of the agrarians as antistatists hamstrung by a constricting "states' rights" ideology.

There were, of course, hard limits to agrarian statism. Constitutional arguments were prominent in late-nineteenth- and early-twentieth-century debates both for pragmatic reasons—as sponsors attempted to design national programs that a nitpicking Supreme Court would tolerate—and because of the prevalent federal argument that sustained a sharp specialization of function between national and local governments. Fortunately for the farmers, most of the new functions they sought to bestow on the national state could be supported as plausible derivations of the interstate commerce or general welfare clauses of Article 1 of the Constitution. Where the Court and conservative opponents remained obstinate, as with the income tax law, agrarians were able to amend the Constitution through determined political action.

Chapter 10 describes labor's legislative successes, principally won in coalition with the periphery Democrats from 1911 to 1917, despite its continuing electoral ambivalence. Chapter 11, the final policy chapter, will examine agrarian and labor antipathy to bureaucracy, one of the central characteristics of native American radicalism and a powerful theme in all American social movements. Preferring a powerful yet nondiscretionary "statutory state," both agrarians and trade unionists nevertheless acquiesced, as a matter of practical politics, in a significant expansion of the national bureaucracy during the years from 1887 to 1917. During World War I, labor leaders forged a corporatist alliance that secured, temporarily, an even greater executive branch control over the U.S. economy.

The assignment of new interventionist functions to bureaucracies with a wide array of discretionary mandates left much of the power to shape property relations in the hands of presidents, administrators, and judges—actors with questionable sympathy for agrarian and labor goals—against whom must be wielded the sword of legislative specification. That weapon could accomplish much (as it did, for example, in railroad regulation); but in policy arenas where legislative majorities were fragile and transient (for example, labor and antitrust law), the damage to movement goals, damage resulting from administrative indifference or judicial fiat, was very difficult to repair.

The agrarians, who had always anticipated such outcomes and attempted to nail down statutory mandates in precise language, could not have been very surprised when portions of the progressive state were thus undermined;

their labor allies, no fans of bureaucracy themselves, had also been wary from the start. The groups compelled to "eat their words" were the urban intellectuals and representatives of diverse agricultural/industrial areas who believed that flexible language and expert discretion were essential to compromise the agrarian animus against industrial and financial capitalism with the capitalists' insistence that all regulatory power lie within their ultimate control. Only a small sector of the American polity positively backed discretionary administrative regulation, but their strategic position between two hostile poles gave them significant power in the design of the new state. The resulting weak legitimacy of administrative institutions and their continued penetration by judges, elected officials, and societal interests made bureaucratic "autonomy" a dubious proposition.

For decades, the struggle in the courts over administrative autonomy revealed the inherent weakness of American bureaucracy. Then, in the late 1930s, judicial oversight was finally tamed to a degree that allowed the progressive administrative ideal to flourish. By the 1970s, however, the pathologies of New Deal–style discretionary bureaucracy had come to be widely acknowledged. In inaugurating a new era of regulatory reform, Congress resurrected the agrarian weapons of statutory specificity and binding rules so that legislative majorities might prevail over a weak or hostile administration.[13] Thus the agrarian legacy in the American state lies not only in its regulatory content and adversarial animus but also in a characteristic *method*, revived whenever the popular urge to constrain capitalism crests in the most democratic forum, the legislature.

PART I
The Political Economy

2

Core and Periphery in the American Economy

Because of its continental breadth, the United States has always encompassed within its boundaries several quite distinct regional economies. The original settlement of North Atlantic seaports and their role as entrepôts for European commerce conferred an early preeminence on the eastern seaboard, and as the struggle over ratification of the Constitution revealed, the coastal cities (particularly their bankers and merchants) had political interests distinct from those of the rural hinterland.[1] Nevertheless, the development of *regionally* distinct economic systems (and intense regional political rivalries) was not clearly evident until the 1820s, with the emergence of conflict over slavery.

In the South, spurred by development of the cotton gin, a plantation economy based on slave labor was steadily expanding toward the Southwest. Ultimately, southerners would oppose rapid western settlement unless it was followed by the slave economy, but this mode of production was not well suited either to the land or to the preferences of the European settlers of the West and Midwest. Furthermore, as cotton cultivation expanded into the Southwest and as the South became the major supplier to European looms, the region became firmly wedded to the principle of free trade and thus unsympathetic to cries for protection from the infant industries of the Midwest and mid-Atlantic states. Nor, with its fields turned to cotton and its port connections well established, was the southern political elite very sympathetic to demands for further internal improvements. In addition to these budding economic differences, a growing revulsion against slavery made clear the potential of the issue to divide South and West.[2]

Taking advantage of these emergent differences, New England's political representatives embraced the protective tariff, cheap land, and the military expenditures demanded by the western sections and turned these policies to their own region's advantage. Northeastern cities became suppliers of financial services and industrial goods to the rural South and West and provided brokers and shippers for the growing southern export trade. In return, they would consume the food, leather, and staple products of the interior. Thus the once-threatening westward flow of population became an advantage. Linked by the steamship, and later the railroad, distant markets were opened to northeastern banks and industries. The new settlements also helped to keep peace in elite-dominated New England by draining off malcontents from the older cities of the East.[3] Meanwhile, the South's adherence to staple agriculture and slave labor doomed it to political isolation and economic backwardness.

The Rise of the American Manufacturing Belt

In the two decades before 1860 there emerged in the North a swath of commercial and industrial cities whose economic hegemony would remain unchallenged for more than one hundred years.[4] The mushrooming industrial cities emerged along three major water and rail transportation routes.[5] Two of these converged in New York City, the queen city of U.S. commerce and industry. The first, and oldest, industrial pathway followed the seaboard from southern Maine south through the great commercial and banking centers of Boston, Providence, New York, and Philadelphia. Baltimore, with its steel, shipping, and machinery industries and strong periphery ties, marked the southern terminus. A second pathway reached inward from New York up the Hudson River valley to Albany and then west to Buffalo—a natural transshipment node on Lake Erie and an early site of flour mills and iron foundries. From Buffalo this industrial highway skirted Lake Erie through Cleveland and Toledo, reaching up to Detroit and across to Chicago and Milwaukee. The rise of a great industrial and commercial city at the southern tip of Lake Michigan was inevitable, since rail lines pushing west ran along the lakeshore and since the rich agricultural areas to the south would naturally look to Chicago for market outlets. The third industrial pathway began at Philadelphia, moving west to Pittsburgh and then north to Lake Erie. The availability of high-quality coal gave Pennsylvania an early preeminence in iron and steel manufacture and the second-highest rank (after New York) in value of manufactures in both 1860 and 1910.[6]

On the eve of the Civil War, then, there was a marked geographical specialization in the American economy. In the northeastern/north-central region bounded on the south and west by the Potomac, Ohio, and Mississippi Rivers, prominent industrial corridors linked the large and dynamic cities of the manufacturing belt. Industrial production had entered a period of rapid expansion, marked by the use of power-driven machinery, burgeoning coal and pig-iron production, and dramatic railroad expansion. Cities of the manufacturing belt concentrated on economic activities for which their locations and their human and natural resources conferred particular advantages. New England cities became early centers of banking, insurance, and shoe and textile manufacture; Pennsylvania and northern Ohio cities excelled in iron and steel; and New York and Chicago exploited a host of locational advantages to achieve prominence in diverse manufacturing as well as in trade and finance. Communication and transportation links were forged between the cities of the industrial belt, serving as channels for the diffusion of technological innovations and providing a basis for the emergence of large industries with national markets.[7]

Outside the antebellum manufacturing belt there were other cities of regional (as opposed to national) importance, which had not entered the ranks of the great industrial cities producing for national markets. Some of these— such as Cincinnati and St. Louis in the Midwest and San Francisco, Seattle, and Portland on the Pacific coast—had significant amounts of local manufacturing but were handicapped by their relative isolation. But the cities most notably absent from those ranks were southern. With an economy based on the production of a staple crop, the South preferred to import its manufactures from the European nations to which it exported. Because of the low skill level and purchasing power of its population and the considerable self-sufficiency of the plantation system, there was no foundation for a modern industrial economy in most of the South. Transportation routes linked coastal ports to their cotton-producing interiors, with relatively little intercity contact. Thus southern cities participated in few of the technological and communication links forged among cities to the north during the antebellum decades and were increasingly isolated from the domestic industrial economy.[8]

The three most notable characteristics, then, of the American manufacturing belt were its westward spread from the Atlantic seaboard, its concentration in the northeastern/north-central regions and along the major transportation arteries, and its inertia after 1860. The dominance of the antebellum manufacturing belt was maintained by its heavy capital investment, the self-generating economic growth associated with large concentrations of population, and the economic relationships forged among cities and between cities and hinterlands during the emergence of the industrial economy.[9]

Urbanization was a major by-product of this regional economic revolution. Well over 40 percent of the New England and mid-Atlantic population lived in cities by 1860, compared with less than 10 percent in the South and well under 20 percent in the plains and mountain states. Further, the *role* of cities in the core was fundamentally different from the role of cities in the periphery. The great industrial cities of the manufacturing belt existed as loci of factories and of those who worked in and otherwise supported them. There were, and are, agricultural areas within the manufacturing-belt states, but they are dependent on the industrial cities for their raison d'etre and not the reverse. The dairy, truck, and poultry farms outside the industrial cities existed to supply city residents with foodstuffs, particularly perishables. In the agriculture/extraction-based periphery, on the other hand, the engine of economic growth lay in the surrounding countryside. Cities here existed to supply surrounding farms, ranches, mines, and forests with banking, storage, and transportation services and essential commodities.[10] Although there might be significant manufacturing in the periphery, it was for a very localized market in which transportation costs or perishability (bakery products, for example) made local manufacture viable. What surplus production was exported from these cities was taken out of the ground or shipped with relatively little processing. Because of these differences in city functions, the urban-rural distinction per se has limited explanatory power in American politics. The cities of the periphery backed their rural hinterlands on major national economic policy questions in the early twentieth century, and farm areas of the manufacturing belt were likewise carried along with the great metropolis—however alien they might find the social life of the city—in major debates on economic policy.

The rapid industrialization of the post–Civil War period brought profound changes in the structure of manufacturing-belt industries. The major geographical shift was that of heavy metals and machinery into the Great Lakes region along the routes heretofore described. Most remarkable in this migration from the eastern to the western half of the belt (which entailed an *addition* to the balance, without significant loss of industrial status in the older eastern region) was the emergence by the early 1900s of the Michigan-Ohio-Indiana automobile industry. Destined to be an American industrial giant, the new auto industry spurred midwestern steel, glass, textile, and rubber production as well. The 1910 censuses of manufacturing and population confirmed the persistence of regional specialization. The New England, mid-Atlantic, and Great Lakes states contained over 70 percent of the U.S. manufacturing workforce (only 10 percent down from its 1870 share) and produced 77 percent of value added in manufacturing. Regional urbanization figures ranged from 19 percent in the Southeast to 73 percent in New England. Seven of the eight U.S. cities with populations over 500,000 were found in the Northeast–Great Lakes industrial region.[11]

Late-nineteenth-century changes in industrial structure not only enhanced the economic power of manufacturing-belt corporations but inevitably aggravated core-periphery political tensions. Beginning in the 1880s, the completion of a national railroad and telegraph network and the development of coal and oil fuel technologies made possible the emergence of huge corporations with established national and budding international markets. The new, vertically integrated, horizontally coordinated firms emerged particularly in capital- and energy-intensive areas amenable to high-volume, standardized production (especially food, chemical, machinery, oil, and metals). In the late nineteenth century and the first few years of the twentieth, a remarkable wave of mergers produced the giant firms whose names became household words: Standard Oil, U.S. Steel, Quaker Oats, Diamond Match, Campbell Soup, American Tobacco, Carnation, DuPont, Kodak, International Harvester.[12] Surpassing the railroads in size and complexity, the new corporate giants were equally unpopular in the rural periphery.

Mixed and Nonindustrial Regions

Outside the manufacturing belt, other economically specialized regions were clearly defined at the turn of the century (see map 2.1).[13] In closest proximity to the great industrial cities were the Appalachian and central mining districts, the Minnesota-Wisconsin dairy region, and the midwestern corn belt. The mining areas of eastern and southwestern Pennsylvania, southern West Virginia, southeastern and western Kentucky, and the western corner of Virginia, along with the lesser coal-mining areas of southern Illinois, southeastern Ohio, and western Indiana, were the principal suppliers of fuel to the railroads, utilities, blast furnaces, and homes of the manufacturing belt. The lake-country dairy belt owed its emergence to a function shared with New York and Pennsylvania dairying districts: supplying the cities of the manufacturing belt with foodstuffs.

The Corn Belt

On the two-hundred-mile-wide strip of exceptionally rich prairie that stretches from eastern South Dakota and Nebraska through northwestern Missouri, northern Illinois and Indiana, and western Ohio, there exists the greatest concentration of corn and meat production in the world.[14] Its proximity to the Great Lakes industrial cities again suggests an economic interdependency with the manufacturing belt, but this prosperous and productive farm area long ago exceeded the consuming capacity of proximate urban markets. By the early twentieth century, its truly national market encouraged political independence from dominant northeastern urban-industrial interests. As a

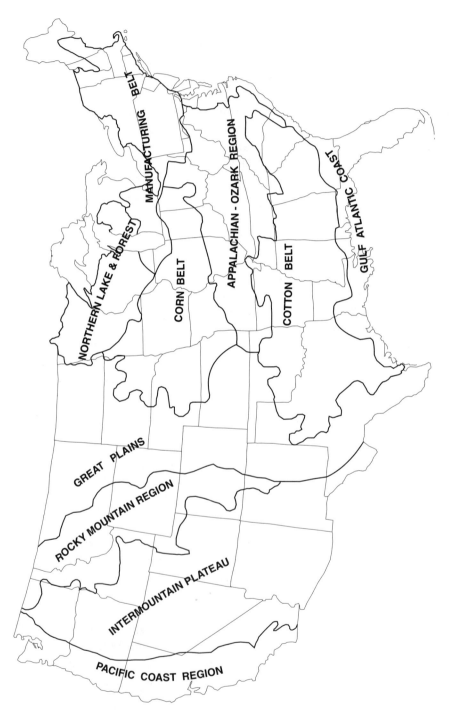

Map 2.1 Economic regions of the United States. *Source:* Slightly modified from Harold Hull McCarty, *The Geographic Basis of American Economic Life* (Port Washington, N.Y.: Kennikat Press, 1940), vol. 1, frontispiece.

result, the corn-belt economy imposed a dual identity on the area's principal marketing center: Chicago. Not only a great industrial city, Chicago owed much of its economic dynamism to its relationship as banker, supplier, and distribution center for its agricultural hinterland.[15] This interdependency with the corn, hog, and cattle belt gave Chicago a different character—and Illinois a different politics—from New York, Massachusetts, or Pennsylvania. In Chicago, in contrast to most other American trading areas, neither the urban center nor the immediate hinterland has clearly dominated the region.

The Periphery: Cotton, Wheat, Wool, and Mining Areas

South and west of the manufacturing, dairy, coal, and corn districts stretches a vast area long characterized by its agrarian and extraction-based economic system. The oldest of these regions, from the standpoint of settlement, and the most truly "peripheral" to the modern industrial economy to the north was the cotton South. This region produced the nation's most valuable cash crop, more than 60 percent of which was exported in the early twentieth century. Other important crops included rice and tobacco—the latter also an important American export. Harold Hull McCarty's map of the cotton belt, published in 1940, needs only a slight tug of its northeastern boundary to match that on the drawing-room wall of a southern planter in 1860. Throughout the first third of the twentieth century, the political imperatives of the South were predetermined by its cotton economy. The South was "peripheral" because it was cotton.

On the eve of the Progressive Era, there were only two notable industrial areas within the eleven-state region of the old Confederacy. The Birmingham iron and steel industry was established toward the end of the nineteenth century and came under the control of J. P. Morgan and the U.S. Steel combine in 1907. The Birmingham mills were handicapped by the low quality of local coal and iron ore and by the low demand in their immediate market area. They were unable to compete nationally because of relatively high transportation costs—a portion of which represented discriminatory pricing by both their parent steel company and the railroads.[16] In the southern piedmont areas of North and South Carolina and Georgia there was substantial cotton textile production by 1910. The southern mills represented the "most important migration ever experienced by a major branch of American manufacturing industry."[17] These mills were originally developed almost entirely with local financing and at first produced only the coarser grades of cotton cloth; within a few decades, piedmont boosters would exploit their energy resources and low-wage workforce to lure away the bulk of the New England cotton textile

industry. However, in 1914, New England still accounted for 55 percent of
U.S. cotton textile production.[18]

In addition to Birmingham, the major cities of the South in 1910 were
Atlanta, New Orleans, Dallas, Richmond, and Memphis. Only New Orleans
exceeded 150,000, and only Birmingham could be described as an "industrial"
(rather than commercial, hinterland-servicing) city. Granted Federal Reserve
status in 1914 as a result of political pressure to decentralize the new national
banking system, the Richmond, Atlanta, and Dallas banks were painfully un-
dercapitalized in comparison with northern reserve banks—further evidence
of their peripheral status.[19]

Stretching through the center of the country, from Texas and New Mexico north to the Canadian border, is the Great Plains region. Its principal
crop for export was, and is, wheat. Although most of this exportable surplus
went to other states, wheat was also the second-most-valuable agricultural
export (after cotton) in U.S. foreign trade during the period from 1909 to
1940. Large quantities of wheat were also grown in alternation with other
crops in the corn belt and even in Pennsylvania and Ohio, where much of
the crop was fed to poultry and livestock. But wheat was the *primary* (in some
cases, the exclusive) crop of the plains region and also of eastern Washington
and Oregon. The hinterland-dependent "capitals" of the wheat belt have historically been Minneapolis, Kansas City, and Spokane.

In the sparsely populated mountain regions lying between the Great Plains
and the Pacific Coast states, the major products with national markets in the
early twentieth century were cattle (for meat and hides), sheep (wool), miner-
als (copper, lead, zinc, silver, and gold), and sugar beets. Spokane, Denver,
and Salt Lake City were the major commercial centers of these regions, but
only Spokane had reached the 100,000 mark by 1910.

The Diverse Economies of the Pacific Coast

At the western edge of the continent, the three Pacific states grew rapidly
throughout the nineteenth and early twentieth centuries. By the Progressive
Era, they wavered between industrial and periphery status. Certainly San
Francisco was an important industrial city by 1910, with a population approaching half a million. But the great bulk of its manufacturing production
was for local consumption (this was even more true of Los Angeles), and
the state remained a net importer of manufactured goods through the 1930s.
Although the canning and aircraft industries would become nationally significant in the next decade, California cities on the eve of the Progressive Era
remained largely service centers and producers of essential consumer goods

for their agricultural and mining hinterlands. Fruit and vegetable production for domestic markets would rapidly propel California into the highest ranks of the farm states by the 1920s, based on the value of agricultural production. Lumber and wood products, though significant in California, were of much greater importance to the economies of Oregon and Washington. The most significant exports from the Northwest (sent mainly to the eastern states by sea or rail but with some export trade to the Orient) provided at least half the total income of Washington and Oregon through the 1930s. Like California cities, Portland and Seattle were, in the early twentieth century, commercial centers for their agricultural/extraction-based hinterlands. Although their physical isolation from eastern production centers made diverse light manufacturing inevitable, only the canning of fruit and vegetables and the processing of timber provided an exportable "industrial" surplus of significant value in 1910.[20]

Economic Regions and Political Constituencies

Political rivalries and alliances rooted in the divergent economic interests of the old manufacturing belt, the agrarian/extractive periphery, and the diverse Midwest/Pacific regions were critical determinants of the scope and institutional structure of early federal intervention in economic markets. The essential economic differences must, then, be traced into the political constituencies of the representatives and senators who wrote the laws and oversaw their enforcement by the executive branch. The value of manufacturing is probably the single best indicator of economic system type in this period. Table 2.1 summarizes aggregate and per capita value added in manufacturing for states. It clearly distinguishes between the New England, mid-Atlantic, and Great Lakes states, which composed the industrial core of the country, and the southern, plains, and mountain states, which had minimal industrialization in the early twentieth century. Connecticut, Rhode Island, New Jersey, Michigan, Massachusetts, Ohio, New York, and Pennsylvania stood at one extreme, with per capita industrial product value of over $400, while North Dakota, New Mexico, South Dakota, Oklahoma, Mississippi, Arkansas, Kentucky, Texas, Nevada, Alabama, Nebraska, Kansas, Tennessee, and Georgia all had under $100 per capita.[21]

The 1919 census of manufacturing has been used here, since the 1910 census did not provide the county industrial data that were needed to construct congressional district measures. Close to the end of the period encompassed by this analysis, the 1919 data reflect an intensification of industrial production for World War I, but the geographic pattern of economic special-

Table 2.1 Value Added in Manufacturing by States, 1919

Region[a]	State	Value Added per Capita	Gross Value Added
Core	Rhode Island	548.21	331,333,655
Core	Connecticut	511.72	706,494,421
Core	Massachusetts	454.39	1,750,468,496
Core	New Jersey	444.40	1,401,591,708
Core	Michigan	421.69	1,546,945,240
Core	Ohio	379.96	2,188,360,857
Core	New Hampshire	378.43	167,677,317
Core	New York	377.82	3,923,790,987
Core	Delaware	357.13	79,640,076
Core	Pennsylvania	356.11	3,105,294,239
Diverse	Illinois	298.67	1,936,974,248
Diverse	Wisconsin	273.44	719,709,346
Core	Washington	270.12	366,445,453
Core	Maine	263.35	202,253,260
Diverse	Indiana	247.00	723,802,819
Periphery	Maryland	223.91	324,597,395
Diverse	California	222.46	762,346,183
Core	Vermont	206.95	72,935,491
Diverse	Oregon	204.98	160,576,586
Periphery	Wyoming	201.62	39,194,866
Periphery	North Carolina	162.91	416,901,768
Periphery	Missouri	157.97	537,751,174
Periphery	Minnesota	140.35	335,039,958
Periphery	West Virginia	137.34	201,030,281
Periphery	Louisiana	136.10	244,785,903
Periphery	Florida	124.57	120,646,587
Periphery	Virginia	117.78	271,970,788
Periphery	Colorado	107.23	100,752,060
Periphery	Utah	104.09	46,778,722
Diverse	Iowa	93.69	225,231,890
Periphery	Kansas	92.46	163,579,107
Periphery	South Carolina	91.15	153,466,600
Periphery	Tennessee	90.46	211,486,432
Periphery	Nebraska	88.92	115,268,376
Periphery	Georgia	87.28	252,747,039
Periphery	Idaho	84.66	36,562,244
Periphery	Arizona	84.16	28,123,675
Diverse	Nevada	82.47	6,383,694
Periphery	Alabama	81.79	192,066,605
Periphery	Montana	81.10	44,512,594
Periphery	Kentucky	66.19	159,944,791
Periphery	Texas	64.08	298,824,898
Periphery	Mississippi	56.44	101,069,116
Periphery	Arkansas	55.64	97,499,881
Periphery	Oklahoma	43.76	88,757,040
Periphery	South Dakota	30.14	19,184,912
Periphery	New Mexico	28.11	10,129,119
Periphery	North Dakota	19.92	12,884,123

Source: Computed from U.S. Department of Commerce, Bureau of the Census, *Abstract of the Census of Manufacturers, 1919* (Washington, D.C.: GPO, 1923), 573, and *Fourteenth Census of the United States,* vol. 1, *Population* (Washington, D.C.: GPO, 1921), 16.

[a]States are assigned to regions based on the per capita manufacturing value added for the trade areas in which they are located (see text).

ization should not differ much from the patterns of earlier years. Map 2.2 fits these county data into congressional district lines for the first Wilson (63rd) Congress (1913–15), providing a delineation of the national political constituencies expected to champion industrial interests. Only a handful of industrial districts are found outside the traditional manufacturing belt, and probably less than half of their production moved in interregional trade.

While county- and district-level measurements may provide suitable indicators of industrialization, reliance on this data alone would imply an extremely localistic focus that is probably not realistic for U.S. congresspeople addressing broad regulatory issues. The symbiotic relationship between an industrial metropolis and farm areas dependent on nearby metropolitan markets encourages political alliances on economic policy questions. Similarly, politicians from cities like Chicago, Cincinnati, and San Francisco, which functioned as service and distribution centers for large, important agricultural areas, could be expected to show more sensitivity to agrarian interests than representatives of industrial centers without extensive, interrelated agricultural hinterlands. One way to tap these regional economic interdependencies (which often span state boundaries) is to group the political constituencies into economic "trading areas." As economic units, trading areas combine major cities with their hinterlands—that is, with the expanse of territory whose residents look to the city to market goods and to purchase other goods and services. For example, the commercial trade area series published annually by Rand-McNally relies on transportation links, retail sales, newspaper circulation, and so forth to describe the fifty major trade areas into which the country is divided.[22]

Although the Rand-McNally series is not available for the Progressive Era, a similar conception of the trade area is provided by banking districts. When the Federal Reserve System was constructed in the Wilson administration, local bankers and businesspeople were polled to ascertain which cities they preferred to have provide central banking and clearinghouse services. Comparing these preferences with the assets and capabilities of urban center banks, transportation and communication links, and other relevant data, the Federal Reserve Board designated twelve cities as Federal Reserve cities (the maximum number provided by the 1914 law) and subsequently selected twenty-two other cities to serve as branch bank subregions within the twelve districts.[23] Adding to each of these urban financial centers its economic hinterland, we can divide the country into thirty-four trade areas. Both states and congressional districts can then be attributed to these economic regions. This is the methodology used in Richard F. Bensel's *Sectionalism and American*

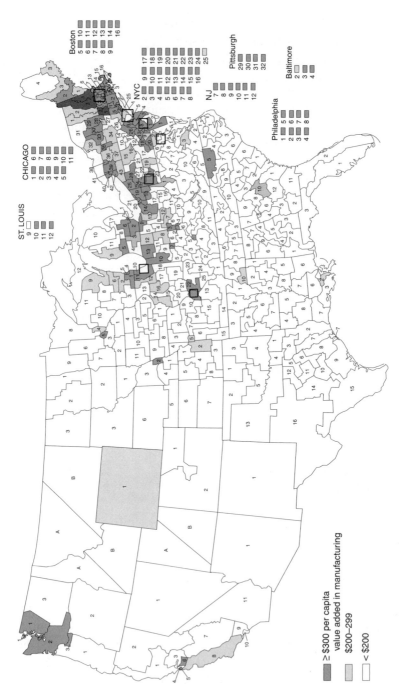

Map 2.2 Industrialization by congressional district, 63rd Congress. *Source:* Congressional district map from Kenneth C. Martis, *The Historical Atlas of United States Congressional Districts, 1789–1983* (New York: Free Press, 1982), 147. At-large congressmen are omitted. Manufacturing and population data are from *1919 Census of Manufactures* and *1920 Census of Population*.

Political Development (1984), and trade-area groupings of House districts are coincident with Bensel's for the period covered here.

Map 2.3 displays the thirty-four economic subregions, shaded according to level of (per capita) value added in manufacturing in 1919. Again, the Northeast–Great Lakes manufacturing belt stands out in sharp relief. The Cincinnati, Chicago, San Francisco, and Portland areas fall into the "diverse" industrial category, reflecting the extensive agrarian hinterlands that distinguish them from the more "autonomous" national and internationally focused cities of the industrial and commercial "core." Before 1918, Seattle was comparably situated as a service center for the trade of the Columbia plateau, but Spokane's aggressive businesspeople and politicians managed to secure for their city both a favorable railroad rate revision from the Interstate Commerce Commission and a designation as a Federal Reserve branch bank city. Subsequently, Spokane took from Seattle some of the banking and retail trade of the wheat-growing "Inland Empire."[24] The result is that the Federal Reserve district line artificially contracts Seattle's rural hinterland and enhances its industrial classification above that of the other Pacific coast cities—a politically driven anomaly in an otherwise economically predictable regional pattern.

The reserve bank regions having a per capita value added in manufacturing of $300 or more composed the upper rungs of the interregional division of labor, here labeled "core" (see table 2.1). Regions below $200 are classed as "periphery," with the intermediate $200–299 group labeled "diverse." The lefthand column of table 2.1 applies the same labels to states. Reflecting the importance of regional economic systems, a state is labeled "core" if the majority of its population falls within a *trading area* with at least $300 per capita value added in manufacturing, and so on. In the Senate, there were, in 1913, thirteen core states in the Northeast, Midwest, and Pacific regions, seven diverse states in the Midwest and Far West, and twenty-eight periphery states. Maryland was still the northeastern boundary of the periphery in the Progressive Era (the Baltimore trading area was largely agrarian, with a value added in manufacturing of less than $200 per capita). All eleven states of the Confederacy were included in the periphery, along with most of Kentucky, Missouri, and the plains and mountain states. Nevada, because it was in the San Francisco trading area, was classified "diverse." In the House, congressional districts were assigned to the trading area that contained a majority of the district's population and were labeled "core," "diverse," or "periphery" according to the trading area's value added in manufacturing. The relatively few congressional roll calls analyzed for the late nineteenth century employ the same regional designations or rely on conventional regional categories.

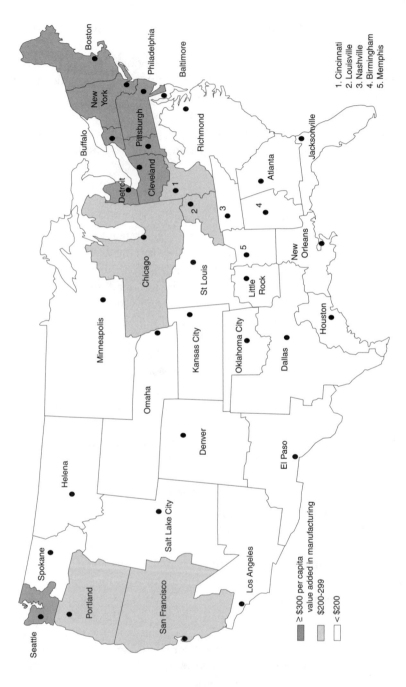

Map 2.3 Industrialization by trading area in the early twentieth century (Federal Reserve Bank territories). *Source: Eighth Annual Report of the Board of Governors of the Federal Reserve System, 1921* (Washington, D.C.: GPO, 1992), 693–99; *1919 Census of Manufacturing; 1920 Census of Population.*

The regional count of House districts in the 61st Congress (1909–11) was core, 131, diverse, 77, and periphery, 183. Beginning in the 63rd Congress (1913–15), the number of House districts was increased to its final size, 435, and the regional totals were 150, 81, and 204. Slight variations in regional totals for the 62nd and 64th Congress totals resulted from the entry of New Mexico and Arizona into the Union and from redistricting. The trading areas of the historical (eleven-state) South composed just under half of the periphery House seats in the 63rd and 64th Congresses (1913–17); in the Senate, about 40 percent of the periphery was southern. Though not a numerical majority, the South constituted the largest and, economically and politically, the most cohesive of the periphery's component regions. By virtue of its size and the intensity of its grievances in the national political economy, the South almost inevitably led the periphery voting bloc in Congress. However, as the voting tables will demonstrate, periphery cohesion was often disrupted by divergent interests in the national political economy, as well as by the powerful pull of party affiliation and the force of historical experience.

As can be seen in the congressional district maps, there are areas of high industrialization within the "diverse" regions in the early twentieth century and even a few highly industrial House districts within the periphery (the St. Louis, Minneapolis, Baltimore, and Greensboro/Winston-Salem districts), just as there are agricultural areas within the core.[25] With the expectation that such differences would be reflected in congressional roll-call voting, each broad region was further subdivided into high-industrial/low-industrial subregions for the voting analysis. However, the few industrial districts and states in the periphery seldom deviated from the agrarian majority; likewise, most rural core districts followed the industrial-district majority on the bulk of the roll calls examined. To highlight the more important (as it turned out) core-diverse-periphery and party divisions, such detailed regional breakdowns are not included in the tables of part 2. Where such intraregion divisions are important in roll-call voting, they are noted in the text or in footnotes.

Table 2.2 shows the distribution by state of farmers and workers in 1900. There are, of course, workers and farmers in all regions. The modest number of workers in the periphery shared many class interests with northern core workers; however, they were less ethnically diverse, and as recent migrants from the country (and with many relatives there), they likely did not sharply distinguish their interests from those of farmers, as did labor in the metropolitan core. This is one of the reasons why the Knights of Labor assemblies in the periphery were so occupationally diverse and why the Populists were so

Table 2.2 Farmers and Workers as a Percentage of the Employed Population over Ten Years of Age, 1900

State/Territory	% Farmers	% Workers	State/Territory	% Farmers	% Workers
Mississippi	75.6	6.9	Vermont	36.4	30.5
Oklahoma	71.4	7.9	Wisconsin	35.8	27.9
Arkansas	70.1	10.3	Utah	34.1	28.6
Indian Territory	68.7	10.5	Michigan	33.2	29.5
South Carolina	68.7	11.8	Oregon	32.4	25.2
Alabama	67.1	12.7	Wyoming	29.6	35.1
North Carolina	63.5	14.4	Arizona	29.4	36.3
Texas	62.0	10.7	Nevada	28.9	32.0
North Dakota	60.8	11.7	Maine	26.8	35.1
South Dakota	60.2	12.9	Ohio	26.4	33.7
Georgia	59.9	12.6	Delaware	25.8	33.9
Tennessee	56.2	14.8	Illinois	25.3	30.7
Louisiana	54.1	13.0	Montana	23.7	40.8
Kentucky	53.8	17.1	Washington	23.1	34.6
Kansas	53.1	17.5	California	21.6	30.4
Nebraska	49.6	16.8	New Hampshire	20.8	46.7
Iowa	46.7	19.9	Maryland	20.4	31.8
West Virginia	45.7	26.0	Colorado	19.9	37.6
Virginia	44.9	18.8	Pennsylvania	13.3	44.7
Florida	44.8	20.6	New York	12.2	38.7
Idaho	42.3	27.6	Connecticut	11.1	49.1
Missouri	40.8	23.1	New Jersey	8.6	44.6
New Mexico	40.5	20.1	Rhode Island	5.3	55.8
Minnesota	39.1	23.3	Massachusetts	5.2	50.6
Indiana	37.1	26.3			

Source: U.S. Department of Commerce and Labor, Bureau of the Census, *Special Reports: Occupations at the Twelfth Census* (Washington, D.C.: GPO, 1904), table 41. The category "farmers" consists of agricultural pursuits *minus* gardeners, lumbermen, and woodchoppers. The category "workers" consists of manufacturing and mechanical pursuits (which includes miners) *minus* fishermen, manufacturers and officials, and photographers, *plus* draymen, teamsters, boatmen, packers and shippers, railroad workers and porters from the trade and transportation category, and lumbermen and woodchoppers from the agricultural pursuits category. In all cases, males and females were added together. The major category of workers omitted here was domestic and personal service, particularly the nonspecific category "laborers," which could be either agricultural or unskilled industrial or other workers.

comfortable with a farmer-labor alliance. Farmers, also, show regionally distinct orientations. The term "agrarian" is used here to reference those agricultural regions, largely coincident with the designated southern-plains-western "periphery," that were devoted to one or two cash crops produced for national and international (as opposed to local) markets. These farmers—particularly, but not exclusively, growers of cotton and wheat—were enmeshed in an economy quite distinct from that of the dairy and truck farmers producing for nearby, steadily expanding urban markets, as well as from the more favorably situated corn, hog, and diverse grain farmers on the rich and well-watered soil of the midwestern corn belt (see map 2.1). The periphery agrarians were more bound to the fate of a single crop (whose price was set in a world market); more distant from crop marketing, storage, and distribution centers; more likely to be dependent on a single rail line and monopolistic or oligopolistic purchasers; more starved for credit in the long months between planting and harvest; and more vulnerable to drought and, especially in the warm and humid South, to insect damage.

These were the conditions that predisposed periphery farmers to define their interests as antithetical to those of large industrialists, bankers, and railroads and to look to the national state for solutions to their difficulties. As their distress intensified in the 1880s and 1890s, they undertook a broad reevaluation of changes in the late-nineteenth-century economy and of what those changes meant, not only for farmers but also for other vulnerable groups. In particular, the agrarians reached out to factory, mine, mill, and railroad workers, who shared both their vulnerability to concentrated economic power and their vision of a more decentralized and egalitarian society in which the producers of the nation's wealth would share more fully in its bounty. In the process, they constructed the most original and searching critique of industrial capitalism that American history has yet experienced and a political movement that mounted the broadest challenge to the foundations of the new economic system. But for an effective challenge, they needed allies who were similarly mobilized.

3

Labor Organizations and the State, 1873–1912

The three great workers' organizations of the late nineteenth and early twentieth centuries were the Knights of Labor (KOL), the Socialist Party (SP), and the American Federation of Labor (AFL). The Knights viewed political education and the exertion of political pressure on lawmakers as natural outgrowths of worker solidarity and the broad social alliance of "producers." Socialists were committed to an electoral strategy for bringing about the end of capitalism. At the other extreme, the leaders of the AFL had little interest in political reform and devoted their efforts to wringing discrete concessions from capitalists through workplace militancy. Yet even the AFL was necessarily political. Its directors recognized that workplace goals such as union organizational rights and the abolition of child labor would require state action, for which they were willing to lobby and, on occasion, campaign. What distinguishes these three wings of labor is not a dichotomous political/apolitical orientation but the willingness to mount or support third-party efforts, the breadth of the political program endorsed, and the inclination to effect alliances with nonworkers. On these three dimensions, the AFL clearly ranks third, with Knights and Socialists alternating for the first two spots.

For a broad-based reform movement to succeed, then, either the KOL or the Socialists had to prevail among workers. The Socialists more closely matched the farmers' avid commitment to politics; but farmers, however much the poorest in their ranks might flirt with socialism, would always be repelled by the leading role played in the party by urban intellectuals contemptuous of the "petit-bourgeois" agrarians and committed to the socialization of land. It was, therefore, the success of the Knights and their willingness to forge a farmer-worker alliance upon which the triumph of democratic populism depended. The decline of the KOL after 1886 was thus a more critical turning point for both the labor movement and the shape of American democracy than the ebbing of electoral socialism after 1912. The forces that contributed to the Knights' demise would continue to plague the labor movement and would propel the surviving AFL into a narrow, defensive, and apolitical craft unionism that, in turn, contributed to its political ineffectiveness.

By the Progressive Era, both farm and labor organizations had experienced a transformation from social movements to interest groups—that is, from sustained, organized protest by marginalized groups outside formal centers of power, pressing their (relatively radical) grievances on the state or economic elites,[1] to more conservative and institutionalized lobby groups with sufficient formal access to regularly present their moderate demands to political authorities. But organizations of farmers in the periphery retained two qualities of late-stage social movements that distinguished them from organizations of industrial workers: they continued to press relatively radical demands, embedded in a broad reform program, on the national state; and as mature social movements of the disadvantaged have generally done, they looked outward, to other marginalized groups for allies.[2]

Social movements in American politics have historically faced the following set of strategic choices:

1. A "purist" organization strategy emphasizing only collective action, with a localistic focus. Common economic (e.g., cooperatives, strikes) and social activities would draw members to the movement. The more members there were, the more success in the core activities. The organization would then, presumably, become so large and cohesive that *politicians would come to it* and court its members' votes by endorsing whatever political demands they put forward. Those demands would center on the removal of obstacles to movement organization and activities. The organization would endorse no political party and would largely ignore the partisan proclivities of the membership. Presumably, members would exercise their rights as individual citizens and, as informed voters, would back candidates favorable to the cause. This was the preferred strategy of the AFL before 1906 and of the KOL and the Farmers' Alliance (FA) in their early years.

2. Work for the election of whichever major-party candidates pledge the greatest support for the goals of the movement while maintaining the principle of flexible nonpartisanship. Inevitably, one party will prove more sympathetic than the other (though not necessarily the same party in each state, making national endorsements problematic). Such electoral alliances represent tactical cooperation, not a permanent alliance. The maintenance of a Washington, D.C., lobbying organization usually accompanies this nonpartisan "friends and enemies" strategy. The Farmers' Alliance and the KOL in the 1880s, the AFL in 1906, 1908, and 1916, and many late-twentieth-century social

movements of consumerists, feminists, environmentalists, and pacifists have used this strategy.

3. Combine with one of the major parties through a formal merger, "fusion," or massive infiltration. Many southern and midwestern agrarians endorsed this course. The national Populist-Democratic fusion of 1896 is illustrative.

4. Mount an independent third-party effort, as did local Knights and farmers in the 1880s, Populists in 1892–94, and Socialists after 1900.

Each choice brings its own risks and calculation of benefits and costs, and different strategies may appeal to a movement at different stages of its existence. In the early stages, social movements of the disadvantaged are typically skeptical of any close affinity with the major parties, which, after all, have not been very attentive to their needs. Since a movement's leadership will naturally be more educated, with wider experience and connections than the bulk of the membership, it is plausible that some movement leaders will be attracted to overtures from the major parties (Terrence Powderly of the Knights of Labor is a good example here) and that the entry of the movement into politics will attract political activists with prior experience in major or minor parties, predisposing them to fusion. Such activists will often also have policy interests that diverge from those of the membership (or other leaders). Tensions, then, will inevitably emerge among leaders, and between leaders and followers, when a movement "goes political." Further, as the leaders' energies become focused on the political process, they will inevitably have less time (and inclination) for direct communication with members or organization-nurturing activities.[3] The movement's dynamics, then, will change, and its force may well be dissipated by the move into politics. If the movement's adherents constitute a minority in the relevant electoral units—as is usually the case—-coalitions must be effected with other social groups whose position in the political economy promises some hope of mutual support on common issues (or relatively low-cost logrolling). If the potential allies find some aspects of the movement's program objectionable, there will be pressure to sideline or jettison those positions. Inevitably, some movement members will object to the new demands adopted on behalf of allies. Movement esprit will be dissipated.

These are serious risks; and yet, a movement that is stymied at the first level may see the move into politics as the only alternative to protect its members from further erosion of their life chances and to win some tangible benefits. The farmers' movement of the late nineteenth century tried all four strategies, moving from number one to two to four and ending up in three as the diminished movement came to rest in a Democratic Party that both captured and was transformed by the agrarian movement it had swallowed.

Labor organizations confined their strategies to numbers one, two, and four; the AFL, to one and two. The difficult social, economic, and political conditions in which labor had to navigate—rendered even more severe by the surge of immigration, corporate consolidation, and conservative political mobilization of the 1890s onward—would reinforce labor's organizational and strategic choices, making a reform alliance with farmers increasingly problematic. These choices were premised on finding a way around partisan legislative politics. And yet by the Progressive Era, it became clear that the rising hurdles to labor organization could be surmounted only through national political mobilization. This was the conundrum in which labor found itself in the early twentieth century. The following description of the three workers' organizations and their interrelationships will help to clarify the choices with which labor was confronted and the implications of those choices for a farmer-worker alliance.

The Knights of Labor

One of the most remarkable of American reform movements (and clearly a "movement" as well as a national organization), the Knights of Labor had its origins in the revival of trade unionism in the late 1860s and early 1870s. After its beginnings in the Philadelphia area, local assemblies of the Knights proliferated in the Pennsylvania, Illinois, and Ohio coalfields in the second half of the 1870s.[4] Local assemblies (LAs) were either "trade" (limited to one occupation) or "mixed" (involving members of various trades in a geographic area). LAs were joined in district assemblies (DAs) or, in some cases, were linked directly to a state assembly or to the national body, the General Assembly. Unlike the earlier national labor organizations it succeeded—the National Labor Union of 1866–72 and the Industrial Brotherhood of 1874–75—the KOL grew from the bottom up, that is, from a local worker base, rather than from a national organization of labor and reform leaders down. The program enunciated by its leadership conceived of society as divided between the "producing classes" of workers, farmers, and small manufacturers and an emerging parasitic and exploitative class of financiers, speculators, bondholders, and monopolists who were steadily appropriating a larger and larger share of the wealth created by producers. To counter the exploiters, the KOL hoped to build worker solidarity across craft lines and to cooperate with other producer groups, particularly the more numerous farmers.[5]

The first great national corporations to emerge in the post–Civil War era

were railroads; thus it was the railroads that occasioned the first national uprising of labor as well as the earliest confrontations between workers and the
state. Precipitated by the Panic of 1873, which triggered the country's longest
economic depression to date, railroads began to cut workers' wages, both on
the roads and in the coal mines that were rapidly falling under railroad control.
Other industries followed suit. Pinkertons and similar private police forces
were used by employers to put down the resultant strikes, and most national
trade unions were destroyed in the four years following the panic. In the
cities, unemployment demonstrations were met with harsh police repression.
The routing of the railroad brotherhoods and the formation of a great trunk-
line pool emboldened rail executives to implement further wage cuts in 1877.
But this proved to be the last straw for workers. Spontaneous strikes spread
across the Baltimore and Ohio and Pennsylvania Railroads to other roads and
into adjacent mines, reaching as far north as Michigan and west all the way
to San Francisco. When townspeople and local militia proved sympathetic to
the strikers, troops were called in from distant cities, and scores of strikers
were killed or wounded. Ultimately President Rutherford B. Hayes ordered
in federal troops, and the nation's first national strike was finally suppressed,
with considerable bloodshed.[6]

The "Great Upheaval" of 1877 jolted the nation. It revealed a hitherto
unknown depth of discontent among workers and demonstrated to employers
and the public the power of an aggrieved workforce to disrupt the nation's
commerce, now integrated by a web of railroad lines. Public officials responded with a revival of "conspiracy" doctrines in court proceedings and
state laws and with discussions of the need for stronger and more centralized
militias. Workers responded by going into politics and joining the Knights
of Labor.[7]

The vehicle that drew the organizers of the Knights' first General Assembly into local and national politics was the Greenback-Labor Party. Several
labor leaders who would later be active Knights had participated in earlier
greenback conventions, and the labor and middle-class reformers of the National Labor Union held greenbackism as a central tenet. In fact, working-
class intellectuals like printer Andrew C. Cameron and William Sylvis of the
Iron Molders Union (coeditors of a Chicago labor paper) were among the
earliest and most influential converts to the monetary philosophy. Originally
devised in the 1850s by a failed New York dry-goods merchant, Edward Kel-
logg, and elaborated fifteen years later by a Pennsylvania iron manufacturer
named Alexander Campbell, greenbackism was welcomed by labor leaders
such as Cameron and Sylvis, Richard Trevellick of Detroit, and Robert Schil-

ling of Cleveland (both of whom became KOL organizers). These labor activists were discouraged by the failure of strikes and cooperative ventures in the post–Civil War deflation era. Like Campbell, they came to believe that the workers' well-being—indeed, the prosperity of "producers" generally—depended on low interest rates and a steady expansion of the currency to meet the needs of a growing population and commerce.[8] In Sylvis's words: "A high interest rate is the mill-stone around the neck of labor; it cripples the energy of the whole people, and retards production[;] . . . reduce the rate of interest to three percent, and give us a national currency made of paper, and new enterprises will be started, machines now idle will be put in motion; there will be work for all."[9]

The policy of postwar Republican governments led in the opposite direction. It embodied a determination to retire the wartime greenbacks, support gold payments to holders of war-issue bonds, and allow private bankers to create money. These policies appeared to be taking their toll in unemployment and agricultural distress, particularly in the iron, coal, and farm districts of Pennsylvania, Ohio, Indiana, and Illinois. That so many currency and labor reformers hailed from these regions thus reflected not only local economic conditions but also a resurgent resentment of the political dominance of northeastern, capital-rich cities and of the banker, bondholder, and mercantile interests concentrated there. The overlapping of personnel and a liberal borrowing of platform language and principles from earlier labor and farmer organizations (particularly the Patrons of Husbandry, or the Grange, and midwestern antimonopoly movements) explain the continuing thread of greenback philosophy in labor/reform movements of the 1870s—including the Knights—and the naturalness of broad farmer-labor political alliances for these labor leaders. Representatives of farmers' societies had participated in the second convention of the National Labor Union in 1867, and Robert Schilling urged in the 1874 Industrial Congress that a national labor organization be modeled on the Grange and seek "intimate cooperation with the Farmers' movement."[10]

Independent workers' parties sprang up in local and state elections in 1877, and alliances were effected between labor reformers and greenbackers. Leaders of the Knights of Labor—Uriah Stephens, Terrence Powderly, Robert Schilling, George Blair, Ralph Beaumont, John M. Davis, James L. Wright—all ran for office on Greenback-Labor tickets in Pennsylvania, Ohio, and New York; Powderly was elected mayor of Scranton in 1878, the same year he replaced Stephens as Grand Master Workman of the KOL. Several of these men were among the eight hundred delegates who participated in a National

(Greenback-Labor) convention in Toledo in 1878.[11] Demonstrating the appeal of greenbackism to both urban workers and farmers, the National Party's congressional candidates garnered over one million votes in state and congressional elections. In fifty-six congressional districts, Greenbackers (either alone or in fusion with a major party) won 30 percent or more of the total vote. Thirty-three of these ran in the Midwest and South and twenty-three in the Northeast (Maine, Vermont, Pennsylvania, New Jersey, New York, and Massachusetts). Of the fifteen elected, five had run in the Midwest, three in the South, three in Pennsylvania, two in Maine, and one each in Vermont and New Jersey.[12]

As a measure of the support base for the Greenback reform movement in national politics, these fifteen districts merit a closer examination. Eight of them were overwhelmingly rural, with less than 20 percent of the population (ranging from 3 to 18 percent) living in towns or cities of over 4,000. However, one of these (Maine's fourth district) did have a modest industrial base in its collection of small towns, and another, in central Pennsylvania, contained several important coal-mining counties along with a fair wheat production. These two, then, may not be aptly classed as "agrarian." Another district (the Texas fifth), with an urban population of 24 percent, nevertheless had high cotton production, low value added in manufacturing, and a strong agrarian cast, despite enclosing the state capital at Austin. This district contained, in fact, the sparsely populated central Texas county that gave birth to the Farmers' Alliance. In all, seven of the fifteen Greenback districts appear, from their rural and economic profiles, to represent an agricultural milieu. Only four of the fifteen—those in Philadelphia, Indianapolis, coastal Maine, and southern New Jersey—had over 30 percent urban populations; the addition of less-urban districts with relatively high value added located in Pennsylvania and Maine brings the number of plausibly "labor" districts in the Greenback group to seven. The remaining district, in northwestern Missouri, had substantial farm output, very modest industrial production, and an urban population of 26 percent.[13]

The picture, then, is genuinely mixed. Among the Greenback congressmen were at least two with working-class occupations or identified with labor causes (Thompson Murch of Maine and Hedrick Wright of Pennsylvania), the former president of the Illinois Grange (Albert Forsythe), and an Iowa Greenbacker known both as an agrarian reform leader and a friend of labor (James Weaver). On a very small scale, the Greenback movement had managed to achieve a farmer-labor reform coalition in national politics. The problem, of course, was scale.

The year 1878 proved to be the electoral high point for the Greenback movement, and the fate of the party revealed two aspects of labor's political tendencies that would prove enduring: as individuals, national labor leaders, some of whom entertained political ambitions in their own right, might support major or third parties locally, but they were unwilling to commit their *organizations* and thus to attempt national labor electoral mobilizations; and the rank and file, aware of their leaders' ambivalence and pressured by employers, long-standing party loyalties, and their own assessments of labor advantage, could not be counted on to sustain a national reform campaign.

Several KOL leaders were on hand at the 1880 Greenback convention (one was named chair of the Chicago nominating convention in June), but the enthusiasm of Powderly and others had notably waned. Despite the adoption of a vigorous reform program that included more labor demands than any earlier platforms, the KOL made little effort for the Greenback presidential candidate, and his labor vote was minimal.[14] Commentators have suggested that the lifting of the depression in the fall of 1880 and the nomination of Iowan James Weaver rather than Gen. Benjamin Butler of Massachusetts contributed to labor's disenchantment with greenbackism.[15] Butler, now a wealthy lawyer and Greenbacker, had cultivated a labor following in Massachusetts. But Weaver was a loyal friend of labor and, as the 1884 campaign would demonstrate, enjoyed far more national popularity than Butler (if the South had to swallow a Union general for president, better a man of agrarian sympathies like Weaver than the "Beast of New Orleans"). Certainly the 1880 Greenback platform promised much more to labor than did the Democratic and Republican versions. At any rate, the falloff of labor support left the agrarian Greenbackers high and dry.

The expansion, in the early 1880s, of an antimonopoly movement centered in the midwestern farm belt got little overt response from the KOL. Driven by antirailroad animus and led by many former Greenback activists, an 1883 convention adopted a platform calling for railroad regulation, a government-operated telegraph and postal savings system, tariff reductions, an income tax, and direct election of senators. To this, an Antimonopoly Party formed in 1884 added a section incorporating labor demands. Eventually, a revived Greenback Party and the Antimonopolists settled on the same presidential and vice-presidential candidates: General Butler and Absalom M. West of Mississippi, an old antisecession Whig planter and ex-Confederate general who had been converted to Greenbackism by—as implausible as it may sound—labor leader Sylvis, who had met West during a union organizing trip in Mississippi.[16]

Despite the pairing of Union and Confederate, agrarian and labor, with labor ostensibly at the head, the ticket drew very little support at the polls. Though its best showing came in the Northeast and probably rested on worker support, the feebleness of that support and the reluctance of agrarians to back Butler (an anti-Cleveland Democrat who was rumored to be, and probably was, on the Republican Party payroll) doomed the ticket to a mere 175,000 votes. There was little sign of KOL effort; Powderly was ostensibly neutral. The Order (KOL) did, however, take over for its own constitution several Greenback-Antimonopoly planks: the income tax, postal savings, and government ownership of the telegraph.[17] The last was especially appealing to the KOL after Jay Gould's Western Union Co. crushed the Order's national trade assembly of telegraphers in 1883.[18]

The Knights' leaders meanwhile turned their energies to organizational development. Membership grew from around 28,000 to 104,000 between 1880 and 1885 (see table 3.1). The percentage of trade-based assemblies steadily dropped, reflecting the Order's philosophy and the growing diversity of its membership, and the proportion of local assemblies that were occupationally mixed grew to 54 percent by 1886.[19] As a result of the expansion into manufacturing and transportation from the earlier coal-mining base, the majority of LAs organized from 1882 to 1886 were in cities.[20] At the same time, the Order spread rapidly outside its northeastern bastions. Between 1878 and 1886, the percentage of existing LAs located in the North Atlantic states fell from 53 to 41 while the percentage in the South Atlantic, south-central, and western states grew from 13 to 24.[21] However, because urban LAs were generally much larger than rural ones, 38 percent of Knights were in large cities, with another 28 percent in cities with populations between 8,000 and 100,000, and the large majority (60 percent) of members were still found in the North Atlantic states in 1886.[22]

In theory, the KOL was highly centralized and emphasized education, cooperation, collective moral suasion of employers and legislators, and mediation of industrial disputes by the national leadership. The reality however, was much more complicated. Producer and consumer cooperatives were often attempted and did secure some financial backing from the national office. However, they suffered from the well-known difficulties of raising contributions, securing credit, arranging marketing, managing business enterprises, and securing workers' patronage. The largest such undertaking, a KOL-owned coal mine at Cannellburg, Indiana, was an enormous financial drain. Cooperation was not a significant aspect of the KOL by the mid-1880s.[23]

Members joined the Knights during and after successful strikes and boy-

Table 3.1 Membership in Labor Organizations, 1879–1917

Year	Knights of Labor	AFL	Total Union Membership	% Nonagricultural Workforce
1879	20,151			
1880	28,136			
1881	19,422			
1882	42,517			
1883	51,914			
1884	60,811			
1885	104,066			
1886	702,924	138,000		7.3 (KOL & AFL only)
1887	510,351	160,000		
1888	259,518	175,000		
1889	220,607	210,000		
1890	100,000	225,000		2.4 (KOL & AFL only)
1891		238,000		
1892		255,000		
1893	74,635	260,000		
1894		275,000		
1895		270,000		
1896		265,000		
1897		264,000	447,000	
1898		278,000	500,700	
1899		349,000	611,000	
1900		548,000	868,500	4.8 (all union members)
1901		787,000	1,124,700	
1902		1,024,000	1,375,900	
1903		1,465,000	1,913,900	
1904		1,676,000	2,072,700	
1905		1,494,000	2,022,300	9.2
1906		1,454,000	1,958,700	
1907		1,538,000	2,122,800	
1908		1,586,000	2,130,600	
1909		1,482,000	2,047,400	
1910		1,562,000	2,184,200	8.4
1911		1,761,000	2,382,800	
1912		1,770,000	2,483,500	
1913		1,996,000	2,753,400	
1914		2,020,000	2,716,900	
1915		1,946,000	2,607,700	9.2
1916		2,072,000	2,808,000	
1917		2,371,000	3,104,600	

Source: Leo Wolman, *The Growth of American Trade Unions, 1880–1923* (New York: National Bureau of Economic Research, 1924), 31–33, for columns 1, 2 (until 1897), and 3. Wolman's 1888 figure for the KOL, taken from John R. Commons et al., *History of Labor in the United States* (New York: Augustus M. Kelley, 1966), has been corrected. For column 2, 1897–1917, see Philip Taft, *The AFL in the Time of Gompers* (New York: Harper & Brothers, 1957), 233, 362. For column 4, figures in column 3 were divided by nonfarm gainful workers ten years old and older in U.S. Department of Commerce, Bureau of the Census, *Historical Statistics of the Untied States* (Washington, D.C.: GPO, 1960), 72. The 1886, 1905, and 1915 denominators were computed by extrapolation. Note that "workforce" used here is larger than "wage earners," since it includes the self-employed, managers, and supervisors. "Workforce" is used to permit long-term comparison. As a percentage of nonagricultural wage earners, the 1915 figure would be about 12.2.

cotts.[24] The great spur to KOL expansion was the railroad strikes that broke out spontaneously in early 1885 when shopmen on the Missouri Pacific, the Wabash, and the Missouri, Kansas and Texas Railroads, all controlled by Jay Gould, quit work en masse to protest wage cuts. A KOL emissary was sent to offer assistance and recruit strikers for the Knights. With growing sympathy strikes and strong community and state government support for the strikers in the Southwest, Gould backed down, and the reductions were withdrawn. A short time later, however, layoffs and lockouts of KOL members were ordered on the Wabash, and the KOL executive board ordered a strike and freight boycott. In subsequent negotiations between the railroad managers and the KOL board, the former agreed to rehire locked-out workers, and Gould announced that he was not opposed to worker organization. These victories were an enormous energizer for the labor movement, and the KOL's membership surged. From just over 100,000 in 1885, the Order grew to over 700,000 by mid-1886. From January through May, aided by the return of prosperity, over 500 new LAs were formed every month.[25]

In 1886, the KOL was an exceedingly diverse and geographically widespread organization. It had 2,700 LAs in the Northeast, over 2,000 in the north-central states, almost 1,300 in the South, and 260 in the Far West. Its penetration into the South and other farm states was remarkable. Kansas ranked second (after New York) in number of LAs organized in 1883; in 1885 the impact of the southwestern strikes put Texas in third place, and rail, sugar, and lumber workers, coal miners, farmers, and farmworkers poured into the Order all across the South.[26]

The KOL enrolled the skilled and the unskilled, native and foreign-born, men and women, blacks and whites. At its peak in 1886, its numbers included an estimated 30,000–35,000 women (concentrated in the textile and shoe industries and including a scattering of temperance advocates, suffragettes, and farm wives). Separately organized black locals numbered 120, all but 18 of them in the South, but some local assemblies had biracial membership. Black Knights were estimated to number between 15,000 and 20,000.[27] Grand Master Powderly made a point of having a black member introduce him at the 1886 General Assembly in Richmond, Virginia, and the flaunting of the city's segregation codes by the convening Knights brought threats of violence there. Powderly was forced to disavow any intent to disrupt southern racial relations, but the KOL's commitment to enroll blacks did just that. It was, in the 1880s, "a beacon of racial enlightenment in a dark sea."[28]

The fantastic growth of the KOL in 1885–86 was both a vindication of the Knights' inclusive and idealistic premises and a source of serious difficulties. It brought the KOL to the attention of the press, which purveyed exaggerated notions of the Knights' power over the country's economy. It also aroused strong and increasingly organized business opposition and aggravated long-standing difficulties with the Catholic Church (particularly in French Canada, where the KOL was making rapid gains).[29] Expansion of the number of mixed assemblies and rural LAs brought into the KOL a large membership inclined both to oppose trade-based organization and to mount independent political campaigns. Both tendencies were also supported by KOL socialists who, emboldened by the rapid expansion, took the offensive against trade unionism in 1886 and provoked an irreparable split within the labor movement.

The Knights of Labor and Trade Unions

Skilled craftsmen, although quite numerous within the KOL, were never completely comfortable with the Knights' inclusive membership policies, the attention to broad theorizing and politics, and the unpredictable support for local strikes and nitty-gritty union concerns such as wages and hours. In 1881, a disaffected group of big-city trade unionists formed a rival order, the Federation of Organized Trades and Labor Unions (FOTLU). The federation created a legislative committee headed by Samuel Gompers of the Cigar Makers International Union (CMIU). Its platform endorsed the protective tariff (an issue the KOL declined to touch), trade-union organizational rights, compulsory education, a ban on child labor, enforcement of the eight-hour law for government employees, a mechanics' lien law, a national labor statistics bureau, and an end to convict and foreign contract labor and to the use of the conspiracy laws against trade unions. Its formative convention specifically ruled out planks dealing with broad national issues such as federal land policy and nationalization of railroads and the telegraph—issues central to the Knights' political program. FOTLU was a weak organization based on nationally organized trade unions; its membership never exceeded 24,000. It suffered from lost strikes and the greater dynamism of the KOL. Its main legacy for the labor movement was in providing an organizational shell that could be absorbed by the AFL in 1886 and in calling—as a desperation measure in its declining years—for a national strike on May 1, 1886, to demand the eight-hour day. This event became a rallying cry for trade unionists, Socialists, and anarchists and provided the stage for the Chicago Haymarket bombing that would prove momentous for labor's mid-1880s development.[30]

There were "vast and essential differences between our Order and the Trades' Unions," affirmed the KOL Grand Master Workman, since the

Knights "contemplate[d] a radical change in the existing industrial system," whereas the trade unions, in the view of Powderly and most labor historians, had accepted the modern wage system and pressed only for practical material gains.[31] FOTLU's 1884 convention explained: "We do not hold with those theorists . . . who strive to direct the labor movement in pursuit of some will-o'-the-wisp millennium grounded neither upon the capabilities of human nature nor the dictates of common sense. We must walk before we can fly and we believe the gaining of higher wages and shorter hours to be the preliminary steps toward great and accompanying improvements in the condition of the working classes."[32] The contrast with the idealistic, transformative republicanism of the Knights was stark. There was also a fundamental difference in strategy. The KOL believed that narrow, exclusive craft unions divided and weakened the labor movement. The trade unionists believed the core strength of labor to be in workplace militance, organized by homogeneous crafts.

The break between the two groups came in 1886. The Order's rapid growth in 1885–86 inevitably caused friction with the trade unionists; not only did the KOL compete with the unions for skilled workers, but its recruitment of the unskilled led to charges that the KOL succored "scabs." Matters came to a head in New York City. There, KOL District Assembly 49 was controlled by an aggressive and secretive group of Socialists rabidly opposed to "pure and simple" trade unionism. DA 49 encouraged politically minded cigar makers to desert the Cigar Makers International Union for the Knights, and it organized tenement-house cigar workers at a time when the CMIU was working to shut down such production. In late 1886, CMIU leaders engineered the formation of a new trade-union federation that was, in comparison with FOTLU, even more narrowly craft-based and more aggressively hostile to the KOL and everything it stood for: the American Federation of Labor. In succeeding years, the Knights often made overtures for peaceful coexistence with the AFL. Federation leaders, however, were committed to the defeat of the KOL and, particularly after their own membership surpassed the declining Knights (in about 1890), scorned such gestures.[33]

Knights in Politics in the 1880s

Under Powderly's leadership, the national KOL discouraged independent labor (or labor-farmer) political campaigns. On their own, however, local and district KOL assemblies across the country carried on a multitude of campaigns targeting local, state, and national offices during 1886. Independent labor parties made impressive showings in Chicago, St. Louis, and New York.

The Milwaukee People's Party elected a mayor, seven state legislators, and a congressman. A labor reform slate, backed by white workers and black Republicans, swept municipal elections in Richmond, Virginia. Southern congressional candidates did especially well as labor and vigorous new farmers' movements joined forces. Knights were elected to Congress in Virginia's fifth district and in North Carolina's fourth. In Ft. Worth, Texas, the Southern Farmers' Alliance and the KOL carried a relationship developed during the southwestern railroad strike into politics, demonstrating an electoral threat that pushed Republicans and Democrats into united opposition. In Arkansas's fourth district, a Greenback Knight sponsored by the Agricultural Wheel and the KOL also ran a strong second, and in Kentucky's sixth district, Knights almost unseated the Speaker of the House, a Bourbon free-trade Democrat unsympathetic to labor.[34] The spontaneity and geographical diversity of the 1886 efforts and the considerable strength they demonstrated against all the odds discouraging independent parties and candidates—especially those of the Left—appear to justify Leon Fink's description of this as "the American worker's single greatest push for political power."[35] But the political outpouring had no national organization and failed to build on the promise of 1886. Workers' interest in politics subsided even as that of farmers quickened.

Rather than support independent labor candidates, national KOL leaders urged their followers to exercise the franchise to punish labor's enemies and (less frequently) reward proven friends. In the 1886 congressional elections, the Knights' Washington representative, Ralph Beaumont, urged a massive labor turnout against Republican Rep. Thomas B. Reed of Maine's first and most urban district and his colleague Wilson Dingley of the second. However, in a harbinger of an AFL campaign twenty years later, both Reed and Dingley won, by even larger margins than two years earlier, apparently with the votes of many (if not most) of the workers of their districts. Beaumont took heart from the victories of fourteen of seventeen other incumbent congressional candidates, mostly Democrats, who had the Knights' endorsement, but labor support was not the decisive factor in most of these races. For example, James Weaver of Iowa had the nomination of both the Democratic and the Greenback Parties and, like most of the other fourteen victors, had strong farmer support.[36] The core of the group identified as labor's best friends in Congress was, in fact, agrarian.

One 1886 "labor victory" that revealed the dangerous dynamics of labor's position in national politics was the defeat of Democratic Rep. William Morrison of southern Illinois. The chairman of the House Ways and Means Committee, Morrison had not been considered friendly to KOL-backed legislation, but his defeat was actually engineered by Pennsylvania iron magnates and the Republican National Committee, who resented Morrison's free-trade stance. As part of their campaign against him, they arranged to have a Pittsburgh labor leader (John Jarrett of the Iron and Steel Workers) who belonged to a manufacturer-led high-tariff association speak against Morrison in his district. Though Powderly himself—reflecting his Pennsylvania origins— had protectionist sympathies, he studiously avoided any public personal or organizational commitment on the divisive tariff issue. This was, however, fast becoming the paramount issue in congressional and presidential politics. The Knights' Washington representatives watched in dismay as conflicts over the tariff monopolized legislative attention in 1887–88 and split the KOL-backed cohort into partisan antagonists.[37]

The looming tariff issue worked against both the Democratic Party (which must have regretted having pressed it) and independent labor politics even as it benefited the party of protection. In the national elections of 1888, the Republicans trumpeted the benefits of the tariff for labor and put Jarrett and other labor leaders on the stump for the GOP. Pittsburgh LA 300 contributed money and volunteer labor to Benjamin Harrison, and Charles Litchman of Massachusetts, elected general secretary of the KOL in 1878, resigned his post to campaign for the Republican ticket. The GOP offered Powderly the newly created Commissioner of Labor post in Washington if he would agree to speak out in defense of protection, and the KOL leader apparently gave serious consideration to the secret offer. Meanwhile, the GOP distributed an early favorable speech of Powderly's, much to the dismay of the Knights' strongholds in the South.[38]

The Union Labor Party (ULP) was formed in 1887 by members of the Farmers' Alliance, Agricultural Wheel, Greenbackers, Grangers, and a small and unofficial delegation of Knights. The majority of delegates were farmers. The convention's platform endorsed virtually the same combination of currency, land, transportation, election, labor, government ownership, and income-tax proposals as the earlier Greenback and Antimonopoly Parties. The purpose of the new movement, said delegate Alson J. Streeter, was "to organize labor [in the broadest sense as 'producers'] as capital is organized."[39] ULP candidates ran in state and local elections in 1887, doing best in rural areas and small municipalities but with a far less impressive showing than in the independent campaigns of 1886, when the labor movement was more unified and more politically mobilized at the grass-roots level. Locally, internecine strife within the labor movement and conflict with middle-class allies derailed independent labor politics in several big cities where the Socialists were strongest.[40]

In the 1888 national elections, the ULP ran Alson Streeter—a Greenbacker, a northern Farmers' Alliance leader, and a Knight to boot—for president and Charles E. Cunningham of Arkansas for vice-president. The ticket received 147,000 votes, 30,000 less than the 1884 Greenback candidate. Its support base was overwhelmingly agrarian, with the largest vote registered in Texas, Kansas, Missouri, Arkansas, and Iowa. Illinois manufacturer Robert H. Cowdrey, the candidate of the remnant of the urban labor reform organization, the United Labor Party, got a mere 2,800 votes for president, most of them in New York. In a political campaign polarized around the tariff, important northern labor allies who were affiliated with the Democrats—Albert Anderson and James Weaver of Iowa, Isidor Rayner of Maryland, Henry Smith of Wisconsin, and Timothy Tarsney of Michigan—were defeated by Republicans, and Knight John Nichols, who ran as a Republican in North Carolina, lost to a Democratic opponent.[41] As prospects for an independent labor block faded, the congressional agrarians were left as the diffuse custodians of labor's political agenda.

The Labor Lobby

Considering the divisiveness of the tariff issue and competing major-party loyalties for the KOL, Powderly preferred to concentrate the Order's political force on legislative lobbying. In the mid-1880s, state and local KOL assemblies made abundant use of their right to petition Congress, and the *Congressional Record* abounds with memorials presented on the Knights' behalf by senators and representatives. Sen. Benjamin Harrison, for example, introduced eight petitions from Indiana Knights during one session. Representative Weaver of Iowa presented seven, from Iowa and several other states.[42] A KOL-backed proposal for the creation of a federal bureau of labor to gather and analyze labor statistics was passed in 1884.[43] In the same year, KOL leaders made their first appearance before a congressional committee to argue for an end to foreign contract labor. Headquarters asked members to write Congress on behalf of the limitation and presented petitions with thousands of signatures.[44] The recommended bill passed easily in 1885 and was strengthened with more elaborate enforcement mechanisms in 1887.[45]

At the peak of KOL membership in 1886, the General Assembly voted to create a three-man Legislative Committee to reside in Washington when Congress was in session. Powderly appointed Ralph Beaumont, a labor journalist and shoemaker from Elmira, New York, along with James Campbell, a Pittsburgh glass blower, and John J. McCartney, a Baltimore carpenter. Beaumont was the major figure on the committee and shared Powderly's policy leanings. The list of bills the KOL committee decided to target must have delighted the Knights' agrarian supporters. Of the eight proposals endorsed, six involved land concerns: government reclamation of railroad and other land grants, repeal of timber and desert land acts that favored large syndicates, settlement of a portion of the Sioux Indian reservation and of Indian Territory, and a prohibition on landownership by aliens. The other two bills would have declared federal election days to be holidays and would have prescribed that $100 million of the current Treasury surplus be disbursed and U.S. Treasury notes be substituted for retired national bank notes (measures designed to expand the circulating medium and shift the control of money issue from private banks to the federal government).[46] These were controversial proposals, even within the Democratic Party.

In the politically momentous year of 1886, the attitude of the southern faction of the agrarian block toward federal power was still in flux and its implication for labor unclear. John Reagan of Texas was intent on establishing the right of Congress, under the interstate commerce clause, to regulate railroad freight charges and practices. When the Knights, beginning to lose a mammoth railroad strike in 1886, petitioned Congress to investigate labor conditions and create a federal mechanism to foster arbitration of labor disputes, Reagan argued that labor conflicts, unlike freight charges, were local matters that could, and should, be handled by the states—a position that opponents of his regulation bill found surprising and hypocritical.[47] Reps. James Morgan of Mississippi and John Rogers of Arkansas joined Reagan in opposing the arbitration bill on constitutional grounds, and twenty-two southern Democrats voted against the federal arbitration bill on final House passage.[48]

This opposition represented an antebellum constitutional position now rapidly being eroded. Most members of Congress were unwilling to let constitutional scruples stand in the way of a positive government effort to deal with the growing problems of an industrial age, particularly when those problems involved railroads, the lifelines of commerce. Nor were they willing to ignore the petitions for action that were flowing in from an organization of seven hundred thousand workers distributed around the country. Even Senator Harrison, not a prominent friend of labor, presented the KOL arbitration petition to his chamber, and other representatives voiced the opinion that the wishes of such a massive organization could not be ignored. During floor debate on the investigation, Rep. Andrew Curtin of Pennsylvania announced, "I hold in my hand a letter from Mr. Powderly," to which the cry went up, "Read it!" He proceeded to read into the *Record* Powderly's request for an investigation of labor conditions, to which the House promptly agreed.[49] The KOL-endorsed bill provided for federally supported arbitration boards with three members—one each chosen by labor and capital and a third chosen by them jointly—to settle railroad disputes. The bill passed the House 199 to 30; though, as noted, 22 southern Democrats composed the bulk of the small opposition, the majority of the South's vote went for the bill. The delegation from Texas—one of the states most affected by the 1886 strike and the locus of a budding collaboration between members of the KOL and the Farmers' Alliance—voted 6 to 1 for the federal arbitration initiative, leaving Reagan alone in opposition.[50]

When the bill reached the Senate floor, Richard Coke of Texas kicked off the debate with an impassioned defense of labor unions as the necessary counterpart to organized capital. Labor organizations of the day might be "crude and untrained," Coke admitted, "but time will bring them the wisdom of experience and discipline." His own bias was clear and, in contrast to Reagan's position, hinted at the potential for a farmer-labor alliance.[51]

The strike was over (and lost) before the Senate could pass the arbitration bill. However, the bill was passed in the next session, only to be vetoed by President Grover Cleveland.[52] Cleveland opposed the creation of the voluntary ad hoc arbitration boards favored by labor and demanded a permanent, presidentially appointed commission. Senator Coke had spoken out against this alternative in 1886, arguing that presidential control and location in Washington would deny labor its right to participate in the construction of the boards and might well make the arbitration commission "a tool of corporate interests."[53] Nevertheless, to avoid another veto when it revisited the issue in 1888, Congress appended to the ad hoc arbitration mechanism a provision allowing the president to appoint three commissioners (including the commissioner of labor) to investigate railroad labor disputes. In other respects, the arbitration section of the 1888 law was essentially the same as the measure endorsed by the KOL two years earlier. It passed Congress easily, with only a few mild constitutional objections and now with the strong support of John Reagan.[54]

Congress meanwhile continued to conduct its own investigations of labor disputes and to issue reports much more sensitive to the conditions of workers, and favorable to their organizations, than the reports of executive commissions or the dicta of judges.[55]

"The Three Great Questions of the Future":
Land, Transportation, Finance

With the exception of the strike arbitration bill, the remarkable feature of the KOL political agenda in 1885–87 was its limited "labor" content and the pervasive agrarian character of most of the bills endorsed. Powderly himself has been described as a "land crank." Influenced by the dispossession of the Irish in their homeland, he often emphasized the land question in his addresses to the General Assembly and persuaded that body to adopt various land proposals during the 1884–89 period.[56] Federally owned land should be reserved for actual settlers, not sold to corporation speculators or alien landlords. Land that was granted to railroads and that was not actually used for railroad purposes should be reclaimed and distributed to settlers. Lawrence Goodwyn has described Powderly in this period as having fallen "almost wholly under the ideological sway" of Charles Macune, leader of the Farmers' Alliance, whom he had gotten to know during the two men's Washington lobbying efforts.[57] However, Powderly had his own reasons for supporting these policies.

Edward T. James suggests that the focus on land and other agrarian issues might have been perceived as a way of enlisting farmer members in the KOL, especially as the conflict with the trade unionists escalated and urban membership began to decline. Beaumont estimated that recruitment in the rural sections could bring the Order one million new members within a year.[58] It is plausible that an agrarian strategy would have appealed to a KOL leadership beset by hostile trade unionists, lost strikes, and urban membership losses at a time when the farmers were just getting fired up and when rural organization of workers and farmers into the KOL was undergoing a remarkable expansion.

However, the KOL leaders themselves were steeped in the Greenback and antimonopoly reform movements of the 1870s, and they and their members shared in the broad national debates on land, railroads, and banking and currency—"the three great questions of the future," as Beaumont labeled them in 1886.[59] Even FOTLU had passed a resolution against landownership by foreigners and added a platform plank on railroad land forfeiture, and New York's Central Labor Union agitated on land and money questions in the 1880s.[60] There was widespread recognition that the Homestead, Timber Culture, and Desert Land Acts had encouraged speculation and had handed over vast tracts at a pittance to large corporations, western cattle barons, and absentee landlords. Although farmers had the most direct grievances here, the urban worker too was victimized, both as a worker and as a citizen.

Similarly, the volume of money in circulation, the flexibility of its supply, the level of interest rates, and the control of note issue were burning public questions, widely believed to be intimately connected to the degree of prosperity and broad distribution of wealth the country might enjoy. Why should not organized labor have its say on such questions? Were these issues not, in the long run, at least as important as eight-hour bills and the like? The railroad debate shared this broad aspect. The availability of fair and dependable rail service affected the viability of the smaller towns and cities where many workers resided and the disposable income of the farmers and town dwellers who purchased their products. More directly, a million rail workers had reason to expect that federal control or ownership would net them better treatment than they received at the hands of Jay Gould, Tom Scott, and Cornelius Vanderbilt.

The Decline of the Knights of Labor

To maintain the loyalty of its members, the KOL had to deliver more than education and solidarity. It must, from the workers' perspective, help them win strikes against recalcitrant employers. The number of strikes went up almost 50 percent from 1884 to 1885 and more than doubled from 1885 to 1886 as the recession lifted. Over four hundred thousand workers were involved in strikes in 1886.[61] Even though this mid-eighties strike wave ballooned the Order's membership, the Knights could not possibly amass sufficient resources to support a large number of strikes in a given year, so its panicky leadership was determined to discourage such actions.[62] The appeal to Congress to establish federal strike mediation machinery in 1886 was one aspect of this effort.

In the spring of 1886 another strike broke out in Gould's southwestern railway empire. This time, however, the skilled engineers, firemen, brakemen, and conductors of the craft-based railroad brotherhoods refused to join. Public support rapidly waned with the inconvenience of traffic paralysis. Local Knights ignored Powderly's order to go back to work as a prelude to possible mediation, and violence flared. With the help of state militias, local police, and Pinkertons, the strike was finally crushed by May 1886. By late summer, there was very little left of the KOL on the southwestern railroads; four-fifths of the strikers were discharged, never to work the Gould system again.[63]

A few weeks after the southwestern capitulation, a special KOL assembly was called. The KOL's officers persuaded the General Assembly to forbid strikes, absent a two-thirds secret ballot vote of the local or district members and (if the Order's financial assistance was hoped for) approval by the general executive board. Powderly himself admitted that employers took advantage of the new policy, ordering over two hundred lockouts with perceived impunity, since the KOL locals were thus hamstrung. Still, he refused to support Chicago packinghouse workers in their strike for the eight-hour day, and he took actions that undercut the striking workers. In the following year the Order's national strike assistance fund was abolished altogether, leaving local and district assemblies to their own devices.[64] The "no strike" policy did untold damage to the KOL's standing among workers, and the Knights' reputation was further damaged by Powderly's steadfast refusal to participate in the movement for clemency for the accused Haymarket anarchists (one of whom was a Chicago Knight).[65]

The combination of lost strikes, the Haymarket furor, the bitter competition with trade unionists, and an organized counteroffensive by employers was disastrous for the KOL.[66] Membership declined as meteorically as it had risen. From 703,000 in 1886, it dropped to 510,000 in 1887, 260,000 in 1888, 221,000 in 1889, and about 100,000 in 1890. Membership estimates become quite unreliable at this point, but Jonathan E. Garlock posits figures of around 74,000 for 1893 and just over 50,000 in 1896.[67] Norman J. Ware, Philip S. Foner, and other labor historians have perceived inexorable decline after 1886; in Ware's opinion, the KOL was "dead" by 1893.[68] The formation of new local assemblies tells a somewhat different story. The number of LAs formed was up 25 percent between 1886 and 1887, even as aggregate membership dropped. As Garlock shows, three thousand new LAs were organized between 1888 and 1896.[69] What is clear is that membership size and structure changed drastically after the 1886 peak, and KOL politics evolved in the unmistakable direction of agrarianism.

In 1886, a bare majority of the new LAs formed were in small to medium-sized cities and large metropolitan areas; by 1890, 76 percent of new LAs were organized in villages and hamlets. Collaboration with the Southern Farmers' Alliance (both white and colored wings) was a spur to rural organization. Many mixed-occupation and farmer-farmworker LAs were formed in the strong Alliance states of Texas and North Carolina, and in 1887 one-third of all new LAs organized had farmer or farmworker bases. Revived organization among coal miners also contributed heavily to the post-1886 "ruralization" of the KOL, with particular successes in the more isolated coalfields, where mine, farm, and railroad workers formed common organizations.[70]

In part, this shift in geographic balance indicated the better fit between the KOL's philosophy and the small-community ethic; in part, it reflected the greater organizational competition for the workers' allegiance in larger cities, as well as the cross-pressures arising from the metropolitan political economy and perhaps a stronger employer counteroffensive there.[71] It is clear, Garlock has written, "that the Knights were especially suited to organizing in non-metropolitan communities where an inter-trade focus had special appeal . . . and where the order's penchant for political solutions to labor problems had practical significance, especially in conjunction with alliance to agricultural movements."[72] In large cities, the KOL appealed to the unskilled and industrial workers largely ignored by the trade unions.[73] It was here that the Order's inadequate strike support and increasingly macroeconomic and agrarian legislative focus were probably most costly in the long run, though the contribution of local factionalism and organized employer hostility as factors in the KOL decline in urban areas cannot be ignored. Within a year of its summer 1886 peak, the KOL had lost 176,000 members in nine northeastern cities—118,000 in Boston, Philadelphia, and New York alone.[74] Table 3.2 suggests a hierarchy of regional losses: most severe in large industrial cities; slower in smaller cities (and the Midwest); slowest in the periphery.

John R. Commons and his coauthors argue that the geographic shifts in the KOL's membership base left it "an organization predominantly of country people, of mechanics, small merchants and farmers" and that this membership transformation "serves, more than anything else, to account for the subsequent close affiliation between the Order and the Farmers' Alliance, as well as for the whole hearted support which it gave to the Peoples Party."[75] However, this argument misrepresents both membership structure and the Order's programmatic trajectory. The distribution of total LAs was about evenly divided between urban and rural (defined as less than eight thousand population) in the mid-1890s, but the average size of urban LAs far exceeded that of rural units, so that membership no doubt remained predominantly urban.[76] Thus, despite its rural tilt after 1886 as rural organizing helped to counteract urban decline, the KOL could still claim to be the voice of organized urban workers until at least 1890 (when the more regionally and occupationally concentrated AFL surpassed it in membership), and it remained more urban-industrial than rural even in the last phase of its life. It was simply a much more diverse and inclusive organization than any other American labor body before or since. Its ideology and politics were, indeed, more "agrarian" after 1886, but a broadly reformist republicanism and concern with land and money issues had characterized the KOL well before its presumed ruralization and would understandably have received renewed emphasis in the late 1880s and early 1890s, when farm organizations took the lead in organizing a national reform movement.

Table 3.2 Membership Decline in Selected Knights of Labor District Assemblies

DA	Location	July 1886	July 1888	Percentage decline
1	Philadelphia	51,557	2,314	
3	Pittsburgh	8,472	6,103	
24	Chicago	12,868	3,507	
30	Boston[a]	81,191	9,179	
49	New York City	60,809	15,421	
51	Newark, NJ	10,958	491	
57	Chicago	7,389	761	
95	Hartford, CT	14,148	1,379	
99	Providence, RI	11,512	556	
	Total	258,904	39,711	84.7
63	Rochester, NY	606	809	
68	Troy, NY	9,520	2,730	
77	Lynn, MA	10,838	358	
90	Trenton, NJ	1,867	857	
130	Reading, PA	5,360	1,065	
168	Harrisburg, PA	1,480	582	
	Total	29,671	6,401	78.4
47	Cleveland, OH	3,576	2,469	
48	Cincinnati, OH	6,458	4,527	
50	Detroit, MI	4,615	1,356	
53	San Francisco, CA	1,618	226	
72	Toledo, OH	2,109	1,252	
108	Milwaukee, WI	7,724	595	
	Total	26,100	10,425	60.1
69	Cherryvale, KS[b]	2,646	1,043	
78	Galveston, TX	7,423	3,678	
79	St. Paul, MN	7,535	3,490	
82	Denver, CO	4,663	2,120	
84	Richmond, VA	2,934	495	
98	Butte City, MT	896	437	
102	New Orleans, LA	3,539	4,659	
105	Atlanta, GA	2,551	365	
107	Kansas City, MO	1,990	719	
132	Chattanooga, TN	1,808	546	
145	Texarkana, TX	555	133	
	Arkansas State Ass'n	2,645	3,035	
	Total	39,185	20,720	47.1

Source: Knights of Labor, *Proceedings of the General Assembly, 1886* (Richmond) and *1888* (Indianapolis).

[a] DA 30 was merged into a Massachusetts State Association in 1888; the 1888 figure is for the state assembly.

[b] Listed as Scammonville, KS, in 1888.

In the years after 1886 the *Journal of United Labor* devoted increasing attention to land and money questions and to national politics generally, printing congressional vote breakdowns on bills in which it had an interest. The KOL collaborated with the lobby of the Southern Farmers' Alliance, and except for its campaign for an effective eight-hour law on government work (which labor waged without the support of farm organizations), it mostly pressed demands that coincided with the Alliance's.[77] The Knights' General Assembly meeting in Atlanta in November 1889 gave an enthusiastic welcome to FA officers, who regaled the Knights with the farmers' economic woes and solicited their help in the coming battle against concentrated wealth. Powderly's reply rang with emotion as he pledged that the "ranks of organized producers" would fight together.[78] He, Beaumont, and A. W. Wright accepted the farmers' invitation to attend their convention in St. Louis the following month. Out of this meeting emerged a KOL endorsement of the program of the Southern Farmers' Alliance (now renamed the National Farmers' Alliance and Industrial Union in deference to its labor alliance ambitions)—a program centered on bimetallism, greenbacks, land for settlers, an end to commodity speculation, and nationalization of communications and transportation.[79]

The *Journal of United Labor* hailed this "treaty of the tillers and toilers" as a combination of two and a half million voters that would "cause monopolies to shudder before its mighty power . . . destined to unite the industrial forces in one great army of reformers that will sweep away the last robbing combinations from the face of this country."[80] But despite local enthusiasm for the farmer-labor alliance and a growing support (as measured by local assembly petitions and memorials printed in the *Journal*) for the farmers' financial program, Powderly kept his distance as the farmers' movement built toward a third party.

National KOL officers and local delegations did attend the Alliance-sponsored conventions of reformers that met in 1891–92 to agonize over national political strategy; the KOL thus differed from the AFL, which would have nothing to do with the Alliance, northern or southern. However, Powderly continued to emphasize that such participation was by individuals only, with no implied organizational commitment. Although the Knights' presence was dwarfed by representatives of farm organizations, the resultant platforms and resolutions did reflect labor concerns.[81] The *Journal of United Labor* printed the Populist Party platform and its ringing preamble on page one, highlighting Powderly's enthusiastic welcome by the Populist delegates at Omaha.[82] Yet despite open endorsement of Weaver by the KOL leaders, Powderly did very little to mobilize labor votes for the Populist ticket. Instead, he expended his political energies in local Pennsylvania politics (where he backed GOP candidates) and in delivering occasional anti-Democratic harangues that delighted the Republicans.[83] On the eve of the 1892 election, Powderly agreed to address a Populist rally in New York City, but his speech there constituted more an attack on the Democrats than an endorsement of populism.[84]

It is doubtful that a strong effort by Powderly—who now presided over an organization of around eighty thousand members—would have made any difference in the 1892 results. The Populist ticket drew less than 2 percent of the vote in the northeastern industrial states, which meant that only an insignificant percentage of urban workers had responded to the party's appeal for a producer alliance against capital. But there were reformers of national vision within the KOL, as well as politically minded local assemblies convinced that the KOL could still make a difference in national politics, and the onset of severe depression in 1893 strengthened their position. At the November 1893 General Assembly, Powderly was deposed by a coalition of New York Socialists led by Daniel De Leon (of DA 49) and other politically inclined delegates whom labor historians have labeled "agrarian."[85] James R. Sovereign, a labor journalist from Iowa who had worked as a cattle driver, marble carver, and labor statistician, was elected Grand Master Workman.[86]

Powderly's political timidity had been a major reason for his overthrow, and under Sovereign the Populist sympathies of the KOL blossomed. Crusades against bondholders benefiting from federal monetary policy and against worker oppression by injunction-issuing courts took the headlines of the *Journal of United Labor*. Attention to politics increased, along with stories detailing the increased concentration of wealth and much more favorable coverage of the People's (Populist) Party. Much outrage was expressed over the use of government troops against strikes and Jacob Coxey's "Army" of the unemployed, and great play was given to the Pullman strike, in which the KOL actively backed Eugene V. Debs and his American Railway Union (ARU).[87] A formal organizational affiliation was arranged with the ARU, and attempts were undertaken to unite, in a common front, the KOL, the AFL, the ARU, railroad brotherhoods, and the Alliance, both northern and southern.[88]

The KOL's devotion to populism was now unqualified. In 1896 the *Journal of United Labor* trumpeted its endorsement of William Jennings Bryan and a "Call to Action" by Ignatius Donnally. A huge headline in the last issue before the 1896 election asked: "How Can Any Workingman Vote for McKinley?"[89] In contrast to Powderly's reticence in 1892, Sovereign stumped the country for Bryan. But the contrast was sharper than that. Powderly

stumped for William McKinley in 1896,[90] and the majority of industrial workers, ignoring the call of the much-diminished KOL, apparently followed his
lead.

Socialists: Urban and Rural

Every thinking Socialist in this country ought to be glad that
the farmer element of America is revolutionary, and apt to
listen to new ideas.

      Victor Berger to Henry Demarest Lloyd, January 11, 1897

As the Knights of Labor and then the Farmers' Alliance and the Populists
declined, the Socialist Party appeared to inherit many of their members, their
broad reform spirit, and their programs. But before that could happen, it was
necessary to steal socialism away from the isolated and doctrinaire leaders of
the Socialist Labor Party (SLP) and "Americanize" it by moving it west and
south.

    The SLP, founded by mostly German immigrants in the mid-1870s, re-
fined its doctrinaire tendencies with the ascension to leadership of Daniel De
Leon. De Leon, born in Curaçao, had come to the United States by way of
Germany in the early 1870s. He studied international law and became a lecturer at Columbia University. In 1890, he joined the Socialist Labor Party
as a national lecturer, and in 1892, he assumed leadership of the party and
editorship of its English-language newspaper, *The People*. After taking over
the SLP, De Leon set out to use his New York Socialist base to gain control
of the Knights of Labor. With the aid of the city's United Hebrew (garment)
Trades and other Socialist-led unions, De Leon got himself elected delegate
to the 1893 KOL General Assembly from New York's DA 49. There he led
the Socialist Knights into a short-lived alliance with pro-Populist forces and
helped to elect James Sovereign as Grand Master Workman. When Sovereign
refused to appoint De Leon's SLP ally to the editorship of the KOL journal,
the New Yorker "declared war" on the Knights. By 1895 tensions had reached
the point that members of the De Leon clique were refused seats at the
Knights' General Assembly. De Leon then ordered the thirteen thousand
members of the unions he controlled to leave the KOL.[91]

    Even before the break with Sovereign, the New York Socialists had shown
little regard for populism. In 1892 the SLP had run its own candidate for
president, drawing 21,157 votes (86 percent coming from New York State).[92]
In the summer of 1893 the SLP had declared the "misnamed People's Party"
merely an attempt "to transfer to the small farmers a considerable portion of

the plunder heretofore chiefly levied by the plutocratic class upon the wage working masses." Farmers represented a "hybrid and transitory class that is doomed to dispossession and disappearance through the action of economic forces evolved by the modern system of production," along with a faction of "precarious" landowners and "small adventurers in manufactures and commerce." Workers must resist the appeals made by this doomed class.[93] The People's Party was a "middle class corruption." "Nothing short of Socialism" was the SLP's slogan in politics.[94]

Outside the Northeast, socialists were not so scrupulous. In the Great Lakes region, industry and agriculture met, unleashing, in hard times, a melange of reform forces from which socialists found it difficult to remain aloof. Populism was much milder here than to the south and west, as farmers were generally less hard-pressed; but in the devastating depression of 1893–96, downstate farmers looked to urban workers for political allies. With their large and well-organized voting base, Chicago workers were not shy about pressing their demands on farmers. When Illinois Populists invited the state Labor Federation to a reform conference at Springfield in the summer of 1894, a Chicago labor delegation headed by Englishman Thomas J. Morgan accepted the call. Like the trade unionists who ignored the AFL leadership's warning not to traffic with Populists, the Chicago socialists went to Springfield in defiance of the New York SLP leadership. But Morgan was determined to secure from the Populists endorsement of a socialist political agenda as the price of SLP support.[95] The program, modeled on that of British trade unionists and influenced by the 1892 Populist Party platform, advocated independent political action and listed eleven demands to be pressed on the local and national state: (1) compulsory education; (2) direct legislation (the initiative); (3) a legal eight-hour workday; (4) sanitary inspection of workshop, mine, and home; (5) liability of employers for injury to health, body, or life; (6) abolition of the contract system in all public works; (7) abolition of the sweating system; (8) municipal ownership of streetcars and of gas and electric plants; (9) nationalization of the telegraph, telephones, railroads, and mines; (10) the collective ownership by the people of all means of production and distribution; and (11) the principle of referendum in all legislation. The Populist conference endorsed ten of the socialist planks but adamantly refused to accept the critical plank, #10. Morgan went home in disgust.[96]

However, this was not the final blow for farmer-labor-socialist politics in Illinois. The Illinois State Labor Federation called a second "industrial conference"—attended, like the first, by Knights, trade unionists, Populists, socialists, anarchists, and single taxers. Morgan again presented his socialist platform, but plank #10 was defeated 59 to 49, with the farmer, single-taxer, anarchist, and conservative trade-union delegates in opposition. That might have been the end of the experiment, but this region had long been home to a class of public intellectuals skilled in connecting farmer and labor radicalism. Henry Demarest Lloyd, a well-to-do Chicago journalist, labor advocate, and Fabian socialist, devised a compromise. In lieu of plank #10's unambiguous commitment to collectivization, his substitute pledged the constituent organizations to "vote for those candidates of the People's Party . . . who will pledge themselves to the principle of the collective ownership by the people of all such means of production and distribution *as the people elect to operate for the commonwealth*" (emphasis added). This the farmers and the more conservative unionists interpreted as requiring an explicit electoral authorization (as in a referendum), and they assumed it would lead only to selective nationalization or municipal ownership of utilities. The socialists, however, could interpret the plank as a commitment to socialism. It was accepted, and the political alliance was forged.[97]

Labor-farmer conferences followed in other states, primarily in the midwestern, southwestern, and mountain regions. These efforts permitted Philip Foner to argue that in 1894, "A.F. of L. trade unionists, Socialists and Single-taxers worked wholeheartedly for the labor-Populist cause, each ignoring the warnings of their top leaders, Gompers, De Leon, and Henry George, to remain aloof from the third party movement."[98] But such unionists and Socialists were too few, and too unrepresentative of working-class sentiment nationally, to make a difference, and the Populists made a poor showing in most of the urban labor-Socialist strongholds. Though their electoral strength certainly increased from the 1892 level (and even reached one-fifth to one-third of the vote in Milwaukee and Minneapolis), the Populists drew only 12 percent in Chicago, 8 percent in Cleveland, and 3 percent in Detroit. Farther east, Boston registered 6 percent; Pittsburgh, 4 percent; Philadelphia, less than 1 percent.[99] In the state of New York, the Populist candidate for governor also got less than 1 percent of the vote. In New Jersey as well, the Populist gubernatorial vote was negligible. The industrial working class was, it seemed, immune to populism and, in all but a few local polities, to socialism, even in the midst of a severe depression.[100]

The Greening of American Socialism

De Leon's attacks on the AFL and formation of a rival Socialist trade-union organization led to a revolt among Socialists in the late 1890s. In New York, Morris Hillquit formed a new socialist party that repudiated De Leon's ban on Socialist membership in the AFL and took steps to join forces with other dissidents.[101] In Milwaukee, Austrian emigré Victor Berger had established an independent socialist party allied both with local trade unions and with a Milwaukee "People's Party" started by local Knights of Labor. In 1895 Berger forged a critical connection when he visited Eugene V. Debs in prison at Woodstock, Illinois, bearing as a gift Marx's *Das Kapital.*[102]

The figure who would merge—in his own persona—populism and socialism and become an apostle for a socialism rooted in American republican ideals, Debs had grown up in Terre Haute, Indiana (pop. 26,000 in 1880), and had been an active railroad unionist, journalist, and Democrat from his youth. By 1895 he had abandoned the Democratic Party for populism, had been expelled from his old union (the Brotherhood of Locomotive Firemen), and was scorned by the AFL. His broad-based American Railway Union was crushed by the General (railroad) Managers Association in concert with the federal government, and Debs was imprisoned for interfering with the mails and disrupting interstate commerce during the ARU's strike against the Pullman Company. Thus he came to socialism via trade unionism, midwestern Democracy, populism, and industrial unionism. Debs was the kind of broad-gauged, inclusive reformer, steeped in republican ideals, who could build into socialism the traditions and values of native American radicalism. The only credential he lacked in that respect was an early Greenback affiliation, but the Greenback-Populist animus against corporate monopoly was ingrained in his thought by 1895, sharpened by his own experience.[103] What is more, as his biographer Nick Salvatore has shown, he shared the agrarian zest for electoral politics. Strikes might be crushed by the combined power of the giant corporations and their allies in the state, but the ballot was the worker's birthright, "a weapon that executes a free man's will as lightning does the will of God." Speaking to the wildly enthusiastic crowds that greeted him on his release from prison, Debs preached the redemptive power of the ballot. "There is nothing in our government," he argued, "that it cannot remove or amend."[104]

In 1894 Debs endorsed the People's Party, from which the ARU had received support during the Pullman strike. In 1896 he was the first choice of the mainline Populists for their party's presidential nomination, and at least a third of the convention delegates were pledged to support him. However, in the interest of unity among the reform forces, he demurred and urged his supporters to back Bryan. Debs was, in fact, the most prominent labor leader (besides Sovereign) to endorse Bryan. Even as Gompers remained studiously neutral and Berger condemned Bryan's program, Debs undertook an extended speaking tour for the Nebraskan in the month before the election.

With scarcely a word about socialism, he argued that bimetallism was the immediate solution to the problems of unemployment and industrial conflict that beset labor.[105]

After the election, Debs publicly embraced socialism and, with a remnant of his followers from the ARU, joined with Berger and his allies to form a new Social Democratic Party in 1898. The party's thirty-three founding members were from Illinois, Indiana, and Wisconsin; the membership base lay among SLP defectors in Milwaukee, Massachusetts, and St. Louis. The midwestern and northeastern factions (including Hillquit's New York SLP group) managed to unite behind the presidential candidacy of Debs in 1900 and ultimately consummated a merger as the Socialist Party in 1901, with headquarters in St. Louis.[106] Spurred by recession following the panic of 1907 and a swelling urban and rural reform tide inadequately addressed by the major parties, the SP grew rapidly in the 1908–12 period. It would reach its peak electoral significance in 1912 with just under 6 percent of the national vote and a membership of over 113,000 (see table 3.3). At this point the party could boast over 1,000 state and local officials and one U.S. congressman.[107]

Table 3.3 Socialist Party Membership and Vote, 1900–1916

	Reported SP Membership	Vote	
		SP	SLP
1900	5,000	96,931	33,405
1901	10,000		
1902		223,494	53,765
1903	15,975		
1904	20,763	408,230	33,546
1905	23,327		
1906	26,784	331,043	20,265
1907	29,270		
1908	41,751	424,488	14,021
1909	41,479		
1910	58,011	607,674	34,115
1911	84,716		
1912	113,371	901,062	30,344
1913	95,401		
1914	93,579	874,691	21,827
1915	79,374		
1916	83,284	597,000	14,398

Source: American Labor Year Book, 1916 (New York: Rand School of Social Sciences), 94–97; *1917– 18*, 340. The 1900–1901 membership figures are from Morris Hillquit, *History of Socialism in the United States*, 5th ed. (New York: Dover Publications, 1971) 304, 308.

The presence of Debs at the head of the ticket, expounding a political rhetoric more derivative of Jefferson, Lincoln, and Protestant Christianity than of Marx, brought to the national party many homegrown socialist organizations and thousands of individual voters and political activists who were veterans of the Farmers' Alliance, the KOL, the Populist Party, and the American Railway Union.[108] Although he was inevitably drawn into intraparty conflicts, the role Debs set out for himself was as an evangelist for socialism rather than an architect and manager of a political organization. His métier was to storm the country in the party's "Red Special" train in the weeks before a national election and to inspire crowds in places as geographically and culturally distant as New York's Cooper Union and Socialist encampments in rural Oklahoma and Texas. Berger, the SP's consummate organization man, ensconced in his Milwaukee city machine, was contemptuous of Debs's evangelical activities and the eclectic doctrine on which they were based. Berger represented the "right-wing" faction in Socialist Party debates on such issues as the relationship with the Industrial Workers of the World (IWW), racial and ethnic equality, criticism of Gompers's leadership of the AFL, and promotion of industrial unionism; Debs was aligned with the left wing, and the radical tendency in the SP was strongest in the South and West.[109]

The SP, like the KOL and the Populist Party, was receptive to women and African Americans, who were largely ignored by the craft unions. In Oklahoma the SP fought against suffrage restriction, and everywhere the party campaigned to enfranchise women. Socialists were not, however, immune to racism. In the South and Southwest, race was one of the two issues (the other being landownership) that sorely tested Socialists. Although blacks were admitted to mixed locals in Texas and Oklahoma, most southern parties were afraid to actively recruit blacks for fear of losing white supporters, and the northern SP organizers who held prominent positions in the southern parties often had stronger race prejudices than their southern counterparts. For their time and place, one may say that the southern Socialists were remarkably, even heroically, progressive.[110] At the national level, Debs was a strong voice for biracial organization and racial brotherhood; Berger, on the other hand, was a strident racist. Racial and ethnic bias also infected the party's stance on immigration. Socialists in the Pacific Coast region were strongly opposed to Asian immigration, and most national SP leaders accepted racial arguments against admitting "unassimilated coolie" labor. In 1910, after a heated debate, the party convention endorsed a resolution by Morris Hillquit that avoided overt racial exclusion but backed legislation "to prevent the immigration of strike-breakers and contract laborers and the mass immigration from foreign countries brought about by the employing classes for the purpose of weakening of American labor."[111]

Debs's appeal to farmers, miners, railroad, and timber workers set the stage for a remarkable expansion of socialism in states west of the Mississippi. Hardened in violent conflicts with powerful corporations, western miners and lumberjacks were militant, class-conscious unionists. Though sympathetic to the KOL and populism, the westerners were more inclined to anarchosyndicalism than to political action, and they saw the electoral process more as a check on the use of local and state police against strikers than as a means toward socialism or immediate legislative reforms. Because of his belief in industrial unionism, and his frustration at the AFL's reluctance to organize the unskilled, Debs was an early supporter of attempts by the Western Federation of Miners (WFM) to form a new umbrella labor organization. In 1905, a group of western labor leaders and left Socialists (including Debs and De Leon) met in Chicago to form the Industrial Workers of the World. The IWW connection brought thousands of coal and metal miners, southwestern timber workers, and other unionists to socialism. However, the IWW and the SP soon clashed over the possibilities for political reform, the IWW's raiding of other unions, and its refusal to condemn violence and sabotage. In 1912, the SP adopted a constitutional amendment to expel any member who advocated such tactics, and the following year Bill Haywood, the leading IWW organizer, was recalled from the Socialist Party Executive Committee because of his refusal to disavow sabotage. The votes against Haywood came mainly from the northeastern states and Wisconsin, but even Debs, who had long defended the IWW in SP councils, concurred in Haywood's removal.[112]

In the Southwest, the growing impoverishment of farmers and the industrial-union organizing by the WFM and IWW engendered a growing radicalism that swelled the Socialist vote. After the decline of populism and then the Farmers' Union, many agrarian radicals in Oklahoma, Texas, Louisiana, Alabama, and Missouri found a new home in the Socialist Party. The rise of large-scale timber operations, the western spread of the cotton economy, and the expansion of farm tenancy—the latter reaching 54 percent in the Southwest by 1910—provided fertile ground for a native socialism. As James Green has shown, Debs's strongest support here came from the poorest farm and piney woods districts in southern Oklahoma, north-central and northeastern Texas, and western Louisiana and from the farm and coal-mining counties of southwestern Kansas and western Arkansas. Like the Populists, Socialists were found disproportionately among single-crop producers in small, poor, and isolated communities. Both movements were fed by deep class resentments against landlords and bankers, lawyers, and merchants in the towns. Within its most successful state (Oklahoma), the SP vote was correlated positively with rurality, tenancy, and membership in fundamentalist churches and negatively with urbanization and value of farm property.[113]

Recruitment and communication in such areas were sustained to some extent through industrial unions such as the biracial Brotherhood of Timber Workers (which joined the IWW), the United Mine Workers (UMW) union, and the Renters' Union (of white tenant farmers). But the most important links were camp meetings and a dynamic regional Socialist press. The summer encampment—an activity common to rural religious revivals and to populism—was first appropriated by a Texas Socialist who was a veteran of such Populist affairs. The first Socialist camp meeting in rural northeastern Texas drew 4,000 people and lasted a week. By 1908 such meetings, featuring prominent regional and national Socialist speakers, along with study groups, barbecues, and Socialist skits and songs (put to old Populist tunes), were drawing up to 10,000 people and had become a major organizing device.[114]

By far the most successful Socialist newspaper in the United States was the *Appeal to Reason,* founded by Julius A. Wayland in 1895. Published in Girard, Kansas, and sold by an "Appeal Army" of some 80,000 volunteer salesmen, it had an average weekly circulation of almost 762,000 by 1913; the five major New York Socialist papers together reached only 252,000.[115] The *National Ripsaw,* a "semi-populist" Socialist magazine edited by Debs, Kate O'Hare, and Oscar Ameringer in St. Louis, enjoyed a national circulation of 150,000 and was popular with southwestern farmers and workers. The *Rebel,* a Socialist newspaper published in Halletsville, Texas, had, at over 26,000, a circulation that rivaled that of the *Milwaukee Leader.*[116]

Yet the more orthodox Socialists of the northern industrial states looked askance at the naivete and religious fervor of their rural comrades;[117] more fundamentally, they were disturbed about the whole notion of socialist farmers. Although Socialist organizers who spent any time in the region soon became aware that impoverished tenants and debt-laden yeomen farmers hardly fit the conventional Marxist description of petit-bourgeois capitalists, many of the party's urban Marxists were never able to bend their doctrine to accommodate a genuine rural outreach. This was even true of Socialist theoreticians who supported the party's endorsement of "immediate demands" and an evolutionary transition to socialism. At the SP unity convention in 1901, the delegates voted 82 to 30 to include immediate demands in their platform, but they quarreled bitterly over a proposal to include a list of "populist-tainted" farmer planks. The party's acknowledged "farm expert,"

Algie Martin Simons of Illinois, argued that farmers did not own the great national "tools" of production and transportation and that most had very low incomes; further, it was "absolutely ridiculous . . . to hope that you can ever accomplish anything without the [votes of the] farmers."[118] But for the majority of delegates, every farmer belonged to "the possessing class," and the interest of rural farmers and urban wageworkers were inherently antithetical. The Socialist Party, they thought, should not spend its energies in an attempt to save a class doomed to extinction. All mention of farmers was avoided in the first platform.[119]

For years, the most that official SP doctrine could offer farmers was government ownership of industry and transportation and the presumed advantages of collective farming over tenancy. After being fully proletarianized, they could become trade unionists and true Socialists. However, the *Appeal to Reason* and state parties in the Southwest maintained that the SP's commitment to the public ownership of "all means of production, distribution, communication and exchange" did not imply nationalization of all farms, only of certain monopolistic landholdings. The Oklahoma party appealed to both tenants and landowning farmers with a program of state-owned grain elevators and warehouses, tax exemptions for basic farm equipment and dwellings, state insurance against disaster, maximum interest rates, and loans to pay off mortgages. A group of southwestern and Wisconsin Socialists and farmer advocate A. M. Simons continued to lobby within the national organization for recognition of the farmer's plight and endorsement of programs geared to its amelioration. But at the 1908 SP convention, these delegates were unable to win acceptance for a set of farmer demands. Instead, the delegates voted 99 to 51 for a resolution pledging complete socialization of all land and urging the farmer to "study the economics of the cooperative social system."[120]

The 1908 platform was, in its concrete proposals, a program geared entirely to the perceived needs of urban labor. It condemned private ownership of land and mentioned the farmer only once, as someone "indirectly" exploited by large capital. The platform contained a long list of demands for workers: an eight-hour day and prevailing union wages on government work; unemployment assistance paid to labor organizations; loans to state and municipal governments for extensive public works; in industry, a shorter workday, a guaranteed day and a half of rest, and public health and safety inspection, prohibition of child labor, and compulsory health, life, and unemployment insurance. Railroads, telephones, telegraphs, steamship lines, mines, forests, oil wells, water-power facilities, "and all land" were to be collectivized; yet only those *industries* that were "organized on a national scale" and in which competition had "ceased to exist" were to be socialized, despite the fact, recognized in many convention speeches, that "trustification" had proceeded much more slowly in agriculture than in industry.[121]

In 1910 the southwestern Socialists again tried to win the national party's approval for their farm program. Delegate Oscar Ameringer presented the rationale of the Oklahoma Socialist Party's farm program and revealed the basis of its considerable appeal to the region's farmers—among whom, as his colleague Kate O'Hare emphasized, even the most revolutionary, class-conscious renters were "fighting tooth and nail to get forty acres of land":

> [The farmer] is exploited by the owners of the large means of production and distribution. He is exploited through the usury of the banks that are farming the farmer, and he is exploited by the owner of the land. Now, what we Socialists want to do is to put an end to exploitation. Do we not? Therefore we want the farmers to own the farms. We want them to be the owners of the means of production. We want to make it so that the farmer also can get the use of capital without being robbed by a usury class. . . . Do we want the common ownership of all land? No. What for? We have the common ownership of land in Oklahoma—of three million acres of school land. It is common property, and the farmer is a renter on the state land. The relationship is the most unsatisfactory you can imagine, for the farmer does not hold the land long enough to improve it by dwellings. All he does, is to exploit the soil and then move off afterwards. . . . The thing we want to do is to give the land to the man who uses the land. The fellow who doesn't use land—God bless his heart, he doesn't need any. . . . We in Oklahoma want every farmer who owns land and farms his land to keep it, and the more he works and produces, the better for us, and the more he improves it the better for mankind.[122]

But most of the delegates could not square the southwestern program with Socialist principles, which simply required, as Thomas Morgan insisted, that "private property [be] wiped out for the farmers as well as for every other class."[123] Even Berger, who had argued the political necessity of a farm program, opposed the demands, charging that the grant of long-term occupancy rights on public land to tenant farmers constituted "a long step toward permanent private property."[124]

Finally, in 1912, the national convention expressed some sympathy for farmer demands. A new section appeared in the platform's preamble, acknowledging that farmers in every state were "plundered by the increasing prices exacted for tools and machinery and by extortionate rents, freight rates and storage charges." The "working class" was defined to include those who worked on the soil. Several farm-oriented planks were added to the long list of immediate demands that constituted the SP's "working program." One proposed that cities, states, or the federal government take over all grain elevators, stockyards, and storage warehouses. The government should also take an active role in land reclamation and flood control. Finally, the platform called for "the collective ownership of land *wherever practicable*" (emphasis added) and, where not practical, for "confiscatory taxation of the profits of land held for speculation." This, then, was the substance of the Socialist "farm program," and significant parts of it would be gone by 1916.[125] As the election results showed, the program was not very competitive with what the Democrats—pushed to the left by the same social ferment—offered the farmers. And the winner-take-all electoral system operating in federal elections encouraged all but the most intensely committed to shift their votes to the closer major party.

Although the national farm program was not its long suit, the Socialist Party did share certain important orientations toward the state with earlier agrarian organizations. For example, and despite the predictable expansion of bureaucracy that would attend widespread socialization, the SP was quite enamored of direct democracy. Its platforms repeatedly endorsed (as had those of the Farmers' Alliance and the Populist Party) direct election of senators and the initiative and referendum. The SP extended the demand for direct elections to the presidency and vice-presidency and called for abolition of the presidential veto and of the Supreme Court's power to declare legislation unconstitutional. The lower federal courts were to be abolished, with state courts to assume jurisdiction over cases arising under diversity of citizenship. To these extensions the agrarians would doubtless have been sympathetic; for example, periphery congressmen preferred state jurisdiction over corporate abuses and had often proposed it in railroad regulation and antitrust initiatives. In 1917, the Socialists would join William Jennings Bryan in calling for a national referendum before a declaration of war. Urban Socialists and periphery agrarians were the factions most opposed to U.S. imperialism in general and to World War I in particular, and both opposed the creation of a professional continental army.[126]

The Socialist vote in the rural periphery was impressive in 1912 (see table 3.4), a measure of the appeal of the SP's strong stand against capitalist privilege and of the distress of the small farmer. Indeed, what is striking about the map of American socialism is its relative weakness in the northeastern industrial areas. Although, by virtue of its large population, New York usually held the largest number of party members, the percentage of the state's vote

Table 3.4 Socialist Strength by State (for 14 states with over 2,000 members)

State	Members 1914	% of SP Total	Presidential Vote, 1912	% of SP Total
New York	10,717	11.4	63,381	7.2
Pennsylvania	7,648	8.2	83,614	9.6
Oklahoma	7,039	7.5	42,262	4.8
Illinois	6,562	7.0	81,249	9.3
California	5,252	5.6	79,201	9.0
Minnesota	4,965	5.3	27,505	3.0
Massachusetts	4,830	5.2	12,662	1.4
Ohio	4,626	4.9	89,930	10.0
Wisconsin	3,885	4.2	33,481	3.8
New Jersey	3,364	3.6	15,928	1.8
Washington	3,241	3.5	40,134	4.6
Michigan	2,943	3.1	23,211	2.6
Texas	2,893	3.1	24,884	2.8
Indiana	2,222	2.4	36,931	4.2

Ranking by Percent State Vote for Debs, 1912

1 Oklahoma	(16.6)	9 Florida	(9.3)
2 Nevada	(16.5)	10 Ohio	(8.7)
3 Montana	(13.6)	11 Wisconsin	(8.6)
4 Arizona	(13.4)	12 Texas	(8.4)
5 Washington	(12.4)	13 Minnesota	(8.2)
6 California	(11.8)	14 N. Dakota	(8.0)
7 Idaho	(11.3)	15 Utah	(8.0)
8 Oregon	(9.7)	U.S.	(6.0)

Source: Part 1, *American Labor Yearbook,* 1916 (New York: Rand School of Social Sciences), 94–98. Part 2, *World Almanac and Encyclopedia, 1914,* 725.

given to the SP in 1912 was, at 4 percent, significantly below the national average and far behind the electoral enthusiasm of the plains and western states and of Florida, Texas, Louisiana, and Arkansas in the South. Oklahoma stands as the most Socialist state, with a 16.6 percent vote for Debs in 1912; two years later it boasted almost 53,000 Socialist voters (21 percent) and 38,000 *Appeal to Reason* subscribers—a record that few large industrial states approached. Oklahoma also had the most extensive state organizational network, with as many as 12,000 party members in 961 locals.[127]

There were four major regions of Socialist voting strength in 1912. From a wide fulcrum in the Pacific and Rocky Mountain states, one prong swept north through timber and mining counties to Lake Superior; another cut south through mining, agricultural, and piney woods counties to Florida. The fourth Socialist region was centered in the Midwest, with an urban-industrial gradient hugging Lake Michigan, Lake Erie, and the upper Mississippi River (Minneapolis) and a more diffuse and small-town/rural, manufacturing, and coal-mining cluster in eastern Ohio and west-central Pennsylvania. While the southern and western prongs had roots in populism and agrarian radicalism, Ohio and Pennsylvania Socialists, like their comrades in Minneapolis, Chicago, California, Wisconsin, and New York, had close connections with organized labor.[128]

In 1910 Berger's party won control of the Milwaukee city government with the help of the city's trade unionists; Berger himself was elected to Congress for the first of five terms. By the end of the 1911 state and local elections, 1,141 Socialists held office in some 324 municipal governments in thirty-six states. Several major cities had Socialist mayors or high-ranking city officials in this era: Milwaukee; Berkeley, California; Butte, Montana; Flint and Kalamazoo, Michigan; and Schenectady, New York.[129] But the more typical Socialist victories came in far smaller cities and towns: Winnfield, Louisiana; Conneaut and Martin's Ferry, Ohio; Hazeldell and Roulette, Pennsylvania; Coeur d'Alene, Idaho; Nederland, Colorado; Winslow, Arkansas; Tukwila, Washington; Antlers, Oklahoma; Pillager and Ten Strike, Minnesota; Red Cloud, Nebraska; and Arma, Kansas (surely towns with such names were destined to have Socialist governments!). In 1910, of 190 communities registering Socialist victories, 136 (72 percent) had less than 5,000 population; 77 (41 percent) had less than 1,000. In 1911, more urban states held elections, but 58 percent of Socialist victories came in places with under 5,000 population.[130]

About a third of the communities registering Socialist electoral successes in 1910–11 could be described as agricultural.[131] Most of the others, like Coshocton, Ohio, and New Castle, Pennsylvania, were home to paper, flour, or steel mills, coal mines, or other industrial and transportation enterprises whose technological innovations and distress in business recessions had a great impact on the community. In such towns scattered across the land, but particularly in the Midwest, the SP served as a vehicle for protests by workers, farmers, and not a few middle-class citizens outraged at local corruption and elite callousness in the midst of economic dislocation.[132]

At the 1912 national peak, 174 Socialist candidates ran in U.S. congressional races (for 435 House seats).[133] Of these, 61 got 10 percent or more of the vote, including 27 who ran in highly industrial districts (defined as $300 or higher per capita value added in manufacturing) and 12 in districts with barely any industry (less than $100 per capita). In the core industrial states of Massachusetts, Connecticut, New Hampshire, Rhode Island, New Jersey, and New York, only one Socialist candidate (Meyer London of New York

City) breached the 10 percent threshold, and he did so by abandoning unpopular Socialist doctrine and adopting the ward-heeling strategy of his Tammany opponent.[134] In fact, the party's performance in these core states was upstaged by its much more robust showing in a number of periphery and diverse states. In Oklahoma and California, every congressional race featured a Socialist candidate and all but two reached the 10 percent threshold. Nationwide, only sixteen Socialist congressional candidates got as much as 20 percent of the vote in 1912. Of the sixteen, half ran in urban industrial districts in the New York, Chicago, Milwaukee, Pittsburgh, Cincinnati, and San Francisco Bay areas. The other eight significant Socialist candidates ran in agricultural, timber, and mining districts of southern Kansas, southern Oklahoma, central Louisiana, western North Dakota, northwestern Minnesota, and Nevada, and in a rapidly growing Los Angeles, California.[135]

The difficulty of developing a national political program for this geographically sprawling party is obvious. From across a continent and from vastly different life experiences, urbane New York and midwestern intellectuals, proud of their mastery of Marxist dogma and their familiarity with European Socialist Party debates, confronted a rough-and-tumble southern and western contingent. The latter were more radical on *action*—being, for example, much more skeptical of gradualist, one-step-at-a-time socialism and craft unionism and more favorable to the IWW—but were less orthodox on *dogma*. And one of the most rigid tenets of Marxist dogma was its treatment of farmers. Periphery state parties that combined radical activism with a recognition of landholding rights and other practical populist-tinged state benefits for farmers and workers pushed at the upper limits of success for American socialism. But for workers and farmers attracted to political solutions, the SP offered a very constricted choice. The "constructivist" or "right-wing" Socialists, who believed profoundly in the possibilities of electoral politics but made little effort to bolster industrial unionism or to recruit excluded minorities, were wary of endorsing farmer demands and generally opposed cooperation with other reform movements or labor parties. The ideological left wing shared this refusal, if it found politics credible at all, and endorsed a drastic and rapid transition to socialism that few workers, and fewer farmers, were ready to accept.[136]

Among the proximate causes of the decline of socialism after its 1912–14 peak,[137] the most often cited are the winner-take-all electoral system, the preemption of reform by the Democratic Party, the repression by local and national governments, the alienation of important labor and intellectual allies provoked by SP opposition to World War I, and intraparty factionalism. The drop in presidential voting from 1912 to 1916 was surely related to the record of the first administration of Woodrow Wilson, when favorable legislation and appointments made the Democratic Party a more plausible reform vehicle for workers and farmers previously attracted to socialism.[138] When Wilson campaigned as the peace candidate in 1916, the Socialist presidential vote, without Debs on its ticket, dropped from 900,369 to 589,924 (from 6 to 3 percent).[139]

Under the Espionage Act of 1917 the federal government was empowered to censor and ban from the mails those newspapers that opposed the war effort, and Postmaster Albert Burleson construed his powers liberally. The ban on papers like the *Appeal* and the *Rebel* was devastating to rural Socialists with few alternative means of communication.[140] Strong resistance to the war in the periphery, involving thousands of active draft resisters, brought the full power of the state down on the rustic radicals.

A telling example of southwestern radicalism and its reception by both the authorities and the SP leadership can be seen in the "Green Corn Rebellion" that took place in Oklahoma in 1917. Several hundred poor farmers plotted a people's uprising against the war. They would march to Washington, gathering recruits along the way (it had been rumored that in Chicago alone, 190,000 industrial workers were ready to join their ranks). The rebels managed to dynamite a few railroad bridges and pipelines before being rounded up by local authorities. The organizers of the aborted uprising were convicted under the Espionage Act and sentenced to long prison terms. Although the Oklahoma SP had played no role in the affair (except to try to prevent it), thousands of Oklahoma Socialists were arrested in the aftermath. In a panic because Berger and the national SP executive committee were also on trial for their antiwar efforts, the state SP leadership decided to disband the Oklahoma Socialist Party in the hope of severing any connection between the national leaders and an actual antiwar conspiracy.[141] Thus was the party's most dynamic state organization mortally wounded by prowar hysteria and then sacrificed for the national leadership.

Even as rural Socialist organizations atrophied, big-city branches expanded as a result of immigration (see table 3.5). Thousands of new eastern European recruits tipped the balance in the SP once again toward a more northeastern, urban, and doctrinaire socialism. Although the Russian Revolution provided an emotional stimulus to Socialists everywhere, it created, in combination with the arrival of thousands of Russian, Finnish, Polish, and Hungarian Socialists, serious new tensions in the SP. The party had always been factionalized, but the effects of the war sharpened the differences be-

Table 3.5 Socialist Elected Officials

	Socialist State Legislators			
	1910–1915		1916–1921	
	N	%	*N*	%
Core	8	11.1	29	34.9
Diverse	42	58.3	42	50.6
Periphery	22	30.6	12	14.5
Total	72	100.0	83	100.0
	Towns and Cities Electing Socialist Mayors or Major Officials			
	1910–1915		1916–1920	
Core	51	36.2	15	45.4
Diverse	30	21.3	12	36.4
Periphery	60	42.5	6	18.2
Total	141	100.0	33	100.0

Source: Computed, using my regional designations for states, from data in James Weinstein, *The Decline of Socialism in America, 1912–1925* (New Brunswick, N.J.: Rutgers University Press, 1984), tables 2–3, pp. 116–18. Core states are New England, mid-Atlantic, Michigan, Ohio, and Washington; diverse states are Wisconsin, Illinois, Indiana, Iowa, California, and Nevada. The remaining (southern, plains, mountain) states are periphery.

tween the more cautious right wing, which was devoted to achieving socialism step by step at the polls, and a newly constituted left wing, which disparaged political action in favor of revolution (after all, the more recent arrivals could not vote). By 1919, foreign-language federations accounted for 53 percent of SP membership. Reversing the 1900–1914 Americanization of the party, the new Socialist recruits put the success of the Russian and other European revolutions at the top of party priorities and adapted domestic dogma and strategy to that end.[142] This program had little appeal for the mass of workers or farmers, and the European immigrants who swelled the left wing after 1914 had little interest in or knowledge of the traditions of native American radicalism, traditions that the party had earlier been able to tap.

When Debs made his last race for the presidency from federal prison in 1920, Minnesota was the only periphery state to rank in the top ten for the SP. Wisconsin was now first (up from eleventh in 1912) and New York third (up from thirty-first). The Socialist share of the presidential vote in 1920 was only 3.4 percent. Of the total 914,000 votes (swollen by women's suffrage), periphery states contributed just over one-fifth, compared with almost one-third in 1912. New York and Wisconsin had accounted for only 11 percent of Debs's vote in 1912 but accounted for 31 percent eight years later.[143] The SP was now a very minor party; six years before, with significant strength among farmers and industrial workers, spread over much of the country, it could have been called a movement.

The tendencies that produced the Communist-Socialist split in 1919 had long been evident among America's urban Socialist intellectuals, whose concern for "getting it right," in terms of German or Russian Marxist dogma, had led to debilitating personal attacks and wholesale expulsions. A dogmatic exclusiveness in the Socialist leadership had contributed to the wreck of the KOL, the SLP, the IWW, and the SP. The Socialist theoreticians' contempt for the rural citizens who had always been at the center of dynamic reform impulses in the United States was destructive to both populism and socialism. Leaders like Debs, who arose from the heartland and maintained constant touch with a wide array of workers and farmers, had allowed the party to escape the isolation of its urban intelligentsia and had subjected dogma to a degree of healthy reality testing. Without such linkages, dogma became sterile, inflexible, and incapable of mobilizing the masses. When the Socialist Party lost its rural wing, it lost a vibrant diversity as well as the geographic reach necessary for a political party with national ambitions.[144]

In the midwestern and northeastern enclaves where the party retained some strength, that strength rested on a close cooperation with unions, most of them AFL affiliates. As the AFL increasingly occupied the constricted field of American organized labor, the much smaller SP could hardly afford to alienate the labor federation. Yet for the SP to depend exclusively on the AFL meant forgoing significant inroads into the vast numbers of unorganized workers, particularly the unskilled and semi-skilled workers whom the AFL made little effort to reach; it meant, in addition, yoking itself to an organization whose leadership was hostile to socialism and held only a weak and opportunistic commitment to electoral politics.

The American Federation of Labor

The character of the American Federation of Labor, which by 1916 encompassed almost three-fourths of all trade union members, has been summarized by Marc Karson as follows:

> It steadily opposed the formation of an independent labor party . . . [and]
> it viewed the idea of the welfare state with suspicion and actively lobbied
> only for legislation that would permit trade-unionism to make effective use
> of its economic power through organizing, through collective bargaining,

and through the use of the strike. Its racial and nationalistic politics were indistinguishable from the prejudices of the nation in general. The Federation created no workers' education movement, it hired no academically and professionally trained people for specialized staff work in its offices and it made no serious effort to increase its political strength by alliances with progressive groups outside its fold.[145]

The AFL managed to distance organized labor from the reformist zeal of intellectuals and farmers and to withhold labor support from "debilitating" national political crusades. In the process, it accepted a marginal role for labor in national politics.

The questions that continue to engage labor scholarship concern how highly class-conscious labor leaders, their early careers steeped in Marxism, ended up atop such a conservative organization and to what degree the ideologies and personalities of individuals shaped its orientation. How much choice, in other words, did the AFL leaders have? Did the choices they made represent the best plays from a bad hand or a submission to a business-dominated power structure that closed off real alternatives?

Early-twentieth-century scholars, impressed by the AFL's persistence through the depression of the 1890s and persecution at the hands of trusts, employers' associations, and the state, considered the AFL's strategy a great improvement over that of the Knights and Socialists. Trade-union leaders such as J. P. McDonnell of the New Jersey Federation, Adolph Strasser and Samuel Gompers of the Cigar Makers, and P. J. McGuire of the Carpenters—immigrant workers who gradually lost faith in the socialist "panaceas" that had appealed to them in their youth—developed a restricted workplace militancy that produced a better fit with both the American worker's psychological predispositions and the limitations imposed by the external political and economic environment. At the same time, in the view of University of Wisconsin Professors John R. Commons and Selig Perlman and others, the tough class consciousness of these former socialists "acted as an inseparable barrier against middle-class philosophies such as greenbackism and cooperatives." Further, "their foreign birth and upbringing kept them from contact with the life of the great American middle class, the farmers and the small employers." To the Wisconsin school, the AFL had thus emancipated labor from the "producer consciousness" of the native American labor movement, whose antimonopoly conceptions "denoted a mental subordination of the wage earner to the farmers, a labor movement in the grip of rural ideology."[146]

A later generation of labor historians would excoriate the AFL leadership for taking labor out of the ranks of progressive reform, devoting its energies to the service of an elite group of skilled craftsmen, and ignoring the mass of unskilled workers.[147] Even those sympathetic to Gompers's "common denominator" argument—that a commitment to trade unionism represented the strongest tie binding workers whose long-standing partisan attachments and issue positions could only pull them apart in politics—have argued that he pushed the denominator too low, overly constricting the scope, political power, and legitimacy of the labor movement.[148]

AFL leaders touted "voluntarism" for its pragmatism and potency. This was a purist, "labor for itself" strategy that aimed at harnessing the undeniable workplace militancy of the American worker, building workers' collective power to the point where employers would be compelled to grant better wages, working conditions, and job control. The state, at the mere threat of retaliation by organized workers through commercial obstruction or at the polls, would grant whatever (presumably few) political dispensations might be needed. To maximize workplace power, cohesive and autonomous national trade unions had to be promoted. Such organizations, AFL leaders assumed, required craft-based unions with clear jurisdictions, preventing union competition for the same group of workers. Dissident unionists who broke off from existing craft unions or attempted to form broad-based general unions in industries already organized by craft unions would be strongly discouraged by the national federation.

The "pure job consciousness" of the AFL was in part a reaction to the philosophy and political program of the federation's older rival, the Knights of Labor.[149] It also reflected the cultural gulf that separated the immigrant AFL leaders from the native producerism of the Knights. For Gompers and his colleagues, the strategy simply registered political learning. They had seen other labor organizations flounder on the shoals of partisan politics and divisive national issues. Workers had been voting for half a century before the AFL appeared on the scene, and the national political economy, ethnic ties, and links to local machines predisposed them to a party affiliation, usually Democratic or Republican. The ties that bound the metal trades to the Republican Party and the brewers and needle trades to the SP were features of political economy and ethnic community that the AFL could do little to change.

The point of mounting an independent political effort (which might imply support for its old antagonists, the Socialists) or endorsing Democratic or Republican candidates was to obtain legislation. But the American courts had ordained that federal law could not constitutionally touch many areas of labor relations. This meant that labor had to conduct legislative campaigns in a multitude of states—which had reason to compete for industrial locations by denying labor claims. Even if the campaigns were successful, continued pressure would have to be exerted to secure favorable executive enforcement. And, of course, even if a legislative initiative (say, a limitation on hours) passed, chances were good that it would be voided in the state or federal courts as an unconstitutional trespass on the right to contract. It made sense, then, to propound a doctrine of economic self-help. Unions should confront business in the workplace and obtain their goals by collective action there.[150]

But once the precepts of voluntarism were accepted, they propelled the AFL into a distinct organizational logic that heightened its conservatism and its marginality in national reform politics. National conventions structured representation in a way that privileged national and international union organizations over state and local federations, which were more inclined to politics,[151] and the Executive Council was tightly controlled by craft unionists of the Gompers persuasion. As Gary Marks has written:

> From its establishment in 1886 to the 1920's, the AFL was dominated by relatively closed [craft] unions, to an extent that was unparalleled in any other major union movement. These unions were, above all, committed to the sectional defense of their members' job territory[;] . . . closed unions could be militant in the defense of their members' interests, but their militancy was directed to preserving their special position in the division of labor rather than reforming the basis of the wage system.[152]

Skilled craft workers were relatively successful in controlling the supply of labor in their occupations by defending apprenticeship regulations and other barriers to entry, a workplace power that contrasted with their political weakness at the state and national level. On the other hand, the greater labor-market vulnerability, combined with large potential membership, of industrial unions encouraged those unions to pursue political strategies.[153] The one was satisfied to maintain the privileged status of a small, exclusive membership; the other sought the widest possible membership but recognized that it needed state assistance to recruit and maintain that membership. Furthermore, the skilled craft unions were dominated by second-generation Irish Americans who often looked with disdain on the newer southern and eastern European immigrants, Asians, and African Americans who represented the majority of the industrial working class by 1910. The Irish were Catholic as well, and the profound hostility of the Catholic Church to socialism undoubtedly influenced the political tendencies of the Irish-Catholic-dominated AFL.[154]

Reliance on craft organization not only diminished support for the organization of unskilled workers but also immersed the national organization in endless jurisdictional disputes. The Executive Council often refused charters to industrial unions that did form, on the grounds that they competed with existing craft unions; or it might subsequently charter separate craft unions that broke the solid industrial front. At some points, AFL craft affiliates even collaborated with and provided "scab" workers for companies struck by industrial or rival craft unions. Such internecine warfare was, needless to say, very detrimental to working-class unity and trade-union effectiveness. The extent to which craft-versus-craft conflicts spent the energies of labor is reflected in the estimate that 95 percent of all strikes in the construction industry originated in jurisdictional disputes between unions.[155] The mediation of jurisdictional disputes was the principal activity of the national organization; it was, Gompers complained, "the most destructive, most time consuming of anything else in our work."[156]

There were, however, a few large industrial or "mixed" unions in the AFL. The United Mine Workers, the most powerful single union in the AFL, represented a relatively stable membership of 251,000–289,000 coal miners in the 1904–12 period and constantly pressed the Executive Council to support open unions.[157] Other AFL-affiliated unions organized on an industrial or open-craft basis included the Brewers, the Ladies Garment Workers, and the Western Federation of (metalliferous) Miners, the last of which returned to the AFL after a stint with the IWW. These four unions constituted about 18.5 percent of AFL membership in 1912.[158] The industrial unions composed a radical caucus within the AFL, providing the bulk of votes received for the Socialist political program of 1894 and for later propositions endorsing independent political action, opposing leadership affiliation with the elite National Civil Federation, and supporting government regulation of hours— propositions that drew, on average, about 40 percent of votes cast. Strong socialist currents could be found among the miners, brewers, and garment workers, as well as in some craft unions besieged by technological change and employer antiunion campaigns (for example, the Boot and Shoe Workers and the International Association of Machinists).[159] In 1912, when socialist agitation in the AFL was at its peak, party member Max Hayes ran against Gompers for the presidency of the federation, garnering 27 percent of the votes cast.[160] However, despite the continued agitation of socialists and industrial unionists, their political tendencies, social policies, and organizational preferences had little impact on the national direction of the AFL.

In eschewing national political-party commitments, the AFL left its local unions free to make their own accommodations with local power structures. As Michael Rogin points out, "A national policy of nonpartisanship meant they could be Democratic in Democratic cities and Republican in Republican cities."[161] For craft unions, good relations with urban machines were necessary to secure the favorable building codes, licenses, and apprenticeship regulations that enabled the unions to control job access.[162] Such ties also enabled union leaders on limited salaries to supplement their incomes by securing political appointments to city jobs or nominations to electoral office.

The best practitioners of this pragmatic, local-power-oriented politics were the building-trade unionists, who by 1912 composed 29 percent of the AFL membership and held a commanding position in its direction, but the lucrative opportunity structure of local politics was exploited by other trades as well. The unfortunate results of this free-wheeling, nonprogrammatic union politics can be seen in a few examples. The Amalgamated Association of Iron, Steel, and Tin Workers opposed independent labor politics in the core steel regions and exerted most of its political energies in support of the protective tariff, in alliance with the Republican Party. This collaboration enabled a number of Amalgamated leaders to secure political offices in Pennsylvania, Ohio, and New York and (perhaps) protected steel workers' jobs by limiting imports. But it also yoked the craft-union leadership to the great trust that decimated the union movement in the steel industry after the Homestead strike of 1892.[163] Similarly, the leaders of the four railroad brotherhoods formed an alliance with railroad executives—the American Railroad Employee and Investors Association—to lobby against government limitation of rates and discrimination in favor of large corporations.[164] For mine workers in Pennsylvania, Illinois, and Ohio, the AFL nonpartisan policy allowed union leaders to reward sympathetic Republican politicians like Sen. Marcus Hanna, long known as an enlightened employer and advocate of cooperative labor-management relations. But the outcome of such relationships was also pressure to support conservative Republicans for Congress in opposition to "labor" tickets and to minimize labor strife that might endanger Republican candidates. An alliance with President Theodore Roosevelt apparently prevented the UMW's John Mitchell from supporting the AFL's indictment of administration policy in its 1906 "Bill of Grievances" (see below). In San Francisco, building-trade unionists achieved a remarkable local political dominance, developing after 1906 a stranglehold over construction and creating their own independent political machine in the Union Labor Party. Although the labor government undoubtedly achieved considerable wage and hour benefits for its craft-union constituency and supported some policies of broader interest to labor, the ULP maintained itself on corruption, patronage, and a campaign of virulent race-baiting against Asians.[165]

Having turned away from a broad political organization of the working class toward local economic advantage, the AFL was in no position to constrain unionists' various accommodations to local political economy and ethnic bias. Federation policy strongly discouraged membership revolts against union leadership and eschewed interference in the "internal affairs" of unions. Thus even union leaders who accepted bribes from businessmen to pursue policies seemingly against the interests of their members, or who became virtual dictators, were unlikely to be disciplined by the national organization.[166] In practice, the voluntarism espoused by the AFL was not so much antipolitical as politically opportunistic. The absence of a coherent ideology permitted local labor leaders to make their own accommodations with the political and economic power structure, to the disadvantage and often discredit of the labor movement nationally. Further, the multitude of local accommodations and issue alliances made a large-scale political mobilization even more difficult, when and if such an effort became necessary.

As voluntarism shaded into "business unionism," "labor for itself" became "each craft for itself," and the path of least resistance for many skilled workers' unions seemed to be collaboration with capitalists. At the top, AFL leaders set an example by their membership alongside leading capitalists in the National Civic Federation and their pronouncements on the merits of trusts. Below, individual union leaders fell into the force fields of the national political economy as the political significance of the tariff and other sectional issues enabled capital to woo a major segment of the labor movement, keep it apart from other reform forces, and ensure its neutrality or acquiescence on regulatory issues. Thus metal workers aligned with the tariff policy of their Republican employers, and the railroad brotherhoods joined with management to oppose expanded regulation of railroad enterprise. Having freed itself from producerism and the agrarian alliance, labor appeared, by the first years of the twentieth century, to have become ensnared in the political agenda of capital. This was the consequence of the organizational logic produced by the choices of trade-union leaders, operating atop the powerful polarization of American politics between export-oriented agrarianism and industrial capitalism.

This was a vicious circle, but it did not deny organized labor all elements of choice. A strong, independent labor politics, on the British model, might have enabled the trade-union federation to extract important benefits from one or the other pole. Instead, with a weak organization and unable (because of its feeble penetration into the masses of unskilled workers) to deliver many votes, labor reaped scant benefit from the unions' support for capital's tariff, trust, and railroad policies. And after 1906, when the AFL began to tilt toward the agrarian Democratic pole in national politics, those same organizational and political weaknesses made it a rather uncreative and undemanding appendage to the agrarian coalition. It was prepared neither to form an independent left party or to make this one its own.

Growth and Distribution of Trade-Union Organization

At the turn of the century the AFL's leadership must have believed that its strategy had been vindicated. The trade unions had prospered (even as the Knights disappeared), and the AFL had survived the depression years of the 1890s with no net loss of members.[167] Then, between 1897 and 1900, the AFL claimed a membership growth of over 100 percent, followed by a 200 percent climb between 1900 and 1904, bringing it to 1,676,000 (see table 3.1). The rapid growth of unionism and the AFL coincided with an economic boom, a sharp decline in the unemployment rate, and a remarkable upsurge in strikes.[168] Workplace militancy and the consolidation of the AFL were in no sense incompatible, although the *nature* of that militancy (militancy for what?) is difficult to characterize, since so many strikes were about craft jurisdictions and workforce composition.[169]

After 1904, a fierce employer counterattack and the recession triggered by the 1907 Panic and European war anxiety held gains to a minimum, but the federation reached two million by 1914. Although it grew less rapidly than the nonagricultural workforce from 1904 to 1916, its size and persistence made it the exceptional American labor organization.

In terms of geographic reach, the AFL's membership was concentrated in the industrial core regions and the cities of the diverse Midwest and Pacific regions. AFL membership figures are not available by state for this period, but a rough index of state strength can be gleaned by tallying the addresses of delegates to the 1910 AFL convention and the number of votes they were allotted (an indication of membership size). As can be seen in table 3.6, almost three-fourths of convention votes were cast by five contiguous states—Illinois, Indiana, Ohio, Pennsylvania, and New York. In regional terms, about half of AFL member strength came from the core northeastern and Great Lakes states, with another 40 percent from the diverse areas. By comparison, the KOL probably drew a similar, or even larger, percentage of its members from the core industrial states (the Midwest and Pacific states then being less

Table 3.6 Delegates to the 1910 AFL Convention and Votes Alloted Them (state totals only)

State	Number of Delegates[a]	Number of Votes	State	Number of Delegates	Number of Votes
Illinois	76	2,977	Arkansas	4	57
New York	62	2,806	Mississippi	2	30
Indiana	21	2,164	Maine	1	25
Ohio	29	1,321	Minnesota	4	23
Pennsylvania	18	1,269	Georgia	4	14
Massachusetts	20	932	West Virginia	1	8
Missouri	28	735	Montana	3	6
California	11	358	Texas	5	5
New Jersey	8	226	Oklahoma	4	4
Wisconsin	4	215	Tennessee	3	3
Colorado	5	203	Alabama	2	2
Kentucky	5	197	Maryland	2	2
Michigan	5	166	Florida	1	1
Nebraska	6	129	Iowa	1	1
Louisiana	2	123	Oregon	1	1
Vermont	3	114	South Dakota	1	1
Connecticut	3	100	Utah	1	1
Washington	4	94	Virginia	1	1
Rhode Island	3	73	Wyoming	1	1
Kansas	5	58	Total	360	14,446

Delegate Voting Strength by Region[b]

	Number	Percent
Core	7,126	49.3
Diverse	5,716	39.6
Periphery	1,604	11.1
Total	14,446	100.0

Source: Tabulated by number and address of delegates, *AFL Thirteenth Annual Convention, 1910,* iii–xii.

[a] Twenty-eight District of Columbia, international, and women's delegates are omitted.

[b] Regions are the same as Senate categories, based on value added (per capita) in manufacturing.

industrialized relative to the core), but its periphery component was twice as large.[170]

The AFL membership, then, was less diverse in terms both of region and of occupational skill level than was the membership of its older rival. The approximately two million trade union members in 1910 (almost three-fourths of whom were AFL-affiliated) constituted 10.9 percent of all nonagricultural

Table 3.7 Union Membership in 1910 by Sector

Sector	Percent of Employees Organized	Percent of All Union Members	Largest Union
Mineral Extraction	27.3	12.6	United Mine Workers[a]
Transportation	17.1	22.0	Railroad Trainmen
Building Trades	16.4	21.0	United Carpenters[a]
Manufacturing[b]	11.6	29.9	International Association of Machinists[a]
Public Service	2.5	2.7	Letter Carriers

Source: Leo Wolman, *The Growth of American Trade Unions, 1880–1923* (New York: National Bureau of Economic Research, 1924), tables 7, 14, pp. 62, 86.

[a] Designates AFL affiliate, 1910.

[b] Obtained by summing metal, machinery, shipbuilding, food, beverage and tobacco, paper and printing, chemical, clay, glass and stone, leather, clothing, textile, and lumber and woodworking categories.

wage earners. By 1916 their numbers had risen to almost three million (about 13 percent).[171] However, union density varied greatly by sector, occupation, and region. As table 3.7 shows, mining, transportation, and the building trades were the bulwarks of the American trade-union movement; manufacturing lagged, and trade, clerical, and public-service workers hardly knew unions. Within manufacturing, the overall density of around 12 percent was exceeded in specific industries: brewing, with almost 90 percent union members in 1910; printing and bookbinding, with 34 percent; cigars and tobacco, with 27.3 percent; and clothing, with 17 percent. On the other hand, less than 4 percent of pulp and paper and textile workers were organized (with the South practically untouched) and less than 10 percent of iron and steel workers, with most union members here representing machinists and molders. Similarly, within the transportation sector, barely 2 percent of unskilled construction and maintenance workers were organized in trade unions, compared with 29 percent among longshoremen and 22–24 percent among electric and street railway and steam railroad employees.[172] Large mass-production industries dominated by one or a few firms were quite successful in preventing or destroying the trade-union organization of their employees. Leo Wolman lists the U.S. Steel Corporation, National Biscuit, International Paper, and American Tobacco as examples of this phenomenon.[173] There was also little union penetration in the highly concentrated chemical, petroleum, and rubber industries.[174]

A comparison of unionization in the American and British steel industries also suggests that the sheer size and concentration of American industry were factors in the weak unionization here. Whereas the U.S. workers had been more highly organized than the British in the early 1890s, by 1914 the British steel industry was heavily organized, but the open shop prevailed in the highly "trustified" U.S. industry. Multiplant organization enabled Carnegie Steel to maintain full production while shutting down plants where strikes were in progress.[175] The resources of this huge corporation also allowed it to easily hire strikebreakers and a private detective force to battle the Amalgamated Association of Iron and Steel Workers at Homestead and to mount a costly legal offensive quite debilitating to the union.[176] The formation of U.S. Steel in 1901 (taking over the Carnegie, Federal, and National Steel companies, among others) sounded the effective death knell for the Amalgamated union.

Of course, one cannot divorce industrial structure from the broader social and political context of American unionism. Leadership ideologies and a large, diverse immigration slowed the organization of the unskilled here, as did the stubborn craft focus of the AFL. Had the American iron and steel unions been as broadly encompassing as their British and German counterparts, it might have been easier to sustain a strike *and* to mount political action, had the union leadership been so inclined.[177] It is noteworthy that Great Britain experienced a burst of trade-union expansion from 1911 to 1913, just after the political victory of 1910 and at a time when U.S. unionization was relatively stagnant. And British labor's political mobilization had rapidly secured from the Liberal government (in 1906) a law immunizing unions from damage judgments occasioned by strikes; this law, in turn, removed a powerful obstacle to unionization and strike action.[178] A wide and sustained political mobilization on the part of American unionists might have overcome some of the powerful economic advantages of the trust, secured a more favorable judiciary, and/or overturned unfavorable court decisions through legislation. Political and economic power were more interrelated than the AFL recognized.

The AFL in Politics, 1886–1912

The attachment to voluntarism and the avoidance of national political commitments did not emerge full-blown in the reorganized AFL of 1886. In that year of broad and spontaneous labor upheaval, the federation was caught up in the political movement. Gompers and other trade-union leaders joined the New York campaign for Henry George, and the first convention having sanctioned such activity, local AFL affiliates around the country joined in support of independent labor tickets in the fall elections. However, after the New York movement disintegrated in squabbling among Socialists, single taxers, and trade unionists, Gompers and his colleagues began to affirm their opposition to independent politics. Irish unionists in New York drifted back to Tammany Hall (which had backed George's opponent), and agrarian forces took over the leadership of independent farmer-labor politics. Further, Gompers's New York Cigar Makers Union had seen its successful campaign to outlaw tenement-house cigar manufacture voided by state supreme court decisions in the mid-1880s. In the short space of a few years, the major difficulties attending labor politics had been sharply revealed, and AFL leaders would not forget the lesson.[179]

The Panic of 1893 and the onset of severe depression renewed the debate about labor politics. The national leadership was unmoved, but the AFL was a loose confederation of unions, and in particular unions and regions there was a new flurry of trade-union political activity in 1894–96, despite discouragement from headquarters. In California, workers who had shown little interest in populism in 1892 had different predilections in 1894. The Populists, always antagonistic to railroads, had strongly backed the Pullman strikers and condemned the governor's use of the state militia against Southern Pacific workers. Further, the Populist Party had endorsed all the demands drawn up by a farmer-labor convention sponsored by the San Francisco trade unionists and had nominated a carpenter and a printer for high state offices on its ticket. In the midst of the depression, the Populists' monetary policy had enhanced appeal as well. Under these circumstances, the city registered a large increase in its Populist vote between 1892 and 1894, and the percentage in working-class precincts was twice that of more middle-class neighborhoods. Nevertheless, the Populist labor vote was under one-fourth of the total, and San Francisco County fell well below the party's success in a number of farming counties (as well as in Alameda and Los Angeles). In subsequent years, the San Francisco building trades hardened their opposition to independent politics (beyond the narrow confines of the city) and to the broad coalition movements of populism and progressivism. The city's sailors and unskilled workers, however, would become an important base of support for Progressive Hiram Johnson by 1914.[180]

In theory, the greatest potential for a Populist alliance lay with the coal miners. Theirs was a broad-based industrial union supportive of independent political action. High vulnerability to cyclical unemployment (no other industry was more devastated by the 1893–94 depression than coal) heightened political sensibility, as did the need for legislation to deal with unsafe mines and extortionary company stores. Further, coal mines were located in rural areas, where miners and farmers were "kith and kin," and many had direct experience of each other's work. It was not surprising, then, that many coal miners were attracted to populism and that the Populists made programmatic outreach to the miners.[181] The coal strike of 1894, in which the great majority of midwestern and Pennsylvania coal miners were involved, collapsed in June, leaving a broken UMW and thousands of angry and impoverished miners in its wake. In the next few months, several UMW leaders participated in Illinois and Ohio farmer-labor conventions (see above), and the union president, John McBride, declared for the Populist ticket.[182] The *United Mine Workers' Journal* printed entreaties for farmer-labor unity at the ballot box against corporate monopoly and "this monster, the money power."[183]

However, the results in the midwestern coalfields again demonstrated labor's weak and fragmented political commitments and the disjunction between the union's "amorphous radicalism" and its political quiescence.[184] All but one of the fourteen leading coal counties in Illinois (measured by number of coal-mine employees) registered below the Illinois statewide Populist average of 7 percent, although most did increase their Populist percentages over 1892; half averaged 5 percent or less. In southwestern Illinois, which John Laslett has described as "the center of radicalism" in the UMW, the average Populist vote in the five largest coal counties was 4.9 percent. All fourteen leading coal counties went Republican. In the coal districts of Pennsylvania, closely tied to the eastern steel and railroad corporations, the Populists registered an even weaker vote, averaging 3.8 percent in the thirteen major bituminous-coal counties and 1.1 percent in the seven main anthracite counties. The UMW was stronger in Ohio and the state political context perhaps more favorable. In the 1894 congressional elections, the Ohio Populists averaged 8.3 percent in the fifteen other districts where they fielded candidates, but in the northeastern district that included Stark and Columbiana—major coal counties—Populist Jacob Coxey won 21 percent of the vote. In state elections in 1895 Coxey, as the Populist gubernatorial candidate, surpassed his statewide average of 6.2 percent in nine of the eleven leading coal counties— reaching almost 14 percent in Columbiana. Though all eleven went Republican, these nine eastern Ohio counties presented some of the best evidence of the possibilities for labor populism in the Midwest, comparable to the party's urban showing in Chicago, Milwaukee, and Minneapolis.[185]

The Populist cause in Ohio was aided by the fact that a Republican governor, William McKinley, had sent the militia to deal with strike-related violence in Ohio, whereas a Democratic official (Governor John Peter Altgeld) had done so in Illinois; thus miners in the latter state had dual economic and political grievances that impelled them toward the Republicans. In fact, the economic reaction against the Democrats in 1892–94 dwarfed the movement toward populism and would greatly burden the reconstituted "popocrats" in

1896.[186] By that year, the UMW had returned to its nonpartisan stance, and the momentum of labor populism had dissipated.[187]

In these states there was no relationship between level of labor militancy (as measured by the number of people involved in all strikes, from 1893 to mid-1894, stated as a percentage of county population) and 1894 populism *or* the Bryan vote in 1896. The five most strike-prone counties in Ohio averaged 10.7 percent Populist in 1895—considerably above the state average—but in Illinois, the five most militant counties registered only 6.2, below the state average. In both states the overall correlation between county strike rate and Populist percentage was essentially zero. Only three of the top-ten strike counties in Ohio went for Bryan in 1896; in Illinois, only one. All four had cast majorities for the "Old Democracy" in 1892.[188]

The AFL and Populism

At AFL headquarters, Gompers's opposition to populism (as to socialism) was unambiguous. The AFL leader refused to have anything to do with the Farmers' Alliance and in 1892 disparaged the Populist Party as an organization "mainly of *employing* farmers without any regard to the interests of [agricultural wage labor] of the country districts or the mechanics and laborers of the industrial centers." A union with the farmers was impossible because it was fundamentally "unnatural."[189] The agrarians, he warned, "simply do not understand and are woefully ignorant upon the underlying principles, tactics and operations of the trade unions."[190] He steadfastly maintained that the AFL should remain independent of all parties and attend only to trade-union organization and occasional lobbying.[191]

However, at the 1893 AFL convention, the political actionists succeeded in having the Morgan (independent action) program submitted to the member unions for their consideration and put the federation on record for the free coinage of silver. In the following year, as midwestern unionists were lured into Populist-Socialist alliances, official AFL delegates worked to stanch the movement into politics. At labor conferences called by the KOL, they voted to reject proposals for a third-party movement backed by the KOL and the Farmers' Alliance. As the winter of 1894 approached, Gompers had reason to dread the annual AFL convention. Powderly had been deposed by the KOL for his political timidity the year before, and most AFL unions had voted in favor of some or all of the Morgan political program. There was widespread criticism of Gompers and the "pure and simple" leadership, both for their stubborn political reticence and for their refusal to support the American Railway Union in the Pullman strike. Furthermore, the convention was to be held in Colorado, strong Populist territory.[192]

As it turned out, Gompers's forebodings were justified. The political faction succeeded in replacing Gompers with the UMW's McBride, who had backed the Populists in November, and moved the AFL headquarters to Indianapolis. The convention also reaffirmed its support for the free coinage of silver.[193] The political coup proved to be a temporary aberration, however. By late 1895 a modest recovery had set in, and what enthusiasm had existed for populism or other independent politics was fading among trade unionists. At the annual convention, held in New York this time, Gompers regained the federation presidency from McBride. The assembly inserted in the AFL constitution a declaration that "party politics shall have no place in the conventions of the American Federation of Labor."[194]

In 1896 Gompers and the majority on the AFL Executive Board held steadfastly to the apolitical stance. In his autobiography Gompers revealed that "Mr. Bryan sent a number of messages that he was anxious to meet me to which I made no reply." When the two men happened to attend a dinner in Chicago, Bryan announced that, if elected, he would appoint Gompers to his cabinet. The labor leader promptly responded that he would under no circumstances accept.[195] Pressed by many unionists to declare for Bryan, Gompers would only say, disingenuously, that he was "for William" (the two presidential candidates having the same first name).[196] According to Philip Foner, the "vast majority of A.F. of L. affiliates" nevertheless declared and worked for Bryan.[197] Gwendolyn Mink also assumes a solid trade-union vote for Bryan while arguing that the nonunionized working class, particularly new immigrants from southern and eastern Europe, flocked to the Republican banner, attracted by McKinley's promise of a return to prosperity and his downplaying of ethnic and religious issues.[198]

It is, however, impossible to make such distinctions on the basis of available empirical evidence. It is plausible that union *leaders*, at least, would find Bryan's support for trade-union organizational rights attractive and that unskilled, nonunion, new immigrants might have been less interested in such rights, more easily intimidated by employers, and even more attracted to the Republicans' "full dinner pail" appeals. Since there were so few trade unionists in this period (less than 4 percent of the nonagricultural workforce), they could all have voted for Bryan without making much of an impact. But given the silence of the national AFL leadership, the widespread urban Democratic defections, and the fact that very few new immigrants voted, it seems safer to assume a generalized disaffection of industrial workers from the "populized" Democratic Party, regardless of skill level or union membership. There *was* evidence of class-differentiated voting in the cities, and the bulk of big-city Democratic votes were most likely cast by workers. However, many of those votes represented ethnic traditions or maneuvers to gain control of local party organizations—as in the case of the Irish—rather than endorsement of the 1896 platform.[199] It is clear from the returns that the urban core working class found the rhetoric and program of the reconstituted Democracy significantly less attractive than the conservative Democratic Party of 1892. With the voting patterns of the Pennsylvania and midwestern coal counties in mind, we can say that even where unionism flourished and reached broadly, encompassing men of diverse ethnic origins and skill levels, the politics of protection and monetary conservatism won out over the uncertain promise of farmer-labor "producer" democracy.

The Republicans offered the workers nothing in return for their votes except a signal, implicit in the election results, for capital to resume investment. At the same time, the GOP raised the price of consumer goods with a new high tariff in 1897, condoned a remarkable wave of mergers that ballooned corporations in major industries into anti-labor monoliths, and backed employers and the courts in their legal assault on trade-union organization. That northern urban workers continued, into the early twentieth century, to support the GOP in national politics and eschew the party that opposed trusts and high tariffs and offered the workers everything that leading labor spokesmen said they wanted simply underlines the extent to which workers in politics were locked into a political economy and organizational logic they felt powerless to change.

The AFL Lobby after 1896

Within the AFL, the postelection convention of 1896 appeared to ratify Gompers's apolitical stance by reelecting him unanimously, for the first time. It also moved to establish the federation's headquarters permanently in the East, at Washington, D.C.[200] As the move to Washington illustrated, the federation had abjured parties but not all political influence. In fact, the AFL, following in the footsteps of the Farmers' Alliance and the KOL, helped to pioneer the form of the broad-membership, national legislative "lobby." Andrew Furuseth of the Seamen's Union was appointed the AFL's legislative agent in 1896 and presented the federation's views on legislation pending in Congress. In 1897 the Executive Council paid McKinley a visit and later memorialized the new president and Congress. Its recommendations included a government employee eight-hour bill, a seamen's bill, and an anti-injunction measure.[201]

The labor lobby urged that the federal government become a "model employer," in particular by fixing an eight-hour day on federally funded public works, including projects carried out by contractors or subcontractors.[202] Eight-hour bills for federal employees had been passed as early as 1868; the law was extended to letter carriers in 1888 and, ostensibly, to government contracts in 1892. Its effect was greatly weakened, however, by lax federal enforcement, subcontractor evasions, and court decisions that limited applicability; legislative repair had been a major political goal for both the KOL and the AFL.[203]

Within the states, local and state labor bodies were often active lobbyists for social insurance and welfare programs, as well as for political reforms favoring direct democracy.[204] However, the national federation strongly opposed legislation on wages, hours, unemployment benefits, or health insurance. Such benefits had to be won by unions for their members, and the "short-cut" political path had to be resisted; for, in Gompers' words, "it has been demonstrated that when the achievement of economic ends is entrusted to governmental agents, economic organization is weakened." Without economic action, employers would not abide by the laws, and states would not enforce them. *With* such organized workplace power, laws were unnecessary.[205]

Exceptions were made, however, for certain classes of workers—women, children, the elderly, and government employees—who were not in a position to protect their interests through private economic actions. Children were "wards of the state" and must be protected from the greed and ignorance of employers and parents by child-labor laws (which the AFL strongly supported at the state level). By the 1890s, federation support for "protective" legislation for special classes of employees was extended to women. The eight-hour day and prohibition of work with certain types of machinery served ostensibly to protect the "weaker sex" but also limited women's competition with male workers.[206] In 1908 the Supreme Court, generally hostile to legislation on wages and hours, ratified the exception for women.[207]

Since few exceptions were granted for men, the AFL's objection to general wage and hour laws perhaps spared it some arduous and futile political campaigns. However, the experience in the states suggests that women's hours laws were a good place to begin campaigns for general labor laws and to demonstrate labor's political clout.[208] It was also possible to exploit cracks in the wall that the Court was inclined to erect against general labor legislation, especially on health and safety arguments or for workers clearly in interstate commerce. The justices, by a 7-to-2 majority in 1898, upheld a Utah statute fixing an eight-hour day in mines and smelters. Although a 5-to-4 majority overturned a ten-hour law for bakers in 1905, the latter decision (*Lochner v. New York*) was "practically overruled" by a 1917 decision, and in the same year the Court also confirmed the right of states to establish workmen's compensation laws even if they placed the entire burden of payment on employers.[209] Even minimum-wage laws (for women) were possible and might raise the general wage scale. Massachusetts enacted one in 1912, followed by California and nine other midwestern, western, and southern states by 1916.[210]

There is no doubt that the Court's laissez-faire, anti-labor bias and its remarkably powerful institutional position put labor at a huge disadvantage in the United States relative to other western democracies. But the experience of farmers' and of workers' organizations in the states showed that persistent political pressure could win some important benefits, though statutes might require repeated, creative reenactment or even constitutional amendment. *Had* the national trade-union federation committed itself to political action and sustained a nationally coordinated effort, who can say what might have been achieved in the Progressive Era, when the reform tide was high and labor had influential allies in agriculture and the middle classes? The passage of women's minimum-wage laws *without* much support from organized labor demonstrates the favorable climate for reform in this period, a climate that union leaders might have exploited for a broader agenda.[211] But all these "might-have-beens" depended on a political mobilization that national labor leaders would not or could not mount.

As it was, the domination of Congress and the executive branch by the party of capital stymied the modest labor lobby. Islands of sympathy in the Republican Party were gradually submerged by conservative orthodoxy, even as the pro-labor tendencies of the "populized" Democratic Party intensified. A leading example of the hardening GOP stance came in the AFL's campaign for an effective eight-hour bill on public works. In 1898 a strong bill passed the House under the guidance of Rep. John J. Gardner (R, New Jersey), chair of the Labor Committee. In the Senate, however, Republican leaders sidetracked the measure, to Gompers's bitter disappointment. By the next Congress, Representative Gardner's interest appeared to be flagging. He was chastised by House Speaker Joseph Cannon for allowing the bill to be reported and, according to Gompers, blamed his failure to obtain a New Jersey Senate seat on his sponsorship of the eight-hour bill. In later years, Gardner would boast that he had helped to bottle up labor measures in the House. In the Senate, the Labor Committee was also unfriendly, and it fell to the committee's fifth-ranking Democrat, Thomas Turley of Tennessee, to serve as the bill's champion. Steel companies, shipbuilders, and the National Association of Manufacturers (NAM) were strongly opposed. With the Republican stalwarts in firm control of the Senate and with House Speaker Cannon unabashedly negative, there was no chance of passage. Not until the Democrats took over the House in 1911–12 would an effective government eight-hour bill finally be passed.[212]

On other issues too, the party balance defeated the labor lobby. One proposal strongly advocated by Gompers and Furuseth was a measure to improve the Dickensian conditions of sailors—in particular to ban corporal punishment and various "allotment" schemes through which seamen lost their wages, to require better conditions on board, and to abolish the penalty of imprisonment for sailors who broke their contracts. Sailors, like government workers, were already under federal jurisdiction, and improvement of conditions required national legislation. Action was triggered by a Supreme Court decision in 1897 that upheld the draconian powers of the shipmasters. Predictably, only a relatively weak bill could pass muster with the Republican Congress in 1898. Though corporal punishment was banned and penalties for jumping ship lessened, an amendment by Rep. Levin Handy (D, Delaware) to eliminate both the possibility of imprisonment for desertion and the "allotment" system failed on a 107-to-125 vote in the House. On this tally, 80 Democrats, 15 "hyphenated" Democrats, 2 Populists, 2 fusionists, 7 Republicans, and 1 silver Republican were opposed by a solid Republican majority. Here too, legislative victory waited on Democratic control of the government; the effective law would not come until 1915.[213]

By the early years of the twentieth century the principal national political demands of the trade-union federation centered on two negative goals: exclusion of immigrants and exemption of labor from the antitrust law. Both were perceived as critical to the success of union organizing and the improvement of wages and labor conditions. The older federation had embraced Pacific Coast unionists' demand for an end to Chinese "coolie" immigration, and AFL leaders were spirited defenders of the policy inaugurated in 1882 and reaffirmed in the Chinese Exclusion Act of 1902. In the late 1890s, attention began to turn to the masses of Italians, Hungarians, Poles, and Slavs pouring into the United States. Between 1899 and 1907 the number of immigrants rose from 312,000 to 1.3 million per year. In industry after industry, unions saw strikes defeated by immigrants herded, often under armed guard, into strike locations. It was difficult (though certainly not impossible) to organize the new immigrants, given language barriers, the inexperience of southern and eastern European peasants with unions, their dependence on labor suppliers or *padrones,* and the short time horizon of the substantial percentage who intended to amass a stake and return to their homelands. A docile, mobile, and constantly expanding supply of labor was clearly an advantage to employers; Andrew Carnegie referred to the late-nineteenth-century immigration influx as "a golden stream."[214]

On the other hand, support for restriction clearly was not confined to labor, and so the possibility of success was greater here than on other labor issues. Both agrarian Democrats and Republicans were sympathetic to immigration restriction, as revealed by the robust congressional majorities in support of restrictive legislation from the 1880s through the Wilson era. Although the National Association of Manufacturers, the U.S. Chamber of Commerce, and individual mining, shipping, and industrial firms opposed any large-scale restriction, middle- and upper-class disdain for the new immigrants and fear of "anarchists" and other radicals among them countered the economic utilitarianism of the large employers. Further, it often pleased high-tariff Republicans to emphasize the consistency of their protectionist ideology by opposing the importation of both labor and goods; this "dual protectionism" supported the party's claim to be a friend of labor.[215] Thus, while House Speaker Cannon sided with the NAM in opposition to a literacy requirement for immigrants (the preferred method for restricting the influx of the poor and unskilled), Representative Gardner and Sen. Henry Cabot Lodge were strong champions of the bill.[216]

The great institutional hurdles for this labor objective were the White House and the courts. The latter exploited ambiguities in the contract labor laws of 1885–87 to render them ineffective. Presidents, hesitant to give offense to other countries and eager to maintain discretion in their diplomatic functions, resisted the insulting and restrictive language of the anti-immigration bills. Hence Roosevelt opposed a Japanese exclusion law, and both William Howard Taft (once) and Woodrow Wilson (twice) vetoed literacy requirements passed by large congressional majorities.[217]

The immigration issue also influenced labor's position on U.S. imperialism in the 1896–1905 period. Although the AFL did not actively contribute to the anti-imperialist movement, it did pass resolutions against expansionism in 1898 and in favor of Philippine independence in 1899. Labor papers that voiced opposition to Hawaiian annexation in 1896–97 and to retention of control over Cuba, Puerto Rico, and the Philippines after the Spanish-American War were concerned about the domestic uses of an expanded U.S. Army and the prospect that the incorporation of these islands would bring an influx of cheap goods and cheap labor. Employers were suspected of plans to evade the Contract Labor and Chinese Exclusion Acts through the "back door" of Hawaii and the Philippines, and a flood of Cuban cigar makers was anticipated. Further, U.S. manufacturers might locate in the new territories to take advantage of cheap and abundant labor, and shipping companies could recruit docile, low-wage seamen there. The leading anti-imperialist unions were the cigar makers (CMIU), seamen, and shoemakers. Gompers, once a cigar maker himself and still close to the union's leaders, was sympathetic to the arguments of the CMIU and to West Coast unionists' adamant opposition to Asian immigration. However, the strong support for imperialism among some unions— in particular the railroad brotherhoods, typographers, bricklayers, and masons—and the apathy among many unionists who perceived no direct material interest caused Gompers to keep a low profile on the issue. Once assured that the contract labor and Chinese exclusion laws would be upheld and that imports from the new territories would be limited by tariffs and quotas, organized labor rapidly dropped most of its opposition to U.S. domination of overseas territories.[218]

By the early twentieth century, then, organized labor was conspicuous for its silence on the major issues of national politics—money and banking, transportation regulation, tariff reform, trusts—and its voice on imperialism was weak and contradictory. Except where existing federal jurisdiction placed workers in the realm of the national state (as with public employees and seamen), it did not seek to expand the reach of the national state in the economy. Rather, it emphasized the negative aspects of state power: exclusion of immigrants and contraction of the reach of the antitrust laws.

The officers of the AFL clung to private action as a means of advancing labor's cause. Gompers and Mitchell joined the National Civic Federation (NCF), an organization of advanced capitalists, philanthropists, and professionals who sought to construct nonviolent solutions to labor conflicts. The preferred methods were trade agreements between union representatives and employers and informal mediation of industrial disputes.[219]

Gompers and Mitchell believed that their membership in the NCF would encourage capitalists, as well as the public, to see organized labor as an equal partner in industrial enterprise. If the large employers and financiers of the NCF could be prodded to endorse unions and collective bargaining, others, they hoped, would follow.[220] The NCF did achieve some success in the acceptance of trade agreements among its members before 1907, and its mediation work filled a vacuum. However, the organization's activists were concerned to establish industrial peace, not to promote unionization, and even their modest efforts brought sharp criticism from anti-labor employers both within and outside the NCF. The involvement of NCF members in the formation of the U.S. Steel Corporation did nothing, apparently, to stop the corporation's successful campaign to crush the steel unions, and the 1902 UMW strike against the anthracite coal "trust" (whose principals also had NCF ties) yielded no trade agreement and was settled only after intervention by the president of the United States.[221]

Whether because of the AFL officers' membership in the NCF or simple resignation to the inevitable, the federation's attitude toward industrial concentration mellowed significantly in the early twentieth century.[222] Gompers himself had accepted the large corporation as an inevitable and probably beneficial development and did not support legislation to control it. Perhaps thinking of his NCF contacts with enlightened industrialists such as Mark Hanna, rather than labor's actual experience to date, Gompers told the 1907 Chicago Conference on Trusts: "The greatest and most enlightened combinations of capital in industry have not seriously questioned the right and indeed, the advisability of organization among employees. . . . Organized labor has less difficulty in dealing with large firms and corporations today than with many individual employers or small firms."[223]

Given capitalists' anxiety about the potential danger that the Sherman Antitrust Act posed to business practices, Gompers hoped to use the forum of the National Civic Federation to revise the antitrust law in a way favorable to both labor and large corporations. Both must be allowed to form combinations, he argued. In return for an exemption from antitrust prosecution for its own activities, labor would support relaxation of the law and perhaps other business legislative goals as well. Gompers issued both an offer and a warning: "If the captains of industry expected any assistance from labor, they must see to it that the same rights of organization were accorded to labor which they demanded for themselves and they must make common cause with us for the full rights to which we as labor unions were entitled. Otherwise, what happened to them under the antitrust laws was of no concern to us."[224]

In pursuit of this exchange, Gompers threw the AFL's support behind a 1908 bill developed in the Roosevelt administration and backed by the NCF. The Hepburn bill would have instituted a voluntary system of federal licensing through which corporations would put themselves under the supervision of a presidential agency empowered to legalize their restraints of trade where those were deemed "reasonable." Trade unions could also avail themselves of the benefits of registration and were granted specific leave to strike or engage in other peaceful collective activities. The bill was never brought to a vote, since hearings revealed vociferous and generalized business opposition to the labor section (even after it was significantly modified) and to the unprecedented executive supervision that corporations must endure in order to achieve Sherman Act waivers.[225] It is ironic indeed that a labor organization committed to voluntarism and a minimal state threw its support to an extraordinarily statist measure anticipating a large centralization of discretionary power over business enterprise in the executive branch of the national government. But the AFL's support for the Hepburn bill represented no change of heart on statism. It was simply a measure of the organization's desperation before an employer counterattack that, aided by federal court decisions, threatened the very existence of labor unions.

The Injunction and Labor's Political Turn

In the decade after 1896, labor had enjoyed considerable success with its principal organizational weapons: the strike and the boycott. Both increased dramatically in frequency, and AFL membership more than tripled between 1898 and 1902. These successes triggered a massive antiunion movement by business.

In 1902, in the face of a damaging boycott by the United Hatters Union against several Danbury, Connecticut, hat manufacturers, one of the latter, D. E. Loewe, took the lead in organizing the American Anti-Boycott Association. Other antiunion employers' associations sprang up in a variety of industries to assist each other with "employer intelligence" about unionists, strategies for opposing unionization, and strike funds. The National Association of Manufacturers dedicated itself to combating unionism in the workplace and in politics. By 1907 it had taken the lead in forming the National Council for Industrial Defense to coordinate an expanded anti-labor lobbying campaign in Washington.[226]

Meanwhile, Loewe had initiated a court case that was to be of signal importance for labor. Resisting a closed-shop agreement, which the hatters had won in 187 firms (with only 12 nonunion holdouts), Loewe and Co. filed suit for damages against the United Hatters Union, charging that its effective secondary boycott, directed against wholesalers and retailers, constituted a combination in restraint of interstate commerce, an action prohibited under the Sherman Act.[227]

Careful legislative histories of the Sherman Act have concluded that congressional supporters of the 1890 law intended it to outlaw only *business* restraints and monopolies.[228] Nevertheless, a federal district court in 1893 declared that a New Orleans general strike violated the act, thus creating a powerful new resource for employers. This reformulation of the Sherman Act as an anti-labor weapon paralleled other judicial coups of the era. Federal judges (including William Howard Taft) discovered that although the Interstate Commerce Act intended no strict regulation of railroads, it could be used to punish railroad strikers or boycotters. In 1894, Cleveland's attorney general secured sweeping injunctions against the officers of the American Railway Union for obstructing rail traffic during the Pullman strike. Eugene V. Debs and other strike leaders were found guilty of contempt for violating an injunction, and a federal circuit judge in Chicago ruled that the rail workers' actions fell under the Sherman Act's prohibitions, as a "conspiracy against travel and transportation by railroad." In this case, however, the Supreme Court found the 1887 railroad act a sufficient statutory vehicle to halt such "obstructions" of commerce and to send strike leaders to jail.[229] The Court that had earlier transformed the Fourteenth Amendment from a civil rights measure to a shield against state regulation of business was not hesitant to twist landmark federal regulatory statutes into anti-labor juggernauts.

The decisive blow came in 1908, when the Supreme Court unanimously reversed a circuit court dismissal on an appeal financed by the American Anti-Boycott Association and made the first proclamation by the nation's highest court that the Sherman Act did apply to labor, whose activities would be broadly scrutinized for their effects on the flow of trade and commerce. The case was then returned to the lower court, which tripled the company's damages and fined the United Hatters Union of Danbury, Connecticut, $232,000. Union members were held liable for the fine, and their property was attached to pay it.[230]

A second injunction case struck directly at the AFL. In 1907 the Buck's Stove and Range Company obtained an injunction in the District of Columbia against AFL officials for publishing the firm's name in a "We Don't Patronize" list as part of a boycott. Gompers and two other AFL officers were sentenced to jail terms of six to twelve months for contempt of court. Although the Supreme Court later dismissed the contempt case on technical grounds, the case affirmed, in principle, labor's liability to Sherman Act prosecutions, even for mere speech or the issuance of printed matter supporting boycotts.[231]

These cases raised fears not only that the ordinary tactics of trade-union organization and mass pressure might be outlawed but also that the unions themselves might be threatened with financial ruin through oppressive fines. It was against this backdrop of employer militancy, judicial defeats, and stagnant membership that the AFL made its first organized foray into politics in 1906.

For over a decade, the federation had lobbied Congress for statutory exemption from Sherman Act prosecution. As early as 1892, such a bill was introduced in the House by a Staunton, Virginia, Democrat (Rep. Henry Tucker) hard-pressed by the Populists in his district. In the summer of 1900, an Arkansas Democrat (Rep. William Terry) introduced for the AFL a similarly worded exemption amendment that the Republican Judiciary Committee had refused to consider: "Nothing in this Act shall be so construed as to apply to trade unions or other labor organizations organized for the purpose of regulating wages, hours of labor, or other conditions under which labor is to be performed." The amendment passed, to loud applause, with only eight negative votes. But Republican votes were apparently aimed at symbolic election-year advantage. The antitrust bill that carried the amendment was quickly buried in the heavily Republican Senate, for this and three subsequent Congresses.[232]

The AFL leadership decided that its organizational goals now depended on a conversion or reconstitution of Congress via electoral politics. In 1906, without abandoning its independent nonpartisan stance, the organization mounted a large-scale campaign to mobilize state and local labor bodies, to pressure sitting members of Congress into passing the desired legislation, and to marshal labor votes against congressional enemies. A special political fund was raised, a modest $8,000. However, many local leaders responded heartily to the call from AFL headquarters to lend their support, and the federation's Washington staff was thrown into the political campaign.[233]

The AFL drew up a "Bill of Grievances" that encompassed its legislative demands. Preeminent among these was a statute prohibiting injunctions in labor disputes. Other demands included the following: effective workmen's compensation for accidents, an eight-hour day, and petition rights for government employees; an end to competition from convict-made goods; immigration restriction; a postal savings bank; improved working conditions for merchant seamen; and reconstitution of the House Labor Committee. The document—presented to the president of the Senate, the Speaker of the House, and President Roosevelt—elicited mostly unfavorable responses from the Republican leaders. Gompers thereupon mailed copies to all House members and to a group of Democratic and Republican Party leaders, requesting written replies.

The replies were reproduced in the September *American Federationist*, with the intention of guiding union voting in the districts. Of the 386 mem-

Table 3.8 Congressional Responses to Labor's Bill of Grievances, 1906

Region	Democrat		Republican		Both Parties	
	Pro	Vague/Con	Pro	Vague/Con	Pro	Vague/Con
Core	9	0	3	29	12	29
Diverse	1	0	4	20	5	20
Periphery	31	8	8	8	39	16
Total	41	8	15	57	56	65

bers of the House, 121 sent replies—a response rate of about 36 percent for the Democrats, 29 percent for the Republicans. A number of the Republicans, and a handful of periphery Democrats, returned very brief and vague responses. Republicans, in particular, tended to make vague promises to "give serious consideration to" or "consult with my colleagues about" labor demands. Gompers often appended his own editorial comments after the published replies, characterizing many as "haughty," "indefinite," or "condescending." When the length and the specificity of the responses are considered, especially on the critical issue of the injunction, 41 of the Democratic replies can be categorized as positive and 8 as either negative or too vague to characterize. For the Republican replies, the figures are 15 and 57.[234] The party and regional breakdown is given in table 3.8.

Though the periphery (mostly southern) Democrats, who constituted the great bulk of the party, were less unanimous than the small number of core Democrats, they nevertheless constituted by far the largest pro-labor bloc in the House, and this pattern is consistent with roll-call voting on labor bills, as will be demonstrated in chapter 10. Periphery Republicans as well were much more favorable than their core- and diverse-area copartisans. Together, periphery representatives composed thirty-nine out of the fifty-six favorable responses (70 percent).

Such patterns reveal the benefits to be gained by replacing hostile core Republicans with labor-backed Democrats, but this proved extremely difficult. As Gompers put it in his autobiography, "It was a serious question whether those who had been identified with the Republican Party organization could be brought to see that their interests as workingmen made it necessary for them to vote against that party because of its attitude on labor's paramount interests."[235] In both the 1906 and the 1908 campaigns, the AFL solicited funds for its political activities and distributed the legislative records of congressional members to further its "reward your friends, punish your enemies" strategy. Whereas local organizations were often more interested in positive support for friends of labor, the AFL leadership was reluctant to make endorsements, emphasizing the negative "punish your enemies" side of the adage.[236] Particularly targeted in 1906 was Republican Charles E. Littlefield of Maine, chair of the House Labor Committee. Littlefield's district was heavily industrial and contained an estimated three thousand AFL unionists. Gompers made numerous speeches in the district, blasting the congressman's anti-labor record.[237] Although Littlefield's victory margin was reduced in 1906, labor's enemy returned to Congress, and his party continued to hold the seat after he retired in 1908. The Republican-dominated Congress elected in 1906 proved to be even less sympathetic to labor than the previous one.[238]

In 1908, the union movement was beset by the Supreme Court's judgments in the Danbury hatters, *Buck's Stove and Range*, and *Adair* cases. Unemployment rose sharply after the Panic of 1907, and the growth of real wages ceased for several years. The NAM appealed to its members for a fund of $1.5 million to fight "industrial oppression" by trade unions.[239] In an outreach remarkable for the AFL, federation leaders called a special political conference to which they invited representatives of the Farmers' Union (FU), along with heads of all AFL national and international unions and the railroad brotherhoods.[240] It was clear, Gompers wrote later, that the AFL "had the cooperation of the farmers. . . . Our common interest was an amendment to the antitrust law excluding our organizations."[241]

Finally conceding the importance of party politics to judicial outcomes, the AFL decided, for the first time in its history, to urge that workers rally behind a presidential candidate. Going through the motions of impartial lobbying, the federation presented its list of legislative demands to both parties as they constructed their platforms in the 1908 presidential nominating conventions. The principal demands were exemption from Sherman Act prosecution and trial by jury in contempt cases flowing from injunctions; other sections called for extension of the eight-hour day to all workers on federal government contracts, an employers' liability law for workers in federal jurisdiction, a separate department of labor with a secretary in the cabinet, a federal bureau of mines, a postal savings bank, and a constitutional amendment for women's suffrage.[242]

The Republican convention rebuffed labor's petition. In Louis Koenig's account, Gompers "was rejected and humiliated by shouts of 'go to Denver'" (the Democratic convention site). He did, and Bryan and the agrarian Democrats welcomed the labor emissaries and incorporated most of the AFL demands into their platform.[243] Immediately after the platform was adopted by the convention, Bryan telephoned Gompers to get his reaction and invite the AFL leader to his home.[244] To cement his appeal to labor, Bryan selected as his running mate John W. Kern of Indiana, who as Democratic leader in the state senate had worked closely with the AFL.[245]

The prospects for a farmer-labor electoral alliance were seemingly enhanced in September when Gompers accepted the invitation of the Farmers' Union, the principal southern farmers' organization, to address its annual convention in Ft. Worth, Texas. As the AFL president was pondering the invitation, he received a warm letter from Farmers' Union officials informing him: "We desire to tell you that we have always looked forward to a visit from you; that we have always felt that much good would come of a visit from you, and that we will do everything in our power to make your visit a pleasant one. We need you; we want you. We will do all in our power to make you know that we want you."[246] Gompers warmed to the idea of an alliance of the two bodies, which represented, in aggregate, five million members. The AFL leader was greeted by great tides of applause as he entered the FU convention hall and as he concluded his address to the farm delegates. He focused his remarks almost entirely on the injunction issue and labor's need for legislative relief. In return, he pledged labor's reciprocal support for the farmers' legislative agenda, inciting wild cheers with the following words: "And whither thou goest, there will we also go. The ties that now bind the conscience and heart and intelligence and purposes and principles of the agricultural laborers and the industrial laborers are indissoluble for all time to come."[247] Gompers departed in a rush of good feeling, with the unanimous pledge of the farm organization to render him "loyal support in his efforts to get justice."[248]

Given the worsening of labor's position in 1907–8, the ringing endorsement of the Democratic Party, and the clearer party preferences of the national labor leadership, one would have predicted that the 1908 political mobilization of unionists would exceed that of 1906 and have a more dramatic effect. However, the reality epitomized labor's political fragmentation and vacillation. Analysis of the local labor bodies' response to the 1908 campaign shows "much less enthusiasm and energy than in 1906 and the emergence of great opposition within the AFL to Gompers's increasingly pro-Democratic strategy. Some unionists preferred the Socialist Party or a newly constituted independent labor party; however, there was also strong support for the Republican presidential candidate, despite that party's record on injunctions. Some members of the AFL Executive Council remained loyal to the GOP, as did many local unionists. John Mitchell, the head of the largest industrially organized union of unskilled workers, had enjoyed a close relationship with Roosevelt and worked to prevent a full Democratic commitment by the AFL. Another member of the AFL Executive Council, Daniel J. Keefe, announced his active support for Taft. The Steam Shovel and Dredge Men made an honorary union member of the Republican candidate, whom Gompers condemned as "the originator and specific champion of . . . government by injunction." Republican unionists wrote Gompers and angrily objected to his attempt to tell them how to vote. It was probably a Republican protectionist who returned one of Gompers's mailings after scrawling across it: "We vote as we please. Prosperity First."[249] When labor politics moved from the local stage to the national political arena, the internal contradictions arising from labor's uncertain position in the national political economy were sharply visible.

To commit the federation to the Democratic campaign thus implied riding roughshod over numerous dissenters. Hence the AFL campaign effort in 1908 was highly centralized and marked by much less local activity than in 1906, and many unionists complained of national dictation. Dissension in the ranks permitted the Republicans to deny that AFL pronouncements against the party represented labor sentiment and to berate its leaders for trying to "deliver the labor vote." AFL leaders with Republican leanings were singled out for praise in Taft's speeches.[250]

In his official pronouncements, Gompers frequently denied that the AFL had become politically partisan; positive endorsements were muted in favor of criticism of the Republicans' labor record.[251] However, cooperation between the AFL's national offices and the Democratic Party was extensive in 1908. The federation placed six of its organizers in the labor bureau of the Democratic National Committee, and the party paid for printing and distributing pamphlets drawn up by the AFL.[252] Bryan frequently consulted with Gompers in preparing his positions on labor issues, and the Democratic candidate's speeches, in turn, were often reprinted in the *American Federationist*.[253] Within the constraints of a small and fractured labor movement, it would seem that Gompers did about as much as he could to deliver a labor vote to the Democrats. Although the AFL's directors might be described as elite "business unionists," its grievances, adopted by the Democrats, had implications for the entire labor movement. The Republicans in 1906–8 left no doubt where they stood on labor issues, and as Gompers said of Taft, "It would have been impossible for the party to find a more effective representative of its policy."[254]

Business leaders in the industrial states also saw the contest in no uncertain terms and went all out to defeat the Democratic presidential candidate and pro-labor congressmen. As the AFL's leading antagonist, James van Cleave (head of Buck's Stove and Range and the National Association of Manufactures), put it, "The result of the [1908 Democratic] convention has made it the duty of the employing classes regardless of party to bury Bryan and Bryanism under such an avalanche of votes that the work will not have to be done over again in 1912. [255]

The results of the election belied the notion of a labor vote. Taft won handily, with a large popular vote in the northeastern states, where the AFL membership and campaign effort had been concentrated. Gompers, who "found himself in the awkward position of urging the unionists to assume a role he had always deprecated . . . discovered that the membership clung too well to the antipolitical dogma."[256] The Republicans maintained control of Congress, losing only three seats in the House and two in the Senate and winning over three-fourths of core House districts. Workers, it seemed, had again chosen the promise of Republican prosperity over the class appeals of the opposition.[257]

Bryan and the congressional Democrats had had great hopes for the farmer-labor alliance in 1908 and were bewildered by Taft's decisive victory. Bryan carried only the South, Kentucky, Oklahoma, Nebraska, and three mountain states. The Democrat lost even New York, which he had managed to carry, with Tammany's cooperation, in 1900. Though both Bryan and Gompers tried to put the best face on the results, it was clear that the labor vote "had simply not materialized."[258]

Chastened by the 1906–8 experience, the AFL seemed to revert to the political quiescence of the pre-1906 period. Very little effort was made to rally workers in the 1910 elections, short of providing legislative voting records to unionists who requested them.[259] Ironically, the retirement of organized labor from its brief foray into national politics coincided with the Democratic Party's first victory in House elections in almost two decades. The 1910 elections, followed by the Democratic sweep two years later, would bring the Progressive Era to high tide—and would yield many legislative benefits to a labor movement that could not plausibly claim any significant role in the outcome.

4

Farmers in Politics, 1873–1896

The farmer's orientation toward politics was much less ambiguous than the worker's. Though farmers, too, often differed among themselves on political questions, political activity was a natural outgrowth of organization, and the need for it was seldom disputed. In the post–Civil War industrial transformation, farmers constituted by far the most numerous class in the workforce, still a majority by 1870, compared with around 30 percent for workers in manufacturing, trade, and transportation.[1] So large an interest—broadly enfranchised, undisturbed by sharp cultural differences, and imbued with a long-standing republican ideology—was strongly predisposed to political action when confronted with the powerful economic dislocations of the late nineteenth century. Decades earlier, when workers' numbers were much smaller, they had lost the autonomy of the independent artisan; most workers, both native and foreign-born, were resigned to the status of dependent wageworkers. But farmers in the 1870s, 1880s, and 1890s were determined to hold to or regain the autonomy of the independent small producer in the new industrial economy and saw politics as a logical strategy to that end.[2] Because they were geographically dispersed and bound up in powerful flows of interstate and foreign commerce, local economic collective action could not provide the alternative for farmers that it might for workers. The farmer's enemy was not an employer but a *system*—a system of credit, supply, transportation, and marketing. To reorder such a system required political action at the highest level. Thus, while nineteenth-century industrialization appeared to offer labor a workplace alternative to political action, the commercialization of agriculture made politics all the more urgent for farmers.

The economic context of the farmers' political revolt is indicated by the data in tables 4.1–4.4. During the 1870s, 1880s, and 1890s, a lag in the growth of gold production for the world's money supply and expanding international competition in grain and textile fibers contributed to a sharply falling agricultural price level. While the number of farms more than doubled, farm income lagged the 130 percent increase in total national income, and its share of that

Table 4.1 Crop Prices and Percent of Domestic Production Exported, 1866–1900

	Wheat/bu.		Cotton/lb.		Corn/bu.	
1866	$1.53		0.32		0.47	
1870	0.94	(21%)	0.17	(73%)	0.49	(.2%)
1875	0.90		0.13		0.37	
1880	0.95	(40%)	0.11	(70%)	0.40	(6%)
1885	0.77		0.09		0.33	
1890	0.84	(22%)	0.09	(68%)	0.51	(5%)
1894	0.49		0.06		0.46	
1895	0.51		0.08		0.25	
1900	0.62	(34%)	0.09	(67%)	0.36	(10%)

Source: U.S. Department of Commerce, Bureau of the Census, *Statistical Abstract of the United States, 1909* (Washington, D.C.: GPO, 1910), 125, 126, 585–87.
Note: Average farm value for wheat and corn; for cotton, value per pound for average grade of upland cotton.

Table 4.2 Farm Mortgage Interest Rates and Tenancy by Region

	Effective Interest Rate		Sharecroppers and Tenants as Percent of All Farmers		
	1890	1915	1880	1890	1900
Northeast	5.6	5.7	16.0	18.4	20.8
East-North-Central	7.1	6.1⎤	20.5	23.4	27.9
West-North-Central	8.6	7.2⎦			
South Atlantic	7.4	7.4	36.1	38.5	44.2
South Central	8.2	8.7	36.2	38.5	48.6
West	9.1	9.1	14.0	12.1	16.6

Sources: 1890 interest rates: Kenneth A. Snowden, "Mortgage Rates and American Capital Market Development in the Late Nineteenth Century," *Journal of Economic History* 47 (September 1987): 675, table 1 (rounded to one decimal). 1915 interest rates: C. W. Thompson, "Interest Rates Paid by American Farmers," in Edwin G. Nourse, *Agricultural Economics* (Chicago: University of Chicago Press, 1916), exhibit D, 705 (regional figures were computed by averaging states in region). Tenancy: Fred A. Shannon, *The Farmer's Last Frontier: Agriculture, 1860–1897* (1945; reprint, White Plains, N.Y.: M. E. Sharpe, 1973), table, 418, appendix.

total declined from one-fourth to one-fifth.[3] For the two-thirds of U.S. farmers who lived in the southern, plains, and mountain states, the contrasts were more glaring. Whereas northeastern farmers had secure and rapidly expanding urban markets to supply with a diverse produce, over easily accessible and competitive transportation lines, periphery farmers faced severe credit stringencies, transportation monopolies, and the vulnerabilities of one-crop dependency. The growth of world markets in staple commodities brought

Table 4.3 Total Bank Deposits by Region, 1909

Region[a]	Total Deposits	Per Capita
Northeast	3,872,445,250	$139.81
South	225,729,394	7.68
Midwest	1,188,236,824	39.76
West	387,449,638	56.79
U.S.	5,678,735,380	61.74

Source: U.S. Department of Commerce, Bureau of the Census, *Statistical Abstract of the United States, 1909* (Washington, D.C.: GPO, 1910), 621; *1913* (Washington, D.C.: GPO, 1914), 25–27.
[a]Northeast here includes New England and mid-Atlantic (including Delaware, Maryland, and the District of Columbia); South includes south Atlantic, east- and west-south-central states; Midwest includes east- and west-north-central states; West includes mountain and pacific states. Alaska and island possessions are included in U.S. total but not in the regional figures.

great and hitherto unknown price fluctuations in those products, with often devastating results for cotton and wheat farmers. Producers of corn, most of which was used for domestic animal feed, and dairy, truck-crop, and livestock producers faced a much better price calculus. Arguments that railroad rates were falling and that overall relationships between farm and general price levels were not deteriorating in the 1865–1900 period[4] ignore sectoral and regional variations; although many cash-crop southern and midwestern farmers were extremely hard-pressed, a considerable segment of the farm population was relatively unaffected by the grievances that produced the 1870–96 wave of farm protest and thus remained outside the agrarian reform movement.

At the extremes of the credit spectrum, Alabama, Arkansas, Montana, New Mexico, Texas, and Wyoming farmers paid 9 to 11 percent interest for a farm mortgage loan in the early twentieth century—if they could get one at all—while northeastern farmers paid 5 to 6 percent.[5] Some of the premium reflected the higher risk of lending in distant, newly settled areas of variable rainfall. However, recent studies have concluded that risk alone cannot account for the interest-rate differentials. For residents of the southern and west north central states, dependent on out-of-state lenders for 43–67 percent of mortgage lending, these differentials smacked of monopoly and exploitation.[6] American mortgage companies reaped high profits in the late nineteenth century, and competition was limited by the fact that Congress in 1863 had prohibited the national banks from loaning money on real estate. Farmers in the periphery were at the mercy of agents or brokers who charged their own hefty commissions on top of the company interest rate.[7] State usury laws were common by the early twentieth century but had little beneficial effect where

Table 4.4 Railroad Freight Rates by Section, 1870–1900 (gold prices per ton-mile)

	East of Chicago				Chicago to Missouri River					West of Missouri River				Southern			
	a	b	c	d	e	f	g	h	i	j	k	l	m	n	o	p	q
1870	1.27	1.27	1.23	4.10	1.95	2.32	2.61	2.38	2.03		3.60			4.34	2.51	4.53	
1875	0.89	0.99	0.97	1.30	1.69	1.69	1.71	1.83	1.66		2.16	2.12	4.51	2.53	1.69	3.06	4.67
1880	0.75	0.92		0.87	1.54	1.21	1.49	1.75	1.08	3.15		2.38	3.09	2.47	1.59	2.16	3.11
1885	0.55	0.70	0.58	0.55	1.31	1.04	1.19	1.28	0.96	2.25	1.42	1.75	1.56	1.62	1.16	1.95	3.60
1890	0.64	0.66	0.69	0.56	0.94	1.00	0.98	1.00	0.81	1.53	1.14	1.13	1.25	1.39	0.97	1.31	3.13
1895	0.57	0.57	0.64	0.43	0.81	1.08	1.14	1.08	0.77	1.33	0.97	1.05	1.21	1.08	0.83	1.05	1.95
1900	0.49	0.50	0.58	0.34	0.65	0.99	0.84	0.93	0.77	1.11	1.05	0.93	0.97	1.14	0.75	0.92	1.77

Source: Fred A. Shannon, *The Farmer's Last Frontier: Agriculture, 1860–1897* (1945; reprint, White Plains, N.Y.: M. E. Sharpe, 1973), 296–97.

Note: Railroads: [a]Lake Shore and Michigan Southern; [b]Pennsylvania; [c]Pittsburgh, Fort Wayne, and Chicago; [d]Chesapeake and Ohio; [e]Illinois Central; [f]Chicago, Rock Island, and Pacific; [g]Chicago and Northwestern; [h]Chicago, Milwaukee, and St. Paul; [i]Chicago, Burlington, and Quincy (east of Missouri River); [j]Chicago, Burlington, and Quincy (west of Missouri River); [k]Union Pacific; [l]Atchison, Topeka, and Santa Fe; [m]Texas and Pacific; [n]Georgia; [o]Louisville and Nashville; [p]Southern; [q]Galveston, Houston, and Henderson.

money was scarce and may well have aggravated the shortage. The bottom line was that where debt burdens were already high, sharply falling prices and/or more than one bad harvest presented a high risk of foreclosure, and the pattern of agrarian unrest reflected that vulnerability to loss of income and independence.[8]

The Granger Movement

The Patrons of Husbandry, or the Grange, was founded in 1867 by Minnesota farmer Oliver H. Kelley, who had served as a clerk in the U.S. Department of Agriculture. A tour of the war-devastated South had convinced him of the need for a fraternal and self-improvement organization of farmers. Kelley and his farmer correspondents developed an organization open to both men and women, with a secret, colorfully labeled ritual following the fraternal enthusiasms of the times. From chapters in the mid-Atlantic states and Washington, D.C., the organization quickly took root and blossomed in the Midwest. In Minnesota there were, by the end of 1869, thirty-seven active chapters and a state organization prepared to embark on the cooperative purchase of agricultural supplies. Such cooperation, in both purchasing and marketing, and agitation against railroads became the principal activities of the early organization.[9]

The Grange began to grow rapidly in 1872 as Grangers plunged into cooperative projects, arranging the shipment of wheat to foreign ports, operating grist mills, offering life and fire insurance, and even manufacturing their own farm machinery and organizing a few banks.[10] By 1875, at its peak, the organization counted 758,768 members in nearly 19,000 granges (see table 4.5) This

Table 4.5 Membership in the Patrons of Husbandry (Grange) at Its 1875 Peak

Region/State	No. of Members	No. of Granges	No. of Granges per 100,000 Agr. Pop.
North Atlantic			
Maine	8,247	189	230
New Hampshire	2,528	69	152
Vermont	10,193	198	350
Massachusetts	3,825	98	142
Connecticut	480	16	36
New York	11,723	275	73
New Jersey	4,495	94	154
Pennsylvania	22,471	536	191
Total	63,962*	1,475	144

Table 4.5 (*Continued*)

Region/State	No. of Members	No. of Granges	No. of Granges per 100,000 Agr. Pop.
South Atlantic			
Delaware	503	23	136
Maryland	5,635	153	179
Virginia	13,885	663	266
West Virginia	5,990	280	309
North Carolina	10,166	342	109
South Carolina	10,922	342	136
Georgia	17,826	545	142
Florida	3,804	83	164
Total	68,731	2,431	168
North-Central			
Ohio	53,327	879	221
Indiana	60,298	1,485	498
Illinois	29,063	789	194
Michigan	33,196	605	283
Wisconsin	17,226	446	251
Minnesota	16,617	456	441
Iowa	51,332	1,164	452
Missouri	80,059	1,901	613
Dakota	1,178	53	341
Nebraska	8,177	289	508
Kansas	40,261	409	293
Total	390,734	8,476*	357
South-Central			
Kentucky	52,463	1,549	535
Tennessee	37,581	1,092	389
Alabama	17,440	531	158
Mississippi	30,797	645	216
Louisiana	10,078	315	182
Texas	37,619	1,203	457
Indian Territory	450	15	...
Arkansas	20,471	631	388
Total	206,899	5,981	331
West			
Montana	946	26	787
Colorado	2,098	63	629
Arizona	0	0	0
Nevada	378	15	481
Idaho	390	16	602
Washington	2,169	66	800
Oregon	8,233	186	926
California	14,228	263	413
Total	28,442	635	442
United States	758,768*	18,998*	279

Source: Solon J. Buck, *The Granger Movement* (Cambridge: Harvard University Press, 1913), table between 58 and 59.
*Totals corrected from the original.

membership constituted 11.2 percent of the entire male and female population over ten years old engaged in agriculture, making the Grange far and away the most successful "producer" organization of its time.[11]

Although Minnesota, Illinois, and Iowa were the early organizational leaders (and Illinois was the locus of the most extensive Granger political campaign), Missouri, Indiana, Ohio, and Kentucky had surpassed the pioneers by 1875, and the ratios of Grangers to agricultural population were highest in the mountain states. In 1874, Kansas and Nebraska had one grange for every one hundred people on farms.[12] In the South, Solon J. Buck points out, density of membership by the *white* population (blacks were not admitted) was even higher than in the Midwest.[13]

The Grange declared itself a "nonpolitical" organization and discouraged partisan pronouncements, but it encouraged members to be politically active as individuals. Many Grangers were involved in the farmers' conventions and mass meetings triggered by the 1873 panic, and many belonged to parallel farmers' clubs and state farmers' associations that made open political nominations and endorsements.[14] Farmers' uprisings in 1873 preceded the enactment of a strong railroad-commission law in Illinois (replacing an 1871 rate-setting law declared unconstitutional by the state supreme court), as well as a similar commission bill in Minnesota and the enactment of maximum statutory rate and antidiscrimination laws in Iowa and Wisconsin in 1874. Illinois farmers not only held mass meetings to demand a new railroad law and created a Farmers' Club in the legislature to press their demands but also defeated for reelection the chief justice who had presided over the voiding of the 1871 law.[15]

In the same elections, farmers' independent "antimonopoly" tickets were successful in fifty-three of the sixty-six counties in which they ran.[16] Similar movements by farm organizations were mounted against conservative Republican dominance in Iowa, Minnesota, and Wisconsin, with the Democratic parties there endorsing or fusing with the independents under the Antimonopoly or Reform label. By 1874, farmers' independent political movements were in operation in Kansas, Nebraska, and California, and a state-level party had developed in Illinois. By 1876, the movement encompassed eleven midwestern and western states. The principal concerns of the latter were enforcement of the railroad laws, civil-service reform, and economy in government—the latter two representing thrusts against widely perceived corruption in the one-party-dominant Midwest. There was also the beginning of an affinity for a soft-money ("greenback") policy in Illinois and some rumbling against high tariffs. In state and national elections in the fall of 1874, the Illinois Independent Reform Party elected (with the help of the Democrats) the state superintendent of education, three congressmen, and a swing bloc in the state legislature.[17]

The outcome of the seventies midwestern reform movement was a spate of state laws regulating railroads and warehouse facilities, through independent commissions or legislative rate-setting or both. This legislation, upheld in 1877 by the Supreme Court, established the right of governments to institute close supervision of the most powerful corporations in the country. The original "Granger laws" of 1870–74 were subsequently repealed or weakened in Minnesota, Iowa, and Wisconsin after a determined counterattack by the railroads. However, these precedents stimulated subsequent state regulatory efforts across the South, Midwest, and West, and midwestern experience under the Granger laws would inform the drive for federal railroad control. The first such bill to pass the U.S. House of Representatives (in 1874) was sponsored by an Iowa congressman and drew its principal support from states where the Grange was strongest.[18]

The Grange was the first large-scale, national, reform-oriented occupational organization, and it left its imprint on subsequent labor and farmers' organizations, particularly the Farmers' Alliance.[19] In politics, the state and local Independent, Reform, and Antimonopoly Parties spawned by the Granger movement were overtaken by a nationally organized protest party focused on financial reform. The National Greenback Party absorbed the independent reform movements in Illinois and Indiana in mid-decade.[20] From the Midwest, the soft money ideology swept south and west, embraced by many credit-starved farmers who saw it as the essential remedy for their economic distress.

Agrarian Greenbackism

It is notable that all of the political movements which have had origin among those who claim to be the "producing classes"—the Trades Unionists, Knights of Labor, Farmers Alliance, People's Party, etc.—have regarded banks as their natural enemies and financial methods as a point for successful attack upon the bulwarks of money and privilege.
            Ellis B. Usher, *The Greenback Movement*
                    of 1875–1884 (1911)

The decline of farm commodity prices and the rising debt burden indicated in tables 4.1 and 4.2 reflected economic factors such as rising international competition and increased production, but they were also the results of political decisions made by the national government: (1) to create a national banking system tied to government bonds and biased against agriculture; (2) to return to a currency based on gold, the production of which was not keeping pace with the growth of population and commerce; (3) to pay interest on and redeem Civil War bonds, which had been purchased in depreciated money, in gold rather than in greenbacks; (4) to take a large portion of the latter out of circulation; and (5) to demonetize silver. To working men and women in the late 1870s, but particularly to farmers, these decisions came to represent a colossal "fraud against the people" perpetrated by the national state on behalf of a financial elite.

The primary function of the national banks created under the 1863–64 banking acts was to provide a market for government bonds issued to finance the war. National banks had to purchase those bonds as security for their note issues. State bank notes were effectively abolished by a 10 percent tax. Whether because of legal requirements or because of low interest rates on their bond backing, the national banks before 1900 put into circulation only about 30 percent of the notes their bondholdings permitted.[21] Thus, the two major forms of circulating currency in 1867 were (1) national bank notes produced in rather constricted volume, concentrated in the Northeast and extremely scarce in the South (the latter was out of the Union when the system was inaugurated, the poverty of the South made the conditions set for chartering such banks difficult to meet, and the region had, of course, seen its national currency made worthless overnight with the collapse of the Confederacy);[22] and (2) greenbacks, or U.S. government notes issued during the war as an "emergency" currency backed by nothing but the government's word that they were legal tender. By a law of 1866 the amount of greenbacks in circulation was reduced from 449 million (at its 1865 peak) to 356 million. Greenbacks could not be exchanged for gold (specie exchanges for paper money having been suspended in 1861) until the provisions of the Resumption Act of 1875 went into effect in 1879. After 1875, the treasury secretary, a diehard deflationist, further retired greenbacks in tandem with a national bank note issue, aggravating the mid-seventies depression. The government also moved to retire $240 million in other wartime U.S. currency. Furthermore, as a result of an 1873 statute that very few people (except its deflationist authors) understood, the minting of silver dollars was discontinued.[23] The purpose of these actions was to return, as soon as (politically) possible, to the gold standard. The outcome was a drop in the total amount of money in circulation from $30.35 per capita in 1865 to $19.36 by 1880.[24]

As Milton Friedman and Anna J. Schwartz have pointed out, deliberate currency contraction and the slow growth of the gold supply did not prevent a remarkable postwar industrial expansion.[25] However, the lurching toward a monometallic currency standard produced very uneven costs and benefits and was increasingly contested in the political arena as its effects were felt. Creditors who could have debts repaid in appreciated currency and long-term-bond holders who could receive interest in gold and exchange, for "dear" money, bonds purchased in "cheap" money were the direct beneficiaries. On the other hand, some businessmen and manufacturers away from the seacoast cities were convinced, at least in the late 1860s and the 1870s, that monetary contraction denied them sufficient credit to expand and caused financial panics and prolonged recessions.[26]

A much larger number of workers subscribed to these theories as they felt the pain of layoffs (see chapter 3). There was a decline in wage levels in 1877, and throughout the decade of the seventies, when labor greenbackism was at its height, real wages were essentially flat. However, the effects of deflation were less severe for workers than for staple-crop farmers because wage cutting lagged the fall in prices (and falling farm prices increased real wages). The average daily wage in manufacturing increased about 7 percent between 1865 and 1890. Steep price declines, combined with wage increases secured in the militant 1880s, produced a real wage increase of almost 50 percent over the period.[27] Even in periods of significant improvement, however, the purchasing power of wages increased at a much lower rate than profits.[28] Furthermore, late-nineteenth-century unemployment was higher and fluctuated more sharply in the United States than in other industrial countries. There was severe unemployment in midwestern coal- and iron-producing regions in the mid-seventies, and data for the 1890s, when reliable statistics first became available, show unemployment levels of 15–17 percent in manufacturing and of over 30 percent in the coal-mining and building industries.[29] This insecurity must have underlain labor leaders' early enthusiasm for "soft" money and the repeated endorsements of bimetallism by AFL conventions in the depressed 1890s.

Farmers were not significant among the earliest advocates of soft money, a fact that Robert Sharkey attributes to the relative well-being of nonsouthern farmers amid still-high price levels in the late 1860s.[30] But a decade later, farmers were the principal soft-money constituency and would remain so well into the twentieth century. The key to the spread of agrarian greenbackism was the extreme disadvantage of the South in the political economy of the late nineteenth century, a position that turned even locally conservative "redeemers" into radicals on issues of national monetary and regulatory policy.[31]

The shortage of money in the postbellum South had thwarted the establishment of a wage-labor system. What emerged instead was the only plausible alternative in the circumstances: sharecropping. Under this system, a landless farmer unable to pay cash rent took up residence on a parcel (say, fifty acres) of a landowner's estate and paid "rent" with a share of the crop, keeping the rest for himself. Whether his share was one-fourth, one-third, or one-half depended on what the tenant brought to the bargain. If he had his own mule, plow, and tools, his share was bigger and the degree of supervision less. In the old plantation areas in the immediate aftermath of the war, the system had clear advantages for the large landowner, who was desirous of binding his newly freed labor force to the land and who was himself hard-pressed to come up with cash for wages.[32] Newly freed blacks also preferred independent sharecropping to tightly controlled gang-labor for wages; they hoped to be able to buy their own land, and remarkably, the percentage of black farm operators who did own their land grew from zero to one-fourth by 1900. For white farmers, movement was in the other direction. As the cotton economy spread into the upcountry and the southwestern frontier, the furnishing merchant and crop lien followed, with diminishing prospects for small farmers to acquire or hold deeds to the land. From a South-wide tenancy rate of about one-fifth before the war, dependence reached 37 percent of white farmers by 1900 (by which point the majority of southern tenants were white). This was, of course, still well below the 75 percent black tenancy rate. And among the tenant class, black farmers were found much more often in the lowest order of "croppers" working on half shares.[33]

The notorious crop-lien system entrapped both black and white tenants and small farm owners and would oppress southern staple-crop producers well into the 1930s. To secure essential supplies for farming and household sustenance, cash-poor farmers were forced to go to a merchant (sometimes their actual landlords), who advanced the supplies in return for a share of the crop. In this transaction, borrowers paid extraordinary interest rates, ranging from 40 to 110 percent—and most found themselves burdened with increasing debt. When the merchant or landlord finished the tallying up of what was owed him (an accounting that took place directly at harvest time, denying the farmer the flexibility of holding his crop for a better price), very little cash was left to the tenant. Indebtedness and cash-crop dependency were aggravated by the "furnisher's" frequent insistence that cotton be planted on all available land, crowding out space on which the tenants might have grown their own food or raised other crops or livestock for a better diet and additional income. This ensured the lender a readily marketable cash crop as security for the loans while putting the borrower more and more in debt for the ordinary food and feedstuffs in which farmers had once been self-sufficient.[34]

The shortage of banks and money in the South was responsible for the monopolistic position of the merchant-landlord and diminished the ability of young farmers to purchase land. Only the wealthiest farmers, with high land values, chattel, and other assets, could qualify for even an 8 percent mortgage. Most paid multiples of that rate to purchase basic provisions from a supply merchant. With little industry, a small middle class, and a high regional debt burden, few citizens had sufficient means to charter public or private banks, few towns were large enough to house them, and only very small accumulations of deposits were available to be lent out. Many local lenders were in or near monopolistic positions.[35]

Thus a complex of economic and political factors emanating from the effects of the Civil War and the anomalous position of an export-based agricultural economy in a rapidly industrializing nation trapped the South in a downward spiral of poverty and near-colonial dependence. Most southerners were farmers. With little regional opportunity for industrial employment and with limited skills and education to seek their fortunes outside the South, the only means to a decent life was ownership of a farm, a goal increasingly out of reach in the late nineteenth century. Even the one significant southern industry—textiles—depended on limited local funds, being unable to attract any significant outside capital.[36] The South as a *region* was starved for credit. Not surprisingly, it became the core of the movement for money and bank reform in the 1880s and remained so for the next three decades.

As roll-call analysis by Carl V. Harris has shown (see table 4.6), southern Democrats in Congress moved away from their hard-money northeastern co-partisans to align themselves with midwestern and western soft-money advocates as early as the 43rd Congress. Numerous attempts were made by the southern-midwestern-western bloc to repeal the Resumption Act passed by the lame-duck Republican Congress in 1875 and to restore silver to the place it had held before its demonetization in 1873.[37]

Midwestern representatives had taken the lead on monetary issues while the South was still under Reconstruction. Farmers in newly settled regions of the north central states, having incurred heavy debts to purchase land and supplies, had been hard hit by depression and were attracted to soft-money doctrines in the 1870s.[38] The sympathies of many of the region's manufactur-

Table 4.6 Party and Regional Patterns on "Soft Money" Issues (Yea-Nay)

	Republicans	Democrats	Total
House of Representatives			
Pass Inflation Act (1874)			
Northeast	17–53	0–17	17–70
Midwest Far West	61–11	14–11	75–22
South	34–6	24–13	58–19
Remonetize and Coin Silver (1876)			
Northeast	2–26	11–18	13–44
Midwest Far West	27–8	33–5	60–13
South	4–6	40–5	44–11
Pass Bland Silver Coinage Bill (1877)			
Northeast	4–32	9–11	13–43
Midwest Far West	62–4	33–0	95–4
South	6–1	68–4	74–5
Pass Bland Free Coinage Bill (1886)			
Northeast	2–51	1–30	3–81
Midwest Far West	22–40	37–12	59–52
South	5–3	57–28	61–31
Senate			
Pass Silver Coinage Bill (1890)			
Northeast	1–16	1–2	2–18
Midwest	0–9	5–0	5–9
Far West	16–3	1–0	17–3
South	—	24–1	24–1

Source: Carl V. Harris, "Right Fork or Left Fork: The Section-Party Alignment of Southern Democrats in Congress, 1873–1897," *Journal of Southern History* 42 (November 1976): table 4, pp. 482–83. Harris includes announced pairs in his vote count and, on House voting, combines the few representatives from the Far West with those from the Midwest before 1890. Only major-party stands are included in the "total" column.

ers and businesspeople propelled even the Republican Party in the Midwest to vote overwhelmingly for the 1874 Inflation Act, against a large opposing vote from northeastern Republicans (see table 4.6).[39] However, as the monetary debate intensified, manufacturers in western Pennsylvania and Ohio, who had earlier been attracted to the program, began to turn away from the radical potential of Greenbackism. They did so amid Republican charges that inflationists were inciting class war. The greenbackers of the mid-seventies became the first in a long line of American reformers to be branded "communists."[40]

After 1876, as silver's price in relation to gold dropped, soft-money forces became more receptive to the remonetization of silver as an alternative strategy. Silver, a precious metal seen as possessing "intrinsic value," had once enjoyed a place alongside gold in the nation's currency. Hence restoration of silver was a more moderate way to oppose contraction than the greenback printing so loathed by the creditor class. Taking their place in the House after the landmark elections of 1876, southern Democrats voted 68 to 4 for a silver-coinage bill sponsored by another rural Democrat, Rep. Richard Bland of Missouri. Midwestern Democrats cast a unanimous vote for the bill, as did the handful of western Democrats. Republicans from these regions were almost unanimously for the bill as well. In the same pattern that runs through all the votes in table 4.6, the industrial Northeast backed hard money—the Democrats with some division, the Republicans almost without exception. However, when Iowa Republican Sen. William B. Allison devised a milder version in the midwestern vein, making the silver dollar legal tender again but saving the gold standard by sharply limiting the amount of silver to be coined, midwestern representatives flocked to the compromise. A majority of southern and the few western Democrats held out for unlimited silver coinage.[41]

The ease with which southern Democrats responded to agrarian demands and embraced silver in the 1870s helped to blunt the appeal of a radical third-party movement in the region. The outburst of southern Greenback and other "independent" campaigns in 1877–78 was thus directed more against local political monopolies and the conservative state policies of the "redeemer" governments than against national economic policy. The local issues included taxation, support for public schools, lien laws and the plight of the sharecropper, land grants to and regulation of railroads, and the convict lease system— issues that divided small farmers and workers from planters. There were also hotly contested proposals to "readjust" or even repudiate the inflated state debts incurred (often in subsidizing rail lines and public improvements that never materialized) by Reconstruction governments.[42]

Though coalitions were messy because of the tendency of southern Republicans to join any crusade against Bourbon Democrats, the animus behind readjustment, as that behind the other reform issues, came mostly from small farmers. The Virginia Grange played an active role in the agitation; the business and conservative political establishment led the "funder" defense. The campaign for readjustment led to competition for the black vote and farmer-labor appeals, demonstrating the power of financial issues in the late nineteenth century to sweep up social protests among the have-nots. The readjust-ment issue was bound up with other social issues because the stringency of state finances had led to painful cuts in public education and asylums and to the hiring out of convicts to save prison money. After the Readjuster Party won control of the Virginia legislature in 1879, it repealed the poll tax, re-duced land taxes, attempted to raise the corporate tax, pursued state claims against railroads while empowering local school boards to tax them, increased funding for public schools, provided for the chartering of labor and other "benevolent and fraternal" organizations, and established legal wage-payment rights for workers.[43]

National attempts to organize a greenback party had not originated with farmers' organizations but grew out of the labor-reform movement in the Mid-west in the early 1870s. However, in the wake of the panic of 1873 and President Ulysses S. Grant's veto of the inflation bill, farm leaders became increasingly active in monetary reform, including the formation of an independent party in 1875. In the momentous presidential election of 1876, the new Independent (Greenback) Party, with New York philanthropist (and former iron manufac-turer) Peter Cooper as its presidential nominee, polled only 80,000 votes, mostly in the midwestern Granger states. However, deepening agricultural depression and the great railroad strikes of 1877 unleashed the diverse Independent-Green-back political campaigns described above and in chapter 3.[44]

The political reformers who worked to build the national Greenback Party came to the effort by way of earlier experience in the midwestern and Pacific Coast labor movements, the Grange, and farmer-backed independent-party movements. They envisioned a broad-based reform movement, welcoming delegates from the National Women's Suffrage Association and the Socialist Labor Party.[45] But the key to their hopes and strategy was a farmer-labor coalition. To that end, Greenback platforms incorporated virtually the whole of labor's political agenda. The 1880 platform declared

> that labor should be so protected by National and State authority as to equal-ize the burdens and insure a just distribution of its results; the eight-hour law of Congress should be enforced, the sanitary condition of industrial establishments placed under rigid control; the competition of contract labor abolished, a bureau of labor statistics established, factories, mines, and work-shops inspected, the employment of children under fourteen years of age forbidden, and wages paid in cash . . . [and as] the importation of Chinese serfs tends to brutalize and degrade American labor, therefore immediate steps should be taken to abrogate the Burlingame Treaty.[46]

But the heart of the Greenback critique of American politics and capitalism lay in its radical proposals for government appropriation of the money-creating power.

> Corporate control of the volume of money has been the means of dividing society into hostile classes, of the unjust distribution of the products of labor, and of building up monopolies of associated capital endowed with power to confiscate private property. It has kept money scarce, and scarcity of money enforces debt . . . [and] ends in the bankruptcy of the borrower. Other results are deranged markets, uncertainty in manufacturing enterprise and agriculture, precarious and intermittent employment for the laborers, industrial war, increasing pauperism and crime, and the consequent intimidation and disfranchisement of the producer and a rapid declension into corporate feudalism; therefore we declare:
>
> *First*—That the right to make and issue money is a sovereign power to be maintained by the people for the common benefit. The delegation of this right to corporations is a surrender of the central attribute of sovereignty, (void) of constitutional sanction, conferring upon a subordinate and irresponsible power absolute dominion over industry and commerce. All money, whether metallic or paper, should be issued and its volume controlled by the Government, and not by or through banking corporations, and when so issued should be a full legal-tender for all debts, public and private.[47]

It was logical that a state that was to be entrusted with such fundamental economic powers should have other responsibilities as well. Hence, in addition to the labor provisions, it was the duty of Congress that "all lines of communication and transportation should be brought under such legislative control as shall secure moderate, fair and uniform rates for passenger and freight traffic." To support its increased responsibilities, the state required a graduated income tax. But the expanded functions of the national state were to be limited to domestic affairs: "We are opposed to an increase of the standing army in times of peace, and the insidious scheme to establish an enormous military power under the guise of militia laws."

With respect to citizenship rights and the form of the expanded democratic state, the platform denounced efforts to restrict suffrage and urged the states to ensure "that every citizen of due age, sound mind and not a felon, be fully enfranchised." "Absolute democratic rules for the governance of Congress" were demanded, abolishing committee "veto power."

A Jeffersonian republicanism for a new industrial era, Greenbackism in 1880 caught up the major strands of political reform in the post–Civil War era. The party's standard-bearer, James B. Weaver of Iowa, became the first presidential candidate to conduct a genuinely popular campaign, traveling, by his own estimate, some twenty thousand miles across the country and addressing large crowds.[48] When the ballots were counted, however, the Greenbacker had garnered only 3 percent of the vote. The farmer-labor reform impulse ran up against entrenched major-party loyalties and, as it happened, not only a bountiful harvest at unusually stable prices but also an upturn in business conditions.[49] Except for the weakness of the southeastern vote, the county-level Greenback vote was highest where per capita bank deposits were lowest.[50] A study of the 306 counties where the party won 10 percent or more of the vote found them to be an overwhelmingly agricultural group, concentrated in the midwestern- southwestern interior, with high debt burdens and low value added in manufacturing.[51] The highest votes in absolute terms were cast in Missouri, Michigan, Iowa, Texas, Illinois, Pennsylvania, and Kansas, in that order.[52] Clearly, Greenbackism was a movement whose time had not yet arrived. A decade later, its doctrines and farmer-labor coalition project would find a new life in populism and, through that movement, in the Democratic Party; however, the failure of urban labor to respond to Greenback Party appeals in 1880 was an omen of things to come.

The Farmers' Alliance

The Southern Farmers' Alliance had its beginnings in north-central Texas. In the late 1870s, it was another self-help organization for the "agricultural classes," taking root in several frontier counties with a surprising (to twentieth-century urban dwellers) density of social organization. Its founding members were dissatisfied with the Grange but well acquainted with its cooperative activities. They were also attracted to greenbackism—so much so that one wing of the early organization was destroyed by Greenback-Democratic contention. Rebuilt in 1879, the early Farmers' Alliance (FA) devoted itself to the needs of the small yeomen farmers and husbandmen who were its members. Its activities included recovering stray animals and chasing rustlers, avoiding eviction by unscrupulous "land sharks," and participating in vigilante action (fence cutting and post burning) against the large ranchers who were rapidly enclosing the open range. The FA managed, within a few years, to create a complex organization with great missionary potential, drawing on the experience of rural churches, fraternal organizations, and the Grange. Like the last and like the contemporary Knights of Labor, the Alliance heightened camaraderie (and it was a fellowship of both sexes) by secrecy and ritual.[53]

Whether because the time and place were ripe for agrarian mass mobiliza-

tion or because the Alliance supported broad economic programs, unique outreach activities, and ambitious cooperatives, the FA was destined to become
one of the most remarkable social movements in American history. It would
be the progenitor of the Populist Party, and the Populists' fusion with the
Democratic Party in 1896 would plant the agrarian radical ideology in that
organization, giving it an extended life and the means to make a profound
impact on the national state decades later.

By the end of 1882, about 140 "suballiances" (the local unit, consisting
of five to twenty farm families) were joined in a Texas state alliance. Membership was open to men and women, over sixteen years of age, who were farmers
or farm laborers, country school teachers, doctors, and ministers. In later
amendments, "mechanics" were added and lawyers, bankers, and merchants
excluded. Blacks were also denied membership because, it was stated, white
women (who constituted about one-fourth of the membership) could not attend meetings at which black men were present. As a result, a separate Colored Farmers' Alliance (CFA) was organized. However, black farmers were
permitted, and were sometimes encouraged, to participate in the FA cooperatives, to attend outdoor rallies, to listen to speeches, and to partake of the
food (after the whites had eaten). The Alliance's modest outreach to black
southerners and the commitment of individual leaders to protect black rights
and foster class unity were bold enough to violate the region's hardening racial
mores and to provoke outrage and ridicule from Bourbon Democrats. By late-
twentieth-century standards these efforts were, of course, quite limited and
imbued with condescension.[54]

The FA began its rapid growth in 1884. The key to the new dynamism
was its system of "lecturers." Appointed by the state organization, they were
drawn disproportionately from the class of modest rural professionals—ministers, teachers, and doctors. Most were also farmers and had unimpressive
formal education, but they possessed experience and abilities above those of
their rustic neighbors. The lecturers spread the Alliance "gospel" of political
education, social criticism, and economic collective action to remote rural
settlements. In the words of Robert C. McMath Jr., "[The lecturer] was to
the Alliance what the circuit rider had been to early Methodism."[55]

The man responsible for establishing the network was the first "Traveling
Lecturer," S. O. Daws. An energetic lay preacher and small farmer, Daws
was a stirring orator with a self-constructed philosophy that emphasized the
reform role of the yeoman farmer in a time of growing monopoly and concentration of wealth. His strategy for the Alliance was twofold: to build, through
the lecturers, a network for economic and political education; and to use

the county alliances as the basis for a new cooperative movement designed to break the hold of the furnishing merchant. The alliances organized by Daws might contract with one merchant who agreed to fair prices and credit in exchange for Alliance business; but increasingly, they also organized their own stores, their own cotton grading, weighing, and storage yards, and their own cooperative marketing ventures. The last involved "bulking" cotton and seeking buyers willing to make the highest bid. These activities taxed the capabilities of unschooled farmers with little cash or business acumen and provoked the wrath of merchants and cotton brokers, but they mushroomed Alliance membership. By the fall of 1885, there were over 500 suballiances, each with its designated lecturer and each bound in county organizations, which were also headed by lecturers. A few months later, the number of suballiances reached over 1,650, with membership pegged at over 92,000.[56]

The year 1886 proved momentous for the Texas Alliance. A severe drought struck the plains, causing extensive crop and livestock losses. After President Grover Cleveland vetoed a bill appropriating $50,000 for seed grain, the Alliance coordinated an extensive relief effort.[57] Solidarity was not limited to farmers, however. Labor organization in Texas was also growing rapidly in 1885–86, and to many Alliance members it seemed logical that the FA and the KOL make common cause. Though some leaders (including the current president) opposed the move, Daws's protégé William Lamb proclaimed an Alliance boycott in support of the Knights, who were battling with the Gould railroad colossus and a Dallas mercantile company. Joint political meetings were held, and Alliance farmers shared food and funds with the railroad strikers.[58] Farmer-labor political coalitions formed in at least twenty Texas counties in 1886, and the political rhetoric of the Alliance moved from a focus on the yeoman to appeals directed at the "laboring class" of farmers and workers. The FA was beginning to move into class politics.[59]

At the 1886 state convention at Cleburne, Texas, the majority political faction won the adoption of a set of legislative demands conceived as the basis of a political alliance of "the industrial classes . . . now suffering at the hands of arrogant capitalists and powerful corporations."

> We demand: The recognition by incorporation of trade unions, cooperative stores and such other associations as may be organized by the industrial classes to improve their financial condition, or to promote their general welfare . . . [and] the substitution of legal tender Treasury notes for the issue of the national banks; that the Congress of the U.S. regulate the amount of such issue, by giving to the country a per capita circulation that shall increase as the population and business interests of the country expand.

. . . the establishment of a national bureau of labor statistics [to] arrive at a correct knowledge of the educational, moral and financial condition of the laboring masses of our citizens. And further, that the commissioner of the bureau be a cabinet officer of the U.S.

. . . the enactment of laws to compel corporations to pay their employees according to contract, in lawful money . . . and the giving to mechanics and laborers a first lien upon the product of their labor to the full extent of their wages.

. . . the passage of an interstate commerce law that shall secure the same rates of freight to all persons . . . according to distance of haul, without regard to amount of shipment. To prevent the granting of rebates, to prevent pooling freights to shut off competition; and to secure to the people the benefit of railroad transportation at reasonable cost.

. . . that all convicts shall be confined within the prison walls and the contract system be abolished.

. . . a call for a national labor conference, to which all labor organizations shall be invited . . . to discuss such measures as may be of interest to the laboring classes.

The Alliance convention also demanded that public lands and lands forfeited by railroads or other corporations be sold in parcels of limited size to actual settlers, on easy terms; that fences unlawfully erected by corporations or cattle companies be removed from public lands; that corporations be compelled to pay taxes due; that futures dealing in agricultural commodities be abolished; and that aliens be prohibited from owning land in the United States (a demand aimed at Scottish and English cattle syndicates). The president of the Alliance was authorized to appoint "a committee of three to press these demands upon . . . the legislators of the State and nation."[60]

The program, in other words, incorporated "the greenback critique of American finance capitalism"[61] and interwove the specific demands of farmers and workers. Its radical tone and the break it seemed to portend with the Democratic Party almost led to the secession of a minority faction wedded to a nonpolitical posture. A split was averted by the efforts of the man who was to become the principal economic theorist and publicist of the organization: Charles Macune. Another of the remarkable "rural professionals" attracted to the Alliance, Macune was self-educated in medicine and law, was editor of an Alliance newspaper, and possessed unusual writing and organizing talents. He convinced the new FA leadership and the antipolitical dissidents that, without abandoning the Cleburne political program, the organization should dedicate its energies to renewing and expanding economic cooperation and to seeding new branches and merging with similar progressive farm organizations in other southern states.[62]

One of those organizations, the Arkansas Agricultural Wheel, had an estimated membership of 75,000 in that state alone, was represented in almost every county, and had chartered branches in Alabama, Kentucky, Missouri, Mississippi, Tennessee, Texas, Wisconsin, and Indian Territory. The total membership of the Wheel was estimated at several hundred thousand in 1887. The parent Arkansas organization has been described by Carl C. Taylor as "equally active in economic projects and more militant in its political attitudes than the Texas Alliance." Like the Alliance, it had pledged itself to concerted action with labor unions. In 1887–88, after a whirlwind of organizing activity, the Alliance merged with the Wheel, with the smaller Louisiana Farmers' Union, and with the North Carolina Farmers' Association, led by Col. Leonidas L. Polk, a former Granger and editor of *Progressive Farmer*. The combined organization called itself the Farmers' and Laborers' Union of America, indicating the outreach to labor.[63]

Although the Wheel and some other allied groups had accepted black members, at the time of merger the segregation policy of the FA prevailed. Given the weight of southern racist sentiment, divergent party attachments, and also blacks' considerable skepticism of white farmers, separate organizations seemed inevitable. Richard M. Humphrey, a white Allianceman and Baptist minister who had worked with black churches, played a prominent role in the founding of the Colored Farmers' Alliance and the establishment of its cooperative exchanges; both black and white organizers aided the black organization as it spread into the southeast from Texas. Less is known about the CFA than the FA, since secrecy protected its members from landlord and merchant retaliation. Humphrey, who served as its national spokesman, claimed over one million members for the organization by 1890, but Lawrence Goodwyn puts the figure closer to a quarter million.[64]

In the upper Mississippi Valley, another farmers' alliance had also begun to take shape in the late 1870s; like the southern FA and the Wheel, it combined local cooperative efforts with antimonopoly political demands. Spurred, like the Texas movement, by drought, grievances against the railroads, and the hard times of the mid-eighties, the organization grew rapidly in the old Granger states of the Midwest. A convention in Minneapolis in 1887 drew delegates from seven states, the most active representing Kansas and the Dakotas.[65] A Minnesotan with some fame in antimonopoly politics, Ignatius Donnelly, served as official state lecturer and general promoter. The "northwestern" alliances around this time claimed about 27,000 members. In Illinois, the Farmers' Mutual Benefit Association, known for its well-run grain cooperative in the corn belt, claimed several thousand in 1887, spurting to perhaps 40,000 members by the end of 1888. It held itself aloof from the larger regional organization, as well as from the earnest entreaties to merge with the southern FA.[66]

The southern and northwestern alliances agreed to hold a joint meeting in St. Louis in 1889 and to seek an expanded confederation of all the farmer organizations and organized labor. The hoped-for union, however, could not be consummated. The ostensible barriers were the northwestern alliance's objections to the southern organization's secrecy and rituals, its exclusion of blacks, its adherence to Macune's radical "subtreasury" plan (see below) introduced at the St. Louis meeting, and southern opposition to a proposed federal law banning a cottonseed oil product (oleomargarine) in competition with the butter and lard produced in the Midwest. The southerners were willing to drop the race stricture from the national constitution, but they held secrecy essential to the success of the cooperative movement. More important to the failure of the merger, in the view of recent scholarship, was the organizational weakness and programmatic timidity of the northwestern alliance.[67] The much smaller northern organization lacked the strong grass-roots base of the southern suballiance cooperative and lecture system and had not developed a comparable critique of capitalism around which to rally the "producer" forces. Its leaders, in Goodwyn's view, hesitated before the organizational and ideological zeal of the Farmers' and Laborers' Union because "the [southern alliance] had a program which produced both internal structure and external purpose, while the Northwestern group did not." Further, the northern leaders "had no intention of participating in an organized revolt against the structure of Gilded Age politics and did not do so."[68]

Surrounding all these differences, there must have been a substantial cultural alienation between the two organizations, reflecting the different life-worlds of the northern and the southern farmers. There were also different and deeply rooted partisan traditions. Macune, for example (himself strongly attached to the Democratic Party), believed that the secretary of the northwestern alliance, an Iowa Republican, "wanted nothing to do with an organization composed largely of southern Democrats."[69]

At St. Louis, representatives of the more radical Kansas and South Dakota chapters broke away from the Northwestern Alliance and joined the southern group in a renamed National Farmers' Alliance and Industrial Union (NFA&IU). Representatives of the KOL, its membership by now much diminished but increasingly politicized, joined with the NFA&IU delegates in an endorsement of a seven-point platform devoted to banking and currency and "land to the tiller" demands, along with a call for nationalization of the means of communication and transportation.[70]

After St. Louis, the NFA&IU continued to expand into the Midwest but also attracted a substantial membership in the Pacific Coast states and even chartered small groups in the mid-Atlantic region.[71] The southern-based but now genuinely biregional Farmers' Alliance claimed about 1.5 million members in forty-three states and territories by 1891.[72] Michael Schwartz gives a lower estimate, pegging membership at no more than 964,000. Even the lower figure, he points out, would imply that the FA reached at least 25 percent of the adult male population of the rural South, 50 percent in Texas.[73] Thousands of women also poured into the organization, which actively recruited them.[74] A state-by-state breakdown of FA membership, compiled in early 1890, is given in table 4.7. The source of these figures, the 1891 *Appleton's Annual Cyclopedia*, reported estimates that the combined total of the colored and white alliances might have reached 3 million by the end of the year.

The lifeblood of the FA was its system of collective education. Meetings were devoted to the study of political economy, broadly conceived, based on "lessons" printed in Macune's paper, the *National Economist*, and led by the unit's lecturer. Topics of the lessons in the first six months of 1892 included

Table 4.7 Estimated Membership, by State, of the National Farmers' Alliance, 1890

Alabama	75,000	New Jersey	500
Arkansas	100,000	New Mexico	5,000
California	1,000	New York	500
Colorado	5,000	North Carolina	100,000
Florida	20,000	North Dakota	40,000
Georgia	100,000	Ohio	300
Illinois	2,000	Pennsylvania	500
Indiana	5,000	South Carolina	50,000
Kansas	100,000	South Dakota	50,000
Kentucky	80,000	Tennessee	100,000
Louisiana	20,000	Texas	150,000
Maryland	5,000	Virginia	50,000
Mississippi	60,000	West Virginia	2,000
Missouri	150,000		
		Total	1,271,800

Source: Appleton's Annual Cyclopedia and Register of Important Events of the Year 1890 (New York: D. Appleton & Co., 1891), 301.

the British class structure, the Russian peasantry, and the position of million-
aires in American life. The underlying theme, in Theodore Mitchell's words,
was "a warning that the centralization of wealth and power . . . always leads
to the repression by the rich and powerful of the poor and powerless." The
lecturer led the discussion and guided those farmers present through exercises
designed to drive home points of the economic analysis (Macune helpfully
provided the lecturers with hints on pedagogy). Meetings concluded with
rousing Alliance songs and group prayer.[75]

The *National Economist* had a circulation of over 100,000, and many copies
were undoubtedly shared, but the Alliance movement had other organs as
well. The Texas *Southern Mercury* and the Kansas *Advocate* together had
about 110,000 subscribers, and the North Carolina–based *Progressive Farmer*,
the *American Nonconformist*, and the *Kansas Commoner* were also among the
more important communication mechanisms. Macune organized a National
Reform Press Association of over one thousand newspapers, and the National
Economist Publishing Company produced a "torrent of pamphlets, broad-
sides, and books" on the concentration of wealth, "the financial question,"
and other Alliance issues.[76]

One of the most important functions of the communications network was
to promote economic cooperation in order to free the farmer from the crop-
lien system. Statewide cooperative enterprises were undertaken to store and
market cotton and tobacco and to buy wholesale, at the lowest prices, everything the farmer might need. To help the poorest farmers, Macune designed
an ingenious "joint note" credit plan. Each suballiance would amass its members' mortgages, crop liens, and available cash and send them to the state FA
business agent, who would use them as security for credit purchases, in bulk,
of all supplies requested by the members. In the fall, the Farmers' Alliance
Exchange would sell members' crops (stored at local FA warehouses) in huge
lots directly to manufacturers and exporters. The FA exchanges, "the most
ambitious counterinstitutions ever undertaken by an American protest movement," aimed to "replace much of the supply and marketing systems of cotton
tenancy, while returning huge savings to the local farmer." And, for a few
years, they worked. In Texas, North Carolina, Louisiana, Tennessee, Georgia, and South Carolina, the exchanges indeed generated large savings for
farmers and posed a formidable threat to the economic power structure.[77]

While the exchanges flourished, the FA was also able to mount a successful
boycott against a national cartel formed to monopolize the supply of the jute
that was used to wrap cotton bales. After the cartel doubled the price of jute
in 1888, Alliance members across the South substituted cotton wrapping for

jute and persuaded New York and New Orleans traders to accept the substitute without penalty (the Liverpool cotton exchange refused that concession). Concerted action finally forced the "Jute Trust" to lower prices to pretrust levels—a significant victory for the farmers. However, the shortage of cotton bagging and Liverpool's insistence that cotton-wrapped bales be discounted made the boycott impossible to sustain.[78]

The threat the exchanges posed to the merchants, landlords, banks, and middlemen brought massive resistance, and the dependency and cash shortage of members provided no cushion to weather setbacks. Banks in Dallas, Fort Worth, Houston, Galveston, and New Orleans refused to lend money to the Texas Exchange. Manufacturers declined to sell to the exchange on credit, since its notes could not be easily redeemed. Heroic effort got the organization through its first year, but the concerted attacks and rumors of exchange insolvency in the conservative press ultimately produced a climate of such pessimism that members became unwilling to make further contributions. The effort collapsed after twenty months.[79]

Similar catastrophes befell other Alliance cooperatives in 1889. "Locals in the Southeast discovered in early 1889 that all the wholesalers in Norfolk, Virginia, had agreed to boycott the Alliance coops. Manufacturers all over the country boycotted the Alliance: Mississippi locals could not get wholesale farm implements, clubs in North Carolina were denied wholesale prices on shoes . . . Alabama and South Carolina banks foreclosed on Alliance mortgages. Virginia railroads refused to give discount shipping rates available to other large customers."[80] As economic conditions worsened for the farmers, fewer and fewer could pay their dues. The Florida, North Carolina, and Kansas state exchanges went bankrupt in 1891.[81] The Georgia Exchange, one of the strongest, survived an agent's sticky fingers and continuous external opposition until 1893.[82] The Dakota Farmers' Alliance Company apparently experienced less-devastating credit problems. It had developed the strongest and most diversified cooperative enterprise outside the South, including a unique crop, fire, and life insurance program for members. Nevertheless, the Dakota Exchange was also going under by 1891. Desperate schemes to unite all the tottering state exchanges came to naught. As the cooperatives declined, so did Alliance membership.[83]

As the Texas and other state exchanges began to experience severe difficulties, Macune made another bold leap. He developed a plan by which the federal government would construct warehouses in every significant agricultural county. At these "subtreasuries," farmers could safely store their produce rather than sell at depressed harvest-time prices and could receive from the government loans of up to 80 percent of the stored crop's value at the time of entry. At any point, they could sell the subtreasury certificate of deposit for whatever the commodity would bring and repay the loan, forfeiting a small fee for grading, storage, and insurance costs.[84] By this mechanism, the farmers would escape the snares of the crop-lien system, avoid the dishonest warehouseman, and receive the best price for their crops; and the nation would benefit as the major demand for currency, triggered each year by the need to transfer money from northeastern banks to the interior "to move the crops" at harvest, would be met by this highly flexible, automatic money-creating system.

Half a century later, such federal government mechanisms for agricultural credit and money creation would be accepted public functions. But in the late 1880s, Macune's proposal was by far the most radical idea placed on the political agenda by a major social organization. The subtreasury plan posed a clear threat to existing creditors, commodity brokers, warehousemen, and speculators. Critics also argued that it would centralize power in the federal government and necessitate a great expansion of federal employment to man the warehouses.[85] And it was, after all, a scheme for creating the dreaded fiat currency, although Sen. William A. Peffer of Kansas liked to point out that U.S. bank notes carried notices that they were secured by U.S. bonds held in vaults; why was it so radical to base a currency on wheat, corn, or cotton held in government warehouses?[86]

But radical it was. The subtreasury promised not only the emancipation of farmers from the merchants and landlords to whom they were indebted but also a source of credit and currency creation outside the control of the nation's bankers. The amount of new currency to be added, estimated at around $550 million, exceeded the peak greenback circulation and thus promised a significant inflation. Further, the *National Economist* argued, the plan would create hundreds of local markets for cotton, keeping at home the profits and opportunities that now flowed to middlemen in the great entrepôt cities.[87]

At the 1889 meeting in St. Louis, a committee of southern Alliancemen presented the subtreasury plan to the assembled delegates, who adopted it with surprisingly little discussion. No longer president of the Alliance (Leonidas Polk of North Carolina was elected at St. Louis), Macune threw himself into the campaign for the new program. As editor of the *National Economist*, he tirelessly prepared materials for use by the Alliance lecturers, who now fanned out across the country with the message of agricultural salvation through the subtreasury.[88]

The Alliance communication structure was harnessed to press its demands on candidates for office and endorse those who pledged support to the St. Louis platform. Across the South and Great Plains, the farmers surged into politics in 1890. The FA president, Polk, accompanied by Ralph Beaumont of the Knights of Labor, traveled to the western plains to preach radical economics, political mobilization, and an end to sectionalism.[89] In Washington, D.C., the Alliance leaders, coordinating their efforts with the KOL, lobbied for their program. Representatives from North Carolina and South Dakota introduced the subtreasury bill, but it was buried in the Republican Congress without even coming to a vote. The Alliance therefore set out to elect sympathetic legislators and seemed to have achieved impressive successes in the 1890 elections. Candidates pledged to the Alliance program (many of them FA members) appeared to control the legislatures of seven southern states and 70 percent of the congressional seats from Georgia and the Carolinas.[90] In Kansas, an independent Alliance/Populist ticket narrowly lost the governor's race but elected five congressmen and a senator and gained control of the House on an electoral base consisting of disaffected Republicans joined by Democrats, 1888 Union Labor voters, and Prohibitionists.[91] As many as forty-four Alliance-endorsed candidates took their seats in the U.S. House of Representatives, contributing to the GOP rout there; in addition, several senators were elected from the South.[92] Polk spoke exuberantly of "the coming revolution."[93]

Midwestern and western Alliance members, as the Kansas case demonstrates, had been much less reticent about independent party politics than their southern colleagues. Sectional traditions lay behind both tendencies. In the Midwest, Antimonopoly and Greenback parties had broken the ice, and the continuing power of "bloody shirt" rhetoric made the minority Democratic Party an inappropriate vehicle for Alliance demands. In the South, of course, the reverse held. The Democratic Party was the seat of southern nationalism and white supremacy and was extremely difficult for the average southerner, even a member of the Alliance, to abandon. There was great hope that the existing party apparatus could simply be captured by the Alliance, and in 1890, this goal seemed attainable.[94]

However, the southern Democrats who had courted the Alliance proved disappointing. Texas Governor James Hogg refused to support the subtreasury and responded weakly to demands for a state commission, free school textbooks, and mechanics' lien and usury laws. Many congressional endorsees—even Zebulon Vance of North Carolina, who introduced the bill in the

Senate—were lukewarm to hostile toward the subtreasury. Across the South, the officeholders elected with Alliance votes proved much more conservative on the range of Alliance issues than the FA membership.[95]

At the organization's December 1890 convention at Ocala, Florida, delegates drew up a platform that consisted of the financial, land, and transportation/communication planks adopted at St. Louis (the last being softened to call for a trial period of tight regulation before moving toward nationalization); to these were formally added the subtreasury, a graduated federal income tax, direct election of senators, and removal of tariff duties from "the necessities of life." The radical political faction within the Alliance, centered around Texans William Lamb, James Perdue, Evan Jones, H. S. P. Ashby, and R. M. Humphrey, Arkansan W. Scott Morgan, and Kansan Cuthbert Vincent, insisted that the best hope for securing these demands was through an independent party. Macune, always opposed to the third-party route, could, at this point, do little to restrain the drive. But the National Reform Press Association that he chaired provided, in 1891–92, "the basic internal communication agency through which greenbackers [Alliance leaders committed to the subtreasury and independent politics] labored for the third party."[96]

The People's Party was tentatively launched at a National Union Conference in May 1891. It was a diverse gathering of fourteen hundred reformers including Prohibitionists, women's suffrage advocates, Greenbackers, and "hundreds of habitual reformers." The modal number came as Farmers' Alliance members, but almost all were from the Midwest and West; though Lamb and Humphrey were there, fewer than forty represented the southern alliance. Macune attended, but as one of a hundred or so members of the National Reform Press Association and not as a third-party advocate. The Kansas delegates took the lead, with a more cautious group, around FA President Polk and James Weaver of Iowa, counseling delay. Since little could be done without the enlistment of the southerners, the conference only appointed a provisional national party committee headed by H. E. Taubeneck of Illinois and endorsed the St. Louis and Ocala demands.[97]

The southern alliances were committed to politics, though not uniformly to the third party. Across the South in the summer of 1891, county and district lecturers addressed open rallies to explain and promote the subtreasury and the other Ocala demands. Whereas the cooperative movement operated mostly in segregated farmer institutions, the political movement that grew out of it required broad collaboration across racial and occupational lines. Alliance officials now urged an outreach to the Colored Farmers' Alliance members, and in 1891–92 it was possible to envision a new era in southern race relations, one based on a politicized movement of *farmers* as a class.[98] This was a vision held, on both sides of the racial divide, by those most committed to the People's Party. In Georgia, Tom Watson spoke fervently of the common economic problems of black and white tenant farmers and of the efforts of elites to keep them apart by racial demagoguery.[99] The Georgia Alliance opened the state exchange to black Alliancemen and attempted to woo them away from their traditional Republican loyalties. Similar overtures took place in North Carolina.[100] At its Dallas organizing meeting, the Texas Alliance elected two black men to the statewide executive committee of the Texas People's Party.[101] An Alabama newspaper dared to endorse racial solidarity in the "war against trusts."[102] However, efforts toward biracial politics were interrupted by events of September 1891. R. M. Humphrey, the white superintendent of the Colored Farmers' Alliance, called for a South-wide strike by black cotton pickers, with the goal of doubling their daily pay. FA President Polk denounced the strike, reminding the CFA that the price of cotton had dropped to seven or eights cents a pound. A number of prominent CFA members also opposed the strike, and except in the Arkansas delta, it seems not to have taken place. Nevertheless, the incident was a brutal reminder that white and black farmers did not occupy the same rungs on the economic ladder.[103]

This was by no means the end of the experiment in biracial politics, however. In its state platform, the Arkansas Populist Party declared for policies on behalf of "the downtrodden regardless of race," establishing, Goodwyn argues, "the clearest record of racial liberalism" in the South. In neighboring Texas, he notes, the 1894 Populist platform "offered a nineteenth century version of 'black power.'" Alabama populists (who called themselves "Jeffersonians") also declared for the protection of black voting rights in 1892. The Democrats conducted a virulent attack on this "Negro plank," and their own platform pledged "the passage of such election laws as will better secure the government of the State in the hands of the intelligent and virtuous."[104]

It was the Democratic counterattack on the Alliance, unleashed in 1891, that drove many southern Alliance members to the third party. However, whereas the southerners moved reluctantly, the midwesterners were much bolder. In December 1891, five Alliance congressmen from Kansas, three from Minnesota and Nebraska, and Tom Watson of Georgia formed "the first distinctive political body" of the People's Party by organizing a House caucus that nominated Watson for Speaker. The decisive event, however, was a huge conference of "industrial organizations" in St. Louis in February 1892.

About eight hundred delegates from twenty-two reform organizations were allotted seats, with the southern alliance (NFA&IU) holding about a third. Polk was elected chairman. The conference adopted a ringing reform platform with a preamble, written by Ignatius Donnelly, that condemned the injustices and corruption of American society. The platform demands were based on the previous lists of the NFA&IU; in a logroll among the northern and southern Alliance and labor delegates, the conference accepted the subtreasury (which had little support outside the South) and reinstated government ownership of railroads, for which the southerners were less enthusiastic.[105]

Within a month after the St. Louis meeting, "grass roots Populist organizations were springing up from Alliance seedbeds across the South," and county alliances were meeting to endorse the St. Louis demands.[106] But opinion on the wisdom of a third-party campaign was still sharply divided, and although strong Alliance networks in Alabama, North Carolina, and Texas spawned vigorous populist parties, not all vibrant alliances did so.[107] Nor was a deeply rooted Alliance organization *necessary* to agrarian populist politics. As Scott G. McNall has shown, the Kansas Alliance had barely been organized in 1889–90 when the independent party took off. There, the state alliance leadership was dominated by men and women with previous third-party (mainly Greenback and Union Labor) experience; they easily made the transition to independent politics and took the Alliance with them.[108]

Schwartz, sympathetic to the Alliance goal of building economic "counterinstitutions," has described the political turn of 1892 as a fateful move that "destroyed the Farmers' Alliance as a protest group."[109] For Goodwyn, the problem was not politics per se but a compromised, *superficial* politics, the kind that seemed inevitable in states where political action did not grow from a cooperative base. Without the "movement culture" incubated in the cooperatives, Goodwyn has argued, the farmers' discontent could all too easily be harnessed to a pallid "shadow movement" focused on the single cause of free silver rather than the rich tapestry of Greenbackism, and led by southern and western politicians not adverse to fusion with the Democrats.[110]

In response to these arguments, it should be noted that the political activists in the Alliance were the ones who reached out to black farmers, creating an unprecedented recognition of biracial class similarity and mutual need. It was the political activists too who adopted the grievances of the Knights of Labor as their own. The cooperative purchasing and marketing movement promised benefits only for farmers, whereas the political arena was the natural meeting place for occupationally dissimilar producers with the same class and institutional antagonists. It *was* the case, apparently, that the move into politics led to the abandonment of most of what remained of the cooperative movement and the withering of the Alliance organizational structure.[111] A movement's participants have only so much energy and their leaders only so much time. But the accounts of Goodwyn, McMath, Schwartz, and Donna A. Barnes all make clear that the cooperative movement was doomed anyway. Only political action could salvage its goals of emancipating the farmer from bondage to bankers, trusts, railroads, merchants, and land barons; and it might even save the cooperatives themselves. State legislation was important, and Alliance members did what they could at that level.[112] But national politics was clearly the key to the greenback-antimonopoly program.[113]

The People's Party platform endorsed at Omaha in July 1892 called for a "union of labor forces" to redeem democratic politics in a polity corrupted and oppressed by unchecked capitalist power. It condemned, as before, the demonetization of silver and called for free and unlimited silver coinage at the traditional sixteen-to-one ratio. It affirmed the power of the national government to create and distribute money through the subtreasury plan "or a better system," increasing the circulating medium to $50 per capita. The platform also called for a system of postal savings banks where people could safely deposit their earnings; nationalization of the railroads, telephone, and telegraph; government reclamation of unused railroad, corporate, and foreign-owned lands and their designation for actual settlers only; and a graduated income tax. Finally, it declared: "We believe that the power of government—in other words, of the people—should be expanded . . . as rapidly and as far as the good sense of an intelligent people and the teachings of experience shall justify, to the end that oppression, injustice, and poverty shall eventually cease in the land." Appended to this agrarian-greenback platform were ten resolutions. These encompassed labor's demands for abolition of the Pinkerton "mercenary armies"; enforcement of the eight-hour day on government contracts and restriction of immigration; tax reductions for producers; support for "fair and liberal" military pensions; opposition to corporate subsidies; and electoral reform through adoption of the Australian ballot, the initiative and referendum, direct election of senators, and limitation of the president and vice-president to two terms.[114]

This was to be the last flowering of native American greenback radicalism in its pure form—that is, before its dilution and absorption into the Democratic Party. Its philosophy was anticorporate, though not *anticapitalist*. It sought, as recent scholars have established, not to turn the clock back on industrial development but to harness the new technological power for social good, to use the state to check exploitative excesses, to uphold the rights and opportunities of labor (farm and factory), and to maintain a healthy and creative business competition.[115] The program was profoundly opposed to concentrated corporate power. Where concentration seemed inevitable, and for the vital economic functions on which the well-being of the entire society depended, it was best that complete government control be established. This applied to money and probably to railroads and communications as well.

Norman Pollack has attributed to the midwestern Populists a statism more transcendent and transformative than that of their southern brethren. He describes the subtreasury plan, though massively interventionist, as narrowly economic in character, lacking in "philosophical dignity." The southern Populists, in Pollack's view, suffered an "ideological shortfall" in failing to appreciate the full potential for the redistribution of wealth through the income tax (which they backed for rather pragmatic reasons), in advocating nationalization of railroads only as a last resort, and in perceiving nationalization as "a self-contained measure which did not promise further collective activities."[116] To these charges the southern Populist leaders and most Populist voters would undoubtedly have pleaded guilty. They wanted to use the state to restore what they envisioned as the freer and more egalitarian relationships of an earlier democratic republic and to redress the accumulated grievances of farmers and workers. They hoped to tame capitalism, to deconcentrate it, but not to destroy it. They were, undoubtedly, radical reformers, but not socialist revolutionaries. Their view of the state was both idealistic and pragmatic. The Populists did not relish bureaucracy. They elevated direct democracy and specific statutes and surely would have felt, to use Pollack's words, "dimly menaced" by the notion of an expansively powerful, transformative state (a conception he does find in the ideas of Senator Peffer of Kansas, Alliance lecturer and novelist Donnelly of Minnesota, and particularly, the patrician Illinois intellectual Henry Demarest Lloyd). However, at a century's remove, the Populists' pragmatic willingness to use public power to balance and constrain market forces, coupled with uneasiness about an unconstrained national executive power, seems more prudent than intellectually deficient.

The theorists of the Populist movement appear to have believed sincerely and strongly in the commonality of interests between farmer and worker. By virtue of the dominance and exploitation of large corporate and financial interests, farmers and workers occupied similar positions in the social and economic order. The redemption of the state to serve the interests of ordinary people, and its use to effect the democratization of the industrial and commercial economy, would serve the interests of both, argued Populists like Peffer, Weaver, Watson, Morgan, and Lamb.[117] Although there was, at this point, little evidence among trade-union leaders of a similar probing analysis of social conditions and the effects of large-scale economic change on class positions, the guiding figures of the agrarian movement had thought long and hard about these processes. They wrote books in which they drew out the political implications of the convergence of farmer and worker interests. It was an alliance on which they pinned all their hopes.

Populism at the Polls

Laboring men of America! The voice of Patrick Henry and the fathers of American Independence rings down through the corridors of time and tells you to strike. Not with glittering musket, flaming sword and deadly cannon; but with the silent, potent and all-powerful ballot, the only vestige of liberty left. Strike from yourselves the shackles of party slavery, and exercise independent manhood.

Strike at the foundation of the evils which are threatening the existence of the Republic.

Strike for yourselves, your families, your fellow man, your country and your God.

Strike from the face of the land the monopolies and combinations that are eating out the heart of the Nation.

Let the manhood of the Nation rise up in defense of liberty, justice and equality. Let the battle go on until all the people, from North to South and East to West, shall join in one loud acclaim, "Victory is ours, and the people are free!"

W. Scott Morgan, *History of the Wheel and Alliance and the Impending Revolution* (1891)

The Omaha convention nominated as its standard-bearers the ex-Greenbacker James Weaver of Iowa and James G. Field of Virginia. The combination of Union and Confederate generals could not overcome sectional feeling, however. When General Weaver took his campaign to the dusty country towns of Georgia, Democratic opponents pelted him with words and rotten eggs for alleged Civil War atrocities. General Field, likewise, was vilified in Iowa for his Rebel past. A reversal of position, with a respected southerner like Leonidas Polk at the head, might have produced better results in the South without a corresponding northern handicap. Though a Rebel officer himself, Polk had strongly opposed secession in North Carolina (for which he suffered considerable abuse in the 1860s) and had long campaigned against sectionalism. Unfortunately, the Alliance president died a month before the convention.[118]

Along with the "bloody shirt" and racial demagoguery, the Populists' opponents charged that the Omaha platform was a program of unthinkable radicalism. The *New York Times* branded the subtreasury plan "one of the wildest
and most fantastic projects ever seriously proposed by sober man."[119] The
New York Sun supplied a campaign ditty: "Why should the farmer delve and
ditch? Why should the farmer's wife darn and stitch? The government can
make 'em rich, And the People's Party knows it."[120]

In both North and South, the Populists appealed for the votes of the
weaker major party. In Kansas, North Dakota, and the western silver-mining
states, effective fusion with the Democrats brought electoral advantage.[121] In
the South, alliances were made with Republicans, leading Democrats to
charge that the Populists had betrayed sectional interests and undermined
white supremacy.

In North and South Carolina, Georgia, and Texas, the Democrats fought
populism by imitating it in their own platforms. Populists in Texas had criticized the Democratic governor, James Hogg, for the limited nature of his
railroad reforms, but many supported the Democratic ticket rather than risk
Hogg's defeat by a powerful conservative rival. In Alabama, Reuben Kolb's
independent "Jeffersonian" ticket was backed by Populists, Republicans, and
a Democratic faction opposed to the regular Democratic machine; when the
ticket seemed headed for victory in state elections, the Democrats responded
with massive vote fraud. The black vote was still formally unrestricted, but
economic dependence allowed Kolb's opponents to pile up huge votes against
him in the plantation counties.[122] In Georgia, as in five other southern states,
the beginning of suffrage restrictions aimed at blacks had already reduced the
potential anti-Bourbon vote. But here, as in Alabama, the greater effect was
achieved by hauling black farmworkers to the polls and murdering a number
who had allied with the Populists.[123] Predictably, the 1892 Populist vote in
the Alliance heartland was a disappointment.

Considering the multiple handicaps of a third-party campaign, the results
were not unimpressive: 1,024,280 popular votes (about a fifth of that received
by each of the major-party candidates) and, thanks largely to the western silver
states, twenty-two electoral votes. At 8.5 percent, the Populist percentage of
the popular vote was more than twice the 1880 Greenback ratio; since 1860,
it has been exceeded only by Theodore Roosevelt (Progressive) in 1912, Robert M. La Follette (Progressive) in 1924, George Wallace (American Independent) in 1968, and Ross Perot (Independent) in 1992. Weaver got over one-
fifth of the vote in nine periphery states and Oregon. In Kansas, the Populists
swept five of seven House seats, the state senate, and the governorship. Ne-

Table 4.8 Populist Vote, 1892 (%)

Top Ten States		Bottom Ten States	
[a]Nevada	66.8	Delaware	.0
[a]Colorado	58.1	Vermont	.0
[a]Idaho	54.3	New Hampshire	0.3
[a]Kansas	50.2	New Jersey	0.3
North Dakota	49.0	Maryland	0.4
Wyoming	46.2	Rhode Island	0.4
Nebraska	41.6	Connecticut	0.5
South Dakota	37.7	Massachusetts	0.8
Alabama	36.6	Pennsylvania	0.9
Oregon	34.4	New York	1.2
Texas	23.9		

Source: Walter Dean Burnham, *Presidential Ballots 1836–1892* (Baltimore: Johns Hopkins University Press, 1955), table 4.
[a]Carried by James Weaver (several states divided their electoral votes).

braska and Colorado also elected Populist governors, and in all, thirteen Populists (including the hyphenated ones) were sent to the U.S. House of Representatives; Nebraska and North Carolina also chose Populist senators.[124]

The minuscule urban labor vote was a great disappointment, its implication evident in the second column of table 4.8. If workers unhappy with the Republican regime had bolted, it appeared that they had thrown their votes to the conservative Democrat Grover Cleveland rather than to the party whose platform incorporated the sum of organized labor's political demands.[125] In Allegheny County, Pennsylvania, where the Homestead steel strike had been crushed a few months earlier, the Populists got only 578 votes out of a total of 78,504, slightly below the Pennsylvania average of 0.9 percent.[126] The party of protection carried the steel county and the state.

Two years later, the depression was deep, the tide of greenback-silver sentiment was high, and there was no presidential election to bolster party regularity. The Democratic president's rigidity and conservatism, particularly his insistence on repeal of the 1890 Sherman Silver Purchase Act,[127] were in fact producing massive defections across the South and West. President Cleveland demonstrated his lack of sympathy for labor distress by meeting the bedraggled protest march of "Coxey's Army" with mounted police and arresting its leader, Jacob Coxey, and by calling out federal troops against the Pullman strikers.[128] A context more favorable to a radical third party could hardly be imagined.

Efforts to forge an alliance with labor intensified in 1894. While conservatives in the two major parties condemned strikes and the protest marches of "industrial armies," prominent Populists backed the dissident workers, and a Populist convention in Kansas collected money for the unemployed marchers.[129] In Alabama, Kolb's "Jeffersonians" condemned the state's governor for calling out the militia against strikers and adopted a platform that demanded an end to convict labor, a lien law for miners, state inspectors, limitations on the employment of children, and even a tariff policy "to protect the laborer."[130] Populists in Tennessee backed the miners in their successful campaign to abolish the convict-lease system in that state; throughout the South, the party campaigned to end the practice. In Congress, Populists took prominent, and lonely, pro-labor stances.[131] Widespread sympathy was expressed for Eugene Debs and the ARU in the Pullman strike.[132] The *Dallas Mercury* ran editorials about "the bitter and irrepressible conflict between the capitalist and the laborer" and, after Debs's arrest, declared, "With Debs in jail, no American is a freeman."[133] In view of this record, and the incorporation into the Omaha platform of the demands expressed by the political voices of labor, the familiar criticism that agrarian Populists "simply did not know what to say" to industrial workers seems wide of the mark.[134] The fact is that while farmers struggled to run the gauntlet of the two-party system, and lost many of their troops along the way, northern urban labor scarcely responded at all to the inducements of the Omaha program or to local Populist appeals.

The most impressive percentage gains in 1894 came in the South. With "no Union general yoked to their tickets," the third party had become a real threat to the Democrats.[135] The ten leading Populist states in this year's elections were North Carolina, where fusion with the Republicans boosted the total to 53.8 percent, Nebraska (49), Alabama (47.6), Georgia (44.5), Colorado (41.4), Washington (39), Kansas (39), Texas (36.1), South Dakota (35.5), and Montana (30.9). In the Midwest and West, Populist totals dropped wherever the party, either out of independence or rejection, did not ally with the Democrats. In Kansas, Colorado, Nevada, North Dakota, Wyoming, and Idaho, these losses were severe.[136]

Despite the western losses, the party's national vote had increased 42 percent, to almost a million and a half, despite repeated massive vote fraud by the Democrats in Alabama and Georgia. Donnelly was sure that the Democrats would soon go the way of the Whigs, leaving the Populist Party in contention with the party of the plutocrats.[137] However, pragmatists within the party viewed the difficult terrain of the South, the western losses, and the failure of the labor outreach as signposts of a dead end for the third party. The Populist Party needed to pick a different road, either to *become* a major party or to take over the one most ideologically compatible. Either way, these pragmatists reasoned, the party had to deemphasize its more radical demands (especially fiat money and the nationalization of railroads) and raise the flag of silver to broaden its electoral base.[138]

The farmers' movement thus confronted the same set of political alternatives and agonizing choices that labor and, indeed, all social movements before or since have had to reckon with in the American political system (see chapter 3). There were single-member-district, territorial elections, overlain by, in those years and for a long time thereafter, the powerful sociohistorical divide of the Civil War. This system produced two major parties, to which attachments were strong. A movement with genuinely national ambitions would plausibly attempt to avoid major-party alliance because of the inevitable watering down of its program and loss of members with strong prior attachment to the other party. But was there a genuine alternative for the farmers? The purist collective action (cooperatives) had met a dead end. Tactical alliances had borne little fruit, and the third party had not done well nationally in a year in which economic conditions were dismal (hence presumably most promising for a party of the disadvantaged). In the aftermath of the 1894 elections, as Goodwyn himself acknowledges, Populist leaders had to confront the fact that

> the People's Party had done its best to convince American voters of the need for the Omaha Platform. After four years the party had gained a following of anywhere from 25 to 45 percent of the electorate in twenty-odd states. . . . Politically, the mathematics of the situation were fatal. The People's Party needed to broaden its base or see the cause of reform die completely. One did not have to be a populist politician to accept the fact that reformers had to be in office to enact reforms.[139]

Free silver was not greenbackism, not a program on which to build a *movement,* but it was more than an empty panacea. It proposed to found the nation's monetary system on a metal in expanding production (and *domestic* production at that). Friedman and Schwartz have written: "As between the early adoption of silver as the standard . . . and an early commitment to gold, it seems likely that on the whole, the adoption of silver would have been preferable, though this is clearly a difficult and complex judgment. Adoption of silver by the United States would certainly have moderated or eliminated deflationary tendencies here. It would also have moderated and might have eliminated deflation in the world at large."[140]

Stable general price levels might have saved many thousands of farmers from crushing debt loads and descent into tenancy and sharecropping. The "automatic" aspect of coinage on demand also promised to wrest control of money creation from banks and bondholders and their allies in the Treasury Department. These were no small aims.

As a common denominator on which to build a winning national coalition, silver was probably unmatched. It was "hard money," the "dollar of the daddies," and could accomplish many of the purposes of greenback printing without the "fiat money" ideological baggage. Specifically, silver was an entrée to the following voting blocs and campaign resources: (a) southern, western, and midwestern Democrats; (b) those farmers, particularly in the North, who felt the effects of high interest rates, mortgage-debt burdens, and declining cash-crop prices but found the subtreasury program of the southern Farmers' Alliance too radical; (c) miners and mine owners, the latter able to put up significant sums of money for the educational phase of the national campaign; and (d) urban workers. The last group, of course, was the most critical and problematic. However, the currency-expansion remedy had first caught on with northern labor leaders, and more recently, AFL conventions had repeatedly endorsed free silver. In 1895, Samuel Gompers, John McBride, James Sovereign, Max Hayes, and five carpenter and railroad union chiefs had signed a petition to Congress demanding free coinage. Illinois Governor John Peter Altgeld, a prominent (and aptly named!) friend of labor, was already a leading campaigner for bimetallism, and labor advocate Clarence Darrow also endorsed the silver strategy. Thus the agrarians could reasonably hope that the silver issue would be the key to victory for a national farmer-labor reform coalition.[141]

1896: The Farmer-Labor Alliance Miscarries

Wherever there has been an effort on the part of laboring men
to secure any legislation on their behalf, where have they
found their friends? They found their friends on farms, and not
in Wall Street among the advocates of the gold standard. . . .
[Applause.] The laboring men know that they cannot separate
themselves from the tillers of the soil . . . and they know that
the great toiling masses have got to stand together or, if I may
use one of the early jokes, they have got to stand together or
they will hang separately.

William Jennings Bryan, speech at Hornellsville,
New York, August 29, 1896

The fate of the Populists in 1896 is well known and need not be recounted in detail. Chairman Herman Taubeneck and his allies in the People's Party assumed that the conservative, Cleveland wing of the Democratic Party would maintain control of the presidential nominating convention. The silverites would then bolt to the People's Party. The latter would win a three-way election and thereafter take its place as one of the two major parties (the gold Democrats would ultimately vanish as their adherents bled off into the Republican Party). Instead, reform forces took control of the Democratic Party, nominated the buoyant young silverite William Jennings Bryan, and wrote a platform condemning "government by injunction" and federal repression of strikes, demanding stronger railroad regulation and a constitutional amendment to restore the income tax, and of course, declaring for free coinage of silver. The Populists, who had scheduled their convention *after* the Democrats in order to receive into their fold the dissenting reformers, were left with no real choice but to nominate Bryan.[142] The Democrats then became the only plausible party of reform, the vehicle of the farmer-labor alliance.

The 1896 election has been described as "the first modern class-struggle political contest" of industrial America.[143] The Bryan campaign attracted the enthusiastic support of the country's diverse reform leaders, ranging from the fiery South Carolina Sen. "Pitchfork" Ben Tillman to the genteel Illinois factory inspector Florence Kelley. Eugene Debs lent his masterful oratorical gifts to woo labor audiences, arguing that free silver was "the only solution to the problem now staring us in the face, as to how to open the mills and factories to the working men."[144] As Debs wrote later: "I supported Mr. William J. Bryan and the platform upon which he stood, not because I regarded the free coinage of silver as a panacea for our national ills . . . but because I believed that the triumph of Mr. Bryan and free silver would blunt the fangs of the money power. . . . The free silver issue gave us not only a rallying cry, but afforded common ground upon which the common people could unite against the trusts, syndicates, corporations, monopolies—in a word, the money power."[145]

This was certainly the way Bryan viewed the issue, and the early enthusiastic response to his campaign appearances by huge crowds of workers and farmers belies historians' post hoc judgment that the Democratic candidate made a fatal mistake with silver. The Republicans had intended to make the tariff the central issue of the campaign. It was a natural decision, considering the tendency of the northern public to accept the argument that the Wilson-Gormley Tariff of 1894 had deepened the depression.[146] But Bryan would not be drawn into the trap. Assiduously refusing to discuss the issue, he emphasized a stable, steadily expanding money supply as the key to raising employment and prosperity. Farmers and workers could never thrive on an appreciating currency, he argued; the impoverishment of the millions of cash-crop farmers would, by shrinking the market for the urban worker's goods, impoverish the latter as well.[147] He supplemented this argument with more targeted discussions of autocratic courts, the need for an income tax and trust regulation, and the abuse of injunctions, along with support for greater use of mediation in labor disputes.[148] The program was well received; by early August, the enthusiastic response to Bryan's fast-paced campaign tour had the GOP in a panic.[149]

Mark Hanna's oft-quoted boast—"Bryan's talking silver all the time and that's where we've got him"—was misleading bravado. The GOP recognized the breadth and appeal of the Democratic challenge, and it "got him" by pulling out all the stops, harnessing the vast (one can hardly avoid the term "hegemonic") material and cultural resources of northern capital to defeat the insurgency. A fund estimated at $4 to $16 million, secured from corporations and wealthy individuals, enabled William McKinley's campaign to mount a massive and unprecedented "educational" campaign, targeting northern farm, labor, and middle-class groups vulnerable to Bryanite seduction and developing multilingual pamphlets warning of the dire consequences of Democratic policies.[150] Big-city newspapers kept up a drumbeat of alarmist rhetoric. The *New York Times* quoted business predictions of "the worst panic the world ever saw" if the candidate of "tramps, deadbeats and anarchists" should win.[151] Considerable effort was made to link Bryan to anarchism, communism, treason, and revolution. Particularly stressed were his ties with three great bugbears of the northeastern establishment: Debs, Tillman, and Altgeld (who, as governor, had pardoned the remaining Haymarket "bombers").[152] Northeastern academicians and scholarly journals were almost uniformly antagonistic to the free coinage of silver, which, they argued, would bring economic disaster.[153] In addition to the massed hostility of the academy and the press, "torrents of abuse poured forth from the clergy who beheld Bryan and the Chicago platform as equivalents to the Devil and the Great Temptation."[154] Three prominent New York ministers described Bryan as "a mouthing, slobbering demagogue" with a platform that "was made in hell" and that would bring a "revolution, the destructive consequences of which no man can picture."[155]

The Democratic platform had excoriated the federal courts for overturning the income tax and for oppressing labor via injunctions and seemed to advocate an end to life tenure for judges as well as other civil servants. The eastern press was particularly incensed by this "dangerous attack" on a sacrosanct conservative institution, and the breakaway gold Democrats, in drafting their own platform, took pains to distinguish their position, condemning "all efforts to degrade that [Supreme Court] tribunal or impair the confidence and respect which it has deservedly held."[156]

In addition, businessmen mounted a vast, diverse, and decentralized effort to convince their employees and customers of the dangers of a Bryan vote. Eastern insurance companies warned midwestern farmers that mortgages would be refused or foreclosed and insurance policies devalued if Bryan won. Northeastern newspapers carried many accounts of factory closings related to anxiety about the monetary, tariff, and social policies of a Bryan administration. The Southern Pacific Railroad in California sent its workers pamphlets forecasting inevitable wage reductions following a Bryan victory, and it transported workers into San Francisco for a huge pro-Republican rally; the Pennsylvania Railroad hauled one thousand employees into Canton, Ohio, to demonstrate their "spontaneous support" for McKinley (they followed a delegation of now unionless steelworkers from Homestead, Pennsylvania, marching up the street "with military precision behind its own squad of Homestead policemen," according to an enthusiastic newspaper account).[157] Some historians have discounted the impact of this employer "persuasion" on the vote; after all, the secret ballot was in wide use in 1896, and besides, the Republicans continued to win northern elections without such extraordinary employer mobilization. It seems plausible, however, that workers were influenced by this powerful regional elite consensus and the demonstrated threat of withheld investment. The efforts of the press, intellectuals, the clergy, and employers rose to a crescendo in the early fall, choking the initial momentum of the Democrats, whose woefully inadequate treasury simply lacked the resources to counter the Republican "educational" campaign.

Lack of money had dictated the Democrats' campaign strategy.[158] The near-solid hostility of the northeastern middle and upper classes, and the dubious prospect of winning over the more economically secure farmers of the core, argued against putting scarce resources into a northeastern campaign.[159] Taking New England and the mid-Atlantic states for granted, the Republicans were concentrating on the critical, silver-sympathetic Midwest, but that region was also the necessary addition to Bryan's southern-western heartland. Thus the Midwest became the major battleground in 1896, and it was here that Bryan concentrated his efforts to woo labor.

However, despite the urging of advisors to waste little time in the Northeast, Bryan refused to concede the region and insisted on presenting the party's cause first "in the heart of what now seems to be the enemy's country, but which we hope will be our country before the campaign is over."[160] He began the intensive postconvention campaigning in early August with a speech in Madison Square Garden, followed by a trip to Albany, where he addressed an enthusiastic crowd of ten thousand. From there Bryan turned toward the critical Midwest, but en route to the campaign's Chicago head-quarters, he delivered speeches in Syracuse, Rochester, Buffalo, Erie, Cleveland, Columbus, Toledo, South Bend, Milwaukee, and Chicago, with stops in many small towns and hamlets in between.

The next leg of the campaign circuit, lasting from September 11 to September 30, took him south to Kansas City, St. Louis, Louisville, Lexington, and Knoxville. Then Bryan turned north, traveling through Asheville, Richmond, Washington, D.C., Baltimore, Wilmington, and Philadelphia and reaching Brooklyn, New York, on September 24. His punishing speaking tour subsequently carried him to several Connecticut cities. In New Haven, an aggressively hostile audience of Yale University students heckled the candidate off the platform. Undaunted, he forged on to Worcester and Boston, where he addressed a crowd of about seventy-five thousand before heading back again to New York and urban New Jersey.

The next campaign swing began with an early October foray through West Virginia and Maryland en route to St. Louis, then turned back to the Midwest. October was spent once more in the cities and towns of that critical region, with major appearances in Cincinnati, Indianapolis, St. Paul, Minneapolis, Grand Rapids, Detroit, Terre Haute, Peoria, and Chicago. After addressing large rallies in the last city and meeting with Democratic clubs and ethnic and labor organizations, Bryan concluded the campaign with visits to Wisconsin before heading back to Nebraska to vote and await the results. By his own account, he had traveled eighteen thousand miles and made an unprecedented six hundred speeches in twenty-seven states.[161]

The crowds were large and enthusiastic, judging by the reports of a hostile press.[162] The common theme of the speeches offered bimetallism as a means both to steady economic growth and to democratization of the economy, a "bottom-up" strategy to counter the Republicans' gold-and-protection "trickle-down" theory.[163] But the supply of money did not always dominate Bryan's discourse. In a major address to nine thousand Chicago workers and their families on Labor Day, Bryan did not speak of silver at all. Instead, he used the occasion to describe his philosophy of government and of labor: "It is the duty of government to protect all, if possible, without injustice to anyone . . . government must restrain men from injuring one another. That is one of the most important duties of government . . . and the government that fails to restrain the strongest from injuring the weakest is a government that fails to do its whole duty." Though there were evils in government, there were no necessary evils. A critical public, through the ballot box, could redeem government and use it to restrain the destructive tendencies of grasping capitalists. "Discontent," Bryan argued, is "the foundation of all progress." Next to the power of the ballot, the greatest protection the common people enjoyed was the power of association, and labor organizations were singled out as first "among all the agencies . . . improving the condition and protecting the rights of this country."[164]

In his "Cross of Gold" speech at the convention, Bryan had appropriated the language of northeastern conservatives in arguing for a more just distribution of wealth and power:

> When you come before us and tell us that we shall disturb your business interests, we reply that you have disturbed our business interests by your course. [Great applause and cheering.] We say to you that you have made too limited in its application the definition of businessman. The man who is employed for wages is as much a businessman as his employer. . . . The farmer who goes forth in the morning and toils all day . . . is as much a businessman as the man who goes upon the board of trade and bets upon the price of grain. The miners who go 1,000 feet into the earth . . . are as much businessmen as the few financial magnates who in a back room corner the money of the world.[165]

Bryan

At Chicago, he stretched the term "middle class" to encompass "the struggling masses" of producers who created all wealth and, quoting Lincoln, declared labor superior to capital. A society polarized between the great wealth of a few and the extreme poverty of the many would be dangerously unhealthy, Bryan argued. Toward the end of his speech, which was held in a large park, a listener sitting on a tree limb fell to the ground when the limb broke—giving the candidate the opportunity to joke that at least the fallen man "did not make the mistake that some men are making; he did not saw off the limb he sat on, like some men who are trying to destroy the production of labor." It was an eloquent speech, squarely in the Jeffersonian-Greenback republican tradition, and judging by the size of the crowd and the reports of frequent and spirited applause, it was well received. "Labor Unions All Right: One of the Few Things in This Country Mr. Bryan Likes," grumped the *New York Times*.[166]

Was Bryan's message, as a number of historians have suggested, inherently defective? Paul Kleppner finds the Democratic program backward-looking (in contrast to the more modern ring of McKinley's politics of growth) and

Bryan's appeal to workers rooted in a "jarringly anachronistic perception" of urban laborers as "petty entrepreneurs" rather than wage earners. Bryan's plea for recognition of the fundamental contributions of farmers to the nation's prosperity was hardly an appropriate tack to take with urban labor, Kleppner argues. Further, Kleppner and others have contended that the campaign's revivalistic style, as well as the presence of some elements among Bryan's rural supporters (particularly the midwestern Prohibitionists), was offputting to urban Catholic workers.[167] The neutrality to hostility of the big-city machine leadership was, along with the aloofness of Gompers, a cue to the "alien" nature of the Bryan campaign for urban workers, and endorsements by Debs and Sovereign—neither of whom had large or enthusiastic followings in the Northeast or organizational bases competitive with that of Gompers—could not have carried much weight against the hegemonic sectional program of the Republicans.

Bryan himself assiduously counseled tolerance and avoided divisive social issues. Indeed, as Robert F. Durden and Samuel T. McSeveney have reported, it was the conservative opposition that consistently invoked moral and religious judgments, and it was the Republican spokesmen who exploited sectional antagonisms to discredit Bryan and his Populist supporters.[168] And, as even Kleppner acknowledges, it was Bryan's mission and strategy to supersede the old ethnic, religious, and sectional politics and to persuade urban workers to see the new Democratic Party not simply as a pluralist amalgam, or a "preserver of their religious value system . . . , but as a vehicle through which they could implement *class* objectives."[169] That this appeal failed does not constitute evidence that cultural perceptions were all-powerful but may indicate that at the ballot box, workers simply (with a lot of prodding from their "betters" and with considerable anguish) gave less weight to the predicted long-term advantages of class-based, redistributive politics than to the capitalist-led politics of growth offered by the other side.[170]

The itinerary described above and the campaign coverage of the *New York Times* evidence Bryan's unprecedented efforts to mobilize urban workers behind a farmer-labor ticket and leave little doubt that the campaign struck a powerful chord. Although the *Times* editorially insisted on Bryan's weak and fading support among workers, stringers on the campaign trail sent in reports of frenzied enthusiasm for the Democratic candidate. Bryan was "wildly cheered" in Pittsburgh, the heart of protectionist sentiment (September 11). At Toledo, Ohio, a torchlight procession led the candidate to the high school square, where he addressed an audience estimated at 30,000 to 40,000 (September 3). At Canton (McKinley's home), "the enthusiasm of the crowd was manifested in every conceivable way" (September 11). "Never before has the present generation seen so large a crowd assembled in Albany, and seldom has there been more enthusiasm displayed" (August 26). "No public man ever received a heartier reception in Buffalo" (August 28). "The audience [of 8,000 working people at a Brooklyn skating rink] was a scene of wild enthusiasm" (September 24).

The last assembly joined in the chorus of a song dubbed "the American Marseillaise" and "liberally applauded" a speaker who urged, "Let us not fear the word 'revolutionist.' Franklin, Paine and Jefferson were revolutionists." A "howling, pushing, good natured, police-resisting crowd" of about 75,000 greeted the candidate at Boston Common—"Probably the Biggest Crowd that Ever Gathered to Hear a Speaker on that Classic Ground" (September 26). A noisy audience of 15,000 greeted his speech at Paterson, New Jersey, "with tremendous outbursts of applause" (September 29). When, at a later speech to 5,000 working people in New York City, Bryan collapsed from exhaustion and had to be taken away in a carriage, "a wild mob of men and women and boys followed through the drenching rain as fast as they could run" (September 30). In a round of speeches in Grand Rapids, Michigan, where the crowds swelled to 25,000, Bryan was "the recipient of a continuous ovation" (October 16). At his midwestern campaign stops, workers' organizations gave him symbolic gifts made of gold and silver, and a group of Jewish Democrats presented him with a silver star. The "cheering multitudes" that greeted the candidate during his last visit to Chicago included "a Negro free silver club, and Bryan clubs composed of Germans, Irish, French, Polish, Bohemians, Hebrews, and other foreign nationalities" (October 28).

Such reports belie the conventional assertions about the Bryan campaign's parochialism and weak outreach to workers. The contrast between this enthusiasm and the weakness of the final labor vote on November 3 suggests that even though many workers were sincerely drawn to the "Popocrat," the powerful economic warnings of the core establishment and charges that the "sectional" program of periphery farmers would bring ruin to the northern industrial economy were ultimately persuasive on election day.

Part of this calculus must have included, as Walter Dean Burnham suggests, considerable skepticism among urban working- and lower-middle-class voters about the advantage to them of the agrarian inflation program.[171] Although the silver strategy was a plausible counter to the Republicans' gold-and-protection politics of growth, all such common denominators are inherently problematic. The Republican protection program carried dubious benefit for working-class consumers in a mature and actually quite internationally competitive industrial economy, and the labor-capital contradiction of the GOP was at least as great as the labor-farmer disjuncture for the Democrats. However, such coalition strategies are essential in large and diverse societies with broad-based two-party systems. A more narrowly focused group-benefit politics, such as some historians have retroactively urged on Bryan, would not have been considered legitimate in the nineteenth century and would hardly have improved the chances of a candidate already accused of "class politics."

The charge that Bryan's appeal to urban labor was inherently flawed echoes the complaint, discussed above, that the Populists "simply did not know what to say to the industrial worker," and one may find merit in the charge without laying all the blame on Bryan and his agrarian constituents. As McNall puts it, the workers "did not develop a radical class language that farmers could appropriate. So conservative, in fact, was the language of workers that it inhibited the development of a common organizational structure for farmers and workers."[172] What was true in 1894 also held in 1896 and through the first two decades of the twentieth century. If the preeminent labor organization asked so little from the state, what could the agrarian Democrats do but try to recruit workers into the farmers' program while offering them legal emancipation to pursue the trade-union organization project and restricted immigration (the dual foci of labor's limited national demands), along with a promise of economic expansion through a steadily expanding money supply?

In sum, Bryan's problem in the industrial cities lay not in a weak or misguided appeal to labor. Rather, it was rooted in sectional political economy, the intense and monolithic hostility of elites to the Democratic-Populist program, the inadequacy of the AFL as a vehicle for labor political mobilization, and the fact that Bryan was compelled to spend most of his time in this unprecedented grass-roots campaign defending, to audiences of workers, as a universal value what the periphery farmers so desperately needed—a more plentiful, publicly controlled currency. The Democrat defended this fundamental Greenback premise with more eloquence and wit than any previous politician, but it was an idea whose time had not come—and would not come until, step by step, in 1913, 1933, and 1971, the United States finally abandoned the gold standard and gave itself the "fiat currency" that had so terrified nineteenth-century bankers.[173]

Bryan came very close to winning—in spite of the enormous elite opposition and the charge of Democratic responsibility for the depression—on the basis of a highly sectional South-West-Midwest (periphery plus diverse region) vote. Despite his failure to carry a single core industrial state, a shift of under 20,000 votes in states contiguous to his periphery bastions—in closely contested California, Oregon, North Dakota, Indiana, Kentucky, and West Virginia—would have brought the Democrat within two electoral votes of victory. Another 1,700 votes in Delaware would have put him over.[174] Had Bryan won, the reform Democrats would have been the party to benefit from the rising farm prices that attended crop failures abroad and the imminent expansion of gold production (which would have increased the money supply even before, or without, the restoration of unrestricted silver minting). Whether a victorious Democratic coalition would have inaugurated an agrarian-led social democracy, and what that would have meant for American capitalism, can only be a subject of speculation. What is clear is that the chance for a bottom-up, farmer-labor coalition led by a sympathetic populist president was lost in 1896. Disfranchisement and industrialization would gradually undermine southern populism. And future Democratic presidents would be closer to northeastern capital, more weakly committed to labor and domestic reform, and more strongly attracted to the augmentation of national military power than was William Jennings Bryan.

5

Agrarian Politics
and Parties after 1896

The American farmer is the most learned farmer in all the
world about politics.

Rep. William H. Murray of Oklahoma,
Congressional Record, 63rd Congress, 2nd session (1914)

It is a widely accepted view that 1896 marked the end of agrarian-led reform.
With the Populist dissenters vanquished, the two major parties are said to
have become sectional vehicles of elite dominance. In a tacit bargain, the plantation elite controlled the South, and the industrial and financial elite dominated the North. Competition and voter turnout declined sharply; most congressional seats became safe regional sinecures.[1] Within the southern Populist
heartland, the restoration of elite hegemony began with the passage, in state
after state, of new constitutions and electoral laws that made it all but impossible for African Americans to vote. Populists generally resisted the imposition
of electoral restrictions but without enough force to block them. Frustrated
after their own electoral defeats at the hands of a manipulated black vote, a
minority of southern Populists were beguiled by the Bourbon Democrats'
argument that if only the electoral process could be "purified"—by the elimi-
nation of the black franchise—white southerners could divide among themselves without fear of corruption or loss of white social supremacy.[2]

The results of the Bourbon electoral coup are well-known. Registration
requirements, poll taxes, literacy tests, and new ballot forms proved devastating to the poor-white electorate as well as the black. The new institution of
the white primary, offered as a sop by the Bourbons, was not a "purified"
arena in which class politics could thrive: it gave rise to a politics characterized
by short-term and personalistic, rather than programmatic, factions and to a
new breed of racist demagogues.[3] In spite of these developments, the South
was washed by a new reform tide in the first decade of the twentieth century,
but in both South and North, reform, in the conventional telling, was now
very much an urban, middle- and upper-class phenomenon.[4] Agrarian radical-

ism had presumably died at the polls in 1896 or been buried under a mound of suffrage restrictions.

The problem with this account is that it ignores the continuity across the 1896 divide and the fact that most of the national legislative fruits of the Progressive Era had their unmistakable origins in the agrarian movements of the 1870s, 1880s, and 1890s. Given the indisputable facts of suffrage restriction and resurgent racism, how can we explain the apparent afterlife of populism? One might, of course, deny the paradox and interpret the national legislation of 1909–17 as a conscious program of the bourgeoisie,[5] but this interpretation is difficult to sustain empirically, as the evidence set out below will demonstrate.

The alternative approach, followed here, distinguishes intrastate and national political processes and argues that the decline of interparty competition and voter turnout and the tragedy of racist politics within the South did not destroy the agrarian impulse in national politics. That impulse retained significant organizational and institutional support in the agrarian areas, and its rationale in the national political economy was not significantly undermined after 1896, despite the improvement in farm prices and currency volume. There were, in particular, four factors that sustained the agrarian reform program in national politics after 1896: a new wave of farmer organization; the direct primary; the national Democratic Party leadership of William Jennings Bryan; and most fundamentally, regional political economy.

The Farm Organization Revival

Even as the Farmers' Alliance consumed itself in politics in the 1890s, the older Grange began a modest revival. By 1900 it had a dues-paying membership of almost 190,000.[6] Another source puts the Progressive Era peak at about 300,000 in 1917.[7] Writing of the Grange revival in western Washington, Marilyn Watkins observes that the farm organization became a vibrant focus of rural life, combining social, political, and educational activities in a manner very reminiscent of the Farmers' Alliance. Like the FA, the western Grange joined farm men and women in a relatively gender-egalitarian association and sought alliances with labor organizations on issues of both state and national politics (including railroad regulation, money, taxation, the eight-hour day, workmen's compensation, the power of the judiciary, and the direct primary, referendum, and recall).[8]

A few years after the Grange began its slow revival, a new farm organization began to take root in the old Farmers' Alliance territory. The years from 1896 to 1900 were marked by a bottoming out of cotton prices and a profound demoralization in the heartland of the old Alliance. In 1902, the price trend turned up, and with that shot of optimism Newt Gresham, a former Allianceman and Populist of very modest means, convinced a few of his neighbors in Rains County, Texas, that the time was right to rebuild a general farmers' organization.[9] Ten charter members—three Populists, one Socialist, one independent, and five Democrats (including Gresham, who had been a Populist and became a Bryan Democrat)—organized the Farmers' Educational and Cooperative Union of America, known as the Farmers' Union (FU), to assist farmers "in marketing and obtaining better prices for their products" and to encourage fraternal and cooperative activities. Some of the early organizers combined hopes of benefiting farmers as a class with a strong dose of self-interest. Gresham, for example, was a man of proven idealism, living more or less off the charity of his friends. The fees collected from organizing must have been quite welcome. In fact, disputes over the handling of fee money eventually led to the dismissal of most of the founders. But the eager enrollment of Texas farmers in the new organization in Rains, a hardscrabble county of small farmers and high tenancy, amazed the early organizers. Soon the tiny post office at Point, Texas, was swamped with inquiries. The desire for a farmers' organization had sprouted again, almost overnight, in the old Alliance soil.[10]

The first state organization was formed in 1904, and the revival spread rapidly from Texas through the Southwest and Southeast. A national organization took shape in 1905, with Charles Barrett of Georgia elected its first president in 1906. The national secretary claimed 935,837 active members in 1907, and Barrett referred to "a membership approaching three million" at the 1908 convention, but there are no accurate membership records.[11] Carl C. Taylor, dividing national dues collected by sixteen cents (the per-member share to national headquarters), derives a much more modest figure of around 130,000 in 1908 and about 136,000 in 1915–19. But, as he reports, the large female membership paid no dues, and given the casualness about national contributions, actual adherents were probably at least four times that number.[12]

A range of 500,000 to 900,000 would yield an organization with a more modest penetration than the 1870s Grange or the 1880s Alliance but comparable in absolute size to the Knights of Labor in the mid-1880s and the AFL in 1900–1901. Structurally, there were about 20,000 locals in twenty-nine states, stretching from the Pacific Coast through the Midwest and South. Growers of cash crops (cotton, tobacco, wheat) were the main adherents. In

1912, three-quarters of the national dues were collected from the twelve states of the cotton belt, the biggest contributors being North Carolina (which had the largest and most militant organization), Texas, Arkansas, Alabama, and Tennessee. However, the wheat regions of the Midwest and West would loom largest after 1915 as the southern cooperative movement ran into the same problems that had stymied the Farmers' Alliance.[13]

Reflecting the established racism of the time and place, the FU was committed to a racially exclusive membership centered on white farmers (both male and female) and farm laborers. In response, black farmers formed their own organization.[14] In addition to farmers, the FU admitted mechanics, schoolteachers, ministers, and doctors, along with newspaper editors who took a pledge to "support the principles of the Order." Bankers, merchants, lawyers, and speculators were excluded.[15] The FU devoted most of its energies to cooperatives, collective control of marketing, and campaigns to withhold crops for a better price. The Texas organization alone built 323 cooperative warehouses between 1905 and 1908, and a 1913 report on agricultural cooperation counted 1,600 FU warehouses in the cotton states at the end of the decade. The FU Jobbing Association in Kansas City, Kansas, was described by *Literary Digest* as "the largest cooperative institution in the world." Throughout the South, Midwest, and West, the FU sponsored a great variety of cooperative enterprises, though the familiar problems of inadequate funds, inexpert management, and the opposition of private business had thrown many of the southern warehouses into bankruptcy by 1916.[16]

It is important to remember that the Farmers' Union was hardly "new." Many of its organizers and members had been active Alliance members and/or Populists, and its goals and methods, as well as its image of farmers as a proud but oppressed class suffering great injustice, were clear links to the old FA. However, chastened by the failure of the Alliance, and with a membership probably less representative of tenants and more of landowners, the FU was more cautious and less radical than the old Alliance,[17] more an organized interest group than a movement (and in this respect it had more in common with the AFL than had the Alliance). Nevertheless, its political agenda was probably the broadest and most "progressive" of any grass-roots organization of this era. There was scarcely a radical reform (in the Progressive Era context)—from nationalizing essential natural resources to outlawing child labor—that the FU did not advocate between 1911 and 1915. The organization clearly manifested an agrarian republican ideology of Greenback/Jeffersonian lineage, with some surprising twists.[18]

The national FU leadership was determined to avoid the party politics that had ended the old Alliance. At the same time, political collective action was seen as essential to the improvement of the farmers' lot, particularly after the cooperatives began to fail. "The Ballot is the deadliest weapon known to modern history," Barrett proclaimed. "The only way to impress your purpose is to shoot them in the neck with your ballot." Trying to solve the farmer's problems without political action would be like "trying to turn over the earth with a toothpick."[19]

To that end, the national and state organizations, from the earliest years, passed resolutions advocating legislation and maintained state and national committees to lobby for their agenda, which centered on facilitation of cooperation, antitrust investigations, railroad regulation, public control of banking and currency, government-supplied credit for farmers, lower tariffs, aid for agricultural and industrial education and public schools generally, direct election of the president and the Supreme Court, and the outlawing of commodity speculation.[20] Like the Alliance, the FU frequently attempted to make common cause with labor unions. FU publications displayed a printers' union label, and officials of the FU and the AFL attended each other's conventions as fraternal delegates.[21] In Texas, trade unionists were "conspicuous by their appearance on the program of all open meetings" of the state FU, and AFL and FU members were urged to buy products carrying each other's labels. The Texas FU passed resolutions opposing convict labor in competition with free labor and advocating an eight-hour day,[22] and workers achieved significant legislative gains in the reform administration of a Democratic governor backed by former Populists, the Texas Federation of Labor, and the FU.[23] Worth R. Miller describes the formation of the Farmers' Union as a critical step in the return of the Populists to the Texas Democratic Party, the strengthening of the Democratic reform wing, and the instigation of a new reform era in that state.[24]

As a result of its organization, legislative advocacy, and close ties with southern members of Congress, the FU acquired substantial political influence as the organizational voice of the periphery farmers in the Progressive Era. State officials and congressmen in the South and (later) the Midwest and West "naturally tried to win Union support by offering to do the farmers' bidding in legislation and government administration."[25] The FU was certainly less frightening to the political and economic elites of its time than the Alliance and the Populist Party had been, but that is a measure not only of the FU's caution but also of the extent to which agrarian positions of the

1890s had been absorbed into a regional ideology. This difference may also reflect the emergence of other, more radical manifestations of collective action by dissenting farmers, such as the Socialist tenant farmers' unions of the Southwest and various "direct action" episodes in the South.[26]

The Direct Primary

In response to the popular demand that control of party nominations be wrested from conservative party bosses, the direct primary swept the southern, midwestern, and mountain states in the first decade and a half of the twentieth century and was part and parcel of the progressive movement for political reform. In the South, which invented it (in South Carolina in 1896), the reputation of the primary is much less salutary than in Wisconsin, which touched off the midwestern electoral reform wave in 1903. In the states of the old Confederacy, this intraparty opening occurred for white men only. It excluded African Americans from what was, in most cases, the only significant election, and the contention that the organization that conducted this election (the Democratic Party) was a private and exclusive association of white citizens reigned until the Supreme Court struck down the white primary in 1944.[27]

Further, as every student of southern politics has learned from V. O. Key, the gathering of almost all political contestation into one socioeconomically diverse party produced factionalized, personalistic, and demagogic politics as individual candidates attempted to distinguish themselves to a confused electorate. Even when a genuine reformer won, the absence of a permanent legislative organization pledged to a program made it extremely difficult to carry reform through the legislature.[28]

On the other hand, southern Democrats, already compelled to adopt major Populist platform stances in order to compete, were also forced to grant the Populist constituency a voice in nominations via the institution of the primary, and the primary did provide a mechanism through which the interests of low-income whites could be pressed. The use of these intra-party elections for the nomination of U.S. senators, a process that the southern states pioneered years before the constitutional amendment for direct election, also introduced an element of popular democracy into the conservative upper chamber. Had the direct primary not also been marked by (or encouraged) race-baiting, the reforms won by poor white farmers might have made primary elections a source of some economic advantage for black citizens as well. But the racist demagoguery that accompanied the rise of Democratic primary politics was an undeniable evil. The best that can be said of the institution by those who stress its constructive aspects is that "the Negro . . . fared the same—no better, no worse"—with the inauguration of primary elections.[29]

The advantage for poor whites lay in the fact that the primary broke the control of the plantation-county Bourbons over the Democratic Party nominating process. To win nomination, a candidate would have to appeal to the masses, and the numerous poor-white voters of the southern hill country and pine flats—where sympathetic local registrars often winked at registration requirements—saw their influence in the party greatly enhanced. The first victor of the new system in Mississippi was James K. Vardaman, who as "a champion of the farmer against the 'predatory' corporate interests" excoriated banks and railroads. As governor, he ended the viciously inhumane system by which state convicts, mostly black, were leased to plantation owners and private industries, increased public school appropriations by almost 20 percent, expanded state regulation of banks, railroads, insurance companies, and monopolies, and improved conditions in state asylums.[30] Elected to the U.S. Senate in 1907 (by a vote highly and inversely correlated with county wealth),[31] Vardaman became one of the leading progressives in that body, a consistent supporter of legislation on behalf of low-income farmers and workers. The Vardaman pattern, combining support for radical economic reform with scurrilously racist rhetoric, was repeated with the election of Theodore Bilbo, who would go on to become one of the strongest Senate supporters of the New Deal.[32] Thus did the direct primary achieve its mixed legacy within the South even as it linked the region's agrarian politics with national progressive reform.

Bryan

In 1896, when we nominated the grandest and truest man the
world ever knew—William Jennings Bryan—for President,
we stole all the Populists had; we stole their platform, we stole
their candidate, we stole them out lock, stock and barrel. . . .
Populists—why I used to hate them; but I did not know as
much then as I do now.

Governor Jeff Davis of Arkansas, 1905

The ideological and organizational leader of the transformed Democratic Party from 1897 through at least 1912 was William Jennings Bryan. Whatever Bryan was in his early political career in the 1890s—perhaps, as his critics charge, an ordinary left-of-center silver Democrat with a flair for oratory—

such a superficial description hardly fit him during the period from 1896 to 1915 (the year in which Bryan effectively ended his political career by resigning his cabinet seat to protest administration policies he believed would lead the country into war). At some point after receiving the nomination of the Populist and silver Democratic Parties, Bryan became, heart and soul, a populist. He was committed to the farmer-labor alliance, to a great expansion of government regulatory functions, and to the democratization of wealth and political power; he opposed militarism at home and abroad; and in all his stands, political principle was cast in the strong moral tones of nineteenth-century republicanism.[33] In his remarkable career, including three presidential races, Bryan's electoral base was periphery farmers. He himself never found a formula with which to win the labor vote of the core and diverse regions, but that was not for lack of trying.

In the 1900 campaign, Bryan played down the monetary issue and stressed opposition to trusts and imperialism and support for labor. The Democratic platform that bore his imprint "condemned two practices inimical to labor's well-being, the injunction and the blacklist; pandered to its fears by opposing Asian immigration; underscored the contradiction between militarism and labor's self-interest; called for a federal 'labor bureau'; and carried Bryan's own pet proposal for avoiding strikes and lockouts, a plan of voluntary arbitration."[34]

None of these propositions, however, could counter the Republicans' "full dinner pail" and Spanish American War victory. The Republican convention had proclaimed, in Chauncey Depew's words, "gold and glory—gold, the standard which . . . had given us the first rank among commercial nations and the glory of our arms, which has made us a world power."[35] Northern intellectuals drawn to Bryan's anti-imperialism were offended by his economic radicalism and his collaboration with Tammany Hall (whose Irish leader, a gold Democrat in 1896, had come over to Bryan for his anticolonialism). Many western silver Republicans, on the other hand, were too nationalistic to stay with Bryan on the imperialism issue. The GOP again funded a propaganda blitz to warn workers of the dangers of a devalued dollar and cuts in the protective tariff, and the northeastern press reported business contracts contingent on McKinley's reelection and attacked Bryan for stirring up class resentments. Though Tammany's endorsement improved Bryan's vote in New York, and anti-imperialism had a similar effect in Massachusetts, McKinley still swept the core and diverse states and took from Bryan's column six states, all west of the Mississippi, that he had carried in 1896.[36]

Though Bryan remained the most influential national Democrat, his demoralized party turned elsewhere in 1904. He had led a progressive reform party twice and lost. Shortly after the 1900 defeat, northern conservative Democrats (centered in New York) and disgruntled southern Bourbons alienated by the party's economic radicalism were emboldened to seek reinstatement. They promised success if the party returned to its pre-1896 "moderation" under their leadership. Emerging victorious out of the internecine party warfare of 1901–4, the conservative "reorganizers" succeeded in nominating the New York gold Democrat Judge Alton B. Parker. However, Bryan attended the convention as the leader of the progressive wing and obtained appointment to the platform committee. There he countered every conservative proposal with a progressive plank of his own, advocating nationalization of railroads and the telegraph, a government-issued currency, an income-tax amendment to the constitution, a strong antitrust plank, anti-imperialism, electoral reform, and several labor planks. Though the convention had seemed stacked against him, Bryan rallied his troops and, by the force of his personality and his standing with the mass of Democratic voters, succeeded in foiling the reorganizers' plan to adopt a conservative platform. He took to the hustings in support of state and local progressive Democrats, attacked Roosevelt for his militarism, and propounded his own progressive program. When Parker lost overwhelmingly, "the Commoner" was ready to pick up the pieces and reconstitute the party. Abandoning its outreach to the "plutocracy," the Democratic Party, under Bryan's leadership, returned to the basics of the farmer-labor alliance and the populist creed.[37]

By 1905 progressive reform was coming into bloom in state and city politics across the West, Midwest, and South, with tentative buds in the Northeast, and even the White House colored in remarkable new hues. Bryan, like a devoted gardener, encouraged all this growth, advertising it in his paper, the *Commoner,* and fighting for the cause in Nebraska, on the Chautauqua circuit, and on the hustings as he campaigned for progressive state and local candidates around the country. He praised Roosevelt's efforts in peacemaking abroad, and in antitrust, railroad regulation, and meat inspection at home, but he criticized the president for not going far enough.[38] Indeed, Roosevelt's progressive transformation may be read as a response not only to the small progressive wing of the GOP but also to the massive support for Bryan's agrarian progressivism in the interior of the country.

Bryan and his hinterland constituents had few serious disagreements on policy; in the case of the southern Democrats' defense of white supremacy, the absence of conflict points to a serious contradiction in the reformer's democratic creed. Indeed, Bryan's greatest flaw as a champion of the disadvantaged stemmed from his compromises with racism within the farmer-labor coalition that he hoped to lead to power. Though he courted black votes, strongly condemned lynching, and advocated equal "citizenship" rights in education and voting, Bryan did little, if anything, to put these ideals into practice and seldom challenged the prejudices of the southern Democrats. Likewise, he took the Gompers/AFL line on Chinese exclusion.[39] On the "woman question," however, the Nebraskan's stand was far more advanced than that of most of his troops, and his public advocacy of government ownership of railroads and telephone and telegraph companies caused great distress for conservative elements in the party.[40]

As one of the many reform enterprises in which he participated, Bryan was one of the fathers of the constitution of the new state of Oklahoma in 1907, advising on its construction and strongly endorsing the resulting document. Not surprisingly for a state soon to host the nation's strongest Socialist Party, the new platform was described in the *Outlook* as "the most radical organic law ever adopted in the Union." It had extensive provisions for direct democracy via the initiative and referendum and contained provisions for the election of administrative and judicial officials, advanced labor and antitrust sections, and authorization for state and city governments to engage in any enterprise they might wish to undertake.[41] When, in the following year, Bryan supervised the drafting of the Democratic Party platform, he combined elements of the Oklahoma constitution, the Nebraska state party platform, and labor planks endorsed by the AFL.[42]

Even after his third defeat in 1908, agrarian and labor reformers rallied around the program Bryan had championed for years, and conservatives in the party were forced to endorse ideas they had long opposed. It was the pull of Bryan's leadership, his de facto control of the party's nomination, and the desire to tap into his mass following that transformed the prim, conservative governor of New Jersey (who had been a Cleveland-gold Democrat) into the candidate of progressive Democrats in 1912. Bryan played a major role in securing the nomination for Woodrow Wilson, wrote the 1912 platform that charted the path of reform for the "New Freedom" years, and coached the candidate through the campaign. And it was Bryan who inspired the congressional Democrats to push the president on antitrust, labor, banking, currency, farm credit, and Philippine independence and who encouraged them to restrain Wilson's momentum toward preparedness and war.[43]

Writing of Bryan's lifelong devotion to political reform, Claude Bowers observed in the early 1950s, "Almost everything we've got today in the way of reforms originated with Bryan."[44] Later scholars and pundits associated him more with the event that immediately preceded his death: the Scopes evolution trial. However, even that involvement, which reflected the aged reformer's commitments to evangelical Protestantism and strong local religious communities, had more to do with the political reform impulse than has been generally recognized. Bryan strongly objected to arguments that drew on the social implications of Darwinism to justify the exploitation of workers and consumers and to discourage reform movements. Against those tenets he wrote in 1921, "Pure food laws have become necessary to keep manufacturers from poisoning their customers; child-labor laws have become necessary to keep employers from dwarfing the bodies, minds and souls of children; anti-trust laws have become necessary to keep over-grown corporations from strangling smaller corporations, and we are still in a death grapple with profiteers and gamblers in farm products."[45] The Antimonoply-Greenback-Populist creed that Bryan embodied was naturally antithetical to Darwinism, whose founder, in *The Descent of Man*, had argued against reforms that checked the salutary process of weeding out the weak and less fit. In addition, Bryan abhorred Nietzsche's Darwinist defense of war as both necessary and desirable for human progress. Such ideas, he believed, were important factors in the development of German militarism leading to World War I.[46]

Agrarianism as a Regional Program

Despite the common description of the progressive reform leaders as representatives of the urban business and professional classes, the farmers were the most numerous constituents for expanded public power in the southern and midwestern states where the reform movements were strongest. In the South, where the social origins of Populist and progressive leaders have been sharply contrasted, the new middle-class reformers embraced and elaborated on the older agrarian agenda. "Under the growing pressure of monopoly," wrote C. Vann Woodward, "the small businessmen and urban middle class overcame their fear of reform and joined hands with the discontented farmers. They envisaged as a common enemy the plutocracy of the northeast, together with its agents, banks, insurance companies, public utilities, oil companies, pipelines and railroads."[47]

This metamorphosis could also be observed in the Midwest, where a relatively young, dissident, middle-class cohort emerged within the dominant Republican Party. These men, many of whom had been anti-Populists in the 1890s, now embraced much of the agrarian program as if they had invented it themselves.[48] To what could the farmers attribute this fortuitous conversion of their old urban antagonists? A major factor was undoubtedly the disappearance of the Populist Party. The return of the Populists to the major parties and the inauguration of primary elections contributed to the new sensitivities in the political leadership class. But principally, the urbanites had come to realize that not only the farmers but also the periphery (and, to a lesser extent, the diverse) regions generally occupied dependent and disadvantaged positions within the national political economy. Their rudimentary industry and commerce suffered the stifling competition of "trusts" grown even larger and more powerful in the unprecedented merger wave of 1897–1903; likewise, they still bore regionally discriminatory freight rates and an increasing tariff tax on the manufactured goods they imported, and the problems of low bank deposits, insufficient credit, and high interest rates had scarcely eased (refer to tables 4.1–4.4).[49] In regions dependent on agriculture, the plight of the farmer reverberated strongly in the small towns and cities. In the cotton belt, the rate of tenancy—which served as a barometer of that region's continued economic distress—continued its inexorable rise. About 38 and 80 percent of white and black farmers, respectively, aged thirty-five to forty-four were tenants in 1910; the numbers would grow to 50 and 81 percent by 1930.[50]

The share of the nation's wealth in the periphery states of the South Atlantic, west-north-central, and mountain regions declined or showed no significant increase between 1890 and 1912;[51] and this measure of "wealth" is a figure that overestimates landed wealth and understates wealth derived from stocks and bonds or embodied in personal property. Further, the mining, manufacturing, and transportation assets counted as "wealth" in these regions were frequently owned by residents of other (mainly core) regions. The South had an estimated per capita wealth of $509 in 1900, compared with a national average of $1,165; in 1919, per capita income in the South remained 40 percent below the national level.[52] Thus the problems to which farmers were peculiarly sensitive were also regional disadvantages perceived as thwarting social and economic advancement.

In view of these regional tendencies, it seems appropriate to recognize the major reform legislation of the Progressive Era—the tariff, banking, income tax, railroad, shipping, and commodity exchange regulation and the antitrust, farm credit, highway, and education measures—as an "agrarian" agenda, albeit one now broadly endorsed in the periphery. The progressive reforms of 1909–17 had their roots in programs advocated by a long succession of Grangers, Antimonopolists, Greenbackers, Farmers' Alliance members, Populists, and Farmers' Unionists. Whatever the social origins of Progressive Era reform leaders (up to and including President Wilson), the periphery regions that provided the necessary votes for these bills had economies dependent on agriculture, forestry, and other natural-resource-based activity, and farmers constituted the largest and best-organized voting blocks there.

However, formal local-interest organization was less important to the shaping of public policy in this formative period than the fact that the Democratic Party, having deposed most of its northern conservative wing in 1896, was an *agrarian* party, itself the foremost political organization of the periphery farmers. In the Republican Party, the bulk of midwestern and western progressive reformers who would break with the eastern capital wing to support the new surge of legislation either represented periphery states and districts or—in the case of some Wisconsin, Illinois, and Iowa legislators—were dependent on farmers for essential electoral support.

Regions, Parties, and Progressive Reform

In sheer numbers of congressional seats, the nonindustrial periphery appeared to possess a decisive political advantage in the Progressive Era. The agriculture, timber, and mining regions held the largest block of members in all four Congresses from 1910 to 1917, with 47 percent of House seats and 57–58 percent of the Senate. Indeed, it is surprising, from this perspective, that the significant political victories finally won in the insurgent Republican and Wilson eras were so long in coming. However, as noted in chapter 2, the interests of the periphery were by no means homogeneous. Despite the fact that this vast region was overwhelmingly rural[53] and depended for its livelihood on products extracted from the soil, the nature of the markets enjoyed by those products propelled some sections of the periphery into political alliance with northeastern capital. The sheep, cattle, timber, and sugar-beet regions of the West produced almost entirely for a domestic market, and their products could be purchased at a significantly lower price from other countries (particularly from Latin American countries, Australia, and New Zealand but also from Canada in some cases). The South, on the other hand, was the world's prime cotton-growing area and the low-cost cotton producer through the 1930s.[54] Sixty percent of the cotton crop was exported in 1910, at prices set internationally. Selling in the world market, the South preferred to buy there as well, so that its customers might accumulate dollars and its necessities might be purchased at the lowest price.

Thus it was that on the tariff issue—which was a fundamental line of political cleavage for much of American history—the South and the West had different interests. The wheat-growing areas, which enjoyed only a modest export trade, and the domestically oriented corn-hog-grain belt in the Midwest were usually reluctant to coalesce with the South. Recognizing the conflicting interests of regions within the periphery, representatives of eastern manufacturing firms years before had crafted a political program that could penetrate the agrarian sections. A high tariff on finished woolen goods produced in the Northeast could be balanced with protective duties for raw wool and sheep. Similarly, the tariff coalition sponsored by the East could embrace a wide variety of other periphery products threatened by imports (for example, sugar, fruits and nuts, hides, lumber, and some metals). Like a balance with a fulcrum somewhere in Iowa, the Republican Party deftly brought eastern and western producer interests into a rough parity and thus dominated national politics, to the broad advantage of eastern capital. Given the unpopularity in the West of the Democratic stand on the tariff issue, it was not surprising that the Populists ignored the issue and Bryan talked mainly of bimetallism in 1896. Currency inflation was an issue on which periphery farmers, ranchers, and miners could agree.

The failure of the Populist-Democratic coalition did not diminish the willingness of the southern periphery to pursue an alliance with northern labor. Just as eastern capital had penetrated the western periphery, southern agriculture sought to penetrate the industrial core.[55] The cities of the manufacturing belt were growing rapidly in the early twentieth century, and the interests of the expanding labor force were generally ignored by the party of capital. The draconian labor policies of the era's capitalists made their arguments for common benefit through the tariff seem increasingly flimsy to the working class (who did notice the rising costs of consumer goods). Since the interests of northern labor could be accommodated at little or no cost to the nonindustrial South, a political alliance against their mutual enemy (northern capital) recommended itself. This alliance formed the basis for a revitalized Democratic Party in the Progressive Era.

In the early twentieth century, then, the most sharply antagonistic interests existed between northern industrial capital and southern agriculture. The two major political parties had formed around these two poles of regional interest. By 1909, the Democratic Party was almost entirely confined to the periphery (see table 5.1). Its strongholds were in the cotton and tobacco states, with a sprinkling of representatives from midwestern and western farm and mining regions. Core industrial areas, on the other hand, elected Republicans by a 3-to-1 margin, despite Bryan's labor strategy in the 1908 election. The tendency of more recently settled immigrant groups in some core cities to vote Democratic for state and local offices produced only a weak echo in national politics. Residents of manufacturing-belt truck-garden and dairy sections were overwhelmingly Republican; the same was true of the corn, hog,

Table 5.1 Regions and Parties in the Progressive Era House of Representatives

Trade Area	Party Balance 61st Congress 1909–1911		Party Balance 62nd Congress 1911–1913		Party Balance 63rd Congress 1913–1915		Party Balance 64th Congress 1915–1917	
	D[a]	R[a]	D	R	D	R-Other[b]	D	R-Other
Core Industrial								
Boston	4	24	7	21	17	14	6	25
Buffalo	1	4	2	3	3	3	2	4
Cleveland	6	8	11	3	14	1	7	9
Detroit	0	5	1	4	2	4	2	4
New York	13	27	28	12	38	9	21	26
Philadelphia	5	21	8	18	14	16	5	25
Pittsburgh	0	11	2	9	2	9	2	9
Seattle	0	2	0	2	0	4	0	3
Total	29	102	59	72	90	60	45	105
Diverse (industry, agriculture, timber, mining)								
Chicago	14	42	21	34	32	26	20	38
Cincinnati	4	8	8	4	8	4	5	6
Portland	0	2	0	2	0	3	0	3
San Francisco	1	6	1	6	2	7	2	7
Total	19	58	30	46	42	40	27	54

Periphery (cotton, wheat, grazing, mining)

Atlanta	12	0	12	0	13	0	13	0
Baltimore	3	5	7	1	7	1	6	2
Birmingham	8	0	8	0	9	0	9	0
Dallas[c]	13	0	14	1	17	0	16	1
Denver	3	1	3	0	4	0	3	1
Helena	0	0	0	1	2	0	2	0
Houston	5	0	5	0	5	0	5	0
Jacksonville	3	0	3	0	4	0	4	0
Kansas City, Ks	2	9	3	8	8	3	9	2
Little Rock	5	0	5	0	5	0	5	0
Los Angeles[d]	0	2	1	2	2	2	2	2
Louisville	7	0	7	0	7	0	7	0
Memphis	8	0	8	0	8	0	8	0
Minneapolis	1	15	1	16	1	18	2	17
Nashville	5	2	5	2	5	2	5	2
New Orleans	9	0	9	0	9	0	8	1
Omaha	3	4	3	4	3	4	3	4
Oklahoma City	2	3	3	2	6	2	7	1
Richmond	23	6	27	2	26	4	26	4
St. Louis	13	8	16	5	19	2	19	2
Salt Lake City	0	2	0	2	0	4	1	2
Spokane	0	1	0	1	0	1	1	3
Total	125	58	140	47	160	43	161	43

[a] Party designations are taken from the congressional directories for the first session, filling vacancies.

[b] The "other" category mainly designates Progressives. In the 63rd Congress, for example, it includes 9 Progressives, 7 progressive Republicans, and 1 Independent. There was 1 Socialist in the Chicago trade area in the 62nd and 1 in the New York trade area in the 64th Congress.

[c] Includes Texas portion of the El Paso trade area, where the majority of the population resided in the Dallas trade-area districts. The remainder of the El Paso trade area went to Los Angeles. Two New Mexico districts are added here in the 62nd Congress.

[d] The Los Angeles trade area includes newly admitted Arizona in the 62nd Congress.

Rep.

cattle, and grain sections of the Midwest (the Chicago and Cincinnati trade areas). The western strategy of the Republican Party was splendidly affirmed by an overwhelmingly GOP vote in the San Francisco, Seattle, Portland, Helena, Spokane, and Salt Lake City trade areas.

However, by 1910, partisan patterns were clearly shifting in the industrial and diverse farm-industry regions. Holding their solid southern base, the Democrats won a majority of the House in 1910 and added sixty-three more seats in 1912. Although population growth in the southwestern periphery accounted for a portion of the Democratic gains, the bulk of the new Democratic seats were won in the manufacturing belt and the midwestern corn belt. In the 61st Congress, 72 percent of Democratic House seats were held by periphery representatives; in the 63rd, the periphery composed just under 55 percent of the Democratic Party. An indecisive Republican president and an intransigent congressional Republican leadership had failed to accommodate rising demands for public control of corporate power and for a more reasonable tariff. In three- and four-way elections contested by Progressives and Socialists, the Republicans temporarily lost their control of the core. As a result, a new reform coalition—consisting of a solid phalanx of southern and other periphery Democrats, joined by a new cadre of northern urban Democrats and a smaller number of progressive Republicans—was now in a position to challenge the Republican regime and construct a new national state.

Who Were the "Progressives"?

Attempts to uncover a single ideology at the root of Progressive Era reform have seemed destined either to fail empirical substantiation or to be so vague ("optimism," "activism," "status anxiety," "social justice") as to defy any effort at empirical demonstration.[56] One way of avoiding the quagmire of ideological labels is to focus on what people *did* during this period, as opposed to what they said or what they (presumably) were *thinking*. If the irrefutable identifying trait of a "reform" period is the large quantity of new programmatic legislation, then analysis should start there—with the new statutes—and work backward to the supporting coalitions that enacted them. Dealing only with federal statutes and formal public behavior (roll-call votes), supplemented by public debates and pronouncements, one may put aside some of the intriguing but frustrating questions about the origin and shape of progressive *ideas* and search for patterns in actual *events*. In this method, it is not "where did the idea come from?" that is most important but "who had the incentive and provided the muscle to put this idea into national law?"

Biographies of "progressives" tend to overemphasize the role of their principles in securing legislation. The favored biographical subjects, of course, have been the Hamlet-like insurgent Republicans. Repelled by the corruption and conservatism of their party's leadership, but equally repulsed by the party of the cotton South, the insurgent Republicans stood apart from the old two-party axis of contention and freely criticized both poles. They collected and developed ideas for solving social problems and helped to mobilize public support for new legislation. Because these insurgents were well-educated, articulate, independent, and accessible, the middle-class "uplift" magazines (*Collier's, Success, McClure's,* and the *New Republic,* for example) found them very good copy. Such publications consciously served as mouthpieces and propagandists for their policy initiatives and indirectly helped the "partyless" insurgents build supporting organizations, both at home and within a larger national arena.[57] Once these Republicans became respected celebrities, non-government activists (such as Louis Brandeis) sought them out as sponsors for reform proposals.

At the turn of the century, widespread corruption permeated the political power structures of the states. In Iowa, for example, two great railroads had built an imposing network of control by distributing free passes to local notables and sponsoring political campaigns for state offices. As a result, the railroads were able to keep their taxes low and avoid rate and service regulation. What the railroads did in the Midwest and California, powerful mining trusts (like the Rockefeller-Guggenheim Mineral Coal and Iron Company) did in western states, along with even more shameless exploitation of their workers. The Republican Party in these essentially one-party states sanctioned and furthered corporate policy goals. The party became, in Thomas J. Bray's words, a "bulwark of plunder and special interests."[58] Because the South had already adopted the direct primary, southern progressives could work more easily within a loosely organized one-party system. In the Midwest, however, it was necessary to reorganize the dominant Republican Party in order to attack "the interests." Electoral reform, particularly the direct primary and the popular election of senators, became the opening wedge in that reorganization. Civil-service laws provided methods for undermining the patronage that supported reactionary incumbents.

Most of those destined to rebel against the Republican Party in the 61st Congress shared two traits, one personal and the other regional: they were ambitious politicians who found their careers thwarted by the Old Guard Republican leadership; and they represented areas of the Midwest where the policy direction imposed by the core GOP was increasingly unpopular. Most began their political careers as straight-arrow Republicans, strongly support-

ive of the protective tariff and contemptuous of Bryan and his party.[59] They
lived in small towns or cities in the Midwest and West, almost all located in
the corn, sugar-beet, and wheat regions. William Borah of Idaho was something of an exception, representing a predominantly mining and sheep-raising
state in the West (such tariff-dependent regions typically produced Republican loyalists).[60] Comfortable, conservative lawyers, the insurgent Republicans
were preeminently good politicians. When the people of their states and districts began to show dissatisfaction with national Republican policies and local
Republican corruption, they seized on that discontent and turned failed or
failing political careers into near invincibility.[61]

Less articulate and often less well educated, the rustic spokesmen for the
South and border states have attracted far less (and less favorable) attention
from Progressive Era historians, and the Democratic Party, in the years before
it acquired a large urban wing, has generally been seen as traditional and
ineffectual. Champ Clark, who led the resurgent Democratic Party in the
House, was ridiculed in the eastern press and treated condescendingly by
historians. Southern members of Congress were less prolific memorialists,
which may explain some of the omission, as David Sarasohn has suggested.[62]
But more important, the most senior southern congressional leaders, men
like John Sharp Williams of Mississippi and Texas Sens. Joseph Bailey
and Charles Culberson, had not been associated with the Populist or Democratic reform factions in their home states. Although from the standpoint of
regional economic imperatives, it was quite possible for politicians representing middle- and upper-class interests in intrastate politics to become ardent
progressives in the national arena, historians have been understandably reluctant to include these regional champions among the ranks of those progressives for whom national reform efforts were logical extensions of state careers
as reform leaders.[63] It was particularly difficult to do so in the 1960s and early
1970s, when much of Progressive Era history was being written and when the
oppressive southern segregation system was finally under concerted attack.

The southern congressmen often performed less brilliantly in debate than
the insurgent Republicans. Few of them had attended universities or law
schools of the first rank,[64] and one suspects that small-town life in the cotton
belt failed to impart a sophisticated understanding of the industrial economy
they were struggling to control. Nevertheless, southern committee leaders
could swiftly graft appealing ideas onto their own legislative proposals, and
the great majority of their rank-and-file colleagues joined the supporting side
on almost all issues commonly designated "progressive" in this era. They did
so not because they were farsighted idealists but because such positions went

over very well with their constituents. The insurgent Republicans were progressive for the same reason.

By 1910 the progressive movement in the states—particularly the states of the Midwest, South, and West—had secured electoral reforms, regulatory restraints on railroads and insurance companies, taxes on powerful corporations, and mitigation of some of the most reprehensible employment practices. However, the effectiveness of state laws was limited. Corporations harassed by state regulators could threaten to move their operations elsewhere, and federal court decisions made it impossible for states to have much influence on corporations heavily engaged in interstate commerce. If a state like New Jersey opened its arms to trusts and holding companies, redress for their abuses of farmers, businesspeople, and consumers in other states was beyond the reach of those victims. When the U.S. Department of Justice refused to act, or pursued the transgressors halfheartedly, the immunity of the offending corporations was almost complete. Where national legislation existed, as in the Interstate Commerce and Sherman Acts, federal court interpretation often rendered it useless or applied it perversely to protect corporations from their workers or would-be competitors. Reformers were compelled to turn their attention to national politics.[65]

While Theodore Roosevelt was president, it appeared that the reform movement could be accommodated within the national Republican Party, in the same way that the movement was transforming state parties in the Midwest. Roosevelt's actions in the *Northern Securities* and other cases gave new vitality to the Sherman Act. His antitrust efforts, his arbitration of the 1902 coal strike, and his support for railroad, conservation, reclamation, and meat-inspection laws convinced reform-minded Republicans that their party had stepped into the vanguard of a popular movement to cure the ills of industrial society.[66] However, with William Howard Taft in the White House, this hope faded. The "standpatters"—senators like Rhode Island's Nelson Aldrich, New York's Elihu Root, Pennsylvania's Boies Penrose, Connecticut's Orville Platt, Massachusetts's Henry Cabot Lodge, New Hampshire's Jacob Gallinger, Utah's Reed Smoot, and Wisconsin's John Spooner and Speaker Joseph Cannon and his circle in the House—balked at serious reform, and the president declined to push them. Under standpat leadership, the Republicans lifted protection to prohibitive levels, provoking cries that high tariffs milked the consumer and nurtured monopolies. When midwestern farmers complained about the tariff, party leaders offered to cut duties on *their* products. When reformers pressed for an income tax, Republican leaders came forward with a corporation tax, easily passed on to consumers. When farmers and small businesspeople complained about railroads, Taft offered them a "Commerce Court" and schemes to facilitate railroad "cooperation." Revolt within the party was inevitable, and it was inevitably most pronounced in regions where the debilities of Republican policy (particularly policy on the tariff, railroads, and trusts) outweighed the benefits.

In the House of Representatives, the first clearly identifiable group of "progressives" among Republicans were those who, in 1909 and 1910, successfully moved (with Democratic cooperation) to strip the autocratic Speaker of his most important powers and to change the rules by which bills were brought to the floor and debated. Some of the insurgents were motivated only by annoyance at what they perceived as Cannon's unfair handling of their committee assignments or legislative proposals, but most insurgents either were or soon would be "progressives" in support of reform legislation previously blocked by the Republican leadership.

Within the Republican Party, it was mainly farm-state representatives who were restless, but agricultural economies alone were not the determining factor. Farm areas within the manufacturing belt remained steadfast under the Republican standard, and western wool and sugar-beet areas, dependent on the protective system, dared not desert the Republican coalition. Among the thirty-three insurgent Republicans in the 61st Congress,[67] only six represented districts in the industrial heartland, and the evidence strongly suggests that the "insurgency" of the latter resulted from personal pique at Cannon's tactics rather than from policy incongruity with the majority (see table 5.2). They were faithful to a man on the tariff and cast only a few sporadic votes with the opposition on other divisive issues. The policy-oriented insurgents came overwhelmingly from the corn and wheat sections of the Midwest. In the West, only Miles Poindexter, from wheat-growing eastern Washington (Spokane), and San Francisco representative Everis Hayes, whose dissent was mostly confined to labor issues, joined the insurgent ranks. The wheat sections of the periphery were more favorable to the southern Democratic position on the tariff than were the corn-belt districts in the Chicago trade area. The latter were both closer to manufacturing centers and less involved in international trade.

Sympathy with labor's legislative goals was expressed by many Republican insurgents, particularly representatives from the Milwaukee and Minneapolis areas, where there were significant numbers of industrial workers. However, as the second labor vote in table 5.2 indicates, this was a "soft" issue for the dissident Republicans. The third vote in table 5.2 provides a measure of support for strong railroad regulation. The most popular issue for the agrarian insurgents (but clearly a zero for the core contingent) was control of corporate malfeasance and protection of small competitors. There are few House roll calls that tap this sentiment in 1909–10, but the fourth roll call reported in the table is indicative. Eighteen of the twenty-seven periphery- and diverse-area insurgents voted with the southern Democrats to keep in state courts all suits against distant corporations—the goal being greater convenience for the local plaintiff and considerably greater chance of conviction.

In the Senate, there was no rules fight to galvanize the intraparty rebellion, but a small group of midwestern senators began to conspicuously oppose the Old Guard during the 61st Congress. The early leaders of the "insurgent" group were Robert La Follette of Wisconsin, Albert Cummins of Iowa, Cummins's colleague Jonathan Dolliver (recently transformed from standpatter to progressive), Joseph Bristow of Kansas, and Albert Beveridge of Indiana. Death and defeat removed Dolliver and Beveridge in 1910, but insurgent ranks expanded with election reforms in the western and midwestern states and the promotion of House insurgents to the Senate. By 1912 the group of rebellious Senate Republicans had gained George Norris of Nebraska, William Borah and James Brady of Idaho, Miles Poindexter of Washington, Moses Clapp of Minnesota, William Kenyon of Iowa, Ash Gronna of North Dakota, and Coe Crawford of South Dakota.[68] The issues that most clearly distinguished the insurgents from the Senate leaders were the tariff, the Mann-Elkins railroad bill, and to a lesser extent, labor issues. As in the House, however, Senate insurgents were not "progressive" on all issues. They were much more consistent on railroad and subsequent corporate regulatory legislation than on labor. It must be remembered that on each of the roll calls reported in the tables, there were about four Democrats for every Republican on the "progressive" side. Republican insurgency seldom involved more than 15 percent of the party (20–30 members) in the House, and it lost considerable momentum in the 62nd Congress even as the Democrats were achieving remarkable cohesion within their own ranks. It was periphery Democrats and their less numerous northern labor allies who provided the foot soldiers for the progressive program.[69]

In table 5.3, a summary of regional and party patterns for 1909–11 has been constructed from data provided in an unpublished Ph.D. dissertation by Jerome M. Clubb. Three-quarters of the "reformers" on these issues (which encompassed tariff, taxation, railroad, banking, conservation, and political reform proposals) were Democrats. The largest bloc came from the South, where reformers constituted almost 80 percent of representatives. The next-largest group was midwestern, mainly Democrats but with a substantial co-

Table 5.2 House Republican Insurgents and Issue Positions

Reps.	District	Region	Defeat Payne Tariff[a]	Labor Exemption[b] I	Labor Exemption[b] II	Defeat Commerce Court[c]	Corporate Suits in State Courts[d]	Put Murdock on Rules Committee[e]
Ames	MA 5	C						
Cary	WI 4	D	X	X	X	X	X	X
Cooper	WI 1	D		X	X			X
Davidson	WI 8	D						
Davis	MN 4	P	X	X	X	X	X	X
Fish	NY 21	C		X	X			
Foelker	NY 3	C						
Fowler	NJ 5	C				X		X
Gardner	MA 6	C						
Good	IA 5	D		X			X	
Gronna	ND AL	P	X	X		X		
Haugen	IA 4	D	X	X		X		X
Hayes	CA 5	D			X			
Hinshaw	NE 4	P		X			X	
Hubbard	IA 11	D	X	X	X	X	X	X
Kendall	IA 6	D	X	X	X		X	
Kinkaid	NE 6	P		X			X	
Kopp	WI 3	D		X			X	
Lenroot	WI 11	P	X	X	X	X	X	X
Lindbergh	MN 6	P	X	X		X	X	X

Representative	State	District	Party	a	b	b	c	d	e	Total by Issue
Madison	KS	7	P					X		
Martin	SD	AL	P							
Miller	MN	8	P						X	
Morse	WI	10	D	X				X		
Murdock	KS	AL	P	X	X	X	X	X	X	
Nelson	WI	2	D	X	X	X	X	X	X	
Norris	NE	5	P	X	X			X		
Pickett	IA	3	D					X		
Poindexter	WA	3	P	X	X	X	X	X		
Steenerson	MN	9	P	X	X					
Taylor	OH	12	C							
Volstead	MN	7	P	X	X			X		
Woods	IA	10	D	X	X	X	X	X	X	
Total by Issue				15	20	12	12	18	12	

Regional Totals	
Core	6
Diverse	13
Periphery	14

a Payne–Aldrich Tariff Conference Report, CR, 61-1, July 21, 1909, 4755.
b Amendment to prohibit the use of federal monies to prosecute labor violations of the antitrust laws, two votes, CR, 61-2, June 21, 1910, and June 23, 1910, 8656, 8852–53.
c Motion to recommit Mann–Elkins bill and strike the provision for a commerce court, CR, 61-2, May 10, 1910, 6032 (a yea vote favors strong railroad regulations).
d Hubbard (West Virginia) amendment to weaken Garrett (Tennessee) amendment facilitating suits against out-of-state corporations, CR, 61-3, January 18, 1911, 1070.
e Motion by Rep. Norris to appoint insurgent Rep. Murdock of Kansas to Rules Committee in place of the regular Republican nominated by the leadership, CR, 62-2, January 11, 1912, 864–65.

Table 5.3 House Supporters of "Progressive" Reform, by Census Region, 61st Congress

	Reformers / All Representatives from Region (%)	Democrats / All Reformers (%)
Northeast	33	20
(New England & Mid-Atlantic)	112 (29.5)	33 (60.6)
Midwest	73	38
(East-North-Central & West-North-Central)	137 (53.3)	73 (52.1)
South	103	98
(South Atlantic, East-South-Central	131 (78.6)	103 (95.1)
& West-South-Central)		
West	7	4
(Mountain & Pacific)	22 (31.8)	7 (57.1)

Source: Jerome M. Clubb, "Congressional Opponents of Reform, 1901–1913" (Ph.D. diss., University of Washington, 1963), table 26, 190–91.

hort of Republicans from the (periphery) states of the west-north-central region. Reform-oriented representatives were scarcer in the northeastern (core) states and were usually Democrats following an agenda set by the majority agrarian wing of the party. In the South, over 80 percent of the reformers represented districts that contained no large cities; but even among the small urban contingent, supporters outnumbered opponents of reform by almost six to one.[70] In the Midwest, rural representatives also dominated the group of reformers, but in the northeastern and Pacific states, rural districts were more conservative than big-city districts.[71] Thus, early progressivism in Congress was not a program of farmers in general but of farmers in the less-industrial regions of the South and Midwest.

PART II
The Agrarian Statist Agenda

Although two extremely important pieces of legislation—the Interstate Commerce Act and the Sherman Antitrust Act—were passed in the late nineteenth century amid intense agrarian political protest, their effective enforcement and legislative strengthening did not take place until the Progressive Era. Particularly during the Taft and Wilson administrations, concentrated in the period between the 1909 revolt against House Speaker Joseph Cannon and late 1916, Congress came to be dominated by a reform coalition whose most numerous members were agrarian Democrats. Allied with an expanded cohort of northern urban Democrats and a group of midwestern and western dissident Republicans, the agrarians were able to establish control over the national government and impose their broad policy agenda on national political development, enacting regulatory initiatives that had been percolating for years.[1]

Another block of legislation represented the agrarians' delivery on the old coalition bargain with labor. Although many compromises had to be made along the way—with presidents, with conservative core Republicans, and with the more nationalistic and bureaucracy-minded congressmen from diverse areas—the agenda of progressive reform nevertheless had clear agrarian origins and, as will be shown below, overwhelming agrarian support.

Long out of power, and probably aware that the opportunity would be of limited duration, the agrarians packed a lot of legislative creativity into these eight years; as a result, the record of periphery leadership is impressive for its range as well as for its novelty. Table II.1 displays the most important legislative results.

Railroad regulation, a long-standing issue for farmers, provided one of the earliest victories. The periphery Democrats joined the Republican insurgents to strengthen a landmark 1906 bill, and the coalition came back in force to take President William Taft's conservative 1910 proposals away from him and reformulate them into an effective federal rate-control statute. A few years later, the coalition established valuation of railroad property as an aid to rate

Table II.1 The Agrarian Statist Agenda: Major Progressive Era Legislation

Transportation	*Commodity Trading, Storage, and Grading*
1910 Mann-Elkins (Railroad Rate Regulation) Act	1914 Cotton Futures Act
	1916 Warehouse Act
1913 Valuation Act (for railroads)	1916 Grain Standards Act
1913 Abolition of Commerce Court	
1916 Shipping Act	*Infrastructure: Social and Physical*
	1914 Smith-Lever Agricultural Extension Act
Trade	1916 Bankhead-Shackleford ("Good Roads") Act
1913 Underwood Tariff	
	1917 Smith-Hughes Vocational Education Act
Taxation	
1913 Income Tax	*The Delivery for Labor*
1916 Revenue Act	1912 Lloyd-La Follette Act (postal employees' organization rights)
Banking and Credit	1912 Eight-Hour Act (federal employees)
1913 Federal Reserve Act (structure, public control, & credit provisions)	1913 Sundry Appropriations Act (no Justice Department prosecutions of trade unions)
1916 Federal Farm Loan Act	
	1914 Clayton Act (labor sections)
Corporate Concentration and Monopolistic Practices	1915 La Follette Seamen's Act
	1916 Child Labor Act
1914 Clayton Antitrust Act	1916 Workmen's Compensation Act
	1916 Adamson Eight-Hour Act

control and prohibited railroads from owning or controlling competing water carriers. Early in 1913, Taft's judicial obstacle to effective administrative rate control (the Commerce Court) was abolished. In the administration of President Woodrow Wilson, attention focused on ocean shipping, inaugurating federal supervision of rates and service and, for a time, even government ownership of freighters essential to the export trade.

The first item on the agenda of the united Democratic government in 1913 was tariff revision. Thwarted during the Taft administration, the export-oriented farmers finally succeeded with Wilson's support and control of both chambers of Congress. Substantial cuts were made in the duties on manufactured goods, and a variety of food products, industrial raw materials, and farmers' machinery and supplies were put on the free list. To replace lost customs revenues and pay for new government functions, the agrarian coalition enacted a federal tax on individual net incomes over $3,000. This tax exempted the great majority of periphery farmer and urban working-class families and collected over three-fourths of its total revenues from the upper classes of the northeastern and north-central industrial states. The new tariff-taxation system not only enacted the traditional trade philosophy of the agrarian periphery but also reversed, at least temporarily, the regional wealth redistribution fostered by the protective system.

The federal reserve system, with twelve regional banks under a presidentially appointed board, was created to facilitate the national movement of funds at harvest time, to generally stabilize the financial system, and to provide for a flexible currency—goals on which there was wide agreement. The design of the new currency system, however, reflected periphery interests and aroused intense opposition in the industrial-financial heartland. It provided for a very decentralized structure and a publicly appointed apex—both features with a long agrarian/greenback genealogy. The Federal Reserve Act also made it easier for farmers to get credit by providing a means for rediscounting agricultural paper and authorizing national bank loans on farmland. The Federal Farm Loan Act of 1916 went further, providing direct federal support for farm loans through a network of land banks.

Reacting to abuses of corporate power long tolerated by the courts and the party of capital, the agrarian coalition wrote a far-reaching expansion of the Sherman Antitrust Act in 1914. It attempted to overcome judicial ambiguity and executive inaction by explicitly outlawing practices that might lead to monopoly and by strengthening the ability of private individuals to take offending corporations to court. On other fronts, the corrupt New York Cotton Exchange, which had blatantly defrauded both buyers and sellers of cotton, was reformed by the Cotton Futures Act, and the Grain Standards Act mandated inspection and grading of grains under federal license. Another regulatory statute intended as a benefit to farmers was the 1916 Warehouse Act, one result of which was a legitimate warehouse receipt that the farmer could use, in a manner reminiscent of the old subtreasury plan, to obtain credit.

As a result of the Smith-Lever Act of 1914, the federal government undertook to provide funds for agricultural education "in the field." In the 1917 Smith-Hughes Act, the farmer-labor coalition secured federal money for agricultural and industrial education in public high schools. The Bankhead-Shackleford ("Good Roads") Act of 1916 took a similarly unprecedented step in providing national funds for local farm-to-market road construction, another long-cherished goal in the periphery.

Labor legislation also proliferated in the Progressive Era as the periphery Democrats made good the political bargain pioneered by the populists and William Jennings Bryan and repaid their northern copartisans for their support on tariff, credit, and business regulatory legislation. Labor's most important gains came in the Clayton Act, which presumed to exempt organized workers from prosecution as "conspirators in restrain of trade" and to limit the issuing of injunctions and jailing for contempt in labor disputes. The federal government was prohibited from bringing Sherman Act suits against labor (a practice initiated by the Harrison administration in 1892). Congress also attempted to ban the products of child labor from interstate commerce (like the Clayton Act guarantees, this measure would be voided by the Supreme Court). With greater success, conditions for sailors in the merchant marine were significantly improved by the 1915 Seamen's Act. Regulation of work hours was made more effective, and compensation for industrial accidents was established for federal employees.

This list does not, of course, encompass all significant legislation passed in this era. The Progressive Era was a time of extraordinary intellectual ferment and social organization, and many policy proposals were put forward by distinctly urban groups and individuals. To what extent can these be said to constitute important, alternative "national statist agendas"?

Middle-class professionals campaigned, as individuals or as directors of public and private organizations, to secure particular reforms. Much of this effort took place in state-level struggles for social legislation, but at the national level, the contributions, for example, of the USDA's Harvey Wiley to food and drug regulation, of Gifford Pinchot to "scientific" conservation, and of Louis Brandeis to business and labor regulation are well-known. Legislation dealing with pure food and with efficient resource use on public lands resulted from campaigns led by committed public intellectuals who were able to convince particular professional associations and a few "enlightened" businesspeople that the legislation would benefit the public as well as their own occupational interests.[2] Both campaigns had to overcome significant opposition from businesses and from congressmen protecting local economic interests (no few of them agrarians).

The diverse policy ideas of these middle-class activists were undoubtedly significant inputs during the pluralistic national legislative debates of the early twentieth century. But their numbers were too few, their mass base was too thin, and their often elitist claims about the need for expert direction of vast areas of American life were too antithetical to reigning public norms to have the impact they hoped for. As in Stephen Skowronek's accounts of the disappointment of those intellectuals who would centralize and professionalize the military and civil service and bring the railroads under rational expert direction,[3] their ideas fell into the force fields of legislative and party politics; for the most part, they found partial success only when adopted by one or the other party coalition for its own purposes.

Capitalists, unlike middle-class intellectuals, *did* control a party—and had undisputed political power. A strong vein of Progressive Era scholarship, cited earlier, imputes a national statist agenda to advanced capitalists and finds evidence of its success in virtually every Progressive Era initiative. As Joel Silbey summarizes these arguments: "The avant guard of the new industrial elite [had] a growing interest in a larger and more sustained government involvement in shaping the economy, a willingness to have the government move in radically different directions. . . . They wanted a commitment to rationalize the economy in more orderly and careful ways than the usual American practice of competitive individualism."[4] Arguments about advanced capitalist statism, which will be confronted in part II, rely on a good bit of creative interpretation from fragmentary and often contradictory evidence. Certainly there were *particular* capitalists who realized (usually when the idea was broached by a passionate, nonbusiness policy entrepreneur) that their own firms' profits might be enhanced by a government mandate for scientific forestry, unadulterated food, and so forth. But the claim of a self-conscious statist agenda on the part of capitalists who engaged in positive, concerted action growing out of a shared philosophy is not easy to sustain in the major Progressive Era policy arenas examined below (with, perhaps, the partial exception of national banking). The large majority of capitalists, even those who perceived advantage to their firms or sectors in a particular form of government intervention, did not trust the legislature to give them the kind of regulation they might welcome. So, for the most part, it was better *not* to expand the regulatory powers of the state, to leave economic concentration to the capitalists themselves. When that seemed no longer possible, when some regulatory juggernaut was building, the wisest among them would, of course, enter the deliberations and attempt to deflect the movement into less dangerous channels. *Defensively,* their power was impressive.

And yet there was a limited *positive* statist agenda widely endorsed among capitalists and prominent in Republican Party dogma: tariff protection; the gold standard; a new, more centralized, privately controlled national bank; and a beefed-up military apparatus to protect American investments at home and abroad. The agrarians provided the major opposition to this agenda and proposed a multifaceted state-expansion program of their own. The following case studies will examine their pursuit of new national policies and the resultant interactions among agrarians, workers, capitalists, public officials, and middle-class reformers.

6

The Transportation System

Farmers, Railroads, and the State

Railroad regulation has generated one of the longest-running controversies in American political development. Writing in 1913, the year that congressional progressives made their final repairs to the railroad regulatory net, Solon J. Buck credited the midwestern Granger movement with laying down, in the early to mid-1870s, the fundamental principles upon which public control of railroad capitalism would be erected.[1] The Progressive Era interpretation came under attack in the 1950s. Influenced by the pluralist paradigm in political science and a broad skepticism about social movements in general—and agrarian movements in particular—that prevailed in urban academic circles, new scholarship debunked farmer influence and discovered the roots of railroad regulation among organized northern business interests. Gerald Nash linked the House interstate commerce bill of 1886 to agitation by independent Pennsylvania oil producers who were resisting John D. Rockefeller's (Standard Oil) exploitations of railroad rate favors to gain a monopoly over the eastern oil industry;[2] Lee Benson placed the impetus farther east, in the commercial center of New York City, where a small group of prosperous merchants criticized the railroad pooling efforts of the late 1870s.[3] In the 1970s, George H. Miller also denied the Grangers, and farmers generally, credit for the (misnamed, in his view) original "Granger laws." He attributed leadership of the early state-level regulatory movement to urban commercial interests in river towns threatened by the new railroad rate structure, pointing out that rural spokesmen in the 1866–72 period often opposed state regulation for fear it would discourage construction in their as yet unserved areas. Although Miller acknowledged that agrarian unrest contributed to a second round of state legislation in 1873–74, he went to great lengths to deny farmers a leading role.[4]

In 1965, Gabriel Kolko stepped beyond the pluralist paradigm to make a provocative argument rooted in the Marxist tradition: the railroads themselves had sought federal regulation as the only solution to their failed efforts at cartelization.[5] With Kolko, the interpretation of the genesis of federal controls over railroads had moved as far as possible from the original agrarian-progressive view. The controversy by no means ended here, however. Writing in the early 1970s, at the beginning of major northeastern-midwestern railroad bankruptcies, Albro Martin returned to older notions of sponsorship by agrarians and small businesspeople but added a strongly negative twist. In Martin's view, these "archaic progressives," far from granting the railroads' wishes, had imposed on a once-vibrant enterprise a repressive and stultifying control that sapped their potential for generating and attracting the necessary new capital investment.[6]

Whereas Martin's refutations of the Kolko hypothesis relied heavily on an evaluation of the economic results of regulation, the criticism offered by Ari Hoogenboom and Olive Hoogenboom rested on the legislative histories of regulation bills. During the long congressional struggles to establish federal control, members of Congress were well aware of the strong opposition of railroad men to antipooling and long/short-haul provisions. Farmers, merchants, industrialists, and railroad men all participated in the debate and helped to shape the bill, but the Hoogenbooms saw a strong sectional cast to the proregulation forces. Opponents, they noted, were concentrated in the Northeast, whereas backers of the most stringent versions of the first Interstate Commerce Act were agrarian Democrats; the compromise 1887 statute, still opposed by the railroads and their northeastern supporters, drew its most enthusiastic backing from the Midwest. In short, they wrote, it was the Midwest and the South that "muscled the bill through; the Northeast and the railroads could not block legislation which had been demanded for nearly two decades." Like Martin, the Hoogenbooms found the Interstate Commerce Commission (ICC) throughout its history more deferential to the political power of shippers and other constituents than to the economic needs of the railroads, and they attributed the railroad failures of the 1970s to overregulation by a shortsighted, politically bound bureaucracy.[7]

The theme of bureaucratic failure resonates also in Stephen Skowronek's 1982 analysis of railroad regulation from the late nineteenth century to 1920. Although Skowronek's legislative history confirms the major role played by agrarians, he does not follow Martin in laying regulatory failure at the door of "archaic progressives." Rather, Skowronek's focus is systemic. The emergence of railroad regulation in a "state of courts and parties" marked by vibrant societal forces, minimum administrative capacity, and a domineering Supreme Court probably doomed from the beginning any possibility for a powerful, autonomous bureaucracy with genuine planning capability over the nation's sprawling transportation network. Such a commission—the vision of a small progressive intelligentsia—required a struggle to establish the new administrative capability and then to free it from the arrogant tutelage of the courts; but given the nature of the American political system, victory in these endeavors succeeded only in tying the ICC more firmly to Congress—and thus to a hotbed of societal pressures whose reconciliation made enlightened regulation impossible. "A state that promoted pluralism promoted a formula for failure," in Skowronek's view.[8]

Recent scholarship, then, has supported the older notions of antirailroad animus as the driving force behind the establishment of federal transportation regulation, but the debate over agency is by no means resolved. In 1988, Martin Sklar's *The Corporate Reconstruction of American Capitalism, 1890–1916* revived the argument for advanced capitalist dominance of progressive reform. Though a few references are made to attempts to assuage the discontents of "antistatist" farmers, the image that emerges from this, as from earlier corporate-liberal arguments, is of an inevitable, corporate-led reconstitution of state-society relationships on (big) capitalist terms.[9] Labor is inconsequential, and farmers are a minor nuisance in the unfolding of a grand capitalist design, the implementation of which takes place largely through presidential action. For Gerald Berk, this presumed victory of corporate liberalism was not an economic inevitability, however, but a political outcome; and the driving force in railroad politics was ideology, not class or regional economic interest.[10]

So there is still more to learn from the saga of American railroad regulation. A new look at the social forces that contended over the shape of the interstate commerce law in Congress may help to solve the muddled "whodunit" of early regulatory state-building, providing a necessary corrective to elite- and executive-centered accounts.

In the late nineteenth and early twentieth centuries, laws were shaped in Congress. It was in the legislature that agrarian promoters of an expanded state contended with the defenders of core capital over its shape and substance. What railroads wanted in the late nineteenth and early twentieth centuries was for the state to either condone or ignore their pooling of risks and revenues and their market-wise discrimination favoring the largest and most urban customers. The farmers just as adamantly opposed such behavior.

Because these two interests, rooted in vastly different political economies, seemed virtually irreconcilable but the agrarian pressure showed no signs of abating, a narrow middle ground was opened up—narrow because its first-line promoters were so few and so sandwiched in between the major contenders. The "middle way" of bureaucratic regulation had the support of a small number of urban intellectuals convinced that expert public administration was the only remedy that could constrain capitalist abuses without damaging the system itself. But ideas are powerful only when they resonate with a political base. The administrative solution ultimately succeeded (in the creation of the ICC) because, in view of the massed agrarian pressure for a much more drastic solution—one that threatened capital accumulation itself—bureaucracy offered a less desperate way out for railroad capitalists. The commission form of regulation attracted critical votes in Congress by virtue of being the first preference of a small group of midwesterners whose diverse economies predisposed them to compromise. The periphery farmers accepted bureaucratization because in the partial democracy of the Gilded Age legislature, it was the best they could get.

Antecedents

Accounts of the struggle for national public control of the railroads normally begin with the Granger movement of the 1870s, but in fact the end of the governmental nurturing period and the beginning of controls imposed on behalf of broad societal and public interests came earlier. During the Civil War, the Union Congress authorized the president to take over rail and telegraph lines, and troop transport was actually placed under military control.[11] In the Confederacy, Postmaster General John H. Reagan prepared for his later career as the father of the Interstate Commerce Act by bringing southern railroads to heel.[12] Nationally, the benefit of mail contracts carried the seeds of rate regulation. Complaints about mail service and charges had led Congress to regulate, as early as 1838, railroad charges for mail transport; by 1872, federal law required District of Columbia and all land-grant railroads to carry mail at government-mandated rates.[13] Thus began the process by which, in Albro Martin's account, members of Congress would milk the railroads for burdensome and often unremunerative mail and parcel-post transport on behalf of their individual and small-business constituents.[14] As Lewis Haney noted, Congress was "trained in regulation" by its increasingly sharp supervision of mail service.[15] The training became more direct in the early 1870s, when widespread farmer complaints prompted Congress to pass a law regulating the conditions of animal transportation. Those conditions, which had become "deplorable and sickening" by the seventies, minimized railroad costs while diminishing the price of livestock to western and southwestern cattle raisers. Over the objections of the railroads and of congressmen who doubted federal jurisdiction over such matters, the regulatory bill passed in 1873.[16]

Most rail traffic was local until the late 1860s, and with little or no competition, high rates prevailed. However, in the decade before 1873, end-to-end combinations of short lines were rapidly effected, and long-distance lines emerged. After 1873, feeder and trunk lines were consolidated into great regional systems. Competition for through traffic over the long-distance routes between major terminal cities intensified, punctuated by rate wars in the depression years of the early 1870s and following the construction boom of the early 1880s. This competition, along with general price deflation and technological advances, brought average ton/mile charges steadily down.[17] However, small and remote shippers were not in a position to benefit from these developments. They could not command the rebates available to large shippers, and at interior locations, distant from major rail terminals and typically served by only one line, farmers remained at the mercy of rail monopolies. In fact, competition over long lines made their situation worse, since "captive" shippers had to subsidize price cutting for shippers in advantageous competitive situations (large and high-value shippers, large cities). The outcome of this virtually unrestricted railroad enterprise was to intensify regional economic differentiations and heighten sectional antagonism from cash-crop farmers, suffering from commodity price deflation and utterly dependent on a single transportation lifeline, toward the railroad capitalists and their favored customers.

The railroad response to the increasing competition for large long-distance customers was pooling. The first and perhaps most successful of these stabilizing ventures was the Iowa Pool. Three railroads competing for Chicago-Omaha traffic formally agreed in 1870 to divide business and cease long-distance competition; informally, they generally respected each other's local territorial monopolies as well.[18] The success of the "Great Pool" in stifling competition and maintaining rates showed the way to Albert Fink and other pool organizers of the 1870s, but it was also a major spur to the midwestern railroad regulation movement. Burdened by high transportation charges and sharply declining farm prices, the Grange and other farm organizations joined unhappy merchant groups in support of strong state regulatory legislation in Iowa, Illinois, Minnesota, and Wisconsin between 1871 and 1875. Wisconsin's law, establishing a fixed schedule of maximum rates, was probably the strongest, though not the longest-lived.[19] But despite ultimate Supreme Court legitimation for these regulatory efforts in the *Munn v. Illinois* decision,[20] the railroads' political power and their claim that the Granger laws contributed to their distress in the post-1873 depression severely undermined the midwestern efforts by the late 1870s.[21]

Midwestern congressmen led the drive for federal control over rates, achieving the first House passage of a general rate-control bill in 1874. This pioneering measure was similar to the 1873 "Granger law" in Illinois. Sponsored by Rep. George W. McCrary of Iowa, the bill prohibited unreasonable and extortionate rates and provided for a nine-member board of presidential appointees to gather information and fix a schedule of maximum permissible rates. The United States or aggrieved parties could sue offending railroads in federal district court, and penalties of $500–$5,000 plus damages and attorney's fees were provided.[22] The McCrary bill passed on a 121–115 vote. Just over half the affirmative votes came from the Midwest; another fourth came from the South.[23]

The latter region, still suffering from the rail devastation of the Civil War, was at this point more concerned with building and rebuilding railroads and harmonizing its narrower gauge with the northern standard than it was with regulation. In the year of the McCrary bill vote (1874), the large majority of the southern congressional delegation was still Republican. Hoping to secure economic-development benefits for their constituents, the region's representatives of both parties had channeled their efforts toward securing national subsidies for railroad construction, as well as for waterway improvement. However, the railroad efforts had largely come to naught, and in the mid-1870s southern Democrats joined their northern party colleagues in opposition to further federal rail subsidies.[24]

The great expansion of southern railroad construction did not begin until the late 1870s; southern mileage east of the Mississippi doubled in the next decade.[25] Railroad rates were significantly higher in the South than in other regions throughout the seventies, and monopolization came earlier and more firmly. The region's oldest railroads were falling under northern financial control in the 1870s and early 1880s (a process that climaxed with J. P. Morgan's organization of the massive Southern Railway in 1893). Successful cooperation among fast-freight lines was first established in 1868, and the formation of the Southern Railway and Steamship Association (SRSA) after the depression of 1873 was a milestone of successful railroad collusion. First administered by master pool-maker Albert Fink, the SRSA gave member roads virtual monopolies in their local territories while severely constraining their long-distance competition. Because of the degree of control exercised by the SRSA after 1874, southern freight charges resisted the sizable declines experienced elsewhere, and southern rail managers could afford to treat with contempt the pleas of small communities for reductions.[26] In this context, it is not surprising that southern congressional members took the lead in the drive for federal regulation in the late 1870s—and, in fact, for half a century thereafter.

The McCrary bill met a legislative dead end; the Senate, as its opponents fully expected, simply buried it. The upper house, populated by powerful politicians sympathetic to the business interests—particularly the railroads—that dominated their state legislative electors and promoted their own careers, was hardly a popular forum in the late nineteenth century.[27] Its posture was strongly conservative and would respond only to massive public pressure.

The Interstate Commerce Act of 1887

The leader of the antirailroad movement in the House from 1877 until the passage of the 1887 Interstate Commerce Act (ICA) was John Reagan of Texas. Reagan undoubtedly gathered ideas from outside his native state in constructing his regulatory proposals, but to give credit for the ICA to Pennsylvania oil men or New York merchants—as do Nash and Benson—one must ignore the fact that those groups had relatively narrow and time-bound interests in regulation and that their support for Reagan's bill had waned by 1886; congressmen from Pennsylvania and New York were notably hostile on the crucial roll calls of that year.[28]

The economic circumstances of the New York region, and of the northeastern seaboard metropoli generally, could never support the kind of specific and punitive regulation anticipated by the Reagan proposal. Northeastern cities were major railroad and shipping terminals, enjoying more favorable and competitive transportation services than anywhere else in the country. They were, furthermore, the headquarter cities of major rail and financial firms and home to the bulk of their stockholders. The existing system of rail rates, despite occasional annoyances, greatly advantaged the Northeast's industries and brought its factories and household consumers cheaply transported food and raw materials from distant farms and mines. It was a system that ensured the core cities' advantage as major industrial, commercial, financial, and export centers. Reagan and the congressional agrarians may well have borrowed some early ideas from New Yorkers, and were certainly glad for any expression of support from a region generally hostile to public control of corporations, but they received little if any tangible support from that quarter.

Reagan's legislative efforts gathered behind his banner a number of distinct and localized reform initiatives and brought to the railroad wars a new standing army from the periphery—where the grievances of economic geography were broadly based and persistent. But there *was* a direct link between the Pennsylvania independent oil producers and Reagan's concerns. James H. Hopkins of Pittsburgh, Reagan's colleague on the House Commerce Committee, championed the cause of local independent producers and refiners against the Standard Oil Co., whose mammoth size enabled it to induce lucrative rebates from the railroads. Hopkins introduced a bill for a federal ban on such rate discrimination and persuaded the House to investigate Standard Oil's efforts to secure a monopoly via preferential railroad service. However, neither Hopkins's bill nor the investigation got anywhere in Congress, and it appeared that Standard Oil had openly influenced committee members to block action. In 1876, Hopkins himself was defeated for reelection, but another Pennsylvania representative subsequently introduced a new antirebate bill prepared by an association of independent oil producers.[29]

When Reagan became chairman of the House Commerce Committee in 1877, the stalemate was broken. He had supported Hopkins's efforts and gave the independents' bill a favorable report, but Reagan's own analysis convinced him that much more was needed than a simple ban on rebates and rate discrimination. In his own state, once-competing lines were now pooling business through the Texas Traffic Association. In the Southeast, the SRSA was demonstrating the effectiveness of railroad self-government, and Albert Fink's Trunk Line Association was restructuring its pooling agreement in the East. In the Midwest, the Iowa Pool was in its heyday.[30]

Pooling operations showed great vicissitudes. In the trunk-line pool of northeastern railroads, for example, agreements on long-distance (Chicago–eastern seaboard) rates were successfully maintained by the cartel from 1871 to 1874, were tenuously revised in 1876–79, were mostly successful in 1880–83, and were largely unsuccessful in the recession years of the mid-1880s, which followed several boom years of railroad construction. The economist Paul MacAvoy, who, like Kolko, argues that the railroads could not control competition without government assistance, also stresses the repeated cartel *failures*.[31] However, one might just as well stress the inevitable *revivals* of collusion. At any rate (no pun intended), small and remote shippers received little if any benefit from the intermittent rate wars. If prices were cut for long-distance shippers from major collection centers (say, Chicago packinghouses or St. Louis grain dealers), the relative disadvantage of the remote shipper was accentuated, since there would be upward pressure on local rates to make up the losses; when long-distance rate agreements were maintained, the short-distance, farm-to-market rates stayed high.

Thus the other major complaint of farmers and small-town businesses—especially in the South—was the long- and short-haul rate differentials that favored competitively situated shippers and receivers at major transportation nodes against interior "captive" shippers. In the Midwest, farmers and small businesses at a distance from the great rail and water junctions of St. Louis and Chicago found their per-mile rates exorbitant in relation to through rates. In the South, the use of "basing points" produced the most flagrant violations of the distance principle, discriminating against southern farmers and businesses distant from major urban centers. The southern rate structure maintained by the SRSA not only produced high rates for agricultural producers and for consumers but also discriminated against midwestern industries, which paid much higher rates for shipments into the South than did more distant, northeastern firms.[32]

Reagan introduced his revised railroad bill in the summer of 1878. It not only prohibited rebates and rate discrimination for similar service, as in the earlier Hopkins bill, but also outlawed pooling and long/short-haul discrimination. It required railroads to publicly post their rate schedules. Violations of the bill's provisions were to be punished by payment of three times the damages sustained by the aggrieved shipper, who could sue in any federal district or circuit court location where the offending railroad did business; in addition, the offender was subject to a fine of at least $1,000 per offense, to be recovered by the U.S. government (with half the sum to go to the people informing the government of the violations). Officers and directors of the rail corporations were liable for misdemeanor convictions carrying personal fines.[33]

Whatever utility the railroads might have seen in a government ban on rebates, the Reagan bill was anathema to them. It outlawed precisely the mechanism—pooling—that they fervently hoped to legalize. However, in spite of this opposition, the bill passed the House 139–104. The largest regional support was registered in the South, which voted about 2-to-1 in favor; the Midwest also cast a majority of favorable votes, although the four Granger states—Illinois, Minnesota, Wisconsin, and Iowa—registered a divided vote (only Iowa and Minnesota cast majorities in favor).[34] In the Northeast, a large majority voted in opposition. Pennsylvania, however, was an exception to the regional pattern. Its representatives had backed the McCrary bill in 1874 and still supported the Reagan bill in 1878. New Yorkers strongly opposed the measure; only six of that state's twenty-four voting members—none of them from New York City—voted for the Reagan bill.[35] Reps. Clarkson Potter and Abram Hewitt of New York led the opposition in debate. "Enforcement of such a law would destroy the commerce of New York, Boston, Philadelphia and Baltimore," Hewitt argued. Whatever grievances New York might have had against railroads, the *New York Times* editorialized, this "revolutionary" measure was not the way to deal with them.[36]

The Reagan bill was passed by the House twice more (in 1885 and 1886), but it was not until 1885 that the Senate finally agreed to take up railroad regulation—and then in a very different mode. As complaints against the railroads multiplied and consensus in the agrarian regions grew, the House minority and Senate conservatives were pressed to develop a less drastic alternative to Reagan's statutory prohibitions. The solution was supplied by railroad expert Charles Francis Adams Jr., first director of Massachusetts' weak railroad commission and later a trunk-line pool official and railroad president himself. Adams designed a bill to establish a three-member Board of Commissioners that would investigate complaints of discrimination in charges or service. Should the railroads ignore its admonitions, the board would, in its next annual report, recommend legislation to make its instructions effective.[37] For Adams, as for Albert Fink and other railroad leaders and sympathetic intellectuals, the principal "railroad problem" was not monopoly or discrimination but an excess of competition. Adams himself had earlier written, "So far from being necessarily against public policy, a *properly regulated combination of railroad companies for the avowed purpose of controlling competition* might prove a most useful public agency" (emphasis added).[38]

Railroad executives and attorneys told the House Commerce Committee that if regulation *must* be initiated, a commission of the sort recommended by Adams—provided it be staffed with men like Adams himself—would be far superior to the provisions of Reagan's bill. The difference between the two bills, opined George Blanchard of the Erie Railroad, was the "difference between knowledge and its lack, between breadth and narrowness, between fairness and prejudice." Albert Fink was more circumspect. "As a rule," he testified in 1883, "the [state] commissions are only advisory, and I think that is a most excellent feature and a very good thing to have these commissions because you can explain to commissioners a great many things that you cannot explain to the people at large."[39] Thus railroad leaders in the 1880s defensively advocated the creation of a powerless federal advisory and educative commission and often voiced the unrealistic hope that government would provide for the judicial or commission enforcement of railroad rate and traffic pooling agreements. Such advocacy constitutes the shaky foundation upon which Kolko builds his argument that the railroads themselves sought federal regulation.[40]

A bill modeled on Adams's proposal was introduced by Republican Rep. Thomas J. Henderson of northern Illinois and, over Reagan's objections, was reported favorably by the House Commerce Committee in 1882, a year in which the Republicans controlled both chambers of Congress.[41] Reagan held out vociferously for his own proposal. The commission envisioned by the Henderson bill would, he feared, represent the interests of the railroads, not the public. In ringing agrarian republican rhetoric, Reagan asked his colleagues:

> If they are to be allowed thus to go on unrestrained and uncontrolled, and if Congress shall continue to disregard the rights and interests of the people through either imbecility, corruption, or the fear of offending the managers of these corporations, how long will it be until they have the complete mastery of our agricultural, mineral, manufacturing, and commercial, indeed of all our material interests; of our governments, State and Federal, including legislative, executive, and judicial departments; until a few railroad magnates shall own the most of the property of the country, while the masses of the people must be reduced to a condition of serfdom, poverty and vassalage? And if we allow this to occur, as it will if we do not act, shall we not have an aristocracy of wealth with monopolies and perpetuities which are forbidden and denounced by all our constitutions; and will we not then be subject to a vassalage more galling and more disgraceful than that of the feudal ages? Will we not be consenting to the breaking down of all the bulwarks of civil liberty, and to the destruction of all manhood; of that personal freedom and independence which is the pride of every American citizen; and of civil liberty itself? And when by our weakness and moral cowardice we have created a class of rulers and masters, shall we not become their subjects instead of being citizens of a great, free republic? There is in this country, at this time, a mournful pathos in the lines:
> Ill fares the land to threatening ills a prey,
> Where wealth accumulates and men decay.[42]

In the next Congress, Reagan resumed as House Commerce Committee chair but could not muster a committee majority for his bill. The Texan therefore offered his bill on the floor as a substitute for the commission bill reported by the Commerce Committee (which had already made some concessions to Reagan's demands for stricter controls).[43] Reagan again stated the agrarian regions' objection to a commission, which would, he predicted, easily be controlled by the railroads through their influence on appointments and representation by "their attorneys, the ablest in the United States." His substitute, in contrast to the provision for an expert, discretionary commission, simply declared "what shall be done and what shall not be done." He stated, "We do not propose to do anything in this Congress which requires, so far as I know, the assistance of any railroad expert."[44]

Core and Chicago-area representatives blasted Reagan's substitute as "ironbound and inflexible," as creating "arbitrary and despotic power" in the state. They defended railroads and warned of the danger of government interference "with certain natural laws of trade." Only a commission of railroad experts, with modest powers like those exercised by the Massachusetts and New York Commissions, should be attempted, they argued.[45] In a small concession to opponents, Reagan offered to substitute his statutory prohibitions for the first seven sections of the committee bill but leave a commission to make investigations and gather information. This substitution was effected in a 142-to-98 vote on December 18, 1884.[46] Further debate on the reconstituted bill followed, and the Reagan bill passed the House, 161–75, early in 1885.[47]

The Senate, although controlled by the Republicans and dominated by railroad interests, could no longer afford to ignore demands for railroad regulation. Shelby M. Cullom, a conservative (but not reactionary) Republican senator from Illinois, became the de facto leader of forces seeking to thwart the Reaganites. Cullom was, according to his biographer, an unimaginative man with neither progressive tendencies nor railroad expertise. However, he represented a state that contained both a major railroad terminus and farmers inclined to the Granger movement, so he had learned the value of intermediate positions. As governor of Illinois, he had appointed the first members of the Railroad and Warehouse Commission and later argued against its abolition. Cullom's willingness to champion commission regulation made him the man of the hour in the Senate.[48]

A member of the Committee on Railroads, Cullom introduced a commission bill in December 1883, though the committee reported an even weaker bill. However, the second House passage of the Reagan bill and rising public clamor convinced the Senate's conservatives that discretion, in the form of a Cullom-style commission, was the better part of valor. In early February 1885, the Senate substituted Cullom's measure for the Reagan bill and passed it 43–12.[49] The 48th Congress ended in stalemate between the opposing House and Senate bills.

In March 1885, Cullom secured the appointment of a select committee to investigate the need for legislation. According to his own account, he met with Albert Fink and found him opposed to "the whole thing"; but when the "arrogant" railroad men realized that a regulatory bill was inevitable, they were anxious to be heard before the committee.[50] The Cullom committee issued its report in 1886, cataloguing grievances against the railroads and describing unjust discrimination as the paramount evil arising from the business.

It noted an "unexpected unanimity of the testimony in favor of such a commission" as it recommended to the Senate.[51]

However, the "unanimity for a commission" meant nothing in substance.[52] The Cullom bill, which passed the Senate in 1886, envisioned a commission significantly stronger than those of earlier commission bills and very different from the advisory body on which railroad men pinned their hopes. In fact, Cullom's bill resembled Reagan's in important respects. Both forbade rebates and discrimination among customers and places and compelled the railroads to divulge their rate schedules. Both enunciated the common-law principle that all charges by common carriers must be reasonable. Criminal penalties (fines) for violations were included in both bills. The method of enforcement, however, was starkly different, and the Reagan bill contained two explicit prohibitions—on pooling and long/short-haul violations—that the Cullom bill did not. Under Reagan's bill, aggrieved shippers were simply empowered, on the basis of clear prohibitions, to take railroads to federal district courts—which were far more convenient, Reagan argued, than a distant Washington agency—and to sue before local jurors to recover damages, with courts directed to assess attorney's fees against a losing defendant. This remedy was less impressive than the triple damages provided in Reagan's original bill but was far superior, he felt, to existing common-law remedies.[53] The specificity of the outlawed practices, the liability for attorney's fees, and the prohibitions against the kinds of discrimination that railroads could ordinarily use to discourage litigation were viewed as powerful deterrents to railroad abuses. In the wake of *Munn v. Illinois*, and before the Supreme Court's turn from regulatory tolerance to the procapitalist activism of the 1890s, the agrarians were confident that this statutory empowerment would be sufficient to tame corporate abuses. In retrospect, this was a naive hope; but the hopes of those who sought redress through administrative regulation would also be dashed by the Court a few years hence.

Although the Cullom bill still allowed individuals to go to court, as permitted under common law, and attached criminal penalties to outlawed practices, one could not, because of the less precise wording, be sure what was outlawed. The new remedy provided, and clearly preferred, by the Senate bill was to seek arbitration by a new administrative commission. The agency would consist of five presidential appointees, none of whom (this must have been galling to the railroads) could own stock in, or be affiliated with, railroads. The commission was empowered to decide which charges railroads must post, to investigate railroad management, and to hear shippers' complaints of abuses under the law, compelling in a courtlike manner the attendance of witnesses and the delivery of books and papers. If the commission asked the railroad to adjust its practices, and the railroad refused, the agency could, after conducting its own investigation, order the carrier to cease and desist from the violation. If this was refused, the commission could apply to the Justice Department to take the defendant to court for damages. However, commission advocates assumed a wide degree of voluntary compliance short of formal court proceedings. The agency's discretion extended not only to actions on behalf of shippers but also to the granting of exemptions from the Cullom bill's principle that charges for short hauls should not exceed charges for long hauls over the same line. It was instructed to investigate the subject of pooling and report to Congress on the need for legislation on that subject.[54]

Both the Reagan and the Cullom bills passed their respective chambers in the summer of 1886. The Senate margin was 47–4, with a large group of abstentions that included both conservative opponents, like Nelson Aldrich and Leland Stanford, and advocates of tougher, Reagan-style regulation.[55] The Reagan bill, whose blunt prohibitions contrasted so sharply with the softer, more modern ring of the Cullom measure, was substituted for the Senate bill when it reached the House floor, by a vote of 134–104; final passage came by the larger margin of 192–41.[56] On the vote to substitute, which posed a clear choice of regulatory methods, the agrarian South and Midwest held for Reagan.[57] The small number of congressional members from the Pacific states, fearing the loss of their cheap long-haul rate advantage, preferred the Cullom bill, thus joining the northeasterners at the other end of the trunk lines. The New York, Portland (Maine), Boston, Hartford, Syracuse, Albany, Philadelphia, Buffalo, Scranton, and Pittsburgh trade areas cast only 13 of 77 votes for the Reagan substitute. The largest block of supporters (5) in the region could be found in Pennsylvania. However, the remaining independent oil producers there had reached an agreement with Standard Oil "which amounted to virtual surrender."[58] Representatives from Pennsylvania no longer demonstrated the outrage that had swept them into Reagan's camp in 1878 and 1884; the great majority preferred the milder approach of the Cullom bill.

Anticipation that the two chambers would again be deadlocked was shattered by an October Supreme Court decision more fateful than was recognized at the time. In *Wabash, St. Louis & Pacific Ry. Co. v. Illinois*,[59] the Supreme Court shifted its stance on the permissible limits of state regulation. In the 1877 Granger cases, the Court had agreed that in absence of congressional action, states could exercise extensive regulation over corporations even when the latter were clearly in interstate commerce. Now, with Chief Justice

Morrison R. Waite in the minority, a new majority led by President Abraham Lincoln's appointees Stephen J. Field and Samuel F. Miller was unwilling to let states control such commerce even where Congress had not acted. The pro-business, nationalizing vision of the new majority signaled the beginning of a new era in Supreme Court jurisprudence.[60] Henceforth, the most important state efforts to regulate business were likely to be voided by an increasingly activist Court, and national regulatory efforts would require extraordinary persistence. At the moment, however, the Court's dictum had an obvious remedy.

Under the spur of the *Wabash* decision, a conference committee meshed the two approaches to railroad regulation.[61] Reagan's strict prohibitions on pooling, rebates, and other discrimination were kept, along with the requirement that all rates be posted locally. The outlawed practices were made crimes carrying personal fines on conviction. However, the ban on charging more for short than for long hauls over the same lines was modified by a Cullom bill phrase—"under substantially similar circumstances and conditions"— that would later prove to be its undoing. The most important contribution from the Cullom bill was, of course, the commission, with its powers to investigate and act on shipper complaints. Individual plaintiffs could still, as in the Reagan bill, bring suit for full damages together with attorney's fees, but if they chose instead to file a complaint before the commission, the option to sue would be forgone.[62]

The railroads and their financial allies found this composite bill intolerable.[63] The *Commercial and Financial Chronicle*, for which the value of railroad securities was a major (indeed, the major) concern, had been a militant defender of railroad pools. In September 1886, it had enthusiastically announced to investors that although the trunk-line pool was still shaky, "roads in the Northwest and South [were] perfecting the details for a pool on the most comprehensive basis ever known."[64] The journal had applauded the *Wabash* decision for bringing an end to state efforts to push all rates down to the lowest competitive level, noting that railroad stock prices had recovered in December 1886.[65] With the announcement that conference action on the Reagan-Cullom bills had been postponed, the *Chronicle* was still hopeful that the Senate would not accept a stronger bill than the one it had passed.[66] The conference bill, in the view of the preeminent financial organ, was "so full of crudities and so totally at variance with all economic and we might almost say moral laws, that it passes comprehension how an intelligent body of men can countenance or recommend certain of its main provisions." The ban on pooling was "unacceptable," the long/short-haul clause "fatal." The railroads were to be placed "under the almost absolute control of a national commission, endowed with summary powers." As the conference bill cleared both houses in January 1887, the *Chronicle* bemoaned: "The Interstate bill is wholly restrictive. It is 'thou shalt' and 'thou shalt not.' It has nothing whatever to offer to the railroads in compensation for laying them under such disciplinary law as is provided for no similar corporations in the world."[67]

The final Senate vote on the conference bill was 43–15. The opponents were overwhelmingly northeasterners and Republicans. All ten senators from New York, Pennsylvania, Massachusetts, Rhode Island, and New Hampshire were either paired or voted against the interstate commerce bill. The final House vote was 219–41, with the bulk of supporters representing the southern and midwestern periphery. About half the House opponents had also opposed the Reagan substitute (another twelve had abstained), and again the opponents were overwhelmingly northeasterners and Republicans. However, eight of the opponents were Reagan bill supporters, obviously disgruntled over the conferees' acceptance of the commission. Reagan himself, having led the House conferees, made a point of being in Texas during the final vote, though his support for the conference report was announced to the House.[68]

Skowronek has emphasized the contradictions in the Reagan bill and the 1887 Interstate Commerce Act. To ban pooling, he points out, was procompetitive, but to ban long/short-haul differentials discouraged competition along trunk-line routes through major rail termini.[69] Both provisions, of course, reflected the position of the periphery farmers. If short-haul charges could not exceed long-haul rates, the presumption was that local rates would be pushed down toward the lower level induced by competition along competitive long-haul routes. Thus, competition would achieve a low rate standard to be applied by regulation to noncompetitive routes. Admittedly, this process would have been devastating to railroad income, but no one has accused the agrarians of being solicitous of the railroads' financial health. In the event of massive bankruptcies, the agrarians would no doubt have advocated public ownership—as did the Farmers' Alliance, the Populist Party, and William Jennings Bryan in later years. As it turned out, the Interstate Commerce Commission *was* concerned about the continued viability of the rail transportation system and used its discretion under the long/short-haul clause to prevent extreme consequences. The railroads, too, found ways to reduce competition after pooling was denied to them.

If local rates could not be pushed down by regulation, the second-best alternative for the hinterland was just to reduce the long/short-haul differential that put the remote shippers at a competitive disadvantage vis-à-vis shippers located in or near major urban centers and ports. Without regulation, supporters of the ICA had argued, the rail system would operate to concentrate population and wealth in a handful of great cities—a vision the periphery and midlands found morally as well as economically abhorrent.[70] At stake in the long/short-haul clause was the very character of the nation. Would population and industry be decentralized, maintaining the degree of competition, reliance on small-scale production, widespread property ownership, and community that agrarians believed was necessary for a democratic republic? Of all the economic forces—banking, tariffs, trusts, commodity speculation, and so on—that the agrarians sought to bring under public control, rail transportation was the most important for the maintenance of the decentralized republic. The fact that centralization of power in the national government was necessary to this goal was an irony produced by the Supreme Court.

[handwritten margin notes: "how could it ever be decentralized?"]

The Commission in Operation: The Failure of Administrative Regulation

As the new commission organized its work under the respected Michigan jurist Thomas M. Cooley, it appeared that this new experiment in "positive government" might succeed in both mollifying the anxious railroads and reconstructing their operations under public supervision.[71] Shippers did not rush to take advantage of the new administrative remedy,[72] leaving the new agency time to sort out its discretionary powers and slowly and cautiously build up a body of federal transportation law. Initial voluntary compliance was sufficient to reduce local rates in many sections; in accordance with the statute's explicit prohibition, pools were disbanded; and efforts to simplify and publicize rate schedules were soon in evidence.[73]

It was not long, however, before the railroads discovered that with a powerful ally in the Supreme Court, the commission could be disobeyed or ignored. The Court's drive to enshrine the laissez-faire principle and establish institutional supremacy over Congress and its new administrative creation was clearly in evidence by the early 1890s. One of the first cases to reach the high court involved rebating, which had continued virtually unchecked even though Congress, in 1889, added imprisonment to the law's available penalties. Since the practice was secret and involved few witnesses, it was very difficult to prosecute. In 1892 the Court held that a large grain dealer who had been offered a special low rate to Chicago could not be compelled to testify because existing law did not clearly protect him from self-incrimination. Statutory amendment and six years of litigation were necessary to establish the ICC's ability to compel testimony against rebating; but railroads easily adapted their methods to circumvent the prohibitions and continued both to offer special freight rates to large shippers and to bribe public officials and leading citizens with free passenger tickets.[74]

Not only did extraordinary judicial scrutiny delay ICC proceedings and encourage the railroads to disregard its authority, but when ICC cases reached the courts, they were, in effect, retried, often with new evidence brought forth by the defendants in this more sympathetic forum. The commission's orders were frequently reversed as a result of changes in the record and legal technicalities and because the justices themselves simply came to a different conclusion and substituted their own judgment for that of the ICC.[75]

What finally devastated the new agency, however, was the Supreme Court's blunt dismissal of its two major discretionary powers: the right to set a new rate in lieu of one found unjust or unreasonable; and its attempt to define the grounds for exemptions under the section-four long- and short-haul provision. The commission had assumed and had exercised for its first decade an implicit power to set a new rate. However, the Supreme Court had warned in state commission cases in 1890 and 1894 that "the question of the reasonableness of a rate is eminently a subject for judicial investigation" and had found "a judicial duty to restrain anything which, in the form of regulation of rates, operates to deny to the owners of property invested in the business of transportation that equal protection which is the Constitutional right of all owners of other property."[76] In 1897 the Court denied the ICC such powers, arguing that they had not been expressly granted in the Interstate Commerce Act.[77]

Regarding its discretion under section four, the ICC had moved very cautiously, taking its characteristically moderate position between railroads and aggrieved shippers. It ruled, at first tentatively and then more firmly, that competition with *unregulated* carriers (water carriers or foreign or intrastate railroads) could be grounds for exemption from the long / short-haul admonition, since not to allow such rate cutting would divert long-distance traffic, to the detriment of both interstate railroads and local shippers; however, any other exemptions would be made only in "rare and peculiar cases"—which would not likely include competition with other regulated railroads.[78] The test case arose in the South, where long / short-haul violations had continued to be common. Again exploiting the ambiguity of Senator Cullom's portion of the ICA, the Supreme Court upheld in 1897 a circuit court ruling that competition among regulated railroads could, indeed, produce the dissimilar conditions that justified exemptions.[79] Since almost any competition could now justify rate disparities, section four was henceforth a dead letter. The commission now had little to do but collect statistics.

The Legislative Repair of the Interstate Commerce Act

The saga of the ICA presents an extraordinary example of legislative persistence against powerful corporations, indifferent presidents, and arrogant courts. At the turn of the century, it seemed clear that the railroads had won and the agrarians had lost. The latter had lost because the regulatory statute contained too few blanket prohibitions; because, where such prohibitions worked, the railroads had adopted other stratagems (as in the case of pooling, for example);[80] because Congress had put too many eggs in the commission's basket, which had been dropped; and because the courts they had counted on to enforce the statute had drastically changed their orientation toward corporate regulation.

The "railroad problem" was bound up with the problem of monopoly power generally. The severe depression that began in 1893 touched off frantic competition, rate wars, massive bankruptcies, and then a thorough reorganization of the nation's railroads. This time the railroad managers and investment bankers succeeded in consolidating control in a small number of rail systems linked by interlocking stock ownership. Where nineteenth-century pools and traffic associations had failed, these new "communities of interest" succeeded in tightly controlling competition and in stabilizing rates. By the late 1890s, railroads exercised monopoly power in their own right and, through common ownership and conferral of special rates, built up other monopolists in the form of warehouses, elevators, grain and cotton dealers, fertilizer and equipment manufactures, and so on.[81] By the early 1900s, the once chaotic, over-built welter of rail lines had conglomerated into seven great systems. Predictably, rates began to turn sharply upward, and the ICC was powerless to do anything about it. As Albro Martin has noted, "After 1902, neither government nor shippers could count on disunity and internecine warfare among the major railroads to maintain 'competition.'"[82] The architects of the new railroad empires spoke openly of their plans to reach as far as the law allowed to consolidate rail transportation into a few, giant continental systems.[83]

However momentous the year 1897—for the decline of populism, the establishment of Republican hegemony, the beginning of the great wave of corporate mergers, and the Supreme Court's decisive blow to the ICC—this was not to be the end of the federal experiment in railroad regulation. The position of the periphery in the national railroad network generated continuing grievances. The enhancement of monopoly power and growing political schism would ultimately bring new recruits—and new success to the cause of railroad control.

The ICC, in the face of judicial attack and the scorning of its orders by ever more powerful rail empires, achieved a status in the periphery that it had not enjoyed in the late 1880s. The reconstruction of its statutory powers now became the focus of those who hoped to bring the railroads under effective control. Democratic platforms in 1896, 1900, and 1904 called for expanding ICC powers. The commission itself, in an early example of bureaucratic entrepreneurship, campaigned tirelessly to remind Congress of its judicially tied hands in the face of mounting railroad abuses and to outline the needed statutory amendments. In its 1897 annual report, after the Court's crippling decisions, the commission reminded farmers of the significance of its protective functions in the modern agricultural marketing system, a system in which "no individual could ordinarily be a match for the vast wealth and power of a railroad corporation."[84]

Even in the conservative 58th Congress, sentiment for strengthening railroad controls made possible the first major ICA amendment. The Elkins Anti-Rebating Act established heavy fines— applicable now to shippers and railroads, as well as to their officers and agents—for any deviation from published tariffs. But this amendment, though favored by small shippers, was sponsored by the railroads themselves, who were thereby protected from the necessity of offering discounts to high-volume customers. At the end of 1903, the railroads were well satisfied with the operation of the interstate commerce law; for their antagonists and for the ICC, however, the Elkins amendment constituted a very mild beginning. In 1904, the commission noted a growing urgency for repair of its rate-making powers, "in view of the rapid disappearance of railway competition and the maintenance of rates established by combination."[85]

Hearings on bills to strengthen ICC powers were held in the House and Senate in 1904–5, after President Theodore Roosevelt signaled his support for strengthening legislation.[86] The president's distaste for the arrogance of the rail barons had been demonstrated in 1902 when the administration went to court to block the consolidation—by J. P. Morgan, J. D. Rockefeller, J. J. Hill, and E. H. Harriman—of the three major northwestern railroads into a proposed Northern Securities holding company. Roosevelt had no quarrel with large-scale enterprise, but he shared the widespread public perception that the railroads and other extraordinarily powerful corporations had gone too far and must be, to some extent, reined in by public bridle. The proper locus of public control was, of course, the executive branch. Congress could never be trusted to find the appropriate balance between the prosperity of vital national enterprises and the demands of the small and vulnerable users of their services.[87] Advocacy of regulation by expert administrators was not an idle intellectual preference for the president. In an era of resurgent reform, when severe limits had been placed on state regulatory capacities, administrative expansion was a method by which the president could respond to agrarian dissidents in his own party and to a growing middle-class audience while protecting both his own institutional prerogatives and those of the large capitalists with whom he was in basic sympathy.

By 1906, agrarian and middle-class discontent had become politically undeniable. In the Midwest, reform governors like Robert M. La Follette of Wisconsin, Albert B. Cummins of Iowa, and Coe Crawford of South Dakota had formed their political strategies around attacks on railroad power. The trail of midwestern Republican reformers who, like La Follette, would follow victories over corrupt state Republican machines into the governor's office and thence to the U.S. Senate spelled trouble for the railroads. Southern politicians of the period were also steeped in the antimonopoly and antirailroad sentiment roiling their regions. Reform governors such as Jeff Davis of Arkansas, Benjamin R. Tillman of South Carolina, James K. Vardaman of Mississippi, and Hoke Smith of Georgia (the latter three would also win Senate seats) exemplified the new political era.[88]

In the congressional hearings and national rate conventions of 1905, agricultural interests—and small shippers generally—were the major advocates of expanded ICC powers. Large shippers and railroad spokesmen opposed regulatory expansion with near unanimity.[89] When the House, toward the end of the 58th Congress, passed a bill granting rate-making powers to the commission,[90] the railroads responded with an unprecedented nationwide publicity campaign against expanded regulation. The effort, however, probably did their cause more harm than good.[91]

In the next Congress, Roosevelt (who had not supported the 1905 House bill) threw his support behind a bill, sponsored by Rep. William Hepburn of Iowa, that embodied the administration's approach. It granted the ICC the power to establish a maximum reasonable rate, subject to an unspecified court review. The commission's jurisdiction was extended to private cars (special refrigerator and oil tank cars, sleepers, etc.) using the lines of common carriers, and the ICC was given greater powers to inspect and prescribe railroad bookkeeping. During House debate on the bill, southern representatives proposed amendments to further expand ICC rate powers, include telephone and telegraph lines in its jurisdiction, and invoke imprisonment for violations; however, the agrarians rallied to the stripped-down administration bill on final passage as the best they could get at the moment, and the Hepburn bill passed the House with only seven votes (all northeastern Republicans) in opposition.[92] The Senate, which had refused to act on the 1905 rate bill, was expected to present a great obstacle to the passage of any strengthening measure.

Roosevelt made a bargain with the Republican Old Guard. In return for staving off the tariff reform being sought by the midwestern wing, he expected them to allow the rate bill to pass.[93] Under pressure from the president, non-core Republicans, and (as usual) the Democrats, continued obstruction by the core Republicans was unsustainable. However, Nelson Aldrich, the leader of the Senate conservatives, was prepared to use all his parliamentary talents to ensure that, under the new bill, the courts retained their power to have the last say on rates. His first extraordinary maneuver was to appoint a southern Democrat—one personally obnoxious to the president—to head floor debate on the bill in lieu of Republican Sen. Jonathan Dolliver of Iowa, who longed to present himself to his constituents as a champion of railroad reform. "Pitch-fork Ben" Tillman of South Carolina thus became the principal floor strategist for the Hepburn bill and for Senate progressives who hoped to strengthen the House version. He worked closely with Texas Sen. Joseph W. Bailey, a politician on the conservative side of most Texas political conflicts but in national politics usually a faithful representative of his state's progressive economic inclinations. The resultant legislative situation was thus peculiar and awkward for the president, since he was compelled to deal with two southern Democrats whose preferences on railroad legislation were far more extreme than his own and with whom he was not on speaking terms.[94]

The Senate became a battleground as Bailey and Tillman, aided by La Follette of Wisconsin, led a struggle to expand the bill's jurisdiction and—the principal issue—to narrow the court's powers to review the ICC's decisions. Bailey, Tillman, and most of the Democrats backed an amendment containing two key provisions: to limit the appellate courts' review to questions of legality and procedure (that is, questions of whether the commission had exceeded its statutory and constitutional powers and whether it had followed the statutorily prescribed method), so that the courts could not reopen the substantive case; and to prohibit the courts from enjoining the new rate during the review period. For a time it seemed that Roosevelt would back at least the first part of Bailey's amendment, in a compromise to be proposed by Republican Sen. Chester Long of Kansas. However, the bipartisan compromise effort collapsed, and the president sided with Republican conservatives against any amendments restricting court review.[95]

The courts had become, as William Ripley noted in 1913, the railroads' "second line of defense."[96] With unrestricted review, their conservative spokesmen were willing to accede to commission rate powers and jurisdiction-expanding amendments. The railroads' southern-midwestern-mountain antagonists, finding the Hepburn bill still a substantial improvement over the status quo, supported it also, and final Senate passage came with few dissents.[97] Both sides could not be right, of course, and this time the railroad bet was the bad one.

Despite the overwhelming approval on final passage, there were hotly contested roll-call votes in the Senate, not limited to the court review issue. An analysis by Jerome M. Clubb of twenty-two controversial amendments to the Hepburn bill found only five Republican senators—from Minnesota, South Dakota, Nebraska, Wisconsin, and Vermont—who supported more-stringent regulation half or more of the time; on the other hand, thirty of thirty-one Democratic senators could be so categorized.[98] All but two—Francis Newlands of Nevada and John Gearin of Oregon—represented southern and mountain periphery states.

Although the agrarians had seemingly lost on the scope of court review, provisions added in the Senate made the Hepburn Act a far stronger measure than the original administration bill. Successful amendments restored prison terms for violations of the rate provisions; expanded ICC regulation to include oil pipelines and express companies, as well as sleeping cars, terminal facilities, spurs, and sidings; eliminated a requirement that ICC rates be "fairly remunerative"; greatly restricted the issuance of free passes; and barred the railroads from transporting goods from their own enterprises (the aim being to make them solely common carriers of independently produced commodities).[99] Free passes, which had been used by the railroads to influence state and local officials, were permitted only to specified beneficiaries. The ICC—expanded from five to seven members with higher salaries—was given fortified powers to elicit information and to impose standardized accounting and reporting formats on the railroads. As a result of its new powers, shipper complaints to the ICC increased dramatically, from 633 in 1905 to more than 5,000 in 1907.[100]

The fate of the commission's principal new power—to set new maximum rates on shipper complaints—hinged on how the Supreme Court would interpret the ICC's unspecified review powers. In 1910 the high court, in an uncharacteristic act of self-denial, issued as dicta a narrow interpretation of its

review powers, the same interpretation that the agrarians had futilely attempted to assert in the Hepburn Act. Its appellate powers did not include,
in the Court's words, "setting aside a lawful administrative order" simply
because the order was not, in the justices' view, a wise one.[101] It has been
suggested that this act of abnegation, a landmark in the development of administrative regulation, revealed that the Court was "searching for a new and
more secure position before the growing democratic attack on the judiciary
got out of hand and caused some real damage to its prerogatives and prestige."[102] Indeed, the critical decision came even as Congress, in a much more
radical mood, prepared once more to take up major amendments to the Interstate Commerce Act. The Court had astutely decided to yield gracefully what
the aroused agrarians were about to take away.

The Final Repair: 1910–1913

The Hepburn Act had confirmed the still-fledgling commission's powers over
the behavior of the nation's most vital common carriers. It had left on the
back burner two simmering grievances held by farmers, small shippers, and
small towns: the power of the federal courts to suspend the ICC's new rates
while they were being appealed by the carriers (which meant that shippers
might have to go on paying the old "unfair" or "unreasonable" rates for years,
even if the case was finally decided in their favor); and the judicially emasculated long- and short-haul clause. By 1910 there were new progressive faces
in both the House and the Senate, and the Republican unity marshaled by
Roosevelt in the 1906 railroad debates had been shattered. The Democrats,
for their part, had repudiated their brief, desperate flirtation with conservative
presidential politics and had gone back, in 1908, to Bryan—who was quite
ready to pursue nationalization if regulation failed to tame the railroads. The
pot on the back burner was about to boil.

President William Howard Taft did not share Roosevelt's ambition to be
seen as a leader of reform. His tariff pledge—to lower the duties now widely
perceived to be exorbitant—had not been kept. He had sided with Joseph
Cannon, Nelson Aldrich, and Richard Ballinger. Now, in 1910, he further
revealed his insensitivity to the cry for reform by introducing a railroad bill
that only a railroad sympathizer could embrace. The bill had, in fact, been
prepared by Attorney General George Wickersham after several conferences
with railroad spokesmen.[103] The bill yielded to the reformers in granting ICC
power to suspend rates pending review (but only for sixty more days) and
to investigate and set new maximum rates on its own initiative; it also granted
additional information-gathering powers to the commission, as well as the

power to change freight classifications and establish alternate through routes. However, what the administration bill gave with one hand it took away with the other. A new Commerce Court was proposed with broad powers to hear carrier appeals and enjoin ICC orders. Furthermore, carriers were permitted to make collective rate agreements so long as they reported such agreements to the ICC within twenty days, and the attorney general was authorized to take over ICC litigation in court. Other sections, ostensibly aimed at establishing federal power over such abuses as stock "watering" and at gaining further supervision over mergers and acquisitions, looked—to southern and western skeptics—like crafty manipulations to reduce competition and evade the antitrust laws.[104] Even if, as Martin reports, the railroads were profoundly disturbed by the new rate and acquisition supervision in Taft's bill, congressional supporters of reform nevertheless saw the bill as a shameless sellout to the rail magnates.[105] With the Republican Party split along a sectional/ideological divide in 1910, a powerful bipartisan reform coalition came together in both chambers and rewrote Taft's bill almost beyond recognition.

In the House, Rep. William C. Adamson of Georgia was the principal spokesman for the antirailroad forces—which included the bulk of the chamber's 172 Democrats and up to two dozen Republican dissidents (half of whom came from the periphery, with nearly all of the remainder from diverse areas). The Republican majority was led by Rep. James R. Mann, chair of the Interstate Commerce Committee. Although Mann was a "regular" Republican, his midwestern roots made him much less resistant to agrarian pressure than his party's champions of orthodoxy. He was willing, for example, to let the House restore the long- and short-haul clause by omitting the old Cullom qualifier that had invited judicial emasculation, so long as the ICC retained some discretion to grant exemptions.

In addition to the long/short-haul revision, the periphery- and diverse-area reformers first amended, with Mann's acquiescence, the section on collective rate agreements by requiring ICC approval before the agreements went into effect; then, on a 110–91 vote, they eliminated that entire section of the bill.[106] A successful amendment by Rep. Charles Bartlett of Georgia brought telephone and telegraph companies under the Interstate Commerce Act.[107] Other amendments would have allowed shippers to sue in their more convenient (and sympathetic) state courts to recover damages set by the ICC and would have empowered the commission to make a valuation of railroad properties in order to facilitate cost-based rate making. Some reformers were inclined to rewrite the mergers section, which, as submitted by the administration, threatened to undermine the Sherman Act. However, Adamson and Rep.

William Richardson of Alabama argued that it was safest to eliminate the section altogether, so that conferees would have no chance of reinserting such provisions. The House voted 131 128 to strike the section.[108] There was some sentiment among the agrarians to strike also the section requiring ICC approval for stock and bond issues. They argued that, like the chartering of corporations, the regulation of capitalization was constitutionally a state function. Their fear seemed to be that national regulation here would preempt strong state supervision, such as that exercised by Texas and Georgia; further, it might choke off railroad construction in the periphery and limit both economic development and competition with established corporate giants. Adamson's motion to strike this section failed 49–87 in the House, but similar arguments in the Senate contributed to its excision there.[109]

The crucial roll-call vote in the House came on Adamson's motion to recommit the bill and delete the Commerce Court sections. It was a partisan division, with only twelve periphery- and diverse-area Republicans joining the mostly periphery Democrats against the court. Because the Commerce Court and various other objectionable features remained, the Democrats opposed the Mann-Elkins bill on final House passage, despite the considerable improvements they had effected.[110]

In the Senate, further surgery was performed. Here the insurgent Republicans led the way, and the southern and western Democrats furnished the bulk of the reform votes. In some cases—as on the addition of a long/short-haul amendment and the time period of ICC rate suspension, for example—fear of a more drastic change forced Aldrich and his conservative faction to agree to provisions they opposed; in other cases, the Republican leaders withdrew sections deemed likely to fail on the floor.[111] The bipartisan reform coalition succeeded in forcing coverage of telephone and telegraph companies, allowed shippers to designate through routes, authorized the ICC and shippers to appear in court proceedings challenging ICC orders (although the attorney general remained in charge of the government's case), directed the ICC to investigate freight classification, and limited federal court injunctions against state laws. The administration-sponsored provisions legalizing cooperative rate making, providing for Commerce Court rulings on mergers and acquisitions, and establishing federal supervision of stock and bond issues were eliminated from the bill. The Senate also eliminated the crippling words "under substantially similar circumstances and conditions" from the long/short-haul section of the ICA. Whereas the House had lengthened the period in which rate increases could be suspended pending ICC review from 60 to 120 days, the Senate stretched the suspension period an additional six months. The major defeats sustained on the floor by the reform coalition came on La

Follette's valuation amendment, on Bailey's amendment strengthening the prohibition of railroads' transport of their own commodities (which the Supreme Court had, after 1906, limited in application), and on Cummins's amendments allowing the indefinite suspension of rates pending ICC review and eliminating the Commerce Court.[112]

These votes clearly reveal the sectional locus of the reform drive (see tables 6.1–6.4). Democratic support for expanding the scope of regulation and maintaining or strengthening antitrust prohibitions was nearly unanimous. On the typical strengthening amendment, sixteen to eighteen Democratic votes, all but two or three coming from periphery senators, constituted the bulk of the reform vote. To that base would be added the votes of four or five diverse-area Republicans and seven or eight periphery Republicans. This was the

Table 6.1 Vote to Table Amendment Adding Telephone and Telegraph Companies to ICC Jurisdiction (Senate, 1910)

		22–37 D 1–16 R 21–21[a]		
% of Seats		% Yea	(N)[b]	% of All Yeas[c]
28.3	Core	80.0	(15)	54.5
15.2	Diverse	16.7	(12)	9.1
56.5	Periphery	25.0	(32)	36.4

Source: The 1909–17 roll calls analyzed in this and subsequent tables were supplied on tape by the Inter-University Consortium for Political and Social Research (ICPSR).

[a]Indicates opposing core and periphery majorities within the party.

Core Republicans	80.0	(15)
Periphery Republicans	38.9	(18)

[b]Numbers in parentheses indicate number of senators or representatives voting in each region (pairs and absentees excluded), reported where table space permits.

[c]This percentage is given to compensate for disproportionate abstentions.

Table 6.2 Cummins Amendment (to Mann-Elkins Act) to Eliminate Commerce Court (Senate, 1910)

		28–37 D 20–0 R 8–37		
% of Seats		% Yea	(N)	% of All Yeas
28.3	Core	0	(20)	0
15.2	Diverse	54.5	(11)	21.4
56.5	Periphery	64.7	(34)	78.6

Table 6.3 La Follette Amendment (to Mann-Elkins Act) for Valuation of
Railroad Properties (to facilitate rate regulation) (Senate, 1910)

		25–30 D 15–0 R 10–30		
% of Seats		% Yea	(N)	% of All Yeas
28.3	Core	5.9	(17)	4.0
15.2	Diverse	42.9	(7)	12.0
56.5	Periphery	67.7	(31)	84.0

hard core of the reform group in the Senate.[113] The willingness of some other
noncore Republicans and a few nonvoting Democrats to be brought in for
somewhat milder provisions was the spur to the reformers' indefatigable offering of amendments and to the consideration that prompted the conservative
leadership to offer less-radical compromises or to withdraw those provisions
of Taft's bill that seemed bound to be destroyed on the floor.[114]

The power of the tariff to define economic and political regions is evident in the fact that the conservative core Republicans could usually count
on ten to twelve periphery Republicans to oppose regulatory expansion.[115]
This group of mountain, midwestern, and border-state Republicans toed the
core-established party line on railroads because insurgency threatened the
tariff that kept their constituents in the wool, hide, sugar-beet, or mineral-
producing areas in business. They had supported the stalwart position on the
previous session's Payne-Aldrich Tariff and assumed that their constituents
would understand the larger gains of party regularity. It was certainly no

Table 6.4 Bailey Amendement (to Mann-Elkins Act) to Strengthen Ban on
Railroads Owning Companies Producing Products They Transport
(Senate, 1910)

		25–31 D 14–0 R 11–31		
% of Seats		% Yea	(N)	% of All Yeas
28.3	Core	0	(15)	0
15.2	Diverse	54.5	(11)	24.0
56.5	Periphery	63.3	(30)	76.0

coincidence that three-fourths of the hardy band of Republican insurgents who backed the fight for a stronger Interstate Commerce Act in 1910 had already thrown off the party traces in the tariff battle of 1909.[116]

The insurgent Republicans, especially the diverse-area Senators Cummins, La Follette, and Albert Beveridge, were inclined in railroad and other regulatory battles to be more favorable to national administrative control than were the agrarian Democrats who fought beside them. The Republican insurgents were more optimistic about discretionary regulation both by the courts and by the ICC. The agrarian Democrats backed insurgent amendments requiring ICC approval of railroad rate agreements and keeping men with railroad interests off the Commerce Court but then pushed to delete the entire sections on agreements and the Commerce Court. In addition, representing states with stronger railroad commissions and fewer competing railroads, the agrarian Democrats opposed federal preemption of stock- and bond-issue supervision. The insurgent Republicans lamented the deletion of both provisions from the bill, insisting that they could have been further improved with floor amendments.[117] But the Democrats remained skeptical, fearing that conservative House-Senate conferees would take advantage of any remaining Taft provisions and that, if the bill passed, the commission and courts might interpret those sections in the interest of the railroads. These differences between the progressive, mainly midwestern Republicans and the progressive, mostly southern Democrats reflected both party ties and political-economy differences. The former meant that Republican insurgents expected to have some influence on the ICC and the judicial appointees who would interpret the act. But a complex of economic and demographic conditions also predisposed the diverse states to support bureaucratic (expert, discretionary) solutions to economic problems, in situations where the periphery representatives preferred specific statutes. These contrasting patterns will be discussed more fully in chapter 8.

Fear that a conference committee headed by Aldrich and Mann would take back the gains won on the floor led 130 Democrats and 26 Republicans to support an unsuccessful motion (by Rep. Irvine Lenroot, insurgent Republican from one of the two periphery districts in Wisconsin) to accept the Senate amendments. The vote on the Lenroot motion, reported in table 6.5, reveals the typical pattern of periphery support for stronger regulation, in a context free of direct party considerations. It thus presents the clearest set of choices of the House roll calls on the Mann-Elkins railroad bill.

Despite the reformers' fears, the conference committee did not materially weaken the major provisions written on the floor of the House and Senate,

Table 6.5 Lenroot Motion to Concur with Senate Amendements to Mann-Elkins
Bill (strengthen bill, avoid conference) (House, 1910)

		156–162 D 130–6 R 26–156		
% of Seats		% Yea	(N)	% of All Yeas
33.5	Core	18.6	(97)	11.5
19.9	Diverse	39.4	(66)	16.7
46.5	Periphery	72.2	(151)	71.8

and the bill thus emerged as a landmark of Progressive Era legislation. The
commission was empowered to set maximum reasonable rates, on its own
initiative, and to suspend rate changes for up to ten months while it studied
them, with the railroads shouldering the burden of proof of reasonableness.
The House version of the refortified long/short-haul clause went into the
bill, along with regulation of telephone, telegraph, and cable companies and
a host of other provisions designed to protect shippers and expand the ICC's
power over rates and services. The only major reform lost in conference was
the valuation provision, and it was passed separately in the next Congress.

The railroads had contributed to their own trouncing by an extraordinarily
impolitic action. In the midst of debate on the Mann-Elkins bill, twenty-
four railroads west of the Mississippi jointly filed rate increases of 13 to 50
percent. Shortly thereafter, the railroads of Official Territory (the Northeast-
Midwest) also filed general rate advances. So great was the outcry—not only
about the size of the advances but also about the fact that they were made
in concert—that Taft's attorney general was compelled to secure an injunction and threaten antitrust prosecution. These actions secured the postpone-
ment (and, ultimately, the withdrawal) of the broad increases, but shippers
were on notice of what awaited them in the absence of a fortified ICC; the
rate filings were often cited in congressional debate as a powerful reason for
strengthening the Interstate Commerce Act.[118]

Of course, the railroads and the administration did not come away empty-
handed. One of the only major Taft administration proposals to remain in
the Mann-Elkins bill was the president's provision for a Commerce Court.
The railroads and their conservative supporters clearly hoped, by the creation
of a new and specialized intermediate court recruited by Taft, to introduce
a new level of substantive review to keep the ICC in check. Democratic reformers charged that the new court could well negate every significant new

Table 6.6 Eliminate Commerce Court Judgeships (House, 1913)

		176–76 D 163–16 R 13–60		
% of Seats		% Yea	(N)	% of All Yeas
34.5	Core	58.8	(51)	17.0
18.9	Diverse	62.5	(56)	19.9
46.7	Periphery	76.6	(145)	63.1

power given the commission, and as a result of this provision, most of them refused to vote for the bill on final passage.[119]

The agrarians' fears about the new court were soon borne out. Inheriting all existing ICC cases in the circuit courts, as well as those initiated after passage, the Commerce Court showed little hesitation in overturning commission orders. It was clear that, in Ripley's words, "the court took itself seriously as a check upon . . . the Commission." Of thirty relevant cases disposed of by the end of 1911, all but three were decided in favor of the railroads.[120] The railroad triumph here was short-lived, however, for the Supreme Court, having established its own modus vivendi with the ICC, looked skeptically on this judicial interloper. Of twenty-two decisions appealed to the Supreme Court, the Commerce Court was reversed in thirteen and modified in two more.[121] But the decisive blow came from the legislature that had, with such misgivings, created the court. The next Congress voted to abolish the Commerce Court, but it was temporarily saved by a Taft veto in 1912. In 1913, the congressional railroad antagonists—most of them periphery Democrats— easily defeated Taft's creation (see table 6.6).

Reagan's Revenge: The Railroads under Strong Regulation

Fortified by its new powers, the Interstate Commerce Commission in the years from 1910 through World War I restrained rate increases and made significant rulings on behalf of shippers. In 1910, accepting the arguments of Louis Brandeis and of Clifford Thorne, the counsel for midwestern farm organizations and state regulators, the commission decided that both the eastern and the western railroads had failed to demonstrate the reasonableness of their proposed rate increases and should employ more-efficient management in order to absorb their increasing costs.[122] A few years later, eastern railroads again filed for an increase, citing significantly higher wage and coal costs, the effect of state laws, taxes, unremunerative rates for carrying the mail (including new parcel-post burdens imposed by Congress), and track-and bridge-repair needs. After fourteen months, the ICC rendered its decision in 1914, allowing only a subset of roads a modest 5 percent increase. By this point, there was widespread sympathy for the railroads' position in the core, as reflected by newspapers there and even by middle-class progressive magazines such as the *Nation* and *Outlook*.[123] During the severe recession and the consonant railroad distress of 1914–15, the ICC consented to extend the 5 percent increase to other eastern roads, but it forced the western roads to get by on less than 1 percent. Passage of the 1916 Adamson Eight-Hour Act (see chapter 10), along with state full-crew and 100-mile-day mandates, imposed new wage costs on the railroads. By the time the United States entered World War I, declining investment and car shortages and traffic tie-ups had made clear the weakness of the nation's rail system. The ICC, however, continued to turn a deaf ear to most petitions for rate relief. The Hoogenbooms' description of the situation in 1911 could be maintained throughout the Progressive Era: "Clearly . . . the ICC was not the captive of railroads; indeed, it was hostile to them and friendly to shippers."[124]

Presidents, however, had always shown more sympathy for railroads than had Congress or "its" regulatory commission. In an address to Congress in 1914, Wilson made clear his concern for the railroads, and a few months later, he caused great consternation among Democrats and progressive Republicans by appointing the archconservative Winthrop Daniels to the ICC. Known in his home state as a reactionary public service commissioner, and bitterly opposed by La Follette and other Senate progressives, Daniels was narrowly confirmed with the help of ten standpat Republicans.[125] Daniels's prorailroad stance pointed up the vulnerability of discretionary regulation to a sharp change in personnel, but his conservatism was not enough to shift the commission's course in the Wilson years.

Epilogue: War and Regulation

By World War I, progressive reformers had clearly brought the railroads to heel. They had used the state to compel competition, break up railroad monopolies and "communities of interest,"[126] compel better treatment of workers, put small shippers on a par with giants, bolster small country towns, and sharply curb the impetus of freight and passenger fares. Martin contends that the "archaic progressives" thus drove the railroads to ruin. But the railroads were not yet ruined in 1917; they limped along, pale shadows of the arrogant and seemingly all-powerful enterprises of 1905, until the 1970s when high labor costs and unremunerative passenger service brought on a wave of bank-ruptcies. Between those years, in an increasingly complex regulatory environment, there occurred several significant milestones of administrative regulation.

In the back of the reformers' minds, it had always been assumed that if regulation did not work, the ultimate remedy would be nationalization. William Jennings Bryan, the standard-bearer of the periphery agrarians, had argued that although regulation under the strengthening amendments of the Progressive Era should be given "a fair trial," in the event of the failure of this regulation to halt the "plunder" of the people by the railroad corporations, the federal government should nationalize the interstate trunk lines and the states should take over control of the intrastate lines.[127] He continued to support nationalization during the 1919–20 debate on the future of the railroads. "If I had to choose between the concentration of all this power in New York in the hands of railway magnates and the centralization of all this power in the hands of government officials, I would without a moment's hesitation prefer to risk concentration in the hands of public officials," he told the House Commerce Committee.[128] But Bryan's position had always been controversial even in the periphery, and the agrarians' experience with federal control of railroads during World War I probably diminished their support for nationalization.

The president's decision to take over operation of the railroads in 1917 was based principally on the war necessity to introduce a high level of coordination into a chaotic rail system compelled by law to compete and not cooperate; however, it was also a way to circumvent the ICC, which, he agreed with Commissioner Daniels, was starving the railroads. The railroads, for their part, did not protest, since they were guaranteed profitable compensation during the period of government operation (mandated by law to terminate within a specified time after the end of the war). The ICC was denied power to suspend rates for the duration, and a federal administrator was given power to initiate rate increases. In the first six months, the Railroad Administration ordered general passenger and freight increases of 18 and 28 percent, respectively, and sharply raised intrastate rates as well. But the biggest beneficiary of federal control was organized labor. The government mandated collective bargaining and pro-rata pay for overtime (beyond eight hours) and ordered wage increases, over the two-year period, of up to 100 percent above the 1916 level—which generated additional railroad costs of $965 million.[129] These wage increases were not drastically out of line with those experienced in other industries, but considering the aggregate impact of federal control, Frank H.

Dixon has observed, "It is no exaggeration to say that the gains made by railroad labor during the 26 months of federal operation in the power of collective bargaining, in the development of union organization, in the standardization and nationalization of practices and policies, were greater than in the entire previous period of their existence."[130] Railroad workers were on their way to an extraordinary protected status in the national state, a status that would last for the entire twentieth century.

For agricultural shippers, deprived of ICC protection regarding rates, long/short-haul discriminations, and the like, the war experience was not a happy one. The federal control episode indicated that a nationalized rail system would subsidize railroad workers but not necessarily farmers. Thus the agrarians hoped to return, after the war, to the status quo ante.[131] But that was not to be. Republicans controlled both houses of Congress in 1919–20, and Wilson was willing to sign almost any bill that returned the railroads to private control.

Like the original Interstate Commerce Act, the Transportation Act of 1920 resulted from two divergent approaches to regulation. Both versions, however, had moved substantially beyond the progressive menu. Southern and western efforts to restore what had by now come to be characterized unflatteringly as "negative" regulation had their greatest (albeit limited) influence in the House. The Esch bill, passed in November 1919, was drafted in consultation with the ICC. It restored ICC rate-making power (although the suspension period was cut to 120 days) and—mainly to help weak roads and water carriers—authorized the setting of minimum as well as maximum rates. It also empowered the commission to approve both extensions and abandonments of rail lines, to overrule state decisions on intrastate rates, and to supervise railroad stock and bond issues. The Esch bill, although less favorable to the railroads than its Senate counterpart, guaranteed them a continued operating income for six months equal to prewar levels and established a two-year revolving loan fund for their benefit. In the clearest break with the past, the House bill authorized pooling and consolidation of railroads by merger or control of stock, on commission approval, and amended a 1912 law that had prohibited railroad acquisition of water carriers. Further, it admonished the ICC to consider railroad revenue needs in establishing "reasonable" rates. Both railroads and railway labor were made liable for damages (via civil suits) for contract infringement—a provision that would fall most heavily on labor. Three Labor Adjustment Boards and a Board of Labor Appeals were provided to hear labor disputes.[132]

The prospects for a drastic Republican turn in railroad policy seemed to revive sentiment for nationalization among some periphery representatives. Leading off debate on the minority side was Rep. Thetus Sims of Tennessee, who had introduced the nationalization bill (the Plumb Plan) favored by the railroad brotherhoods. In a remarkable speech, Sims argued that there had never been "a solution through private ownership," since transportation was an essential service that should be furnished at cost.[133] But in the midst of a Republican resurgence and public anger at an unprecedented strike wave, nationalization was not a viable option. The agrarians thus concentrated their fire on the most objectionable aspects of the Republican ICC bill: its centralization of power in the national government (the new ICC powers gained at the expense of state regulators); the new rate-making standards; the railroad income guarantees; the "encouragement of monopoly"; and the "punitive and unnecessary" labor sections. Neither higher wages nor ICC regulation had ruined the railroads, they argued; they laid the blame instead on stock speculation and mismanagement. Rep. Jared Sanders of Louisiana, after listing his objections to the Esch bill, issued to his colleagues what he called "a solemn word of warning": "If this bill is the best that the brain of men who believe in private ownership can do, then the answer to this bill by an indignant and outraged people is going to be Government ownership. [Applause]."[134]

The major modification made on the House floor was the replacement of the Esch bill's labor sections by a substitute, offered by Rep. Sydney Anderson of Minnesota, creating a voluntary dispute-adjustment apparatus and omitting any provision for strike damages. The bill's remaining provisions, though acknowledged as being far superior to the solutions brewing in the Senate, still evoked unified Democratic opposition on the final House vote.[135]

Meanwhile, the defection of Republican progressives from the agrarian alliance was sharply evident in the Senate bill sponsored by former insurgent Albert Cummins of Iowa. Cummins's bill was far more extreme than the Esch bill in centralizing both government and private power and in subduing labor. Like the House bill, it withdrew regulatory powers from the states to the ICC. But a new executive agency under the president, the Federal Transportation Board, was proposed to take on important new regulatory functions. The board was given continuous investigatory power over the entire transportation system and over most non-rate-making functions of the ICC. It was to serve as an appeals board in labor controversies, to supervise the issuance of securities, and—most significant—to draw up a plan for consolidation of the nation's railways into twenty-five to thirty regional systems, each with a federal charter. Mergers were to be voluntary for the first seven years, then compulsory. The ICC was directed to set rates providing the railroads with at least a 5.5 percent return on investment. Excess earnings were to be "recaptured" in reserve funds from which both railroads and government could draw for improvement of the transportation system. The bill's labor sections used fines and imprisonment to enforce the decisions of the arbitration board.[136]

The ambitious Cummins plan passed by the Senate was not a simple capitulation to the railroads. Postwar plans submitted by railroad executives had asked for pooling and voluntary consolidation authority (by lifting the antitrust laws) and optional federal incorporation. Clearly preferring regulation under the president to control by a commission attuned to the legislature, the railroads supported the creation of a Federal Transportation Board that would take over all but the rate power of the ICC, serve as an appeals forum for labor controversies, supervise stock and bond issues (in preference to the performance of this function by the states), and inform the ICC of the carriers' revenue needs that must be provided for in rate making.[137] Although there are obvious similarities between this agenda and the Cummins bill (which the railroads preferred over the House bill), the railway executives' program seemed animated by a vision of government-assisted reconstruction of early-twentieth-century communities of interest. Their plan left decisions for consolidation and incorporation with the railroads. The Cummins plan, on the other hand, vested such decisions in the government. Cummins's bill, with its highly discretionary, potentially coercive, and firmly centralized national planning authority, had a definite New Nationalist flavor. It represented the strain of progressivism most strongly supported by the representatives of the midwestern and far western diverse areas, where the guiding hand of expert administration was considered necessary both to business rationalization and to the protection of a broadly defined public interest.[138]

Earlier, during the progressive Republican insurgency, this faction had allied with the periphery agrarians, with very different legislative results. In the Mann-Elkins Act, and in the 1914 Clayton and Federal Trade Commission Acts, for example, the periphery's more radical and punitive approach to regulation was softened by bureaucratic discretion, but its fundamentals survived. In 1920, the insurgents had returned to their party. The new dominant alliance of progressive and conservative Republicans, though it still had to make concessions to the radical agrarians and labor, combined expanded bureaucratic discretion with the business nurturing that core Republicans advocated. Of course, times were different for the railroads. The government was now called on to nurture a sick industry rather than regulate a healthy one. For a variety of reasons—overbuilding in the nineteenth century; the burdens and rigidities of government policy on rates, hours, and wages; the blossoming of the motor carrier industry; and decades of mismanagement and irrational rate structures—the general perception now was that the railroads would collapse without intensive public care. Such a situation made inappropriate "the prohibitory or punitive element" dominant in the preceding acts and called for a more "constructive" approach, in the progressive Republicans' view.[139]

The final transportation law produced by a House-Senate conference in 1920 was far less ambitious than the Cummins plan. It contained no provisions for a new transportation board, federal incorporation, or mandatory consolidation, and railroad earnings were guaranteed for only two years. The ICC received the expanded powers contemplated in the House bill. Labor's success in eliminating the punitive features of the House bill was sustained when the conference committee, despite Cummins's insistence, eliminated the anti-strike and criminal penalty provisions passed in the Senate bill. However, enough doubts remained about the impact of the labor sections that the railroad unions joined farm spokesmen in lobbying the president to veto the bill. Despite the opposition of most Democrats, Wilson signed the new Transportation Act.[140]

The 1920 statute was in several respects a milestone of American political development. It signaled the end of the period of agrarian-led, anticorporate, legislatively mandated reform (though not the end of individual efforts). It heralded, as Skowronek has noted, a new era of administrative centralization and autonomy—the first instance in federal economic regulation of a grant of massive discretionary authority not only to constrain business behavior but also to promote the health and development of an industry through indicative planning.[141]

The very generosity of the grant, however, proved the undoing of the ICC. The year 1920 would mark the beginning of the decline of a gutsy agency resented by railroads, cherished by farmers and small shippers, and hailed as a prototype by Progressive Era intellectuals. Dedicated to a single purpose—protection of the most vulnerable shippers—and armed with an explicit statutory mandate, the commission had struggled against powerful corporations and arrogant courts to plant the flag of administrative regulation. But scarcely had it won the critical battles than circumstances—economic and political—changed, and the legislature handed it a complex and contradictory mandate to look after not just shippers but also railroads and, indirectly, labor.[142] And this was but the beginning. Eventually, trucks, busses, and water carriers would also be entrusted to the commission's care and regulation. By the 1960s, the ICC, measured against its impossible mandate to nurture, regulate, and plan virtually all surface-freight transportation, would be considered the prototypical example of regulatory failure.[143] When, in the 1970s, a bipartisan core initiative under presidential leadership succeeded in dismantling most of the regulatory apparatus, railroad regulation had come full circle over a century. Railroads and core congressional members (though most of the latter were now liberal Democrats) rejoiced at the lifting of controls and the restoration of the market. The only strong opposition arose where the interests of captive shippers with limited access to competitive transportation services bemoaned the loss of the ICC's original regulatory functions and sought public protection from market power. The critical votes on railroad deregulation in 1980 echoed the core-periphery battles of the nineteenth century.[144]

7

Trade, Taxation, Banking, and Credit

The Tariff

The protective tariff was a traditional, endemic issue in American politics, one of the economic conflicts that contributed to disunion. But in the early twentieth century it became the opening wedge of progressive reform, catalyzing the progressive-conservative split in the Republican Party and the emergence of new reform coalitions. It was also intimately linked to the broader issue of corporate power and to the search for a more fair, less regressive method for raising federal revenue.

Before 1861, northeastern industrial interests had lacked the political strength to maintain a strong protective system and futilely protested the steady reduction of duties from 1832 to 1857.[1] After the South seceded, manufacturing-belt Republicans were free to raise duties, with the urgent revenue needs of the war effort as justification. At the end of the war, northern capitalists were fearful that the return of southern representatives to Congress would imperil protection (which now averaged about 48 percent).[2] Fear of economic revolution was the mother of political invention. In an ingenious feat of coalition-building to head off a hostile agrarian-based alliance, manufacturing-belt interests reached out to embrace western and midwestern farmers. Long before the war, protectionists had endorsed, in an ad hoc manner, the addition of products like hemp, flax, and wool to the lists of dutiable goods, but the coalition axis was now forged in a formal way and became the linchpin of the Republican Party. The crucial bargain was forged when a convention of wool growers and wool manufacturers met in 1865 in Syracuse, New York, and agreed to support even higher duties for both raw wool and woolen manufactures. Their agreement, "an intricate and detailed scheme of duties, prepared by the producers of the articles," was enacted in 1867.[3]

The wool bargain directly affected the interests of New England and a large sheepherding industry concentrated, at that time, in Ohio, Michigan, California, and New York. Behind the tariff wall, sheep raising rapidly expanded in the West, becoming a mainstay of the economy (and of Republicanism) in the states of Utah, Nevada, Montana, Idaho, New Mexico, Wyoming, and Oregon.[4] Similar bargains could encompass hide producers in the West and the corn belt and footwear manufacturers in the Northeast, sugar refiners in the Northeast and sugar-beet growers in the Midwest and West,[5] and iron-ore extractors in Michigan-Minnesota and steel manufacturers in Pennsylvania and Ohio. In more contentious situations, as in the 1890 McKinley Tariff, Republican leaders were willing to impose duties on wheat, corn, and barley as well, although imports of these commodities were insignificant. Thus interests that would otherwise be antithetical were yoked in the Republican Party in support of its foremost industrial policy.

Whenever the Democrats captured a congressional majority they immediately lowered the tariff and struck at the Republican coalition by putting wool on the free list (as in 1887, 1894, and 1913). When the Republicans returned, they revised duties upward and put wool and hides on the dutiable list (as in 1890, 1897, and 1922). The susceptibility of the western and even the midwestern agricultural areas to Republican tariff seduction encouraged cotton-belt representatives to look to the northern working class for coalition partners. A supplementary mechanism to the protective tariff reinforced this choice.

By the late nineteenth century, tariffs had begun to create treasury surpluses that were embarrassing for the Republican Party, endangering its support particularly in agricultural areas not greatly benefited by protection. In another brilliant political coup, the GOP devised a system for distributing the surplus produced by the tariff: the military pension. Available only to Union veterans (and thus confined almost entirely to the North), military pensions became the first U.S. welfare system. Accounting for 38 percent of the federal budget by 1894, they gave residents of the West and Midwest compelling reasons to support the tariff. For the South, the pension system made the tariff doubly onerous. Not only was the cotton belt penalized by higher prices for the manufactured goods it purchased and by restricted export markets for its cotton and tobacco, but it got back none of its contribution to industrial protection. As Richard Bensel has written: "The tax imposed by the higher costs of manufactured goods was recaptured by regionally repatriated profits, and customs duties were recaptured by the payment of military pensions. The developmental engine left the southern periphery to shoulder almost the entire cost of industrialization. . . . The periphery was drained while the core prospered."[6]

In the manufacturing belt, the group least benefited by the protective system was immigrant labor. Despite the industrialists' argument that the tariff protected them from the competition of foreign "pauper" labor, the opposition pointed out that the Republican Party refused to aid workers by limiting the importation of labor. The Democrats also produced a continuing flow of statistics showing that the most protected industries paid, in fact, the lowest wages and that high prices for the necessities of life easily offset the presumed advantage of protection to labor. Industries benefiting from decades of protection engaged in lockouts and mercilessly crushed strikes.[7] Further, immigrants were not eligible for Civil War pensions and so were excluded from one of the auxiliary attractions of the protective system. This situation enhanced prospects for a political alliance between cotton-belt farmers and northern labor.

The Dingley Tariff of 1897 imposed the highest rates in U.S. history—an average of 52 percent—and was the longest lived of all U.S. tariff policies.[8] In the first decade of the twentieth century, however, the schedules came under widespread attack, mainly because of two concurrent developments that Democrats would trace to the Dingley Tariff itself: a massive wave of industrial consolidations into holding companies or "trusts"; and a sharp rise in the cost of living. The Democrats constantly flailed the tariff as "the mother of trusts." Although economists generally found the connection tenuous (after all, patent abuse, price and service discrimination, and weak enforcement of the Sherman Act also fomented monopoly), high tariffs clearly facilitated both collusion and mergers designed to raise or defend price levels. And as the Democrats predicted, the new oligopolies and near-monopolies were not kinder to their workers than competitive firms. In fact, the attitudes of employers appeared to harden after the turn of the century, with giants like U.S. Steel taking the lead in aggressive antiunion activities.[9] Nor did consumers notice any price advantage from the presumed efficiencies of concentration.

In this set of circumstances, highlighted by an outpouring of literature critical of the trusts and a conviction among economists that tariff levels had reached unjustifiable heights, the traditional southern complaints against protection found a more receptive audience. The midwestern farm belt, in particular, became more amenable to tariff revision. Politicians like Indiana's Albert Beveridge had stumped for the tariff as a principle that "filled the republic with the golden fruit of plenty and the hearts of the people with the very music of joy" and whose support was "a duty . . . to wife . . . children . . . flag."[10] Now, in the presence of rising prices and rapacious trusts, protection seemed less golden. Its benefits accrued mainly to eastern manufacturers and their bankers and, to a lesser extent, to vulnerable wool, fruit, timber, and sugar-beet producers in the West, but the midwestern farmer got little out of the Republican system (particularly as Civil War veterans passed from the scene). Thus it is not surprising that corn- and wheat-belt Republicans were willing, by 1909, to take on the eastern GOP stalwarts and press for tariff revision.

The agricultural products in the best international trade position during the Progressive Era were cotton (which accounted for half the value of agricultural exports and one-fourth the total value of U.S. exports), grain and grain products (mainly wheat and flour), meats, and tobacco. These were southern, corn-belt, and plains products. In manufactures, a number of the "infant" industries sheltered by the tariff were now overgrown adolescents perfectly capable of competing advantageously in a global market. Although older New England cotton and wool industries clearly needed protection if they were to survive, the region's shoe industry was still competitive. The iron, steel, machinery, and vehicle industries of the mid-Atlantic and Great Lakes states were very strong; lower transportation costs and an abundant supply of metal ores had provided a great stimulus to U.S. metal exports.[11]

From the turn of the century to 1914, the percentage of U.S. exports composed of agricultural products dropped from 65 to 48 percent as the industrial system matured. However, core representatives continued to resist tariff reductions on manufactured goods. Despite the growing export potential of U.S. manufactures, the domestic market was still the great mainstay of American industry.[12] There was also the inertia of ingrained beliefs. The myth that the tariff yielded prosperity for all had been inculcated by the Republican Party and its predecessors for half a century, and there was an understandable reluctance to give up the certainty of the domestic market for the riskier benefits of world trade. More important, the tariff was the linchpin of the Republican coalition. It won critical support in the rural periphery for the eastern elite's positions on such issues as transportation, banking, and business regulation. Furthermore, the revenue lost in tariff reduction would have to be replaced somehow. The replacement sure to be adopted was that proposed by the Democrats for the past two decades: an income tax that would fall heavily on the upper classes of the industrial areas.

Thus, even though some large, internationally competitive industries were more receptive to downward tariff revision by 1909, the party that represented their interests in Congress showed little movement, and scholars who attribute Progressive Era reform to business initiative find the tariff a poor case. Business organizations such as the Home Market Club of Boston, the National Association of Wool Manufacturers, the American Protective Tariff League, the Philadelphia Manufacturers Club, and the American Iron and Steel Association were noisy and persistent advocates of protection, and the more import-vulnerable businesses had more votes than the few mild revisionists.[13] Henry Ford and Elbert Gary did not lobby for a protective tariff in 1913, but Republicans from automobile- and steel-producing areas voted resolutely protectionist on the Underwood Tariff. Individually, many manufacturers favored *selective* tariff reduction. Lower duties on lumber, hides, wool, ores, and other raw materials would lower their costs, increase domestic profits, and perhaps improve exports. But revision on raw materials alone would tear asunder the bonds of Republicanism and enable a periphery coalition to move on the other taxation and regulatory fronts that were anathema to the industrialists and bankers of the manufacturing belt.[14]

The Payne-Aldrich Tariff of 1909

In response to the popular clamor for reform, the Republican platform of 1908 had incorporated a pledge to revise the tariff (with the general understanding, strongest among the midwestern sponsors of the plank, that "revision" meant "reduction"). Both parties in the Progressive Era were modifying the rationale for their tariff positions in order to broaden their appeal. The Democrats were careful to avoid advocacy of "free trade," a term that struck terror into northern hearts, or its practical corollary, the "tariff for revenue only." Instead, they proposed a "competitive" tariff. This term seemed to imply maintenance of minimal duties for import-vulnerable industries with large fixed *Dem.* investments but little or no protection for raw materials, for industries with strong trade positions, or for those controlled by trusts. The "competitive tariff" would, the party argued, encourage technological development, discourage monopoly, increase employment, and yield the consumer a wider, less-expensive choice of products. For the Republicans, the necessary modification in tariff philosophy (or at least in rhetoric) implied an abandonment of "excessive" protection and a more "scientific" formulation. To midwestern insurgents, "scientific" meant active participation in tariff formulation by an impartial body of experts. The Old Guard northeastern protectionists resisted any loss of control to a tariff commission; their concession to scientific formulation was to champion a tariff designed so that it equalized "the cost of production at home and abroad, together with a reasonable profit to American industries." Tariff experts like F. W. Taussig were quick to point out that such a scheme ignored the significantly higher productivity of the American workforce and that its strict application meant "simple prohibition and complete stoppage of foreign trade."[15] Nevertheless, the Republican insurgents believed that they had wrung a commitment from both party and president to lower tariff levels.

President William Howard Taft called a special session of the legislature to enact a new tariff in the spring of 1909. By the time the tariff was taken up, however, the Republican establishment had had its close call on the first rules fight, which had necessitated vote trades with representatives whose districts' products had to be protected. Once openly corrupted, the revision process degenerated into rampant localism, with the insurgents and a substantial number of Democrats backing protectionist amendments for their products.[16] Even if the House had passed a more general reduction, however, the protectionist coalition in the upper chamber would undoubtedly have mauled it in the same way.

In the Senate of 1909–10, the older manufacturing industries of the core regions had the dominant voice (members were still chosen by their state legislatures, though a significant group of southern, midwestern, and mountain states nominated Senate candidates in primary elections), and industrial and finance capital still held sway over many legislatures in both East and West. Direct from boardrooms to the Senate came men like Simon Guggenheim of Colorado, Morgan Bulkeley of Connecticut, Henry Du Pont of Delaware, and Stephen Elkins of West Virginia. Nelson Aldrich of Rhode Island was the chamber's dominant figure and chaired the Finance Committee. Aldrich was spokesman and symbol for American industry (particularly its mature, New England branch) and high finance. His opinions on protection had not changed in the slightest since he had entered the Senate in 1881. It was an article of faith for Aldrich and his circle that most Americans (or at least most Republicans) had a stake in protection.[17] Assisted by such stalwarts as Frank Brandegee of Connecticut, Jacob Gallinger of New Hampshire, Henry Cabot Lodge of Massachusetts, and Boies Penrose and George Oliver of Pennsylvania, Aldrich was determined to resist the rising reform tide and to do it in the way his region had always managed: by splitting off those periphery states vulnerable to imports.

Whereas the House bill contained a few modest reductions, the Senate bill reported by Aldrich's committee represented old-style protectionism. Duties were raised beyond the Dingley Tariff level on silk, wool, and cotton manufacturers. Since it was essential to keep the West in the Republican coalition, Aldrich rejected attempts to put raw materials on the free list. Duties cut by the House were reinstated on coal, hides, and iron ore, and the lumber tariff was also raised; manufactured goods using these raw materials were given compensatory duties. Wool and sugar tariffs were left intact. In Aldrich's interpretation, the tariff revision promised in the Republican platform could, and did, mean *upward* revision.[18]

Midwestern Republicans were outraged at both the content of the tariff bill and the secretive way it was prepared. When the Finance Committee and the Customs Bureau denied them information on the complex existing schedules, they laboriously undertook to master the critical schedules and draft amendments for reduction. This effort was necessary, since the corn- and wheat-belt congressmen remained believers in protection. After all, midwestern constituents sold almost all of their meat, grain, and dairy products to residents of the American industrial cities and thus had a stake in the city-dwellers' prosperity. In addition to this dependence on the domestic market, the northern farm sections feared Canadian competition with their own products. For these reasons, they rejected the "meat-ax" approach of the southern Democrats. Rather than drastic reductions and a long free list, the midwestern representatives advocated a moderate lowering of rates—although, in the case of raw materials in short supply in their own states (such as oil, lumber, and coal), free entry was preferred. Rejecting both an across-the-board slashing of duties and the arbitrary and excessive tariffs of the old Republican system, the midwestern insurgents argued for "scientific" reductions that would provide the minimum necessary protection.

On vote after vote, the insurgent Republicans, backed by the more numerous periphery Democrats, attempted to reduce the tariff levels in the Senate bill. The coalition was most cohesive on products like wool, iron, and steel manufactures that were mainly produced in the manufacturing belt and on sugar; it was weakest on lumber, in which the South had some protective interest. The coalition was rarely able to muster more than thirty votes for these moderate reductions. The manufacturing block (all Republicans) prevailed, with the support of the import-vulnerable mountain and Pacific states.[19]

The southern periphery–insurgent alliance also attempted to insert an income-tax amendment in the Aldrich bill. The southern block had previously added an income-tax provision to the 1894 Wilson-Gorman Tariff, but the Supreme Court had declared it unconstitutional in 1895, halting what the Court perceived as the beginning of a "communistic" assault on property. In 1904, the demand for an income tax was omitted from the Democratic platform on the insistence of northeastern party leaders, but in 1908, William Jennings Bryan and his program were back in full force. Now, with support for tariff reduction growing among midwestern Republicans, the southern

Democrats came forward with another income tax proposal, presented by Sen. Joseph Bailey of Texas. Insurgent Sen. Albert Cummins of Iowa produced his own version, and the two agrarian blocks soon mustered a substantial phalanx for a joint tax proposal.[20]

Aldrich and his cohort were alarmed, not only because the proposal raised the prospect of a direct tax on northeastern wealth but also because the tax would constitute an alternative revenue source that would increase the potential for a successful periphery-centered attack on Republican tariff policy (and other Republican policies as well).[21] With the assistance of President Taft, Aldrich devised a clever stratagem. An individual income tax, Taft argued, would probably be declared unconstitutional again by the Supreme Court. Aldrich would, however, agree to support a tax on corporate income as part of the tariff bill (reversing his long-standing opposition to any such tax) if the Bailey-Cummins amendment was dropped. Congress then could pass a Constitutional amendment authorizing an individual income tax.[22] This maneuver by Taft and Aldrich was successful; Bailey's income-tax amendment was defeated by Aldrich's corporation-tax substitute 45 to 31. Following the pattern of previous tariff-reduction votes, Aldrich was supported by twenty core senators and twenty-five periphery- and diverse-area Republicans who were allied with him on the tariff. The bulk of the opposition was composed of twenty-two periphery Democrats and six of the ten insurgent Republicans (all of the small insurgent cohort except Idaho's William Borah were from midwestern farm states). Democrats and Republicans then joined to pass the constitutional amendment, with the Republican standpatters hoping it would fail ratification in the states and the Democrats and insurgents betting they were wrong.[23]

In its final form, the Payne-Aldrich Tariff bill kept high duties on cotton, silk, and wool manufactures and raw wool, duties that were central to the New Englanders and their western allies. The sugar duties beloved of the Philadelphia-based sugar trust and western-midwestern beet-sugar states were left virtually intact. There were some reductions on iron and steel products where the duties were believed to be of little benefit. Hides remained on the free list, with a slight corresponding reduction for leather products. Protectionists inserted in the bill a provision that the stated rates would be *minimums* and that the president was authorized to impose an additional 25 percent ad valorem on products from countries that discriminated against U.S. goods.[24]

Thus constructed, the conference bill drew a comfortable Senate majority (47–31) against southern Democratic–midwestern insurgent opposition. In

Table 7.1 House Support for Payne-Aldrich Tariff, 1909

		Final House		Conference	
		217–161		195–183	
		D 4–160		D 2–163	
		R 213–1		R 193–20	
% of Seats		% Yea	% of All Yeas	% Yea	% of All Yeas
33.5	Core	79.5	46.5	77.2	50.3
19.9	Diverse	76.6	27.2	66.8	25.6
46.5	Periphery	32.8	26.3	26.7	24.1

the House, the vote was much closer (see table 7.1). The midwestern insurgents had backed the original Payne bill as an improvement over the existing Dingley Tariff rates but found the Senate amendments extremely objectionable. As they saw it, this was a tariff bill by and for New England and mid-Atlantic industrial interests. Twenty House Republicans voted against the bill, all but two from districts in the diverse and periphery trade areas of Chicago, Cincinnati, and Minneapolis. Sixteen of the twenty represented nonindustrial districts in the corn, dairy, and wheat sections. Only two periphery Democrats, both from southern Louisiana sugar districts, defected to support the tariff bill on the final vote; none of the twenty-nine core Democrats deserted their party's position.[25]

The Payne-Aldrich Tariff bill cost the Republican Party dearly. It was a major issue in the 1910 elections and contributed to the Republicans' loss of over fifty House seats. The midwestern Republicans were deeply alienated from their party and also from President Taft, who had clumsily defended the conference bill as the "best tariff ever" and had opposed the reelection of its opponents. As if the 1909 tariff fight were not a sufficient test of Republican Party cohesion, Taft proceeded in 1911 to further fracture his party with his Canadian tariff reciprocity proposal. "You want tariff reduction?" he seemed to say to the midwesterners, "then I'll reduce tariffs on *your* products." The president proposed a treaty that would promote sales of Canadian livestock, grain, timber, meat, and dairy products in the United States while lowering Canadian duties on U.S.-manufactured goods. This was an ideal proposition for the manufacturing belt, since it offered free raw materials and cheaper food for northern industries and consumers while maintaining the protected domestic market for U.S. manufacturers. Canadian wool was not included on the free list, in deference to the loyal western states. With strong

Democratic support, the reciprocity proposal passed, but the treaty was defeated in the Canadian Parliament.[26]

The midwestern Republicans did find new support for one of their tariff proposals: the creation of a nonpartisan fact-finding tariff board. Part and parcel of the moderate protectionists' belief in the possibility of a "scientific" tariff, the board was proposed by the insurgents during the Payne-Aldrich Tariff debate. At that time, the high-tariff standpatters were resolutely opposed, agreeing only to let the president appoint individual advisors. By 1911, the frightened standpatters grasped at the tariff commission as a last-ditch stand against the looming victory of the Democratic free traders in 1912, a hedge against Democratic legislative control of the tariff-making process. Thus the tariff commission proposal was framed as a cooperative effort between standpatters (John Dalzell of Pennsylvania and Nicholas Longworth of Ohio) and insurgents (Irvine Lenroot of Wisconsin and James Good of Iowa), and it received unanimous Republican support on the floor. The Democrats opposed it with almost equivalent unity (only twelve of the most protection-inclined core- and diverse-area Democrats voted for the proposal). Presaging subsequent divisions between the two reform blocks, the periphery Democrats argued that they were quite capable of revising the tariff schedules in short order, without the help of expert advisors. The agency died in 1912 when House Democrats blocked its appropriation.[27]

The Underwood Tariff, 1913

The tariff votes of the 62nd Congress were a prelude to Democratic control of economic policy and demonstrated the party's new internal discipline. Even as the Republican coalition fragmented, the periphery Democrats tested the loyalty of their new urban colleagues and found them true. There were few metropolitan defections on the major tax and tariff votes in 1911–12.

By the time the 63rd Congress began in 1913, the southern Democrats had already constructed their tariff program. President Woodrow Wilson, who had made the tariff and trusts his principal campaign issues, pushed for even more ambitious reductions and used all the influence of his office to keep potential defectors in line. The result was remarkable: a tariff bill that made substantial across-the-board cuts in duties on manufactured goods (an average of 26 percent below the Payne-Aldrich Tariff rates) and placed a large number of raw materials and agricultural and consumer goods on the free list (including wool, iron, coal, lumber, meat, dairy products, leather boots and shoes, wood pulp and paper, wheat, and most agricultural implements and supplies). For sugar, the duty was to be gradually reduced, going on the

free list in 1916.[28] The reform pushed tariff rates back to the range of the
pre–Civil War years, when the periphery had last shaped national economic
policy. Federal fiscal policy was permanently altered by the enactment of an
income tax (authorized by the constitutional amendment Congress had passed
in 1909) to replace the revenues lost by tariff reduction. David F. Houston,
Wilson's secretary of agriculture, waxed exuberant over his party's triumph:
"Think of it—a tariff revision downwards at all—not dictated by the manufacturers; lower in the Senate than in the House—one which will not be made
in the conference committee room!! A progressive income tax!! I did not think
we would live to see these things!!"[29]

The outcome was remarkable because the party enlargement that had
made tariff reduction possible had brought into the party's ranks members
who opposed sharp reductions. The Democratic stand on labor and corporate
control had won it new seats in states like Colorado, Montana, and Ohio,
where Democrats were opposed to reductions on sugar and wool. Massachusetts Democrats objected to placing shoes on the free list, and representatives
of other industrial areas were predictably anxious.[30]

Enactment of the centerpiece of the Democratic platform thus required
rigid party discipline. House Democrats, on obtaining their majority in 1911,
had resurrected the party caucus and molded it into an extremely effective
political tool. The caucus hammered out the shape of major legislation behind
closed doors and then bound members to support it on the floor. The only
exceptions were granted to those who had earlier filed with the party a notice
of contrary promises made to constituents before their election.[31] The obvious
advantage of caucus government was that it provided a mechanism for enforcing vote trades between different sections within the party and avoided apos-
tasy on the floor. Its principal cost was that policy-making in closed party
conference alienated the Republican progressives. The insurgents had rebelled against their own party's autocratic control of policy-making and could
not tolerate it from the opposition. They were humiliated and bitter at being
pushed aside in the 62nd Congress. But the insurgents' numbers were too
few, and their tariff-cutting proclivities too mild, to make them reliable allies
for the Democrats. Probably with such considerations in mind, Wilson decided to forgo attempts at building a bipartisan progressive coalition and,
instead, undertook to whip his newly enlarged party into an efficient legislative steamroller.[32] On the tariff, this strategy achieved victory against great
odds.

In the House, only a handful of Democrats voted against final passage of
the Underwood Tariff and income-tax bill in 1913. Of the nineteen remaining

Table 7.2 House Support for Underwood Tariff and Income Tax Bill, 1913

			Final House		Conference
			281–139		255–104
			D 274–5		D 248–4
			R 4–125		R 4–92
% of Seats		% Yea	% of All Yeas	% Yea	% of All Yeas
34.5	Core	60.0	31.0	63.1	32.2
18.9	Diverse	54.4	15.3	59.0	14.1
46.7	Periphery	77.0	53.7	81.5	53.7

Republican insurgents from the 1909–10 class, only William Cary of Wisconsin joined the Democrats and a small group of new Progressives in support for the bill (see table 7.2). In the Senate, passage was more uncertain because the Democratic majority was narrower (51–44, as opposed to 290–127 in the House)[33] and the western protectionist states were overrepresented. Caucus discipline and presidential suasion were ultimately successful, however, and only two Democrats from Louisiana voted with the opposition on the final poll. Some semblance of the bipartisan agrarian alliance surfaced on a few votes dealing with manufacturing schedules but quickly vanished when the debate turned to farm products. Midwestern insurgents George Norris, Joseph Bristow, Moses Clapp, Ash Gronna, Knute Nelson, and Cummins were unwilling to abandon protection here, and miffed at Democratic caucus control, they voted with the core Republican standpatters on most amendments and on final passage.[34] Robert M. La Follette, after losing his intricately constructed amendments to raise the Democratic duties in a "scientific" fashion, cast a principled vote for the Democratic bill, acknowledging it as an improvement over the existing Republican system. Progressive Republican Miles Poindexter of Washington also joined the majority. Republicans throughout the nation once again joined in support for the creation of a bipartisan tariff commission, but their amendment was defeated on a straight party vote, 37 to 32 (see table 7.3).[35]

Although tariff politics caused the Republican insurgents to rediscover their affinity for the Grand Old Party, the income tax was another matter. Here, once more, the agrarians united to extract their pound of flesh from the industrial elite. Anticipating a very close fight in the Senate, the Democrats had incorporated into the Underwood Tariff bill a somewhat more moderate tax than they had proposed in 1894 and 1909. It established a 1 percent

Table 7.3 Senate Votes on Underwood Tariff, 1913

% of Seats in Senate		Raise Auto Duties	Raise Wool/Woolens Duties	Create Tariff Board	Final Senate		Conference	
		21–47	29–41	32–37	44–37		36–17	
		D 0–40	D 0–41	D 0–37	D 42–2		D 34–2	
		R 21–7	R 29–0	R 32–0	R 2–35		R 2–15	
						% Yeas		% Yeas
		% Yea	% Yea	% Yea	% Yea	Cast by:	% Yea	Cast by:
27.1	Core	57.9	58.8	61.1	38.1	18.2	46.7	19.4
14.6	Diverse	30.0	54.5	60.0	57.1	18.2	83.3	13.9
58.3	Periphery	17.9	27.1	36.6	60.9	63.6	70.6	66.7

tax on corporate income and individual income over $3,000 ($4,000 for a couple) and a graduated 1 to 3 percent surcharge on incomes over $20,000. It was a tax that left workers and all but the richest farmers untouched.[36] In the Senate, Borah and the midwestern insurgents pressed for a much more steeply graduated tax on the highest incomes (over $75,000). Nearly all of their amendments, including one to add an inheritance tax, drew twelve to seventeen votes, mostly from the midwestern, mountain, and Pacific insurgents, while the Democratic caucus line for the original proposal held firm.[37] The Democrats feared that such amendments would jeopardize the tariff bill, and they saw no reason to raise a large surplus in the treasury. The potential for a federal welfare state was not at issue in this period; the most likely use for additional revenues would have been an expansion of the U.S. Navy along the lines urged by Theodore Roosevelt and the nationalists in both the eastern and the far-western wings of the Republican Party. Consistent with their antimilitarist tradition, such expenditures were strongly opposed by the Democrats.

There was, however, growing support for a more progressive income tax among the more radical agrarian Democrats (particularly James Vardaman of Mississippi, James Reed of Missouri, Henry Ashurst of Arizona, and William Thompson of Kansas). Responding to this pressure, President Wilson (who favored only a moderate tax) finally agreed to take the tax in increments from 4 percent to 7 percent on incomes over $75,000, and the compromise carried by voice vote.[38] Industrial-state Republicans, hopelessly outnumbered, bemoaned the unfairness and "sectional character" of a tax that would "plunder" the successful families of their region.[39] It was, in fact, a tax that would extract more revenue from the city of Chicago than from the eleven southern states combined; four states—New York, Pennsylvania, Massachusetts, and Illinois—would supply almost 60 percent of the combined income and corporation taxes levied by the Underwood Tariff.[40]

This issue had always been a difficult one for northern Democrats,[41] but House and Senate votes in the 62nd Congress had shown an increasing potential for class politics in the core. In 1912, the four industrial-state Democrats in the Senate and most of the fifty-eight core Democrats in the House joined the agrarian Democrats in an unsuccessful attempt to extend the corporation tax to individuals.[42] Disaffection from the core Republican Party was finally strong enough to permit the election of a significant number of core Democrats willing to desert their regions' traditional positions on taxation and the tariff. The Democratic coalition held again in 1913.

The Revenue Act of 1916

The income tax was made still more obnoxious to the core elite under a revision carried out in 1916. Faced with a revenue shortfall because of war-related trade disruption and administration requests for sharply higher defense expenditures, the White House proposed to make up the difference by lowering the threshold for taxable income and imposing new taxes on oil, gasoline, and automobiles. These regressive tax proposals were met with outrage in farm and labor constituencies, and Democratic congressmen deluged their leaders with protests. An agrarian coalition on the House Ways and Means Committee then took matters into its own hands and radically revised the 1913 tax law. The new bill passed by the House was made even more progressive by Senate agrarians. In its final form, the Revenue Act of 1916 doubled the tax rate on incomes over $40,000, raised the maximum tax on incomes over $20,000 from 6 to 15 percent, added a graduated inheritance tax, and levied an additional tax on the net profits of munitions industries. If the core elite wanted war, the Democrats and dissident Republicans argued, they should be prepared to pay for it.[43] Mobilization for war, strongly resisted in the southern, midwestern, and mountain states, had brought sectional tensions to the boiling point.

The 1916 bill did make several concessions to the protectionists in hopes of winning over progressive Republican votes and minimizing northern Democratic losses in the upcoming national elections. It established, at long last, a bipartisan tariff commission to gather information on domestic and foreign industries. In view of the government's revenue difficulties, the sugar duty was maintained at 70 percent of the Payne-Aldrich Tariff rate rather than being reduced to zero, as anticipated by the 1913 law. In addition, American chemical and dye manufacturers were granted a moderate increase in duties (to protect them against German competition), and a penalty against dumping "with intent to injure" American competitors was incorporated into the revenue bill. These provisions did little to improve the reception of the Revenue Act among core Republicans, who complained that the antidumping clause with its "intent" provision was worthless, that the duty on dyestuffs was too low to maintain the industry, and that the tariff board would inevitably serve Democratic trade purposes.[44] For these members, the taxes on wealth overrode all other considerations and damned the bill. Industrial-state Democrats, on the other hand, were enthusiastic about the tariff commission and hoped that its creation would bolster sagging party fortunes in the North.[45] Beneath the "protectionist" window dressing, however, this was essentially an agrarian tax law, with overwhelming support in the cotton, wheat, and forest regions. In the House, thirty-seven Republicans (80 percent of them from the midwestern wheat, corn, and forest districts) joined an almost unanimous Democratic Party. In the Senate, midwestern insurgent Republicans La Follette, Cummins, Clapp, Norris, and William Kenyon joined the Democrats behind the bill while a core-centered Republican block opposed it (see table 7.4).[46]

President Wilson's sponsorship of mild protectionist measures in 1916 had come as an unpleasant surprise to periphery Democrats, although he had begun to distance himself from the traditional Democratic trade and regulatory programs as early as 1914. Majority leader Claude Kitchen of North Carolina refused to sponsor the tariff commission bill in the House, leaving the responsibility to Rep. Henry Rainey of Illinois. But for the most part, the congressional agrarians accommodated the tariff concessions and other such shifts out of political necessity. They owed a great debt to Wilson for

Table 7.4 Support for 1916 Revenue Act

	Final House		Final Senate	
	238–142		42–16	
	D 196–1		D 37–0	
	R 37–139		R 5–16	
	% Yea	% Yeas Cast by:	% Yea	% Yeas Cast by:
Core	31.0	16.8	27.3	7.1
Diverse	56.9	17.2	92.3	28.6
Periphery	87.7	66.0	79.4	64.3

his important part in earlier legislative victories, and they realized that their programmatic interests were closely linked to the president's reelection and to the electoral success of their urban copartisans.

Banking and Credit

I have a plan the details of which I cannot work out tonight;
but it is one that will make the United States the financial
centre of the world, which it is entitled to be. [Great Applause]
                                Sen. Nelson Aldrich of Rhode Island, 1909

The second item on the Democratic agenda in 1913 was a far-reaching reform of the nation's banking and credit institutions. As with the tariff, there was a broad consensus by 1909 that reform had become imperative. And again there were profound differences over the shape of reform. These differences typically pitted the agrarian periphery against the corporate and financial elite of the core and left the midwestern corn and wheat sections to agonize, Hamlet-like, between those polar alignments. Labor interest and involvement in these banking struggles was not significant.

Tariff reform had been the traditional program of Democrats in the South and in the less-prosperous southern reaches of the corn belt. They had been ready in 1913 with a program and a philosophical commitment to see it through. There was no question about the role of government. This "industrial policy" was accepted by all as a fundamental role of the national government. The question was not whether or to what extent government would act but only which of the contending programs the government would enact. However, with banking and credit reform, as with transportation, antitrust, and labor policies, the legitimacy and the scope of national government intervention in the economy were at issue. Logically, then, the politics of banking reform would be more complicated and unpredictable than was the case with the tariff.

Postal Savings System

The postal savings legislation enacted during the Taft administration permitted small savers to maintain government-secured accounts in local post offices, constituting a minor victory for residents of small-town and rural areas of the West and Midwest. The initiative was also favored by northern urban Democrats, though they made no important contribution to its enactment by a Republican Congress and administration. A post-office savings system had been endorsed by the Populists and the American Federation of Labor in the 1890s and had been included in labor's "Bill of Grievances" in 1906.[47]

The legislative history of the bill illustrated the fundamental dilemma of the agrarian Republicans. With their own party in power, the dominant bloc of standpat representatives of eastern capital would always attempt to twist "reforms" to their own advantage. To salvage their alternative proposals, the insurgent Republicans thus would have to ally with the block of agrarian Democrats, but success here risked presidential vetoes. On the other hand, to work within the Republican Party inevitably brought subordination to core elite goals. This was the story of postal savings.

The "bankers panic" of 1907 had spurred demands for some sort of government protection for small depositors. Texas, Oklahoma, Kansas, Nebraska, and South Dakota had already enacted state guarantees, and the 1908 Democratic platform called for a federal deposit-insurance system, endorsing a postal savings system only if the former could not be realized. Midwestern Republicans backed the more modest postal savings plan, for which they managed to win Taft's approval and a plank in the 1908 Republican platform. The American Bankers' Association strongly opposed the plan, predicting that its passage would make every rural post office a target for robbers and that the South and West would be "overrun with bandits."[48] In the House, Speaker Joseph Cannon branded the idea "a step toward populism" and a part of "the everlasting yielding to the popular outcry against wealth."[49]

To conservative fellow Republicans, Taft and the insurgents defended the establishment of secured savings depositories in post offices as a method for promoting thrift and discouraging hoarding by the lower classes. In rural areas, with widely scattered and often unsound banks, the bill would provide a secure receptacle for small deposits and would increase locally available capital. (The postal depositories themselves, it was assumed, would place accumulated funds in sound local banks at only a slightly higher interest rate than that offered postal savers.) In urban areas, the postal depositories would capture the small savings of immigrants who distrusted banks and were accustomed to postal savings systems in Europe—to the extent that immigrants were said to be shipping $90 million a year to European depositories, a loss to U.S. industrial development.[50]

Realizing the broad support for postal savings and finding the plan preferable to the Democrats' more radical deposit-insurance proposal, Senator Aldrich and other standpatters decided to imprint the program with their own objectives rather than block it. Aldrich anticipated that the resulting small deposits might be nationally aggregated and used to purchase some of the large stock (over $730 million) of old-issue government bonds held by national banks to secure their currency. Marketable only at a discount if they would not serve as the basis for issuing U.S. bank notes (because their 2 percent interest rates were below current market rates), these bonds had become a major stumbling block to currency reform because denial of the circulation privilege would entail large losses for the national banks that held them. If the postal savings system could be used to bail out the banks (buying up the 2 percent bonds), it could pave the way for the new national central-bank and currency plan on which Aldrich was working.[51]

In the Senate, an alliance of agrarian Democrats and insurgent Republicans opposed both Aldrich's developing central-bank plan and mechanisms by which local postal savings could be siphoned off, either by the government itself or by large metropolitan banks. Senators Cummins of Iowa and Borah of Idaho led floor fights for amendments requiring the deposit of postal savings funds in local banks, restricting presidential authority to withdraw the funds for investment in U.S. bonds, and requiring that deposits earn at least 2.25 percent interest (a rate still below prevailing commercial rates but high enough to block Aldrich's bond-purchase scheme). The alliance succeeded in enacting a provision requiring that 65 percent of local postal savings funds be deposited with local banks at no less than 2.25 percent interest. However, with Taft's support, the Republican regulars in the Senate beat back limitations on the president's ability to withdraw all of the local funds whenever he judged that the "general welfare or interests of the United States" required; and in the House, the regulars struck the Senate-passed requirement that those funds be invested at more than 2 percent. The postal savings bill then passed the House with unanimous Republican support; twenty-four Democrats—mostly from northern and western areas with large foreign-born populations—also voted in favor. The southern periphery had a minuscule immigrant population and was reluctant to back any scheme that might drain away scarce local funds; it remained hostile.[52]

The midwestern insurgents in the Senate were bitter that their postal savings project had become a vehicle for an elite-controlled mobilization of the nation's financial resources. When the "nationalized" House bill returned to the Senate, Cummins proposed to restore Senate provisions establishing depositories in every town above a uniform (and presumably low) population threshold and requiring more than 2 percent interest on funds withdrawn by presidential order. Georgia Sen. Augustus Bacon proposed to strike altogether the provision authorizing the withdrawal of local funds for the purchase of U.S. bonds. None of the amendments passed.

Table 7.5 Senate Votes on Postal Savings, 1910

% of Seats in Senate	Bacon Amend.: Strike Provisions for U.S. Withdrawal of Funds	Cummins Amend.: Require Local Depositories	Cummins Amend.: Pay 2¼ Interest on Nationalized Deposits	Final Senate Vote: Accept House Amendments	
	24–34	28–34	22–37	44–25	
	D 18–0	D 19–0	D 15–1	D 1–22	
	R 6–34	R 9–34	R 7–36	R 43–3	
					% Yeas
	% Yea	% Yea	% Yea	% Yea	Cast by:
28.3 Core	0	0	0	100	43.2
15.2 Diverse	44.4	60.0	54.5	63.6	15.9
56.5 Periphery	62.5	62.9	51.6	46.2	40.9

(The three amendments reported here are Senate amendments to House amendments, occurring after original passage by both chambers.)

The Senate votes in table 7.5 offer a window into Progressive Era party and regional dynamics, revealing the dependence of the Republican insurgents on the periphery Democrats for their reform initiatives and, likewise, the importance of the western periphery to the core Republican conservative agenda.[53] All three amendments elicited the alliance of periphery Democrats and corn- and wheat-belt Republicans but were defeated by the classic Republican coalition of core industrial-state senators and their tariff-yoked allies in the mountain and Pacific states. Under pressure from President Taft, all Republicans but three (Bristow, Cummins, and La Follette) swallowed their objections and backed the Senate acceptance of the conservative House version, but southern opposition placed the majority of periphery representatives and senators against the program.

By 1916 postal savings deposits had reached $86 million—still a far cry from the hundreds of millions anticipated by Aldrich and Taft. Scattered among more than eight thousand post offices, the number of depositors per capita was highest in the mountain and Pacific states and the Northeast and was negligible in the South. The great bulk of deposits were concentrated in large cities of the manufacturing belt; New York alone held 24 percent of the national total.[54] The opposition of bankers gradually diminished as it was demonstrated that the system did indeed draw out the hidden savings of distrustful immigrants and offered no real competitive threat to banks. Still, the postal savings program was not a victory for banks, which had opposed it, or for poor immigrants, who were furnished secure local depositories but at an interest rate far below market and far below that offered by European postal savings institutions. Instead, this legislative achievement of the Taft years was a modest victory for the New Nationalist vision. A program advocated by rural and labor spokesmen for the benefit of their constituents had been imprinted with the grander designs of Republican officials to centralize the nation's financial resources and enhance executive discretion. It not only removed a barrier to the erection of a new central bank and provided a new source of financing for Panama Canal construction but also integrated the physically isolated and urban working-class immigrants into the modern industrial system and harnessed their meager savings for national economic expansion.[55] Such were the limits and conditions of financial reform in the Republican era.

The Federal Reserve Act: "Bryanizing" Finance

Passage of the Federal Reserve Act in 1913 elicited powerful, antithetical sentiments, as the following quotations from three representative protagonists illustrate.

Sen. Elihu Root (R, New York):

> I say that this bill presents the financial heresy twice repudiated by the people of the United States. I say that the central reserve board appointed under this bill will have to represent that very heresy. If this bill passes as it stands, America stands to lose all we saved when Grant vetoed the inflation bill, all we saved when Grover Cleveland abolished the silver purchase, all we saved when we elected McKinley, all the Republicans, all the gold Democrats saved when they helped in the repudiation of the vital principle which has been put into this bill.[56]

Rep. Irvine Lenroot (R, Wisconsin):

> I shall vote for the adoption of this conference report. [Applause on the Democratic side.] I shall do so, Mr. Speaker, because the bill as agreed upon establishes the power of public control over the finances of this country by a Federal board similar to the control that is now exercised over the interstate commerce of the country through the Interstate Commerce Commission. . . . [It] takes the reserves of the banks of the country that are now piled up in the city of New York and used to aid stock speculation upon the New York Stock Exchange and distributes those reserves back to the different parts of the country from whence they came. [Applause on the Democratic side.] . . . In addition to that, the bill provides for an elasticity of currency that, in my opinion, will meet the needs of different parts of the country

during the seasons of the year when crops are moved. Another reason is that . . . it does provide substantial assistance to the farmers of this country in the making of farm loans. And last of all, Mr. Speaker, I will vote for it because when this bill is put into operation, in my judgment, it will insure against purely financial panics in this country, such as occurred in 1907. [Applause.][57]

Rep. J. Willard Ragsdale (D, South Carolina):

Many of the provisions that we find in the bill at this time were met with strong disapproval at the time they were offered by me in the committee. Then I was denounced as a rebel and insurgent . . . and now, to-day, it seems to me that we have before us a currency bill that we can all safely hand to the people of the United States and say the power of the Money Trust is broken and that the people have come into their own. [Applause on the Democratic side.] . . . Mr. Speaker, the time has come, and it has been written into this statute for the first time in this country, that farm lands are a basis for credit in America, and that the owners of them who produce the wealth of this country shall share in that financial system. . . . The time is here when farm products are a basis of credit and subject to rediscount in the national reserve banks of America, and the men on whose shoulders rest the feeding of the masses now have some recognition at the hands of the Nation through the Democratic Party. [Applause.] . . . [W]e can go home and say to our people, "At last we have given you a system by which you shall control and take charge of the financial system of this country." [Applause.][58]

In retrospect, one may wonder at the pride of achievement voiced by the congressional agrarians on passage of the Federal Reserve Act (FRA) and at the dire forebodings of core Republicans. The Federal Reserve Board today is rarely viewed as a great democratic institution,[59] and the recent argument that the campaign for banking reform culminating in the FRA represented the formative experience in the development of a modern, self-conscious corporate elite has a ring of plausibility.[60] Of course, any evaluation of legislative winners and losers must acknowledge that the system evolved in ways not anticipated by the act's proponents (or opponents, for that matter) and that, however conservative the ultimate outcome, the "producer classes" might still have fared better with the new national banking law than without it, at least until the Federal Reserve Board stumbled and exacerbated the post–World War I deflation. Still, there is no doubt that a group of people resembling a corporate and financial elite spearheaded, with their intellectual allies, the movement for a new national bank in the decade before 1913, and so for scholars who attribute Progressive Era state expansion to elite instigation, the FRA would seem to be the best possible case. If there can be said to have existed a "statist agenda" among the core elite, the creation of a national central bank was at the top of the list.

There is, nonetheless, a significant burden of proof for those who would argue that the agrarians were cowed or duped into backing a central bank very like that envisioned by corporate and financial leaders. Although the technical details of FRA note creation, check clearing, rediscounting, investing, and intrasystem relationships may bear strong resemblance to provisions in the earlier plans of elite financial activists,[61] the Federal Reserve System differed from the latter in areas that both agrarians and core capitalists considered fundamental: public versus private control; degree of centralization; capitalization of local reserve banks; treatment of agriculture in the banking and credit system; and potential for inflation. It was in those areas that the FRA resonated with the agrarian "financial heresy" presumably vanquished in 1896 and 1900, and most of the leading advocates of the elite-sponsored Aldrich plan for a national central bank viewed the FRA with disgust and foreboding.

To be sure, they learned to live with it and prospered under it, the collective sigh of relief probably beginning with Wilson's surprisingly conservative appointments to the Federal Reserve Board in 1914. But speculation about such accommodations could not override the fear of most large capitalists at the time of enactment. Looking, then, at the *creation* of this vastly expanded state intervention into critical banking and money-creating functions, James Livingston's claim that the genesis of the FRA cannot be understood "apart from the emergence of a modern ruling class"[62] must (even if one accepts the claim) acknowledge a dual conditionality: the path taken by banking reform in 1913 also cannot be understood apart from the active hostility of agrarians to the central-bank designs of the core elite or the power of the agrarian interest in the legislature to challenge those designs. The agrarians, with their vastly different preferences for banking and currency policy, not only succeeded in grafting those preferences onto the central-bank mechanisms drafted by others but also, by the fact of their legislative power, induced great fragmentation in the ranks of the elite reformers. The latter then faced, in 1913, the choice of adamant resistance or a scramble to mitigate, wherever possible, the obnoxious features of a Democratic bill. There simply is no straight line from the capitalist-led banking-reform movement of the early 1900s to the Federal Reserve Act of 1913.

Debate over national banking policy had been sectionally polarized at least since the 1820s. So great was the periphery's hostility and distrust toward northeastern banking centers that no national banking system existed from the expiration of the second Bank of the United States in 1836 until 1863. The National Currency Act of 1863 and the subsequent National Banking Act of 1864 did not create a third Bank of the United States but, instead, just a system for federally chartered and supervised national banks. Banks in three cities (New York, Chicago, and St. Louis) were designated to hold the reserves of the outlying country banks and act as their redemption agents. National banks were permitted to issue limited amounts of notes, using U.S. bonds for collateral. Unlike state banks, they were prohibited from making loans secured by farm or other real estate.[63]

Regional bias permeated the war-created Republican banking system. It institutionalized and encouraged the dependence of country banks on northeastern—particularly New York—banking houses and the flow of funds out of the farm regions. This system was highly beneficial for the reserve-city banks. By 1900, deposits from country banks composed one-third of the total assets in New York national banks (for Chicago and St. Louis, the proportion was about one-fourth).[64] High minimum capitalization rates for national banks created barriers to entry in small towns, discouraging competition. Furthermore, there was a dearth of bank notes in the South and West, but the northeastern states were amply supplied.[65] The regional maldistribution of money and credit was reflected in short-term interest rates and average discount rates that remained twice as high in the South and West as in New York and New England at the end of the nineteenth century.[66] Credit stringencies, of course, reflected the risks of lending to farmers at a distance from money centers, risks imposed by climate, poverty, and information deficiencies. But they also stemmed from monopoly, deflation, banking restrictions, and other forces that were in large part the result of federal government policy. It was apparent that the system was not designed to accommodate the credit needs of periphery farmers and that it performed this function poorly, exacerbating the "natural" financial debilities of the rural hinterland.

With no provisions for routine clearance, pooling of reserves, or emergency lending, and with limitations on credit and note issuance, the banking system produced a severely inelastic currency and periodic liquidity crises (as in 1873, 1893, and 1907). Periphery farmers, falling further into debt, bankruptcy, and peonage, saw the nation's money supply increasingly concentrated in New York banks, where the aggregated reserves of outlying banks were commonly used for speculation on the New York Stock Exchange—a practice that contributed to recurring financial crises. After the turn of the century, the animus against the northeastern capitals of finance was exacerbated by a surge of financial consolidations and the growing power of investment bankers over industrial, transportation, and communication corporations. By 1910, the House of Morgan and its associates controlled the nation's ten great railroad networks and the three largest life-insurance companies, plus U.S. Steel, General Electric, International Harvester, Western Union, and American Telephone and Telegraph.[67]

Thus debate over currency reform triggered the primordial forces of regional competition—competition for control over the fundamental regulatory processes of economic life and, ultimately, over the distribution of wealth. As with the struggles to control the railroads and corporate competitive practices, the goal of periphery representatives in congressional battles over banking reform was to use the national government against regionally concentrated market power—power that had arisen "naturally" within the confines of public law.

Since the Republicans were in power during the 1907 panic, they were forced to respond to the mounting outcry for currency reform. The Aldrich-Vreeland Act of 1908 represented a compromise effort to provide for voluntary pooling of reserves during financial crises and the issuance of emergency currency backed by bonds or short-term commercial paper. To develop a plan for long-term reform, the act created a National Monetary Commission (NMC) to study the banking question and report to Congress. The commission was headed by Senator Aldrich, who had personal connections to the New York financial community and relied for advice on the prominent northeastern bankers, lawyers, and economists long concerned about the absence of central-bank mechanisms in the United States. The NMC banking-reform plan itself was drawn up in late 1910 at a secret meeting of Aldrich and the New York bankers Paul Warburg (the principal author), Frank Vanderlip, and Henry Davison and the Harvard economist A. Piatt Andrew.[68]

The NMC or "Aldrich bill" thus reflected the preferences of the New York financial community, though it already embodied certain necessary political compromises. It called for the creation of a single National Reserve Association (NRA) with fifteen branches whose managers would be appointed by the central NRA directorate. The latter would set a uniform national discount rate, issue currency, and control open-market operations, as well as supervise the work of the branches. The NRA was to be owned by subscribing banks (which would join voluntarily) and controlled by a forty-six-member board of directors that would be composed largely of bankers and businesspeople, along with three cabinet members and the comptroller of the currency serving ex officio. The governor would be appointed by the president (for a ten-year term) from a list of three names submitted by the NRA board; by a two-thirds vote, the board could remove the governor. This was to be a "nonpolitical" bankers' organization. It would provide for mobilization of the reserves of the country's scattered banks during times of stringency and would rediscount (through its branches) the paper of member banks. It would also issue a more elastic, asset-based currency whose quantity would be curbed by a graduated tax after it reached a specified amount ($900 million) or whenever reserves fell below a certain level. The new paper currency, issued on the basis of gold and short-term commercial paper, would be backed by the privately owned NRA and not by the federal government.[69]

The Aldrich plan represented the culmination of what might be viewed as an elite social movement, spurred by the 1907 panic and centered in New York and Chicago, to prepare public opinion for the establishment of a new national bank and a new currency. Both bankers and academic economists had been active in generating ideas for banking reform. Almost all endorsed a highly centralized, privately controlled system, but the most politically astute tailored their recommendations to their perceptions of political reality. Victor Morawetz, a Harvard-educated lawyer with Morgan connections, recognized that no central-bank plan was likely to survive in the regionally combative American political process, so he developed a plan for a banking system with decentralized private control of reserves but with central coordination of note issue. Warburg, the principal theorist behind the NMC plan, favored a broadly empowered national central bank on the European model but settled for the more limited "reserve association" that emerged in the Aldrich bill. Proponents of the Aldrich plan created, at Warburg's instigation, a "businessmen's monetary reform league" to promote it via publications, speeches, and conferences. The National Citizens League for the Promotion of a Sound Banking System was headquartered in Chicago and led by a midwesterner (J. Laurence Laughlin, a University of Chicago economist) as a conscious political strategy; any movement visibly controlled by Wall Street would have been doomed from the start. In fact, there was considerable tension between Laughlin and the New York group; the League, according to Laughlin, did not support "a central bank as urged in the Aldrich bill" but backed a more general concept of national monetary reform.[70]

There were also latent theoretical disagreements within the elite reformers' ranks, and these had important reverberations in the political process. Laughlin, who became the League's principal publicist, accepted the reigning doctrine to which all the leading banking reformers subscribed—namely, that a properly elastic paper currency should be based on short-term commercial paper (bills of exchange, promissory notes, etc.). Such paper represented transactions based on "real production" and was self-liquidating (expiring within, say, thirty days). As a result, the credit supplied and the currency issued on this basis would automatically expand and contract with the needs of business, causing neither inflation nor deflation.

This "simpleminded" version of the "real-bills" theory was, according to scholars Robert Craig West and James Livingston, accepted by the midwestern economist Laughlin and, even more persistently, by his student H. Parker Willis. West and Livingston argue that major New York bankers such as Warburg, Vanderlip, and Davison and more sophisticated economists like A. P. Andrew and O. M. W. Sprague at Harvard and E. W. Kemmerer at Cornell had a fuller understanding of banking and currency and recognized that such credit was *not* self-limiting. This group, the original and consistent partisans of the Aldrich plan, apparently had an organic fear of inflation and, in Livingston's argument, of wasteful, competitive domestic investment. Their central-bank plan thus advocated that only solidly capitalized banks should participate in paper-currency creation and that a central, banker-controlled body dominated by the largest banks and presided over, presumably, by men like themselves should have the power to control the type of paper eligible for rediscount and note issue. Further constraints on the quantity of money in circulation would be effected through discount rates, reserve requirements, statutory limits on the volume of notes, taxation of "excess" notes, and open-market operations.[71]

In the context of American politics—that is, given the power of agrarian and small-business interests in the legislature and the hatred of monopoly that infused the Progressive Era—the centralized private structure charted by the Aldrich bill was dead on arrival. The Laughlin-Willis assumptions, however, found favor with the congressional periphery Democrats who controlled the House after 1910. Even the more conservative Democrats like Carter Glass of Virginia represented capital-starved regions with a deep aversion to concentrated economic power and big bankers. Though Bryan and his followers had traditionally opposed a currency based on bank assets in favor of a less-restrictive metallic and paper currency issued directly by the government, the Laughlin-Willis real-bills doctrine was potentially attractive, especially if it could be modified to include agricultural paper. The doctrine implied that no strong central control or anti-inflation mechanisms were necessary and that the issuing of paper currency could be quite decentralized.[72] The automatically expanding money supply envisioned by the old

Greenbackers, subtreasury proponents, and silverites might be achieved by this modern mechanism.

As luck and geography would have it, the young Willis had taught, at Washington and Lee University, a class in which Glass's sons were enrolled, and they brought their teacher to Glass's attention.[73] Working with Willis, Glass cautiously inaugurated the Democrats' banking-reform strategy: to attack the Aldrich bill's obnoxious features and to graft onto the mechanisms of that plan the essential elements of a Democratic-periphery banking reform. Although President-elect Wilson and the Democratic leaders in Congress and the cabinet knew relatively little about the intricacies of large-scale banking, they knew that their party would not accept either a centralized banking system under the control of large northeastern banking houses or a currency and credit mechanism that defined "assets" as commercial transactions, excluding the farmer's land and produce. In this, the periphery Democrats found allies among agrarian Republicans.

In 1912, Republican insurgent Andrew Volstead of Minnesota attacked the Aldrich plan on several fronts: it left monetary control in private rather than public hands; it limited the class of paper that could be discounted by member banks (only short-term commercial paper, not agricultural transactions); and it left the concentration of reserves in New York, where they could be tied up in "gambling" in stocks and bonds.[74] These were criticisms on which there was broad agreement in the agricultural sections. In the 1910 postal savings fight, midwestern corn- and wheat-belt Republicans had joined southern and border Democrats in favor of the decentralization of deposits. As on the tariff question, however, the midwestern insurgents found themselves between the polar extremes. They were skeptical of the eastern "money trust" and Wall Street but not as hostile as the cotton-belt representatives; in addition, they favored more decentralization of financial power than currently existed but could not go along with the southern Jacksonians in the latter group's atavistic refusal to establish a more centralized banking system. Although credit was tight in the corn belt, it was not nearly so stringent as in the cotton belt and the mountain states. Representatives from the more isolated regions clamored for a banking system that would put the farmer and small-town banker "a day's train ride away" from loan approval. For much of the corn belt, this condition already existed, since Chicago and St. Louis were central reserve cities under the 1864 National Banking Act. Thus, even though midwestern representatives also condemned an inflexible, speculation-ridden banking system that ignored the farmers' credit needs (not even rich corn-belt land could be used for loan security at a national bank), they were definitely more amenable than were southerners to reforms that promised centralization and stability without undue inflation of the currency. To ward off Wall Street influence, they advocated—as did the Progressive Party platform of 1912—public control rather than extreme decentralization. As usual, the midwestern progressive Republicans were critical of the alternatives advanced from both (core and periphery) ends of the political spectrum.

In the 62nd Congress, the southern Democrats used their new control of the House to lay the groundwork for the party's bank-reform alternative. The House Banking Committee established two subcommittees. One, under Glass (assisted by Willis), began to develop the structural intricacies of a Democratic banking and currency proposal; the other subcommittee, which aroused much more enthusiasm in the periphery wing of the party, launched a far-reaching investigation of the "money trust." Headed by Rep. Arsene Pujo of Louisiana, the latter subcommittee employed Samuel J. Untermeyer to probe the evils of concentration and speculation in the existing banking system and to recommend public solutions. The investigation was wide-ranging, delving into nefarious dealings on the New York Stock Exchange as well as the manipulative, anticompetitive practices of New York's larger banks and such institutions as the New York Clearing House. The subcommittee's charts and diagrams revealed the structure of the financial and industrial empire controlled by the directors of a half dozen New York and Boston banks (principally, J. P. Morgan, John D. Rockefeller, and George F. Baker).[75]

In early 1913, the Pujo Committee recommended a range of legislation to diminish elite domination of the financial system. Because of Pujo's retirement, opposition by Glass and core Republicans, and the perceived exigencies of the European war, the committee's major recommendations for regulation of banking practices and securities transactions were set aside (and not enacted until the New Deal). However, as the committee had suggested, in 1914 the Clayton Act banned interlocking bank directorates and prohibited banks and corporations from purchasing stock in competing firms where the effect might be to substantially lessen competition. Even before passage of the Clayton Act, the unfavorable publicity of the investigation led Morgan himself to voluntarily shed his interlocking directorates.[76] The publicity achieved by the Pujo Committee confirmed the political impossibility of the Aldrich bill and facilitated passage of the Democratic alternative that became the Federal Reserve Act.

On the eve of its sweeping 1912 victory, then, the Democratic Party, dominated by its periphery wing, took a public stand in opposition to concentrated financial power and the Aldrich plan, which, it argued, would only institutionalize the "money trust." However, although the Democratic platform contained a section arguing the need for expanded credit in rural areas, it was completely devoid of specific positive suggestions for comprehensive banking-reform legislation. By contrast, the Republican platform listed a number of principles—most of them compatible with the Aldrich plan—to be served by currency reform. The Progressive Party, while condemning the Aldrich plan, was more specific in locating the plan's principal deficiency: the failure to lodge control of credit and note issuance in a public body.[77]

The process of "Democratizing" the available proposals for reform took place in two stages, the first controlled by Glass and his expert advisor, Willis. The second unfolded in response to Bryan and the radical agrarian Democrats, with President Wilson playing the strategic role. In the fall of 1912, Glass set Willis to work on a draft banking-reform plan that met the party's principles as Glass interpreted them.[78] In early 1913, their committee held hearings to "test public opinion," with agriculture, labor, banking, and business spokesmen, along with economic experts, invited to testify. Only organized labor failed to send representatives, despite repeated efforts to solicit their views. Farm interests were represented by the Farmers' Union and the Grange, whose delegates registered their opposition to the Aldrich plan and advocated federal government control of clearinghouse and currency-issue functions. They also urged that farmland and commodities be included in the "assets" base of the new currency, and the Farmers' Union delegate detailed the need for a new system of land banks like those existing in several European countries.[79]

The original Glass-Willis plan, which had taken shape before the hearings were held, resembled that of the NMC in establishing a private bank-owned and -controlled system, with note issue based only on short-term commercial paper partially backed by gold. However, the Glass bill rejected the central premise of the NMC plan: the centralization of reserves under a single stockholder-owned reserve association. Like the rest of the southern Democrats, the Virginian was firmly committed to decentralizing the country's bank reserves and to finding an antidote to the long-standing Wall Street dominance of banking. To that end, the Glass-Willis plan would have established not one bank, with regional branches subscribing to its capital (as in the Aldrich plan), but twenty or more independent regional banks with low minimum capitalization put up by local member banks. These regional banks would discount the paper of member banks (thus creating and loaning money where it was needed) and conduct their own open-market purchases of government securities and investment paper. They would even conduct foreign financial operations. Coordination of the regional institutions would be effected by a large board "without resources or capital," composed mostly of delegates chosen by member banks but also including several executive-branch officials operating under the general supervision of the comptroller of the currency. The regional reserve banks would take over the functions of holding the reserves of country banks and of holding federal government deposits—functions performed at the time by large reserve-city banks. The country bank reserves that had "piled up" in New York and in the other two central reserve cities (but mostly in New York) would then shift from large private banks in those cities toward the new regional reserve banks. Thus, southern and western reserves would be "repatriated," and government funds would be distributed more evenly around the country.[80]

The agrarian Democrats in Congress lauded the projected decentralization of financial resources but strongly opposed other features of the Glass bill, in particular the reliance on private control, the note issue by the reserve banks, and the inadequate attention to rural credit needs. The radicals were represented on the House Banking Committee by Joseph H. Eagle of Texas, J. Willard Ragsdale of South Carolina, Otis Wingo of Arkansas, and George A. Neeley of Kansas. Another radical, Robert Henry of Texas, chaired the Rules Committee. Their leader and spokesman in the administration was Secretary of State Bryan. In the Senate, Robert Owen of Oklahoma, the chairman of the Banking and Currency Committee, was also closely allied with Bryan.[81] This was the group of actors who provoked the second-stage "Democratization" of the banking-reform bill.

When Glass and Willis went to Princeton, New Jersey, to discuss their bill with the president-elect, they were shocked to hear him suggest that the regional bank system needed a "capstone"—a smaller supervisory board empowered to effect the degree of centralization that was, Wilson felt, necessary to the system's functioning. Though both Glass and Willis considered such a board objectionable, they acquiesced and revised the bill. The minimum number of districts was lowered to fifteen, and a new Federal Reserve Board was created consisting of only three representatives of the reserve-system banks and six directors chosen by the president. Wilson is said to have been delighted with this modification.[82]

It is impossible to know whether the president-elect's motives in advocating a more powerful, publicly controlled central board derived from his own internalization of Democratic principles, from his knowledge that public control was necessary to win his party's acceptance for banking reform, from an informed concern for the efficacious functioning of the new financial system, or from a desire to have this potentially very powerful institution under a degree of presidential control (something a highly intelligent, activist president who had been a professor of government would plausibly have considered). All four considerations were probably important, though well-informed opponents of the changes (such as Aldrich, Warburg, and Willis) tended to attribute them to the influence of the Bryan Democrats. Some years later, Willis told the *New York Times:* "Mr. Wilson wished even stronger centralization than the draft of the [Glass bill] provided. He adopted a proposal of Bryan to make the Federal Reserve Board a government body rather than simply a group of bankers. This was in order to win Bryan's support for the bill."[83] This statement, of course, does not rule out mixed motives on Wilson's part.

The superimposing of a two-thirds public board atop the regional reserve system was far from sufficient to satisfy the radical agrarians. In a tense meeting between Wilson and Bryan in mid-May, Bryan, speaking for the Democratic left wing, insisted that the board be composed entirely of public officials and that the new currency be the obligation of the federal government, not of the privately owned district reserve banks. In the Senate, Owen seemed poised to join the secretary of state in a Democratic rebellion against the House banking bill.[84] As Owen later recounted, he argued to the president: "The Government should control every member of the Board on the ground that it was the function of the Government to supervise this system and no individual, however respectable, should be on this Board representing private interests."[85] As to note issue, Owen argued—against Glass as well as advocates of the Aldrich bill—that the new currency must be U.S. treasury notes guaranteed by the government and backed by its taxing power. The currency should not be under the control of private persons. In these arguments he had, of course, the "active assistance" of Secretary Bryan.[86] After consultation with Bryan and Samuel Untermeyer, counsel for the Pujo investigation, Owen produced his own banking bill.[87]

Owen found that the treasury secretary, William Gibbs McAdoo, was on his side of the public-control issue. The southern-born McAdoo had a populist streak reinforced by his strong desire to win national political power in his own right.[88] In addition, government control would inevitably mean a major role for the treasury secretary in the operation of the banking system. Hearing the bitter arguments of both Democratic Party principals and the banking community against the Glass bill, the secretary determined to join the debate, convinced that only bold action from the administration could put together a banking-reform measure acceptable to the party and capable of passing Congress. McAdoo conferred with Bryan, selling him on the merits of the real-bills doctrine in its new Democratic variant and discussing with him the role of a presidentially appointed Federal Reserve Board. McAdoo also conferred with Owen, Untermeyer, Comptroller John S. Williams, and "some of the leading bankers," who, as he had expected, condemned his tentative ideas. McAdoo then put together his own banking plan, the most radical alternative yet offered. It proposed a central reserve bank wholly owned and controlled by the government. It would be a bureau of the Treasury Department and would be headed by an Owen-style, presidentially appointed Reserve Board (which would include the treasury secretary). The government, of course, would create and control the issue of paper money. McAdoo seems to have considered, rather naively, that since members of the financial community objected so strongly to the Glass bill's independent regional reserve banks, they might appreciate the degree of centralization his plan embodied. Its essence was, however, thoroughly "Bryanized," and the bankers and Glass were appalled.[89]

Years later, perhaps embarrassed about this radical 1913 proposal, McAdoo claimed that he had made it as part of a "scarecrow" strategy: by staking out such an extreme position, he hoped to frighten the bankers, who were almost unanimously opposed to the Glass bill, into acquiescence.[90] Arthur Link, however, believed McAdoo to have issued his proposals in all sincerity.[91] At any rate, the treasury secretary's offering provided yet another indication that these were very creative times; the policy cauldron was boiling, and the character of the soup was quite indeterminate. The nation's leading bankers sat anxiously at the table, wondering what (probably indigestible) meal they would be served next.

McAdoo's plan was not seriously taken up for debate, but Glass and the president did accept the Owen-Bryan demands on structure and on note issue. To the great bankers, both were anathema. Warburg, surely one of the most reasonable and flexible of the elite banker-reformers (and one who might well have anticipated that his reasonableness would win him a place on the first Federal Reserve Board), had lobbied long and patiently against independent regional banks. Now he found the "Bryanization" of notes and structure "deeply alarming and distressing"; these were "fatal changes" leading toward a politically controlled banking and currency system.[92]

Even as Glass and Wilson presented the revised plan to Congress and the country, bankers were waging an intense campaign against the bill.[93] The level of panic they felt now seems quite remarkable, but in 1913 the proposal, as Link reminds us, constituted an unprecedented level of "government intervention in the most sensitive area of the capitalistic economy."[94] Meeting in Chicago, the country's leading bankers demanded, essentially, a return to the Aldrich plan, while in Boston the House bill was denounced as socialistic by a convention of the American Bankers' Association.[95] Prominent conservatives such as Frank Vanderlip of National City Bank, the railway magnate James J. Hill, and Senators Aldrich and Root condemned the Democratic bill as the embodiment of populist schemes, a generator of "fiat" money, and a step toward socialism. Academic opinion in the core was also hostile. Yale President Arthur D. Hadley, a respected economist, wrote President Wilson that the Glass-Owen program would "involve the country in grave financial danger." Prominent professors concurred with Aldrich at a meeting of the Academy of Political Science, condemning the bill's dangerous absence of limitation on note issue.[96] The result of such legislation, editorialized the *New York Times*, would be the opening of "a fathomless abyss of inflation."[97] The *Banking Law Journal* editorialized that the bill constituted "a proposal for the creation of a vast engine of political domination over the great forces of profitable American industry. . . . The fight is now for the protection of private rights and to be successful it must be waged to enlist public opinion against unwise legislation with tendencies to financial disaster to all the people." The Wall Street–oriented *New York Sun* was less restrained. In June 1913 it blasted the bill as "this preposterous offspring of ignorance and unreason" whose "provisions for a Government currency and an official board to exercise absolute control over the most important of banking functions is covered all over with the slime of Bryanism."[98]

To be sure, there were some bankers who saw it as the better part of wisdom not to burn their bridges to the Democrats. Considering the climate of hostility toward the country's financial leaders and the much more radical alternatives being tossed around, some were willing to negotiate and work to make the bill less objectionable. After all, the country needed a new banking and currency system, and the Democratic version represented political reality. Intransigence would mean loss of influence and might yield an even worse bill. Warburg was one of the conciliationists, but they were not numerous in the Northeast. Members of the core financial elite were almost uniformly hostile. On the other hand, some prominent bankers in the Midwest, South, and West took a pragmatic approach, and country bankers in those regions, like the smaller businesspeople there, were on the whole inclined to be favorable.[99]

Those who displayed a moderately conciliatory tone were courted by Democratic leaders anxious to contain the bankers' opposition. After meeting with a group of New Orleans, Chicago, St. Louis, and Los Angeles bankers, Wilson, Glass, and Owen made several modifications designed to mitigate banker hostility. These included a provision for the gradual conversion of the 2 percent bondholdings of the national banks, more regional bank control over discount rates (which fit the Democratic urge to decentralization anyway), and an "advisory council" of regional bankers to meet with the Federal Reserve Board several times a year. Some bankers and businesspeople took heart from these concessions and appeared to rally around the Glass bill as a less dangerous alternative to other Democratic proposals.[100]

Meanwhile, the periphery radicals in Congress were criticizing the bill as far too conservative. In July 1913, rebellion flared in the House committee as the radicals pressed for amendments putting farm and labor representatives on the Federal Reserve Board, for a statutory ban on interlocking bank directorates (as recommended by the Pujo Committee), for a much longer maturity (120 days) for agricultural paper to be rediscounted by the reserve banks, for federal insurance for bank deposits (to protect depositors in weak country banks), and for an alternative currency partly based on warehouse receipts. Representative Henry of Texas proposed a modern version of the old populist subtreasury plan, calling for $200 million in new currency to be loaned to farmers on the basis of stored corn, wheat, and cotton, receipts for which would be presented by farmers to their banks. Another $500 million would be created on the basis of commercial needs and state and local bonds.[101] Opposed by Wilson, Glass, and the northern Democrats on the committee, the agrarian amendments were said to draw varying degrees of support from about seventy representatives in the House.[102] The *New York Times*, predictably, greeted these proposals with contempt,[103] but the Democratic president and his allies could hardly ignore them—particularly when the radicals took control of the House Banking Committee and proceeded to approve one of the amendments.[104]

The most serious phase of the rebellion was ended only after a long and unruly Democratic caucus meeting that forced the Democratic leadership to agree to provisions extending agricultural paper maturity to ninety days (twice the length for discounted paper in the original Glass bill), extending maturity for loans based on farmlands (newly authorized in the Glass bill) from nine to twelve months, and permitting the Federal Reserve Board to classify bills of exchange based on warehouse receipts as eligible for discounting by the regional reserve banks. Wilson also pledged support for a separate rural credits measure and a ban on interlocking bank directorates in the upcoming antitrust bill. Most of the radicals then agreed to support the federal reserve bill. The House caucus finally made it a binding party measure in late August.[105]

Bryan now urged the agrarians to back the bill as the best measure capable of passage—since it was clear to all that acceptance of the Henry amendments as written would almost certainly have meant defeat. Rep. Rufus Hardy of Texas argued for passage of the revised bill, praising its potential for decentralizing financial power and expanding agricultural credit. In defense of this unprecedented program to enlarge federal government power, he told his colleagues that it was necessary to "surrender to society" some portion of individual freedom "in order to preserve the remainder of it":

> This banking system will give our farming community, our working peo-
> ple—the small man—everywhere an opportunity to make paper that can
> be rediscounted by the local bank with the reserve bank. By such rediscount
> the local bank can get further money in order to extend further credit. This
> system when put into operation will revolutionize the banking conditions
> of the country banking communities and of the great masses of our people.
> . . . It will break down the tyranny of the money power in the great centers,
> which grows every year more potent for evil. A new era will come to our
> people who have nestled down in their homes without any conception of
> the subtle influences undermining the independent status and individualism
> of the average man. It will give them a new and, I trust, a right conception
> of the power and beneficence of our great Government. It is a measure that
> will help our people and take away no shred of their liberties. It is a measure
> that will help our banks, while it subjects them to the power of the Govern-
> ment and subordinates them to the welfare of all the people. [Applause.][106]

Moving to final passage, Glass and Bryan accepted a symbolic Republican amendment that reaffirmed support for the gold standard. That amendment passed 299 to 68. Its opponents, almost all of them Democrats, presented a rough delineation of the radical agrarian phalanx in the House. Fifty-six of the sixty-eight (82 percent) represented districts in the agrarian periphery as we have defined it.[107]

Only three Democrats opposed the bill on House passage, with thirty Republicans and ten assorted Progressives joining the Democratic majority (see table 7.6).[108] The large majority of the Republican and Progressive supporters represented midwestern and Pacific periphery and diverse districts. These Republicans, though shunted aside by the Democrats' partisan strategy and embittered at their loss of influence, were nonetheless hesitant to swell the ranks of the standpat Republicans in opposition to a federal banking program

Table 7.6 Federal Reserve Act Votes, 1913

		House Votes			
		Final		Conference	
		287–85		298–60	
		D 248–3		D 248–2	
		R 30–80		R 38–58	
% of Seats in House		% Yea	% Yeas Cast by:	% Yea	% Yeas Cast by:
34.5	Core	66.9	27.5	76.9	31.2
18.9	Diverse	73.1	19.9	75.0	15.1
46.7	Periphery	85.8	52.6	90.4	53.7

	Senate Votes[b]						
	Resolution to Meet 13 Hours/Day Until Vote	Hitchcock Substitute		Final Senate Vote		Conference	
	41–18	41–44		54–34		43–25	
	D 31–0	D 1–44		D 48–0		D 39–0	
	R 10–18	R 40–0		R 6–34		R 4–25	
% of Seats in Senate	% Yea	% Yea	% Yea	% Yea	% Yeas Cast by:	% Yea	% Yeas Cast by:
27.1	Core	47.1	69.6	41.7	18.5	53.3	18.6
14.6	Diverse	88.9	53.3	57.1	14.8	58.3	16.3
58.3	Periphery	75.8	32.2	72.0	66.7	68.3	65.1

[a] Core and periphery majorities split: core 7–28, periphery 20–15.
[b] Sen. Miles Poindexter of Washington is counted here as a Republican.

that finally incorporated agrarian interests. The Democratic Party's minority core faction, including those closest to organized labor, loyally supported the banking bill on the floor but played no creative role in its passage.

In the Senate, the bill was made even more favorable to the periphery, but not without a prolonged struggle. While maintaining the general structure of the House bill, Oklahoma Senator Owen and his faction on the Senate Banking Committee proposed a number of amendments that enhanced the agricultural credit provisions and the potential for currency inflation. However, a committee rebellion growing out of personal grievances against the administration created an opening for a drastically different banking-reform proposal designed to block the revised House bill.

Three Democratic members of the committee were involved: Gilbert Hitchcock of Nebraska, James O'Gorman of New York, and James Reed of

Missouri. Each had idiosyncratic reasons for opposing the banking and currency bill backed by Wilson and Bryan.[109] The three dissident Democrats were persuaded to join committee Republicans in support for a plan devised by the banker Frank Vanderlip. An original proponent of the Aldrich (NMC) bill, Vanderlip shared the core financial community's distaste for the Democratic bill. One of the most active and influential opponents, he had circulated pamphlets describing its defects.[110] Recognizing that adoption of the original central-bank plan of the NMC was impossible, Vanderlip tried to find common ground with Republicans (both standpatters and progressives) and with the three Democratic dissidents on the Senate committee.

That common ground was established when Vanderlip drafted an alternative plan for a single central bank (with twelve regional branches), owned— and here his plan departed from the Aldrich/NMC plan—by the "public," who would buy its stock, and controlled entirely by a federal government board.[111] The outspoken New York banker considered decentralization the major flaw in the present banking system and blamed country bankers' hoarding for the panic of 1907.[112] Like other Wall Street financiers, he favored a single central bank controlled by bankers, but facing a Democratic plan that offered neither centralization nor banker control and having little hope that the country would ever accept the latter, Vanderlip apparently decided to trade private control for centralization. This interpretation credits the National City Bank president with sincerity in his proposal; it is more likely, however, that he injected this alternative plan into the Senate deliberations merely to ensure that no legislation would be passed.[113]

Vanderlip's proposal contained several provisions applauded by the core metropolitan banking community. Aside from its unitary structure, national bank membership in the system was made voluntary rather than compulsory; currency was to be backed by a more conservative 50 percent gold reserve (as contrasted to 33.3 percent in the Glass-Owen bill) and redeemable only in gold (the Glass-Owen bill contained the phrase "or lawful money," which raised cries of "greenbackism!" in the core); the national bank was directed to repurchase at par the 2 percent U.S. bonds that would become a burdensome liability for the private banks; and dividends of 6 percent were given to the bank's stockholders (the Democratic bill offered 5 percent).[114]

The Vanderlip scheme was embraced by Republicans, as well as by the three dissident Democrats on the Senate Banking Committee. The appeal of the plan to such disparate personalities as John Weeks of Massachusetts, O'Gorman of New York, and agrarian radicals such as Bristow of Kansas and Reed of Missouri was indeed remarkable. Some corn-belt senators praised the proposal's government control and broad stock ownership, whereas core Republican senators were attracted by its centralization and "hard-money" features. Democratic defenders of the Glass-Owen bill found themselves harangued from both sides, accused both of "Bryanism" and of surrender to the "money trust" (for their reliance on member-bank ownership of the regional banks and the selection of six out of nine of the regional bank directors by local member banks).

A month of intricate legislative coalition-building followed the introduction of the Vanderlip plan. During this period, Wilson threw all of his influence behind the Glass-Owen framework while the two banking committee factions vied for support in the Senate at large. Competition between the two sides brought important benefits to the agrarian regions. Both the Owen-Democratic and Hitchcock-GOP factions added federal deposit insurance to their programs—a goal that had eluded agrarian radicals in the House because of opposition from Glass, the president, and core representatives. Both sides extended the time period for national bank loans on farm assets (to five years from nine months, as passed by the House). Whereas the Glass-Owen bill specified a 90-day maturity for discounted agricultural paper, the Hitchcock plan went further, allowing half the paper discounted to bear a maturity of 90 to 180 days). Hitchcock and his allies also felt compelled to replace the single central bank with four regional banks, probably to be located in the existing central reserve cities and in San Francisco.[115]

Core bankers objected most strongly to the potential for currency inflation and the decentralization of reserves (which would cost the metropolitan banks both influence and profits formerly earned on country-bank deposits), but the House-passed bill's compulsory membership, government control, and unfavorable treatment of 2 percent bonds were features broadly resisted throughout the banking community. In addition, the country banks (like their clients) objected to the House-passed bill's too-short maturity for discounted paper and to the denial of charges for out-of-town checks, an important source of income for many small banks. The Owen committee bloc and the Democratic caucus, even while moving to rally agrarian votes, made a number of changes designed to dampen banker hostility, particularly on those points opposed by both rural and urban bankers. The percentage of capital required for membership in the federal system was significantly lowered, more favorable treatment for 2 percent bonds was instituted, and a higher dividend was allowed for reserve-bank shareholders. The revised Senate bill also conceded to the country bankers their exchange charges and, to make the Federal Reserve Board less political, removed the secretary of agriculture and the comptroller of the currency. In other concessions that tilted toward the Hitchcock position, Owen agreed to increase the gold backing for notes in circulation from 33.3 to 40 percent and to provide for eight to twelve regional banks rather than the minimum of twelve required by the House version. The revision also enhanced the power of the Federal Reserve Board over the regional banks by allowing the former to remove directors of the latter at its own discretion. Although major aspects of the Democratic banking bills were still extremely abhorrent to the country's financial leaders, a number of the "technical" modifications made in the Senate succeeded in reducing the hostility of a banking community that had been in a state of great anxiety about this legislation for more than half a year.[116]

By mid-November the Republican-Progressive coalition was in retreat. In caucus, the Democrats endorsed the revised Senate bill (after adding other amendments) and made it binding.[117] The first Senate test of support for the bill came in a vote on December 6, 1913, proposing that the Senate agree to meet thirteen hours a day until the final vote was taken on banking reform, be it the Hitchcock or the Owen program. Well over half the affirmative votes were cast by periphery senators, with ten (mostly periphery- and diverse-state) Republicans joining the Democrats (see table 7.6). All amendments to the Senate bill offered by Hitchcock and the Republicans were defeated, though some of them quite narrowly, on partisan votes. On December 19, the Hitchcock substitute for the Owen bill was defeated 44 to 41, with only Hitchcock himself crossing party lines.[118]

A stronger and less partisan defeat was administered to an amendment offered by Senator Root to substitute the currency provisions of the old Aldrich plan for relevant sections of the Owen bill. These provisions would require 50 percent gold backing for circulating notes (as opposed to 40 percent in the revised Senate bill), make them obligations of the banks rather than the government, and limit, via a punitive tax, the amount of notes in circulation. In a precise and eloquent statement of the elite reformers' objections to the Democratic measure, Root voiced his faction's skepticism of the real-bills theory it embodied. The New York Republican argued that the structural limitations of the Aldrich bill were absolutely necessary to prevent an ultimately "catastrophic" expansion of currency and credit. The Glass-Owen bill, he contended, would produce not an *elastic* currency but an *expansive* one, furnishing "everybody who can draw and sign a bill currency that has behind it the credit of the American people." What seemed the fulfillment of an old dream to the agrarians was clearly a nightmare to the New Yorker: "Little by little business is enlarged with easy money. With the exhaustless reservoir of the government of the United States furnishing easy money, the sales started, the spirit of optimism pervades the community. Bankers are not free from it. They are human." But, he cautioned his "friends in the West, the farmers of the West," this expansion would inevitably lead to a gold drain and financial ruin.[119]

Senator Owen and Sen. John Sharp Williams of Mississippi answered Root with a restatement of the automatic safeguards inherent in the real-bill-backed currency, supplemented by powers the board might call on and the general supervision that would be exercised by the president.[120] The Root proposal was defeated 49 to 22. Core senators backed his amendment 14 to 8 while periphery- and diverse-area senators (among them nine midwestern Republicans) opposed it 41 to 8.[121] On final passage, five Republicans and one Progressive joined the Democrats to pass the Owen federal reserve bill 54 to 34 (see table 7.6).[122] The bank reform bill in the Senate was, finally, a program that revealed major agrarian influence, and it drew the most overwhelming support in those regions. The small contingent of core Democratic senators loyally cooperated in its enactment, joined by a roughly equal number of Republicans from farm and mixed farm-industrial states. The manufacturing regions, still dominated in the upper chamber by the party of capital, opposed the bill by a large majority.

Agrarian members of the House much preferred the Senate bill to their own and thus instructed their conferees to give way to the Senate provision on maturity for agricultural loans and discounted paper. The final bill, as reported from conference and passed by both chambers, kept the generous Senate provisions for agricultural credit but eliminated that chamber's provision for deposit insurance. The conference bill passed the Senate 43–25 and the House 298–60. In the latter a majority of periphery Republicans and all voting Progressives joined the Democrats in support for the bill (see table 7.6).[123]

The Federal Reserve Act provided for the creation of up to twelve regional institutions to serve as "bankers' banks" for member state and national banks (holding their deposits, clearing their checks, and loaning them money by rediscounting their paper), as well as to deal in government securities and foreign currency. The act created a new currency, Federal Reserve notes, to be issued by a Federal Reserve Board agent to the regional banks. For the notes issued, the reserve banks would offer as collateral an equal amount of eligible notes and bills of exchange—drawn for commercial, industrial, or agricultural purposes—from member banks. The regional banks would hold reserves of gold and lawful money equal to 40 percent of their notes in circulation.[124]

The new currency was made an obligation of the United States (not of the banks of issue) and was redeemable in gold at the U.S. Treasury or in gold or "lawful money" at the regional banks. The (twelve) regional institutions were given nine-member boards of directors: three members to be chosen by member banks (who would own the stock of the reserve banks, except for any capitalization deficiency that might be subscribed by the public); three directors to be chosen by the banks to represent various business, agricultural, and "community" interests in the district; and three members to be selected by the Federal Reserve Board in Washington, D.C., which could also designate the chair and remove any regional bank director. Only three of the nine could be directors, employees, or stockholders of banks.

The Federal Reserve Board itself was composed of the comptroller, the treasury secretary, and five other geographically distributed, presidentially appointed members with ten-year terms.[125] This central board was empowered to supervise and control the issuing of notes (with the power to deny a request for issue or demand more security), to approve regional-bank discount rates, to exercise general supervision over the regional banks and examine member banks, to require that the regional banks rediscount each other's notes (so that a region short of currency could tap resources elsewhere), and to exercise a host of other powers—consequential in the aggregate—over reserve requirements, state bank memberships, and compliance of reserve and member banks with the law's provisions.

After passage of the bill, Republicans attempted to dampen the majority party's exuberance at its accomplishment by claiming that all the good features of the act had been copied from the Aldrich plan (the "bad" features, of course, were contributed by the agrarian Democrats). A number of scholars have supported the arguments attributing paternity to Aldrich, Warburg, Laughlin, or Morawetz; others have gone beyond individual and party to interpret the Federal Reserve Act as a victory for the New Nationalist ideology[126] or for a newly coherent corporate capital class.[127]

In view of the legislative history, however, it seems reasonable to characterize the Federal Reserve Act as a result not of the *dominance* of capitalists, farmers, or state officials but of their *interaction*. Each interest played a major role in shaping the legislation, and each seemed to derive some significant benefit from the new system, compared with the status quo. Farmers benefited from the money and credit expansion that followed enactment;[128] bankers and businesspeople profited from the clearinghouse and reserve-sharing functions; and the president and members of the new Federal Reserve Board gained impressive powers.

The president's victory was perhaps the most notable, since the new legislation enacted a preference held by so few people in the United States at the time—the creation of a government agency with great discretion to control the supply of money and credit. Only a few midwestern senators had shown genuine enthusiasm for such an agency. Capitalists had wanted a large-scale clearinghouse managed by bankers who would own its stock; farmers had preferred, as usual, some virtually automatic mechanism to supply money and credit as needed. Both were afraid of the new Federal Reserve Board, the bankers more so than the farmers in 1913.

In December of that year, the *Commercial and Financial Chronicle* had been relieved that, given the crazy ideas batted around in Congress, things had not turned out worse. The capitalists had finally gotten the central banking system that all other industrial countries had and that the farmers had denied them for eighty years. But they got it on the farmers' terms, and the old anxiety about a politically controlled banking agency was still current in New York financial circles:

> The purpose [of the Federal Reserve Act] has not been concealed. It is to get control of the banking and credit facilities of the country with the view to putting every one on a plane of equality as far as obtaining credit and money supplies is concerned. No one doubts that the President will appoint high-minded men to the Federal Reserve Board, but what intelligent people fear is that these men may be responsible to the popular clamor and be more anxious to carry out Mr. Bryan's and Mr. Wilson's ideas of how credit facilities should be dispensed than to act in absolute fidelity to correct banking principles.[129]

The farmers, of course, were afraid that those high-minded men, likely to have banking and business connections themselves, would *not* be responsive to popular clamor. Given the choices they faced, they had opted for a new, powerful public bureaucracy, preferring, in Owen's phrase, "to trust their own president and officials rather than turn the functions of the reserve system over to the genial and attractive gentlemen who have charge of a few big banks of the country."[130] This was essentially the same choice faced on railroad regulation, and the same path was taken, with the same reservations (perhaps somewhat less intense because of the favorable experience with the Interstate Commerce Commission—the farmers, one might say, had been "state-broken" by the Interstate Commerce Act).[131] But when agrarian congressional members defended the Democratic Party's new financial creation, they were more likely to emphasize its "automatic" currency mechanism and agricultural-credit provisions than its discretionary powers. The latter were worrisome, and Rep. Oscar Callaway of Texas no doubt voiced the anxieties of many when, a few days before the House passed the Glass bill, he reminded his Democratic colleagues that they had always opposed a central bank yet were now creating one. And, he added, their faith in presidential appointment as a means of democratic control seemed very shortsighted, to say the least.

> The proponents of this measure assure us that the President will not abuse this power. . . . I am glad it was not left for me to say how absolute and far-reaching the power given by this bill to the President's board would be. . . . You, the proponents of this measure, can not answer by saying this power has got to be lodged somewhere, that it is now lodged in Wall Street, and that we are commanded by our platform to take it away from there. . . . We are commanded by the platform to obtain banking and currency accommodations on terms of absolute security to the public and under complete protection from the misuse of power. What protection have we here from the misuse of power? Faith, faith, faith; faith in man, fallible man, swept by all the passions, prejudices, and ambitions, mental misgivings, short-sightedness, and misconceptions of man. You may have such faith and confidence in the present Executive that you are willing to put such power in his hands, with an absolute faith that he will never abuse nor misuse it; but he is not always to be President. . . . When he is gone the control of this board becomes the greatest prize . . . the financial interest of this country ever . . . fought for. . . . The money trust can take advantage of these possibilities for their own interest if they see fit. You can safely count on the bankers not overlooking anything that is to their interest, and you ought not to doubt that they will take advantage of all possibilities.[132]

In the long run, Callaway's fears were better predictors of the Federal Reserve Board's tendencies than were the *Chronicle*'s. In the long run, the agrarian influence on banking policy and the course of American political development generally would be much diminished. But in the Progressive Era, the Federal Reserve Act was not just a feather in the capitalist homburg.

Farm Credit Legislation

Even though the agricultural-credit provisions of the Federal Reserve Act constituted a major victory for the farm bloc, the agrarians immediately began to push for a more extensive, government-supported credit system. In this drive, however, they were stymied by the active hostility of the president and his agriculture secretary. Wilson would not countenance "class legislation" that put government directly at the service of a single "interest." He did agree to appoint a commission to study and recommend solutions to the problem of inadequate rural credit, and from this resulted a modest bill to establish privately owned rural banking institutions under federal supervision. However, farm organizations insisted that a direct infusion of federal money was necessary to promote agricultural development in the capital-poor agricultural regions.[133]

Early in 1915, agrarian representatives risked a presidential veto to accomplish their objective. Senate passage of a government-subsidized land-bank system resulted from a surprise amendment, offered by Republican Sen. Porter McCumber of North Dakota. Democratic leaders, sure that Wilson would veto the proposal, hastily brought out a more moderate scheme backed by Henry Hollis of New Hampshire, now chairman of the Senate Banking Committee. A motion by Representative Wingo of Arkansas to substitute the McCumber plan was defeated 239 to 89, and the House went on to pass the Hollis proposal by voice vote.[134] However, the bill died when the session ended before conferees could complete their work.

Public pressure favoring a large, government-subsidized rural banking system continued to build in the interior. The demand cut across both parties and was "nearly universal in the agricultural regions."[135] Finally, with party leaders warning of the danger of alienating the midwestern farm vote in an election year, Wilson capitulated and threw his support to the rural credits bill developed by Hollis and Rep. A. F. Lever of South Carolina.[136] Though the administration and Representative Glass opposed "burdening the government" with such a measure, as Willis put it, "it was thought best to yield to radical sentiment."[137] The bill (the Federal Farm Loan Act) passed both houses by large margins in 1916. In the House, the vote was unanimous in the periphery and nearly so in the diverse trade areas, and voting participation was high in both regional delegations. Core representatives yielded to the inevitable, but their indifference led almost two-thirds to abstain on House passage.[138] In the Senate, only five votes were cast against the rural credits bill, all by core Republicans. Expressing the distaste of capital-rich New England for the program, Brandegee of Connecticut complained: "This bill will do my section of the country no good whatsoever, in my opinion. There is no demand for it there. The loans are obtainable on good farm security from the insurance companies and the savings banks and, in my opinion, this bill will not be availed of at all."[139]

The Federal Farm Loan Act created a network of twelve Federal Land

Banks, following the pattern of the Federal Reserve System. Each bank was capitalized at $750,000, with the government contributing to the startup by purchasing any stock not subscribed by the public. The banks operated under the supervision of a five-member board in the Treasury Department. Farmers, organized in cooperative farm-loan associations, could buy stock worth 5 percent of the amount they wanted to borrow, at which point they were eligible for five-year loans on their lands or improvements, at interest rates no higher than 6 percent. The Farm Loan Banks created to purchase the mortgages obtained capital by selling tax-exempt bonds, but low-interest Treasury Department loans of up to $6 million a year were authorized to meet bond-sale deficiencies.[140]

Rushed into operation by election day 1916,[141] the land-bank system became a major source of farm credit, after surviving a constitutional challenge by a group of mortgage bankers; within a decade it held mortgages worth over $1 billion.[142] The agrarians' victory on this unprecedented infusion of federal funds to the capital-starved farm regions constituted a major breakthrough in federal government policy. It was, in Harold Faulkner's judgment, "a far more important step than even the Federal Reserve Act in the breakdown of laissez-faire."[143]

Epilogue: To Whom Did the Federal Reserve Board Respond?

Before 1922–23, the Federal Reserve System had no integrating philosophy or strong sense of mission. The decentralist and real-bills theories on which the act's major proponents had relied encouraged public officials, including those on the Federal Reserve Board ("the Fed"), to conceive of the system as a public utility whose basic money, credit, and clearinghouse functions would proceed rather automatically through its regional institutions.[144] Its most important policy manipulations would be the age-old function of U.S. banking: to manage the movement of metropolitan funds into the countryside in the crop-moving season.

The first significant uses of its discretionary powers to affect monetary policy were motivated by concerns that we may describe as statist and bureaucratic, along with the banker's traditional abhorrence of inflation. A complex of decisions revolving around discount rate levels in 1919–20 composed the Fed's first colossal blunder—and in the aftermath of that blunder and the harsh criticism it provoked, the Fed began to acquire both political wisdom and an informed sense of bureaucratic mission. The principal agents of this political learning were those who suffered most from the system's malfunction and had the organization and energy to demand changes: the farmers.

Just as the Interstate Commerce Commission had to struggle with the courts to establish its bureaucratic autonomy, the Federal Reserve Board had to struggle with the Treasury Department. The motives of the latter were both statist and political, concerned with government finance and with the maintenance of electoral support for the administration. The treasury secretary was the ex-officio chair of the Federal Reserve Board, which also included his subordinate, the comptroller of the currency, and in the Wilson years, an assistant treasury secretary named by the president as "governor" (chief administrative officer). These constituted a "Treasury bloc" on the board. It was opposed in the early years by a more conservative and autonomy-seeking faction of the board consisting of the Wall Street financier Warburg, the economist Adolph Miller, and the railroad president Frederick A. Delano. An Alabama banker held the swing vote.[145]

Treasury Department officials dominated the board's actions soon after its organization, successfully pressuring the Fed to help finance the war by keeping interest rates low. When the war ended, the Treasury Department pressed for continuing low rates in support of another Victory Loan issue to cover the war-generated deficit;[146] in addition, the treasury secretary (now Carter Glass) surely recognized that a continued economic expansion would be more propitious for the Democratic Party than would a monetary contraction in the 1920 election year.

As concern mounted about inflation and, in particular, about speculation in the New York stock market, Glass advocated that the Fed use its discretion over discounts to curb credit for stock purchases but not for other purposes— a discrimination that had been practiced during the war period. Benjamin Strong, governor of the New York Reserve Bank, opposed such "direct action," arguing that there should be only one, higher discount rate and no distinction among the uses of credit.[147] The New York Reserve Bank insisted on raising its rate, and finally the Treasury Department and the Federal Reserve Board assented in late 1919. There followed a general rise to 6 percent in early 1920 and, led by the New York Reserve Bank, an increase to the then remarkably high level of 7 percent in June. The result was a collapse of prices and a sharp rise in bank failures as the economy fell into recession. Despite rising demands that the Fed ease up on its deflation policy, Governor Strong insisted that high interest rates should be maintained until wage rates, which had resisted the general decline, had also fallen decisively.[148] The New York and other reserve banks were also influenced by their desire to rebuild the system's reserves, which had fallen during the war years to a low level vis-à-vis deposit and note liabilities. High rates were thus maintained into 1921, despite their severe depressing effect on prices and employment.[149]

The prime mover in the Federal Reserve System's swing from appendage of the Treasury Department to "public-be-damned" autonomy in 1920–21 was Benjamin Strong. A prominent New York investment banker of great intelligence and conservative vision, Strong had been a leading supporter of the Aldrich central-bank plan and a powerful opponent of the Glass-Owen bill. However, when he saw that passage was inevitable, Strong counseled other bankers not to try to sabotage the new system. In late 1914, on the entreaties of Paul Warburg and Henry Davison, he agreed to take the helm of the New York Reserve Bank and help establish the federal banking institution. Strong's acumen and the vast financial resources controlled by the New York Reserve Bank assured him a leading role in the development and operation of the system.[150]

Though the twelve regional banks had the power to conduct their own open-market purchases of bills and securities, by 1915 they were already calling on the experienced and strategically located New York Reserve Bank to manage these operations for them. In the face of Treasury Department complaints that the banks' uncoordinated purchases and sales of government securities interfered with its financial planning, the governors of the regional banks formed an open-market committee, with Strong as permanent chair, to recommend purchase and sale strategies. In practice, the committee made other important policy recommendations as well, and Strong's prestige and power gave them considerable weight. Jealous of the governors' committee and prodded by the Treasury Department, the Federal Reserve Board reconstituted the body (with the same membership) as an arm of the board rather than of the regional banks. However, Strong quickly became the dominant force on the new open-market committee as well.[151]

Warburg, as it turned out, had been right when he had warned Glass and Willis that a highly decentralized system capped by a relatively weak board would do little to thwart, and might even encourage, New York's continued dominance of the nation's banking. To Glass's disgust, it was not long before Europeans came to think of the New York Reserve Bank as *the* U.S. central bank and of Strong as the governor of the entire system.[152] Strong's close friendship with the head of the Bank of England and his efforts to nurture the international gold standard and link the U.S. and European economies fortified that impression.[153]

The three-cornered power struggle among the Federal Reserve Board, the Treasury Department, and the regional banks (of which the New York Reserve Bank was the dominant force) produced an unwise credit acceleration policy in 1919 and a "too late, too long" braking in 1920–21. The severity of the recession provoked a strong public outcry against the Fed, led by farm organizations and periphery congressmen. Fuel was added to the fire when the former comptroller of the currency charged that the board, the bankers' Advisory Council, and certain banker directors of the regional banks in 1920 had conspired to achieve a rapid deflation and to divert millions of dollars to New York banks, oblivious to the injury caused to farmers and the country banks.[154]

Having promised relief to the farmer during the 1920 election campaign, President Warren Harding and his treasury secretary pressed the board for lower interest rates, against the opposition of the New York Reserve Bank.[155] Strong wrote his friend Montagu Norman at the Bank of England:

> Enormous pressure has been felt in Washington from the agricultural sections of the country that measures be taken to ease up credit conditions. So far as I can discover, the demand comes from no other class than those engaged in agriculture. They made an impressive showing and their complaints reached all classes of congressmen and executive officers of the government right up to the President. This was all put to me most earnestly by my friends and associates in Washington, and the feeling generally prevailed that the New York Bank was causing the deadlock.[156]

Though clearly reluctant, the New Yorker finally withdrew his opposition in May 1921, and the discount rate at the New York Reserve Bank was lowered to 6.5 percent. Strong explained to Norman, "A bullheaded resistance in this situation is always liable to invite political retaliation, and I finally concluded that the wisest course was to meet, in part at least, the demand for lower rates." Subsequent reductions brought discount rates down to 4.5 percent by November 1921.[157]

The threats of political retaliation loomed very large over the Fed in the summer of Strong's strategic retreat. In Congress a Joint Commission of Agricultural Inquiry, created in January, opened hearings on monetary policy and the farm situation in July and August, at which representatives of farm organizations and Fed and Treasury Department officials were almost the only witnesses.[158] A new Rural Credits Act, passed in 1923 to ease the farmers' long-term credit problems, contained another mandate for a far-reaching inquiry into the policies of the Federal Reserve banks.[159]

Strong's biographer writes, "There can be little doubt that he came to be deeply distressed by the plight of those who had been injured [by Fed policy], especially farmers." But, the author adds in an understated addendum, Strong "was also probably influenced somewhat by the large number of 'cheap money' proposals generated by the deflation."[160] Between December 6, 1920, and December 7, 1924, fifty-nine bills were introduced in the Senate and seventy-five in the House to amend the Federal Reserve Act. Seventy-three percent of the senators offering these bills and 75 percent of the bills introduced in that chamber came from the periphery. In the House, the comparable figures were 73 and 56 percent. The bills sought to expand agricultural credit mechanisms, to limit the height of discount rates (to 5 percent), to prohibit "usurious" interest rates at member banks, to scrutinize the reserve system's finances, to open Federal Reserve System meetings to the public, and to prescribe distribution of the system's income.[161] Among the bills that passed was a 1922 measure repealing the clause that required at least two members of the board to have banking experience and enlarging the board to eight members in order to add an agricultural representative (a dairy-farm spokesman was duly appointed).[162] In the face of opposition from farmers, President Harding also refused reappointment to a Federal Reserve Board member associated with the deflation policy.[163]

The discretion-limiting bills introduced by agrarian members of Congress would have tied Fed policy to the congressional majority and would have placed its policy-making squarely in the national political process—something all bureaucracies, but particularly this banking institution, abhorred. Early in 1922 the New York governor wrote his friend at the Bank of England that "the most dangerous menace now before the Federal Reserve, and the country generally," was the formation of a political coalition advocating easy credit.[164]

It was in this context that the Federal Reserve System between 1922 and 1924 began to acquire its new wisdom and purpose. The political outcry of 1920–23 brought home to the Fed the consequences of its actions for the nation's economy and, as a result, for national politics. The outcry encouraged Federal Reserve System officials, with Strong in the lead, to develop theories and concerted action mechanisms that would help to maintain a smooth economic growth, avoiding episodes of wild inflation and sharp economic downturns. The Fed was prompted to use its credit and money creation powers (chiefly discount rates and open-market operations) for the purpose of promoting "high and stable levels of business activity and employment and stability of price levels . . . [and] curbing excessive uses of credit for stock market speculation."[165] The new orientation was first clearly manifested in 1924 when, in a recession much less severe than that of 1920–21, Strong promoted an aggressive policy of open-market purchases and discount-rate reductions to spur recovery.[166] The Fed thus embarked on a new era of "positive regulation," with a degree of success that earned it a rather high level of public approval in the years before 1929.[167] The development of its bureaucratic capacity and mission is today generally perceived as a natural evolution in a still-young public agency, or as the fortunate result of Strong's leadership. However, it seems clear that the Fed's creativity was a response to political necessity—and that the mothers of invention were largely agrarian.

Bureaucratic learning was not linear, however. In 1927 the board embarked on an expansionary policy, urged by mild recessionary indications and by the preferences of Strong. Maintaining constant communication with European central bankers, Strong desired to ease credit in order to help the Bank of England improve its reserve position.[168] Unfortunately, the Fed waited too long to tighten credit, and once again the New York Reserve Bank opposed any targeted actions to restrict credit for stock speculation. And again, when the Fed began braking the supply of money and credit, it cut back too sharply and too long, exacerbating the collapse of the stock market and the ensuing depression. Strong's admirers, numerous among economists and historians, speculate that had he lived (the New York Reserve Bank governor died in 1928), Strong would have recognized the danger and would have applied credit-easing measures earlier; however, it appears that the Fed was generally following Strong's policies from 1927 well into 1929.[169]

The widespread perception of the Fed's drift and incompetence and its domination by the New York Reserve Bank made new legislation inevitable after 1932. On its own, Congress acted to insure bank deposits and divorce commercial and investment banking. The congressional agrarians also rallied to the Roosevelt administration's bill to regulate the stock market. When Marriner Eccles, the enterprising new Fed governor, proposed in 1935 that the Federal Reserve Board be strengthened vis-à-vis emergency lending, discount rates, open-market operations, and loans for stock purchases, the agrarians went along.[170] It seemed to them still the only politically acceptable way to wrench control of banking from the New York financiers whose sympathies had so seldom lain with farmers or workers. The new laws, of course, did not produce a "democratic" Federal Reserve System. Rather, with the exception of presidential pressure to mitigate the electoral liabilities of deflation and, on occasion, to pump up the economy during election periods,[171] the Federal Reserve System is among the two or three least democratically accountable central banks in the democratic world. Along with the Pentagon, the Fed stands as the most "autonomous" of American bureaucracies, in the sense of claims to possession of complex and important expertise and removal from popular pressure. It was the passage of agrarian radicalism from the American political scene that permitted this evolution.[172]

8

Antitrust and the Structure of the Marketing Network

Resolved: That we are opposed to all combinations of capital,
in trusts or otherwise, to arbitrarily control the markets of this
country to the detriment of our own productive industries.
Proclamation of the Farmer's Congress,
Montgomery, Alabama, 1889

Antitrust law in the United States—framed in the Sherman, Clayton, and Federal Trade Commission Acts and their subsequent amendments—established a policy toward industrial concentration and business practices that set the United States apart from other industrial democracies. In Europe and Japan, large-scale industry was long perceived as a national asset, and although particular abuses might be condemned at the government's discretion, emotional antibigness rhetoric and statutory prohibition of monopolistic practices were and are largely absent.[1]

The American enthusiasm for antitrust has shown a marked periodicity, however. Waves of antimonopoly feeling crested in the 1880s and the Progressive Era (particularly in 1909–14) and, with the exception of minor ripples in the late 1930s and late 1940s, did not emerge again until the 1970s, only to subside again in the 1980s. The laws that marked the high points of the first two antitrust cycles were the Sherman Antitrust Act (1890) and the Clayton Antitrust and Federal Trade Commission Acts (1914).

The search for an explanation for the characteristic features of American antitrust law—its legalistic and punitive character, its supporting ethos of potent symbolism regarding the evils of concentrated economic power, and its periodicity—leads, once again, to the fundamental, economically centered forces that have shaped American political development. All three characteristics have their roots in the endemic competition between distinct and antithetical economic systems that characterized the American experience in the late nineteenth and early twentieth centuries. Antitrust policy, with its multi-industry jurisdiction and generalized thrust against concentrated, presumably exploitative economic power distilled this conflict in a unique way. The Amer-

267

American antimonopoly impulse, rooted in agrarian republican ideology, was sustained by the antagonism of the nonindustrial periphery toward the marauding rail, industrial, and financial corporations of the northeastern–Great Lakes manufacturing belt. The antitrust law of the Populist and Progressive Eras grew out of the agrarian effort to restrain those predations and the regional maldistribution of wealth they entailed.

Antimonopoly Politics: Origins and Early Victories, 1880–1896

In the 1880s, farmers already reeling under the burden of high interest rates, declining farm prices, and railroad rate abuses were struck with another ominous business development: a wave of industrial consolidations. The first great "trust"—Standard Oil—had been formed out of forty separate companies in 1882, but imitation of this new corporate structure proceeded slowly until business recovery from fitful depression got under way in 1887.[2] The new national mass-production industries then began to combine in earnest—first horizontally, in explicit attempts to eliminate competition, and then vertically. When state court decisions applying common-law antimonopoly principles called into doubt the legality of the trust, lawmakers in New Jersey discovered a way to enrich the state treasury and oblige consolidation-minded industrialists at the same time. An 1889 statute allowed companies incorporated in New Jersey to hold the stock of other corporations, both within and outside the state. New York soon passed similar legislation, and Connecticut, Maine, and West Virginia competed with their own statutes to attract the great combinations.[3]

Small producers in the hinterland, who derived little or no benefit from the tariff and sold their produce in a highly competitive market, were now compelled to buy from and sell to giant oligopolies like American Harvester, American Tobacco, Swift, and Standard Oil—not to mention the transportation combines on which the farmers depended. In the South, particularly, the antimonopoly impulse was fervid and bitter, intensified by the region's long perception of itself as an economic colony exploited by northern capitalists.[4] The antitrust agitation that led to passage of the Sherman Antitrust Act in 1890 was clearly rooted in the political crusades of the Grange, the Farmers' Alliance, and the Antimonopoly, Greenback, and Union Labor Parties of the 1870s and 1880s.[5] A national antitrust law was the logical sequel to the Interstate Commerce Act of 1887, indicating the broadening of antimonopoly concerns that presaged the Populist and free-silver movements of the 1890s. Though it is true that, by 1890, the agrarian revulsion against trusts was shared by a broad array of other groups nationwide—including some small businesspeople, journalists, and assorted middle-class "reformers"—the agrarians numbered in the millions (not thousands) and their votes could not be discounted by their political representatives. In addition to the demands of farmer organizations, the geographic patterns of sponsorship of antitrust bills and the existence of state antimonopoly laws before 1890 also testify to the agrarian origins of the antimonopoly impulse.[6]

That impulse was sharply at odds with the social Darwinism and laissez-faire ideologies that prevailed in intellectual circles, in the "high" Protestant clergy, and among the protagonists of industrial consolidation. Prominent economists and capitalists agreed that industrial concentration was both inevitable and beneficial and that attempts at legal prohibition were doomed to failure.[7]

Leading the charge against monopoly, the agrarians had no clear idea of the specific methods that were best suited to curtailing "trusts." Nor could anyone predict with assurance what the Supreme Court, becoming steadily more intolerant of business regulation, would accept. There was, however, some evidence on the techniques used by particular trusts. An 1888 inquiry by the New York State Senate shed light on the activities of combinations in the sugar, oil, and eleven other industries. In Congress, the Democratic House had conducted in the same year an investigation of Standard Oil and the sugar, whiskey, and cotton-bagging trusts, and in 1890 a select committee of the Senate opened an investigation of the Chicago-based meat combines. These investigations undoubtedly contributed to the momentum for a trust bill.[8]

In 1888, both Sens. John Sherman of Ohio and John Reagan of Texas introduced antitrust bills, of which Reagan's bill was the more elaborate and better drafted. These became the two leading drafts for congressional consideration, although agrarian representatives introduced about two dozen antitrust bills in the 50th and 51st Congresses. The remedies proposed by southern representatives tended to be specific and severe, whereas Sherman and other northern Republicans who contributed to the ultimate form of the law were inclined to rely on more ambiguous common-law formulations. In the House, for example, Texas Rep. Charles Culberson proposed the most popular Democratic remedy—denial of all tariff protection for trust-made products. Senator Reagan's bill contained a highly specific definition of "trust" and applied criminal penalties to its participants. Sen. James Z. George of Mississippi continually criticized Sherman's bill as unconstitutional (in part anticipating the Supreme Court's distinction between manufacturing and commerce) and, even if constitutional, ineffective. George proposed that trust products be banned from interstate commerce and denied use of the U.S. courts to collect their debts. He also proposed that the antitrust law incorporate a clause specifically exempting labor unions and farm cooperatives from the act's jurisdiction and that Congress pass a constitutional amendment to prohibit combinations in restraint of production as well as trade.[9] Unfortunately perhaps for effective antitrust regulation, none of these suggestions except the provision for criminal penalties were incorporated into the antitrust law of 1890.

Bills introduced by Senators George and Reagan, as well as by a number of representatives, languished in the Republican-led Senate and House committees, but Senator Sherman's Finance Committee reported his revised bill to the Senate floor early in 1890, and debate began in earnest. The willingness of the Republican Old Guard, staunch defenders of unrestrained capitalism, to suffer passage of an antitrust act, was testimony to the strength of public demand for such action in the agrarian areas. Some scholars have also suggested that the Sherman Act was a quid pro quo to win farm-state Republican backing for the strongly protectionist McKinley Tariff bill. With the Democrats making such a noise about the connection between tariffs and trusts, it was no longer politic to raise the former without some apparent commitment to control the latter.[10]

When it became clear that the Republican leadership would permit an antitrust bill to be passed, the agrarians pushed for a strongly worded measure. In the Senate, a Reagan amendment imposing harsh criminal penalties on the trust-makers passed 34–12, with the southern, midwestern, and western farm states arrayed against a mostly New England, New York, New Jersey, and Ohio opposition.[11] Reagan's proposal allowing antitrust suits to be filed in both state and federal courts passed by voice vote, as did an amendment by Republican Sen. John J. Ingalls of Kansas to suppress dealings in options and futures.[12] Senator George of Mississippi and Sen. John T. Morgan of Alabama argued that the bill as written could be interpreted by the courts to suppress labor unions and farmers' organizations, persuading Sherman to accept George's clause exempting these groups from the act's jurisdiction.[13] Sen. Richard Coke of Texas proposed an amendment to substitute for all of Sherman's bill *except* the George and Ingalls amendments (a) a specific trust definition; (b) a ban on interstate shipment of trust-made products; and (c) tariff suspension. His amendment was tabled 26 to 16, with only farm-state senators in opposition.[14]

Subsequently, with apparently few senators present, a number of qualifying amendments were incorporated into the bill, transforming it into an ineffective hodgepodge.[15] At this point Senator George, a member of the Judiciary Committee, pleaded with the Senate to refer the bill to his committee for redrafting. Friends of the bill agreed, but fearing that Judiciary Committee conservatives would stall the bill, they instructed the committee to report within twenty days. The referral proposal passed 31 to 28. Twenty-one of the thirty-one senators voting for the motion represented southern and western states (along with four others from the then overwhelmingly rural states of Maryland, Delaware, and Michigan). The opponents were a mixed, mostly Republican group of northeastern conservatives (including Judiciary Committee Chairman George F. Edmunds of Vermont and fellow member George Hoar of Massachusetts), midwestern farm-state senators (including Ingalls) who probably feared loss of the futures prohibition, and Sherman himself.[16]

There has been considerable debate, among both scholars and the politicians originally involved, about the "authorship" of the Sherman Act. Most of the drafting of the "clean" bill in the Senate Judiciary Committee fell, logically enough, to the Republicans who constituted the committee majority. Both Hans Thorelli and William Letwin attribute the wording of most of the bill's sections to Edmunds, with George and Hoar being responsible for one section each.[17] However, Edmunds and Hoar had shown no prior enthusiasm for an antitrust law and had both voted against referral to the Judiciary Committee. Edmunds particularly opposed the southern senators' attempt to exempt labor and farm co-ops and probably played a major role in scrapping that clause. The core Republicans ultimately consented to reworking the bill into a plausible antitrust law acceptable to agrarian antimonopolists of both parties but without the specificity and severity of sanctions championed by the agrarians. Senators George, Reagan, and George Vest (D, Missouri, also a member of the Judiciary Committee) played major roles in strengthening the bill, and Sherman, for whom the bill was named, deserved more credit for fostering antitrust legislation than did the Judiciary Committee Republicans who reluctantly accepted the task of rewriting his bill.[18]

The bill reported from the Judiciary panel was practically identical to the version enacted a few months later. The Senate defeated attempts by Reagan and George to strengthen the criminal penalties and damages sections and to reinsert dual state-federal court jurisdiction,[19] and it passed the bill 52 to 1 (the sole dissenter was Rufus Blodgett of New Jersey, a banker, railroad man, and Democrat). In the House, debate was led by Democratic Representative Culberson of Texas, although the House Judiciary Committee chairman was Ezra Taylor, a Republican from Ohio. The House passed the Senate Judiciary Committee bill with only one amendment—a provision sponsored by Rep. Richard Bland (D, Missouri) and strongly backed by the agrarians—to specifically ban anticompetitive acts by railroads and meatpacking firms. When

the Senate proved unwilling to accept Bland's amendment, the House receded, and the Senate-constructed bill passed with no dissents on June 20,
1890.[20]

The Sherman Act outlawed "every contract, combination . . . or conspiracy in restraint of trade or commerce" both interstate and foreign. It provided
for confiscation of the offending combination's property and incorporated
Reagan's criminal penalties—a fine of up to $5,000 and a jail term of up to
one year—for those attempting to restrain trade or create a monopoly. In
another improvement on Sherman's original bill, the act gave the U.S. attorney general and district attorneys the duty to institute court proceedings to
prevent and restrain violations of the act, as well as allowing for a degree of
self-enforcement by permitting individuals injured by restraints of trade to
sue for triple damages plus attorney's fees. The act brought into national
public law, in an unequivocal formulation accompanied by criminal penalties,
common-law strictures against monopoly. Yet, as its sponsors pointed out,
it was anchored in the commerce power of the Constitution and did not rest
entirely on ascertaining intent. The Sherman Act was, in Letwin's words,
"as good an antitrust law as the Congress of 1890 could have devised."[21] The
agrarian representatives had failed in their attempts to make the bill more
specific and punitive, to extend its scope, to provide for dual state-federal
court jurisdiction, and to exclude labor unions and farmer cooperatives from
its purview. They could, nonetheless, take credit for the establishment of an
embryonic antitrust policy, at a time when Europe was moving in the opposite
direction on the issue of public policy toward concentrated economic power.

The Sherman Act's major flaws soon became apparent. Because Judiciary
Committee Republicans insisted that George's amendment was unnecessary,
the Sherman Act did not explicitly exempt labor from prosecution against
attempted restraints of trade. A second, less avoidable weakness was Justice
Department enforcement. Given the great expense and difficulties incurred
by farmers or small businesspeople who might take on the trust magnates,
only government action was a realistic remedy for monopoly. When the administration was disinterested, as was the case for at least the next decade,
combinations in restraint of trade were practically unimpeded.

President Benjamin Harrison had taken no part in the drafting of the Sherman Act and scarcely seemed to have noticed its passage. His successor, Grover Cleveland, represented the Democratic Party's conservative northern
wing, which appeared yoked to the periphery only by a common view on the
tariff. His attorney general, Richard Olney, was openly contemptuous of the
act and discouraged district attorneys in the field from initiating prosecutions.

Like his predecessor, who had used the act to enjoin a general strike in New Orleans, Olney found the antitrust law applicable to labor activities that might interfere with interstate commerce.[22]

Without presidential leadership, and with a minuscule Washington staff to enforce it, the law had little effect on business behavior. The Justice Department instituted only nine antitrust cases in the first four years and only seven more by the end of the decade.[23] Most initiatives originated with district attorneys in the field, but the Justice Department's disinterest (or active discouragement) allowed important cases to be ignored or to go to court poorly prepared. In one such case, the Supreme Court delivered an apparent coup de grâce. Decided in 1895, *U.S. v. E. C. Knight* threatened to emasculate the statute, finding that it could not reach the American Sugar Refining Company's near-total monopoly of U.S. sugar manufacture because the contracts under which the trust was assembled concerned only "production" and not "interstate commerce."[24]

Core Political Hegemony, Accelerated Economic Concentration, and Antitrust Revival, 1897–1912

William McKinley's presidential victory in 1896 set the stage for a second and greater wave of capital consolidation. The merger movement had slowed dramatically from 1894 through 1896 for a number of reasons, including the business depression, anxiety over the Sherman Act, and the lower Wilson-Gorman Tariff levels. The election of 1896 was the signal that capital had been waiting for. Populism was defeated, the Supreme Court had severely limited the applicability of the Sherman Act, and the Republican platform had not mentioned trusts at all. When the Republicans came to Washington in 1897, they immediately redeemed their unabashed commitment to protectionism and, in the Dingley Tariff, raised duties on manufactured goods to historic highs. The way was now clear for a massive resumption of the consolidation movement. From 1897 to 1903, frenzied trust-building, undertaken more often by the great financial houses than by the manufacturers themselves, transformed American industrial structure. The merger movement peaked in 1901 with its most elephantine example: the formation, as a New Jersey holding company, of the world's first billion-dollar corporation, United States Steel. J. P. Morgan's most ambitious project, U.S. Steel absorbed several existing trusts (which themselves had swallowed hundreds of once-independent companies) and controlled half of American production. A few years later U.S. Steel would buy up a budding southern competitor, Tennessee Coal and Iron, and through its "Pittsburgh Plus" pricing, consign the

Birmingham, Alabama, steel works to permanent peripheral status. U.S. Steel was but one of the great industrial combinations put together between January 1897 and 1903. The list of new "trusts" also included Eastman Kodak, Amalgamated Copper, Borden's, Quaker Oats, United Shoe Machinery, International Harvester, United Fruit, and two smaller steel trusts: Jones and Laughlin and Republic Steel. Over one thousand firms disappeared in mergers in 1899 alone. A few years later, over one hundred industrial fields were each dominated by a single firm.[25] This awesome change in industrial structure and the incumbent party's unwillingness to do anything about it finally lifted the antitrust issue above the tableau of largely agrarian economic grievances. Now the issue became a distinct and urgent question of government action.

The familiar agents of antitrust reasserted themselves with increased vigor. The Democratic Party platform of 1900 committed the party to "unceasing warfare" against private monopoly. In Congress, a number of bills were introduced to make the Sherman Act more effective, the great majority of them sponsored by agrarian representatives.[26] State legislatures and governors, particularly in the South and West, zealously attacked "foreign" trusts.[27]

There were new elements as well. Outside the farm states, significant local antitrust actions were brought against out-of-state corporations. Ohio, for example, took on Standard Oil, and New York filed suits against the sugar, tobacco, and coal trusts. In the Northeast, however, neither formal law nor public opinion supported a vigorous generalized antitrust campaign. The middle class, though often appalled by corporate excesses, was cross-pressured by the job opportunities and stockholding benefits provided by big business. Labor leaders found credible the contention that restraint of "destructive" competition held advantage for workers, and they resented the use of the Sherman Act against strikes and boycotts. Thus, the AFL gave no support to the antitrust movement.[28] Without strong working- or middle-class support, core capital's opposition to antimonopoly legislation pulled core political representatives to the conservative position.

However, in the face of growing public anxiety about industrial concentration, intellectuals and businesspeople were compelled to acknowledge the issue. The Civic Federation of Chicago convened a large conference on the trust problem in the fall of 1899. The much-publicized conference was attended by leading political and academic figures and delegations sent by various states. As the *New York Times* reported it, the thrust of the "scientific" testimony at Chicago was the familiar opinion that industrial concentration was an inevitable and probably beneficial development. The "unscientific" testimony from the state and movement delegations was in quite another vein:

With the progress of the speaking it became evident that many of the delegates had come with firm convictions for or against trade combinations. The speech of Mr. Wooten of Texas, delivered in the afternoon, attacking trusts in a merciless manner, aroused the wildest enthusiasm in the ranks of the labor representatives and the delegations from many Western and Southern states, while the Easterners generally smiled critically and kept their arms folded.[29]

The Republican Party platform of 1900 subscribed to the easterners' view: condemning the occasional abuses of "bad" trusts, the party nevertheless recognized the "necessity and propriety of the honest cooperation of capital to meet new conditions."[30] In 1903, the House passed, without dissent, a modest strengthening bill sponsored by Republican Rep. Charles Littlefield, but Senate Republicans refused to bring the bill to the floor.[31]

Theodore Roosevelt became the first president to throw the weight of his office behind the Sherman Act and to demonstrate that the act had teeth after all. His initiatives, beginning with the Northern Securities prosecution in 1902, "institutionalized" antitrust policy (in Thorelli's words). Prosecutions initiated by the Department of Justice rose in number from three under McKinley to forty-two in Roosevelt's seven years.[32] But Roosevelt's highly selective policy, based on a distinction between "good" and "bad" trusts, maximized his discretionary power. He was in no way opposed to corporate concentration per se but was determined that the national government—or at least *his office*—possess power that matched (and, in a showdown, exceeded) that of the corporate giants. He supported only new legislation that entailed generous grants of executive discretion, and he condemned the Sherman Act itself because "its full enforcement would destroy the business of the country."[33]

The centerpiece of Roosevelt's strategy was the creation of the Bureau of Corporations (a component of the new Department of Commerce and Labor) with powers to gather information on which to base decisions to prosecute. The enabling act incorporated a vague mandate allowing the president to suppress data he preferred not to make public. Southern Democrats failed in their attempts to give the bureau more-detailed investigatory power and to make more of its information public. Nevertheless, even while urging a discretionary softening of the antitrust law, Roosevelt initiated three dozen prosecutions, including charges against the unpopular corporate giants Standard Oil, American Tobacco, and the Beef Trust.[34] The new executive vigor continued, with less fanfare but more-substantive results, in the administration of William Howard Taft, dampening some of the demand for additional legislation. This belated enforcement could not, of course, reverse the impact of the massive combination movement that had preceded it. But it did slow the pace of economic concentration and, in a few cases, achieved a partial dismantling of industrial combines.[35]

As presidents discovered that jousting with corporate giants produced favorable public reaction and expanded executive power, corporate leaders began genuinely to fear the use of national law against their economic designs. To reconcile their intense distaste for competition with the now widely accepted need for a government role in determining the structure of the economy, business leaders began to agitate for revision of the Sherman Act to render it less threatening. In 1907 the National Civic Federation (NCF) called a new conference on the trust problem, at which speakers condemned the evils of competition and urged amendment of the antitrust law in light of "existing economic reality." Subsequently, an NCF subcommittee (which included NCF President Seth Low, U.S. Steel President Elbert Gary, economist Jeremiah Jenks of Cornell, and Morgan partner George Perkins) drew up amending legislation in consultation with House and Senate committee leaders, the head of the Bureau of Corporations, and the president. The bill, on which hearings were held in 1908, constituted the first formal presentation of a regulatory program potentially acceptable to big business. Its key provision allowed corporations, on disclosure of certain information, to register with the Bureau of Corporations. Registered businesses could then submit to the bureau, for its approval, copies of agreements made with other businesses. If the bureau found the proposed restraints "reasonable," or if it failed to come to a decision in thirty days, the government forfeited the right to prosecute under the Sherman Act. The proposal, called the Hepburn bill after its House sponsor, would also have legalized railroad pooling, dropped the triple damages penalty in favor of actual damages only, and granted amnesty for past restraint-of-trade offenses. As a concession to labor—Samuel Gompers was affiliated with the NCF and was involved in early discussions of the bill—the Hepburn bill also limited the applicability of the Sherman Act in labor disputes.[36]

Such a transformation of the antitrust law fit Roosevelt's conception of a desirable national response to the trust problem: a program that allowed the "inevitable" march toward industrial concentration to proceed under the thoughtful supervision of the federal executive—whose responsibility it would be to guard against abusive methods and "unnatural" monopoly. This was the crux of the New Nationalist position on the trust problem; it apparently enjoyed wide support among intellectuals and drew some backing from corporate and financial leaders in the industrial North. However, business objections to the modest labor provisions and fears of the vast executive discretion that Roosevelt insisted on incorporating into the NCF measure soon dissipated Republican support for the bill. It is doubtful that the bill ever had much support in Congress.[37]

Meanwhile, the periphery party had devised a very different program. The Democratic platform of 1908, constructed by William Jennings Bryan and his allies over the objections of the eastern conservative wing, advocated vigorous enforcement of a Sherman Act amended to include specific prohibitions against price discrimination and interlocking directorates, along with provisions safeguarding labor unions. It also called for federal licensing of interstate corporations above a certain size and denial of licenses to corporations controlling over 50 percent of production in their lines or capitalized with watered stock.[38] Thus severity, specificity, and a preference for what the New Nationalists derided as "atomistic competition" marked the periphery approach to the "trust problem," in contrast to the Roosevelt program's reliance on discretionary executive (and judicial) supervision of an increasingly concentrated industrial economy. Divergent attitudes toward centralization of enforcement also distinguished the core and periphery positions. Unwilling to leave the regulation of corporate behavior to the national executive and courts, the agrarians pushed for expansion of their states' powers to protect local citizens and businesses from the economic giants. In the 61st Congress, for example, rural representatives made several attempts to restrict the ability of corporations to have suits against them removed from state to federal courts on grounds of diverse citizenship. On the resulting votes, a dozen or so progressive Republicans joined the mainly periphery Democrats to back the "states' rights" (and presumably stronger) position on suits against corporations.[39]

The antitrust drive gained further momentum in 1911–12 as a result of two significant events: the achievement of a House majority by the periphery party;[40] and the Supreme Court's decisions in the Standard Oil and American Tobacco cases. In its decisions, the Court found for the government but without endorsing the government's argument that the Sherman Act banned (as the words said) *all* contracts or conspiracies in restraint of trade. Rather, the court argued that "the words 'restraint of trade' at common law and in the laws of this country at the time of the adoption of the Antitrust Act" applied only to actions that "operated to the prejudice of the public interest by *unduly* restricting competition" or which, by the purpose or nature of the act committed, "*injuriously* restrained trade" (emphases added).[41] In these decisions, the

Court reversed its recent willingness to entertain a stricter interpretation of the law (an interpretation that had been manifested in the *Trans Missouri Freight, Joint Traffic Assn., Addyston Pipe* and *Northern Securities* cases of 1898–1903) and once again threw into doubt the ability of the Sherman Act to reach large industrial combines.[42]

The "rule of reason" enunciated by the Court fit comfortably into the New Nationalist view of antitrust policy and found Taft and Roosevelt in agreement. For hard-nosed agrarians, however, the rule of reason misconstrued the Sherman Act and threatened to emasculate it. Bills to reverse the Court's interpretation were immediately introduced by Democratic Reps. William Smith of Texas, William A. Oldfield of Arizona, James Reed of Missouri, and Adolph J. Sabath of Illinois and Sens. Thomas P. Gore of Oklahoma and Charles A. Culberson of Texas. Only one Republican, Sen. Wesley L. Jones of Washington, introduced a similar bill.[43] Although there seemed to be faint prospect of enacting strengthening amendments while the Republicans held the Senate and the White House, the House Democrats prepared the way with a series of investigations targeted at U.S. Steel, the American Sugar Refining Company, and the banking, beef, and shipping "trusts."

House and Senate committees held hearings on proposed antitrust amendments in 1911 and 1912. Testimony at the hearings revealed sharply diverging positions on the proper governmental response to economic concentration. Elbert Gary, Seth Low, and George Perkins advocated federal licensing and the establishment of an executive commission under the president to oversee business consolidations and trade agreements designed to overcome "ruinous competition." Repeating the apparent consensus in their profession, prominent economists argued that industrial concentration should not be discouraged by government policy. They and business spokesmen concurred that federal incorporation and a new trade commission could remedy whatever abuses might accompany concentration.[44]

At the other end of the spectrum, agrarian representatives adamantly opposed federal administrative control of licensing and trade agreements and continued to advocate statutory specification and stronger sanctions. The most detailed presentation of the periphery position was given by John Sharp Williams of Mississippi, formerly Democratic minority leader in the House and now a senator. Williams condemned "Hamiltonian" proposals for trust regulation by bureau. Although the Democratic platform only a few years earlier had advocated federal licensing of corporations in interstate commerce, the agrarians (particularly the southerners) were now having second thoughts. Their licensing proposal had prescribed specific standards and apparently automatic denial for corporations above a certain size, as well as for those corporations found guilty of stock watering or antitrust violations. Now the new enthusiasm of big business and Republican presidents for federal incorporation threatened to produce a discretionary federal licensing mechanism that would forestall state antitrust efforts. Williams thus proposed, instead, that a set of minimum requirements be contained in all state charters granted to corporations that desired to do business across state borders. Corporations that violated charter provisions (which would include prohibitions against interlocking directorates, watered stock, and price discrimination) would be denied access to interstate commerce. In addition to the specification of punishable abuses, Williams proposed heavier fines and expanded rights for aggrieved parties to sue.[45]

Both core and periphery approaches would have resulted in an expansion and centralization of national regulatory power. A key issue separating the two strategies was the scope of executive discretion, but behind that issue lay expectations about the substantive outcomes of antitrust policies. Both core capitalists and periphery agrarians seemed to anticipate that a discretionary bureaucracy would condone anticompetitive agreements and stock purchases. Whether this sympathy for the largest core firms would arise from presidential influence or through recruitment to the agency from the ranks of a largely sympathetic business and academic community was not clear. Experience with national regulatory bureaucracy was, of course, very thin. But periphery representatives could point to the early Interstate Commerce Commission for evidence that even a relatively well-intentioned agency could be reduced to impotence in the absence of specific statutory standards (given courts hostile to its regulatory purpose). Thus, the agrarian position, as voiced by Bryan and Democratic congressional leaders, would have specified competitive abuses in the law and denied offenders tariff protection and access to interstate markets—or, at the least, it would have imposed hefty fines and jail terms. The first preference of core capitalists was to be unconstrained by government in their anticompetitive activities, but fearful of statutory specificity as a weapon in the hands of agrarian radicals bent on dismembering large enterprise, they advocated a discretionary bureaucracy along the lines sketched by the National Civic Federation (Hepburn) bill of 1908. Two such bitterly polarized policy alternatives invited attempts at compromise.

The intermediate position that emerged in 1911–12 sought to discourage the most flagrant competitive abuses and to restrain further economic concentration but not to threaten all existing consolidations. It would, as the periphery Democrats proposed, ban certain specific practices that led to monopoly, but it would not legislatively reverse the rule of reason and apply the Sherman Act to *all* restraints of trade. Instead, the judgmental power would be transferred to an independent administrative body that would be composed of people both more expert and more impartial than federal justices or presidents. This intermediate position, as was so often the case, was backed most strongly by congressmen from the economically diverse midwestern and Pacific trade areas.[46] Albert Cummins of Iowa and Francis Newlands of Nevada, who would become the legislative fathers of the Federal Trade Commission, and Robert La Follette of Wisconsin already had come to this synthesis of trust policies by 1912.

When there is widespread dissatisfaction with the status quo, the middle ground between two polarized positions can generate a dominant policy alternative even though its content represents the first preference of relatively few legislators. Only a small sector of American society backed the creation of a genuinely autonomous and expert bureaucracy with power to compel information and order changes in business structure and practices. Although some articulate lawyers, social science professionals, and journalists were advocates of expert commission regulation, as a group they had little electoral clout. Members of Congress represent territorial, not sectoral, constituencies, and for that reason, ideas must find regional audiences if they are to penetrate the policy-making process in the legislature. Intellectuals such as Louis Brandeis influenced the course of antitrust law by working not only with Woodrow Wilson but also with legislators who were disposed, by the political economy of their states or districts, to seek a middle ground between the core and periphery alternatives. Before 1912 Brandeis had found a sympathetic audience among midwestern progressive Republicans who represented mixed industrial-farm constituencies (Wisconsin, for example) or farm economies dependent on domestic, industrial-city markets (like Iowa). Such congressmen were reluctant to back the southern agrarians' drastic measures, which might severely damage the industrial economy on which their own producers were dependent for markets. On the other hand, they would not allow core corporations to victimize their farm and small-business constituents. For these congressmen, regulation by a commission independent of party, president, and corporate influence (as they themselves professed to be) suggested an ideal solution.[47]

To sum up, then, by 1912 three distinct positions had crystallized on antitrust policy. These are summarized in table 8.1, along with the more limited labor stance, which was concerned almost exclusively with trade union prosecutions under the Sherman Act (and not with antitrust policy generally).

Table 8.1 Alternative Antitrust Policies and Their Bases of Support in the Progressive Era

Held by:	Goal	Method	Strong Regulatory Agency
Core Capital	Preserve existing large enterprise and allow further cooperation and consolidation to rationalize production and limit "wasteful" competition	Replace Sherman act with discretionary national commission to advise on and approve business agreements and practices and take over licensing functions from states on a voluntary basis	Opposed
Labor	Remove trade union activity from jurisdiction of antitrust law; avoid excessive wage-reducing competition	Write explicit labor exemption into the law	Preferred to rigidly enforced competition but this position subordinate to labor exemption
Diverse Areas	Allow existing and future business cooperation and consolidation only where demonstrably in the public interest; restrict abusive practices that injure competitors and customers	Supplement Sherman Act with nonpartisan, expert commission to investigate and prosecute business practices that unfairly and unjustifiably restrict competition	Favored
Periphery	Break up monopolistic and oligopolistic industrial and financial enterprises; prevent such future consolidations	Supplement Sherman Act by strengthening penalties and adding sections outlawing specific anticompetitive practices; lower tariffs to increase foreign competition	Opposed

On the right, spokesmen for core industry and finance proposed to replace the criminal sanctions of the Sherman Act with a new business-government advisory and consultative process under the aegis of a presidentially appointed commission empowered to issue federal licenses to corporations and approve their trade agreements and practices. On the left, periphery representatives called for amendments strengthening the prohibitions and punishments of the Sherman Act and supplementing it with legislation denying offending corporations tariff protection and even, if possible, access to interstate commerce, while exempting labor and farm organizations from prosecution. Between these two poles, congressmen from diverse industrial/agricultural trade areas advocated a genuinely independent and powerful executive agency to prosecute (an open list of) abusive practices and take over the judiciary's self-ascribed role of distinguishing "reasonable" from "unreasonable" business behavior. The "strong commission" alternative reflected not only the diverse regions' ambivalence about the goals of regulation but also their relative institutional weakness in the business-dominant courts and the legislative stronghold of the periphery. The intermediate position was most sharply presented in the Senate, where statewide constituencies incorporated both industrial and extensive farm economies.

Antitrust in the New Freedom: The Saga of the Clayton Act

The Democratic sweep of Congress and the executive branch in the 1912 elections seemed to set the stage for the periphery alternative in antitrust policy. Mobilizing their biregional coalition through caucus deliberation and discipline, the Democrats had swiftly enacted a revolutionary tariff and income-tax bill, abolished the pro-railroad Commerce Court, and then moved to establish a new, regionally decentralized, publicly controlled banking system. Early in 1914, they moved to the next item on the party agenda: antitrust policy.

The early legislative victories had come at a price, however, making succeeding accomplishments more difficult. Insurgent periphery- and diverse-area Republicans were infuriated by their exclusion from the policy-formulating process—the result of the Democrats' decision to use caucus government—and most also abhorred the Underwood Tariff. When, in early 1914, the economy fell into recession, Republican progressives were quick to join their manufacturing-belt colleagues in the charge that the Democrats were pursuing a ruinous business policy. Thus, as the antitrust debate proceeded in 1914, bipartisan cooperation among periphery- and diverse-area legislators was wearing thin, and economic conditions were increasingly unfavorable to radical business reform. More conservative members of the president's cabinet urged him to attempt no further regulatory initiatives; Bryan, on the other hand, insisted that the antitrust plank in the platform be redeemed.[48]

Despite the dissension, the periphery Democrats might have maintained their party juggernaut and carried along a sufficient number of agrarian Republicans to enact the radical periphery antitrust program had it not been for two related events: the outbreak of world war in the summer of 1914; and the conversion of President Wilson to the commission alternative. Until 1914, the president had thrown the weight of his office behind the regulatory program of the congressional Democrats. But the eruption of war in Europe, combined with business depression at home, impelled the president to seek compromise on a middle ground—which he found in the small camp of the progressive Republicans and their intellectual mentors. This break in party ranks presented periphery Democrats with a painful choice: to hold out, virtually alone, for the periphery alternative, at the cost of losing the president's invaluable aid for further farm credit and transportation legislation, or to accept the strong commission and fight to have it accompany, not replace, a tough antitrust bill drafted by House Commerce Committee Chairman Henry Clayton of Alabama. Under the circumstances—of depression, war, and anxiety within party ranks (particularly among the marginal northern Democrats) about the coming elections—insistence on an undiluted version of the periphery antitrust policy would probably have been self-defeating.

As a result of compromises in 1914, the agrarians secured strengthening legislation—the Clayton Act—at what was probably the last possible political moment for doing so, given that a nation at war is unlikely to attack business concentration, and the nonindustrial regions were never again to dominate the national government as they did in the Wilson years. The cost of this accomplishment was acceptance of an institution loathed by the periphery: regulatory bureaucracy. However, that price had been paid before, in the Interstate Commerce Act, and periphery interests had not fared badly. Settling for half a loaf must have seemed better than none.

Wilson's conversion to the "strong commission" alternative has often been attributed to the influence of Louis Brandeis, but the president's receptiveness to the idea was obviously conditioned by the national and international situation in 1914 and his desire to mend his ties with the business community. Brandeis had turned his attention to Wilson after the failure of La Follette's campaign for the Progressive Party nomination in 1912. After the Democratic convention, he wrote to congratulate the New Jersey governor on his nomination, and a meeting was arranged for late August. According to a biographer of Brandeis, the lawyer found Wilson "an apt pupil" and had "a powerful and decisive influence" on the Democratic president's subsequent antitrust program.[49] Brandeis's conversation and writings persuaded Wilson to make the distinction between the Democrats' approach of "regulating competition" and Roosevelt's "supervision of monopoly" a major theme of the 1912 campaign.

Brandeis's connection with antitrust policy is a fascinating example of the influence of policy intellectuals on legislation. Although many scholars have highlighted the eminent lawyer's role, what one might describe as a "political economy of ideas" is almost completely missing in these accounts. They rely heavily on Brandeis's presidential links and have little to say about the reception of his ideas in the legislature or about the reverse flow of influence—to Brandeis from congressional antitrust initiatives, investigations (such as the Pujo hearings), and Democratic Party platforms.[50] In fact, the earliest and most enthusiastic "Brandeisians" were in Congress, but two distinct groups seized different aspects of his argument to bolster their own positions. Periphery representatives—who would provide overwhelming support for him as a Supreme Court nominee in 1916—welcomed Brandeis's Jeffersonian arguments about the need to break up concentrated economic power and his refusal to concede either the inevitability or the greater efficiency of large corporations. They also appreciated his support for outlawing, by statute, specific anticompetitive practices. The agrarians were less interested in his arguments about the need to permit some restraints on competition to protect small and medium-sized firms, particularly when this position implied a need for discretionary bureaucracy to apply different standards in different situations. Brandeis, perhaps influenced by the experience of his business clients (and his legal training), was a strong believer in utility-style regulation, a position to which his admirers in the midwestern diverse states were much more sympathetic. Both progressive factions invited Brandeis to testify in congressional antitrust hearings during 1911–14 and freely appropriated his ideas for their legislative proposals. Though they could never share his enthusiasm for expert guidance of corporate behavior, Brandeis's commitment to economic decentralization won favor with the periphery Democrats and would ultimately make him an acceptable conduit for the trade commission idea—in the midwestern, not the core version—to Wilson and, through the president, to his southern partisans.

The president's endorsement of competition and his condemnation of monopoly during the campaign represented a contemporary polishing of the old agrarian Democratic doctrine. Wilson's views on economic regulation had been formed with a view to winning the Democratic Party's nomination in 1912 and, before the emergence of his presidential ambitions, had included no apparent enthusiasm for antitrust.[51] The party's 1908 platform had advocated the main features of what would become the Clayton Act. The 1912 Democratic platform, written by Bryan before Wilson won the nomination, had drawn on the revelations of the Pujo hearings and had argued for "such additional legislation as may be necessary to make it impossible for a private monopoly to exist in the United States" and to "restore to the [Sherman Act] the strength of which it has been deprived by [Supreme Court] interpretation." Specifically, the platform noted, "We favor the declaration by law of the conditions upon which corporations shall be permitted to engage in interstate trade, including, among others, the prevention of holding companies, of interlocking directorates, of stock watering, of discrimination in price, and the control by any one corporation of so large a proportion of any industry as to make it a menace to competitive conditions." These federal remedies, the platform continued, "shall be added to, and not substituted for state remedies." [52]

In the 1912 campaign for the presidency, Wilson eloquently defended the periphery's antitrust program using recent Brandeisian arguments. Whereas his Republican and Progressive opponents accepted economic concentration as the inevitable result of economic development, Wilson argued that trusts were neither "natural" nor efficient but were simply manifestations of unrestrained greed and bad public policy. He pledged legislation to restore competition, contrasting his program with Roosevelt's acceptance of monopoly under governmental supervision. Roosevelt responded with ridicule for the Democrats' backward-looking Jeffersonianism, charging that enforced competition in absence of an extensive national administrative apparatus would "turn the industrial life of this country into a chaotic scramble of selfish interests." Despite the hyperbole, it was a campaign pitched at an unusually high theoretical level. A broad national readiness for action on the problem of financial and industrial concentration had elicited articulate and distinct programs, passionately argued by their advocates and bolstered by widely read intellectuals such as Herbert Croly and Louis Brandeis. [53]

When, after extensive conversations with and memoranda from his party's southern and western legislative leaders, Wilson outlined his antitrust recommendations to Congress in January 1914, those proposals were cast in a traditional Democratic mold. In his January 20, 1914, speech on the principles of antitrust legislation, Wilson recommended (as had the 1912 platform) a new law prohibiting—"explicitly and item by item"—monopolistic practices, such as interlocking directorates and holding companies, and backed a proposal of Rep. Sam Rayburn giving the Interstate Commerce Commission supervisory power over the issuance of railroad securities. He also adopted a suggestion by Brandeis to let private litigants base their antitrust suits on the factual record and final judgments resulting from government-initiated antitrust cases, and he endorsed the principle of individual responsibility and punishment of corporate directors—a principle that had broad support among agrarians. [54]

Since Democratic congressional leaders strongly opposed the creation of a trade commission with broad discretionary powers, the president's recommendation was for a commission with only investigatory and informational functions. These powers would be stronger than those of the existing Bureau of Corporations, and in addition, the proposed commission would have the capability to aid the courts in "directing and shaping such corrective processes" as might be ordered in an antitrust judgment. Although Wilson hinted in his address that businesspeople would find useful "the guidance and information which can be supplied by an administrative body," he opposed (or at least interpreted "the opinion of the country" as opposing) a commission empowered "to come to terms with monopoly" (presumably, to approve trade agreements). In a letter to Senator Williams of Mississippi (who had written the president strongly urging "the regulation of these trusts by uniform, prescribed law and not by the operation of bureaucratic discretion"), Wilson defended his trade commission proposal, saying that he had conducted his own "canvassing." He noted: "I find that the businessmen themselves desire nothing so much as a trade commission. It is quite possible to gratify them without launching out upon a dangerous experiment."[55]

In the House Judiciary Committee, Chairman Henry Clayton of Alabama, Charles Carlin of Virginia, and John Floyd of Arkansas drafted the legislation that would become the Clayton Antitrust Act. Targeting the methods by which trusts had been built and operated, it prohibited price discrimination, interlocking directorates, intercorporate stockholding (for banks and corporations above a certain size), and tying contracts, and it made corporate directors and officers personally liable for antitrust violations by their firms. Fines and jail terms were provided for violators of the price discrimination, tying, and holding company sections and for violators of a section prohibiting railroad acquisition of interests in supplier firms. In addition, injured individuals were authorized to bring triple damage antitrust suits in federal district courts and, in bringing their charges, to use the evidence amassed by the federal government in its successful prosecutions to establish the defendant's guilt.[56]

Of the three alternative approaches to the trust problem—the business-government partnership, the autonomous regulatory commission, and the specific punitive statute—the House Clayton bill clearly represented the third. Most Republicans rejected it, but for two very different reasons. Core Republicans, predictably, found it "revolutionary and destructive," whereas midwestern progressive Republicans condemned it as old-fashioned and inflexible. There remained one other major faction seriously unhappy with the original House bill: northern industrial-city Democrats with labor constituencies. It was impossible for the agrarians to woo the core or commission-backing Republicans without sacrificing principle. The agrarian-labor trade, however, was essential to the maintenance of the Democratic majority and had, for the agrarians, a long and honorable history. Labor, therefore, had to be accommodated.

Sixteen current or former union members (eleven Democrats and five Republicans) had been elected to the House in 1912, a subset of whom served as labor spokesmen in that body.[57] Neither the labor bloc nor big-city Democrats generally saw any particular advantage in additional antitrust laws. After several recent prosecutions for Sherman Act violations, the attitude of labor officials toward the antitrust laws was particularly jaundiced.[58] A statutory exemption from Sherman Act prosecution was, of course, labor's foremost political goal. Congressional Democrats were eager to oblige; House Democrats in 1910 and 1912 had attempted to grant legislative relief but were blocked by Senate Republicans and the White House. The advent of complete Democratic control in 1913 should have brought easy passage, but this was one of the congressional Democrats' legislative goals that President Wilson did not endorse. Stung by an outpouring of business criticism, he almost vetoed a bill forbidding use of Justice Department appropriations for prosecution of trade unions, but he was compelled to sign it for fear the labor Democrats' defection would imperil the Underwood Tariff bill. A bill to accomplish statutory exemption, sponsored by two Georgia congressmen (Sen. Augustus Bacon and Rep. Charles Bartlett), still languished in committee, however, probably as a result of the president's strong opposition to such "class legislation."[59]

The Democratic labor representatives in the House, who had loyally backed the agrarians on the tariff and banking bills of 1913, now rebelled. Unless the Clayton Act included the requisite relief for trade unions, they threatened, there would be no antitrust law.[60] The southern Democrats quickly agreed to incorporate into the Clayton bill provisions limiting the use of injunctions and providing for jury trials in contempt-of-court cases arising out of labor disputes—provisions that, in two bills sponsored by Representative Clayton, had previously passed the House. After further conferences involving the president, labor, and southern Democratic representatives, the committee added a further provision "that nothing contained in the anti-trust laws shall be construed to forbid the existence and operation of fraternal, labor, consumers', agricultural or horticultural organizations . . . or to forbid or restrain individual members of such orders from carrying out the legitimate objects of such associations."[61]

The labor representatives were not satisfied with the wording of this exemption, which they perceived as weaker than the Bacon-Bartlett bill. The president, however, was adamant; he would approve no further attempts to release union activities from Sherman Act prosecutions. For their part, the labor representatives threatened to join the Republicans in opposition to the bill if labor's demands were not met. The antitrust program was stalemated.

At this point (mid-May 1914) the southern agrarian leaders, who apparently had a greater stake in the bill than did the president, resumed negotiations on their own. Reps. Robert Henry of Texas and Claude Kitchen of North Carolina drafted a new compromise. In addition to the sections prohibiting injunctions against peaceful picketing and other communication activities, granting jury trials in contempt-of-court cases arising out of labor injunctions, and limiting injunctions in labor disputes to situations where they were necessary to "prevent irreparable injury to property, or to a property right . . . for which injury there is no adequate remedy at law" (the threatened property must be described "with particularity"), a clause was added to section seven (later six) of the bill: "nor shall such organizations . . . or the members therefore, be held or construed to be illegal combinations or conspiracies in restraint of trade, under the antitrust laws." Representative Henry, chairman of the House Rules Committee, announced that he stood "squarely behind" labor's demand for outright exemption and brought in a rule prohibiting any roll-call votes during committee of the whole debate, in order to protect supporters of the labor amendment from inevitable conservative criticism.[62] Conservative Republicans were outraged at the new language. Rep. Hampton Moore of Pennsylvania shook his fist at the AFL secretary watching from the House gallery and blasted the Democrats for doing labor's bidding. The *Wall Street Journal* praised Moore's speech for telling "the cringing poltroons of the House of Representatives what their squalid dicker with the labor-union leaders really means," predicting that the Supreme Court would "promptly throw such a law into the waste basket."[63]

The southern Democrats who drafted the compromise amendments undoubtedly believed that they had exempted trade union activities from the Sherman Act. The labor representatives, after conferring with their counsel (Alton B. Parker, former presidential candidate and now a federal judge), agreed and consented to support the package. The only remaining obstacle was Wilson. However, the framers had couched the exemption in the language of past Democratic platforms, and this stratagem, along with appeals to consider party needs in the upcoming congressional elections, made it difficult for Wilson to withhold his approval.[64] In the end, he acceded to the compromise but stubbornly refused to reverse his earlier position. This he accomplished by publicly stating that the amendment did no more than "exclude the possibility of labor and similar organizations being dissolved as in themselves combinations in restraint of trade."[65] Since it was not the *existence* of unions that was threatened by judicial interpretation but rather the *activity* incident to strikes and labor disputes, the president implied that the amendment was a meaningless affirmation of already existing rights. The floor leader, Edwin Webb of North Carolina (who had replaced Clayton as Judiciary Committee chairman when the latter moved on to the Senate), supported the president's face-saving effort, narrowly interpreting the effect of the amendment during floor debate on the labor sections.[66] Although this interpretation conflicted with that of the amendment authors[67] and that of Gompers and the AFL, the statements by Wilson and Webb introduced a note of ambiguity that an anti-labor court could subsequently exploit in interpreting the legislative history of the Clayton Act. Against this cost may be weighed the possible advantage of the president's interpretation. He and Webb might have believed that a clear exemption would stir up enough conservative outrage to block passage of the bill.

With the labor compromise in place, the Clayton Act passed the House easily. The Democratic Party was almost unanimous on this package of long-sought farmer and labor goals. Fifty-two of the fifty-four opposing votes were Republican, but that party was sectionally divided (see table 8.2). On the same day (June 5, 1914), the House passed without recorded vote the Judiciary Committee's "adjuvant" trade commission bill creating an agency (in the place of the Bureau of Corporations) with expanded information-gathering and investigatory powers. It was a weak commission, designed to assist the Justice Department in preparing for antitrust prosecutions and to aid the courts in designing divestitures after successful prosecutions.

Table 8.2 1914 Clayton Antitrust (and Anti-injunction) Act, House Passage

% of Seats		277–54 D 218–1 R 47–52[a] % Yea	(N)	% of All Yeas
34.5	Core	71.8	(110)	28.5
18.9	Diverse	83.3	(72)	21.7
46.7	Periphery	92.6	(149)	49.8

[a]Indicates opposing core and periphery majorities within the party.

Core Republicans	23.7%	(38)
Periphery Republicans	64.5%	(31)

The Bureaucratic Turn in Antitrust

Even as House Democrats were celebrating their victory, the president was shifting to a significantly different antitrust policy. When the adjuvant trade commission bill was under consideration in the House, a Democratic representative from a heavily industrial district, Raymond Stevens of New Hampshire, had proposed an alternative. The proposal, drafted by his friend George Rublee, a New Yorker active in the Progressive Party, would have substituted a simple declaration outlawing "unfair methods of competition" for the Clayton bill's specific prohibitions and criminal penalties and would have left the definition and enforcement of "unfair competition" to a new trade commission. Unlike the original information-gathering and advisory body, this commission would have genuine regulatory (conduct-prescribing and -judging) powers. As Rublee later described the sponsors' sentiments:

> It seemed to us that enactment of the [Clayton and adjuvant commission] bills in their then form . . . would add to the existing uncertainty and also subject to criminal penalties business activities which in certain circumstances might be legitimate. . . . So I suggested to Mr. Stevens that the right way to legislate would be to strike out of the Clayton Act the objectionable and insufficient definitions and instead to declare unfair competition to be unlawful and give the Trade Commission power to prevent it.[68]

The agrarian Democrats rejected Stevens's alternative in the spring of 1914, but the sympathy of northern Democrats and midwestern Republicans kept the idea alive. Business reaction to the final draft of the House Clayton bill had been virulent, and newspaper editorials now resounded with demands that the business and financial community, still reeling from the Underwood Tariff and Federal Reserve Acts, be given a "resting space" before any new regulatory experiments were tried. The agrarian Democrats, charged the *New York Times,* were "pandering to what they still suppose[d] to be the prevailing sentiment of the country, hatred of corporations."[69] In the same vein, Republican Rep. Martin Madden of Chicago charged:

> The dogs of war have been unleashed to tear and cripple the fabric of business and industrial life . . . to satisfy the clamor and the malcontents within the party. . . . The measure is so drastic, so utterly ruinous, that in order to save the country from the confusion and destruction it would produce, I am perfectly willing, if within my power, to persuade the Democrats from supporting it, in their own party interests, even if from no higher considerations.[70]

President Wilson's ambivalence about the Clayton bill grew as the outcry mounted and the business recession deepened. Early in June, Brandeis, Rublee, Representative Stevens, and Sen. Henry Hollis of New Hampshire had a conference with the president and found him very receptive to the "strong commission" alternative.[71] Wilson publicly endorsed the commission proposal shortly after House passage of the Clayton bill. Southern and western Democrats were stunned at the president's reversal but could not hold out alone for the increasingly unpopular Clayton approach. Thus, in the summer of 1914, the agrarians reluctantly stepped to the sidelines as Francis Newlands (chairman of the Senate Commerce Committee) and Albert Cummins (the second-ranking Republican on the committee) rewrote the trade commission bill.[72]

The major contribution of periphery senators (of both parties) to the final trade commission bill came in votes on two amendments offered on the floor of the Senate. Industrial-state Republicans were bitterly disappointed that the commission had been granted no authority to exempt business trade agreements from the Sherman Act and saw no reason to take the function of overseeing business competitive practices from the courts (in which they had the utmost confidence) and transfer it to a new administrative body. However, when Sen. Henry Lippitt of Rhode Island offered an amendment to allow the commission to exempt trade agreements from the antitrust law, an avalanche of periphery and diverse state votes buried the proposal; only fourteen Republican senators, mostly from core industrial states, supported it (see table 8.3).

Republicans and a few conservative Democrats also attempted to alter the

Table 8.3 FTC Act, Lippitt Amendment (let FTC approve business agreements), Senate, 1914

			14–47 D 0–37 R 14–10[a]	
% of Seats		% of Yea	(N)	% of All Yeas
27.1	Core	60.0	(15)	64.3
14.6	Diverse	11.1	(9)	7.1
58.3	Periphery	10.8	(37)	28.6

[a]Indicates opposing core and periphery majorities within the party.

Core Republicans	100.0	(9)
Periphery Republicans	33.3	(12)

Table 8.4 FTC Act, Cummins Amendment (narrow court review of FTC orders), Senate, 1914

		33–25 D 20–16 R 13–9[a]		
% of Seats		% Yea	(N)	% of All Yeas
27.1	Core	46.2	(13)	18.2
14.6	Diverse	77.8	(9)	21.2
58.3	Periphery	55.6	(36)	60.6

[a]Indicates opposing core and periphery majorities within the party.
Core Republicans   37.5   (8)
Periphery Republicans   63.6   (11)

Senate Commerce Committee bill to allow broad federal court review of the "cease and desist" orders of the Federal Trade Commission (FTC). To this end, they rallied behind a broad judicial review amendment drafted by Democratic Sen. Atlee Pomerene of Ohio and approved by President Wilson. Cummins, the Senate's leading "strong commission" advocate, then drafted an alternative amendment that permitted court review but confined it to interpretation of the law, compelling deference to the commission's judgment on the facts of the case (this would put the FTC on the footing now established for the Interstate Commerce Commission). Cummins scored a coup by getting his amendment to the floor first. With the help of periphery senators of both parties, the narrow-review amendment succeeded.[73]

As can be seen in table 8.4, the most overwhelming support for a strong and autonomous trade commission came from diverse-area senators, but they were too small in number (with seven votes in favor) to secure passage; that was accomplished with the votes of thirteen periphery Democrats who deserted their president and committee leaders to back the Cummins amendment. They were joined by seven periphery Republicans. Ironically, this momentous vote, a landmark in the development of regulatory bureaucracy, was carried by senators who were deeply troubled by discretionary law and preferred the specificity and self-enforcing approach embodied in the Clayton bill. They apparently reasoned that as long as a regulatory commission was to be created, it might as well have some teeth. There was no advantage to be gained from allowing the pro-business courts to destroy the agency's effectiveness, on the off chance that it might do some good as an auxiliary

Table 8.5 FTC Act, Senate Passage, 1914

			53–16 D 41–2 R 12–14[a]	
% of Seats		% Yea	(N)	% Yeas Cast by:
27.1	Core	50.0	(16)	15.1
14.6	Diverse	100.0	(9)	17.0
58.3	Periphery	81.2	(44)	67.9

[a]Indicates opposing core and periphery majorities within the party.

Core Republicans	11.1	(9)
Periphery Republicans	57.1	(14)

to the Clayton Act. The fortified commission bill passed easily, over core Republican opposition, on August 5 (see table 8.5).

However, both the "strong commission" advocates and the opponents of any new antitrust law saw the FTC as a substitute, not an auxiliary, for the Clayton Act. In keeping with this philosophy, the Senate Judiciary Committee proceeded to rewrite the Clayton bill, striking its criminal penalties and giving the major responsibility for enforcement of the prohibited practices to the FTC. Several antitrust sections were notably softened, others were omitted altogether, and in the labor sections, workers' rights were made more ambiguous by insertion of the words "lawful" and "lawfully" to modify workers' collective actions.[74] By the time Senate debate began on the Clayton bill in mid-August, however, committee leaders appeared to doubt that even this "defanged" version of the antitrust bill could be passed.

The final chapter in Progressive Era antitrust policy was written in extraordinary times. On June 28, the Austrian archduke was assassinated at Sarajevo. On July 28, Austria declared war, and frantic efforts to avert a general European conflagration dominated the headlines. On August 5, the day the FTC bill passed the Senate, England declared war on Germany. World financial markets were thrown into turmoil. International shipping came to a standstill, and panic spread through the South as cotton, the nation's chief export crop, piled up on the docks (the important German market being effectively closed by a blockade). Rates for scarce shipping services rose 300–1,000 percent. In this situation, with mail pouring in from the region's farmers, merchants, and bankers pleading for federal help, cotton-belt senators predictably gave less attention to the antitrust debate than they had earlier. Mississippi Senator Williams had devised a plan whereby the government would purchase and operate foreign-built ships to relieve the shipping crisis. The controversial plan could not possibly succeed without the president's strongest efforts. Perhaps for this reason, Williams, whose own preferred antitrust program was so different from that being composed in the Senate, kept publicly silent and generally voted the administration position on Clayton bill amendments (as did most other southern senators).[75]

In this situation, one may wonder that the Clayton bill survived at all. The president had apparently lost all positive interest in the antitrust bill some time ago and had just experienced the death of his wife. Leaderless, besieged by business and the press to let the issue drop, and preoccupied with the rapidly falling price of cotton and the shipping crisis, southern Democrats fell back on party loyalty, supporting the committee's weakening amendments while opposing those, offered by conservative Republicans and noncommittee Democrats, that would have weakened the bill even further.[76] The few northern labor-backed Democratic senators—notably Henry Hollis of New Hampshire, William Hughes of New Jersey, and John Kern of Indiana—also voted loyally with the committee-administration position. For both farmer and labor representatives, the goal at this point was to get some version of the Clayton bill passed in a very unpropitious situation. Only a few Democrats—most notably Reed of Missouri—persisted in trying to restore the bill to its stronger, House-passed form. For the Republicans, whose party was in disarray, there was no "party position" at all. Some insurgents seemed to delight in offering hopeless strengthening amendments to embarrass the Democrats, who were now committed to the weaker but enactable bill endorsed by the committee majority and President Wilson. A few core Republicans occasionally joined in, apparently for strategic reasons, and voted to strengthen a bill that was anathema to them and that they opposed on final passage. But most of the standpat Republicans declined to participate in the Clayton debates, realizing that the committee version could pass in spite of their opposition.

In a number of cases, strengthening amendments were accepted by the committee and passed by voice vote, so that the picture gleaned from recorded votes is overly bleak. For example, the holding company prohibition was strengthened when the Senate accepted motions by Senator Reed and Sen. John Shields to change section eight so that it prohibited intercorporate stock purchases "where the effect of such acquisition *may be* to lessen competition" (the House version had said "*is* to *substantially* lessen competition"). Similarly, AFL-proposed language declaring that "the labor of a human being is not a

Table 8.6 Clayton Act, Senate Passage, 1914

		46–16		
		D 38–0		
		R 8–16		

% of Seats		% Yea	(N)	% Yeas Cast by:
27.1	Core	41.2	(17)	15.2
14.6	Diverse	100.0	(10)	21.7
58.3	Periphery	81.9	(35)	63.0

commodity or article of commerce" was accepted by Culberson and added at the beginning of the labor exemption (section 7) by voice vote on the Senate floor, an event that caused great rejoicing among the labor leaders watching from the gallery.[77] On final Senate passage, the unanimous Democrats were joined by eight Republicans (see table 8.6). Only two of the Republicans represented a state (Washington) classified here as "core industrial."[78]

The House and Senate bills were then sent to conference. The legislation reported from the conference committee was a straightforward compromise of the two disparate bills, and its provisions fell between the two.[79] House conferees reinstated major provisions dropped by the Senate but agreed to omit criminal penalties for the prohibited anticompetitive practices. The labor sections kept the clauses approved by the AFL but also included the potentially troublesome wording ("lawful" and "lawfully") favored by the Senate.[80] As for the trade commission bill, the Senate version was accepted with only minor adjustments by the House conferees. It outlawed "unfair methods of competition," against which the commission could proceed by complaint and, subsequently, by cease-and-desist orders enforced by the courts. The most creative and significant elaboration by the conferees was the insertion into section five of new language broadening the FTC's mission. The Senate language had said, essentially, that whenever the commission believed that unfair competition had occurred, "it shall issue and serve upon the defendant a complaint." The conference added, before the quoted section, the following words: "and if it shall appear to the commission that a proceeding by it in respect thereof would be to the interest of the public." This insertion, for which Rublee claimed responsibility, was essential to the progressive vision of administrative regulation because it allowed the commission to define the national interest in business competition and to select cases according to that definition.[81]

When the conference bills came to the floor of the House and Senate, Republican criticism was scattershot and vociferous. Standpat Republicans insisted that this was no time for dangerous experiments that might seriously damage business. Some progressive Republicans, like Sen. William Borah and Rep. Andrew Volstead, denounced the omission of most criminal penalties in the Clayton Act, whereas others, like Rep. Frederick Stevens of Minnesota, condemned the act's attempt to specify offenses at all, seeing that as weakening the jurisdiction of the FTC.[82] As a group, progressive Republicans harbored contradictory impulses. They were unwilling to admit that the new antitrust bills added any strength to the Sherman Act (or, if they did, credit was due only to the Republicans themselves, who had long championed commission regulation). At the same time, they argued, it would have been good to have some tough new sanctions against anticompetitive practices; but this strategy was impossible, since the Democratic tariff had caused a severe recession and public opinion would not countenance "strong medicine" in such uneasy times.[83]

On this discordant note, the legislative deliberations on the new antitrust program were brought to an end. Democrats closed ranks around the bills, obviously chastened by the compromises they had felt compelled to make but relieved that they had been able to redeem major platform commitments to strengthen the Sherman Act and guarantee labor's organizational rights. In the end, the party voted unanimously for the Clayton conference bill in the House and registered only three dissents in the Senate. Twenty-three Republican and six Progressive representatives, but only one Republican senator (Miles Poindexter of Washington), cast affirmative Clayton votes. The conference version of the trade commission bill drew nine votes from Senate minority party ranks, only one of whom (again, Poindexter) represented a core state.[84]

The establishment of the United States' distinctive antitrust policy was thus the product of several decades of agrarian agitation, somewhat tamed and diffused by a small, strategically positioned set of political actors. The latter were determined both to prevent the agrarians from mortally wounding the dynamic industrial economy and to bring big business under some kind of effective public control. Gabriel Kolko to the contrary,[85] the capitalist class played no significant creative role in this process. One has only to compare the texts of the Clayton and Federal Trade Commission Acts with the National Civic Federation's proposed antitrust amendments of 1908 to realize that although enlightened capitalists had indeed advocated a trade commission, what they wanted—a discretionary partnership in which consensus reached by the powerful few would be enforced by governmental authority—was not what they got. Instead, a statutory framework was created (in the Clayton Act) that forbade precisely what the large firms wanted to legitimate: collusive horizontal agreements to suppress competition, holding-company purchases of stock in competing businesses, and mergers between significant competitors "in any section or line of commerce."

After 1914, periphery-based interests were able to extract some benefit from the Federal Trade Commission they had originally opposed, even as court decisions dismantled several key provisions of the Clayton Act. Before Republican appointees took it over, the FTC conducted investigations of meatpacking and grain-trade operations, laying the foundation for remedial legislation in the Packers and Stockyards and Grain Futures Acts of 1921–22.[86] The nonindustrial regions, as well as second-rank manufacturing cities of the diverse areas, also gained from the commission's investigations and actions against basing-point pricing in the steel, cement, paper, and other industries in the 1920s and 1940s,[87] and it was congressmen from these (non-core) regions who spurred the FTC in its mammoth investigation of public utility holding companies, culminating in 1935 legislation against "utility trusts." However, conservative Republican appointees induced a major reorientation of the commission after 1925, and much of the force of the Clayton and Federal Trade Commission Acts was undone by the Supreme Court in the period between its passage and the arrival of the New Deal. Many of the commission's rulings were reversed, and its authority was defined so narrowly that businesspeople were encouraged to defy its orders.[88] Brandeis, now sitting on the Supreme Court, must have been chagrined to hear the conservative majority argue that since the words "unfair competition" were not defined in the law, it was for the Court, not the FTC, to decide what they meant.[89]

A major loophole was opened when the Court ruled that a company might acquire stock in a competitor and then use the stock to get control of the other firm's material assets before the FTC could issue a cease-and-desist order. The labor exemption in the Clayton Act also fell victim to an activist court. In 1921, the Supreme Court overruled two lower courts to deny that the Clayton Act forbade injunctions against peaceful strikes and boycotts.[90] One may blame the bill's drafters (as did many later scholars) for not making the bill airtight, but it would have been extraordinarily difficult to draft antitrust legislation that could preclude intervention by a Court determined to uphold corporate prerogatives.

Other Business Regulatory Legislation

In addition to antitrust legislation, a host of other laws were enacted in the Wilson administration to effect new and unprecedented federal controls over business practices. The Warehouse, Grain Standards, and Cotton Futures Acts of 1914–16 and railroad and shipping legislation of 1910–16 steadily expanded the reach of the national state into economic transactions and laid the foundation for broader controls in the 1930s. Analysis of the legislative histories of these bills again reveals how much of this early expansion of the regulatory state was due to the agitation of the rural population.

Like the antitrust laws, this regulatory legislation was enacted in the face of strong opposition from business leaders, prominent economists, and metropolitan journalists. This opposition partly confounded the agrarian political representatives, most of whom lacked the expertise and self-confidence to design pathbreaking national controls and defend them articulately against charges that they were unconstitutional and destructive to the complex modern economy. As a result, the laws enacted were far less radical than the original proposals. Nevertheless, the legislation was clearly rooted in past and contemporary agrarian movements and reflected the interrelated goals of the periphery farmers to establish some control over the flow of credit for planting and holding their crops and over the storage, transportation, and marketing systems that determined their level of income.

Warehouses, Marketing, and Credit

Crop-storage warehouses were critical nodes in the pricing and distribution of farm commodities. Their centrality had been recognized in 1877 when Illinois farm organizations won from the Supreme Court an acknowledgment that such businesses, which "stand at the very gateway of commerce and take toll from all who pass," were "affected with a public interest" and might properly be subjected to government regulation.[91] Illinois and other major midwestern grain states had instituted such regulation, but in the eyes of many agrarian spokesmen, the state systems were woefully inadequate for the three major functions that they served in the agricultural economy: uniform grading (especially important for exported crops); secure storage; and (on the basis of their receipts) bank credit. Related to these functions was another of great interest to the farmer: stored crops were the basis of the "real" and the "purely paper" futures markets—markets that both contributed to price stabilization and enriched a host of commodity speculators, against whom the farmers bore great animosity.

Public warehousing had been a central element in efforts by the Southern Farmers' Alliance to restructure agricultural marketing. After the demise of populism, political attention shifted to other portions of the marketing system—futures trading, railroad abuses, credit availability. Still, the problems surrounding warehousing remained, and warehouse building for cooperative crop bulking and holding operations continued to preoccupy the Farmers' Union and other farm organizations.[92] There was too little competition and too little publicly available (and reliable) information about charges, commodity prices, and crop sizes. Grading varied from warehouse to warehouse, and farmers were victimized by lower-grade labeling than their crops merited, while the ultimate buyers complained of overcharges for commodities of lower quality than the stated grade—the notorious system of "strict inspection in, easy inspection out," which inflated warehouse profits and damaged the reputation of U.S. exports. Warehouses often lacked sufficient insurance and failed to protect stored crops from pest or weather damage. A number of farm states had no warehouse regulatory statutes before passage of the federal law, and in states that did, enforcement was usually lax. Where local boards of trade did the overseeing, they were accused of discrimination against out-of-state farmers. Large warehouses in major port cities such as New York, Chicago, Minneapolis, Duluth, Boston, and Baltimore were accused of monopolistic exploitation of interior producers. Worst of all, arbitrary and unreliable grading and storage depressed commodity prices and made banks (particularly the large clearinghouses at a distance from the producer) reluctant to accept warehouse receipts as collateral for loans. Thus, the agrarian victory in making agricultural paper eligible for discounting in the new Federal Reserve System produced little actual improvement in crop-secured credit before 1916.[93] Rep. James F. Byrnes of South Carolina summarized the warehouse problem in the cotton economy as follows:

> The cotton crop of the South is marketed during two or three months. . . . All debts of the cotton farmer fall due within a period of 60 days in the fall of the year. The banks and the lien merchants call upon him to pay his debts and the farmer is forced to meet his obligation, even though the price at that time may be depressed to the point that he will receive no profit for his year's work. If he could hold his cotton for even 60 days, he would receive a higher price. But he must sell in order to meet the obligation and because he has no opportunity to warehouse his cotton and borrow money on it at a rate of interest which, together with the storage charges, will leave him any profit. Even where cotton has been stored in private warehouses, the investing public has been slow to lend money upon warehouse receipts

for cotton, because there was no guarantee of the reliability of the ware-houseman; no certainty that should the farmer not pay the loan and the lender endeavor to secure the cotton, that he would find it there; no certainty that if he did find it that it would be in good condition or . . . as represented in the warehouse receipt.[94]

With the outbreak of the European war in 1914, storage facilities and credit on stored products became absolute necessities. Southern cotton farm-ers lost over a quarter of their foreign market as a result of British interdiction of trade with Germany and Austria and a general shortage of merchant ship-ping facilities. The loss of traditional markets in the face of a larger-than-usual American crop brought a sharp drop in the price of cotton, creating an urgent need to store the surplus until something like normal demand resumed and to secure credit on the stored crop, which was virtually the only source of cash income for southern farmers. Cotton-state congressmen responded to the region's economic disaster with a slew of relief measures. Texas Represen-tative Henry introduced a bill under which the United States would deposit $500 million in southern banks, which then would lend cotton farmers the funds at 3 percent interest against stored cotton assessed at ten cents a pound (the price had already dropped from twelve cents to nine cents by September 1914). Another southern proposal would have mandated a quarter-million-dollar bond issue for a direct U.S. purchase of five million bales of cotton and a prohibitive tax on all cotton produced in excess of half the 1914 crop level. A much more moderate proposal, but one that, nevertheless, repre-sented a significant increase in federal regulatory powers, was sponsored by Rep. Asbury Lever of South Carolina and Sen. Hoke Smith of Georgia to establish federal regulation of cotton warehouses so that reliable storage could be secured and valid, standardized receipts could provide a basis for bank credit.[95]

The more radical proposals found almost no support outside the cotton region. The administration publicly branded them "perfectly wild and ridicu-lous"; it consented to support only a token credit expansion and the Lever warehouse bill.[96] Despite Wilson's endorsement, however, the warehouse bill faced strong opposition and could not be passed until 1916. Part of the opposi-tion lay within the farm regions. Some grain-state representatives, particularly in the Dakotas, wanted their crops added to the bill, and the southerners quickly agreed. However, there were strong objections from states (such as Minnesota and Illinois) where the great terminal elevators were located, as well as from other states (like Iowa, Wisconsin, and Missouri) where state warehouse-regulation systems were in place and were apparently operating to the satisfaction of local farmers.[97] Congressmen from the latter states were willing to support regulation for the great terminal markets so long as it did not apply to their own states, but the bill's southern sponsors argued that a system affecting only the large port facilities would "concentrate all of the cotton, all of the grain, all of the agricultural products of this country in great central warehouses."[98]

The strongest objections came from core representatives, who protested any expanded business regulation likely to work against their own regional interests and set a precedent for further interventions. Reps. John Fitzgerald (D) and William Bennet (R) of New York objected that yet another regulatory tirade had targeted the alleged abuses of the New York market, whose seventy miles of warehouses were adequately and properly regulated by state and municipal law.[99] Representative Moore (R) of Pennsylvania complained of yet "another effort to fasten unnecessary law on the people of the country."[100] The warehouse bill was subjected to five roll-call votes before finally becoming law in 1916, and on each vote, the core registered by far the strongest regional opposition. On the first House vote, the bill failed to secure the two-thirds majority necessary under suspension of the rules despite overwhelming periphery support; both parties were regionally divided (see table 8.7). The last vote on Senate passage is shown in table 8.8. The Warehouse Act was finally passed in 1916, together with a Grain Standards Act and a reenactment of the Cotton Futures Act.[101]

Constitutionality was an obvious stumbling block in this early period of regulatory state expansion. If regulation was not confined to the great terminal

Table 8.7 Suspend Rules and Pass Warehouse Regulation Bill (House, 1914)

	164–109		
	D 139–57[a]		
	R 22–52[a]		
% of Seats		% Yea	(N)	% Yeas Cast by:
34.5	Core	25.0	(76)	11.6
18.9	Diverse	55.8	(52)	17.7
46.7	Periphery	80.0	(145)	70.7

Note: Passage under suspension of the rules requires a two-thirds vote.
[a]Indicates opposing core and periphery majorities within the party.

Core Democrats	31.9	(47)
Periphery Democrats	84.4	(122)
Core Republicans	3.8	(26)
Periphery Republicans	56.5	(23)

Table 8.8 Warehouse Act (Senate, 1916)

		40–10 D 32–0 R 8–10[a]		
% of Seats		% Yea	(N)	% Yeas Cast by:
26.1	Core	33.3	(8)	5.0
17.4	Diverse	63.6	(9)	17.5
56.5	Periphery	93.9	(33)	77.5

Note: The Warehouse Act, the Grain Standards Act, and a reenactment of the Cotton Futures Act were packaged as amendments to an agricultural appropriations bill. Separate votes were demanded for the Warehouse amendment. Here, a vote to strike the amendment was recorded as opposition to the Warehouse Act; "% Yea" indicates votes opposed to striking the amendment and thus in favor of regulation.

[a]Indicates opposing core and periphery majorities within the party.
| Core Republicans | 16.7 | (6) |
| Periphery Republicans | 75.0 | (8) |

markets where the power of Congress to regulate interstate and foreign commerce enjoyed a strong presumption, then upon what provision of the Constitution could it be based? Opponents claimed to find no justification for national intervention in an implicitly local function like crop storage. On this issue, several Republican progressives—Albert Cummins of Iowa, Knute Nelson of Minnesota, and Irvine Lenroot of Wisconsin—were among the most vocal opponents of expanded national power, whereas the southern Democrats impatiently pushed aside states' rights arguments with "general welfare" rationales. As Lever of South Carolina professed, "When there is a great general good to be accomplished by legislation, I am not so squeamish about the Constitution."[102]

The solution for warehouse regulation was to make it "voluntary." Warehouses could apply for federal licenses, but they were not obligated to do so. Those who did apply would have to submit to federal inspections and audits and to meet a list of statutory standards promulgated by the U.S. Department of Agriculture (USDA)—including asset and bond requirements, nondiscrimination, reasonable and posted charges, suitable storage facilities, competent management, employment of inspectors and graders licensed by the USDA, and issuance of warehouse receipts in a prescribed format (listing product specifications and certifying that the specified crops were indeed present in the warehouse, stipulations that served as vital protections for both the farmer and his creditors).[103] It was recognized at the outset that the great credit value of a receipt from a federally licensed warehouse would create a preference for those over other storage facilities, but the absence of compulsion avoided direct state-federal conflict and apparently overcame some of the reluctance to expand federal regulatory power in an area of mixed interstate/intrastate transactions. The 1916 law provided for licensing of warehouses storing cotton, grain, wool, and tobacco. Other storable products subsequently were added; by 1924 there were 722 federally licensed facilities, over half of them devoted to cotton.[104]

Setting National Grain Standards

The 1916 Grain Standards Act, passed as a companion measure to the Warehouse Act, extended to grain growers a federal regulatory benefit won by cotton producers in 1914 (see below): the promulgation (by the USDA) of uniform national grades and the right to appeal unfair grading to the secretary of agriculture. Plains and mountain wheat growers had long complained of underweighing, undergrading, and fraudulent grain mixing by the great grain syndicates of the terminal markets.[105]

The Grain Standards Act of 1916 anchored the federal power to regulate grading in the commerce power in Article 1 of the Constitution, prohibiting interstate and foreign shipments of grain using other than the federally established grades. Its passage was delayed from 1914 to 1916—despite intense efforts by Great Plains representatives and the southern leaders' willingness to accommodate them—because the Midwest was divided on the issue.[106] As with warehouse regulation, some representatives objected that their own states had satisfactory grading systems that would be destroyed by federal regulation. Some Illinois and Minnesota congressmen strongly defended the status quo in deference to the great elevator interests of Chicago and Minneapolis. Critics bemoaned the inflationary potential of the new warehouse receipts, the dangerous precedent of usurping state functions, and the expense of a large bureaucracy of federal inspectors.[107] To partially accommodate those objections, the Grain Standards Act provided for USDA licensing of state and private grain inspectors who would remain nonfederal employees but be subjected to federal control.[108] The act prohibited licensing of grain inspectors with any financial ties to grain elevators, warehouses, or merchants, and it empowered the USDA to suspend or revoke licenses for incompetence or malfeasance. Willful misgrading or other violations of the act's provisions subjected the violator to criminal penalties (fines and/or imprisonment), and corporations were made liable for their employees' conduct.[109] Although the new standards and sanctions of the Grain Standards Act applied only to grain shipped in interstate and foreign commerce, the companion Warehouse Act of 1916 compelled all federally licensed warehouses and elevators to specify U.S. standard grades in their receipts (and to employ U.S.-licensed inspectors) whether the crop was destined for interstate commerce or not, as soon as the standards had been promulgated by the USDA.

Commodity Speculation

After antitrust legislation, the most difficult and controversial proposal for expansion of federal business regulatory powers was regulation of futures contracts. The affected commercial interests were fiercely opposed, intellectual opinion was derisively negative, and the president was unmovable. This opposition, and the agrarians' nagging doubts about the wisdom of completely outlawing processes that (the experts insisted) might indeed be vital to the functioning of the new national and international markets, meant, in the end, that less was accomplished here than in other portions of the farmers' policy agenda.

The agrarian animus against speculation extended to contracts traded both on and off the major exchanges. The different voting patterns of core and periphery congressmen (and state legislators) on antispeculation measures arose from the position of these areas in a national and international political economy in which both money and influence over commodity pricing had gravitated into a few hands in the country's major cities. Bank reserves directly or indirectly drained out of the periphery were used to "gamble" in stocks and commodities, and the remote farmer suffered both from credit tightness and from price manipulation of his crop. Thus, whether the issue was banning or controlling commodity futures contracts, outlawing "bucket shops," [110] or bringing the exchanges under public control, the agrarian regions were pitted against the core cities where these functions of the modern industrial and commercial economy were concentrated. This pattern held from the heyday of populism through the regulatory surge of the New Deal. [111]

In the post–Civil War period, commodity speculation soared, so that from 1872 on, the amount of cotton and grain sold on the exchanges exceeded actual production, extending, toward the end of the century, to seven times the volume of the annual crop. [112] In the last session of the 52nd Congress (1892–93), an antispeculation measure reached the House floor at a time when periphery farmers were beset by declining prices and credit contraction. Sponsored by Rep. William Hatch of Missouri, Democratic chairman of the Agriculture Committee, the bill proposed to levy a prohibitive tax on sales of cotton and grain not actually owned by the seller. Backed by the Farmers' Alliance and the Grange, the Hatch bill passed both the House and the Senate by substantial margins, but the two chambers failed to resolve differences before the 52nd Congress expired. A subsequent attempt in 1894 again met with success in the House but failed to come to a vote in the Senate. Congressmen from the region that Cedrick Cowing labels the "Anti-Speculator Tier" (actually a "column")—the Dakotas, Nebraska, Kansas, and Texas—supported the first Hatch bill with near unanimity in both chambers, bolstered by southern, western, and other midwestern farm regions. At the other pole, the "Speculator Seaboard"—Maryland, Delaware, Pennsylvania, New York, New Jersey, Connecticut, Rhode Island, and Massachusetts—voted overwhelmingly against the bill.[113]

The terms of debate on this and subsequent antifutures bills changed little in succeeding decades. In committee hearings and in floor debate, representatives of wheat, cotton, and corn districts complained of price volatility and deliberate efforts by speculators on the exchanges to "bear" the market. This was accomplished, they argued, by disseminating false information about price movements, crop volume, and so forth and by issuing offers to buy or sell large quantities of a commodity at a low price, sometimes in connection with "wash sales." By driving down the price, speculators could buy cheap and later sell dear to the miller or spinner.[114]

The New York Cotton Exchange (NYCE) was a particular villain. Although the South's cotton crop was traded on the New Orleans and other smaller regional exchanges, the volume traded, the proportion of purely speculative transactions, and the level of reported abuses were much higher on the NYCE. Soon after its founding in 1870, the NYCE obtained, by virtue of its access to port facilities and huge credit markets, "a preeminent position as a national agency for the marketing and distribution of the American cotton crop."[115] Its charter, granted by the state of New York in 1871, imposed no external regulation. Rather, it made the NYCE a self-governing entity, subject only to a brief admonition that its rules and practices were not to violate the New York or U.S. Constitutions. It had no local competition, since no charters were issued by the state to establish competing cotton exchanges. Like the New York Stock Exchange, the Cotton Exchange was run very much like a private club; it had complete control over the admission of members and over trading rules. Its internal practices not only discriminated against nonmembers but also held competition among trader-members to a minimum while maximizing members' profits.[116]

The NYCE established its own set of cotton grades, sometimes listing up to thirty separate categories. Cotton buyers—usually New England or foreign textile mills—bought futures contracts on the exchange in order to spread their purchases over the year and hedge against price increases. When the time came for ultimate delivery, however, the buyer had to accept whatever grade of cotton the exchange speculator chose to deliver from the NYCE's warehouses. This would frequently be low-quality (dirty, stained, weak, or short-staple) cotton, overgraded by the NYCE's own inspectors and often unsuitable for the spinners' purposes. Furthermore, the price difference between the "middling" grade specified in the futures contract and the labeled grade of the delivered cotton would be settled not by affixing spot market prices to the two grades but by the NYCE's Revisions Committee arbitrarily setting "fixed differences" at its biannual or triennial meetings. As a result, buyers anticipating receipt of cotton they could not use (or could not sell at a profit to cover purchases on the spot market) discounted the value of the cotton, driving down its price.[117]

It is thus not surprising that the commodity exchanges—and preeminently the New York Cotton Exchange—aroused so much antagonism among the agrarians. The exchanges colluded with affiliated inspectors and warehouses to misgrade the farmers' produce; they drew into speculation bank deposits (including those that country banks were required to keep in big-city correspondent banks) desperately needed for crop financing; and they manipulated commodity prices to make fortunes for speculators. To the Farmers' Union, it was clear the NYCE had "dictated the price of cotton for almost forty years . . . and held the South in practical slavery" and that the NYCE would "not, if possible, permit the Southern farmers anything more than a bare living."[118]

After the failure of the Hatch bill, a number of grain and cotton states had passed laws outlawing futures contracts and bucket shops within their own borders, although such laws could not touch the major exchanges, which were the prime culprits.[119] During debate on the Payne-Aldrich Tariff in 1909, Senator Bacon of Georgia introduced an amendment to levy a prohibitive tax on bucket shop operations. It was defeated 44–34 on a tabling motion offered by Sen. Nelson Aldrich, the vote marked by sharp core-periphery polarization. Despite some sympathy among the major exchanges to suppress bucket shop competition within their own states, national legislation of this sort was viewed in the core as dangerous radicalism.[120]

The following year, Kansas Rep. Charles Scott introduced a bill to ban futures contracts in interstate commerce. It was brought to the floor when two hundred representatives signed a discharge petition, and it passed the House 160–41 (without a roll call), only to die in the Senate.[121] The Scott bill became the standard against which the more radical agrarians would measure the numerous subsequent futures-regulation bills generated in Congress, but 1910 was the high point for outright abolition of futures trading.

In the next Congress, the attainment of a Democratic majority in the House and the Pujo investigations of the "money trust" spurred another effort to control commodity speculation. The agrarians, ever inventive in their search for methods to constitutionally anchor such unprecedented measures, now sought to ban speculative futures contracts from use of the "interstate commerce" in telephone and telegraph messages. Southern Democrats, who led the proponents in debate, met scornful opposition from Representative Fitzgerald of New York and Rep. James R. Mann of Illinois, both of whom defended their local commodity exchanges. The bill (H.R. 56) passed 95–25 but, as usual, died in the second chamber.[122]

In 1913, as the Underwood Tariff was moving toward passage, Sen. James Clarke of Arkansas proposed, as a rider to the tariff bill, a tax of fifty cents per bale on cotton futures contracts in which one party did not own the cotton. The Farmers' Union strongly backed the Clarke amendment, and it won the approval of the Senate Democratic caucus.[123] The New York Cotton Exchange was outraged, and the metropolitan press (particularly in New York) condemned the proposal as "vicious" and "idiotic," indicative of the agrarians' inability to appreciate the useful role played by speculation.[124]

These were, on the whole, also the opinions of leading economists. In their writings and testimony before congressional committees, they touted the benefits of speculation and opposed calls for government intervention. Henry Crosby Emery, a Columbia University Ph.D., had written a dissertation in 1896 that became the standard work on the subject. The exchanges, Emery wrote, were "the nerve centers of the industrial body, and are themselves as necessary institutions as the factory and the bank."[125] In the Wilson years, when bills for regulation of stock and produce exchanges had again risen to the legislative agenda, Emery (now a Yale economist) joined other contributors at an American Economic Association symposium in condemnation of the agrarian proposals.[126]

The elite consensus apparently persuaded Wilson to oppose both the Clarke amendment and the Owen bill for securities regulation, postponing the latter for two decades.[127] The agrarian sentiment for regulating the commodities exchanges was much harder to repel, however. Clarke's anti-futures bill was added to the Underwood Tariff bill in the Senate and survived its first test in the House on a 203–137 vote, thanks to solid support in the periphery and diverse farm sections (see table 8.9). Because it was not a caucus measure in the House and because Chairman Oscar Underwood, as well as

Table 8.9 Concur with Senate (Clarke) Amendment to Underwood Tariff
to Levy a Punitive Tax on Cotton Speculation (House, 1913)

		203–137 D 157–84[a] R 38–50		
% of Seats		% Yea	(N)	% Yeas Cast by:
34.5	Core	40.0	(125)	24.6
18.9	Diverse	72.7	(55)	19.7
46.7	Periphery	70.6	(160)	55.7

[a]Indicates opposing core and periphery majorities within the party.
| Core Democrats | 43.0 | (79) |
| Periphery Democrats | 74.4 | (122) |

the White House, opposed it, Democrats felt free to vote their own inclinations. The vote split the Democratic Party, with periphery members voting three-to-one in favor and with a substantial majority of core members in opposition. Periphery Republicans were split evenly, while core Republicans opposed the amendment by better than two-to-one.[128]

At this point, Underwood introduced as a substitute for the Clarke amendment a proposal drafted by the Department of Agriculture. The substitute levied a tax of one cent per pound (the contemporary price of cotton was fourteen cents a pound) on contracts for future delivery of cotton. However, the tax would be reduced to an insignificant level if the contract adopted standard grades, which were to be promulgated by the USDA. Exchange traders would be compelled not only to adopt U.S. standard grades and settle contracts according to market prices but also to keep, and make available to USDA inspectors, records of all futures transactions, on pain of fines and possible imprisonment.[129] The clear aim was to preserve futures markets but to outlaw the nefarious practices of the exchanges, particularly the NYCE.

The ensuing debate took place mostly among periphery representatives. Core Republicans, as their votes revealed, overwhelmingly opposed both the Clarke and the Underwood amendments. Nor did core Democrats offer any supporting comments. Clearly unenthusiastic about either approach, they preferred the milder Underwood version to the Clarke amendment. Representative Fitzgerald, the only core Democrat to speak, strongly opposed any federal interference with futures trading.[130]

Within the periphery there was considerable anxiety about the employment, in both versions, of the taxing power to destroy a condemned activity (see below). The agrarian radicals argued for the method of the earlier Scott bill: an outright prohibition of futures contracts in interstate commerce. Beyond that objection, of course, lay the fundamental distinction between the Underwood and the Clarke measures: one proposed to regulate, the other to abolish, speculation in commodities. The Underwood substitute carried on a narrow 171–161 vote.[131] Core Democrats voted for it 58–17; more significant, 48 periphery (mainly southern Democrat) representatives of the 113 who had previously backed the Clarke amendment now voted for the Underwood substitute. Some agreed with Representative Lever of South Carolina, who argued, "By proper regulation we can force the cotton exchanges to render a useful service to the cotton trade."[132] Others probably feared that abolition would disrupt an established marketing system, to the disadvantage of producers (as the experts insisted would happen).

The Senate's refusal to accept the Underwood substitute stalled the measure in the first session. The USDA's alternative, however, became the basis for the 1914 Cotton Futures Act (CFA). The CFA settled the debate about commodity speculation in favor of regulation rather than prohibition, although advocates of the latter continued to press the issue through the 1920s.[133] The only roll call on the 1914 bill, the House vote on the conference report, found the large majority of Democrats in favor of passage, though sixteen disgruntled agrarian Democrats refused to support a regulatory measure that "legalized gambling" (see table 8.10). Although textile interests have been described as leaders in the movement for regulation, those who represented the interests of the New England mills in Congress were overwhelmingly opposed to the 1914 bill on final passage.[134] In fact, as Robert Wiebe points out, the most outspoken advocates of exchange controls among manu-

Table 8.10 1914 Cotton Futures Act (Conference, House)

		146–77		
		D 132–27		
		R 14–43		
% of Seats		% Yea	(N)	% Yeas Cast by:
34.5	Core	60.3	(58)	24.0
18.9	Diverse	56.5	(46)	17.8
46.7	Periphery	71.4	(119)	58.2

facturers were *southern* textile manufacturers,[135] and they joined a regional position established by the growers.

In 1913–14, as momentum grew for a cotton futures law, the NYCE was finally persuaded to reform its operations. After years of adamant opposition, the exchange finally consented to adopt standard USDA grades and to make more frequent revisions of grade price differences, as well as to restrain speculation and market manipulation in several minor ways. These changes, it was hoped, would "end the movement to enact federal laws to curb operations on the Exchange."[136] They did not have the intended effect, however, and the exchange finally was saddled with the unwanted provisions in 1914: USDA regulation of the terms of futures contracts; settlement according to extant spot-market price differences; reporting requirements; broad appellate and investigatory powers in the hands of the Department of Agriculture; and criminal penalties for violations. Reflecting NYCE reactions, an alarmist *New York Times* greeted House passage of the 1914 CFA with the headline: "PASSES BILL CURBING GAMBLING IN COTTON, AIM TO END EXCHANGE HERE By Taxing It Out of Existence—Will Save $100,000,000 to South, Says Lever."[137]

The Search for Methods

In this fledgling period of state growth, and under the eagle eye of an extremely conservative Supreme Court, there was much concern about the methodology and constitutional anchoring of the federal regulatory power. Southern distaste for using the taxing power to regulate was deeply rooted.[138] In 1893, Mississippi Senator George had attempted to amend the Hatch futures bill in favor of an outright prohibition, and the same arguments were heard in 1913–14.[139] Once Congress had decided against outright prohibition, however, the taxing power was again the favored method. Another possibility, to which the southerners were partial, was to use the postal power and the commerce clause to prohibit the use of the mails, telegraph, or other interstate communications systems to advertise or effect the sale of futures contracts that did not conform to the mandated standard. This was the method used in the unsuccessful Owen bill for the regulation of stock exchanges and in the Scott antifutures bill.

The communications ban raised two serious problems, however. On the one hand, as the *New York Times* pointed out, it placed a great burden on newspapers and telegraph companies to screen ads and financial reports from the exchanges.[140] In addition, the fact that the U.S. Post Office was a highly politicized department raised fears of "political" administration of the law. The Owen bill had given jurisdiction over securities fraud to the Post Office because "under our Constitution the authority to regulation through the Post Office is less open to question" than if jurisdiction were placed elsewhere in the still-rudimentary federal executive branch.[141] Conservative critics were outraged at the idea that Postmaster Albert Burleson, Wilson's patronage chief, would be in command of the proposed system, particularly since Burleson's "special line of activity as a congressman was regulating business."[142] The Senate version of the Cotton Futures Act employed the interstate communications ban because, as Sen. Ellison D. Smith of South Carolina related in the committee report, doubts had been raised about the constitutionality of directly interfering with (futures) contracts.[143] The NYCE, drawing on the Supreme Court's narrow view of the commerce power, claimed that its business consisted of locally negotiated contracts beyond the reach of federal law.[144] Asked during floor debate if the mail ban had any precedent, Smith cited an 1895 law banning lottery tickets, or advertisements for them, from the mails. The lottery ban, upheld by the courts, was often cited by advocates of futures regulation or prohibition, with the observation that the NYCE had a far greater negative impact than the lottery.[145] However, the mail ban also posed constitutional problems by requiring the press to censor communications from exchanges that did not comply with USDA standards. The House approach, which used a steep tax on nonconforming futures contracts, ultimately seemed the safer bet and was adopted by the conferees. The methodology was never successfully challenged, but a federal district court in New York voided the law on a technical point of improper legislative procedure (the final version had been passed first in the Senate, and tax legislation must originate in the House). The CFA was reenacted, with only minor modifications, in 1916.

The limits of the taxing power were revealed a few years later when agrarian legislators sought to bring grain futures contracts under similar controls. The 1921 Futures Trading Act levied a prohibitive tax on a class of purely speculative transactions (known as "privileges," "bids," "offers," "puts and calls," "indemnities," or "ups and downs") and on all futures contracts made neither by actual owners nor by boards of trade designated and supervised by the USDA. On the same day that it voided the second Child Labor Act with the same argument, the Supreme Court declared the Futures Trading Act to be an unconstitutional use of the taxing power to effect business regulation. To allow a wide range of regulation to rest on the taxing power, in the Court's words, would "break down all constitutional limitation of the powers of Congress." However, the Court hinted that its objection might be overcome in this instance by a shift in wording and method emphasizing the need to remove obstructions to interstate commerce. Thus Congress passed, in 1922, a new Grain Futures Act advertising itself as "an Act for the prevention and removal of obstructions and burdens upon interstate commerce in grain by regulating transactions on grain futures exchanges" and solemnly declaring that grain futures were "affected with a national public interest." The new law abandoned the tax in favor of making it "unlawful for any person to deliver for transmission through the mails or in interstate commerce by telegraph, telephone, wireless or other means of communication any offer to make or execute, or any confirmation of . . . or any offer to make, or any quotation or report of the price of, any contract of sale of grain for future delivery," except by owners or on boards of trade designated and supervised by the USDA. Enforcement was given to the USDA and the Justice Department, not the Post Office. Thus reconstructed, the Grain Futures Act survived Supreme Court scrutiny.[146]

Where actual goods (rather than contracts or offers) were being transported in a "stream of commerce," the Court was more charitable to regulatory efforts, even though the processes and facilities targeted by regulation were themselves contained in one state. Thus the Grain Standards Act of 1916 was not problematic. The Court also upheld the 1921 Packers and Stockyards Act, despite the appellants' claim that their business was not in interstate commerce.[147] Still, it was clear from the Court's peevish scuttling of the Futures Trading Act (not to mention the more ominous—from the Court's perspective—Child Labor Act) that the justices sympathized with the plaintiffs' alarmist query: If this use of the tax or commerce power is upheld, where will it all end? That virtually all manufacturing and commercial operations might someday be considered proper subjects of federal regulatory power was still an unthinkable proposition in the Progressive Era and one on which Court opinion would significantly lag behind public and congressional disposition.

Conclusion: Agrarian Radicalism and the Regulatory State

In the Progressive Era, the angry farmers of the hinterland played out the struggles launched by their nineteenth-century counterparts to bring the dynamic but brutal forces of capitalism under public control. They managed to accomplish what the earlier agrarian radicals could not: they put on the books laws whose enforcement would succeed in remedying many of the evils of which the farmers complained. Because the affected businesses and those who represented their interests in Congress were either hostile or indifferent toward these initiatives (as were most of the core middle classes), passage must be attributed to the determined efforts of the farmers. This is not to say that the forces of agrarian discontent were not channeled and tamed in the process, because clearly they were. In the most common use of the term, those who accomplished the channeling and domestication have been seen as the "true" state builders. It was they who designed the bureaucracies that administered the legislation resulting from farmer agitation. More will be said about this interactive state-building in chapter 11.

9

Federal Aid for
Practical Education:
Farmers First

Between 1908 and 1912, both farm and labor organizations championed the inauguration of an ambitious program of federal aid to agricultural and mechanical education in the nation's high schools. Yet vocational education became enmeshed in complicated partisan and committee maneuvers, was sidetracked by a more powerful legislative juggernaut pushing agricultural "extension" work, and was not passed until 1917, three years after the agricultural bill. The saga of these practical education movements in agriculture and industry reveals much about the nature of the farmer-worker political alliance and the distinctive orientations of the two "producer classes" to politics and the positive state.

Previous accounts of the development of federal policies in support of applied agricultural and industrial education have interpreted these seminal pieces of legislation as the direct outcome of efforts by middle-class professional organizations and social scientists, assisted by powerful business groups.[1] But such an interpretation is plausible only if one comes into the story relatively late—say, around 1912. At that point, it is true that the National Society for the Promotion of Industrial Education (NSPIE) and the Association of American Agricultural Colleges and Experiment Stations (AAACES)—both led by professional educators with powerful, self-interested agendas—had become major players in the struggles for federal aid to vocational education and agricultural extension. But the legislative struggles did not begin in 1912. Their origins go back to around 1903 (with even earlier precedents in agriculture), and as a matter of fact, both of those middle-class professional organizations came into the movements for federal legislation *defensively*, concerned about the thrust of bills introduced in Congress by representatives who were responding to local and regional demands.

Businesspeople were also among the constituents who supported particular forms of agricultural extension and vocational education, but labor played a more direct and active role in the formative years of the legislative struggle for a national vocational education policy, and farmers' organizations were

314

early and active champions of federal support for both forms of practical education. The agricultural regions produced the first such legislative proposals, and as the names of the Smith-Lever Agricultural Extension and the Smith-Hughes Vocational Education Acts reveal, periphery congressmen played major roles in their final enactment.[2] These two legislative sagas are thus far more complex than is suggested by accounts emphasizing the role of professional and business organizations. We *are* in the domain of pluralist politics here, but there were larger and more fundamental processes at work than interest-group politics—processes involving regional political economy, partisan coalition-building, and the troubled alliance of farmers and workers.

The stories of the agricultural and industrial education bills are intimately intertwined. Farm-state congressmen were, in fact, responsible for both, but some agrarians later came to perceive distinct farmer interests and used their legislative power to secure their bill first. In doing so, they made an argument that illustrates a continuing theme in this book: although the AFL's interest in federal aid for practical education was recent and episodic (arising in about 1908 and peaking in 1911–12), farmers could trace their advocacy in a continuous line back to the antebellum period. They could thus claim credit for the steady expansion of a policy system that began in 1862 (with the Morrill Act and creation of the Department of Agriculture) and could cite the nineteenth-century Grange and Farmers' Alliance as the spiritual parents of the Progressive Era extension movement. The agrarians had created an unusually responsive federal bureaucracy and kept close tabs on it. They had also kept up social-movement pressure on the land-grant colleges to discourage what seemed to be the professional educators' natural tendency to distance themselves from the common folk. The result had been the creation of successful public policies that expanded the realm of useful scientific knowledge to improve the lives of men, women, and children on the nation's farms. They thought it would be a good thing to expand the education opportunities of city children too, and farm organizations and representatives insisted that they wanted to. But since labor lacked the farmers' activist history, its program was more controversial and constitutionally tricky. It would take more time and could not be allowed to delay the culmination of the agricultural education movement.

During the Civil War, that movement had scored its first victory with passage of the Morrill Act "to promote the liberal and practical education of the industrial classes" (that is, the "producing classes," farmers and workers). The 1862 act donated eleven million acres of federally owned lands to the states to endow and support "agricultural and mechanical" (A&M) colleges.

The bill, first introduced in 1857, was a response to widespread antebellum agitation by freelance "educational reformers," state and local agricultural societies, state college officials, and others to win government support for the creation and maintenance of institutions that would provide *useful* and *relevant* scientific education for the children of the agricultural and artisanal classes—in contrast to the elitist private and state universities of the time, which emphasized law, literary, and classical studies for the preparation of the urban professional classes.[3] Objections by southerners then committed to a states' rights ideology and an impotent national government did not prevent the bill's passage by a narrow margin in Congress, but President James Buchanan vetoed the measure in 1859. Two years later, the dynamics were starkly different. In the midst of the Civil War, Rep. Justin Morrill "sweetened" the bill with a provision requiring that military tactics be taught at the land-grant colleges established under the act (hence the origins of the Reserve Officer Training Corps). With its southern opponents out of the Union, the Morrill Act was signed into law in 1862.[4]

Ironically, after the Civil War, southerners became the most numerous and enthusiastic proponents of federal aid to education. Southern Democrats argued against the states' rights constitutional objections of their northern copartisans and provided strong support for the Blair bill for federal aid to elementary education.[5] They also enthusiastically backed an 1887 act, sponsored by Rep. William Hatch of Missouri and Sen. James Z. George of Mississippi, that provided annual grants (derived from the sale of public lands) of $15,000 each to the states for the support of agricultural experiment stations run by the land-grant colleges. The amounts provided for agricultural research were subsequently doubled and appropriated directly from the Treasury in the 1906 Adams Act.[6]

The Hatch Act reflected the insistence of the Grange, the Farmers' Alliance, and other farm organizations of this highly mobilized decade that federal funds be used for the production and dissemination of "useful and practical information" relevant to increased agricultural productivity. Distrustful of the colleges nurtured by the Morrill Act of two decades earlier, sponsors made the terms of the 1887 act more specific and authorized inspections and monitoring by the U.S. Department of Agriculture (USDA).[7] The Morrill Act amendments that followed three years later continued this effort to specify precisely how the recipient institutions should use the funds, incorporating a restrictive amendment proposed by the National Grange.[8] Farmers were intent not only on expanding federal support for practical education but also on making sure it *was* practical.

Both the Grange and the Farmers' Alliance were intensely interested in education. Farmer education was the principal reason for the founding of the Patrons of Husbandry (the Grange), and the Farmers' Alliance considered itself a "great national university" for the education of the rural masses; so, in a less radical sense, did the later Farmers' Union.[9] All three groups campaigned for support for public schools at all levels of government, and all were supportive of the expansion of the land-grant colleges. The Grange and the Farmers' Alliance, however, were highly critical of the way the land-grant colleges had evolved in their first two decades; as a result, the development of these institutions during and after the 1880s was "profoundly shaped by efforts to ward off the 'investigation' and attacks of angry farmers and the state legislators who represented them."[10]

What provoked these attacks was the tendency of the land-grant colleges to mimic the curriculum of the established literary colleges and offer very few courses in agriculture or "mechanic arts" or means by which rural and other underprivileged youth could be admitted, remedy their preparatory deficiencies, and support themselves while studying.[11] Farm organizations were sometimes successful in persuading state legislatures to withdraw Morrill Act support from such universities and establish new agricultural colleges; elsewhere, as in Wisconsin and Minnesota, the universities were compelled to redesign their programs. In Minnesota, for example, a spirited campaign by the Farmers' Alliance and the Grange forced the state university to create a new branch campus with a farm outreach program and an agricultural high school as well.[12] Once the militant farm organizations succeeded in redirecting the land-grant colleges, they then rewarded the colleges with political support—beginning with a second Morrill Act in 1890.[13] The process of movement-driven democratization and outreach by the land-grant universities would continue through the Progressive Era, winning them ever wider support among the rural population. That support, however, was clearly contingent on their relevance to the improvement of farm life.

The poorer farm states of the southern and north-central regions had little wealth to tax, and farmers already bore much of the burden of property and excise taxes. Thus, there was a natural progression in these regions from local educational reforms to proposals for national aid. Alabama, Georgia, and Minnesota, having pioneered the creation of agricultural high schools at a time when access to schooling beyond the elementary level was rare in the rural periphery, produced strong supporters of federal aid to vocational education. The earliest proposals for such aid seem to have originated in the South. Shortly after the Georgia legislature, in 1906, provided for the creation of agricultural high schools in each of its congressional districts, Reps. Leonidas Livingston and William Adamson of that state introduced bills for federal grants to such schools and for branches of the agricultural experiment stations to accompany them. Rep. Ariosto Wiley of Alabama introduced a bill in the same year to inaugurate federal funding of common and "industrial" schools (the latter term encompassed both agricultural and mechanical vocation-related education for benefit of the producing or "industrial" classes). However, the southern proposals went nowhere in the Republican-dominated Congress. Instead, two legislators from the northern periphery states of Nebraska and Minnesota introduced the measures that would frame the later policy evolution.[14]

The 1901 Nebraska legislature, in which a narrow Republican majority struggled against the cohesive Populist-Democratic "fusionist" coalition that was William Jennings Bryan's legacy,[15] passed a bill requiring certified public-school teachers to pass examinations demonstrating a certain level of scientific agricultural knowledge. The legislature's action reflected a growing dissatisfaction with the quality and orientation of rural schools. But the state quickly learned that its attempted upgrading of vocational agricultural education could make little headway because of the inadequacy of teacher training. State officials and teachers then drafted a bill to secure federal aid for state normal schools, to be used for education in agricultural and mechanical subjects and "domestic science." Sen. Elmer J. Burkett, eager to demonstrate his progressive credentials, introduced the bill in the Senate; Rep. Ernest M. Pollard, also of Nebraska, proposed it in the House. After it was introduced, the bill won an endorsement from the National Education Association, which testified in its favor before the Senate Committee on Agriculture and Forestry the following year. The Utah State Legislature, facing difficulties similar to those experienced in Nebraska, also appealed for its enactment, and representatives from Kentucky and Missouri introduced similar bills.[16]

Whereas the funding approach and the justification for the bill relied on the precedent of the Morrill and Hatch Acts, the ultimate recipients specified in the bill were the state normal schools. This apparently alarmed land-grant college educators, who felt a proprietary interest in agricultural and mechanical education. The Association of American Agricultural Colleges and Experiment Stations (AAACES) thus set to work to include the A&M colleges in the vocational education movement. Ten months after the introduction of the Nebraskans' bill, the AAACES drafted a measure to double the Morrill Act appropriations to the states (from $25,000 to $50,000) over five years so that the land-grant colleges would have resources for training teachers for the expansion of high-school vocational education. Sen. Knute Nelson of Minnesota proposed the measure as an amendment to an agricultural appropriations bill early in 1907 and actively promoted it.[17]

The congressional agrarians apparently cared little about which set of educational institutions administered the federal aid, but having the land-grant colleges do it struck most as entirely appropriate. Nelson's amendment passed the Senate easily, without a recorded vote.[18] In the House, however, there was a fight. The Agriculture Committee chairman, Rep. James W. Wadsworth of New York, and the other House conferees refused to accept the amendment. Wadsworth and other standpat Republicans objected to the increased expenditure and the far-reaching precedent that such federal aid would set. Reps. Charles R. Davis of Minnesota and Henry D. Clayton of Alabama, on the other hand, strongly defended the measure.[19] Representative Clayton stated: "Mr. Speaker . . . we propose to pass this measure in order that poor boys may have the full benefit of a good education in scientific agriculture and the most useful and common mechanic arts. . . . We are going to have this legislation now. I appeal to the farming districts to stand with me."[20] Against the "dangerous centralization" argument raised by opponents, Clayton responded, "Nobody is afraid that the government is going to be ruined and centralized on account of this small contribution to the agricultural and mechanical colleges of the country." It was too late to debate the policy, he argued. The policy had been set in 1862.[21]

Clayton's motion that the House recede from its objection and concur in the Senate (Nelson) amendment passed on a 120–87 roll call.[22] Because party discipline had broken down on an amendment proposed by a Republican but opposed by the Republican committee chair and because no other such bill was currently before Congress, the vote provides a good test of sentiment on federal aid to vocational education. As can be seen in table 9.1, the Nelson amendment was carried in the House by the periphery Democrats, who contributed the largest block of yea votes. Periphery Republicans diverged from their party majority to back the measure, but a substantial minority of core Republicans (thirty of seventy) were also willing to endorse it. What is most surprising, in view of later labor support for public vocational training, is the opposition of the small group of core Democrats. Rep. William Wilson of Pennsylvania, an officer of the mine workers' union and the AFL, voted against the amendment, as did four Massachusetts and four New York Democrats.

The lack of support among labor Democrats hardly slowed the drive to secure federal aid. In the same year that the Nelson amendment was passed,

Table 9.1 Support for Federal Aid to Train Vocational Education Teachers (House, 1907)

		120–87 D 61–15[a] R 59–72[a]		
% of Seats		% Yea	(N)	% of All Yeas
33.5	Core	39.5	(81)	26.7
19.9	Diverse	42.1	(38)	13.3
46.5	Periphery	81.8	(88)	60.0

[a] Indicates opposing core and periphery majorities within the party.

Core Democrats	18.2	(11)
Periphery Democrats	91.9	(62)
Core Republicans	42.9	(70)
Periphery Republicans	57.7	(26)

Representative Davis of Minnesota combined the proposals of Georgia Representatives Adamson and Livingston (for aid to agricultural high schools and branch experiment stations) with provisions for support of mechanical and home economics education in city schools. The following year Davis added to this package a provision (similar to the Burkett-Pollard bill) for teacher training in these subjects at state and territorial normal schools, with a total expenditure of about $8 million a year. This was quite an ambitious program, not only unprecedented in proposing to pay the salaries of local public-school teachers but also costing over twice the amount currently channeled to the land-grant colleges under the Morrill Act. Already showing the progressive tendencies that would make him an anti-Cannon insurgent in the 61st Congress, Representative Davis was kept off the Agriculture Committee by the House Republican leadership. Nevertheless, his bill clearly enjoyed broad agrarian support, and he succeeded in getting a predominantly hostile committee to hold hearings on it in 1908.[23]

From 1906 through 1910, the campaign for federal aid to vocational education was Congress-centered, with representatives responding to a diverse array of grass-roots farmer and labor demands and producing bills designed to yoke farmers, workers, and educators in a broad supportive coalition. It was only after 1910 that the vocational education movement began to break apart into distinct rural and urban components. In 1911–12, a group of agrarian congressmen would move to elbow aside the urban advocates and secure their own bill first, a decision that, in turn, allowed a small group of professional educators to capture the urban vocational education movement. To understand the forces that created this disjuncture in about 1911, we need to leave the congressional arena and review the development of the two great practical education movements that swept the United States in the Progressive Era.

Practical Education for Farmers

The farmer education or "extension" movement was designed to bring the scientific knowledge accumulated in the universities and the USDA to the mass of farmers. Its first nationwide manifestation was the "farmers' institute" movement, which burgeoned in the late nineteenth and early twentieth centuries, spurred by the demands of the Grange and the Farmers' Alliance and by the desire of the land-grant colleges to curry favor with the rural public. The farmers' institute was a public meeting, usually of several days' duration, at which knowledgeable people of both sexes—whether academic and bureaucratic experts or respected farmers and teachers—made presentations, mounted exhibits, and conducted discussions on topics of interest to farm families. The popularity of these "adult farmer's schools" was immense by the turn of the century, but their growth did not peak until around 1912, with over three million people in attendance. The experience of participating in these grass-roots educational events led to the formal organization of outreach activities in the USDA and in the land-grant colleges (forty-three of which had created extension departments by 1912) and promoted a creative search for better methods of communicating useful knowledge to farmers.[24]

The second prong of the farmer education movement involved similar supporters (and some new ones), was inspired by the peculiar conditions of cash-crop southern agriculture, and originated with a remarkable individual. Dr. Seaman A. Knapp had been a farmer, minister, teacher, editor, professor of agriculture at Iowa State College, and one of the drafters of the 1887 Hatch Act. In the mid-1880s he was lured to the South by a land-settlement project on the Louisiana Gulf Coast. Searching for some crop that could be profitably grown there, Knapp hit on rice and persuaded the land company to create "demonstration" rice fields in each parish and to back farmer "demonstrators" whose success would inspire others. This method of teaching farmers new cultivation practices proved spectacularly successful. Midwestern pioneers were attracted to the area, and within five years Louisiana was the country's leading rice-producing state.[25]

In 1898 Knapp was hired to work for the USDA, which, in 1902, appointed him director of a program to improve southern agricultural methods through five model farms in Louisiana and Texas. Knapp's method matured in Terrell County, Texas. Here, building on the Louisiana experience, Knapp put into practice his conviction that lectures, technical bulletins, and model farms could never reach and convince the mass of ordinary farmers. Instead, these farmers, working with trusted advisors and fellow farmers, should be personally guided in applying the new methods on their own land. They needed to see the results with their own eyes and learn by doing—but with a strong support network. Knapp first met with farmers and businesspeople to explain the new method and pick a "demonstration" farmer who would agree to try it on his farm. Bankers and businesspeople were asked to guarantee the demonstrator against losses in the first year, and the USDA, through Knapp, would supply the selected seed, fertilizer, and other necessities. Other farmers would agree to be "cooperators"—observing the new methods, discussing them with the demonstrator and his advisors, and ultimately trying the techniques themselves. When first put into operation in Terrell County, the "cooperative demonstration" method was remarkably successful. The demonstration farmer made $700 more than he had under the old methods, despite an ominous new development: the cresting of the boll weevil infestation of cotton plants in the Southwest.[26]

In the following year, panic gripped Texas in the face of the boll weevil's destructive onslaught. The USDA and Knapp had ideas about cultivation methods that could reduce the insect's damage; the challenge was to get the message out to farmers on a massive scale. In Congress, Texas Rep. Omar Burleson took a jar of boll weevils preserved in alcohol to the House Agriculture Committee and made a dramatic plea for federal aid to combat the menace. After some "slippery slope" arguments, Congress agreed, early in 1904, to allocate $250,000 for the fight against the pest. Knapp sprang quickly into action.[27]

Though an educator himself, Knapp was suspicious and dismissive of college-trained agricultural "experts," who possessed, he believed, scant practical knowledge and little ability to communicate with ordinary farmers. He chose practical farmers to be his "agents," and they fanned out over the southwestern cotton states like missionaries or Peace Corps volunteers, selecting demonstration farmers, attaching to them as many cooperators as possible, and seeking business support in the towns. The Farmers' Cooperative Demonstration Work (FCDW), as it came to be called, aimed not just to control the boll weevil but to improve southern agriculture generally, promoting diversification, crop rotation, better seed, use of livestock, and new cultivation techniques. Knapp linked up with black colleges in Alabama and Virginia and enrolled two black "county agents" in 1906 (one hundred by 1914) to carry the message to African-American farmers. By 1912 he had a total of seven hundred demonstration agents in the field and well over one hundred thousand farmer demonstrators and cooperators. Knapp also persuaded local businesses to contribute resources for support of the work, including southern railroads which helped in the dissemination of information.[28]

The FCDW seemed to mushroom in all directions. Both to inspire rural youth and to provide an avenue to the education of their parents, the FCDW recruited children through "corn clubs" in which youngsters were taught good farming methods on a plot of their parents' land. Such clubs were usually gender-specific but inclusive in the aggregate and involved roughly equal numbers of each sex. The boys typically grew corn or raised hogs, and the girls raised poultry, tended vegetable gardens, and learned canning. A South Carolina teacher who had organized such clubs at her school was recruited to expand the activities for girls. The logical progression was to recruit the farm wife into "home economics" demonstrations, and as the USDA institutionalized the woman-to-woman teaching of nutrition, household management, sanitation, and so forth, a "new profession for women was created— the home demonstration agent." By 1914, about one-fourth of the agents at work in rural counties were women.[29]

A deep-pocketed nongovernmental organization soon joined this dynamic and eclectic system. A million-dollar donation by John D. Rockefeller had created the General Education Board (GEB), chartered by Congress in 1903 "for the promotion of education within the United States without distinction of race, sex or creed." The GEB concentrated its efforts on the South and in its early years made scattered grants for the improvement of rural schools. In late 1905, its director was introduced to Knapp and his cooperative demonstration work, whose promise he immediately recognized. The following year, the GEB entered into an unusual "silent partner" agreement with Knapp and the USDA. Since Knapp's work was funded through the boll-weevil appropriation, it could not, technically, be extended to the central and eastern states of the South, where the pest was not yet a serious problem. In the latter region, the Rockefeller money was made available to fund the work of Knapp's agents, whose nominal one-dollar federal salaries made them government employees under USDA direction. The Rockefeller contribution totaled almost $1 million over a nine-year period. Whatever squeamishness southerners felt about accepting such help from the despised oil baron was perhaps assuaged by USDA control and the fact that state and local governments too, as well as regional businesses and private individuals, were contributing funds for the hiring of demonstration agents in the counties.[30]

Although the cooperative farm and home demonstration work developed much more rapidly and extensively in the South, northern and western rural counties were also inspired by the FCDW. The northern system was rather more sedate and traditional than the southern. Its USDA organizer did not share Knapp's aversion to working with the academic experts of the land-grant colleges, and he preferred that college graduates perform extension work with the presumably more well-to-do and sophisticated northern farmers.[31]

This, then, was the intensely popular rural education movement that prompted periphery congressmen to propose supportive legislation. It was not, however, entirely without opposition. Some resistance came from southern manufacturers and from plantation owners wary of more knowledgeable and self-reliant tenants. But the most organized resistance originated in the land-grant colleges. Knapp had made no secret of his disdain for the educators of the A&M colleges ("academic and military," he scoffed) and for their formalistic and technical "extension" methods. They, in turn, were extremely jealous of Knapp and the mushrooming FCDW, which was rapidly winning the hearts and minds of rural southerners. Their marginalization by a movement on its way to becoming "the largest single adult educational enterprise in the world" presented a clear threat to the colleges' public support. "It was a movement," notes Joseph C. Bailey, "that had to be killed, captured, or accepted" by the professional educators.[32] Since they were unable to kill it, they attempted to capture it.

The first obvious "capture" attempt came in 1909, when defensive activists within the AAACES finally overcame internal resistance and drafted their own bill for federal aid to agricultural extension channeled through and controlled by the A&M colleges. The bill, sponsored by Rep. J. C. McLaughlin of Michigan, went nowhere; in the end, the professional educators had to accept a mixed system in harness with the USDA and the state and local governments and had to adopt the methods pioneered by Knapp. Nevertheless, the colleges were in the game to stay.[33]

Organized Labor and the Vocational Education Movement

Meanwhile, the Davis bill of 1907 was expanding, its progress spurred by the demands of farmer and worker organizations. Labor acquired an interest in the urban vocational education sections in 1909. Whereas the involvement of the farmers' organizations came as a logical progression from their central

education concerns, their struggles over the A&M colleges, and local education efforts (for the improvement of rural schools, the establishment of agricultural high schools, and support for cooperative demonstration movements), labor's involvement was more reactive and episodic.

The AFL had endorsed various education reforms at the state level for
limited, pragmatic reasons; for example, it supported compulsory school attendance as an analog to its interest in outlawing child labor.[34] The organization's attitude toward vocational education was inextricably bound up with
its struggle against manufacturers whose representatives began to actively
champion the promotion of technical and mechanical training in the post–
Civil War decades.

Businessmen had begun, in the 1870s, to criticize the "narrow" cultural
and intellectual absorption of urban public schools and to demand that the
schools incorporate pre-vocational courses teaching basic manual skills. In the
1880s and 1890s the "manual training" movement made great headway as
educators responded to "the voracious manpower demands of an expanding
industrial economy."[35] The AFL at that time opposed the introduction of
such pre-vocational training into the schools, charging that its aim, or at least
its effect, was to turn out large numbers of half-trained "botched mechanics"
who would work for low wages and serve as strikebreakers.[36]

However, the greater threat perceived by the AFL was the proliferation
of *private* trade schools by manufacturing corporations and railroads. These
schools often made their anti-union motives explicit. They aimed not only
at increasing the numbers of skilled workers but also at imbuing them with
a strong sense of loyalty to their employers and overcoming the "artificial"
labor shortages and high wage demands produced by the union apprenticeship
system. Organizers of the new trade schools and groups like the militant antiunion National Association of Manufacturers (NAM) appealed for public
support of privately controlled vocational education by stressing the urgent
need for the United States to match its global industrial competitors—
Germany, England, and France—which had superior mechanical-training
schools. The "outrageous opposition" of labor unions to vocational education
must be overcome, the NAM argued in 1905, and "trade schools protected
from the domination and withering blight of organized labor."[37]

Labor in the Progressive Era was thus confronted with powerful forces
working against its interests. The old apprentice system run by skilled union
men was rapidly breaking down under the weight of mass-production techniques and surging immigration. Manufacturers and their educator allies were
delivering the coup de grâce by building private training institutions openly

opposed to the union movement. In the most industrialized states, moves were afoot to secure public funding for these schools or to create distinct public vocational-training schools in which employers were the primary consultants on curriculum and teacher qualifications.[38]

The vocational education movement in the industrial states reached a threshold of national visibility and organization in 1906 with the issuance of an important report commissioned by the Massachusetts legislature and the formation of a new lobbying group, the National Society for the Promotion of Industrial Education (NSPIE). The NSPIE organizers brought into the group a wide variety of activists, including social workers and representatives of both capital and labor (in addition to the New York educators at its helm). It perceived three great hurdles blocking its goals:

1. The skepticism of employers' organizations such as the NAM, which did not feel that public institutions could turn out the kind of workers they wanted

2. The opposition of organized labor to existing vocational schools under employer domination and labor's fears of a dual educational system, which not only raised the specter of employer control but also might limit the upward social mobility of working-class youth, tracking them permanently into manual occupations

3. The opposition of some public-school educators and organizations to a dual system that would take vocational education out of regular school classrooms and diminish the importance of general education[39]

The NSPIE was, first and foremost, an organization dominated by a particular segment of northeastern professional educators, and both the NAM and the AFL were initially reluctant to cooperate with the group. That the NSPIE ultimately succeeded in winning the endorsement of both labor and capital for a vocational education bill of its own design was a credit to the talents of its leadership and a testimonial to the political faintness of heart of the AFL.

The goals of this segment of core professional educators have often been summed up in the phrase "social control." Professor David Snedden of Columbia University, commissioner of education in Massachusetts at the time of that state's vocational reforms and a mentor of the NSPIE's prime mover, had developed what he called "a science of educational sociology," drawing on the ideas of Darwinist philosopher Herbert Spencer. Seeking institutional designs to improve "social efficiency" and the "enhanced social control of followers by leaders," Snedden saw vocational education as a means to fit children for their appropriate place in society. Charles Allen Prosser, his student at Columbia, followed him to Massachusetts. Prosser shared Snedden's philosophy, his contempt for general education, and his commitment to vocational tracking. Vocational education must impart specific technical skills and industrial discipline rather than broad intellectual preparation and should preferably be conducted in separate schools—a dual system on the model of German education.[40]

This philosophy represented, of course, a great departure from the democratic foundation of American public education, which had traditionally emphasized universality and equality of opportunity. Professional educators in the vocational movement effectively turned the old philosophy on its head. General education might *appear* democratic by exposing all students, regardless of social background and intellectual preparation, to the same training, but in fact it was not. General education was irrelevant to the needs of most working-class children, and they dropped out at an early age. Only half of school-age children completed eight years of schooling, and less than 10 percent finished high school. Separate vocational schools, by providing a relevant and appropriate education for these youngsters, would in fact be more democratic than the existing system.[41] *interesting*

Such arguments might be expected to align the NSPIE more with business than with organized labor, and indeed the group's leadership "privately confided their preference for professionals and moderate businessmen."[42] However, NSPIE activists genuinely desired to provide a forum for the reconciliation of class differences on educational issues and recognized the importance of winning labor's support for public vocational education. When first organized in 1906, the NSPIE extended membership to three trade unionists, including John Mitchell, and invited Mitchell to assume a place on the group's board. However, the United Mine Workers president refused the offer.[43]

In 1908, in the midst of its legal battle with militant employers' organizations over union rights, the AFL decided to establish its own vocational education committee and to speak for itself in the growing vocational education debate. It recognized that the movement for government involvement was becoming unstoppable and that labor passivity might result in the creation of a system potentially hostile to its interests. The AFL committee created the following year included Samuel Gompers, John Mitchell, and Rep. William B. Wilson.[44] Representative Wilson may have drawn the committee's attention to the vocational bill then being strongly promoted by Representative Davis of Minnesota. At any rate, on entering the lists, the AFL decided to ally itself with the Minnesota agrarian, who welcomed support from this new quarter. The labor leaders' instincts, on the heels of the Bryan outreach,

were apparently to ally trade unionists with farmers' organizations and, eschewing middle-class tutelage, to present their case in the legislature.

The Davis bill enjoyed strong agrarian support, with endorsements from
the Grange, the Farmers' National Congress, the Farmers' Union, and the
state of Georgia. The AFL believed that it could have a greater impact by
joining the campaign for a federal program rather than working to block or
channel vocational movements in the individual core industrial states, where
professional educators and employers' organizations exercised great influence.[45] The AFL committee thus simply appropriated the Davis bill and
made a few modifications: it increased spending from $8 to $11 million (keeping expenditures symmetrically apportioned between rural areas and cities),
shifted the major federal supervisory responsibility from the secretary of agriculture to the secretary of the interior, and required that the vocational funds
be administered by the same state education boards that oversaw public education generally. To the section of the bill requiring that federal funds be
used only for "distinctive studies" in agriculture, home economics, and the
trades and industries, the new draft added short courses and part-time "continuation" courses open to those already in the workforce.[46]

The Davis bill fit the AFL's agenda. It established a national program,
bringing vocational education into the public schools, where working men
and women, as citizens and voters, could influence the direction of such education and could counter management's anti-union ideology. The bill kept
urban industrial education in a unitary system, avoiding the separation of
vocational students into separate and culturally impoverished institutions.[47]
Further, it was targeted at children fourteen and over who had already completed eight or nine years of general education, rather than starting in the
elementary grades as favored by the NAM and the social Darwinist professional educators.[48] After the revisions were made, according to Gompers, "a
representative of the Farmers' Organization and a representative of the American Federation of Labor jointly presented this bill on industrial education
to Senator [Jonathan] Dolliver of Iowa," who promptly introduced it into
the Senate in January 1910. Representative Davis sponsored the bill in the
House.[49]

For the next two years of accelerated legislative activity, the AFL was the
leading advocate of federal aid to vocational education. Senator Dolliver allowed an AFL official, Arthur E. Holder, to preside over his committee's
hearings on the bill in April 1910.[50] The AFL undertook an energetic effort
to publicize the measure and to yoke farm and labor organizations behind it,
along with whatever educational and business groups could be persuaded to

join the campaign.[51] With the latter groups there was little success. The NAM refused to participate in the April hearings. Although a few individual educators submitted endorsements, the major professional associations took positions ranging from wary to hostile. The NSPIE refused to support the Davis-Dolliver bill; the group's efforts so far had been directed toward securing state, not federal, legislation, and its leaders had strong objections to many aspects of the measure.[52] The National Education Association for the first time began to take more positive notice of the bill but was not yet ready to endorse it. The head of the federal Bureau of Education opposed the Davis bill, even after it was revised to give his office a major administrative role. Other educators and congressmen objected that it was unprecedented, premature, and probably unconstitutional.[53] In 1910 the movement for federal aid to vocational education had little elite support.

The popularity of the FCDW and the campaign for the Davis-Dolliver bill did, however, spur the professional educators to develop their own bills. As described earlier, the AAACES had drawn up a measure for federal extension aid channeled through the land-grant colleges: the 1909 McLaughlin bill. Senator Dolliver, chair of the Committee on Agriculture and Forestry, early in 1910 became the sponsor of a similar extension bill in the upper chamber. Since agrarians favored federal aid both for agricultural extension and for high-school vocational education (and since the cooperative demonstration movement encompassed both farms and schools), congressional supporters decided in mid-1910 to combine the two measures. The resulting omnibus bill thus contained the three major sections of the former Davis-Dolliver bill (providing $5 million a year for high-school instruction in trades and industries, home economics, and agriculture; appropriating an equal amount for district agricultural high schools and branch experiment stations; and providing $1 million for state normal schools), to which was added a provision authorizing $1.5 million for the state land-grant college extension work. In states with racially separate institutions, a "just and equitable division" between the two was required. Later versions of the bill added additional funds to sweeten this provision for the South and increased the total agricultural extension appropriations to just under $3 million.[54]

The combined vocational-extension bill was favorably reported by the Senate Committee in June 1910. It was endorsed by the Grange, the Farmers' Union, the American Society of Equity (a midwestern farm organization), and the Farmers' National Congress, as well as by the AFL and the National Education Association. The NSPIE, however, refused to support it. Leading NSPIE activists saw the omnibus bill as a hodgepodge that was drafted, in

Professor Snedden's words, "with a view to the needs of the southern and western portions of the country." Administration by the Bureau of Education in the Interior Department, in collaboration with other federal agencies, and the channeling of aid to state education departments threatened to bring vocational education under the influence of the general educators, which was anathema to the "dual-system" enthusiasts of the NSPIE. If there was to be a federal vocational program, it was essential that a central national administrative agency responsive to the NSPIE's distinct technical vision of vocational education be created. Otherwise, responsibility would be fragmented and ineffective, and the general educators could "corrupt 'vocational' education into 'liberal' education."[55]

The NSPIE's opposition to the Davis-Dolliver bill was matched by that of the land-grant college association. The AAACES, like the NSPIE, was opposed to combining the extension and vocational bills. Many of its members feared that the new and unprecedented aid to high schools and state teacher-training institutions and the establishment of branch experiment stations would create powerful rivals for a limited pool of federal aid. Perhaps most significant, the land-grant colleges feared subordination to national authority (the original McLaughlin bill had granted funds to the colleges with very few strings attached). The colleges' association therefore stepped up its campaign for a separate extension bill.[56]

In the 62nd Congress, the Democrats took control of the House of Representatives, and Rep. Asbury Lever became chair of the Agriculture Committee, replacing a Republican congressman notably unenthusiastic about either of the proposals. Lever idolized Seaman Knapp and was intent on securing more federal aid to expand his kind of extension work.[57] Although this interest predisposed Lever to back a separate extension bill—and he promptly introduced his own—it did not make the South Carolina representative a mouthpiece for the AAACES. In fact, the congressmen most enthusiastic about expanding federal aid for practical agricultural education were intent on preventing the colleges from imposing their traditional, limited vision of extension on the federal program. To that end, they insisted on giving the USDA a strong role in the development of the extension system; they also specified in the bill that at least 75 percent of the appropriated funds be expended for field demonstrations and that the existing FCDW be protected.[58]

The colleges' association ultimately became resigned to the conditions imposed by the congressional agrarians—the requirement to "cooperate" with (and submit its extension proposals for approval by) the USDA and to adopt the Knapp "hands-on" demonstration system—in order to secure federal aid through a distinct program in the line of the Morrill, Hatch, and Nelson Acts. Given the probability that Congress would soon provide national underwriting for the farmers' practical education movement, most of the land-grant college officials realized the advantage of linking the new program to a historically legitimated policy in which their institutions had been given the central role.[59]

In 1912, the southern Democrats who controlled the House Education Committee decided to press on with the extension bill rather than endorse the omnibus measure under Republican sponsorship in the Senate. On the death of Senator Dolliver, that bill had been adopted by Sen. Carroll Page of Vermont, a straight-arrow core Republican who, for some combination of personal and political-entrepreneurial reasons, had decided to devote his energies to the cause of vocational education. Representative Lever indicated to Senator Page that he would not oppose having some of the vocational provisions added to his bill when it reached the upper chamber, but he worried that the large appropriation carried by the omnibus bill ($14.5 million when fully implemented, compared with $3 million for the Lever bill) would frighten off potential supporters.[60] Unsure about the degree of meshing of the two bills that might occur later, the core Republican and the periphery Democrat embarked on a friendly competition (its cordiality encouraged by the degree of overlap among the grass-roots enthusiasts of the two measures) to promote their separate bills in the House and the Senate. Both worked to cultivate broad political support within and beyond their own regions.

The Page bill secured the endorsement and publicizing resources of the NAM, which was won over to the idea of a publicly controlled vocational education system by the NSPIE.[61] The latter had, in late 1911, made a decision like that of the AAACES: to prevent the enactment of an objectionable bill, the NSPIE had to move energetically to capture the legislative initiative. When Prosser took over the directorship of the NSPIE in early 1912, the organization moved into high gear. Senator Page at first resisted attempts by Snedden and Prosser to redraft his bill to meet their central concerns, but he was gradually worn down by the professional vocationalists;[62] the Page bill, though its fundamentals were still those of the Davis-Dolliver program, came more and more to reflect the NSPIE's preferences for centralized administrative guidance and a distinct orientation for the local vocational high schools. It is not so surprising that Page, without much support within the core Republican contingent, would come to rely on the professional vocationalists. They, after all, had long led the state vocational movement in the Northeast and now boasted the support of leading capitalists. What is more remarkable is the acquiescence of labor to the NSPIE agenda.

The "capture" of the vocational campaign by the NSPIE in 1912 was facilitated by the withdrawal of the AFL from active leadership of the movement. Why the labor organization was so easily elbowed aside by the professional educators is difficult to understand. One may credit the impressive public relations skills of NSPIE leaders, who worked hard to secure the support of both labor and capital for their particular vision of public vocational education. When the NAM capitulated to NSPIE and ceased to use vocational education as a major forum for its attack on labor, the AFL may simply, as Elizabeth Fones-Wolf argues, have "eased its vigilance because it no longer perceived industrial training as a direct threat to trade unionism." Having "accomplished its primary goals—preventing the growth of trade schools and establishing the general belief that vocationalism was a matter for the public school system"—the AFL ceased to play an active role and left the details of the bill and the responsibility for its promotion to others.[63]

Of course, the devil may lurk in the details, and labor thus gave up the opportunity to shape a vocational bill of genuine benefit to the working class. It also, by not actively pressing for speedy legislative action, allowed a delay of five more years for the inauguration of the program. The legislative campaign was handed over to Page, a core Republican without a pro-labor record, and to the professional educators, and the effort to cultivate public opinion was left mostly to the NAM. Though William Wilson, the AFL's principal spokesman in the House, was the vocational bill's sponsor in that chamber, he seems to have accepted the NSPIE's direction at least as readily as did Page.[64] Perhaps the best explanation is simply that the AFL had never had much inclination to support positive social legislation, particularly at the national level, and that its brief leadership of the federal vocational campaign was an aberration, provoked, as was true of most of its legislative battles, by a defensive effort in its struggle with the enemies of trade-union organization. And in a national election year in which labor was uncomfortable with the presidential choices and played no major role in the political arena, the AFL was not in a strong position to press its claims on the Democratic Party.

The Farmer-Labor Package Fails

After labor had withdrawn from the fray, congressional Democrats had even less reason to cooperate with core professional educators or with Page, an otherwise conservative New England Republican with whom—unlike Dolliver and Davis—they had seldom been aligned in the past. Given the opposition to the unprecedented and expensive vocational bill from influential conservative Republicans[65] and the contrasting broad and enthusiastic support for aid to extension in the farm states, the temptation was great for the congressional agrarian leaders to try to pass their more modest program first while promising subsequent action on the larger vocational project. For the agrarian *followers*, however, the strategy was not so obvious. The Grange had been an early supporter of the vocational bill, and its active women's contingent was very enthusiastic about the expansion of high-school home economics training.[66] The organization, lobbied by both camps, continued to affirm its support for both the vocational and the extension bills.[67] Likewise, the Farmers' Union continued, through 1912, to "heartily endorse all pending legislation in Congress to promote vocational education."[68] The Farmers' National Congress remained steadfastly loyal to the Page bill.[69]

In House debate on the Lever bill, a number of periphery- and diverse-area representatives urged that high-school vocational education be added to the extension bill.[70] However, their amendments were defeated after the bill's advocates argued that although they supported such legislation, its attachment would only slow the enactment of the extension bill.[71] The Lever bill was passed without a roll call on August 23, 1912.[72]

Supporters of the vocational bill were, of course, fearful that separate passage of the extension measure would diminish the rural sections' support for the high-school program. They were thus intent on maintaining the combination. In January 1913, over the opposition of Georgia Sen. Hoke Smith and his allies, and clearly with much support from periphery senators, Page added the vocational sections of his bill to the Smith-Lever extension bill and secured passage of the omnibus package by voice vote in committee of the whole.[73] However, when the Vermont Republican subsequently moved to replace the cobbled-together omnibus bill with his original measure, omitting key provisions of the Smith-Lever bill, he lost most Democratic support. For the southern Democrats in particular, passage of the original Page bill not only was substantively less desirable but also would give all credit for the program's enactment to the Republicans. The Democrats had just won control of Congress and the White House; why hand the GOP an eleventh-hour victory? The Page substitute passed 31–30, but both the vocational and the extension bills died in conference.[74]

Senator Smith subsequently suggested a compromise: the extension bill would be cleared for passage in the new (63rd) Congress, and since the vocational bill still contained badly drafted and controversial features, a commission would be appointed to study and report a plan for national aid to vocational education. With the Democrats in control and with his mentor, Prosser, now actively supporting the commission strategy, Page had little choice but to go along.[75] The AFL, by now concentrating its energies on the antitrust exemption, also accepted the compromise. A commission of nine was appointed in February 1914. The NSPIE lobbied the administration hard for the "right" appointments and was gratified when Prosser and four like-minded vocational activists were chosen for the commission, along with four congressmen. The NSPIE had, of course, prepared well for this assignment, and despite the presence on the commission of Senators Smith and Page, Prosser easily dominated its work.[76]

The extension bill came to a vote in the House on January 19, 1914, the day before the resolution creating the vocational commission cleared Congress. Lever's committee now boasted that the extension bill was "most heartily commended" by the AFL.[77] Though extremely popular among rural legislators, the bill did draw some bipartisan opposition from the core. Rep. John Fitzgerald (D, New York) called the measure "wholly obnoxious to our theory of government": it intruded the federal government into local affairs to an unprecedented and illegitimate extent.[78] Similar objections were raised in the Senate by Sen. Frank Brandegee (R, Connecticut), who warned of the dangers of socialism and chided the southern Democrats for abandoning their historic defense of states' rights and limited government. To this, Sen. James Vardaman of Mississippi responded by arguing, "The highest end of government is the improvement of Man." He added that the good sense of the public could be counted on to secure useful improvements through the state while avoiding the dangers of socialism.[79]

However, the southern Democrats had not completely abandoned the defense of states' rights. When the race issue emerged in the debate over the extension bill, they insisted on the states' authority in social matters. Northern farm-state Republicans attempted to secure language that would, as in the 1890 Morrill Act and the McLaughlin and Page bills, ensure a fair distribution of funds to the black land-grant colleges. Senators Vardaman and Smith fiercely resisted the inclusion of an explicit racial-fairness mandate. After the chamber passed a moderate amendment, by Gilbert Hitchcock of Nebraska, providing that extension work be conducted "without discrimination as to race," the devious Senator Smith arranged to have the provision given up in conference, leaving the bill's funds to be distributed as the state legislatures directed (as in the House version). Over the protest of the advocates of racial fairness, the conference bill was approved and signed by the president in May 1914.[80]

The Smith-Lever Agricultural Extension Act inaugurated a large-scale system of practical education for farmers, conducted by the land-grant colleges "in cooperation with" the USDA. The novel and controversial "cooperative" feature was much protested by the colleges and by northern states' rights defenders in Congress. The USDA, however, was probably more popular than the colleges with periphery farmers, and its supervision was deemed necessary to the institutionalization of the system of participatory learning developed under Knapp.

The USDA was also, not surprisingly, more popular in the farm states than was Rockefeller. An explicit provision was inserted in the bill, at the instigation of Sen. William Kenyon of Iowa, to limit the private funds that might be raised as part of the state's matching share to contributions "from within the state." This provision effectively cut the GEB out of any further role in extension work. Passed at a time when the Standard Oil baron's popularity was at an all-time low because of the massacre of strikers and their families by the Rockefeller-controlled Colorado Fuel and Iron Company, the Smith-Lever Act thus had the virtue of reclaiming extension work from an association with "tainted" Rockefeller money.[81]

The act effected an increase in federal funds for cooperative demonstration from $330,014 in 1913 to $1,080,000 in 1915–16. In addition, states were required to match a portion of the federal appropriation, and total FCDW contributions from within the states rose from $272,569 to $1,695,054. The number of agents engaged in the FCDW increased from 878 in 1913 to 1,136 in 1915. On the eve of World War I, the number of demonstration agents had grown to 1,400; federal and within-state appropriations had increased to $2,719,281 and $3,430,338, respectively. Before the Smith-Lever Act went into effect, there were 100 African-American demonstration agents in the southern and border states; by 1923, there were 294, composing 12 percent of the national total.[82] On the basis of such statistics, one may thus count the 1914 act as a victory for farmers, even perhaps for southern black farmers, whose interests failed to secure any formal protection in the law. In the long term, and particularly after the decline of autonomous agrarian movement organizations, the extension system gave rise to distinct costs that must, in any assessment, be tallied against the benefits. But that is another story, recounted by other scholars.[83]

Meanwhile, the vocational education bill was now firmly under the control of Prosser and his allies. The NSPIE-dominated commission issued its recommendations and a bill embodying them in June 1914.[84] Though the substance of the old Davis-Dolliver-Page bills, shorn of their extension sections, was visible in the commission bill, the latter differed in significant respects from the earlier drafts. The 1910 bill promoted by the AFL had been only two pages long and contained little detail on administration or the nature of the vocational education to be subsidized. The Department of Interior's Bureau of Education had been designated to exercise general oversight, with some unspecified "cooperation" from the secretary of agriculture and the secretary of commerce and labor. State boards for agricultural high schools, general public secondary schools, and normal schools were to receive funds and send to the three cabinet secretaries reports detailing their use of the money. The four-and-a-half-page commission bill, by contrast, created a Federal Board for Vocational Education, which had its own staff separate from the departments. The board was authorized to make its own studies, develop its own guidelines, and scrutinize the plans and subsequent compliance of single state vocational education boards. The nature and types of education to be supported were also specified in much more detail. Clearly, the NSPIE principals were intent on creating a centralized, hierarchical system in which the organization's vision of technical training completely distinct from general education and designed to "fit children for useful employment" could be implemented.[85]

The AFL, in contrast, had advocated the expansion of "supplementary technical and industrial training" programs through the existing public schools in order to provide a high-quality preparation for diverse industrial employment. During the early period of its leadership of the vocational education campaign, and even after it ceded control to the NSPIE, the AFL opposed narrow, job-oriented training intended to supply specific machine-tenders for employers. It also insisted that the children enrolled in vocational classes continue to be exposed to a full palette of civic and cultural education. Labor seemed to anticipate a nationally decentralized but locally unitary public system that would be responsive to local needs. In this system, trade unionists would have had, through their participation on local vocational advisory boards and in their normal capacity as citizens and parents, a good deal of input into the design of vocational courses. The AFL urged that opportunities for working-class youth be expanded, with no door to be closed prematurely, and that control over vocational preparation be lodged firmly in the public sphere.[86] The NSPIE activists on the commission, however, were explicit about their social purposes, which had very different class implications. They urged a federal program to maintain "our position in the markets of the world," to recognize "different tastes and abilities," to introduce "the aims of utility" into public education, and to minimize "industrial and social unrest" by fitting workers for their callings.[87]

The majority in Congress were probably more favorable to the AFL than to the NSPIE vision; some openly expressed fears about the undemocratic aspects of a dual system.[88] Nevertheless, a bill closely modeled on the commission draft was introduced early in the 64th Congress and was enacted, with little opposition, toward the end of the Congress.[89] The reason for the long delay and for the failure to enact the bill in time for the very tight 1916 elections remains unclear. NSPIE officials did persuade Gompers to meet with Senator Smith to urge the bill's passage. With the Georgia senator's belated cooperation, the measure was passed by the upper chamber in July 1916,[90] but the House did not take up the bill until it returned, after the election recess, in December. A great deal of important legislation completing the agrarian agenda and delivering on higher AFL priorities took precedence in the 64th Congress. Further, Congress and the president were locked in debate over preparedness, and President Woodrow Wilson did not make the vocational bill an administration priority.[91] Certainly, it cannot be said that the bill was delayed by business opposition. The NAM and the U.S. Chamber of Commerce had urged its passage for years.[92] But this Congress was not very deferential to business. Democrats were more likely to have noticed labor's reticence than the support of business or, for that matter, the campaign by the NSPIE.

Passage by the House came in the late session after the 1916 elections. President Wilson had recently decided that industrial education was a fitting component of his effort to prepare the country for war with Germany, and he urged enactment of the bill in his end-of-the-year address. The chastened House Democrats gave the bill privileged status and passed it on January 9, 1917.[93] During the debate, there was some grumbling about the federal government exceeding its powers. In response, supporters spoke of a national interest that stretched from enhancing global competitiveness down to securing better homemakers. The representatives closest to organized labor were silent during the debate. It was left to Rep. George Huddleston of Alabama to present the workers' case for federal aid to education. "Education of the masses," he argued, "is the imperative requirement of every democracy." The state in every civilized country assumes responsibility for liberal education, "to fit . . . people for citizenship," to enhance the ability of citizens to earn a livelihood, and to ensure that its people are "secured in a larger wage and shorter hours of labor." But he warned:

In providing for vocational education we should carefully preserve the democracy of the public school. It is the nation's real melting pot, where prejudices of class and caste are broken down and where young Americans learn to respect their fellow citizens of differing types, blood and antecedents. We must be careful to preserve this democracy. Those who expect to enter manual occupations must not be segregated from their fellow pupils, but must be kept in close touch with them so as not to constitute a separate class. We must not make the mistake that has been made by some European countries where children [destined] for useful occupations are from the beginning separated from those who are seeking a . . . liberal education.

The vocational education which I support is not that which would teach a mechanic a trade. . . . The training should be general and fundamental. . . . In dealing with education for industry we should keep in mind as our chief consideration the interest of labor rather than that of the industry itself. . . . We should not interfere with the apprentice system of the trade unions, and in no respect should the labor organizations be antagonized. . . . No system of vocational education can hope to be successful except with the cooperation of organized labor. . . . Above all other things we must be absolutely sure that any system of vocational instruction is not used to oppress labor or to destroy labor's organizations. It must not be possible to train pupils in vocational schools for use as strike breakers or for any other direct effect upon labor disputes.[94]

These had been Gompers's sentiments—certainly not Prosser's—but they were voiced by an agrarian ally rather than a labor spokesman; the AFL had abandoned the field to the middle-class professionals.

After the bill passed, Prosser was appointed the first executive director of the Federal Board for Vocational Education, and he stamped the formative policy with the NSPIE's ideals.[95] The AFL, a late and ambivalent participant in national politics, had not yet learned what the farmers had gleaned from their early experience with the ICC: the cost of ensuring a federal bureaucracy responsive to social-movement goals was careful legislative crafting and eternal vigilance.

With the passage of the two practical education measures of 1914–17, the farmers (*white* farmers in particular) appeared to gain a more solid victory than workers, for reasons summarized in table 9.2. The Smith-Lever Act created a large-scale, publicly controlled, reliably funded, cooperative demonstration program that closely followed the preferences of grass-roots farm organizations and that placed administration in an agency of proven sympathies and under continuing farmer influence. The Smith-Hughes Vocational Education Act required the support of agrarians and the precedents estab-

Table 9.2 Labor Weaknesses and Farmer Strengths in the Legislative Battle for Aid to Practical Education

Labor Weaknesses

1. The nonpartisan voluntarist tradition of hit-or-miss opposition to enemies or support for a few friends willing to endorse particular items on labor's agenda left labor with few consistent standard-bearers in Congress, and several supporters were "deviant" Republicans unable to organize majority support for labor measures. For example, working with Republican Sen. Carroll Page of Vermont on vocational education meant that the measure was hostage to skeptical standpat Republicans when that party controlled Congress, and when southern Democrats were in control, their leaders felt little responsibility to back a "Republican" bill for which they would receive little political credit. The absence of a larger group of labor Democrats in the House and, particularly, the Senate—itself a result of labor's weak and vacillating political strategy—meant that there was no strong, strategically situated group of legislators to press for labor's agenda and bargain with major congressional factions.

2. Organized labor's inability and/or unwillingness to dominate a major party, its small national membership, and its vulnerable position in the political economy encouraged its leaders to seek legitimacy in business-labor-intellectual partnerships (brokered by the last) such as the National Civic Federation and the National Society for the Promotion of Industrial Education. But such alliances resulted in the compromising or watering down of labor's goals (to a greater extent than would have occurred in open alliance with the agrarian Democrats), in order to find a common denominator with business and to serve the agenda of middle-class professionals.

Farmer Strengths

1. Politically mobilized farmers had made the Democratic Party a vehicle for agrarian (especially periphery agrarian) interests. When the Republicans controlled the national state, the Democrats in Congress could ally with agrarian- and diverse-area Republicans and occasionally win; when Democrats controlled the state, the policy agenda was dominated by agrarian interests.

2. Because of earlier legislative victories (the creation of a Department of Agriculture in 1862 and its elevation to cabinet status in 1889, a quarter century before there was a Department of Labor; the 1890–1906 Morrill, Hatch, and Adams Acts in aid of land-grant colleges and experiment stations; and federal support for farm "demonstration work" since 1902), the constitutionality of federal aid to practical education for farmers was easier to defend. Such aid could be supported as merely "completing a system" of agricultural education by adding its logical last step—bringing scientific knowledge to farmers on their farms.

lished by their legislation,[96] but its final drafting was largely the work of middle-class educators. Although the AFL's original goal when it undertook its most active role in federal social-policy debates was achieved through the 1917 legislation—the creation of a public, nationally supported vocational-training system—the new law contained provisions, and embodied a vision, that were in significant respects antithetical to labor's preferences, and it placed administration in a new entity in which labor had very limited influence.

10

The Labor Program of the Farmers' Party

In asserting their political power to reconstruct the national state, the farmers' representatives in the legislature undoubtedly gave first priority to the agrarian agenda. Their major efforts were put forward on behalf of transportation, antimonopoly, banking and currency, tariff, and agricultural extension laws. But this preoccupation did not imply that labor's needs were ignored. To the contrary, the agrarian Democrats, often joined by a minority of Republicans representing the periphery and diverse sections, enacted, by the end of the 64th Congress, almost the whole of the agenda endorsed by national labor leaders. Although labor's electoral support was halfhearted in 1910, 1912, and 1914 the delivery for labor continued to expand from 1911 to 1917 and included some policies whose content and method aroused profound misgivings in the periphery, especially in the South.

Some southern members of Congress made no attempt to disguise their ambivalence, and a few of those most weakly attached to the populist tradition—such as Texas Sen. Joseph Bailey, Georgia Sen. Hoke Smith, and Alabama Rep. Oscar Underwood—were openly hostile to significant portions of the labor program. When such men inveighed against the rationale of an eight-hour bill, impatiently attempted to push aside a labor measure to make more time for a tariff debate, or got caught up in arcane constitutional considerations that delayed a worker-safety bill, they antagonized northern Democratic allies and underlined the cultural gulf that separated farmer and worker.[1] It was thus not surprising that Samuel Gompers seemed to feel ill at ease with the southern Democrats and more comfortable with northern Republican progressives. But despite the opposition of some southerners and the frequent galling reminders of labor's second-fiddle status in the farmer-labor coalition, even the southern agrarians were generally more faithful (and, of course, more numerous) allies than the progressive Republicans. Although individual GOP dissidents played conspicuous roles on some labor measures (Sen. William Borah, for example, was a champion of child-labor legislation), the only insurgent to strongly support labor reform over a broad range of issues was Robert La Follette.[2] The progressive Republicans saw themselves as free agents, and their votes were unpredictable. They were also gifted theoreticians whose speechmaking and reputation for principled action could obscure occasional anti-labor purposes and confound both labor leaders and scholars of the Progressive Era.[3]

The reasons for the agrarian Democrats' persistence in the labor agenda were obvious: the northern urban Democrats from labor districts backed the farmers' program even when it was not obviously in *their* interest to do so, and without support from other regions, the state-expansionist agrarians could not hope to control the national government. Besides, the old Greenback- Populist-Bryan Democratic exaltation of the "producers' alliance" was a powerful ideological commitment. Whenever the commitment faded under the pressure of the party's minority conservative faction (as in 1904), the dismal electoral results provided a sharp reminder of where the most promising strategy lay. Clearly, the agrarians could not expect much support from the urban middle classes (even less from business) or from farmers near urban markets or dependent on Republican tariff policy. Even though political mobilization of workers might never be impressive, the farmer-labor alliance was the only real hope for agrarian reformers.

Dress Rehearsal

Though the national labor organization had played no significant role in the 1910 campaign,[4] the votes of northern workers did make some contribution to the anti-Republican tide that landed the Democratic Party in control of the House of Representatives—and signaled the arrival of a national, Democrat-led progressivism. Sixty House seats shifted from Republican to Democratic hands in 1911. Twenty-six were located in core industrial districts; another six were in industrial sections of diverse trade areas. Of these thirty-two new industrial-district congressmen, seventeen had won with less than 50 percent of the vote and would be particularly anxious to produce a viable legislative record for the 1912 elections.[5]

For the position of Speaker, the 1911 House elected Champ Clark of Missouri, a Bryan ally who represented an agricultural district and was considered a loyal friend of labor. The AFL was also encouraged that fifteen members of the House—eleven Democrats, three Republicans, and Socialist Victor Berger—had trade-union backgrounds. Gompers reported that the fifteen representatives "frequently held conferences with the officers of the American Federation of Labor, counselling with us as to the best methods by which they could be of service to the cause of labor and to the people generally."[6]

Although the labor group did not vote as a block on the floor or feel bound by AFL pronouncements, five of the Democratic unionists did serve as useful spokesmen for organized labor in the councils of the "farmers' party." It was particularly gratifying that William Wilson of Pennsylvania, formerly secretary-treasurer of the United Mine Workers, became chair of the House Labor Committee in the 62nd Congress. A committee that, under Joseph Cannon's regime, had been a graveyard for labor bills now became, in a Democratic House, a seedbed for labor laws.[7]

Another of the "union-card" representatives, textile unionist William Hughes of New Jersey, had already proved a valuable labor champion in 1910. On the AFL's suggestion, Hughes introduced an amendment to an appropriations bill that would bar any use of the scheduled funds for federal government prosecutions of trade unions under the Sherman Act. The provision was incorporated into the House bill but failed in the Senate. It elicited a second House vote when a Republican representative proposed that the House recede from its disagreement with the Senate and abandon the proviso. On this vote, the position of President William Howard Taft and the standpat Republicans carried (see table 10.1).[8] The fate of the Hughes amendment, and the voting pattern it elicited, should have made one thing clear to the trade union federation: on this most urgent and difficult of labor's grievances, the unionists depended on the periphery Democrats; but without a larger contingent of sympathetic core Democrats to supplement their forces and prod party leaders to give high priority to labor legislation (and, of course, without a Democrat in the White House), there was scant hope for the labor exemption. Despite the blossoming insurgency within the Republican Party (a development that Gompers enthusiastically applauded), even minor items on labor's political agenda had languished in the Republican-controlled 61st Congress.[9]

With Democratic control of the lower chamber in the 62nd Congress, a small breach was opened in the Republican dam. The farmers' party used its partial control of the legislature as a "dress rehearsal" for the rise to power that was now anticipated. The agrarians would demonstrate to the country—and, in particular, to labor—that this was the genuine party of reform.[10] The result was a great outpouring of labor proposals, including bills sharply limiting injunctions in labor disputes, providing jury trials in contempt cases, prohibiting Justice Department prosecutions of labor under the antitrust laws, legalizing unions in the postal service, creating a Department of Labor in the cabinet and giving it power to mediate labor disputes, creating a Children's Bureau to investigate and report on child health and living (and working)

Table 10.1 Justice Department Prosecution of Labor Unions
under the Antitrust Law (1910)

	Senate: Remove Hughes Amendment (thus allowing prosecution) 34–16 D 2–11 R 32–5			
% of Seats in Senate		% Yea	(N)	% of All Yeas
28.3	Core	87.5	(16)	41.2
15.2	Diverse	62.5	(8)	14.7
56.5	Periphery	57.7	(26)	44.1

House: I. Instruct Conferees to Keep Hughes Amendment Barring Prosecution 154–105 D 116–2 R 38–103				House: II. Concur with Senate (recede from Hughes Amendment) 138–130 D 3–109 R 135–21	
% of Seats in House		% Yea	% of All Yeas	% Yea	% of All Yeas
33.5	Core	27.0	13.0	76.7	50.0
19.9	Diverse	47.4	17.5	61.4	25.4
46.5	Periphery	83.6	69.5	28.1	24.6

conditions, improving the working conditions of merchant seamen, enacting at long last the eight-hour limitation on all federal government contracts and on river and harbor work, levying a prohibitive tax on unsafe phosphorous matches, and restricting interstate shipments of goods produced by convict labor.[11] The injunction, contempt, and convict-labor laws passed the House but died in the Republican Senate. President Taft vetoed the Justice Department prohibition and the seamen's bill, along with a measure, long sought by the AFL, to restrict immigration.

Organized labor's expressed legislative agenda was moderate and brief. In the main, it comported with the AFL's purist, organization-empowering strategy. That characterization is less apt for the Children's Bureau or the phosphorous match bill, but these were not central concerns for the trade unionists (social workers, academics, and middle-class reformers in the American Association for Labor Legislation played the major role in promoting these bills). The seamen's bill regulating hours, working and safety rules, shipboard punishments, pay practices, and contract requirements also appears to violate AFL voluntarism, but existing federal law and international agreements held merchant seamen in a state of near-bondage for the duration of the voyage, and attempts by seamen to escape in port could lead to arrest and imprisonment or forced labor.[12] These peculiar, near-feudal conditions could be changed only through federal law. The seamen's bill, like most of the other measures on labor's agenda, was not of concern just to the AFL and allied unions. Although one could easily suggest, on the basis of contemporary European legislation, numerous additions to this agenda, most of what labor *did* support was of benefit to American workers generally.

House Democrats did not always pass the precise bills that labor endorsed. In the case of the anti-injunction bill, the AFL backed a measure that Republican Rep. George Pearre of Maryland had agreed to sponsor in the 60th Congress. The bill attempted to limit injunctions—which were issued under the equity jurisdiction of the courts, ostensibly to protect property—by constructing a narrow definition of that term.[13] However, in 1912 House hearings, the lawyer for the American Antiboycott Association ridiculed the idea that Congress could ever, by statue, persuade the courts to overturn numerous precedents and adopt a constricted definition of property rights. The Democratic Judiciary Committee of the 62nd Congress therefore decided on another approach. Under the chairman, Henry Clayton of Alabama, committee Democrats crafted a bill that did not attempt a new and problematic definition of property. Rather, it banned federal injunctions in labor disputes "unless necessary to prevent irreparable injury to property or to a property right" (presumably a very high threshold), and it then went on to list specific acts— the normal activities engaged in by labor unions in the course of disputes with employers or in the process of recruiting members—for which no injunction could be issued.[14] The House passed this bill in May 1912 by a vote of 243 to 31 (with unanimous Democratic support and almost half of core Republicans abstaining rather than casting an overtly anti-labor vote in an election year).

Two months later the House passed a companion bill providing jury trials in contempt-of-court proceedings (see table 10.2).[15] A measure similar to the latter, sponsored by Sen. Augustus Bacon of Georgia, had passed the Senate in 1896. It attacked the obvious injustice of allowing biased judges who had granted injunctions to serve (in Bacon's words) as "judge, jury and prosecutor" and to levy fines and jail terms against union representatives who might not even be aware that an injunction had been issued.[16] Juries, especially those assembled in mining and industrial communities, were expected to be more favorable to labor than were federal judges.[17] The contempt bill had died in

Table 10.2 Anti-injunction and Jury Trial Bills

% of Seats		Clayton Anti-injunction Bill (House Passage, 1912) 243–31 D 166–0 R 73–31		Provision for Jury Trial in Contempt-of-Court Cases (House Passage, 1912) 233–18 D 160–0 R 67–18	
		% Yea	% of All Yeas	% Yea	% of All Yeas
32.7	Core	76.3	23.9	82.1	23.6
20.0	Diverse	85.7	22.2	90.7	21.0
47.2	Periphery	97.0	53.9	99.2	55.4

the overwhelmingly Republican House in 1896, and fifty-three subsequent bills had perished in the committees to which they were referred during the years of Republican control. The jury trial measure that passed the House in the 62nd Congress was, like the companion anti-injunction bill, a long-awaited payoff by the agrarians to their labor allies, endorsed by Democratic platforms since 1896. The timing of passage—in the summer of 1912—made clear the perceived importance of these bills for the farmer-labor electoral alliance, and the large majorities demonstrated the power of such an alliance.[18] Senate Democrats repeatedly tried, unsuccessfully, to discharge the anti-injunction bill from the Republican-led committee in the upper chamber.[19] Both measures would be incorporated into the Clayton Act two years later.

Of the bills signed into law during the 62nd Congress, the greatest significance was accorded by the AFL to a U.S. Post Office bill that guaranteed postal workers the eight-hour day and, most important, the rights of petition and association.[20] Significant increases in workload ordered by the postmaster general, along with a refusal to fill positions authorized by Congress, had resulted in "a great deal of friction and trouble" in the postal service. To forestall workers' complaints to the legislature, both President Theodore Roosevelt and President Taft had issued executive "gag" orders prohibiting all executive-branch employees, either directly or through employee organizations, from appealing to Congress for improvement of wages and working conditions or responding to requests for information, except as authorized by department heads, on penalty of losing their jobs. The AFL pressed hard for a legislative remedy, and the requisite bill was sponsored by insurgent Senator La Follette and Democratic Rep. James Lloyd of Missouri. The major controversy around the bill was whether workers could join organizations affiliated with the AFL and whether they had a right to strike. The version passed by the Democratic House had forbidden punishment of workers for "membership in any society, association, club or any other form of organization" aiming at improving labor conditions. In the Senate, Wesley Jones (R, Washington) proposed to insert the condition that such groups not be affiliated with any outside organization (such as the AFL). Sen. Ellison Smith of South Carolina, who had attacked the "gag" order as outrageously un-American and un-republican, led the opposition to the Jones amendment:

> Is this not an indirect way of saying that membership in certain organizations is dangerous to governmental affairs? . . . it comes with a sinister meaning to me when the Senate of the United States and the lawmaking bodies of this country begin to lay restrictions on the rights of individual citizens. We have no right to inject that here. . . . I, for one, as long as these organizations exist, so long as they are struggling against what they consider the inequalities amongst men, so long as they organize for self-protection, shall not stand here and . . . inveigh against these organizations. . . . It is a shame on the United States Senate; it is cowardice and it is a subterfuge.[21]

Although the Jones amendment was defeated 31 to 20 (see table 10.3), Senate Republicans remained extremely anxious about government employees belonging to trade unions. Even progressive Republicans such as Albert Cummins of Iowa and Coe Crawford of South Dakota opposed any suggestion of a right to strike for government employees. Crawford expressed alarm that workers might join unions like the Industrial Workers of the World and thus come under outside influences that might "have the effect of arousing a spirit of mischief, making a rebellion all along the line." He noted that Senator Smith's opposition to any restraints on worker organization could well lead

Table 10.3 Prohibit Postal Workers from Joining Organizations with Outside Affiliations (Jones Amendment to Lloyd–La Follette Act) (Senate, 1912)

		20–31 D 3–19 R 17–12		
% of Seats		% Yea	(N)	% of All Yeas
27.1	Core	64.3	(14)	45.0
14.6	Diverse	22.2	(4)	10.0
58.3	Periphery	32.1	(28)	45.0

to "chaos" in the ranks of employees.[22] Given the rising sentiment among the Republican majority for some restraint on strikes, Democratic Sen. James Reed of Missouri drafted an amendment declaring that postal workers' associational rights excluded membership in organizations "imposing an obligation or duty among them to engage in any strike against the United States."[23] The AFL did not object to this amendment (which passed overwhelmingly), since it denied imposing any obligation to strike on the part of affiliated unions.[24]

In addition to the eight-hour day for postal workers, individual bills extended the hours limitation to naval contracts, fortification workers, and dredgeworkers.[25] But the most significant of such measures was the enactment of a general eight-hour day requirement on all federally funded public works. (See chapter 3 on earlier attempts to secure such legislation.) The only recorded vote on passage was a 45–11 Senate roll call, with ten Republicans and one Mississippi Democrat in the minority. Over three-fifths of the supporters were periphery senators.[26]

The campaign for a cabinet-level Department of Labor, which finally succeeded at the end of the 62nd Congress, had been carried on by the National Labor Union and the Knights of Labor from the 1860s through the 1880s. The Knights had pushed successfully for state-level bureaus of labor statistics, hoping for "confirmation by a responsible government agency of the existence of the industrial and social abuses which they believed to prevail" and for remedial legislation.[27] The Knights had also secured the establishment of a federal Bureau of Labor Statistics housed in the Interior Department in 1884. In 1888 the bureau was transformed into a department headed by a commissioner with some new responsibilities in railway labor disputes but without the expanded functions or cabinet status urged by the Knights.[28]

The much less political AFL paid little attention to the agency's evolution but was roused to take some position by the introduction of bills to establish a Department of Commerce in which the labor unit would be a subordinate bureau. Subsequently, in 1900–1901, the AFL affirmed its support for an independent Labor Department. However, the Republican Congress and President Roosevelt pushed ahead to create a joint Commerce and Labor Department in 1903. The Democratic minority, now much more committed to labor than it had been in the 1880s, presented "stubborn but futile" opposition to the combination, which labor assumed would subordinate its interests to business. Southern Democrats on the House Commerce Committee gave voice to organized labor's objections in a minority report on the 1903 bill, and the agrarian (mostly southern) Democrats cast almost all of the forty-two votes against House passage.[29]

The AFL continued to push for an independent, cabinet-level department but achieved its goal only when the Democrats took over the House in the 62nd Congress. The bill, sponsored by New York Rep. William Sulzer, passed the House and the Senate on voice votes in the last session. President Taft tried to exchange his approval for a pledge from Gompers to oppose the appropriation rider barring Justice Department prosecutions of labor under the Sherman Act. On the AFL chief's refusal, the president decided to sign the bill anyway, lest the newly elected Democratic Congress and president produce an even more objectionable measure. As passed, the bill created a department containing the Bureau of Immigration (a labor victory) and the newly established Children's Bureau, as well as the core unit now renamed the Bureau of Labor Statistics. A major new function permitted the secretary or his designated agents to mediate labor disputes. The first head of the department (former Rep. William Wilson), appointed by President Woodrow Wilson in 1913, gave great emphasis to the settlement of industrial conflicts, and the department became involved in thirty-three strikes in its first year.[30]

The other two significant pieces of labor legislation passed in the 62nd Congress had bipartisan support and revealed serious tensions in the Democratic agrarian-labor alliance. One was a proposal to abolish, in effect, the production of white phosphorous–tipped matches, which had caused death and disfigurement among match workers and many accidental poisonings of children. Diamond Match Corporation had a patent for a safe substitute but would not shift its production lest it be undercut by its few remaining competitors who might continue to produce the cheaper phosphorous matches. This was, then, a classic market failure that cried out for federal regulation, and the bill had widespread support among progressive reformers.[31] A group of southern Democrats held out against the growing consensus, arguing that the method used—a punitive tax—violated the long-standing Democratic principle that taxation should be used only to raise revenue and not to destroy an industry. For at least one of the southern objectors, Underwood of Alabama, this stance resulted from an extreme aversion to the granting of a federal policy role in social matters;[32] another objector suggested that such a measure might be less objectionable if tied to the commerce power. But for most opponents, references to the tariff and to the outlawing, via taxation, of state bank notes were the worrisome analogies. Georgia Rep. Charles Bartlett, a surprising opponent given his long association with pro-labor legislation, acknowledged the "feeble" and "futile" character of such objections. A long and well-documented rebuttal of Bartlett's position was delivered by Rep. Edward Saunders of Virginia. Saunders focused on the urgency of outlawing a loathsome and dangerous process for the sake of the workers who, because of the obvious disincentive for relevant state action, had no other recourse.[33] In the end, twenty-four southern Democrats (composing three-fourths of the bill's opposition) thumbed their noses at workers and progressive reformers and opposed the match tax; fourteen southerners voted yea.[34]

A southern bloc also breached the emerging Progressive Era consensus on child labor. The southern textile industry, centered in the Piedmont region of Alabama, Georgia, and the Carolinas, was the nation's major industrial employer of child labor. However, even in the region's textile states there were homegrown movements to restrict or outlaw child labor in the early 1900s. These campaigns, led by women's organizations and ministers and strongly supported by labor unions, had achieved some success by 1912 in setting minimum ages and maximum hours for the employment of children.[35] But support for state-level reform did not necessarily translate into advocacy of national regulatory law. Southern officials were swayed by the stubborn insistence of local textile magnates that national regulatory efforts represented a northeastern plot against southern competitors.[36] Although northern textile interests were by no means the driving force behind the child-labor crusade, it was true that otherwise conservative New England congressmen, representing states that already had fairly strong child-labor laws, were abandoning their reflexive opposition to regulatory expansion by mid-decade to back a federal child-labor law that extended such regulations to the South. But other northern business opposition, strong southern resistance, and the reluctance of the AFL to work for a federal (as opposed to state) law at this point combined to stall the national effort, despite support from progressive Republicans and northern Democrats.[37]

In view of the opposition, the child-welfare reformers lowered their sights and focused their efforts on a proposal, backed by Florence Kelley, for the creation of a federal Children's Bureau to investigate conditions and gather statistics relevant to the well-being of the nation's children.[38] The bill's opponents cast their objections in terms of traditional states' rights, government invasion of parental jurisdiction, and bureaucratic duplication, but it was clear that many southern representatives were simply acting on perceived regional interest. They saw the bureau, backed by leading child-labor reformers, as the leading wedge for national regulation and accepted the textile executives' argument that lower labor costs had enabled the South to capture most of the nation's textile production; anything that worked to equalize those costs threatened one of the region's few industries. Such considerations, along with the weakness of southern unions and the apathy or opposition of most mill

Table 10.4 Children's Bureau (Senate Passage, 1912)

		54–20 D 21–12 R 33–8		
% of Seats		% Yea	(N)	% of All Yeas
27.1	Core	77.3	(22)	31.5
14.6	Diverse	83.3	(12)	18.5
58.3	Periphery	67.5	(40)	50.0

workers to regulation that—in the short term, at least—might reduce already painfully low family incomes,[39] made substantial southern opposition a forgone conclusion.

However, with so much support from middle-class progressives and some capitalists, and the benign acquiescence of the AFL, the Children's Bureau bill passed easily in 1912. The Senate backed the bureau 54–20 (see table 10.4).[40] Socially progressive policies with strong regional economic implications reversed the usual congressional voting patterns; Republicans produced the majority of reformers and periphery Democrats the majority of opponents. Still, all three regions supported the bill by large majorities, and even southern senators split 9 to 6 in favor of the bureau. The bill passed the House on a 177–17 vote, most voting southerners joining the national majority. The Farmers' Union, a heavily southern organization, rejoiced at the bill's passage and, in fact, claimed credit for it.[41]

Though passage of these bills was favorably noted by the AFL, neither the phosphorous match bill nor the Children's Bureau had been a high priority for the labor federation,[42] and their passage could not compensate for the loss, to Taft vetoes, of three strongly supported bills: immigration restriction, a seamen's protective law, and a ban on Justice Department prosecution of labor. Immigration restriction has often been portrayed as an aspect of the "dark side" of the Progressive Era, of its Darwinian race consciousness and middle-class concern with social control. In fact, organized labor had always been the strongest advocate of immigration restriction, for purely pragmatic reasons, though labor leaders often couched their arguments in a language of racial and ethnic superiority (of Anglo-Americans and North Europeans)—language that they had reason to assume would be favorably received in the race-conscious culture of the times.[43] Friends of the labor movement (including John R. Commons) and a number of social workers and social-policy intellectuals backed restriction in order to improve the prospects for union organization and for better wages and working conditions and to avoid the broad social costs of unlimited immigration.[44]

As for periphery agrarians, they had two strong reasons to support immigration restriction and few, if any, to oppose it. In the first place, many southern and midwestern rural and small urban communities had tried, without success, to entice more European settlers. Most immigrants settled in cities in the industrial core where, given the region's propensity to vote Republican, their numbers expanded the political power of the farmers' chief rivals. Second, ethnic prejudice led the agrarians, along with most other contemporary American citizens (including AFL and Socialist Party leaders), to argue that the newer immigrants could not easily be assimilated into American society and culture. Even the most idealistic and humanitarian of the agrarian progressives—like George Norris of Nebraska—saw the "immigration problem" of the early twentieth century in these terms.[45] For the agrarian Democrats, the choice must have seemed particularly easy. They were inclined to support immigration restriction anyway, but the fact that the AFL had put the issue so high on its formal agenda[46] made restriction doubly appealing. Southerners could proclaim their innocence of ethnic prejudice (among Caucasians, at least) and couch their support in terms of fraternal solidarity with the industrial working class, as did Sen. John Sharp Williams of Mississippi in 1912:

> I have no racial objection to these people. The Poles, the Magyars are in every sense racially my equals and the equals of my people, but the ignorant man, whatever his race . . . is dangerous. . . . The man who is coming here now comes for the purpose of beating down the price and the standard of American labor. The price of labor is determined by the demand and the supply. . . . Make a scarcity of laborers of the unskilled class in proportion to the demand for labor, and wages will go up in any community as surely as wheat goes up in price with a scarcity of wheat.[47]

The 1912 bill was sponsored by Rep. John Burnett of Alabama in the Democratic House and by Henry Cabot Lodge of Massachusetts in the Republican Senate and was one of the few instances of such cooperation between patrician Republicans and agrarian Democrats in the Progressive Era (an indication of its broad support).[48] The measure followed the recommendations of a Commission on Immigration established by Congress to investigate the subject. It required would-be immigrants to pass a literacy test, barred particular classes of "unfit" immigrants, imposed a four-dollar "head tax," and prohibited transportation companies from soliciting immigrants.[49] The AFL, in view of this prestigious support, was optimistic about enactment. Its ally, the

Farmers' Union, also welcomed the commission's report as a vindication of its own earlier positions and concurred that the documented oversupply of unskilled labor and "the degradation of the standard of living of the workers already here" demanded passage of the immigration bill.[50] The Farmers' National Congress, an annual convention of farm spokesmen (and women) weighted toward the Midwest, also eagerly endorsed the measure.[51]

The immigration bill passed the Senate by voice vote and passed the House 179–52. It was vetoed by President Taft toward the end of his term.[52] In the Senate, the vote to override the president's veto was 72–18. The small number of opponents came from both parties and all three sections. They included Democratic Sens. James Martine of New Jersey and James O'Gorman of New York, who leaned with their immigrant constituents, and periphery Sens. William Stone of Missouri and James Clarke of Arkansas, who condemned the literacy test as unfair and undemocratic. Letters in favor of the bill from the United American Mechanics and the Farmers' Union were inserted in the *Congressional Record* just before the vote.[53] The House came within a few votes of overriding the veto (see table 10.5), with opposition concentrated in core industrial areas, where most of the new immigrants resided and worked. The industrial/nonindustrial distinction was a powerful one. Within both core and periphery, nonindustrial districts strongly supported restriction while industrial districts opposed it. However, the paucity of industrial districts in the periphery gave that region a heavily anti-immigration tilt.[54]

On this issue, then, the agrarians could claim to be the most loyal backers of organized labor's oldest demand. But as the opposition of core Democrats revealed, communities of immigrant workers saw their interests in terms very

Table 10.5 Restrict Immigration/Override Taft Veto (House, 1913)

		213–114		
		D 139–57[a]		
		R 70–56		
% of Seats		% Yea	(N)	% of All Yeas
32.7	Core	47.4	(95)	21.1
20.0	Diverse	55.2	(67)	17.4
47.2	Periphery	79.4	(165)	61.5

[a]Indicates opposing core and periphery majorities within the party.

| Core Democrats | 32.6 | (46) |
| Periphery Democrats | 86.4 | (125) |

different from those of the AFL. Immigration was an issue that separated many urban workers from the trade-union federation, northern from southern Democrats,[55] and both congressional parties from their presidents. Wilson would follow the precedents of Taft and Grover Cleveland before him, vetoing the literary test bill twice before Congress finally succeeded in overriding him in 1917. One might see, in the presidential opposition, a common tendency of the office to support the needs of capitalists and to avoid diplomatic embarrassments. In Wilson's case, however, there were also distinct political reasons for the veto.[56]

Taft's pocket veto of the seamen's bill could also be justified in terms of diplomatic necessity. In prohibiting the arrest of foreign seamen for contract violation when they deserted their ships in American ports, the bill would have violated U.S. treaties with twenty-two other maritime nations.[57] But Taft's position also comported with his general anti-labor attitude and pleased the Republican shipping companies, which had strongly opposed the bill.[58]

The AFL and the International Seamen's Union had campaigned tirelessly for a comprehensive seamen's bill since 1900. Andrew Furuseth, the head of the International Seamen's Union, spent "virtually all of his time in Washington, lobbied incessantly, wrote hundreds of letters and articles, and gradually won Congressmen to his cause."[59] He won, in particular, the strong support of Senator La Follette, who had many trade-union constituents and who was powerfully impressed with Furuseth's passionate expression of the sailors' grievances. The Wisconsin senator introduced Furuseth's bill in 1910 and would be its stoutest defender until final passage early in 1915.[60] The bill, sponsored by AFL spokesman William Wilson in the House, proposed "to abolish the involuntary servitude imposed upon seamen in the merchant marine of the United States while in foreign ports and the involuntary servitude imposed upon the seamen of the merchant marine of foreign countries while in ports of the United States, to prevent unskilled manning of American vessels, to encourage the training of boys in the American merchant marine, for the further protection of life at sea, and to amend the laws relative to seamen."[61]

The bill was clearly drafted to maximize the appeal of a measure whose essential purposes were to raise wages and increase employment of American seamen. By extending to foreign seamen the protection that had been won by American sailors in 1898 against arrest for desertion, it aimed to compel shipping companies to raise wages for foreign and thus for all sailors frequenting U.S. ports. The bill's sponsors argued that it would improve not only the conditions under which sailors worked but also the competitive position of the much-diminished American shipping fleet.[62] Many of the bill's provisions dealt ostensibly with safety: requiring safety drills and adequate numbers of lifeboats on passenger ships, setting new standards for the training of crews and manning of lifeboats and deck watches, and specifying that no less than 75 percent of the crew be able to understand the officer's orders on every ship departing U.S. ports. Arguments for the necessity of such provisions were even more persuasive after the sinking of the *Titanic* in April 1912, but nationalistic and racial arguments were also invoked. This legislation was essential, supporters argued, not only to enhance the competitiveness of the American shipping fleet (by increasing foreign shippers' costs) but also to prevent the complete replacement of American and North European seamen by Asian and other low-wage labor. Furuseth and Gompers repeatedly hammered home the urgent need "to keep the sea for the white race," and the former thanked La Follette on behalf of "the 1,693,000 seamen and coast fishermen in the Caucasian world."[63] These arguments reverberated powerfully on the Pacific Coast, where organized labor was strong and anti-Asian sentiment rampant. But congressmen from the other diverse areas—particularly the Great Lakes region—were also sympathetic. Merchant seamen were important constituents here too, and the opposition of shipping companies could be discounted because the latter were often components of the great steel and railroad corporations, whose managers and stockholders were concentrated in the core.[64]

The opposition to the bill was dominated by core Republicans, but even Democrats in the shipping strongholds of the Northeast found it hard to support the bill. Senator O'Gorman of New York and Sen. Charles Johnson of Maine, two of the five core Democrats in the Senate, were usually counted among the opponents of a stronger seamen's bill.[65] Rather than embrace the argument that regulation would "lift all boats" to the level of the high-cost American fleet, the shipping companies were sure it would put them out of business.[66]

The labor interest was, of course, better represented in the more Democratic and democratic (by virtue of direct popular election) House of Representatives. The agrarian Democrats who chaired the Merchant Marine Committee and subcommittee supported the Wilson-Furuseth bill, and despite the extreme sensitivity of the cotton South to transportation costs, the bill passed easily in 1912.[67] In the Senate, however, committee Republicans significantly weakened the bill, and La Follette's main attempts to restore the more favorable provisions of the House bill failed.[68] The Senate took up the

Table 10.6 Broaden Labor Activity Rights in Seamen's Bill (Senate, 1913)

		28–40 D 17–13 R 11–27		
% of Seats		% Yea	(N)	% of All Yeas
27.1	Core	21.7	(23)	17.8
14.6	Diverse	77.8	(9)	25.0
58.3	Periphery	44.4	(36)	57.1

bill after the election, in the lame-duck third session, and although for each of the amendment votes the majority of La Follette's allies were Democrats, ten to thirteen Democratic senators joined the opposition on three of these amendments. Senator Williams of Mississippi was a strong backer of the seamen's demands, but a majority of voting southern Democrats rejected attempts to extend the law's application to smaller, independently owned vessels. Most of the latter also voted to keep a section of the Senate bill that made it a misdemeanor to "by any threat or force dissuade or prevent . . . any person from taking employment . . . or remaining in the service of any vessel." This provision might have been interpreted by hostile judges to ban key union activities. La Follette thus proposed an amendment to strike this section. The handful of core Democrats backed his amendment 3–2 while midwestern and western diverse-area Democrats supported it 3–0. However, periphery Democrats split 11–11, and with heavy Republican opposition, the amendment was easily defeated (see table 10.6).[69]

Throughout the debate, the strongest support for the seamen's bill was found in the diverse Great Lakes and Pacific Coast states, for reasons discussed above. Taft's pocket veto may have been a blessing from the sailors' perspective, since the bill that passed in the next Congress would be much closer to the draft backed by Furuseth and La Follette than was the compromised version presented to the president at the end of the 62nd Congress.

Another of Taft's parting shots against labor was his veto of the ban on Justice Department prosecution of labor unions under the Sherman Act. The House voted 264–48 to override on March 4, 1913. All but two of the opponents were Republicans, almost three-fourths of them from core districts.[70] The Republican Senate made no attempt to reverse the outgoing president, however, and the veto stood.

Labor and the Democrats, 1912–1914

A month before the 1912 election, the *American Federationist* reported that eleven labor bills had become law in the first two sessions of the 62nd Congress. These included the post office bill, the various eight-hour bills, the Children's Bureau bill, and the phosphorous match bill.[71] None, however, were of great consequence; the more important measures had passed the House, only to stall in the Senate. In the House, as the roll calls show, those sympathetic to labor's cause were overwhelmingly Democrats. Party lines were less clear in the Senate, where the progressive Republican ranks were relatively larger and where at least six of the twenty-two southern Democrats failed to back the labor position on most roll calls. Still, Democrats outnumbered Republicans by more than three to two in the Senate's pro-labor cohort.[72] If the party's control could be extended to the Senate and the White House, labor's fortunes would surely improve. One might thus have expected a robust AFL electoral commitment in 1912. But this was not forthcoming.

As in 1910, the AFL leadership declined to take an active part in the federal elections. There were few public political speeches and, of course, no party endorsements. Though both Progressive and Democratic platforms were favorable to labor, the latter was probably more to the AFL's liking. As Sen. John Kern reminded Gompers, the AFL president had written the labor sections, which were carried over verbatim from William Jennings Bryan's 1908 platform.[73] The Progressive platform was more ambitious in its call for social legislation, but some of its endorsements—for example, the eight-hour day for women and youth and in all continuous-production industries—were not within the power, as then defined, of the federal government; others (like the call for a social-insurance system) went too far in the direction of an active social-welfare state for the voluntarist AFL.[74] Most of what the AFL *did* advocate had already been acted on in the Democratic House, and the Democratic platform had more to say about injunctions, the dangers of federal judicial activism, and labor organizational rights. Furthermore, whatever the Progressive platform might endorse, Roosevelt had not been a friend of the labor movement when he had held the White House. Actions, Gompers wrote in the AFL weekly newsletter, spoke louder than words.[75]

But the AFL leaders could not endorse Wilson. As an academic, he had disapproved of trade unions and declared himself "a fierce partizan [*sic*] of the Open Shop."[76] Among the available Democrats, the federation leaders preferred House Speaker Champ Clark. The rustic Missouri progressive was an astute, well-connected politician who quickly became the Democrats' leading candidate in early 1912. But to Gompers's dismay, Bryan, who was being skillfully courted by supporters of Wilson, turned against Clark and helped move the Baltimore convention to the New Jersey governor. The proximate reason for Bryan's move was Clark's refusal to join him in repudiating the party's conservative contingent, represented at the convention by the Wall Street financiers August Belmont and Thomas Fortune Ryan and the 1904 standard-bearer Alton B. Parker. Bryan considered such formal condemnation necessary to the selection of a progressive platform and candidate, but Gompers had little interest in such ideological squabbles. As a private attorney, the conservative Parker had been willing to defend the AFL leaders in federal injunction proceedings and so had won Gompers's deep gratitude. Unable to sway Bryan, the labor leader was "very much disheartened" when Wilson received the party's nomination.[77]

In the October issue of the *American Federationist*, Gompers outlined labor's political strategy since 1906 and its legislative results so far. He acknowledged the support of both Democrats and progressive Republicans but gave his strongest approval to the work of the small "union-card" contingent in the House. Though he noted that "the National Convention of the Republican Party totally ignored the questions affecting labor's demands for the principles of justice and human liberty," Gompers made no recommendation to workers for the upcoming elections.[78] Those interested in securing the voting records of incumbent congressmen on major labor issues could, as usual, write to the federation. In view of the AFL's wariness, and on the assumption that workers of southern and eastern European extraction were alienated by Wilson's earlier nativist and intolerant writings,[79] it seems unlikely that workers' votes made a very important contribution to the Democratic victory in the presidential race—a victory won with fewer votes than Bryan had garnered in any of his three races.[80] In the congressional arena too, the Democrats' capture of a lopsided majority of House seats owed more to the Republican split than to disproportionate Democratic voting. Half of the seats changing from Republican to Democratic hands in 1912 were in core industrial districts, but in five-sixths of these, the Progressive percentage exceeded the Democratic-Republican margin.[81]

The Antitrust Exemption

Its political weakness did not, however, prevent organized labor from pressing its claims on the new administration and Congress. After Wilson's election, Gompers requested, and was granted, several meetings with the president-elect. In these and subsequent lengthy written communications, the AFL leader strongly urged Wilson to grant the antitrust relief that unions had sought for so long. Two Democratic actions were happily received as evidence of a new era for labor. First, the president granted Gompers's request and named former Democratic Rep. William B. Wilson, who had just been denied reelection by his own mining district in Pennsylvania, to be the first secretary of labor. No other figure in Congress or the administration would be of greater service to the labor movement in the Progressive Era.[82] The second victory had to be wrung from a reluctant president. Soon after the new Congress was seated, congressional leaders had reintroduced a sundry civil appropriations bill with the Justice Department rider forbidding the use of federal funds for prosecution of labor organizations under the Sherman Antitrust Act. Easy passage was expected, and indeed the bill sailed through the House after cursory debate.[83] The closer party division in the Senate ensured more contention, and Republicans were inclined to close ranks around the position staked out by Taft a few months earlier. Whereas agrarian Democrats voted 29–1 to sustain the exemption, farm-state Republicans displayed no such solidarity with labor. Perhaps the pending debate on the "radical" Underwood Tariff bill reminded the rural Republicans of the fundamental interests that kept them in the party of capital. At any rate, only Norris, La Follette, and Jones deserted their party to stand with labor on this vote (see table 10.7).[84]

The president indicated that he would sign the bill, but he had not counted on the "enormous violence" of the business and northeastern press reaction to Senate passage. The National Association of Manufacturers, the U.S. Chamber of Commerce, and other business organizations mounted a large-scale campaign to persuade Wilson to veto the bill. On the other side, the AFL and farm organizations pressed the president to honor the party's platform commitments. Grudgingly, Wilson signed the appropriations bill, averring that he *would* have vetoed the labor proviso had it stood alone and that he

Table 10.7 Keep Appropriations Bill Proviso Prohibiting Justice Department Prosecutions of Labor Unions under Sherman Act (Senate, 1913)

	41–32 D 38–2 R 3–30		
% of Seats		% Yea	(N)	% of All Yeas
27.1	Core	33.3	(21)	17.1
14.6	Diverse	44.4	(9)	9.8
58.3	Periphery	69.8	(43)	73.2

would not allow it to "in any way embarrass the actions of the Department of Justice."[85] The president's attitude did not bode well for the larger battle to come on the Clayton Act. As described in chapter 8, Wilson's opposition to a clear labor exemption in the Sherman Act amendments of 1914 was the principal reason for the act's fatal ambiguity on that score.

The Farmers' New Freedom: A Political Blunder?

The 63rd Congress had unleashed a pent-up tide of agrarian legislation, concentrating its energies on lowering the tariff, enacting an income tax, abolishing the pro-railroad Commerce Court, establishing a new national currency and banking system, regulating commodity trading, enlarging the agricultural extension system, and undertaking a great expansion of the antitrust law. In their enthusiasm for the farmers' agenda, the Democrats seemed at times to have forgotten their labor allies. Workers registered few legislative gains in the first session of the 63rd Congress.

By early 1914, labor's patience was wearing thin. The seamen's bill was being held up because of the president's diplomatic concerns; injunction relief languished in committee; the immigration bill supported by the AFL was pushed aside to make way for tariff and banking reforms; and the president refused to support an effort by northeastern Democrats to ban the products of child labor from interstate commerce. Gompers issued an ultimatum to the Democrats in the January *American Federationist*. They had pledged anti-trust relief and a seamen's bill in their platform and campaign pronouncements. If the party was sincere, now was the time to "give substance to that conviction" in legislation.[86] The final approval of the Clayton Act in October 1914 went a long way toward mending the breach. This was the most pressing item on labor's agenda, and AFL leaders were exuberant at the hard-won passage of labor's "charter of industrial freedom."[87]

Thus, in the fall of 1914, organized labor had some cause for celebration. With a mine worker in the cabinet, a pro-labor Sherman Act revision, and a prohibition on government prosecution now on the statute books, the AFL had achieved a public status it had never had before. And while Congress had been preoccupied with the agrarian agenda, a few other modest legislative victories had been thrown to labor: for example, an eight-hour law for women in the District of Columbia and a new mediation board for railway labor disputes. A Senate investigation of labor repression in the West Virginia coal mines may have, through its publicity of dismal conditions, produced some amelioration.[88]

The more electorally sensitive House of Representatives had tried to do more. In February 1914, it had passed the Burnett immigration bill. In March it passed a bill strongly backed by industrial and mining-area representatives of both parties to create a bureau of occupational safety and health in the Labor Department. In the same month, it had passed another bill high on the AFL's wish list, allowing states to ban the entry of goods produced by convict labor.[89] However, the ease of passage of the convict-labor bill belied the sharp, regionally tinged controversy that would emerge to stall the bill in the Senate. Around the country, prison inmates produced a great variety of products, both in private factories and on farms where owners leased workers from the public authorities that incarcerated them, and in work done directly for the state to defray the costs of their imprisonment. Missouri representatives especially objected to the competition posed to their state's shoemaking industries and workers by prison industries in eleven other states.[90] Whereas some states tried to confine prison produce to public users, others dumped their cheaply produced surplus on the open market. In the South, prison industry was overwhelmingly agricultural, and southern representatives were the most defensive of the system. These states had recently experienced battles to abolish the convict-lease system, whose cruel abuses had been visited mostly on black prisoners.[91] The alternative method adopted in the Progressive Era was work on roads and other public enterprises, including the growing of food and cotton on state-owned farms. These systems were defended as healthier for the prisoners than confinement in cells, and of course, they allowed poor states to generate prison maintenance funds and sometimes even a general surplus from the labor of inmates. Southern officials were pleased with the results of the new system and resisted any law that would ban its products (in this case, surplus cotton production) from interstate commerce.[92]

Southerners supplied ten of the nineteen votes against taking the bill up in the Senate and probably played the major role in sidetracking it there.[93] They were also the principal objectors to a House-passed bill strengthening the prohibition on importation of convict-made goods, whether because it would set a precedent or because it would raise the cost to southern farmers of imported cotton bagging.[94] Though "union-card" representatives in the House made clear their support for these two bills and managed to persuade their southern colleagues to support passage in the lower chamber, both died in the Senate.

Was it the AFL's victory in its key demand (the Clayton Act labor sections) or the failure of the Democrats to do more that led the AFL to put forth so little effort in the 1914 elections? The important role played by the small group of "union-card" representatives in the House and the difficulty of moving labor legislation in the Senate without a comparable labor caucus should have demonstrated the importance of the congressional elections. But the *American Federationist* made no attempt to rally workers; the national body was largely inactive during the campaign season.[95]

The outcome of the November elections was a Republican landslide in the Northeast, with "tidal waves" sweeping away urban Democrats in New York, New Jersey, Pennsylvania, and Connecticut. The *New York Times* blamed the recession and a rising public consciousness that it was time to let up on the "radical" attacks on business.[96] The losses were highly sectional, however. The Republicans carried the majority of House delegations in all of the Northeast–Great Lakes manufacturing belt, but Democratic candidates fared much better in the Midwest and West, and the South, of course, held solid.[97] New Freedom progressivism was clearly a program of the periphery and, to a much lesser extent, the diverse regions. The Democrats' biggest losses, in absolute and percentage terms, came in the core (see table 10.8). The periphery districts (about half of which were southern) returned Democrats by almost the same margin in 1914 (77.4 percent) as in 1912. Within the core and diverse regions, the more rural, less industrial districts were, in proportional terms, even more disapproving than the more industrial districts, but the absolute number of Democratic seats lost in the most industrial dis-

Table 10.8 House of Representatives Democrat-Republican Party Balance

	63rd Congress D-R	64th Congress D-R	Dem. Loss (Seats)	(%)
Core				
More Industrial	78–46	42–84	−36	−46.2
Less Industrial	12–8	4–18	−8	−66.7
Diverse				
More Industrial	22–13	16–21	−6	−27.3
Less Industrial	19–22	10–30	−9	−47.4
Periphery				
More Industrial	13–5	14–6	+1	+7.7
Less Industrial	147–37	144–38	−3	−2.0

Note: The threshold for "more industrial" here is $200 and above per capita value added in manufacturing. Minor parties are excluded in the table. The ICPSR roll-call data identified 13 minor-party representatives (almost all Progressives), distributed as follows in the 63rd Congress: 6 core industrial, 2 diverse nonindustrial, 4 diverse industrial, 1 periphery nonindustrial. In the 64th Congress there were 7: 2 each in the core and diverse industrial regions, 1 diverse nonindustrial, and 2 periphery nonindustrial. Numbers of seats by region change slightly due to redistricting.

tricts was two and a half times greater than in less industrial (42 to 17). The small "union-card" delegation in the House held up well, losing only one of its sixteen members (a Democrat from Pennsylvania). However, the net result of the election was that the large majority of industrial workers now found themselves in districts, and states, represented by conservative Republicans. Labor's legislative interests would be even more dependent on the agrarians.

The Belated Response: 1915–1917

As a dispirited President Wilson reflected on the party's losses and declared the work of reform finished, the lame-duck Congress returned in December after the election, chastened but determined to work through some difficult issues still on the agenda. These included constitutional amendments for prohibition and women's suffrage (both of which ultimately failed in the House)[98] and efforts to deal with ocean-shipping disruptions occasioned by the European war. In addition, several important labor issues remained on the unfinished Democratic agenda.

Northeastern conservatives were pressing for an investigation into the condition of the nation's defenses, as a prelude to recommendations for expansion of the armed forces.[99] However, the periphery agrarians had no desire to embark on "preparedness" that might lead to war. Their immediate concern was to expand the number of ships available to take their exports to Europe and South America and persuade the British to ease their blockade of merchant ships carrying cotton and foodstuffs to Germany. As a result of the shortage and blockade, the cost of shipping wheat and flour to Germany had gone up 500 percent by January 1915; the freight for cotton, of which Germany and Austria had been important prewar consumers, rose over 1,000 percent. Farmers with unexportable surpluses had put fierce pressure on their congressmen to take action, and business groups urged the administration to help allay their export difficulties. Congress responded with bills to encourage foreign ships to register as U.S. flag carriers (to facilitate the purchase by Americans of German ships stuck in U.S. ports) and to authorize federal war-risk insurance. However, none of these measures proved very efficacious, principally because of the very real threat that the British and French would seize German-built ships on the Atlantic regardless of the flag they flew. In fact, it appeared increasingly likely that any trade with Germany would be interpreted as abandonment of U.S. neutrality.[100]

During the anxious winter of 1914, Treasury Secretary William Gibbs McAdoo characteristically came forward with a bold plan to relieve the shipping crisis. He proposed that a government corporation be chartered to construct, purchase, and operate merchant ships. The unprecedented measure found its largest and most immediate support among the periphery agrarians and a few midwestern progressive Republicans seldom troubled by bold state-expansion proposals. Spokesmen for core capital were predictably horrified. A few agrarian Democrats also balked at state ownership of a merchant marine, and many had decided that the dangers of inadvertently getting the country into war outweighed the benefits of the additional ships to their section's immediate material interests. While President Wilson had received hints from British officials that *public* purchase and operation of their opponents' ships was less objectionable than *private* (since the government could be held accountable for violations of neutrality), the tolerance limits of France and Britain were far from clear. Skittishness about getting pulled into the European war thus led both capitalists and agrarians to propose alternative solutions: capitalists favored temporary use of naval ships on trade routes and government backing for bonds allowing private investors to purchase ships; agrarians pressed for government loan programs that would allow farmers to hold and borrow on their crops or for outright federal purchase of the cotton surplus. Wilson and McAdoo resisted both solutions and doggedly stuck with their statist proposal. The government shipping plan passed the House on the strength of periphery support and strong administration pressure but bogged down in the face of a Senate Republican filibuster, tacitly supported by a handful of agrarian Democrats.[101]

The serious and complicated problem of the shipping crisis and its solution roiled Congress in the fall and winter of 1914–15, and the depression in the cotton belt clearly preoccupied the southern agrarians. It is all the more notable, then, that the agrarian congressmen *did* take time out from the shipping debate to deliver on old promises to labor. Perhaps the election results had sounded a wake-up call.

The first (and least contentious) move was passage of the Burnett immigration bill, which had cleared the House in 1914. After Senate passage early in 1915, Gompers and the entire AFL executive council went to the White House to plead for Wilson's signature, enlisting the railroad brotherhoods, farm organizations, and sympathetic intellectuals to back up their arguments. Industrialists, railroad managers, steamship companies, Catholic and Jewish leaders, and spokesmen for various ethnic communities pressed hard on the other side. Wilson ultimately vetoed the bill in late January.[102] The subsequent House vote to override (which fell a few votes short of the necessary two-thirds) followed the pattern of earlier votes (see table 10.5). The urban industrial regions where immigrants lived were reluctant to limit immigration, particularly in districts represented by Democrats. But the periphery districts, regardless of party, overwhelmingly supported limitation, presaging its passage, over the president's second veto, in the next Congress.[103]

A week and a half later, the House took up the child-labor bill. Like the prohibition on Justice Department prosecution, the Clayton labor provisions, the seamen's bill, other more minor labor bills, and of course the immigration bill, the child-labor prohibition was a congressional effort that went forward without the president's support.[104] The bill was drafted by the National Child Labor Committee and sponsored by Democrats A. Mitchell Palmer of Pennsylvania in the House and Robert Owen of Oklahoma in the Senate. By the time it came to a vote in the House in February 1915, forty states had passed legislation to ban or limit the industrial employment of children under fourteen, but with varying degrees of exemptions and enforcement. The Palmer-Owen bill proposed to use the federal commerce power to outlaw (under penalty of fine or imprisonment) interstate commerce in mine or quarry products produced in whole or part by children under sixteen; the limit was fourteen years for manufactured goods—sixteen years in establishments where children worked more than eight hours a day, six days a week, or at night. The bill was endorsed by the AFL, the Farmers' Union, the American Medical Association, and the National Consumers League. It was opposed principally by the National Association of Manufacturers and southern textile manufacturers. Three South Carolina and Georgia Democrats led the opposition in debate.[105]

Despite the controversy surrounding this unprecedented assumption of national power over the conditions of local mining and manufacturing, the child-labor bill passed the House easily (see table 10.9). The opposing votes were concentrated in the Carolinas, Mississippi, and Georgia, with the other southern states divided (Alabama) or in favor. All the periphery Republicans, along with all but one of their copartisans in other regions, and all seven

Table 10.9 Pass Child-Labor Bill (House, 1915)

% of Seats		233–43 D 164–42 R 62–1 % Yea	(N)	% of All Yeas
34.5	Core	96.9	(65)	27.0
18.9	Diverse	98.1	(54)	22.7
46.7	Periphery	74.5	(157)	50.2

voting Progressives supported the bill. In the Senate, however, it was easier for a small number of southern opponents to stall the measure, and so they did.[106] Wilson refused to use his influence to move the bill. When approached by members of the National Child Labor Committee the previous year, he had stated that "he believed that the measure was unconstitutional and would open the door to virtually unlimited national economic regulation."[107]

Presidential opposition almost denied labor another high priority: the seamen's bill. The measure sponsored by La Follette had again passed the Senate in October 1913, despite strong opposition from the shipping companies.[108] For the president, the most immediate concerns were diplomatic. As discussed above, the measure violated existing treaty obligations for the arrest and return of deserting sailors. In addition, the United States had recently participated in an international conference that had drafted a treaty setting uniform safety standards for all ocean shipping, and this treaty was now awaiting ratification.[109]

Furuseth protested, however, that the standards in the new treaty were lower than those of his bill (the La Follette bill), and a majority in Congress took his side. Senate passage came even as State and Commerce Department advisors were urging the president to abandon the seamen's bill and endorse the international treaty without reservations. Nevertheless, the Senate ratified the international Convention on Safety at Sea concurrently with a resolution, offered by Senator Williams of Mississippi, that responded to Furuseth's suggestions. The resolution reserved a U.S. right to ignore international treaties contrary to U.S. policy and to "impose upon all vessels in the waters of the United States, such higher standards of safety and such provisions for the health and comfort of passengers and immigrants as the United States shall enact for vessels of the United States." The House, meanwhile, had passed a somewhat weaker bill by a two-thirds (unrecorded) vote under suspension of the rules. When the result was announced, the chamber erupted in applause.[110] The final conference bill, which generally followed the lines of the stronger Senate (La Follette) measure, was approved by the House and Senate in late February. Northeastern and Great Lakes Republicans had opposed the measure all along, on behalf of the shipping companies. Now, however, a great many people—including the president and his pacifist Secretary of State Bryan—were anxious about the effect of the widespread abrogation of treaties with other nations in the midst of a world war. The export-dependent agrarian regions had both diplomatic and economic reasons to worry about the bill's effects. They were strongly committed to U.S. neutrality and extremely concerned about the shipping scarcity. In this climate, it was remarkable that

Table 10.10 Reaffirm Passage of Seamen's Act (Senate, 1915)

		39–33 D 30–11 R 9–22		
% of Seats		% Yea	(N)	% of All Yeas
27.1	Core	25.0	(20)	12.8
14.6	Diverse	83.3	(12)	25.6
58.3	Periphery	60.0	(40)	61.5

Note: A vote to table Sen. Hoke Smith's motion (to reconsider the vote passing the conference report) is considered a vote to "reaffirm passage." Passage was previously secured by voice vote.

so few southerners opposed the La Follette bill in the Senate on the final conference bill roll call (see table 10.10).[111]

Senator Smith of Georgia, who was obsessed with the cotton crisis, insisted that he wanted to help the seamen, but he pleaded with his colleagues not to be "swept away" by a bill that could bring disaster on the agricultural regions by discouraging foreign ships, on which the nation's commerce depended, from entering American ports. But the majority of southerners apparently agreed with Sen. James Vardaman of Mississippi, who decried the "disgraceful" and "inhuman" treatment of sailors by capitalists who put "the rule of gold" over the Golden Rule. Even if the measure led to a temporary disruption of shipping, Vardaman argued, the benefit to sailors outweighed the risk. Just before the Senate vote on passage of the conference bill, the Mississippi senator inserted into the *Congressional Record* the Democratic Party's pledges, in its 1912 platform and 1914 *Campaign Textbook,* to pass the seamen's bill.[112] Though the bill promised agrarian Democrats little or no benefit and entailed significant economic risk, and even after core industrial workers failed to rally to the party in the 1914 national elections, periphery Democrats voted more than 2-to-1 in favor, carrying the bill over its last congressional hurdle.

The final obstacle was presidential approval, and both Wilson and Bryan were reluctant. But Furuseth and Senators Owen and La Follette made a personal call on Bryan at the State Department, where "the Nebraskan was so stirred by the old sailor's plea that he immediately reversed his position and urged the President to approve the seamen's bill if its advocates would concede an amendment giving the State Department ample time in which to abrogate the commercial treaties." La Follette and Furuseth then visited Wilson at the White House and persuaded the president to sign the bill two days later.[113]

The Seamen's Act was a victory for labor second only to the antitrust relief provided (or so it was assumed) by the Clayton Act. It was one of the earliest measures urged on Congress by the AFL and was hailed by the *American Federationist* as "a great forward step in the march of human freedom and progress" that removed "the last vestige of involuntary servitude in the laws of the United States."[114] After years of struggle, labor had won, through legislation and as a result of concerted political pressure, the final liberation of a segment of the workforce from a set of ancient feudal relationships embedded in the common law and treaties.[115] Legislation in the 1890s had begun the process of freeing merchant seamen from virtual enslavement to their ships and shipmasters.[116] The 1915 act completed the process, outlawing arrest and imprisonment of American sailors for breach of their employment contracts in foreign ports (likewise for foreign sailors in American ports) and setting explicit requirements for their working conditions and for ship-operating safety.

The willingness of the congressional Democrats to pass the bill in these difficult times and the president's final acquiescence signaled a new political opening for labor in American politics. The upcoming national election campaign would magnify this opening and bring farmer-labor progressivism to its highest peak. But the enhanced receptiveness of congressional Democrats to labor legislation did not represent a marked change of position for them, as the series of tables presented in this book have demonstrated. For the president, on the other hand, the shift was dramatic. Faced with having to win reelection in a two-party race, after the ominous results of the 1914 elections, Woodrow Wilson suddenly became a friend of labor.

1916 and the Last Surge of Progressive Legislation

Wilson's biographer Arthur Link makes clear that concern about reelection was responsible for the president's conversion to "advanced progressivism." In 1913–15, the New Freedom years, Wilson had placed the powers of his office and his impressive personal leadership skills at the service of his party's traditional agrarian regulation program. On labor and social policy issues, as well as some of the more ambitious agrarian regulatory proposals, he was more a brake on reform than a leader. In 1916, all that changed. Having aided his party in the completion of the New Freedom agenda, he reached beyond the traditional party consensus to embrace new forms of progressivism hitherto identified with the New Nationalism of the 1912 Progressive Party, Theodore Roosevelt, urban intellectuals, and women social activists.[117]

What has not been appreciated is that the "advanced progressive" turn was urged on Wilson by prominent agrarians and was strongly supported by periphery representatives in Congress. In fact, for the Child Labor and Farm Loan Acts of 1916—measures on which Wilson's abrupt switch from opposition to support signaled his philosophical transformation—overwhelming support in one or both chambers of Congress had already been demonstrated (see chapter 7 and table 10.9). The constitutional issues stressed by the president in defending his opposition to such unprecedented federal intervention had apparently ceased to worry the congressional majority in 1914–15.

The first public sign of Wilson's decision to abandon his former caution and declare boldly for an expanded progressivism came in January 1916, when he nominated Louis Brandeis to the Supreme Court. The appointment of the controversial Jewish lawyer was received with shock and horror by the nation's leading conservatives (including Taft) and the northeastern establishment press. On the other side, labor unions from around the country greeted the president's action with "the most extravagant praise."[118] Though Brandeis had opposed the closed shop and taken other positions with which labor leaders did not agree, he supported trade unions and collective bargaining and had defended labor laws before a skeptical judiciary, at a time when such support from the legal community was rare.[119] It must be noted, however, that the labor endorsements of Brandeis came from individual unions and especially local union federations, not from the AFL directorate.[120]

Several progressive Republicans and Brandeis's co-counsel in a famous railroad-rate case before the Interstate Commerce Commission (ICC) criticized him for supporting even a small rate advance in those proceedings (the outcome of which was denounced by the railroads and generally perceived as a victory for shippers).[121] But despite such grumbling and despite farmers' discomfort with the famous lawyer's advocacy of expert bureaucratic regulation, the latter too must have found Brandeis a powerful intellectual champion of the underdog and of economic decentralization.

The nomination of Brandeis was first urged on the president by Texan Thomas Gregory, his attorney general.[122] Bryan too was an outspoken supporter of Brandeis's elevation to the Court. As soon as the appointment was announced, Oklahoma Senator Owen, the Senate's leading Bryanite, wrote the president to express his delight.[123] Despite intense elite opposition,[124] confirmation was achieved on June 1, with three progressive Republicans joining the almost unanimous Democrats (see table 10.11).[125]

Meanwhile, spurred by farmer and labor opposition to the president's original tax proposals, a periphery-centered coalition with a smattering of progressive Republicans had seized control of revenue policy and written the

Table 10.11 Confirm Appointment of Louis Brandeis to the Supreme Court (Senate, 1916)

		47–22 D 44–1 R 3–21		
% of Seats		% Yea	(N)	% of All Yeas
27.1	Core	31.2	(16)	10.6
14.6	Diverse	75.0	(12)	19.1
58.3	Periphery	80.5	(41)	70.2

sharply progressive "soak the rich" Revenue Act described in chapter 7. The same coalition put through the Federal Farm Loan Act, the Warehouse Act, the Grain Standards Acts, and the landmark "Good Roads" Act of 1916. But the progressive momentum of 1916 was not for farmers only. Two days after clearing the highway bill, the House passed the child-labor bill sponsored in the 64th Congress by Rep. Edward Keating of Colorado (one of the Democratic "union-card" contingent) and Senator Owen of Oklahoma. Again passage was won by an overwhelming margin, with opposition concentrated in the southern textile-manufacturing areas.[126] The Senate committee quickly took up the bill and favorably reported it in April. Here its progress was stalled, however, as Senator Smith of Georgia and a small group of his southern textile-state colleagues were able to keep it off the floor.[127] At this point, President Wilson still did not support the measure. His switch of position in the summer of 1916 would prove to be the deciding factor.

Again, however, the shift to advanced progressivism was urged on Wilson by periphery progressives. Alexander McKelway, originally a minister and editor of a Presbyterian newspaper in Charlotte, North Carolina, had become a crusader against child labor early in the century and had been elected secretary of the National Child Labor Committee in 1904. McKelway undertook to change Wilson's mind on the issue and pointed out, in a series of letters from May to mid-July, that passage of the bill might well be necessary to the Democrats' success in November.[128] McKelway's fellow North Carolinian, Secretary of the Navy Josephus Daniels, also played on Wilson's electoral fears in urging him to use his influence to dislodge the bill. Pointing out that the majority of Republicans backed the child-labor prohibition, Daniels argued that "the failure to pass that bill will lose us more votes in the close states than our southern senators appreciate."[129]

As planning for the Democratic convention got under way, Wilson received several thoughtful communications from Senator Owen. The first, on June 2, emphasized the importance of incorporating into the 1916 Democratic platform the social and industrial reforms advocated by the Progressive Party in 1912.[130] The following day Owen wrote to urge endorsement of a cabinet-level Department of Health "devoted exclusively to the conservation and advancement of human health and physical efficiency," and he again urged adoption of "social and industrial justice" programs.[131] Wilson replied somewhat skeptically but invited the Oklahoma senator to draw up a memorandum laying out such measures as he thought the party might approve.[132] On June 8, Owen complied, providing a draft of a boldly progressive platform plank urging "the larger exercise of the reserve power of the people" to "carry out the spirit of Progressive Democracy in the conservation of human resources through enlightened measures of social and industrial justice." The latter encompassed provisions for

> the prevention of industrial accidents, occupational diseases and overwork; involuntary unemployment and other injurious effects incident to modern industry; the fixing of minimum safety and health standards for the various occupations and the harmonious exercise of the public authority of State and Nation in maintaining such standards; the prohibition of child labor; the establishment of minimum wage standards for working men, women and children, and a living wage scale in industrial occupations; the establishment of an eight hour day for women and young persons, one day's rest in seven for all wageworkers; improved methods of dealing with delinquent citizens in prison and out of it; the preservation of the rights of human beings to the opportunity of labor, self support and development, and the establishment of such social and industrial reforms as will increase to the highest point the efficiency, the self respect, and the happiness of the American people.[133]

Wilson did not, of course, choose to go so far in the direction of advanced progressivism as Senator Owen urged. But at the convention, he presented a platform, adopted on June 16, that was apparently influenced by the Oklahoman's memorandum. It pledged the Democratic Party to a living wage, an eight-hour day, automatic workmen's compensation for accidents, safe and sanitary working conditions, and other reforms for workers in federal employ, to a new Bureau of Safety in the Department of Labor, and to federal child-labor and convict-labor laws.[134] On July 18 Wilson told Daniels that he was prepared to help muscle the child-labor bill through the Senate. The prodding from the president was effective. The ten southern opponents strenuously objected but did not filibuster, and the bill passed 52–12. Over three-quarters of voting senators approved it in all three regions.[135]

Workmen's Compensation for Injuries on the Job

The second major labor bill of the session, the workmen's compensation bill for federal employees, had also been mainly the project of intellectual and social-worker activists but was endorsed by the AFL. Legislation to benefit workers injured on the job had progressed in two waves, with rather different political dynamics. The first wave, a response to workers' political demands in the states, sought to establish the liability of employers for the injury or death of their employees, rescuing workers from what Karen Orren has described as latter-day feudalism.[136] The English and American judiciaries in the nineteenth century had opened up fateful loopholes in common-law doctrines concerning employers' liability for workers' injuries. The doctrines they constructed, which bestowed financial benefit on employers and immeasurable suffering on the working class, justified only partial compensation, or no compensation at all, in the following circumstances: (1) if the injury or death might be at least partly attributed to the action of another employee (a "fellow servant"); (2) if the worker might have avoided harm by being more careful and alert ("contributory negligence"); and (3) if the worker had known of the danger and continued on the job or had been compelled to sign a formal contract relieving the employer of responsibility for accidents ("assumption of risk"). A fourth doctrine held that all rights to collect compensation expired when a worker died; thus, the family left behind could not collect. The last doctrine was commonly perceived as the cruelest and had been abolished by legislation in thirty-nine states by 1904.[137]

The "fellow servant" rule was the first to be challenged by legislatures, however, and the earliest and strongest attacks came in the agricultural states. Railroad accidents were the most numerous and publicly visible harbingers of the dangers of the new industrial age, and railroad corporations were very unpopular in the hinterland. Georgia, with an 1856 law, was the first state to attempt to close the fellow-servant loophole in railroad accidents. After the Civil War, the railroad unions had increasing success in persuading farmer-dominated state legislatures to end such exemptions. Iowa virtually abrogated the fellow-servant rule for railroad accidents in 1862, and Arkansas, Florida, Georgia, Kansas, Minnesota, Missouri, Montana, Nebraska, North Carolina, North Dakota, Oklahoma, South Dakota, Texas, and Wisconsin did so by 1900. Nevada overrode fellow-servant and contributory-negligence defenses for both mines and railroads, and Colorado had abolished the fellow-servant loophole for all industries before the turn of the century.[138]

In the Progressive Era, the struggle reached the national arena. In 1906 Congress passed a law that affirmed the liability of railroads for accidents to their employees. By setting aside the fellow-servant rule and forbidding contractual waivers, the statute made recovery in court by an injured employee or dependents much more likely. The law was declared unconstitutional by the Supreme Court because it was interpreted as covering, in an overbroad manner, some railroad employees not technically engaged in interstate commerce. However, it was reenacted in 1908 (after being modified to meet the Court's objection) and was strengthened by amendments in 1910.[139]

In the same period, Congress also registered its response to a second wave of agitation concerning workplace injuries, considering workmen's compensation bills for federal employees and for railroad workers. Previously, the federal worker's only recourse was to persuade a congressman to sponsor a private bill awarding payment. In the private sector, employers' liability statutes left recovery for injuries or death to the vicissitudes of the legal process. The plaintiff had to expend scarce resources on legal fees, and even if payment of damages was forthcoming, this might take years. It was estimated that less than one-fifth of injured workers ever recovered damages through the courts. Employers also found the system unsatisfactory, particularly as the old loopholes were closed. The system of court-enforced liability encouraged an adversarial relationship with workers and could result in long, drawn-out, and costly proceedings for the employer, as well as onerous insurance premiums. Thus some of the larger businesses had come, by 1910, to favor systems of automatic compensation for death or injury. International Harvester and U.S. Steel had established such voluntary plans, funded by employers' and workers' contributions.[140]

Trade unions were at first very skeptical of such proposals. Benefit levels were typically very low—less than half the weekly wage in cases of injury, with only a few thousand dollars as the maximum death benefit—and the right to sue might be foreclosed by acceptance of the limited compensation system. However, the U.S. workplace accident rate was extraordinarily high in comparison with other industrial countries, and the judicial process was too costly and uncertain for most workers. Thus the labor movement came to agree with middle-class reformers and increasing numbers of employers on the need for an automatic compensation system, and labor leaders took credit for passage of the 1908 workmen's compensation law for federal employees.[141] This first federal compensation law, which provided disability payments and death benefits after workplace accidents, was soon recognized to be quite inadequate. In particular, it covered only government employees in "hazardous" occupations—about one-fourth of the total—and had various other limitations (such as a fifteen-day waiting period, a short time limit for disability payments, and no provision for medical expenses).[142] It was, however, a beginning.

Congress later considered creating an automatic compensation system for railroad employees to replace the 1908–10 liability law. The measure was drafted in 1912 by a special commission consisting of four congressmen and a railroad journalist and had the endorsement of President Taft. It was sponsored in the Senate by Republican stalwart George Sutherland of Utah and in the House by William Brantley of Georgia. Though its benefit levels were fairly low (50 percent of wages for total disability and 40 percent—with a cap of less than $4,000—for a widow in event of death) and of limited duration (thirty to seventy-two months for a lost limb or eye and eight years in case of death),[143] the bill had the support of the railroad brotherhoods, as well as the National Civic Federation, the American Association for Labor Legislation (AALL), and the middle-class "uplift" magazines.[144] There was no strong objection from the railroads. Although it was estimated that the bill would raise the amount railroads paid for workers' injuries by 25 percent, the law would spare them great litigation expenses, since workers subject to the compensation system would be denied recourse to the courts, and a federal agency would bear the administrative costs.[145]

This happy consensus among labor, capital, and professional reformers was soon shattered, however. Some labor publications began to protest that the bill was far more beneficial to the railroads than to their workers, and many congressional progressives—particularly the agrarians—proved very receptive to the criticism.[146] During Senate debate, Smith of Georgia and Reed of Missouri led the opposition to the 1912 bill. Smith denounced the proposed benefits as "trifling" and "utterly inadequate" and particularly condemned the provision making the scheduled benefits an exclusive remedy. He and Reed argued that as a result of the establishment by Congress of strict employers' liability for compensation in 1906–10, the railroads and their supporters had turned, in desperation, to automatic compensation measures like this one. Although the railroad brotherhoods' leadership had "mistakenly" endorsed the bill, Smith argued that the rank and file opposed it. Like the other agrarian opponents, Smith was convinced that he understood the implications of the bill better than did the workers' organizations.[147]

In this conviction there was more than a tinge of self-interest. For many

periphery congressmen—including Smith—personal-injury lawsuits on behalf of railroad workers and other employees of large out-of-state corporations
had represented a significant part of their law practices.[148] This representation
had, in addition to its economic benefits, given the hinterland lawyers knowledge of the burdens borne by workers. It helped them to establish local reputa-
tions as "friends of the workingman" and defenders of community interests
against powerful and predatory "foreign" corporations. They were thus invested in the liability system in more ways than one.

When passage of the compensation bill seemed ensured by overwhelming
Republican support, agrarian Democrats turned their efforts toward amending the benefit schedules to make them more favorable to workers. Democratic
Senators Smith, Reed, Bacon of Georgia, Kern of Indiana, Charles Culberson
of Texas, Gilbert Hitchcock of Nebraska, and Lee Overman of North Carolina offered a number of amendments to strengthen the bill. These would
have (1) made the compensation schedule an optional rather than an exclusive
remedy (maintaining the employer's liability for accidents and the worker's
right to sue, with the statutory compensation thus serving as a minimum but
not a maximum recompense); (2) maintained more convenient and probably
more sympathetic state-court jurisdiction over accidents in states in which
the railroad was incorporated; (3) increased the level of prescribed benefits
by raising the presumed wage base on which they were computed, eased the
injured worker's reporting requirement, and made the benefit level and
time period more generous to the worker's dependents and survivors; and
(4) added 25 percent to the award when the injury resulted from the employer's failure to comply with a public law.[149]

All of these amendments lost by large, highly partisan majorities. They
drew 22 to 30 votes, mostly from a solid phalanx of periphery Democrats.
Progressive Republicans and the few Democrats who had originally backed
the new approach may have sympathized with the thrust of the amendments
but probably feared that the creation of more-generous benefit schedules
would jeopardize conservative Republicans' support for the bill.[150] Though
one could (and the bill's conservative supporters did) charge conflict of interest in the proposals to maintain liability suits, the same group of agrarian
Democrats backed the amendments to make the automatic compensation system more generous to workers and their families. The vote in table 10.12 is
typical of the series of liberalizing amendments.[151]

The debate on workmen's compensation revealed some typical fault lines.
The agrarian Democrats preferred to guarantee litigation rights, shorn of employer common-law defenses, in statutes and to leave enforcement to the

Table 10.12 Workmen's Accident Compensation: Increase Benefits for Surviving Children (Senate, 1912)

		29–49 D 28–6 R 1–43		
% of Seats		% Yea	(N)	% of All Yeas
27.1	Core	21.8	(13)	17.2
14.6	Diverse	20.0	(10)	6.9
58.3	Periphery	48.9	(45)	75.9

courts.[152] Progressive Republicans took the modern approach endorsed by the urban social intelligentsia. This system promised to promote industrial peace and reduce the burden of litigation in the courts. It would make compensation fairly predictable, with a new bureaucracy (in this case, of court-appointed "adjusters") to clarify remaining ambiguities.

On final passage in the Senate, nineteen Democrats (including eight who had backed the failed amendments) joined forty-five conservative and progressive Republicans in support of the compensation bill; fifteen periphery and diverse state Democrats held out in opposition.[153] With similar patterns of support and opposition, the bill passed the House on a vote of 218–81. All eleven "union-card" men who voted backed the bill (though Frank Buchanan, James Maher, and William Wilson abstained); the majority of periphery Democrats opposed it, constituting almost all of the opponents. Republicans and the handful of Progressives were nearly unanimous for the bill.[154] House passage came late in the Congress; as a result, Senator Smith of Georgia was able to prevent a resolution of the House and Senate bills by threatening an indefinite discussion of amendments.[155]

Smith and other periphery opponents were supported in their opposition by railway labor organizations in their home states.[156] The agrarians had apparently succeeded in "educating" these trade unionists to the inadequacies and losses entailed by the proposed compensation system. Gradually, railway workers throughout the country came to share these views and withdrew their support for the policy change. Middle-class reformers repeatedly urged the inclusion of railway workers under the federal compensation system later enacted, but they could not get the railroad brotherhoods to support the change.[157] The agrarian congressmen had, it seemed, firmly persuaded the brotherhoods to stay with the liability system.

Federal employees did not have the right to sue when they were injured on the job, and most were not covered by the rudimentary compensation system created for certain government workers in 1908. The AFL continued to support the change to a compensation system for both public and private workers and particularly hoped for a generous and inclusive system that would cover federal employees and that would serve as a model for the states.[158] However, the lead in drafting and promoting such a law was taken by the AALL, and neither federal government employees nor the northern urban professional reformers of the AALL were important constituents for the agrarian Democrats who controlled Congress after 1912. Neither they nor President Wilson seemed to see any particular urgency in passing the new federal employees' compensation bill that emerged in the House in 1914.[159] Ultimately, however, the delay imposed by agrarian disinterest and the railway compensation fiasco of 1912–13 allowed the gestation of a much stronger bill, one that would create a workmen's compensation system of unprecedented inclusiveness and generosity for federal employees and that would serve as the "gold standard" for future state laws—once the agrarians and President Wilson saw the electoral importance of doing so.

That happened in 1916. The compensation bill was considered the companion bill to the child-labor prohibition and was of similar significance to the winning of the "progressive" vote. When the bill reached the House floor, Rep. Edwin Webb of Georgia immediately yielded to an Indiana Democratic colleague who delivered a recital of all the bills enacted for labor by the Democratic Congress.[160] The compensation bill, drafted by the AALL, was designed to replace the partial and unsatisfactory law of 1908. It was indeed a model bill. Whereas the old system covered only the one-fourth of federal workers deemed to be in hazardous occupations, the new measure (named the Kern-McGillicuddy bill for its Senate and House sponsors) encompassed all federal workers. It also provided reimbursement for medical expenses, and its benefit levels were sharply improved over those of both the old federal employees law and the proposed schedules of the railroad compensation bill considered in 1912–13. In the new bill, disability would result in payment of two-thirds of the monthly wage (up to a total of $66.67 or full pay for workers earning less than $33.33). The waiting period was cut to three days (from two weeks), and payment continued as long as the disability lasted (the Republican law of 1908 carried a one-year limit). Survivors' benefits were likewise far more generous. A fund of $500,000 was established in the U.S. Treasury to pay claims, its size to be expanded as needed.[161]

The federal compensation bill passed the House with only three nays (from Reps. Joseph Cannon of Illinois, Martin Dies of Texas, and Robert Page of North Carolina).[162] In the Senate too, passage was preordained. Senator Smith of Georgia, who claimed to be an enthusiastic supporter of the legislation and to have fought the old common-law doctrines for thirty years, nevertheless offered an amendment to lower compensation proportionately, to a limit of 25 percent reduction, if the employee had been negligent. His amendment was quickly defeated, and the bill passed without a recorded vote on August 19, 1916.[163]

The disposition of the workmen's compensation bill was fraught with political meaning for the Democrats. Its House supporters, on taking up the bill, had flagged it as the crowning addition to an impressive list of "good and wholesome legislation" that had made labor "more prosperous and more independent than ever." They drew a sharp contrast between this legislation and the dismal record of sixteen years of Republican domination. Enactment of the compensation program, Rep. John Adair boasted, would "once more show to the country that the Democratic Party is the real, true friend of labor."[164] In the Senate, Republicans underlined that association by launching, immediately after passage of the compensation bill, an attack on Gompers. Senator Owen and Sen. Ollie James of Kentucky rose to Gompers's defense, and Owen also inserted in the *Congressional Record* a compendium of the Democrats' legislative delivery for labor.[165]

As it turned out, however, the list was not yet complete. The threat of a massive and disruptive railroad strike in the late summer of 1916 gave the Democrats one more chance to come through for labor, with a fiercely contested measure that would become the defining domestic issue of the campaign.

The Eight-Hour Day for Railroad Workers

Although President Wilson is usually given credit for passage of the unprecedented Adamson Eight-Hour Act of 1916, it is no mere coincidence that the bill was named for an agrarian Democratic congressman who had been a leading House advocate of railroad regulation in the Progressive Era. In fact, Congress had always shown more sympathy toward the railroad workers than had presidents and judges. Unsatisfied with the anti-labor intervention of the latter, Congress had conducted its own investigations of labor conditions on the railroads and, beginning with the 1888 law discussed in chapter 3, created machinery for arbitration of railway disputes. Following the wishes of the unions, the resort to arbitration could proceed only if labor agreed, and it could involve only a minimal resort to permanent bureaucracy (though the presidentially supported tendency, with each amendment between 1888 and 1913, was definitely in that direction).

The congressional answer to the ever more creative judicial reliance on injunctions for stopping strikes and imprisoning their leaders and to the president's use of troops for breaking strikes was the 1898 Erdman Act. Like the 1888 Mediation Act, it continued the reliance on ad hoc boards chosen jointly by workers and employers, but it added a provision allowing two bureaucrats trusted by farmers and workers—the chairman of the ICC and the commissioner of labor—to attempt to mediate the dispute at the request of either party and to choose the third member of an arbitration board if the two parties could not agree on such a person. In a clause of great importance to labor, the Erdman Act prohibited "yellow dog" contracts (forbidding employers from requiring agreement not to join a labor organization as a condition of employment) and the blacklisting of workers for union activities.[166] Thus, in Mary O. Furner's words, Congress "sought in the only industry directly under federal supervision to remove one of the obstacles to unionization that the courts had been defining as expressions of corporate property rights and individual free contract."[167]

The national legislature had clearly decided that railroad strikes—like railroad rates—were matters of major national public interest and that employers were expected to negotiate in good faith with workers and to treat them reasonably. The growing success after 1903 of legislation to strengthen the regulation of railroads, in combination with the message and the arbitration mechanism of the Erdman Act (and legislative threats of stronger measures) made large and disruptive strikes unnecessary. The Erdman Act arbitration-mediation provisions "were used very frequently and with astonishing success."[168] After a particular arbitration resulted in a settlement unsatisfactory to labor, and when a subsequent strike was threatened, the act was amended in 1913 (the Newlands Act). A permanent Board of Mediation and Conciliation was created to offer its services to the contending parties, and larger ad hoc arbitration boards were authorized. The new apparatus was highly successful in settling labor disputes, and no important strike took place in the next three years.[169]

By 1916, however, the railroad unions had become more ambitious and less enamored of the arbitration-mediation process. The four brotherhoods representing engineers, firemen, trainmen, and conductors learned to work in concert, presenting their demands to all the major railroads in a region. As the labor market for skilled workers tightened in 1915–16, the brotherhoods became increasingly reluctant to submit to the arbitration procedures that had appealed to a weaker labor movement.[170]

In late 1915, the brotherhoods decided to press for a national eight-hour day (with no wage reduction) for railroad employees. They refused to submit the demand to mediation or arbitration, and when management resistance hardened, the unions threatened a massive railroad strike against almost all of the nation's railroads. President Wilson, horrified at the thought of a paralyzing rail strike, particularly when U.S. entry into the European war was a distinct possibility, personally attempted to bring the two parties together. The railroad presidents were willing to submit the dispute to arbitration but declared that adoption of the eight-hour day would cost them $100 million. If time and a half were required for additional hours, the change could bankrupt them—unless the ICC allowed a concomitant offsetting rate increase. Wilson got the brotherhoods to accept pro-rata pay in lieu of time and a half for work in excess of eight hours and promised to intercede with the ICC on behalf of the rate increase, but the railroads, given their experience with the pro-shipper regulatory commission, were not about to concede the eight-hour demand.[171]

The president thus proposed that Congress enact legislation establishing an eight-hour day for a period of six to ten months, during which time a presidentially appointed commission would investigate conditions on the railroads and make a public report. He also proposed that the ICC be enlarged, that it be instructed by Congress to consider a rate increase to compensate for higher wages, and that the president be authorized to take control of the railroads in case of military necessity and to draft crews and officials to run the roads. The southern Democrat congressional leaders readily agreed to defend the eight-hour and public-report sections but balked at the three latter proposals. A "stripped down" eight-hour bill was hastily brought to the floors of the House and the Senate in an atmosphere of extreme urgency. The brotherhoods proposed to call a nationwide train strike on Labor Day (September 4) if their demand for a shorter day was not met.[172]

The proposal of the Adamson eight-hour bill (named for Georgia Rep. William Adamson, the committee chairman who was the bill's House sponsor) was widely viewed as almost revolutionary. To fix the hours of work of four hundred thousand private employees clearly went beyond any previous federal labor policy, and most attempts to limit the hours of private adult male workers at the state level had been struck down by state and federal courts as an unconstitutional infringement on the right to contract. The agrarian congressmen had few qualms about the bill's constitutionality, however. The regulation of interstate transportation was a steadily expanding net, and its reach to the wages and hours of employees did not shock or offend them. Some, in fact, proposed going much further than the Adamson bill. Senator Underwood of Alabama proposed that the ICC be given broad responsibility to determine wages, hours, and other working conditions of all 1.6 million railroad employees.[173] Senator Norris of Nebraska proposed a substitute bill to extend ICC control to the salaries of railroad officials as well.[174] The right of Congress to act on behalf of railroad workers was settled, Georgia Sen. Thomas Hardwick argued, when Congress passed the Employers' Liability Act in 1907;[175] it was reaffirmed, Representative Adamson pointed out, with subsequent passage of bills mandating that the railroads install safety equipment to reduce workers' injuries and forbidding their employers to compel them to work more than sixteen hours in twenty-four.[176] When the landmark railroad bills of the Progressive Era had been under consideration and Senator La Follette had pressed the Republican-controlled Congress to limit railroad workers' hours, the periphery had provided the lion's share of votes for his proposal, even though it threatened to increase freight rates.[177] In this, the agrarians' oldest and most successful regulatory policy arena, they seemed quite willing to share the mantle of government protection with labor.

Republican opponents condemned the Adamson bill as unfair to railroad investors and fiercely protested having to pass legislation "with a gun held to their heads" by the railroad brotherhoods.[178] It was not so much the intervention of the president per se or his proposal for expanded federal power that upset the Republicans. After all, Presidents Cleveland and Roosevelt had intervened in railroad and coal strikes that had threatened broad economic disruption. What bothered them was, rather, the one-sided nature of the intervention—the failure to make full use of executive power to compel arbitration and punish disruptive workers.[179]

Agrarian and industrial-area Democrats defended the "perfect right" of the rail unions to demand the eight-hour day and of Congress to grant it. They warned that failure to pass the bill would cause widespread economic devastation, particularly for farmers with perishable crops and for the urban poor, who would be threatened with starvation.[180] Several agrarians acknowledged that a rate increase might be necessary to compensate the railroads for increased costs, but others argued that in view of the great increase in rail profits in 1916, and the "fat" present in exorbitant executive salaries, it might well be possible to avoid any significant rate increases.[181] Rep. Thomas Heflin of Alabama gave the most impassioned defense of President Wilson's role. Unlike Roosevelt, who had not attempted to mediate until five months into

Table 10.13 Pass Adamson Eight-Hour Bill (1916)

	Senate 43–28 D 42–2 R 1–26			House 239–56 D 167–3 R 69–53[a]		
	% Yea	(N)	% of All Yeas	% Yea	(N)	% of All Yeas
Core	20.0	(15)	7.0	60.0	(110)	18.5
Diverse	76.9	(13)	23.3	84.1	(44)	19.0
Periphery	69.8	(43)	69.8	96.5	(141)	62.4

[a]Indicates opposing core and periphery majorities within the party.

Core Republicans	39.1	(69)
Periphery Republicans	85.7	(28)

For regional percentages of seats in the two chambers, see tables 10.9 and 10.10.

a great coal strike, Wilson had acted to prevent national paralysis. And his action was certainly superior to that of President Cleveland, who had broken a railroad strike by sending federal troops against workers. Wilson's initiative was, Heflin declared to a roar of Democratic applause, "the bravest act since Andrew Jackson defied the national banks."[182]

The Adamson bill passed the House 239–56 and the Senate 43–28. The Senate vote was highly partisan, with only La Follette joining Democratic supporters. In the House, however, the majority of periphery- and diverse-area Republicans voted for the bill, along with a nearly unanimous Democratic Party (see table 10.13).

All of the "union-card" contingent in the House who voted supported the eight-hour bill, but Representative Buchanan, a major labor spokesman, was clearly uncomfortable. The AFL leaders opposed general eight-hour legislation for male workers in the private sector. This goal, they strongly believed, should be won by union struggle and secured in union contracts. State labor federations, more sensitive than the national AFL to unskilled workers and weaker unions unable to win such advantages *except* by public law, had undertaken legislative campaigns, but they got little support from the national labor body. In both 1914 and 1915, clear majorities of delegates to the AFL convention (which underrepresented the state and city organizations) voted to oppose eight-hour laws.[183]

On the other hand, the four railroad brotherhoods wanted the law, and the AFL wanted the brotherhoods. In the last decade of the nineteenth century, it had seemed likely that the brotherhoods would affiliate with the AFL, but then they became antagonized by the AFL's opposition to the 1898 Erdman

Act. The railroad unions had seen powerful advantages in that law's prohibition of "yellow dog" contracts and other provisions and were not as fearful as the hypersensitive AFL that the act's voluntary arbitration arrangements might prove the "camel's nose under the tent" leading to compulsory arbitration.[184] The AFL leadership was reluctant to oppose the eight-hour goal of the railroad craft unions and also hesitated to go against the president's recommendation. Gompers agreed to accompany the brotherhood officials to the Senate hearing on the Adamson bill, though he could not bring himself to actually endorse it, confining his remarks mostly to underlining labor's opposition to compulsory arbitration.[185]

Representative Buchanan had nothing good to say about the bill and even grumbled that the railroads might well have granted the eight-hour day if government "had kept their hands out of it."[186] This comment was quickly picked up by Republican Rep. Hampton Moore of Pennsylvania, and Rep. William Bennet of New York, also an opponent, cited Gompers's argument in support of his own position.[187]

Thus rural congressmen who desired to please labor must have felt cross-pressured. They had traditionally relied on Gompers to let them know what labor wanted, but he was reticent. On the other hand, the railroad brotherhoods wanted the bill; other railroad unions, hoping it would ultimately be extended to them, also supported it, and working people, along with the socially conscious middle class, probably endorsed eight-hour legislation as well. "Union-card" members in the House (including, ultimately, Buchanan) voted for it, and midwestern senators with large labor constituencies were enthusiastic. Along with the powerful incentive to avoid a catastrophic strike and (for Democrats) to follow the president, such cues from congressional colleagues were ultimately decisive.

A somewhat similar situation would arise in 1917, when socialist Rep. Meyer London sponsored a bill to create a Commission on Social Insurance. The commission, to be composed of the secretary of labor and two representatives each from labor and capital, would be charged with investigating the causes of unemployment and the means by which the federal government might, through a comprehensive unemployment insurance system, remedy this evil. The AFL leadership vehemently opposed the bill in House hearings.[188] However, the House Labor Committee reported it unanimously, and prominent "union-card" and other northern urban representatives spoke strongly for passage. There being no presidential leadership on the issue, the agrarians seem to have followed the lead of the nearly unanimous (twelve out of thirteen) "union-card" group, the Labor Committee, and the northern

Table 10.14 Create an Unemployment Insurance Investigatory Commission
           (House, 1917)

		189–138 D 136–32 R 48–105		
% of Seats		% Yea	(N)	% of All Yeas
34.5	Core	36.5	(96)	18.5
18.6	Diverse	50.7	(19)	19.0
46.9	Periphery	73.8	(160)	62.4

industrial Democrats generally. As a final indication of the pattern of House
support for "advanced" labor legislation—in absence of presidential leadership or AFL endorsement—the vote is presented in table 10.14.[189]

Workers, Farmers, and the 1916 Elections

The federal elections of 1916 constituted a national referendum on the remarkable farmer-labor reform record of the Democratic Party. Although Wilson ran as the president who "kept us out of war" (having finally heeded
public opinion and pulled back from his aggressive "armed and ready" interpretation of American neutrality),[190] domestic issues dominated the campaign.
The Republicans condemned the president and his party for its outpouring
of "class" and sectional legislation for farmers and workers and for their hostility to business, punctuated by the "humiliating surrender" to the railroad
unions. Charles Evans Hughes, the Republican presidential candidate, opened
his September campaign with a tirade against the eight-hour law. In the wake
of that legislation and the progressive income-tax amendments of 1916, "the
great mass of businessmen and bankers closed ranks and poured money into
the Republican campaign chest with generosity unparalleled since 1896."[191]
    The president and his party met this challenge with an unabashed defense
of the record of reform. They had delivered on almost all the promises of
their 1912 platform and on much of the Progressive Party platform as well.
Bryan, exuberant about the legislative accomplishments and the president's
apparent commitment to peace, stumped the Midwest, "carrying the good
news of peace and progressivism to countless throngs."[192]
    The Democrats had responded positively to almost every labor demand,
reneging only on relatively minor items such as convict labor and a bureau
of industrial safety and, temporarily, on immigration (which Congress, at

least, had clearly intended to pass). In addition, the economy was strong, and the congressional agrarians were clearly in line with farmer-labor public opinion in opposing U.S. entry into the war. The standard-bearer of the Republican ticket, who had the strong support of Taft, sounded like a traditional, pro-business Republican, excoriating the Democrats for their "capitulation" to labor while assuming that workers would unhesitatingly vote for the party of the protective tariff. If the Populists and Bryan could be accused of not knowing what to say to workers, that was not the case for the Democrats of 1916. As the campaign developed, Democratic rhetoric on labor issues became "ever more strident in its appeals to class consciousness."[193] Given the party's record and the juxtaposition of choices, did organized labor and workers generally throw aside their voluntarist tradition and long-standing Republican leanings and move strongly into the Democratic column in order to reward that party and maintain these gains? Most scholars have assumed that they did.[194] In fact, however, there is little evidence of a strong labor mobilization for the Democrats in 1916.

To be sure, the railroad-union leadership came out unambiguously for Wilson, and Gompers made what was—for Gompers—a fairly strong endorsement of the president.[195] Polls taken of labor-union officials and of workers and trade unionists in Michigan and Illinois predicted a large labor vote for Wilson.[196] However, the AFL-affiliated trade-union leadership did little to mobilize a worker vote in most states, and what effort was made seems to have centered on the presidential race, not Congress. The most active labor campaigns occurred in states—particularly Ohio and California—where state and local labor bodies had long been politically active, against the AFL grain, and in the western mountain states and Milwaukee, where there were strong populist and socialist traditions. As Julia Greene's history of AFL political involvement describes the 1916 effort, the AFL was "inactive" compared with its efforts in 1908. Its political program was "simply non-existent" in 1916, as in 1914. In this highly significant, fiercely contested election, "there was no mobilizing of AFL organizers, no implementing of the AFL journal for political ends, no gathering of funds, and little discussion among AFL officials about the campaigns." Greene speculates that workers, despite the lack of encouragement from the AFL, nevertheless voted for Wilson, but hard evidence for such a general pattern in the industrial states is not available.[197] Contrary evidence is provided by the Chicago case, where the Irish- and German-dominated Labor Federation campaigned actively against the Democratic president and congressmen out of pique over Wilson's perceived pro-British tilt in foreign policy. The primacy of ethnic over programmatic labor concerns for Irish workers, in particular, contributed to Wilson's defeat (as well as to Democratic congressional losses) in Illinois, New York, New Jersey, and Wisconsin.[198]

Of the eighty-eight counties with a Socialist vote of 20 percent or more in 1912, fifty-four were already in the Democratic column by 1908 or 1912 and remained there in 1916. Forty-six of these counties were in the South or Oklahoma. Elsewhere, providing some evidence for a Socialist-to-Democratic movement, twenty-six of the high-Socialist counties that had been Republican or third party in 1908–12 went for Wilson in 1916. However, the large majority of these counties were in periphery states (Minnesota, with six, had the greatest number).[199]

Clearly, there was not a sufficient working-class Democratic vote to prevent a sweep of the Northeast–Great Lakes manufacturing belt by the Republicans. Wilson, whose victory was in doubt for two days, won the election by only 23 electoral votes and 594,000 popular votes. Of the thirty states he carried, all but five were in the periphery. Outside the southern, plains, and mountain states, he won only New Hampshire (by 56 votes), Ohio, Washington, and California. In the periphery, he carried even the normally Republican states of Kansas, North Dakota, Montana, Wyoming, Idaho, and Utah, losing only South Dakota, Minnesota, and West Virginia. The pattern of congressional voting was similar. Republicans came within a few seats of taking control of the House based on their strength in the core and diverse states. Outside the South, the Democrats would control state delegations in Arizona, Colorado, Kansas, Kentucky, Maryland, Missouri, Oklahoma, and Utah—all in the periphery. Delaware (with one seat) and Ohio were the only core industrial states with a majority of Democratic seats. In the rest of the core, the new House delegations would be overwhelmingly Republican. The Democrats kept control of the Senate—by a reduced margin—because of their strong showing in the periphery (where thirteen of their seventeen victories were won) and the defeat of Republican senators in Delaware and Rhode Island. But the weak labor vote cost the Democrats and the AFL one of labor's best friends in the Senate, Kern of Indiana, as well as three other scarce core- and diverse-state Democratic senators.[200]

Although the president had secured endorsements from a number of prominent urban Progressives, these individuals had little influence on the vote in the regions where their natural constituencies lay. Only in nine periphery states, plus Washington, New Hampshire, and Ohio, was there a significant movement of Progressives into the Democratic column. Overall, it was estimated that Wilson got only about one-fifth of the former Progressive vote.

In the twelve western and midwestern states where women could vote, most seem to have voted Democratic because of Wilson's having "kept us out of war" and, no doubt, because of the party's social legislation as well. It was, then, women and former Progressive Party voters (the latter predominantly middle class) who, alongside the expanded farmer vote in the periphery, provided the Democratic presidential margin of victory in an extremely close race, according to the postelection analysis of the *New York Times*. The labor vote was divided and had probably been decisive for the Democrats only in New Mexico, where the railroad workers were strongly pro-Wilson.[201]

In short, the 1916 election results confirmed the voting patterns of the roll calls analyzed here. The farmer-labor reform program of the Progressive Era was put through and applauded mostly by the periphery sections. As Arthur Link put it, "Wilson had consummated the union of most of the agricultural states, which Bryan had narrowly failed to do in 1896."[202] It was "a Jeffersonian triumph," said the *New York Times*.[203]

11
Farmers, Workers, and the Administrative State

It is accepted as a commonplace that an antipathy to governmental authority lies at the heart of the "American creed." Americans are assumed to be, in the tradition of Locke and the seventeenth-century English religious dissenters, profoundly individualistic and implicitly antistatist.[1] Though a few intellectuals might toy with statist notions, the "masses" are presumed to have retained their Jeffersonian conviction that the *least* government is the *best* government.

The legislative struggles analyzed here belie such conceptions. From the Antimonopolists and Greenbackers of the 1870s and 1880s through the Grange, Farmers' Alliance, Populists, Farmers' Union, Socialists, agrarian progressives, Progressive Party, and Democratic Party of 1896–1917, a great groundswell of demand arose for the expansion of government (continuing through the 1930s and the major social and regulatory surges of the 1960s and 1970s). Though such periods are episodic, they are hardly anomalous. The nonelite segments of American society, whatever their reservations about government power, have shared a powerful belief in community, collective action, and the government's responsibility to remedy market "defects." In the new industrial order of the post–Civil War epoch, a pragmatic recognition emerged that only by "retaking" the state from the corrupt plutocracy could the producing classes create, in the new industrial society, a possibility for widespread economic opportunity and a broad distribution of wealth and power. The Greenback platform of 1880 reformulated the older republican ideology in a new statist variant that winds its way through memory and action into almost every subsequent social movement, from the Cleburne Demands to the Port Huron Statement.

But there is one sense in which the "antistatist" assumption is undoubtedly correct. If "statist" is defined to imply a commitment to *bureaucratic* power, to a discretionary administrative state, then our farmer and worker protagonists *were* antistatist. Indeed, I would contend that *all* social movements (or, at least, all movements of the less advantaged) are *inherently* antibureaucratic. When has one seen protesters marching through the streets carrying signs that read, "Give us an agency!" or "Give us an expert institution to study the situation and figure out what we need!"? No, social movements are mobilized around quite specific demands, and their egalitarian, antielitist tendencies and well-founded suspicions of the policy inclinations of the intellectuals and lawyers who staff administrative agencies reinforce the antibureaucratic ethic. Among the specific demands of the farmer and worker movements that have roiled American history and precipitated political reform are the following:

- Prohibition of monopolies
- No higher freight charges for short hauls than long or for small shippers than large; abolition of railroad pools; prohibition of railroad ownership of products transported or of competing transportation modes
- Prohibition of commodity speculation
- Free coinage of silver at sixteen to one; currency expansion producing $50 per capita; national government (rather than private bank) creation of paper money
- An eight-hour day; employers' liability for accidents; prohibition of child labor; prohibition of arrest of seamen leaving work on ships; specific manning requirements on ships
- Recognition of a right to organize and join trade unions and to strike; prohibition of firing for union activity
- Mechanisms for direct democracy: initiative, referendum, and recall elections and direct vote for senators, presidents, and judges; universal suffrage
- A progressive income tax
- Minimal, legislatively determined tariffs
- Federal money, through specific formula, for rural highways
- Federal money, on a per capita formula, for public elementary or high schools

Though the enforcement of these guarantees, benefits, or prohibitions might require judicial suits and, ultimately, the exercise of federal police power, such goals entail little if any bureaucratic discretion. They have an automatic, relatively self-enforcing quality, as exemplified by the clear statutory standards in the House versions of the 1886 interstate commerce bill and the 1914 Clayton antitrust bill. If bureaucracy (that is, situational discretion) was required, the preference was for local, decentralized, ad hoc arrangements in which movement organizations participated: for example, the labor dispute arbitration boards backed by the Knights of Labor in 1886–88 and the eclectic local organizations of the early agricultural extension program. In general, policy-making should be entrusted to (1) a direct, ballot-box democracy, via the initiative and referendum, (2) the elected legislative representatives of the people, or (3) the people themselves acting through local organizations. Policy-making should *not* be the province of "experts" socially and geographically far removed from farmers and workers and likely to fall under the influence of large capitalists.

Many scholars resist applying the label "statist" or even "progressive" to this agenda. The stereotypical progressive in American historiography is either the cosmopolitan, middle-class intellectual, one of a handful of midwestern Republican senators, or President Theodore Roosevelt; and support for an expansion of expert, discretion-laden bureaucracy has been the defining characteristic of progressivism.[2] To Eldon Eisenach, it is ludicrous even to describe Woodrow Wilson—much less the "parochial peripheries" to whom he was tied by party and region of upbringing—as progressive. The party-legislative state of the agrarian Democrats is, for Eisenach, inevitably a small state that "can never represent the nation as a democracy."[3] Yet the periphery agrarians worked to expand the power of the national state and provided the political muscle for enacting the progressive legislative agenda of 1909–17. The roots of their statism lay not in the writings of the new social intelligentsia but in the antimonopoly agitation of the 1870s, the Greenback movement of the 1880s, the populism of the 1890s, and William Jennings Bryan's Democracy of 1896–1908. Their goal was the broad expansion of the *statutory* state.

Here, then, lies the paradox of Progressive Era state expansion: driven by social movements deeply hostile to bureaucracy, it produced a great bureaucratic expansion (see table 11.1). Why did this happen? The explanation is multifaceted, but the succinct answer is: political necessity.

Farmers were compelled to accept bureaucratic expansion by both their friends and their enemies. Their enemies were mainly core Republicans and the business and financial groups these Republicans represented, who considered discretionary bureaucracy a lesser evil than the extreme statutory remedies advocated by the agrarians. Their friends included the diverse-area (mainly Republican) progressives in the House and Senate, administrators of existing bureaucracies, and the president.   *What about Dem.?*

The Progressive "In-Betweeners"

The midwestern and Pacific progressives, as we have seen, endorsed administrative solutions for reasons embedded in political economy. Positioned between the industrial core and the extractive periphery, their diverse economies shared interests with both poles. They found tariffs too high, railroads and other "trusts" too exploitative, and the money supply inadequate and unstable. But their farm and industrial produce found mainly regional or national

Table 11.1 State Expansion in the Progressive Era: Number of Federal
Employees (Total Plus Selected Agencies)

Selected Agencies	1909	1917	Increase (%)
Dept. of Agriculture	11,279	20,269	79.7
Interstate Commerce Commission	560	2,370	323.2
Dept. of Justice	3,198	4,512	41.1
Dept. of Commerce and Labor[a]	11,999	14,993	25.0
Dept. of the Navy[b]	3,390	6,420	89.4
Dept of War[c]	22,292	30,870	38.5
Dept. of Interior[d]	17,900	22,478	25.6
Federal Reserve Board	—	75	
Civil Service Commission	193	276	43.0
Federal Trade Commission	—	244	
Shipping Board	—	22	
Total			
D.C. and non-D.C.	342,159	497,867[e]	45.5
excluding Post Office	136,799	198,199	44.9

Source: Reports of the United States Civil Service Commission (Washington, D.C.: GPO): 1910, table
19; 1917, tables 9–10; 1919, p. vi; U.S. Department of Commerce, Bureau of the Census, *Statistical
Abstract of the United States, 1917* (Washington, D.C.: GPO, 1918), table 392.
[a] The Departments of Commerce and Labor were combined until 1913. The Civil Service Commission
continued to combine their employees in its subsequent reports through 1917. Separate employment figures for the Labor Department, taken from *The Anvil and the Plow: A History fo the Department of Labor*
(Washington, D.C.: GPO, 1963), appendix, table VI, show an essentially stable personnel level (2,000 in
1913, 2,037 in 1917). The bulk of employees (1,740) were attached to the Bureau of Immigration and
Naturalization in 1917. The Bureau of Labor Statistics was second in importance, with 104. The Children's
Bureau had 103, and increase of 88 from 1913; and the Conciliation Service had only 12, taken from the
secretary's personal allotment. In the next two years of wartime, given new labor-market and conciliation
functions, the departments' personnel would almost triple; however, the number fell back sharply in 1920.
[b] Exclusive of trade and labor employees..
[c] Excludes "ordinance and miscellaneous" categories.
[d] Includes Land, Pension, Indian, and Reclamation Services.
[e] Excludes Panama Canal workforce.

markets; they feared the impact on the national industrial economy of drastic
agrarian policies. They thus preferred to entrust regulation to a body of experts—a tariff commission, the Interstate Commerce Commission (ICC), the
Federal Trade Commission (FTC), or the Federal Reserve Board—and to
trust these experts to find reasonable, moderate solutions to business and
financial pathologies. The diverse regions had large middle classes, good
public-service-oriented state universities, and significant experience with
state-level regulatory bureaucracy. Spurred by a variety of grievances, their
Republicans had fought and defeated the standpat tendencies of the core-

dominated GOP. Thus the aura of neutral competence and political independence attached to bureaucracy in the Progressive Era reflected their own experience. Public intellectuals such as Louis Brandeis and George Rublee, champions of administrative regulation, found their legislative allies among diverse-area congressmen (see chapter 8).

The Bureaucrats

Many middle-class professionals and intellectuals either held public jobs or otherwise saw their careers intertwined with the new public processes. The U.S. Department of Agriculture (USDA) presents a telling example of the role that well-positioned state actors—even in a minimal state—could play, transforming extreme demands into the moderate, discretion-laden programs of an expanding bureaucratic state. Given the importance of agriculture in the U.S. economy and the historic political mobilization of farmers, it is not surprising that the Department of Agriculture was the most dynamic portion of the national state in the early twentieth century. From an agency that endeared itself to the rural public by dispensing free seeds and crop and animal husbandry tips, the department grew to encompass, by the beginning of the Progressive Era, a reservoir of expertise and administrative capability that put it in a position to harvest the fruits of the farmers' discontents, as well as to respond to new middle-class concerns.

The USDA's entrepreneurship was already clearly in evidence when its officials lobbied for, and got, new regulatory responsibilities for forest conservation (1905), pure food and drugs (1906), meat inspection (1906), and additional export inspection and certification functions (1908). Dr. Harvey Wiley, who entered the department as chief chemist in 1883, boasted that his division (which became the Bureau of Chemistry in 1901) contained only six employees when he joined it but that when he left in 1912, after years of service as the chief advocate for expanded food and drug regulation, it employed six hundred.[4] Before 1901, the USDA, which had obtained cabinet status in 1889, had only two bureaus. Between 1900 and 1905 it acquired the Forest Service from the Department of the Interior and created six new bureaus, including a Bureau of Statistics. Expenditures almost doubled, rising from $3.6 to $6.5 million. By 1915, expenditures were $29 million.[5] By comparison, total federal outlays rose 80 percent in those fifteen years while the USDA budget rose 703 percent. In number of Washington employees, the USDA was, in 1917, the second-largest department after the Treasury.[6]

Wilson's secretary of agriculture, David F. Houston, played a pivotal role in charting new progressive missions for the department. A Harvard-trained economist and former university president, Houston brought to the job the prototypical outlook of the Progressive Era intellectual: a broad concern for planning and for the application of expert intelligence to social problems, and a thoroughgoing contempt for "Bryanism" and agrarian radical solutions to farmers' problems, solutions that he perceived as drastic and overly simplistic. When it appeared that cotton futures might be taxed out of existence by the Clarke amendment, Houston quickly developed a proposal to regulate these transactions instead; regulation should not be managed by the postmaster general—head of an older and larger, though less meritocratic and respected bureaucracy—but by the experts of the USDA. Similarly, when old populist schemes for a currency based on warehouse receipts were transformed into the moderate provisions of the Federal Reserve and Warehouse Acts, the USDA was prominently involved. The secretary opposed additional farm credit legislation, but once it appeared inevitable (in the form of the Federal Farm Loan Act), he shrewdly offered to assist in its administration.[7]

In other areas, Houston worked with southern congressmen to significantly expand the service functions of the federal government and, particularly, of his own department. The 1914 Smith-Lever Agricultural Extension Act (discussed in chapter 9) provided for a "cooperative" effort between the federal government and state land-grant universities to carry practical scientific information about farming and home economics to farm families. The "cooperative" twist was inserted in a redrafting by Houston of an earlier bill that had proposed simply to distribute money to the colleges for such purposes. The secretary's intervention, supported by Rep. Asbury Lever over the opposition of the land-grant colleges, ensured a major role for the USDA in planning and supervising extension work.[8]

When a congressional proposal emerged in 1916 to create a new and unprecedented federal role in promoting agricultural, industrial, and home-economics education at the high-school level (the Smith-Hughes Act), Houston and his USDA colleagues again won a major role for the department in the act's administration.[9] The same year, agrarian representatives succeeded in inaugurating an extensive and (expensive) new federal program to support the construction of rural highways. Passed over strong opposition from representatives of the more developed core states,[10] the Federal Aid Roads Act instituted another federal-state "cooperative" venture. It aided the construction and maintenance of rural farm-to-market post roads, the latter designation being the constitutional hinge for the unprecedented program. Because of the USDA's existing administrative resources (which included an Office of Public Roads and Rural Engineering created in 1906) and the range of its rural concerns, the department easily won jurisdiction over the program. In deference to conservatives anxious about the potential for waste and malfeasance, the secretary was given considerable discretion to approve road-building proposals, make rules and regulations for the system, and withhold funds for noncompliance.[11]

After Houston's departure, the department he reorganized and redirected continued to urge the agrarian impulse into more moderate regulatory channels. Thus, for example, congressional proposals for government acquisition and operation of stockyards were superseded by the Packers and Stockyards Act, and bills to abolish all speculation in grain futures were sidetracked into USDA regulation by the Futures Trading and Grain Futures Acts.[12]

With the passage of each new agricultural regulatory and service-expanding statute in the Progressive Era, the USDA gained vital authority to gather information, conduct investigations, and compel divulgence of information by regulated firms and local "cooperating" entities. Its concerns with market regulation were reflected in changing internal structures. The Office of Markets created by Houston in 1913 was upgraded to a Bureau of Markets in 1919 and, in 1922, was consolidated with the department's Office of Farm Management and Bureau of Crop Estimates in a new Bureau of Agricultural Economics, destined to become a linchpin of New Deal agricultural programs.[13] While farmers pressed for and exulted in achieving expanded services and fairer markets, the USDA was irrevocably transforming itself from a rural Santa Claus into an impressive network of information exchange and hierarchical control.[14] And, most remarkable, the bureaucracy-averse agrarians were persuaded to forgo their simple, drastic legislative solutions and entrust their hopes to a discretionary bureaucracy. Theda Skocpol and Kenneth Finegold have quipped that farmers were "state-broken" well before the New Deal.[15] But, as populist demands for regulation, nationalization, and income taxation revealed, the agrarians were not hostile to state expansion per se. They dreaded bureaucracy and government by distant, free-wheeling "experts" or business-dominated commissions. Farmers were not so much "state-broken" in the Progressive Era as they were "bureaucracy-broken."

The bureaucratization of periphery-generated regulatory initiatives made them less threatening to the core elite and won positive approval among the urban intelligentsia. Economists, who generally scorned any proposals for state intervention, finding economic concentration natural and business self-regulation perfectly adequate, were certainly less resistant to USDA jurisdiction than, for example, to proposals for abolishing futures trading.[16] The agrarian representatives themselves, faced with overwhelming opposition to their schemes—and charges from academic experts that the old populist solutions would lay waste the modern marketing system on which the farmer's prosperity depended—yielded, without too much opposition, to the bureaucratic turn. There was much more opposition to the FTC, the Tariff Commission, and (years before) a railroad commission when these bureaucratic inventions seemed to steal away the direct and potent solutions that were within the farmers' grasp. But the Department of Agriculture had been around for a long time and had generally pleased the farmers. It was, at least, *their* bureaucracy (in a way the FTC and the Tariff Commission could never be).

State-centered scholars like Skocpol and Finegold tend to see the unusual administrative capacity housed in the USDA as the result of an extraordinary degree of autonomy. Because the department was created when the South was out of the Union, they argue, its officials were able to construct a capacious and autonomous agency from the top down.[17] But most of the USDA's pre–New Deal programs could more accurately be described as built from the bottom up, in response to agrarian demands. And the surges in capacity experienced by the USDA were registered in a period when the South was in the Union and pressing hard, along with the rest of the periphery, for programmatic expansion. What was extraordinary about the USDA in the early twentieth century was not the degree of expertise of its officials but the degree of participation by a mobilized grass roots in the creation and administration of its programs. The USDA officials' unusual idealism and clientele devotion, which contributed so much to the department's success, was nurtured—one might say, insisted on—by the farmers themselves. This was not classic "interest-group liberalism." The instigation of the new activities resulted from broad social movement pressure and, in programs like the early extension service, featured grass-roots participation in design and administration. Progressive Era agriculture policy was more an early example of the "maximum feasible participation" sought by Great Society programs in the 1960s than a model "iron triangle."

The President

The political force that ultimately persuaded the agrarian Democrats to accept elements of the New Nationalist regulatory program was their party leader and president, Woodrow Wilson. In the first, critical year of the New Freedom, Wilson had put his incomparable "prime ministerial" skills behind a program that was much more the agenda of the agrarian Democratic Party than his own. He served the party nobly on the Underwood Tariff, yielded to Bryan and the agrarians on the Federal Reserve Act, and despite his own very weak record on labor and antitrust policy, saw the bills through to the enactment of the Clayton antitrust and labor-rights program. However, as the recession took hold in 1914 and virulent business criticism poured in, a "new Wilson"—whose principles seemed closer to the original (pre-1908) Wilson—emerged.[18] In Arthur Link's words, the president "worked incessantly . . . to make it clear that he would tolerate no reckless assaults against business" and presented himself as "the sober, constructive friend of business."[19] In this new guise, the president signaled his unwillingness to support securities regulation and backed the weakening of the Clayton Act and its subordination to a Federal Trade Commission. The bureaucratization of antitrust regulation held the promise of increasing support among business and urban progressives; it also expanded the president's power in business regulation.[20]

The president's conservatism was particularly revealed in his appointments to the new and existing regulatory commissions. Wilson's appointment of Winthrop Daniels to the ICC was discussed in chapter 6. Even more alarming to agrarian Democrats and progressive Republicans was Wilson's staffing of the new Federal Reserve Board with conservative bankers and businessmen—clearly not what the Bryanites had envisioned when they had fought for a "publicly controlled" banking system. Opposition centered on Paul M. Warburg of Kuhn, Loeb and on Thomas D. Jones, a former director of the "Harvester Trust." After a bitter confrontation with his own party and Republican progressives, the president finally won Warburg's confirmation, but Jones's name had to be withdrawn.[21]

The historical policy case studies reported here support an argument that the national legislature has been more sympathetic to social movements of the left than has the presidency, even within the same political party. There seems to be a presidential tilt toward the interests of capital—more particularly, toward the interests of advanced, internationally competitive enterprises and finance capital—and away from labor and small farmers. In general, presidents have been (1) more internationalist in trade and finance, (2) more inclined to military intervention, both at home against labor and abroad, (3) less favorable to labor rights guarantees, (4) less supportive of the progressive income tax, (5) less favorable to antitrust policy and other reforms of business regulation, and (6) less supportive of "soft," abundant money than their party's majority in Congress. Further, presidents' executive appointments have incurred displeasure within their own legislative parties more often for their conservatism than for radicalism.

Arguments for a procapitalist tilt in the executive branch arouse little debate among scholars in the Marxist tradition. However, the relationship has been more assumed than empirically demonstrated, and the result has been perceived to flow from an inherent structural (class) dynamic rather than from institutional or electoral forces. Nor do studies focused on class analysis generally pay much attention to legislative behavior that deviates from the structural model.

Congress is dominated by parties, mobilizers of grass-roots electoral coalitions. Closely bound to local constituencies, members of Congress are exquisitely sensitive to the economic pain and moral outrage of their electorates.[22] Further, Congress's institutional stake in control of public policy produces a coincidence of interest with social movements in statutory specificity.[23] In addition, social movements representing minority or marginalized groups, often geographically concentrated, will likely be noticed early by the localistic, territorially bound Congress (provided, of course, that these groups have the franchise), and partisan vote-trading coalitions can then magnify support for the movements, as was true for farmers and workers.

The president's institutional interest in administrative discretion rather than statutory control puts him on the side of both large capitalists and upper-middle-class professionals who, as we have seen, prefer administrative to statutory regulation. The president and business have other interests in common as well. Large capitalists control domestic investment and employment; the public holds the president responsible for macroeconomic policy, and the rate of GNP growth is a strong predictor of presidential reelection.[24] Companies with high export exposure or potential have often demanded (and gotten) military and other U.S. government support abroad, and the president is commander in chief of the armed forces and appointer of diplomats and other foreign policy agents. Presidents have electoral, and advanced capitalists have material, reasons for military intervention abroad.[25] Congress, by contrast, tends to be much more sympathetic to domestically oriented, less competitive business, as well as to labor and agricultural producers. The latter may have great export dependence, but their advantage lies in peaceful trade rather than the military intervention demanded by foreign capital investment; historically, congressional representatives of the agricultural periphery opposed the president on imperialism and foreign military intervention whereas the capital-rich core supported him.[26]

Although Wilson's foreign policy stances did not succeed in winning him much conservative support, in view of even more hawkish tendencies within the Republican Party, his foreign policy and administrative expansion did point the way toward a broad, bipartisan electoral support base with the potential for freeing the president to some extent from his legislative party. As the first president to recognize the full institutional implications of an independent personal electoral base, as well as the enhancement of executive power that would result from a prominent U.S. role in foreign affairs, Wilson is properly seen as the first truly "modern" president.[27]

But dreams of such independence never really came true for Wilson. The overwhelming support of his party in Congress (without much need for additional progressive Republican votes) gave him a remarkable record of legislative successes to campaign on in 1916, and the enormity of the public demand for peace compelled him to run—in the traditional mode of the Bryanite Democrats—as the candidate determined to keep the nation out of war.

Thus the relationship between Wilson and the agrarian Democrats, though not without its tensions, was still a strongly cooperative one. The agrarians grumbled but were ultimately persuaded not to rebel when Wilson initiated his rapprochement with business in 1914 and pulled the nation much farther along the road to war than they (or the agrarian Republicans) were willing to go. They really had no alternative. Victorious through a fluke of three-party politics in 1912, they knew very well that they must broaden their coalition or relinquish power in 1916. For this purpose, they willingly swallowed tariff and trade commissions and other "advanced progressive" flourishes. Without the president's cooperation, the agrarians would have had scant hope of achieving their aims; and his reelection depended, above all, on the rural progressives of the South, West, and plains.

Support for Public Enterprise

At some points, the disparate goals of the president and congressional agrarians were simply fused in a single legislative package. The FTC was made a companion measure to the Clayton Act; and Wilson's tariff commission was combined with the radical agrarian Revenue Act of 1916. When Wilson insisted, in 1915–16, on building up the country's armed forces and merchant marine capacity, the agrarians found opportunities to append some of their projects to the administration's preparedness measures. The voting patterns on these bills and amendments again belie the old conception that the agrarians were "antistatists," because they reveal a strong willingness to support public enterprise. The agrarians had, of course, flirted with government ownership of railroads for decades. In vital sectors of the economy where competi-

Table 11.2 Shipping Act (House Passage, 1916)

		209–161		
		D 196–3		
		R 9–155		

% of Seats		% Yea	(N)	% of All Yeas
34.5	Core	30.0	(120)	17.2
18.9	Diverse	36.8	(68)	12.0
46.7	Periphery	81.3	(182)	70.8

tion was unreliable, public ownership seemed preferable to private monopoly. This was a position that enjoyed some support in the AFL as well.[28]

Thus, during the shipping crisis inaugurated by the outbreak of European war, the agrarians supported not just comprehensive rate and service regulation for maritime shipping (which had been proposed by House Democrats four years earlier) but also William Gibbs McAdoo's controversial plan for the creation of a government shipping corporation to purchase, build, lease, and operate an ocean fleet for the duration of the European war and some period thereafter. Harshly condemned by U.S. shipping companies as a "socialistic scheme," the bill was finally passed on the strength of periphery votes in the summer of 1916 (see table 11.2).[29]

The Farmers' Union at its 1915 convention came down resoundingly in favor of keeping the United States out of war. As one of the measures toward that end, it advocated "government ownership exclusively of all arms and munitions works" so that war support would not be a source of private profit. Pacifist workers supported similar resolutions.[30] During the subsequent congressional debate on a naval appropriations bill—in which the agrarians resisted core nationalists' pressure for a greater buildup—Sens. Benjamin R. Tillman of South Carolina and Henry F. Ashurst of Arizona, along with North Carolinian Josephus Daniels in Wilson's cabinet, led the fight for a government armor-plate factory in order to deny the "steel trust" monopoly profits on navy ships. After the armor-plate manufacturers (Carnegie, Midvale, and Bethlehem) threatened to raise the plate price to an even more exorbitant level, public outrage sped passage of the bill, over strong business opposition (see table 11.3).[31]

Similarly, the agrarians secured passage of a provision creating a federal nitrate plant, ultimately sited in the Muscle Shoals area of northwestern Alabama. Rep. William C. Houston of Tennessee spoke for a large number of

Table 11.3 Build Government Armor Factory (Senate, 1916)

		58–23		
		D 48–0		
		R 10–23		
% of Seats		% Yea	(N)	% of All Yeas
27.1	Core	32.0	(25)	13.8
14.6	Diverse	91.7	(12)	19.0
58.3	Periphery	88.6	(44)	67.2

agrarian representatives when he argued that the bill, "while safeguarding the water power of America from the grasp of monopoly, will provide such development of that power as will enable us to cheaply manufacture nitrate [for explosives], thus freeing us from dependence on Chile. . . . And it is not the less gratifying to me that in thus making provision for a great national military need we may at the same time . . . provide a larger and cheaper supply of fertilizer for the benefit of the farmers of our country."[32]

A government nitrate plant promised triple benefits, since it thwarted monopoly (the "powder trust" of American Cyanamid and Du Pont), provided for public manufacture and sale of cheap fertilizer, and encouraged development in a backward region of the South. In the face of such benefits, the agrarians were not daunted by cries of "socialism!" As Sen. Robert Owen of Oklahoma reminded his colleagues, Congress had recently established an agricultural extension service, authorized government-owned railroads in Panama and Alaska, and spent millions on public works; and, of course, the government owned the U.S. Post Office. The term "socialism" could be applied to these and many other beneficial activities, Owen argued.

> The doctrine which finds its lodgment in the minds of the people of the world of having the powers of the people combined and used in their own service is a wise one and is justified in common sense and on sound principles of government, and no man need be frightened by having the Post Office Department charged with being socialistic, nor the public schools as socialistic, if you please, nor the paving of streets as socialistic. They are all socialistic in one sense—they involve the use of the combined powers of the people for the common benefit of all the people . . . it is high time that the people of the United States should use their combined powers in the public interest for the public welfare; and I want to say that, in my judgment, it is good, solid Democratic doctrine.[33]

Table 11.4 Eliminate Government Nitrate Plant (House, 1916)

	224–180			
	D 44–168			
	R 176–10			

% of Seats		% Yea	(N)	% of All Yeas
34.5	Core	79.3	(145)	51.3
18.6	Diverse	77.8	(72)	25.0
46.9	Periphery	28.3	(187)	28.7

The opposition of the core Republicans and almost half of the core Democrats defeated the bill in the House (see table 11.4), but Owen and his fellow agrarians revived the provision in the Senate, adding it to a military reorganization bill.[34]

A New York Republican pointedly noted that the same people who backed the armor-plate factory had opposed the raising of a continental army,[35] leaving the suspicion that they were far more interested in cheap fertilizer and regional development than in munitions.[36] Indeed, it was the periphery that furnished most of the opposition, in both parties, to Wilson's preparedness efforts, for in this momentous sense, as noted before, the agrarians were not statists: far more than other sections, the periphery opposed war, standing armies, and imperialism.

Labor and the Bureaucratic State

Whereas the agrarians championed state expansion, their junior coalition partners may genuinely be described as antistatists. The major national policy goals of organized labor were negative: to get government off its back via exemption from the Sherman Act and to stem the tide of immigration. "Self-help is the best help" was the AFL's motto. The *American Federationist* often issued alarmed warnings against "the insidious dangers lurking in government by commission"[37] and ridiculed intellectual reformers who, "like the ancient village busybody," were anxious to do things *for* the workers, "anxious to do everything except that which is essential--get off their backs and give them an opportunity to do things for themselves."[38] But the AFL's antistatism was not just antibureaucracy; it extended to statutory state expansion as well. Toward the end of the Congress that passed the Clayton Act and the Department of Justice prohibition on labor prosecutions, the *American Federationist* bemoaned the strange spirit abroad in these times . . . the delusion that the law is a panacea. Whatever the ill or the wrong or the ideal, immediately follows the suggestion—enact a law.

If there is no market for cotton, those interested demand a law.

If there is a financial crisis, a law is demanded to protect special interests.

If the desire for physical strength and beauty is aroused, laws for eugenic marriages are demanded.

If men and women speak ill-considered or unwise words, laws that forbid their speaking in that manner are proposed.

If morals are bad, a law is demanded.

If wages are low, a law or a commission is the remedy proposed.

Whether as a result of laziness or incompetency, there is a steadily growing disposition to shift responsibility for personal progress and welfare to outside agencies.

What can be the result of this tendency but the softening of the moral fibre of the people? When there is unwillingness to accept responsibility for one's life and for making the most of it there is a loss of strong, red-blooded, rugged independence and will power to grapple with the wrong of the world and to establish justice through the volition of those concerned.[39]

There were, however, significant exceptions to labor's antistatism. The AFL endorsed the creation of the Children's Bureau and the child-labor and vocational-education acts. In 1912, it also lobbied for the creation of an investigatory Commission on Industrial Relations. A number of intellectuals and social reformers concerned about the level of violence in labor disputes petitioned President William Howard Taft to create such a commission, and with a tight reelection contest approaching, he acquiesced. Samuel Gompers refused to support the initiative until its promoters agreed that several union leaders would be represented on the commission along with the eminent social scientists the reformers anticipated for the nine-member board.[40] Support for national investigation into labor-management disputes and insistence on direct participation for labor leaders (in numbers equal to those of the representatives of capital) may be seen as old labor strategies going back at least to the Knights of Labor. The Knights had championed public investigatory and research bodies such as the Bureau of Labor Statistics in order to build public support for labor demands. The Knights had also insisted on direct labor representation on ad hoc dispute-mediation boards. But in the Progressive Era such participation acquired a new significance. To be "seated at the table" on a prestigious national board, along with representatives of employers and "the public" (as on the nine-member, three-category Commission on Industrial Relations), was a powerful symbolic victory for organized labor.

Though Gompers had shown no enthusiasm for Wilson's candidacy in 1912, and though Wilson was, before 1916, very reluctant to support labor's key legislative demands, the president found it politically prudent and relatively costless to gratify the AFL leader's request for appointments. The selection of William B. Wilson to head the Department of Labor was the first such gesture, enormously gratifying to Gompers. The adoption of organized labor's list for the Commission on Industrial Relations was another, and President Wilson's designation of Frank Walsh, a friend of labor, to chair the commission ensured that its investigations of major labor controversies would have a pro-labor tilt.[41]

In another exercise of his presidential power, Wilson also displayed an unprecedented evenhandedness toward labor. When he sent federal troops to quell the violence that had erupted in the Colorado mining strike, they did not, as customarily, take the side of management. Not only did the president decree military neutrality, but his emissaries worked actively to persuade the mine owners to bargain with the United Mine Workers.[42] Thus, even before 1916, Wilson had signaled a willingness to accommodate organized labor at the executive level, a willingness that contrasted with his reluctance to support labor legislation.

In 1916, Gompers pressed for and won a presidential appointment to the Council of National Defense (CND). This appointment proved to be the harbinger of a new national recognition and role for organized labor—a high-level corporatist participation that tellingly differentiated the political strategies of farmers and workers. It was in the highest realm of executive power— the power to make war—that Wilson and Gompers would ultimately cement a personal, then institutional alliance.

Labor, War, and Corporatism

Gompers had been, by his own description, a lifelong pacifist. When war broke out in Europe in 1914, he at first spoke out on behalf of the nearly unanimous sentiment of the American working class: the United States should stay out of the war and maintain a strict neutrality. Gompers and the AFL executive council offered to lead a movement for peace negotiations.[43] As the Wilson administration, despite its official proclamation of neutrality, steadily tilted toward the Allied powers—allowing American firms to supply war materiel and capital to that side while disproportionately condemning German violations of neutral rights at sea—many trade unionists became fearful of imminent American entry into the war.

For Irish and German workers in the urban Midwest and Northeast, ethnic concerns weighed heavily in this consideration, but there was also a deep and abiding pacifism and antimilitarism among both workers and farmers. As the administration's pro-British position became clearer following the *Lusitania* sinking, the opposition to war became more active. When Bryan resigned his cabinet post and began to tour the country to preach his antiwar message, many trade unionists applauded his speeches, and New York labor officials sponsored his peace rally at Carnegie Hall. In May 1915, officials of nine international unions attended a meeting at United Mine Workers headquarters to oppose U.S. entry into the war; shortly afterward, the Women's Trade Union League issued a similar resolution. In June, Rep. Frank Buchanan of Chicago—a city that was a hotbed of opposition to U.S. support for the Allies—led the organization of Labor's National Peace Council to bolster the antiwar effort, and a group of labor leaders affiliated with the AFL joined the call for a National Peace Convention to be held in Chicago on Labor Day.[44] The Farmers' Union pledged its cooperation with the labor pacifists "with a view to devising the most effective means of quickly ending the war and securing a permanent universal peace."[45] If there was ever an issue that naturally and spontaneously united farmer and labor organizations, it was opposition to U.S. involvement in World War I.[46]

Meanwhile, both Wilson and Gompers were moving in the opposite direction. While farmers, workers, and congressional agrarians grew steadily more adamant in their opposition to war, Wilson was becoming convinced that entry on the side of the British was in the national interest. Gompers was, if anything, even earlier and more resolute in that conviction.

As early as 1914, Gompers's pacifism had begun to wane, as he later reported in his autobiography. Having furnished the Carnegie Peace Foundation with copies of his pacifist speeches for their publication, he withdrew them.[47] At the annual meeting of the National Civic Federation (NCF) in 1914, six months before President Wilson began to urge expansion of the nation's defenses, Gompers supported a resolution for the formation of a cabinet-led Council of National Defense to promote U.S. preparedness. When such a coordinating body was ultimately established, in the fall of 1916, Gompers secured a presidential appointment to its Advisory Commission.[48]

As peace groups proliferated around the country, Gompers pointedly refused to assist them and pressed other trade unionists to stay away, charging that they were pawns of the German war machine. By the spring of 1915, he had resolved to use "every agency at [his] disposal to send the warning through the ranks of labor."[49] Such means included denial of AFL posts and the possibility of withholding the federation's help for strikes or organizing campaigns. After the AFL became a major supporter of Wilson's foreign policy, Gompers had additional resources at his disposal, since the president made him a conduit for federal jobs, military commissions, and so forth.[50] Dissenters were excluded, isolated, or railroaded at a highly orchestrated convention called by the AFL Executive Council to enunciate "Labor's Position in Peace or War." The resulting document pledged support for the imminent war effort and requested that the government act to uphold trade-union standards during the mobilization.[51]

But the AFL's campaign against the labor pacifists soon took a more ominous turn. Gompers not only impugned the patriotism of those who opposed U.S. entry into the war but repeatedly charged that peace activities and strikes in munitions plants were directly funded and orchestrated by the Germans. In search of evidence to substantiate these claims, the AFL president prevailed on his NCF friend Ralph Easley, who in turn received substantial funds from the J.P. Morgan Co. and various munitions manufacturers for the "anti-sabotage" investigations. Gompers himself was a witness for the prosecution at the sedition trial of antiwar Representative Buchanan, a leader of the "union-card" group in the House of Representatives and one of the principal AFL point men in Congress.[52]

As President Wilson struggled with the pacifists in his own party and with the midwestern and western isolationist Republicans, he naturally came to appreciate Gompers's stand and the potential public support it might win for his controversial preparedness policies. In addition, of course, labor peace would be essential for industrial mobilization in the event of war. The president therefore courted the AFL leader with high-level appointments—beginning with selecting Gompers to represent labor on the important CND Advisory Commission in October 1916—and with frequent consultations. He also paid remarkable presidential visits to the dedication of the AFL's new Washington headquarters and to the organization's 1917 convention. Wilson's support for the landmark labor legislation of 1916 may also have been aimed not only at gratifying labor voters generally but at pleasing Gompers in particular during their budding collaboration on foreign affairs. The two presidents thus came to share a major goal of national public policy. They even used similar methods in dealing with labor and congressional opponents of war.[53]

Why did Gompers, the inveterate foe of state intervention in the struggles of workers, throw aside his voluntarist principles in favor of an active corporatism in 1916? By his own account there were two motives. First, the AFL leader simply despised German autocracy and aggression and desired to enlist the American working class in the struggle to defeat the Entente and defend democratic institutions.[54] His other principal aim was to win recognition and acceptance for labor as an equal partner with capital in the management of the industrial economy—whose mobilization for war was bound to have momentous consequences for workers—and as a body whose interests must be taken into account in the postwar settlement.[55] In this latter sense, Gompers's motives paralleled those of President Wilson. The president became convinced that formal American entry into the war was necessary to enhance his influence with both the Allies and Germany and to ensure that the United States—and Wilson as its leader—would have an important place at the peace conference that would reshape the world.[56] The two leaders used each other as they struggled to obtain their goals in the face of strong internal opposition.

Some historians have suggested that Gompers was manipulated into support for the administration's foreign policy by his colleagues in the NCF. Certainly his function as labor representative and his association with leading capitalists and politicians in that body prepared him for corporatist participation on high-level national boards, and his friendship with Ralph Easley—an early supporter of defense mobilization and a pro-British policy—may well have influenced Gompers. Lewis Lorwin reports that in letters to the AFL president after the outbreak of European war, Easley "influenced Gompers by flattery and by playing on the latter's well known biases [against socialists and intellectuals]. He berated the peace propaganda of the socialists . . . warned against the 'young college men with half baked ideas imbibed from the socialistic professors,' spoke of the need for 'peace with honor' and stressed the advisability of leaving all peace moves to President Wilson."[57] Though it is reasonable to suspect that these elite associations carried weight, one must remember that Gompers himself was a British immigrant and had maintained close ties with the British labor movement (which also sent emissaries to lobby the AFL leader).[58]

Support for preparedness and the Allies could also have been connected with Gompers's organizational interests. The Socialist movement at the polls, in unions, and within the AFL was at the peak of its strength in 1914–15 and loomed as a threat to Gompers's leadership and ideology. Alignment with the labor peace advocates would have meant an uncomfortable association with, and even subordination to, Socialists and their intellectual allies. Support for the Wilson administration, on the other hand, provided powerful resources to fight the Socialists and also his competitors in the Industrial Workers of the World (IWW). Larson, for example, notes that Gompers supported the new espionage and sedition laws and collaborated with the Department of Justice as well as with the NCF's Easley to identify and prosecute "subversives" in the labor movement. Federal funds were obtained (through a "Committee on Public Information") to create a prowar American Alliance for Labor and Democracy to counter the labor pacifists' People's Council, which was working not only for peace but also for a trade-union organizational alternative to the AFL.[59] Unions associated with the People's Council were threatened with loss of government contracts.[60]

Support for Wilson and war need not have entailed the particular corporatist strategy elaborated by Gompers, of course. The tenor of self-congratulation in his autobiography might lead one to suspect that beyond his assessment of labor's collective interest, Gompers's indisputable vanity also drove him to seek high-level positions where he could win personal acclaim in interaction with political and corporate leaders and play the role of world statesman. His leap onto the national and world stage, coming but a few years after labor's nadir during persecution by employers' organizations and the courts, must have been a heady experience.[61] As the labor representative on the CND Advisory Commission, Gompers was empowered to appoint a War Committee on Labor. He chose "the members of the Executive Council of the A. F. of L., practically every International labor officer," John D. Rockefeller, Theodore Roosevelt, Felix Frankfurter, Easley, and other business and intellectual celebrities.[62]

From the CND Advisory Commission, the AFL leader's participation expanded outward. His advice led to the creation of other government mediation, investigation, and labor standard-setting boards, and he appointed all the labor representatives to the War Labor Conference Board and its more applied progeny, the National War Labor Board. One of his AFL colleagues served as the labor commissioner on the War Industries Board. In addition, Gompers and his designees undertook government-sponsored missions to Europe and Russia to win labor support there for Wilson's war aims.[63]

Whatever balance of personal, organizational, and ideological motives lay behind the corporatist turn, Gompers's commitment to this strategy intensified over the course of the war and during peace negotiations, and most of the labor movement—including a number of Socialists—ultimately endorsed the strategy.[64] Despite all the arm-twisting that went into the building of this consensus, trade-union organizations must have shared with Gompers a sense that labor had, by 1917, few choices. The labor movement was so politically fragmented and electorally insignificant that it anticipated little additional national legislation. The AFL had made very little effort in the 1914 and 1916 national elections, and the more radical city centrals had squandered their programmatic influence by voting against the Democrats on ethnic foreign policy grounds in 1916. The result was a more conservative Congress tilting rapidly toward Republican control. Without legislative or institutionalized partisan influence in national politics, collaboration with the president—the trading of war support in the hope of labor advance via corporatist mechanisms—was the only game open to labor. Though Gompers's personal inclinations and organizational rivalries also supported this course, the logic of the political situation was compelling.

Conclusion

Thus both workers and farmers came, by different routes, to support an administrative state they professed to abhor. Farmers accepted bureaucratization because it was forced on them by opponents and allies, though they might have felt some assurance that their legislative power allowed them, through floor and then (as the new system gelled) committee oversight, a way to reign in the agencies most important to them. Labor seized the opportunity of the war to enter into a high-level bargain with the chief executive in hopes of protecting and furthering its Progressive Era gains. But without electoral or legislative power, that bargain hung on a very slim reed.

Support from the administration and a degree of grudging acceptance by corporate managers in rapidly expanding manufacturing, construction, mining, and transportation sectors did win significant gains for labor during the course of the war. To a hitherto unprecedented degree, employers were persuaded to acknowledge workers' rights to join unions and to enter into collective bargaining, arbitration, or government-assisted mediation of labor grievances. The mediation efforts followed strikes and work stoppages that, despite the AFL's attempt to discourage them, reached historically unprecedented numbers during the war years. The standard working day was shortened, and some progress was made in unionizing previously hostile firms.[65] Membership in unions affiliated with the AFL grew from just over two million in 1916 to four million in 1920, and the AFL's percentage of unionized workers increased from three-fourths to four-fifths.[66] Its radical rival, the IWW, was crushed by local and national government prosecutions.[67]

In view of these gains, Gompers was eager to perpetuate and expand the corporatist mechanisms when the war ended. However, Wilson refused to request extension of the war boards or to support the creation of permanent labor-capitalist-public agencies to oversee industrial relations.[68] In the postwar recession, employers resumed antiunion drives, and AFL membership fell back almost to the prewar level by 1926.[69] Thus within a few years after the Armistice, labor's corporatist gains had evaporated.[70]

After a brief flirtation with independent party politics, the AFL would return to voluntarism and political isolation in the 1920s. However, the AFL leadership never lost its taste for a foreign policy alliance with the executive branch. Gompers and his successors would work to encourage the development of U.S.-style unionism abroad and "to support various forms of economic and political imperialism and to oppose revolutionary nationalist movements that imposed too many restrictions on trade."[71] Whatever its difficulties at home, the labor organization continued to pursue the corporatist alliance with government and business abroad.

12

Conclusion

The populist vision of a farmer-worker alliance to redeem, democratize, and expand the state has had a powerful hold on the historical imagination. The agrarian movement of the 1890s became, to make a bad pun, the "gold standard" of social movements. It was a movement of underdogs mobilized by a powerful republican critique of American industrial society. The movement grew rapidly by a sweeping incorporation of diverse older organizations, absorbing their members and their memories of collective action. It propagated a vision and plan of action through a massive grass-roots education project that relied on local and itinerant "lecturers" to stimulate an extraordinary "cognitive liberation."[1] In desperate invention, it tried one strategy after another to aid the credit-starved farmer: building an alternative cooperative economy; endorsing major-party candidates who pledged legislative relief; creating an independent party; and finally, fusing with the national Democratic Party.

The success of the last two strategies depended on winning the support of industrial workers. The entire agricultural sector composed, at the end of the century, about 37 percent of the workforce, and the more prosperous and diversified farmers of the core industrial and mixed regions had little use for the radical legislative schemes of the periphery agrarians. Workers in mining, manufacturing, transportation, and construction made up a sector almost as large but, unlike the farmers, were increasing their proportion of the population. Workers' organizations had also grown like wildfire in the 1880s and had shown considerable strategic inventiveness. Farmers and workers had a common enemy and, presumably, a common need to use their political power to establish economic rights. The capacity of both sectors for social-movement mobilization had been demonstrated, and both had the franchise. If democracy worked in some mechanical way, the two major segments of the "producing classes" should have been able to dominate the political system and use public institutions to their mutual (or logrolled) advantage. As this book has shown, that happened only in a fitful and partial way.

Democracy does *not* operate mechanically, particularly in a large republic, but functions through complex rules, organizations, and institutions—layers of social complexity that work "backward" to shape electoral coalitions and "forward" to channel, contain, and transform their energies into new rules and institutions that may differ significantly from the social-movement agendas that provoke state response. The institutions of federalism, the single-member-district plurality elections, the party and committee systems in Congress, the prerogatives and independence of the president and federal courts, the reservoir of talent and persuasiveness lodged in the fledgling bureaucracies of the early twentieth century—all were powerful sifters and shapers of social-movement success. For scholars who see in these processes a somewhat tardy lurching toward a modern industrial state, the periphery agrarians could be called "agents of modernization," but the state they envisioned was rather less "modern" (by conventional definitions that center on discretionary, insulated, expert bureaucracies) than the state that actually resulted from all the pulling and hauling that the agrarian demands provoked.

The argument that these farmers were nevertheless the principal instigators of progressive reform and of correlative efforts to construct a farmer-labor alliance in the three decades before World War I sets this book apart from most previous works and from popular constructions of the past. Farmers, particularly southern farmers, are presumed to have always been as conservative, "antistatist," and anti-labor as they appeared to be in the late twentieth century. The influence of the Greenback-Populist tradition, that potent wedding of Jeffersonian egalitarianism and industrial age reformism, is only dimly remembered. In perhaps the greatest irony, the term "populism" came to be attached, in the 1980s and 1990s, to a conservative antistatism whose program and class alliances could hardly have been farther removed from the populism of the 1890s. Applied to the policies and followers of Ronald Reagan, Ross Perot, Patrick Buchanan, and even Steve Forbes, the term lost all intrinsic meaning. One of the purposes of this book is to reclaim the agrarian radical heritage and even to suggest that its goals and methods have some relevance today.

The bulk of the book has been devoted to case studies of the legislative process in the late nineteenth and early twentieth centuries—a process through which farmers hoped to build a new, "producer-friendly" state and forge a supporting political alliance. The farmers' goal was to use the expanded regulatory, social, and infrastructure-building capability of the national state to level the economic playing field and effect a more egalitarian

distribution of wealth and power. Farmers took the lead in this political transformation because their grievances were numerous, their commitment to politics unflagging, and their position in the territorially based national legislature
advantageous. In addition, and perhaps most important, they were able to
capture a major political party. The political fluidity of the era, and the seem-
ing availability of a large mass of unhappy workers as potential allies, set the
stage for the reform explosions of the Populist and Progressive Eras and for
a great growth of government. During this period of political ferment, the
owners of wealth were put on the defensive by the rumbling of demands for
change emanating from farmer and labor movements to an extent not matched
before or since.

The two movements were very different. The principal labor movement
organization had a much longer life (and in fact is with us still), but the
farmers' movement had a much greater impact on national state development.
Farmer and labor organizations were internally distinct and were shaped to
fundamentally different purposes. Farmers' organizations attempted first to
create an alternative cooperative economy and, failing that, to press on the
state a great variety of market-shaping powers to be exercised for the good
of the large number of ordinary producers. The AFL, on the other hand,
accepted the concentrated structure of the modern industrial economy and,
as an alternative to politics, focused its efforts on achieving power in the
workplace, vis-à-vis employers—an alternative that farmers, after the failure
of their cooperatives, did not have.

Workers' organizations, repelled by the difficulties of political mobilization
and maneuver that confronted them, were halfhearted and cross-pressured
in their approach to politics and, in the Progressive Era, as likely to spend
political energy on behalf of particularistic ethnic concerns as on more universal working-class benefits. Farmers' organizations were somewhat more inclusive in their occupational definition of eligibility for membership, which recognized only the division between "producers" and controllers, exploiters, or
plutocrats—the latter all grouped together. By contrast, most labor organizations (after the demise of the wonderfully inclusive and producerist Knights
of Labor) were narrowly divided along craft lines and paid little attention to
immigrant and unskilled workers. Farmers' organizations in the South were,
for the most part, racially segregated, though farmer organizations differed
from labor groups in having more gender-egalitarian membership and leadership. This quality lent a considerable advantage to farmers' social and political
mobilization. However, both farmer and worker movements were undeniably

rent by class, ethnic, and regional political economy differences that diminished their capacity for economic and political mobilization and—particularly in the case of southern racial segregation—their moral authority.

The nature of the relationship between leaders and followers also distinguished farmer and worker organizations throughout the period. One cannot tell the story of workers' organizations and their struggles without a considerable amount of attention to individual leaders. Terrence Powderly, Samuel Gompers, and Daniel De Leon loomed large in workers' organizations, compared with the more obscure Oliver Kelley, Charles Macune, or Charles Barrett in farmer organizations. The farmers' movement enjoyed more unity and collective purpose than, in particular, the AFL. The latter combined state and local fragmentation with a national leadership that possessed little capacity to mobilize the membership but significant autonomy to go its own way in high-level, corporatist negotiation and to take political and social positions at variance with the inclinations of the rank and file. There was more political consensus and less distance between members and leaders in farm organizations.

The political differences between farmers and workers were the most striking, however. In the post–Civil War era, farmers were always committed to politics, whereas workers were profoundly ambivalent about the relationship of politics—particularly national politics—to their economic interests and skeptical about their ability to participate effectively in a winning national political coalition. Farmers' interests converged easily and naturally on the national state; workers' goals were strongly local, and the forces of judicially maintained constitutional rules, political economy, and the two-party system worked against their national political mobilization. Particularly at the national level of government, the farmers' expansive political program contrasted with labor's largely negative goals.

Farmers found it easier to dominate the politics of their overwhelmingly agricultural-extractive regions—the agrarian periphery of the South, plains, and mountains—and to participate in legislative coalitions with the mixed urban-rural regions of the Midwest, whose citizens also caviled at perceived exploitation by large northeastern corporations. The farmers' commitment to politics and the relative economic homogeneity of the agrarian periphery in a territorially based political system proved an enduring political advantage to farmers even as their proportion of the population shrank. Legislators could serve, in effect, as organizers or leaders of an agrarian social movement even when, after 1896, the farmers' social-movement organizations declined. The national Democratic Party, having absorbed the Populist Party and rebuffed its own northeastern conservative wing, became the bearer of agrarian demands in national politics. Thus it was that so much of the old populist program could be enacted years after the Populist Party and the Farmers' Alliance had faded away. The politically committed farmer and the extraordinary figure of William Jennings Bryan—at once a national party chief, agrarian social-movement leader, and the country's foremost progressive reformer—made this translation possible.

Workers were concentrated in the core industrial region of the Northeast and Great Lakes, a region dominated by corporate capital through the Republican Party. To win against capitalists in national political contests, they had to make alliance with the periphery farmers, who not only were numerous and determined antagonists of core capital but also enjoyed strategic legislative advantage. But at critical junctures—in 1894, 1896, and 1908—capitalists were able to convince core industrial workers that the interests of farmers were antithetical to the interests of *all* residents of the core industrial regions. The recognition that capitalists might be right, that the politically triumphant farmers might wreck the industrial economy with their legislative program, was profoundly discouraging to workers, for many were undoubtedly drawn to the alliance held out by the farmers' national political leader, Bryan.

Thus the electoral support the workers offered to the farmers' party (in return for the latter's acceptance of labor's limited national political agenda) was always very feeble, never enough to maintain sufficient control of the national state to implement the key protections that workers needed for their organizations and workplace collective actions. The farmer-labor alliance could and did flourish *within* states in the periphery and diverse regions, but it could not sustain an effective cross-regional alliance in national politics. Labor was caught in a political economy that produced and sustained a two-party system, with one party dominated by core capital and the other by periphery farmers. Workers could not comfortably ally with either, and this realization was the major reason for labor's apolitical, voluntarist strategy. The farmers' party desperately needed and avidly courted labor; by the end of the Progressive Era, it had delivered almost every item on labor's legislative wish list. Yet the metropolitan labor vote for the Democrats shrank inexorably in 1914, 1916, and 1918, allowing the GOP resurgence that, even without the mobilization for world war, would have brought the Progressive Era to an end.

In the face of these differences, farmers and workers by the end of the Progressive Era had settled into very different modes of participation in national politics. Farmers worked from the bottom up, through party and legislature. Workers, lacking national party and legislative power, experimented with an "end run" around the legislative playing field into a corporatist arena (the owners' box up above the grandstand seats, in this metaphor). Here they hoped to bargain with large capitalists and to trade support of the president's foreign policy for high-level implementation of labor standards. Unfortunately, the advantage won through this top-down strategy proved to be short-lived. There was just no substitute for political mobilization, party control, and legislative power.

The farmers' natural forum was the legislature. They needed change in the national legal structure, and Congress was much more responsive to grassroots social movements and more willing to deny large capitalists their cherished goals than the executive branch or the courts. Farmers used their party and legislative power to dissuade the president from his more conservative inclinations and to wrestle with the courts for control of regulatory policy.

Scholars like Theda Skocpol, Kenneth Finegold, and Christopher Tomlins argue that by the New Deal era, farmers and workers both saw their interests subordinated to an increasingly autonomous administrative state and their organizations and modes of production thoroughly under the control of the national administration.[2] How could both groups end up in the same place if they were so different, and how could they come to be subordinated to bureaucracy when both movements had traditionally detested bureaucracy? The reasons explored here are different for the two movements but intersect in the inability of farmers and workers to make common political cause, to align their interests in a strong legislative party through which to control the national political agenda at critical political junctures in the late nineteenth and early twentieth centuries when the terms of politics were being renegotiated.

The farmer-labor political alliance worked best *within* the periphery and diverse states, where national partisan, organizational, and political economy differences were less relevant. It was the easy camaraderie of farmers and workers in Texas that sparked the populist vision of a "producers' alliance" in the 1880s. The North Dakota Nonpartisan League (NPL) of 1915–22 revived the populist alliance behind a radical program of farmer-serving state enterprises and labor legislation, and its success spawned a contagion of similar movements in twelve other north-central and western states—including the Minnesota Farmer-Labor Party, which lasted into the 1940s.[3]

Efforts to join this momentum with other currents of labor activism into a national farmer-labor political movement independent of the two major parties flourished briefly in the early 1920s, led by groups of radical statist persuasion: agrarians; socialists; middle-class intellectuals nostalgic for the Progressive Party of Theodore Roosevelt; and in particular, a recent convert to state expansion, railway labor. The last had experienced significant gains under wartime government control of the rails and fought hard for permanent nationalization in 1919–20. Having lost that battle, the railway unions suffered in the postwar depression from both employer wage-cutting drives and unfavorable rulings by the Railway Labor Board created under the pro-railroad Transportation Act of 1920. Their grievances against this law created common ground with farmers. The latter were also in a state of political uproar as commodity prices dropped, credit tightened, and freight rates grew more burdensome.[4]

The leaders of six railroad unions spearheaded, in 1922, a national convention of labor and farmer organizations (including the AFL, the Nonpartisan League, the largest farm groups, and the Minnesota Farmer-Labor Party) along with socialists and religious and civic organizations. This gathering created a Conference for Progressive Political Action (CPPA) to yoke the diverse reformers. The activists did not create a third party (which the AFL and a number of major-party adherents opposed) but supported the election of sympathetic Democrats, Republicans, Socialists, and Farmer-Labor candidates to Congress. In November, the movement saw considerable success, especially in the farm states.[5]

As the presidential elections of 1924 approached, the prospects for an independent farmer-labor party seemed promising, at least from the labor side. The AFL found its reception at the Democratic convention polite but substantively unproductive, and the party's 104th ballot nominee, a courtly lawyer (John W. Davis) with Wall Street connections, was unappealing. The railroad brotherhoods were still smarting from federal labor policy and were disappointed by the shattered prospects of William McAdoo (a popular wartime railroad administrator) for the Democratic nomination. Sen. Robert La Follette, a champion of both farmers and workers and a particular favorite of the railroad unions, was imminently available to lead the independent ticket. The CPPA convention duly nominated the Wisconsin senator and ratified his choice of a running mate, maverick Democrat Burton Wheeler of Montana. It also honored La Follette's choice of label (Progressive) and his decision *not* to create a multilevel party. The candidate managed to get on the ballot in all but one state (Louisiana) using the lines of the Progressive, Socialist, and Farmer-Labor Parties, but he limited his campaign itinerary to the East and the Midwest. He stressed opposition to monopoly as the principal issue, but his platform was replete with specific reforms directed at farmers and workers, an updated Populist-Progressive amalgam.[6]

In the end, confirming the well-known liabilities of third-party candidates (and a radical one at that), La Follette carried only his home state of Wisconsin, though his vote total was almost 60 percent of the Democrat vote and he ran second in eleven western and midwestern states. Kenneth McKay estimates that about 52 percent of the Progressive vote (2,530,000) came from farmers, 20 percent (1,000,000) from socialists, roughly another 20 percent from "various liberal and protest groups [including] the American Federation of Labor," and a few hundred thousand from railroad workers.[7] The labor vote was extremely disappointing to the campaign and was surprising in view of the unprecedented AFL endorsement of an independent ticket and the fact that labor and socialists had organized the CPPA effort. Though several officers of the United Mine Workers, the largest union in the AFL, had been early activists for the CPPA and La Follette, the UMW president endorsed Calvin Coolidge. The AFL itself gave only minimal financial support to the badly underfunded campaign.[8]

Farmers were no doubt wary of a farmer-labor campaign structure in which they composed "the tail of the kite,"[9] and southern farmers, wedded to the Democratic Party, were unlikely to flock to the banner of a candidate who advocated civil rights for blacks and whose campaign pointedly ignored the South. If (midwestern and western) farmers indeed provided the bulk of La Follette's votes, it was a testimony to their politicization and openness to radical reform. However, with so sharp a split in the agrarian vote, the failure of the national political reform movement was preordained.[10]

The 1924 campaign would be the last significant national effort to put together a farmer-labor movement from the grass roots. However, centered on a partyless presidential candidate who called the shots, the Progressive campaign also offered a glimpse of the future of political reform. Franklin Roosevelt and Huey Long would be the next great "movement" leaders, creating and handing down the programs and harnessing the loyalties of the marginalized behind their own presidential ambitions. Where movement strength had previously made itself felt through the legislature, farmers and workers now became components of executive-led coalitions. Such top-down direction was possible because the old movements had now faded into interest groups.

With the decline of indigenous organization for both farmers and workers in the 1920s[11] and the shift of policy initiative definitively to the executive branch, neither farmers nor workers were able to dictate terms in national politics. When the economic crisis of the 1930s arrived, the stage was set for state actors and public-service-oriented intellectuals to propose and *impose* a program that offered to do a lot *for* farmers and workers, according to the interpretation of their interests developed *within* the state, but to grant them little autonomy from national administrative control.

The decline of indigenous labor organizations resulted from state repression of radical trade-union organizations during World War I (repression that the AFL, feeling secure in its corporatist arrangements, did not oppose) and from the failure of workers to wrest definitive organizational rights from the grasp of hostile courts and employers. This failure, in turn, can be traced to labor's weak political mobilization and resulting legislative impotence. Organizational rights would finally be won in the 1932 Norris-LaGuardia Act, a legislative legacy of the farmer-labor alliance. Agrarians had been trying to emancipate labor from antitrust prosecution since 1890, but labor was never able to elect enough industrial Democrats to sustain the alliance or the antitrust exemption. Farmers had provided the crucial lesson that labor would not learn: the Supreme Court would inevitably pick apart your legislation. You had to *keep coming back,* again and again, to patch it up and plug loopholes—as the farmers did with railroad legislation in 1906, 1910, and 1913 and also with antitrust and commodity futures regulation and as the farmer-labor alliance finally did for labor in 1932.

For farmers, the decline of indigenous organizations after 1917 was in part a result of agrarian legislative victories in the Wilson era and the commodity price increases of the war years,[12] but there was another, ironic development. One of the Progressive Era legislative victories of the farmers' movement was the Smith-Lever Act of 1914 creating an agricultural extension service. As the system developed, it created a powerful, state-spawned competitor to the Grange and the Farmers' Union—the groups that had fought for the 1914 act. Faced with the determinedly localistic administrative structure of the act and the food-production needs of World War I, the Extension Service encouraged the growth of local "farm bureaus" to support its agents and then backed their federation into state and national organizations.

Passage of the unprecedented Agricultural Adjustment Act of 1933 proved a second great stimulus to the growth of this peculiar, state-sponsored farmers' organization. By the 1940s, the membership of the staid, conservative American Farm Bureau Federation (AFBF) far exceeded that of the liberal, pro-labor Farmers' Union. The AFBF used its entrenched local administrative network to campaign against progressive political candidates in the South and for abolition of the redistributive Farm Security Administration, which the Grange and the Farmers' Union supported.[13] This development was a distressing and clearly unintended and unanticipated consequence of state expansion. Contemporary antistatists will no doubt respond, "We told you so!" Once erected, bureaucracies acquire a life of their own and may push policy to unwanted, even stifling conclusions for the original sponsors.

Of course, democratic government is a work in progress. One has to keep at it, watch it like a hawk, continually make corrections. Things change. Constant tinkering is necessary. But the more fundamental agrarian answer goes deeper than an admonition to vigilance, mobilization, and participation. The agrarian mode of state expansion did not propose to hand over policy-making to national bureaucracies. It aimed to govern through specific statutes, forged in the legislature for all to observe. The new laws would not set some ambiguous goal for bureaucrats to work out but would say precisely what the government should do and what business *could not* do, on pain of fines or jail terms (or both). The statutes should be as self-enforcing as possible. For example, the law should list—as did the House version of the Interstate Commerce Act of 1886—what railroads must and must not do, specifying that if they failed to comply, any farmer or shipper could take them to court and win triple damages. This was the model too for the House Clayton antitrust bill of 1914 and for countless tariff, tax, money, and labor bills. If an administering agency had to be created, its instructions should be perfectly clear, and private suits to effectuate the law's provisions should be available as alternatives to administrative enforcement.

A strong agrarian undercurrent persisted into the New Deal, and it showed up in laws like the Securities Act of 1933 and early versions of what became the Public Utility Holding Company Act of 1935. There was even, one might argue, a multifaceted "shadow" New Deal, which aimed to combat the Great Depression with the statutorily specific remedies of going off gold and inflating the currency, slashing tariffs, dismantling "trusts," raising taxes on the rich, and effecting a "check in the mail" redistribution along the lines of Huey Long's "Share Our Wealth" program and/or Francis Townsend's pension system. The Roosevelt administration considered these ideas horrifying and dangerous, but it was forced to accommodate them in its own far tamer, bureaucracy-intensive program.[14]

In the 1970s, New Deal–style discretionary bureaucracy and interest-group involvement in agency policy-making came under attack in political science and in a resurgent Congress,[15] and the "agrarian" (specific) statute was resurrected, particularly in the Clean Air Acts of 1977 and 1990. A few Republican "liberals" (though they scorned the title) began to offer a conception of a "statutory welfare state," an expansive, equality-enhancing state that, with minimal bureaucracy, would operate through a "negative income tax" and vouchers for housing, education, and other benefits. However, this tendency was submerged and isolated within the administrations of Ronald Reagan and George Bush and the Republican Party in Congress.[16]

The agrarian model could be seen as a governmental method ideally suited to a society that spawned social movements and strong legislatures but bungled and abhorred bureaucracy. It offered a method for using public law to tame and democratize a lusty market economy. It honored competition by creating it. It reflected the old Greenback republican belief that neither unrestrained business nor autonomous bureaucracy could maintain a broad and democratic prosperity. It was certainly worth trying. Perhaps its time will come again.

Notes

Chapter One

1. A few prominent examples are Lawrence Goodwyn, *The Democratic Promise* (New York: Oxford University Press, 1976); Norman Pollack, *The Just Polity* (Urbana: University of Illinois Press, 1987); Michael Schwartz, *Radical Protest and Social Structure* (Chicago: University of Chicago Press, 1988); Gwendolyn Mink, *Old Labor and New Immigrants in American Political Development* (Ithaca, N.Y.: Cornell University Press, 1986); and Leon Fink, *Workingmen's Democracy* (Urbana: University of Illinois Press, 1983).

2. Three earlier works that do treat the two sectors in conjunction are Nathan Fine, *Labor and Farmer Parties in the U.S.* (New York: Russell and Russell, 1961); Stuart A. Rice, *Farmers and Workers in American Politics* (New York: Columbia University Press, 1924), which provides abundant statistics relevant to questions about the congruence or conflict of farmer and labor politics, emphasizing contemporary midwestern political movements; and Norman J. Ware, *The Labor Movement in the United States, 1860–1895* (New York: Vintage Books, 1964), chap. 17. More recently, Richard M. Valelly has analyzed the evolution of a state-level, radical third party—the Minnesota Farmer-Labor Party—and its influence on state and New Deal politics of the 1920s and 1930s: *Radicalism in the States* (Chicago: University of Chicago Press, 1989).

3. Rural life has indeed seen revived attention, as in James Green, *Grass Roots Socialism* (Baton Rouge: Louisiana State University Press, 1978), and Steven Hahn, *The Roots of Southern Populism* (New York: Oxford University Press, 1983), for example. But the balance still strongly favored labor in the 1990s.

4. Examples of such interpretations include, preeminently, Gabriel Kolko, *The Triumph of Conservatism* (Chicago: Quadrangle Books, 1963), and advocates of the "corporate liberalism" perspective, for example: James Weinstein, *The Corporate Ideal in the Liberal State* (Boston: Beacon Press, 1968); Martin J. Sklar, *The Corporate Reconstruction of American Capitalism, 1890–1916* (New York: Cambridge University Press, 1988); and R. Jeffrey Lustig, *Corporate Liberalism: The Origins of Modern American Political Theory, 1890–1920* (Berkeley: University of California Press, 1982).

5. For example, see Fred Block, *Revising State Theory* (Philadelphia: Temple University Press, 1987).

6. See, for example, Stephen Skowronek, *Building a New American State* (New York: Cambridge University Press, 1982), and Kenneth Finegold and Theda Skocpol, *State and Party in America's New Deal* (Madison: University of Wisconsin Press, 1995).

7. Such is the argument of Sklar, *Corporate Reconstruction of American Capitalism*, 333–430.

8. It is, however, generally acknowledged that agrarian support made possible (though it did not lead) the rise of Scandinavian social democracy. See, for example, Gösta Esping-Andersen, *Politics against Markets: The Social Democratic Road to Power* (Princeton: Princeton University Press, 1985), 71–88. In Canada, much like the United States in socioeconomic profile and political institutions, radical agrarians in the prairie provinces were the bulwark of social democratic reform. See Seymour M. Lipset, *Agrarian Socialism* (New York: Doubleday, 1968).

9. This argument confirms Michael Rogin's suggestion, made three decades ago, that rural insurgency in the United States replaced working-class radicalism as the central dynamic of anticapitalist contention. *The Intellectuals and McCarthy* (Cambridge: MIT Press, 1967), 187.

10. In the terminology of social-movement theory, the institutional constellation produced a more empowering political opportunity structure for farmer than for labor organizations.

11. Subtracting proprietors, managers, officials, and superintendents from gainful employees in these sectors and adding miscellaneous laborers yields a figure of 36.5 percent of the workforce. U.S. Department of Commerce, Bureau of the Census, *Statistical Abstract of the United States, 1913* (Washington, D.C.: GPO, 1914), 229–39. See table 3.1 below for trade union membership.

12. The debate is exemplified by Theda Skocpol and Kenneth Finegold, "Explaining New Deal Labor Policy," and the rejoinder by Michael Goldfield, in the *American Political Science Review* 84 (December 1990): 1297–311.

13. The modern Rule of Law argument on the democratic superiority of specific statutes to bureaucratic discretion was pioneered by Theodore J. Lowi in *The End of Liberalism*, 2d ed. (New York: W. W. Norton, 1978). For a careful analysis of the implications of Lowi's argument, see Richard F. Bensel, "Creating the Statutory State," *American Political Science Review* 74 (September 1980): 734–44.

Chapter Two

1. Jackson Turner Main, *The Antifederalists* (Chicago: Quadrangle Books, 1964); Charles A. Beard, *An Economic Interpretation of the Constitution* (New York: Macmillan, 1937).

2. The following interpretation of New England political and economic strategy and the development of regional blocs relies on Charles Sydnor, *The Origins of Southern Sectionalism* (Baton Rouge: Louisiana State University Press, 1948), 104–222.

3. Eric Foner, *Free Soil, Free Labor, Free Men* (New York: Oxford University Press, 1970), 27.

4. Allan R. Pred, *Urban Growth and City Systems in the United States, 1840–1860* (Cambridge: Harvard University Press, 1980); idem, *The Spatial Dynamics of U.S. Urban Industrial Growth, 1800–1914: Interpretive Essays* (Cambridge: MIT Press, 1966); David R. Meyer, "Emergence of the American Manufacturing Belt: An Interpretation," *Journal of Historical Geography* 9 (April 1983): 145–74; Albert W. Niemi Jr., *State and Regional Patterns in American Manufacturing, 1860–1900* (Westport, Conn.: Greenwood Press, 1974), 29–44.

5. The following description of "industrial highways" is based on Harold Hull McCarty, *The Geographic Basis of American Economic Life* (Port Washington, N.Y.: Kennikat Press, 1940), vol. 2, 499–500, 584–676.

6. On Pennsylvania's iron and steel economy, see Glenn E. McLaughlin, *The Growth of American Manufacturing Areas* (Westport, Conn.: Greenwood Press, 1938).

7. Pred, *Urban Growth and City Systems*, 6–8 and chap. 5. In 1860, six states (Massachusetts, Rhode Island, Connecticut, New York, New Jersey, and Pennsylvania) accounted for 75 percent of the interregional export of manufactured goods in textiles and apparel, paper and printed matter, chemicals, petroleum and coal-based products, rubber, primary and fabricated metals, machinery, transportation equipment, and musical and scientific instruments. Niemi, *State and Regional Patterns in American Manufacturing*, 58–59.

8. Sidney Ratner, James S. Soltow, and Richard Scylla, *The Evolution of the American Economy* (New York: Basic Books, 1979), 192; Meyer, "Emergence of the American Manufacturing Belt," 147–49, 164–69; Pred, *Urban Growth and City Systems*, 167–70.

9. McCarty, *Geographic Basis of American Economic Life*, 484–503.

10. Ibid., 484–85, 505.

11. Harvey S. Perloff, Edgar S. Dunn Jr., Eric E. Lampard, and Richard Muth, *Regions, Resources, and Economic Growth* (Baltimore: Johns Hopkins University Press, 1960), 126–53 (tables); David Ward, *Cities and Immigrants* (New York: Oxford University Press, 1971), 40 (tables).

12. Alfred D. Chandler Jr., *The Visible Hand* (Cambridge, Mass.: Belknap Press, 1977), esp. 287–344, and "The Evolution of the Large Industrial Corporation," *Business and Economic History* 11 (1982): 116–29.

13. The following description relies on McCarty, *Geographic Basis of American Economic Life*.

14. Ibid., 294–95.

15. William Cronon, *Nature's Metropolis* (New York: W. W. Norton, 1991), esp. 81–147 and 303–9; John C. Hudson, *Making the Corn Belt* (Bloomington: Indiana University Press, 1994), 130–35.

16. McCarty, *Geographic Basis of American Economic Life*, 380–81.

17. Ibid., 377.

18. By 1937, the South would account for 60 percent of cotton textile manufacture. Ibid., 376–77. On the early development of the southern textile industry, see Broadus Mitchell, *The Rise of Cotton Mills in the South* (Baltimore: Johns Hopkins University Press, 1921).

19. In capital and surplus, the Richmond, Atlanta, and Dallas banks ranged from $9,484,000 down to $5,900,000. The Boston, Philadelphia, Chicago, and San Francisco banks all had over $40 million; New York had about $250 million. U.S. Senate, *Location of Reserve Districts in the United States*, 63d Cong., 2d sess. 1914, S. Doc. 485, 365.

20. McCarty, *Geographic Basis of American Economic Life*, 55–76. The population of San Francisco in 1910 was 417,000; Los Angeles, 319,000; Portland, 207,000; and Seattle, 237,000.

21. The relatively high Wyoming and Louisiana figures are produced by mineral industries (coal and petroleum); in Florida, the principal "industries" were sawmills. North Carolina, by far the most industrialized of the southern states, had a fast-growing textile industry in the early twentieth century. Of these states, only Wyoming had a statewide value added of $200 per capita by the Progressive Era. However, since Wyoming fell in the Omaha trade area (see map 2.3), it is classified as a "periphery" state.

22. The pioneering work using the trading area as a political unit is Richard F. Bensel, *Sectionalism and American Political Development* (Madison: University of Wisconsin Press, 1984).

23. U.S. Senate, *Location of Reserve Districts;* U.S. House, *First Choice Vote for Reserve Bank Cities*, 63d Cong., 2d sess., 1914, H. Doc. 1134. Final 1921 branch bank and district boundaries can be found in *8th Annual Report of the Board of Governors of the Federal Reserve System, 1921* (Washington, D.C.: GPO, 1922), 693–99.

24. McCarty, *Geographic Basis of American Economic Life*, 169. Spokane later lost its reserve bank designation, leaving it once more in the "diverse" Seattle trade area.

25. For example, in the 61st House, there were 106 high and 25 low industrial districts in the core, 36 and 42 in the diverse regions, and 12 and 170 in the periphery, using $200 per capita value added as the cutoff for "high industrial" in these dichotomizations. This categorization combines my industrialization data with ICPSR district identification.

Chapter Three

1. This definition of a social movement is a modification of that used by Charles Tilly in, for example, *Popular Contention in Great Britain* (Cambridge: Harvard University Press, 1995), 369.

2. In my perception, one of the most important differences between social movements and other forms of collective action (such as interest groups and some identity-based organizations) is precisely that social movements *move*, outward, seeking allies in their struggles for policy change.

3. See Michael Schwartz, *Radical Protest and Social Structure* (Chicago: University of Chicago Press, 1988), 269–83.

4. Jonathan E. Garlock, "A Structural Analysis of the Knights of Labor" (Ph.D. diss., University of Rochester, 1974), xiii, 68–98.

5. Norman J. Ware, *The Labor Movement in the United States, 1860–1895* (New York: Vintage Books, 1964), 6–64; Gerald N. Grob, *Workers and Utopia* (Evanston, Ill.: Northwestern University Press, 1961), 13–36; Edward Topping James, "American Labor and Political Action, 1865–1896 (Ph.D. diss., Harvard University, 1954), 73–157; Chester M. Destler, *American Radicalism, 1865–1901* (New York: Octagon Books, 1963), 25–28, 66.

6. Robert V. Bruce, *1877: Year of Violence* (Indianapolis: Bobbs-Merrill, 1959); Ware, *Labor Movement in the United States*, 45–50; Garlock, "Structural Analysis of the Knights of Labor," 68–81.

7. Bruce, *1877*, 307–19; Ware, *Labor Movement in the United States*, 45–50.

8. Robert H. Sharkey, *Money, Class, and Party* (Baltimore: Johns Hopkins University Press, 1959), 174–220; Irving Unger, *The Greenback Era* (Princeton: Princeton University Press, 1964), 96–114, 299–

302, 347–48; Destler, *American Radicalism*, 32–61; David Montgomery, *Beyond Equality* (New York: Knopf, 1967), 425–47; James, "American Labor and Political Action," 22–30; Jonathan Grossman, *William Sylvis, Pioneer of American Labor* (New York: Columbia University Press, 1945), 189–254.

9. Quoted in Nathan Fine, *Labor and Farmer Parties in the U.S.* (New York: Russell and Russell, 1961), 25.

10. Ware, *Labor Movement in the United States*, 9–10, 16.

11. Ibid., 43, 50–51; James, "American Labor and Political Action," 140–66; Fred E. Haynes, *Third Party Movements since the Civil War* (Cedar Rapids: State Historical Society of Iowa, 1916), 120–23; Unger, *Greenback Era*, 347–49. The platform adopted by the 1878 convention endorsed a national government-issued legal tender currency, silver coinage on the same basis as gold, an adequate supply of money, a national income tax and no tax exemptions for bonds, public lands reserved for actual settlers, reduction of working hours, establishment of state and national bureaus of labor, and prohibition of foreign contract labor and Chinese immigration. Haynes, *Third Party Movements*, 123–24.

12. Compiled from Congressional Quarterly, *Guide to U.S. Elections* (Washington, D.C.: Congressional Quarterly, 1975), 638–41; and U.S. Congress, *Congressional Directory*, 46th Cong., 1st sess. (Washington, D.C.: GPO, 1879). Congressional Quarterly misses fusion and National (Greenback) candidates elected in Illinois and Indiana. Haynes, *Third Party Movements*, 131, counts fourteen elected but misses a New Jersey Greenback-Democrat. His regional table on p. 125 is misleading as a description of the congressional vote. It relies on figures in the 1878 issue of *Appleton's Annual Cyclopedia and Register of Important Events of the Year* (New York: D. Appleton and Co., 1879), 808, which seems to miss many votes for fusion (e.g., Greenback-Democrat) candidates. Kenneth C. Martis counts thirteen Greenbackers (*Historical Atlas of Political Parties in the U.S. Congress, 1789–1989* [New York: Macmillan, 1989], table 46H); my list includes, in addition to those, fusionists Kelley (PA4) and Smith (NJ2).

13. District urban profiles are calculated from the U.S. Department of the Interior, Bureau of the Census, *Compendium of the Tenth Census, Pt. 1* (Washington, D.C.: GPO, 1885). Value added in manufacturing and agricultural production are found in Stanley B. Parsons, William W. Beach, and Michael J. Dubin, *United States Congressional Districts and Data, 1843–1883* (New York: Greenwood Press, 1986).

14. James, "American Labor and Political Action," 167–83. Weaver's vote came mostly from the Midwest and South, with large declines (compared with 1878) in the Northeast and the more urban states of the Midwest.

15. Ibid., 172–75. For a recent analysis of Greenbackism, particularly useful for state/regional contrasts, see Gretchen Ritter, *Goldbugs and Greenbacks* (New York: Cambridge University Press, 1997).

16. James, "American Labor and Political Action," 222–37; Donald B. Johnson, ed., *National Party Platforms*, vol. 1 (Urbana: University of Illinois Press, 1978), 64–70; Haynes, *Third Party Movements*, 148–52, 202–5. On West, see also Montgomery, *Beyond Equality*, 403–4.

17. James, "American Labor and Political Action," 238–47.

18. Ware, *Labor Movement in the United States*, 128–29.

19. Garlock, "Structural Analysis of the Knights of Labor," 37 (table 1). In terms of membership, 50 percent of Knights were in mixed assemblies by 1886 (38 [table 3]).

20. Ibid., 115 (table 22).

21. Ibid., 148 (table 41).

22. Ibid., 139–40 (table 38), 149 (table 42).

23. Ware, *Labor Movement in the United States*, 320–33.

24. The KOL was, according to Ware, "the most successful boycotting organization in the history of American labor." Ibid., 334–45 (quotation at 334). The KOL's *Journal of United Labor* constantly admonished readers to buy union-made goods and boycott products of unfriendly firms, whose names were prominently listed in the *Journal*. See, for example, the issue of November 28, 1889, 1.

25. Ware, *Labor Movement in the United States*, 139–45; John R. Commons et al., *History of Labor in the United States*, vol. 2 (New York: Macmillan Co. , 1918), 368–70; Howard M. Gittleman, "Attempts

to Unify the American Labor Movement, 1865–1900" (Ph.D. diss., University of Wisconsin, 1960), 312–15.

26. Garlock, "Structural Analysis of the Knights of Labor," 140–51, 174–76. Frederic Meyers estimates that there were at least 30,000 southern Knights in 1886. "The Knights of Labor in the South," *Southern Economic Journal* 6 (April 1940): 483–84.

27. Gittleman, "Attempts to Unify the American Labor Movement," 253–60.

28. Leon Fink, *Workingmen's Democracy* (Urbana: University of Illinois Press, 1983), 162–63, 169–72 (quotation at 169).

29. Kim Voss, "Disposition Is Not Action: The Rise and Demise of the Knights of Labor," *Studies in American Political Development* 6, 2 (1992): 306–17; Commons et al., *History of Labor in the United States,* 371–75, 414–15; Ware, *Labor Movement in the United States,* 97–100.

30. Commons et al., *History of Labor in the United States,* 318–31; Ware, *Labor Movement in the United States,* 66 (membership figures), 243–57; Gittleman, "Attempts to Unify the American Labor Movement," 415–35. The most active unions in the organization of FOTLU were the cigar makers, typographers, and iron and steel workers.

31. Gittleman, "Attempts to Unify the American Labor Movement," 347–51.

32. Quoted in Ware, *Labor Movement in the United States,* 251. On the contrasting ideologies of the two organizations, see Grob, *Workers and Utopia,* 7–10, and Victoria C. Hattam, "Economic Visions and Political Strategies: American Labor and the State, 1865–1896," *Studies in American Political Development* 4 (1990): 82–130.

33. Gittleman, "Attempts to Unify the American Labor Movement," 352–84, 461–67; Ware, *Labor Movement in the United States,* 185–89, 277–98; Philip Taft, *The AFL in the Time of Gompers* (New York: Harper and Brothers, 1957), 35–38, 85–93; Commons et al., *History of Labor in the United States,* 411–13.

34. James, "American Labor and Political Action," 295–315; Fink, *Workingmen's Democracy,* 156–57, 198; U.S. Congress, *Congressional Directory,* 50th Cong., 1st sess. (Washington, D.C.: GPO, 1888), 19, 103.

35. Fink, *Workingmen's Democracy,* 26.

36. James, "American Labor and Political Action," 285–91; U.S. Congress, *Congressional Directory,* 49th Cong., 2d sess., 2d ed. (Washington, D.C.: GPO, 1887), and 50th Cong., 1st sess., 2d ed. (Washington, D.C.: GPO, 1888). Eight of the seventeen incumbent candidates endorsed by the KOL ran in the periphery states of Kansas, Texas, Missouri, Kentucky, and Washington Territory.

37. James, "American Labor and Political Action," 291–92, 409–18.

38. Ibid., 418–27. Litchman took with him the KOL mailing lists, which proved very useful to the GOP.

39. Ibid., 320–34 (quotation at 334 n).

40. Ibid., 338–47; Fink, *Workingmen's Democracy,* 201–2; Philip S. Foner, *History of the Labor Movement in the United States,* 7 vols., 2d ed. (New York: International Publishers, 1975–), 147–56.

41. Haynes, *Third Party Movements,* 206–11; James, "American Labor and Political Action," 331, 447–63; Congressional Quarterly, *Guide to U.S. Elections,* 658–61.

42. *Congressional Record* (*CR*), 49th Cong., 1st sess. (hereafter cited in the form 49–1), index, 282, 630.

43. James, "American Labor and Political Action," 220, 249–51. Powderly promptly applied for the job and requested member support, but the directorship went to Carroll D. Wright of Massachusetts. Ware, *Labor Movement in the United States,* 83.

44. Ware, *Labor Movement in the United States,* 196–200, 358; James, "American Labor and Political Action," 216–20.

45. *CR,* 49–2, 1435. The 1885 bill was sponsored by labor Democrat Martin Foran of Ohio.

46. Knights of Labor, *Proceedings of the General Assembly (Richmond), 1886,* 139–41, in Terrence V. Powderly Papers, 1864–1937, and John W. Hayes Papers, 1880–1921: The Knights of Labor, Reel 67-series A, part 4D, Proceedings, General Assembly, 1878–1902; James, "American Labor and Political

Action," 279–84, 358–61. The KOL executive board also endorsed the ultimately unsuccessful bill sponsored by Sen. Henry Blair of New Hampshire, and strongly supported by the South, to appropriate $77 million in aid to elementary education. See chapter 9, note 5.

47. *CR*, 49–1, 3393–95. Reagan had persuaded the KOL lobbyists to include his regulation bill in their legislative agenda. James, "American Labor and Political Action," 281, 288.

48. *CR*, 49–1, 3061–62, 3066, 3393. Rogers stated that he was proud to stand with the only two trade unionists in the House, Martin Foran of Ohio and John Farquhar of New York, both of whom opposed this and other attempts at government involvement in labor relations.

49. Ibid., 3349, 3394–95.

50. Ibid., 3066. Southern representatives split 33–22. For another description of the debate (which emphasizes the constitutional objections of some southerners but ignores the majority's support), see Melvyn Dubofsky, *The State and Labor in Modern America* (Chapel Hill: University of North Carolina Press, 1994), 16–19. The southern Democratic opponents tended to represent an older generation in comparison with regional supporters of the arbitration bill.

51. *CR*, 49–1, 4620–21.

52. *CR*, 49–2, 2375–76.

53. *CR*, 49–1, 4618–24; Gerald G. Eggert, *Railroad Labor Disputes* (Ann Arbor: University of Michigan Press, 1967), 75–77, 103–7.

54. *CR*, 50–1, 3096–109, 8609. The mechanism of the 1888 bill was used only once. It was superseded by a stronger arbitration bill that contained important labor protections, the 1898 Erdman Act. See Eggert, *Railroad Labor Disputes*, 105, 214–25; I. L. Sharfman, *The Interstate Commerce Commission*, 4 vols. (New York: Commonwealth Fund, 1931–37), 1:100n.

55. For three such investigations, see *Investigation of Labor Troubles in Missouri, Arkansas, Kansas, Texas, and Illinois*, 49th Cong., 2d sess., 1887, H. Rept. 4174; *Labor Troubles in the Anthracite Regions of Pennsylvania, 1887–88*, 50th Cong., 2d sess., 1889, H. Rept. 4147; and *On the Senate Resolution in Relation to the Employment for Private Purposes of Armed Bodies of Men or Detectives in Connection with Differences between Workmen and Employers*, 52d Cong., 2d sess., 1893, S. Rept. 1280. On the emergence of pro-labor advocacy in the congressional labor committees, see Mary O. Furner, "The Republican Tradition and the New Liberalism," in *The State and Social Investigation in Britain and the United States*, ed. Michael J. Lacey and Mary O. Furner (Cambridge: Cambridge University Press, 1993), 207–12.

56. Ware, *Labor Movement in the United States*, 88–89, 364–67.

57. Lawrence Goodwyn, *The Populist Moment* (New York: Oxford University Press, 1978), 107.

58. James, "American Labor and Political Action," 381–82.

59. Knights of Labor, *Proceedings of the General Assembly (Richmond)*, 1886, 151. Labor concern with land issues predated the Civil War, and workers supported homestead bills leading to the Homestead Act of 1862. The platform adopted by the 1878 convention of the KOL took over the earlier Industrial Congresses' demand that public lands be reserved for the actual settler. Eric Foner, *Free Soil, Free Labor, Free Men* (New York: Oxford University Press, 1970), 27–28; James, "American Labor and Political Action," 373; Amy Bridges, "Becoming American: The Working Classes in the United States before the Civil War," in *Working Class Formation*, ed. Ira Katznelson and Aristide Zolberg (Princeton: Princeton University Press, 1986), 187; Ware, *Labor Movement in the United States*, 365.

60. James, "American Labor and Political Action," 375–77; Foner, *History of the Labor Movement* 2:33.

61. U.S. Department of Commerce, Bureau of the Census, *Statistical Abstract of the United States, 1912* (Washington, D.C.: GPO, 1913), 288.

62. For an account of the burden placed on the Newark, New Jersey, District Assembly by the undisciplined strike wave, see Voss, "Disposition Is Not Action," 310–11.

63. Foner, *History of the Labor Movement* 2:84–85; Ware, *Labor Movement in the United States*, 145–49; Eggert, *Railroad Labor Disputes*, 60–61.

64. Commons et al., *History of Labor in the United States*, 417–20; Ware, *Labor Movement in the United States*, 150–54.

65. Ware, *Labor Movement in the United States*, 313–19; Richard J. Oestreicher, *Solidarity and Fragmentation: Working People and Class Consciousness in Detroit, 1875–1900* (Urbana: University of Illinois Press, 1989), 198–211.

66. On the devastating effect of the employer backlash, see Voss, "Disposition Is Not Action," 317.

67. Garlock, "Structural Analysis of the Knights of Labor," 231 (table 52).

68. Ware, *Labor Movement in the United States*, 369–70.

69. Garlock, "Structural Analysis of the Knights of Labor," 9–15.

70. Ibid., 45, 105, 115–16, 142 n.

71. Writing of labor strength in the late nineteenth century, Herbert Gutman has argued that in smaller cities the employer's power was "more visible and more vulnerable there than in the larger complex metropolis," and local officials often sided with workers. *Work, Culture, and Society in Industrializing America* (New York: Vintage Books, 1966), 254–57. In "Trade Unions and Political Machines" (in Katznelson and Zolberg, *Working Class Formation*, 241–42), Martin Shefter argues that the more pro-labor climate of smaller cities was, in fact, a stimulus to business relocation to larger cities.

72. Garlock, "Structural Analysis of the Knights of Labor," 190.

73. Ibid.

74. Commons et al., *History of Labor in the United States*, 423n (table).

75. Ibid., 423. Foner's account of a ruralized KOL after 1886 is similar. See *History of the Labor Movement* 2:166–67. For Commons, land and money reform and producer cooperation were "middle class panaceas" (519).

76. Garlock, "Structural Analysis of the Knights of Labor," 115 (table 22), 126–27 (table 29), 140.

77. James, "American Labor and Political Action," 384, 470–75. On the eight-hour bill, which passed in 1892, see *Journal of United Labor*, November 3, 1893, 6, and *CR*, 52–1, 5737. In a pattern that illustrated the weakness of the pre-Bryan Democratic Party's commitment to labor, all of the 31 nay votes in the House were cast by Democrats, most of them from the South (the southern delegation split 23–25 against the bill).

78. Knights of Labor, *Proceedings of the General Assembly (Atlanta), 1889*, 87–96.

79. James, "American Labor and Political Action," 474–75; George B. Tindall, ed., *A Populist Reader* (New York: Harper Torchbooks, 1966), 75–77; Robert C. McMath Jr., *The Populist Vanguard* (Chapel Hill: University of North Carolina Press, 1975), 87–94.

80. *Journal of United Labor*, December 19, 1889, 1, and January 9, 1890, 1–3.

81. John D. Hicks, *The Populist Revolt* (Lincoln: University of Nebraska Press, 1961), 115, 123, 209, 211, 223–26; James, "American Labor and Political Action," 477–80. For example, at the St. Louis Industrial Conference held early in 1892, the Knights had 82 delegates, the National Farmers' Alliance and Industrial (southern, Kansas, and North and South Dakota Farmers' Alliances), 246, and the Grange, National (northern) Farmers' Alliance, Colored Alliance, and Farmers Mutual Benefit Association, another 322. Hicks, *Populist Revolt*, 226.

82. *Journal of United Labor*, July 7, 1892, 1.

83. James, "American Labor and Political Action," 481–84; McMath, *Populist Vanguard*, 144.

84. *Journal of United Labor*, November 3, 1892, 1.

85. Sketchy accounts of the coup can be found in Knights of Labor, *Proceedings of the 1893 General Assembly (Philadelphia)*, 23–61; Ware, *Labor Movement in the United States*, 368–69; Stuart B. Kaufman and Peter J. Albert, eds., *The Samuel Gompers Papers*, vol. 3 (Urbana: University of Illinois Press, 1989), 415; and Foner, *History of the Labor Movement* 2:294–96. What is unclear in these accounts is whether James Sovereign's nonsocialist backers actually hailed from "rural" assemblies or whether the label "agrarian" is just a synonym for "political."

86. *Journal of United Labor*, December 21, 1893, 1.

87. Ibid.: December 28, 1893, 1; January 4, 25, 1894, 1; February 1, 1894, 2–3; April 5, 1894, 1, 4; June 28, 1894, 1.

88. Ibid., June 14, 21, 1894, 1; James, "American Labor and Political Action," 488.

89. *Journal of United Labor*, October 29, 1896, 1.

90. James, "American Labor and Political Action," 489.

91. Foner, *History of the Labor Movement* 2:279–81, 294–96 (quotation at 295).

92. Commons et al., *History of Labor in the United States*, 518.

93. Fine, *Labor and Farmer Parties*, 155.

94. Foner, *History of the Labor Movement* 2:304–5.

95. Ibid., 2:316–17; Chester M. Destler, "Consummation of a Labor-Populist Alliance in Illinois, 1894," *Mississippi Valley Historical Review* 27 (March 1941): 589–602.

96. Fine, *Labor and Farmer Parties*, 142; Destler, "Consummation of a Labor-Populist Alliance in Illinois," 597. Plank #10 was defeated 76–16. Herman E. Taubeneck, the Illinois Populist leader who became national chairman of the People's Party, led the attack on plank #10.

97. Destler, "Consummation of a Labor-Populist Alliance in Illinois," 591, 600–601.

98. Foner, *History of the Labor Movement* 2:319–23.

99. Ibid., 2:326 (from a table furnished by E. E. Witte). The Philadelphia figure is for Philadelphia County, from the 1896 *World Almanac and Encyclopedia, 1896* (New York: Press Publishing, 1896), 453. The disintegration of labor populism in Illinois was sharply revealed in 1895, when a populist mayoral candidate drew only half as many votes in Chicago as had been cast for the party in 1894. James Peterson, "The Trade Unions and the Populist Party," *Science and Society* 8 (1944): 155–56. In Wisconsin and Minnesota, the socialist-labor-populist alliance lasted through the 1896 election (hence the quotation at the beginning of this section), and Wisconsin and Minnesota were the only midwestern states where the Democrat's urban percentage exceeded his rural. Ira Kipnis, *The American Socialist Movement, 1897–1912* (New York: Columbia University Press, 1952), 47–50; William Diamond, "Urban and Rural Voting in 1896," *American Historical Review* 46 (January 1941): 289–90.

100. *World Almanac and Encyclopedia, 1896*, 440, 442.

101. Kipnis, *American Socialist Movement*, 16–42; Morris Hillquit, *History of Socialism in the United States*, 5th ed. (New York: Dover Publications, 1971), 294–301. On the anti-AFL and dual-union crusades of De Leon's SLP, see also Foner, *History of the Labor Movement* 2:285–98; and Gittleman, "Attempts to Unify the American Labor Movement," 492–504.

102. Fink, *Workingmen's Democracy*, 201–6; Roger E. Wyman, "Agrarian or Working Class Radicalism? The Electoral Base of Populism in Wisconsin," *Political Science Quarterly* 89 (winter 1974–75): 825–47; Nick Salvatore, *Eugene V. Debs, Citizen and Socialist* (Urbana: University of Illinois Press, 1982), 150.

103. Salvatore, *Eugene V. Debs*, esp. 100.

104. Ibid., 169, 143–44, 153–54 (quotations at 154).

105. Ibid., 23, 147, 157–60; Louis W. Koenig, *Bryan* (New York: Capricorn Books, 1971), 205, 214, 246; Oscar Ameringer, *If You Don't Weaken* (Norman: University of Oklahoma Press, 1983), 296–97 (Berger's 1896 stance). A poll at the Populist convention showed Debs to be the preferred candidate of twenty-two state delegations, including the entire delegations of Texas, Georgia, Missouri, Indiana, Illinois, and Ohio. Ray Ginger, *The Bending Cross* (New York: Russell and Russell, 1969), 189.

106. Kipnis, *American Socialist Movement*, 50–106; Hillquit, *History of Socialism in the United States*, 301–4.

107. Joseph G. Rayback, *A History of American Labor* (New York: Free Press, 1966), 240.

108. Salvatore, *Eugene V. Debs*, 153, 171; James Green, *Grass Roots Socialism* (Baton Rouge: Louisiana State University Press, 1978), 12–52.

109. Salvatore, *Eugene V. Debs*, 153, 171–77, 197–207, 223–24; Kipnis, *American Socialist Movement*, 107–36, 211–13, 370–90.

110. Green, *Grass Roots Socialism*, 87–115; James Weinstein, *The Decline of Socialism in America, 1912–1925* (New Brunswick, N.J.: Rutgers University Press, 1984), 65–70; Garin Burbank, *When Farmers Voted Red* (Westport, Conn.: Greenwood Press, 1976), 69–89, 170–79.

111. Kipnis, *American Socialist Movement*, 153, 277–84; see also Sally Miller, "Socialism and Race," in John H. M. Laslett and Seymour M. Lipset, *Failure of a Dream* (Berkeley: University of California Press, 1974), 218–31.

112. Salvatore, *Eugene V. Debs*, 202–12, 254–58; William M. Dick, *Labor and Socialism in America*

(Port Washington, N.Y.: Kennikat Press, 1972), 104–7; Kipnis, *American Socialist Movement*, 312–34, 391–420. The IWW claimed around 18,000 members in 1912 and 60,000 in 1916–17. In 1915, a faction controlled by De Leon declared itself a separate Workers International Industrial Union, after a long fight with the organization it labeled "the Bummery." Paul Brissenden, "The I.W.W.: A Study of American Syndicalism" (Ph.D. diss., Columbia University, 1919), 218–37, 159–60, 254, 270, and Appendix IV.

113. Green, *Grass Roots Socialism*, 12–86, 228–69; Burbank, *When Farmers Voted Red*, 6–11, 53–68. See also Grady McWhiney, "Louisiana Socialists in the Early Twentieth Century: A Study of Rustic Radicalism," *Journal of Southern History* 20 (1954): 315–36.

114. Green, *Grass Roots Socialism*, 39–41, 151–62; David A. Shannon, *The Socialist Party of America* (Chicago: Quadrangle Paperbacks, 1967), 26–28; Weinstein, *Decline of Socialism in America*, 17–18. For a discussion of the influence of Protestant Christianity on southwestern socialism and the way biblical images colored this radical turn in the American republican tradition, see Burbank, *When Farmers Voted Red*, 14–43.

115. Green, *Grass Roots Socialism*, 39; Shannon, *Socialist Party of America*, 28–31; Weinstein, *Decline of Socialism in America*, 94–102 (table 1). Conservative opponents dubbed the paper "The Squeal of Treason," and Roosevelt tried to have it banned from the mails; Wilson ultimately did. Green's examination of 103 top *Appeal* salesmen listed in *Who's Who in Socialist America* in 1914 found 43 percent to be farmers and 28 percent workers (268 n).

116. Weinstein, *Decline of Socialism in America*, 86–87 and table 1; Green, *Grass Roots Socialism*, 136; W. Scott Morgan, Arkansas populist and historian of the Agricultural Wheel and Farmers' Alliance, also wrote for the *Ripsaw*. One of *The Rebel*'s features was a "Five Minute Sermon" column written by Rev. M. A. Smith, who "quoted chapter and verse to prove that those who monopolized the earth were sinners of the highest magnitude." Green, *Grass Roots Socialism*, 136–52 (quotation at 151).

117. David Shannon quotes a letter from Berger to Hillquit in which Berger complained that the enthusiastic southwestern socialist Kate Richards O'Hare was sure to "make the American Socialist Party ridiculous" at international meetings. But, adds Shannon, their fears turned out to be unfounded. "Mrs. O'Hare's record of enrolling farmers from the Great Plains in the Socialist cause so impressed European socialists that Jean Juares invited her to come to France to advise the French leaders how to gain strength among the peasants." *Socialist Party of America*, 25–26.

118. Fine, *Labor and Farmer Parties*, 209–11. See also Donald B. Martin, "Answering the Agrarian Question: Socialists, Farmers, and Algie Martin Simons," *Agricultural History* 65 (summer 1991): 53–69.

119. Fine, *Labor and Farmer Parties*, 209–12; Kipnis, *American Socialist Movement*, 69–73, 126–29. The Wisconsin delegates sometimes raised the "farmer question" as a matter of self-defense. Farmers controlled the nation's food supply and could starve the cities; further, they were well-armed and could slaughter unarmed urban socialists. Therefore it was prudent to offer them some accommodation. Socialist Party, "Proceedings of the National Convention, Chicago 1908," 15–21, cited in Kipnis, *American Socialist Movement*, 121–28.

120. Green, *Grass Roots Socialism*, 28–29, 79–82; Socialist Party, "Proceedings . . . 1908," 179–86.

121. Johnson, *National Party Platforms*, 163–66.

122. Socialist Party, *Proceedings of the First National Congress, 1910* (Chicago: Socialist Party, 1910), 182 (O'Hare), 221–23 (Ameringer).

123. Ibid., 223–24.

124. Green, *Grass Roots Socialism*, 83. The midwestern and northeastern socialists, many of them foreign-born, and the highly class-conscious Pacific state delegates had experience of farmers who were relatively prosperous, conservative, often employers of wage labor, and disinclined to cooperation with labor. Ameringer himself, familiar with the more comfortable and conservative farmers of Bavaria and the midwestern corn belt, had been shocked by the situation of Oklahoma farmers when he first arrived there to work with them. See Green, *Grass Roots Socialism*, 37, 45.

125. Johnson, *National Party Platforms*, 188–91, 207–11. The 1916 platform omitted the favorable preamble references to farmers, and the implication of land collectivization was strengthened in 1916 and 1920. Ibid., 208–9, 240.

126. Ibid., 366–78. On the socialist and agrarian preference for direct democracy, see Shannon, *Socialist Party of America*, 90–91, and Hicks, *Populist Revolt*, 406–7.

127. Weinstein, *Decline of Socialism in America*, 24; Garin Burbank, "The Disruption and Decline of the Oklahoma Socialist Party," *American Studies* 7 (2): 134.

128. Dick, *Labor and Socialism in America*, 78; John H. M. Laslett, *Labor and the Left* (New York: Basic Books, 1970), 9–54, 144–91.

129. Shannon, *Socialist Party of America*, 5, 21–22; Robert F. Hoxie, "The Socialist Party in the November Elections," *Journal of Political Economy* 20 (March 1912): 206–7. Minneapolis elected a Socialist mayor in 1916.

130. The list of towns with major socialist officials is taken from Weinstein, *Decline of Socialism in America*, 116–18 (table 2); statistics are from Hoxie, "The Socialist Party," 210.

131. Calculated from data in Hoxie, "The Socialist Party," 210–11. See also Robert F. Hoxie, "The Rising Tide of Socialism: A Study," *Journal of Political Economy* 19 (October 1911): 218–29.

132. Hoxie, "The Socialist Party," 218–29. See also James R. Simmons, "The Socialist Party in Indiana, 1900–1925," in *Socialism in the Heartland*, ed. Donald T. Critchlow (Notre Dame, Ind.: University of Notre Dame Press, 1986), 52–57. The SP had always had a substantial middle-class professional contingent (hence Trotsky's jibe, aimed at the Berger-Hillquit wing, that a gathering of American socialists resembled a convention of dentists). Kipnis's occupational analysis of 293 delegates to the 1912 convention found 32 journalists, 21 lecturers, 20 lawyers, and 12 mayors. Businessmen, authors, ministers, physicians, and (yes) dentists accounted for another 60. There were also 22 white-collar workers and "functionaries," 10 farmers, and 7 housewives. About 100 (37 percent) seem to have been representatives of labor, with less than 30 being unskilled or semi-skilled workers. Hillquit estimated in 1908 that about 66 percent of the party *members* were workers and that about 20 percent of organized labor voted Socialist. Kipnis, *American Socialist Movement*, 396–97; Hillquit, *History of Socialism in the United States*, 354–55. Trotsky's remark is from Shannon, *Socialist Party of America*, 21.

133. The total includes 161 Socialist candidates, 3 Socialist Labor (2 in Illinois and 1 in Utah), 7 Public Ownership (in Minnesota), and 3 Social Democrats (in Wisconsin). The count is from Congressional Quarterly, *Guide to U.S. Elections*, 717–23. None of the socialist candidates won; the four who did best were in Alameda County, California (40 percent), Milwaukee (33 and 36 percent), and northwestern Minnesota (33 percent).

134. Arthur Goren, "A Portrait of Ethnic Politics: The Socialists and the 1908 and 1910 Congressional Elections on the East Side," in *Voters, Parties and Elections*, ed. Joel H. Silbey and Samuel T. McSeveney (Lexington, Mass.: Xerox Publishing, 1972), 246–48. Unlike Hillquit, the Socialist candidate in 1908, London opposed any limits on immigration and took forthright stands on local issues of concern to the Jewish community. He won with 49.5 percent in 1914. Both Hillquit and London ran far ahead of Debs in the district.

135. The manufacturing value added per capita of these eight districts ranged from less than $100 in Oklahoma, North Dakota, Nevada, and Minnesota to $187 in the Los Angeles district.

136. On SP factions, see Kipnis, *American Socialist Movement*.

137. "Decline" is used here to describe the party's relative national electoral strength and must be somewhat qualified by pointing out, as Salvatore and Weinstein do, that *membership* actually increased again (reversing the 1912–16 trend) between 1916 and 1919 (before the Communist split). See Weinstein, *Decline of Socialism in America*, 154–59; Salvatore, *Eugene V. Debs*, 280.

138. Laslett, *Labor and the Left*, 294–324; Weinstein, *Decline of Socialism in America*, 38–39, 105.

139. Congressional Quarterly, *Guide to U.S. Elections*, 284–85.

140. Shannon, *Socialist Party of America*, 109–11.

141. Ameringer, *If You Don't Weaken*, 347–57.

142. Weinstein, *Decline of Socialism in America*, 182–234; Shannon, *Socialist Party of America*, 126–55.

143. Congressional Quarterly, *Guide to U.S. Elections*, 284, 286.

144. By 1922, membership had fallen to just over 11,000. Discontented agrarians who earlier would have turned to socialism now joined the Nonpartisan League and other farmer-labor movements. Shannon, *Socialist Party of America*, 162–63.

145. Marc Karson, *American Labor Unions and Politics, 1900–1918* (Boston: Beacon Press, 1958), 285–86.

146. Commons et al., *History of Labor in the United States*, 308; Selig Perlman, *A Theory of the Labour Movement* (New York: Macmillan, 1928), 197–202. On the relationship of these midwestern intellectuals to the labor movement, see Leon Fink, "Intellectuals versus Workers: Academic Requirements and the Creation of Labor History," *American Historical Review* 96 (April 1991): 395–421.

147. A major critic is Philip Foner—see, for example, his *History of the Labor Movement* 5:3–4. For a discussion of conflicting views of AFL leadership, see Dick, *Labor and Socialism in America*.

148. See Dick, *Labor and Socialism in America*, and Michael Rogin, "Voluntarism: The Political Functions of an Apolitical Doctrine," in *Labor and American Politics*, ed. Charles M. Rehmus and Doris B. McLaughlin (Ann Arbor: University of Michigan Press, 1967), 108–28.

149. Perlman, *Theory of the Labour Movement*, 169, 198–99.

150. Gary Marks, *Unions in Politics* (Princeton: Princeton University Press, 1989), 221; Perlman, *Theory of the Labour Movement*, 169–70.

151. Gary Fink, "The Rejection of Voluntarism," *Industrial and Labor Relations Review* 26 (January 1973): 808–9.

152. Marks, *Unions in Politics*, 204–5. Whereas industrial or "open" unions composed between one-fourth and one-third of total AFL membership before World War I, they made up 55 percent of the British Trades Union Congress by 1913; it was these unions that propelled the TUC toward electoral politics and a socialist program. Ibid., 206–11.

153. Ibid., 205 (table). See also Jill Quadagno, *The Transformation of Old Age Security* (Chicago: University of Chicago Press, 1988), 51–75.

154. Karson, *American Labor Unions and Politics*, 221–40, 324n. It is likely that over half the AFL membership was Catholic, and Catholics held at least half the seats on the AFL Executive Board in any given year in 1900–1918. Irish Catholics were the dominant nationality group in the organization.

155. Foner, *History of the Labor Movement* 3:195–218; on jurisdictional disputes, see also Samuel Gompers, *Labor and the Employer* (New York: E. P. Dutton, 1920), 180. Taft, *The AFL in the Time of Gompers*, 185–212. Within the workplace, there might be ten or fifteen different crafts represented, their contracts all expiring at different times—with obvious consequences for a common workers' front against the employer.

156. Quoted in Foner, *History of the Labor Movement* 3:205. On the rigid separations that craft unions maintained and their implications for both worker solidarity and productivity, see Bruno Ramirez, *When Workers Fight: The Politics of Industrial Relations in the Progressive Era, 1898–1916* (Westport, Conn.: Greenwood Press, 1978), 88–103. The nature of work organization by craft unions may have been responsible for some of the extreme hostility shown by American employers toward unionism. The craft unions insisted on a very narrow and rigid definition of work rules that could severely limit the adoption of new machines and work processes or changes in the job assignments of employees. Industrial unions, less concerned with the jobs of skilled workers, might have been less confining and hence less threatening to the employer's cost calculations. For empirical evidence of the costs posed by unionization in the pre–New Deal years, see Larry J. Griffin, Michael E. Wallace, and Beth A. Rubin, "Capitalism and Labor Organization," *American Sociological Review* 51 (April 1986): 147–67. In another sense too, organization on craft lines may have been self-defeating. Gompers and John Mitchell devoted their efforts to securing "industrial self-government" through the trade agreement, but without much success in the large, mass-production industries. Concentration was one disadvantage—the most notable successes came in highly competitive industries, like the bituminous coalfields, where an industry-wide agreement on labor could stabilize competition (see Ramirez, *When Workers Fight*, 17–29). But where union organization was partial and fragmented, such as on craft-union terrain, it proved very difficult to gain such agreements.

157. Taft, *The AFL in the Time of Gompers*, 198–99. Membership figures are from Leo Wolman,

The Growth of American Trade Unions, 1880–1923 (New York: National Bureau of Economic Research, 1924), appendix, table 1.

158. Calculated from membership figures in Wolman, *Growth of American Trade Unions*. Marks's figures show that only two of the ten largest U.S. trade unions were industrial or general unions in 1916. In Britain, half of the top ten were industrial and in Germany, seven of ten. *Unions in Politics*, 87–89.

159. Marks, *Unions in Politics*, 206–9 and appendix tables. See also Laslett, *Labor and the Left*.

160. Lewis L. Lorwin, *The American Federation of Labor* (Clifton, N.J.: Augustus M. Kelley Publishing, 1972), 114–15.

161. Rogin, "Voluntarism," 127. The autonomy and insulation of political machines and their forthright ethnic brokering reinforced the tendency of immigrant workers to lead, in effect, dual lives. In the workplace, they experienced class-structured identities, but at home they participated in cross-class ethnic and religious activities. In local politics, ethnic concerns—more than class concerns—shaped political loyalties. Ira Katznelson, *City Trenches* (New York: Pantheon Books, 1981), 25–86; Shefter, "Trade Unions and Political Machines," 267–76.

162. Rogin, "Voluntarism," 126–27; Lorwin, *American Federation of Labor*, 424.

163. Horace B. Davis, *Labor and Steel* (New York: International Publishers, 1933), 225–35.

164. Foner, *History of the Labor Movement* 3:145–46. The four brotherhoods were not affiliated with the AFL, although they enjoyed a loose cooperation. The Engineers, Trainmen, Firemen, and Conductors, who had traditionally held themselves aloof from the rest of labor, constituted the largest block of unionists outside the AFL, though their craft exclusivity was in tune with the AFL.

165. Michael Kazin, *Barons of Labor* (Urbana: University of Illinois Press, 1987); Gwendolyn Mink, *Old Labor and New Immigrants in American Political Development* (Ithaca, N.Y.: Cornell University Press, 1986), 71–112.

166. Foner, *History of the Labor Movement* 3:136–73. On trade-union corruption and its impact on public opinion, see also Rayback, *History of American Labor*, 221–22, and David Montgomery, *The Fall of the House of Labor* (New York: Cambridge University Press, 1987), 298–99.

167. Lloyd Ulman, *The Rise of the National Trade Union* (Cambridge: Harvard University Press, 1955), 6; table 3.1. Further, unionists secured significantly higher wages and shorter hours than nonunionists in the late nineteenth and early twentieth centuries. Ibid., 20–22 (citing Douglas, *Real Wages in the U.S.*).

168. U.S. Department of Commerce, Bureau of the Census, *Statistical Abstract of the United States, 1913* (Washington, D.C.: GPO, 1914), tables 168 and 171, 288–89. The number of strikes almost doubled between 1900 and 1903, and the percentage of strikes that were organized by labor unions showed a significant increase compared with those in the late nineteenth century. P. K. Edwards, *Strikes in the United States, 1881–1974* (New York: St. Martin's Press, 1981), 13 (table).

169. In the early strike data collected by the commissioner of labor, major causes of strikes are listed as (1) "wage increase," (2) "wage increase and hour decrease," (3) "hour decrease," (4) "recognition, wages, and hours," (5) "sympathy" strikes, (6) "recognition, union rules, and other," and (7) "miscellaneous." Strikes in the last two categories include job-control issues and some controversies over which union should represent which employees—issues of great concern to craft unionists. The "miscellaneous" category also includes "demands for or against discharge of certain employees or foremen, objections against working with Negroes and foreigners, etc." Categories six and seven accounted for, on average, 26.5 percent of strikes in the KOL years of 1881–87. From 1895 to 1905 (the early AFL years), these categories composed 42 percent on average and in 1904 and 1905, over half of all strikes. Florence Peterson, *Strikes in the United States, 1880–1936*, Bureau of Labor Statistics Bulletin #651 (Washington, D.C.: U.S. Department of Labor, 1937), 33 (table 8). See also Edwards's discussion of the peculiar, and continuing, emphasis of American unions on job-control issues and the equally intense opposition of employers to this challenge to their "right to manage" in the production process. Edwards, *Strikes in the United States*, 233–46.

170. Computed using the location of LAs, DAs, and state assemblies from the Knights of Labor,

Proceedings of the General Assembly (Richmond), 1886 (326–28) and the "Report of the General Secretary" in the 1888 *Proceedings* (2–5). The periphery component of the KOL (state-listed assemblies) was 14.1 percent in 1886, 23.2 percent in 1888.

171. Wolman, *Growth of American Trade Unions*, 85. The 1916 figure extrapolates from his 1910–20 wage-earner figures for the denominator and uses the figure in table 3.1 for the numerator.

172. Ibid., 86; Leo Wolman, "The Extent of Labor Organization in the United States in 1910," *Quarterly Journal of Economics* 30 (1916): 505, 515, and appendix table 2.

173. Wolman, "Extent of Labor Organization," 507.

174. Alfred Chandler lists these three industries, along with steel, electrical machinery, transportation equipment, instruments, and tobacco, in the *most* concentrated group ("over 50 percent oligopolistic"). Applying Wolman's union density figures to Chandler's industry names (where categories could be matched) yields a mean unionization level of 11.7 percent in the most concentrated group, and that percentage is pulled up by the rather high figure (27 percent) for tobacco. In Chandler's *least* concentrated group (leather, publishing and printing, lumber and wood, furniture, and apparel), the mean 1910 union density was 19.1 percent. See Alfred Chandler, "The Structure of American Industry in the Twentieth Century: An Overview," *Business History Review* 43 (autumn 1969): 258–59 (chart 1).

175. James Holt, "Trade Unionism in the British and U.S. Steel Industries, 1880–1914: A Comparative Study," in *Labor History Reader*, ed. Daniel J. Lieb (Evanston: University of Illinois Press, 1985), 166–96. Kim Voss, in her study of the New Jersey Knights of Labor assemblies, also found small firms more willing to settle strikes on union terms because they could ill afford to have production disrupted. Voss, "Disposition Is Not Action," 311.

176. Foner, *History of the Labor Movement* 2:206–18, 3:32–34.

177. The preference in Britain at this time was for the "general union" either achieved through amalgamation of discrete existing unions or started anew. Eric Hobsbawm, *Workers: Worlds of Labor* (New York: Pantheon, 1984), 161.

178. T. O. Lloyd, *Empire to Welfare State* (Oxford: Oxford University Press, 1970), 12–19; Henry Pelling, *A Short History of the Labour Party* (New York: St. Martin's Press, 1968), 11–28; George Dangerfield, *The Strange Death of Liberal England* (New York: Capricorn Books, 1935), 225–98.

179. Taft, *The AFL in the Time of Gompers*, 289–90; Fine, *Labor and Farmer Parties*, 41–53; Samuel Gompers, *Seventy Years of Life and Labor*, 2 vols. (New York: E. P. Dutton, 1925), 1:194–98.

180. Alexander Saxton, "San Francisco Labor and the Populist and Progressive Insurgencies," *Pacific Historical Review* 34 (November 1965): 421–38; Michael Paul Rogin and John L. Shover, *Political Change in California* (Westport, Conn.: Greenwood Publishing, 1970), 16–19; *World Almanac and Encyclopedia, 1896*, 417 (table).

181. Laslett, *Labor and the Left*, 197–201. On midwestern coal miners and populism in 1894, see also Richard Jensen, *The Winning of the Midwest* (Chicago: University of Chicago Press, 1971), 238–60, and Paul Kleppner, *The Cross of Culture* (New York: Free Press, 1970), 234–49.

182. Laslett, *Labor and the Left*, 197–201.

183. *United Mine Workers' Journal*, October 5, 1894, 5, and November 1, 1894, 5.

184. Peterson, "Trade Unions and the Populist Party," 157.

185. Voting percentages are calculated from *World Almanac and Encyclopedia, 1896*, 423, 451–53, and Congressional Quarterly, *Guide to U.S. Elections*, 675. Leading coal counties were identified from U.S. Department of the Interior, *Report on Mineral Industries*, Eleventh Census, 1890 (Washington, D.C.: GPO, 1892), 370, 397 (tables). The Illinois 1894 statewide race was for treasurer; the Pennsylvania race was for governor.

186. Kleppner, *Cross of Culture*, 238–49.

187. *United Mine Workers' Journal*, October 22, 1896, 4, and November 5, 1896, 1.

188. For these computations, the number of strikers was totaled for each county from strike data in U.S. Commissioner of Labor, Tenth Annual Report, *Strikes and Lockouts*, vol. 1 (Washington, D.C.: GPO, 1896). In the case of coal strikes listed as occurring in "various points," strikers were apportioned to counties according to the county's proportion of coal miners, using data from the U.S. Department of

the Interior, *Report on Mineral Industries.* Total strikers in 1893–94 were divided by county population from the 1890 *Census of Population* to compute strike rates.

189. Samuel Gompers, "Organized Labor in the Campaign," *North American Review* 155 (July 1892), reprinted in Kaufman and Albert, *Samuel Gompers Papers,* 201. After the election, the Executive Committee rebuffed another overture for common cause from Ben Terrell of the Texas Farmers' Alliance. See ibid., 262–63.

190. Quoted in Foner, *History of the Labor Movement* 2:306.

191. Kaufman and Albert, *Samuel Gompers Papers,* 419.

192. Ibid., 442, 606–7.

193. Ibid., 613–62.

194. Lorwin, *American Federation of Labor,* 40.

195. Gompers, *Seventy Years of Life and Labor* 2:88.

196. Lorwin, *American Federation of Labor,* 40. Years later, Gompers would claim to have voted for Bryan in 1896, but if so, he kept his choice to himself at the time.

197. Foner, *History of the Labor Movement* 2:338–39.

198. Mink, *Old Labor and New Immigrants,* 129–57. Debs worried that southern and eastern European workers "do not hesitate to vote according to the orders they receive." Robert F. Durden, *The Climax of Populism* (Westport, Conn.: Greenwood Press, 1965), 142. Kleppner and Jensen hammer home the point that Bryan failed to "polarize the toiling masses" in midwestern cities, with the Republicans often making large gains over 1892 in poor areas. Both see an 1896 working-class vote immune to Bryan's class appeal and often alienated by the moralism of his campaign. Kleppner, *Cross of Culture,* 287–90, 303–6; Jensen, *Winning of the Midwest,* esp. 296–305.

199. In 1896 the *New York Times* (an anti-Bryan paper) reported surveys of local workers purporting to show a growing sentiment in favor of gold and McKinley (see July 19, 8, July 20, 4, July 22, 9, July 24, 9, July 25, 9, August 3, 2, October 19, 5, and October 29, 9). The greatest Republican tilt was reported among skilled labor, like well-paid Brooklyn hatmakers, brass workers, pattern makers, bookbinders, cigar makers, printers and paper workers, and press and die makers. Metal workers, conductors and motormen, poor and unskilled laborers, "ignorant voters," presumably Irish "in lockstep with Tammany," longshoremen, and drivers were more likely to see Bryan as "the workingman's friend." German and Jewish workers (the latter organized in AFL garment unions) were particularly hostile to the Democrats' soft-money views, according to the *Times* (see, e.g., the assembly district canvasses reported on October 19, 5, and reports of German Tammanyite defections on October 29, 12). McSeveney's analysis of the 1896 New York City vote confirmed the Democratic loyalty of Irish voters but found "no evidence of *unusually* heavy Jewish or German defections to McKinley," in view of the general city-wide losses. Bryan became the first Democratic presidential candidate since 1848 to lose both New York and Kings Counties. His losses were heaviest in middle- and upper-class, old-stock neighborhoods in Manhattan. Samuel T. McSeveney, *The Politics of Depression* (New York: Oxford University Press, 1972), 178, 198–99. On the advantage to the Irish of Democratic loyalty in 1896, see ibid., 175–76.

200. Lorwin, *American Federation of Labor,* 41.

201. Taft, *The AFL in the Time of Gompers,* 292–94; Gompers, *Seventy Years of Life and Labor* 2:525.

202. Taft, *The AFL in the Time of Gompers,* 292–94.

203. *Journal of United Labor,* November 3, 1892, 6; *American Federationist,* May 1898, 57–59.

204. Fink, "Rejection of Voluntarism," 805–19; Quadagno, *Transformation of Old Age Security,* chap. 3; Elisabeth Clemens, *The People's Lobby* (Chicago: University of Chicago Press, 1997), 118–34.

205. Gompers, *Labor and the Employer,* 101; *American Federationist,* August 1898, 110–12.

206. Gompers, *Labor and the Employer,* 118–21; Bettina Berch, *The Endless Day* (New York: Harcourt Brace Jovanovich, 1982), 40–51. By 1890, women constituted 38–56 percent of workers in the clothing, textile, and tobacco industries and 25 percent in printing (Berch, *Endless Day,* 42). Since many AFL unions excluded women and since the organization as a whole was unsympathetic to the concerns of female

workers, a national Women's Trade Union League was founded in 1903, with critical backing from upper-class women. It became a major supporter of protective legislation. Berch, *Endless Day*, 45–46.

207. *Muller v. Oregon*, 208 U.S. 412 (1908). On passage of hours laws for women, see Elizabeth Brandeis, *Labor Legislation*, vols. 3 and 4 of Commons et al., *History of Labor in the United States* (1935), 457–59.

208. Brandeis, *Labor Legislation*, 474–78.

209. Loren Beth, *The Development of the American Constitution, 1877–1917* (New York: Harper and Row, 1971), 183–89.

210. The movement for minimum wages was led not by organized labor (which either opposed or only nominally backed the state campaigns) but by "public spirited middle class individuals and groups," particularly women. The National Consumers League and Women's Trade Union League were the prime movers on this issue. Brandeis, *Labor Legislation*, 501–18.

211. Theda Skocpol and Gretchen Ritter, "Gender and the Origins of Modern Social Policies in Britain and the United States," *Studies in American Political Development* 5 (spring 1991): 36–94; and Theda Skocpol et al., "Women's Associations and the Enactment of Mothers' Pensions in the United States," *American Political Science Review* 87 (September 1993): 686–701.

212. Gompers, *Seventy Years of Life and Labor* 2:231–38; Albert K. Steigerwalt, *The National Association of Manufacturers, 1895–1914* (Grand Rapids: University of Michigan Bureau of Business Research, 1964), 98; *CR*, 55–2, 4984–88, 6691–92, 6788, and 55–3, 403, 2532, 2716–17. Every Democrat on the House committee was said to favor the eight-hour bill in the 56th Congress while the bill again passed on a voice vote, though Rep. Joseph Bailey of Texas dissented in floor debate. *CR*, 56–1, 5802–3, 5805. In the Senate, Richard F. Pettigrew of South Dakota moved to discharge the Education and Labor Committee of both the eight-hour and a convict-labor bill, but a motion to table his discharge motion passed 33–28. The 28 supporters of the discharge motion included 13 Democrats, 8 Republicans (only 1 from the Northeast), 3 populists, 3 silverites, and 1 fusionist. All but one of the votes to table were cast by Republicans. *CR*, 56–1, 6800; see also *American Federationist*, August 1898, 120.

213. *American Federationist*, January 1899, 217; Gompers, *Seventy Years of Life and Labor* 2:229–30; *CR*, 55–3, 129–32, 157.

214. Gompers, *Seventy Years of Life and Labor* 2:151–68; *American Federationist*, December 1902, 932–37; Kitty Calavita, "The Anti-Alien Contract Labor Law of 1885 and 'Employer Sanctions' in the 1980s," *Research in Law, Deviance, and Social Control* 5 (1983): 52–56 (quotation at 55). By 1910, Gutman estimates, eastern and southern European immigrants and African Americans composed two-thirds of the workers in twenty-one major mining and manufacturing industries. In 1908–10, forty-four southern and eastern European immigrants went home for every one hundred that arrived—a "revolving door" that presented obvious problems for union organizers. Gutman, *Work, Culture, and Society in Industrializing America*, 22, 30. See also Mark Wyman, *Round Trip to America* (Ithaca, N.Y.: Cornell University Press, 1993), esp. 66–70, 74–98; Robert D. Parmet, *Labor and Immigration in Industrial America* (Boston: Twayne Publishers, 1981), 27–152; Ramirez, *When Workers Fight*, 132–37; Mink, *Old Labor and New Immigrants*, 63–111; and A. T. Lane, "American Trade Unions, Mass Immigration, and the Literacy Test: 1900–1917," *Labor History* 25 (winter 1984): 5–26. Among economic historians there is considerable agreement that immigration held down wages in the 1890–1914 period. See, for example, the discussion in Albert Rees, *Real Wages in Manufacturing, 1890–1914* (Princeton: Princeton University Press, 1961), 3–5, 13–16, 126.

215. Calavita, "Anti-Alien Contract Labor Law of 1885," 57–63.

216. Gompers, *Seventy Years of Life and Labor* 2:167, 171; Wyman, *Round Trip to America*, 99ff.

217. Gompers, *Seventy Years of Life and Labor* 2:165–73; Parmet, *Labor and Immigration in Industrial America*, 155–89. Wilson's veto would be overridden in 1917 (see chapter 9).

218. John C. Appel, "The Relationship of American Labor to U.S. Imperialism: 1895–1905" (Ph.D. diss., University of Wisconsin, 1950). See also *American Federationist*, September 1898, 136–40; Richard E. Welch, *Response to Imperialism* (Chapel Hill: University of North Carolina Press, 1979), 84–88; and Karson, *American Labor Unions and Politics*, 145–46. Gompers served for a time as a passive vice-president

(one of forty-one) of the American Anti-Imperialist League. John Hayes of the KOL occupied another such position, but the KOL's opposition to war and imperial control appears to have been stronger, more consistent, and less concerned with material considerations than that of the AFL. See Appel, "The Relationship of American Labor to U.S. Imperialism," 28–29, 45, 180–81, 216–18, 304–23. Federation spokesmen often used racial arguments in their objections to imperialism, as in *American Federationist*, September 1898, 136–40.

219. Marguerite Green, *The National Civic Federation and the American Labor Movement, 1900–1925* (Washington, D.C.: Catholic University Press, 1956), 2–13.

220. Gompers, *Seventy Years of Life and Labor* 2:105–10; Green, *National Civic Federation*, 33; Ramirez, *When Workers Fight*, 73–75.

221. Ramirez, *When Workers Fight*, 68–71, 137–39; Lorwin, *American Federation of Labor*, 83–84; Martin J. Sklar, *The Corporate Reconstruction of American Capitalism, 1890–1916* (New York: Cambridge University Press, 1988), 258–66; Green, *National Civic Federation*, 25–36, 314.

222. A content analysis of the *American Federationist* by Louis Galambos found that the AFL's hostility to big business peaked (with 82 percent unfavorable references) in the mid-1890s. By 1901 the figure had dropped to 55 percent, reaching 50 percent by 1915. Galambos, "The American Federation of Labor's Concept of Big Business: A Quantitative Study of Attitudes toward the Large Corporation, 1894–1931," *Journal of American History* 57 (March 1971): 849–52.

223. Quoted in Florence C. Thorne, *Samuel Gompers: American Statesman* (New York: Philosophical Library, 1951), 127. See also Gompers, *Seventy Years of Life and Labor* 2:129, 256.

224. Gompers, *Seventy Years of Life and Labor* 2:112.

225. Sklar, *Corporate Reconstruction of American Capitalism*, 238–85; see also Gabriel Kolko, *The Triumph of Conservatism* (Chicago: Quadrangle Books, 1963), 132–38. Farmers, of course, were very cool to proposals for watering down the Sherman Act. The NCF's director pressed Gompers to try to win the endorsement of Charles Barrett, president of the Farmers' Union, with no success. Nor was Nahum Bachelder, Grange president and an NCF member, willing to endorse the bill on behalf of his organization. Sklar, *Corporate Reconstruction of American Capitalism*, 254–55.

226. Lorwin, *American Federation of Labor*, 76–80; Karson, *American Labor Unions and Politics*, 33–37; Sarah L. Watts, *Order against Chaos: Business Culture and Ideology in America, 1880–1915* (New York: Greenwood Press, 1991), 143–55.

227. Edward Berman, *Labor and the Sherman Act* (1930; reprint, New York: Russell and Russell, 1969), 77–78.

228. Ibid., 11–54, is a leading example.

229. William Letwin, *Law and Economic Policy in America* (Chicago: University of Chicago Press, 1965), 157–61; Felix Frankfurter and Nathan Greene, *The Labor Injunction* (New York: Macmillan, 1930), 6–7, 18–20. The Court decisions of 1893–1908 and the justices' willingness to hear local economic disputes involving citizens of different states enabled the federal judiciary to join the explosion of injunction activity by state courts in the 1890s. See ibid., 5–15, 20–23, and William E. Forbath, *Law and the Shaping of the American Labor Movement* (Cambridge: Harvard University Press, 1991), 59–79. Forbath estimates that the total number of labor injunctions issued by state and federal courts grew from 105 in the 1880s to 410 in the 1890s, to around 850 in the 1900s and 1910s, and up to 2,130 in the 1920s. The percentage of strikes enjoined rose from about 1 percent in the 1880s to about 5 percent by 1914–19 and to 25 percent in the 1920s. The percentage for sympathy strikes and boycotts was much higher, rising from 10 percent in the 1880s to around 25 percent in 1900–19 and to 46 percent in the 1920s. Ibid., 197–98.

230. Lorwin, *American Federation of Labor*, 81 n; Berman, *Labor and the Sherman Act*, 77–87. *Loewe v. Lawlor*, 208 U.S. 274 (1908).

231. *Gompers v. Bucks Stove and Range Company*, 221 U.S. 418 at 438–39 (1911). See also Lorwin, *American Federation of Labor*, 81–82, and Berman, *Labor and the Sherman Act*, 87–90. In another decision, *Adair v. United States*, 208 U.S. 161 (1908), the Court overturned a provision of the 1898 Erdman Act that had prohibited the firing of railroad workers for the mere fact of union membership. Karson, *American Labor Unions and Politics*, 52–53.

232. Frankfurter and Greene, *Labor Injunction*, 140 and n. 18; Gompers, *Seventy Years of Life and Labor* 2:238–39; *CR*, 56–1, 6501; U.S. Congress, Senate, *Bills and Debates in Congress Relating to Trusts* (Washington, D.C.: GPO, 1903), 481; Hans J. Thorelli, *The Federal Antitrust Policy* (Baltimore: Johns Hopkins University Press, 1955), 514. The 1892 bill (H.R. 6640, reprinted in *Bills and Debates*) exempted both agricultural and labor organizations, as did a subsequent omnibus bill introduced by Terry.

233. Lorwin, *American Federation of Labor*, 88–91; Karson, *American Labor Unions and Politics*, 29–49; Julia Greene, "The Strike at the Ballot Box: The American Federation of Labor's Entrance into Election Politics, 1906–1909," *Labor History* 32 (1991): 169–82. According to Greene, over a fourth of all congressional districts, concentrated in the mid-Atlantic and Great Lakes states, registered at least a minimal level of union participation in the AFL campaign.

234. *American Federationist*, September 1906, 643–88. Karson gives the party figures as 23–50 ("acceptable" and "unacceptable" to Gompers) for Republicans and 47–3 for Democrats. He does not indicate how he arrived at these figures. Karson, *American Labor Unions and Politics*, 46. Obviously my threshold for a "favorable" response was somewhat higher. I have not counted two replies sent by party officials who were not members of the House. Most friends of labor sent detailed replies (often citing voting and bill sponsorship evidence) affirming their unconditional support for labor's demands in the "grievances" list. A few obviously friendly respondents sent vague but warm replies. (For example, James M. Griggs of Georgia replied, "I agree fully with you in every demand therein made." Gompers characterized this as "brief, but unqualifiedly in approval of labor's bill of grievances.") When Republicans mentioned specifics on which they agreed, the most numerous by far concerned opposition to immigration, especially by Chinese.

235. Gompers, *Seventy Years of Life and Labor* 2:266.

236. Greene, "Strike at the Ballot Box," 174–79, 190.

237. Karson, *American Labor Unions and Politics*, 47; Irving Greenberg, *Theodore Roosevelt and Labor: 1900–1918* (New York: Garland Publishing, 1988), 286–88.

238. Greene, "Strike at the Ballot Box," 178–80. Karson, *American Labor Unions and Politics*, 46–49; Lorwin, *American Federation of Labor*, 90–91; *American Federationist*, May 1908, 341. In this issue the AFL printed a table (p. 353) showing that fifteen more anti-labor congressmen could have been defeated had their opposition not been split into Democratic, independent, and Socialist factions. However, the reluctance of the national AFL leaders to make endorsements (as opposed to just urging votes against the incumbent) probably contributed to this result.

239. Karson, *American Labor Unions and Politics*, 50. On wages, see Rees, *Real Wages in Manufacturing, 1890–1914*, esp. table 44, 120.

240. Greene, "Strike at the Ballot Box," 170 n.

241. Gompers, *Seventy Years of Life and Labor* 2:271.

242. Karson, *American Labor Unions and Politics*, 54–58; *American Federationist*, May 1908, 341–53.

243. Koenig, *Bryan*, 432–33, 438; Arvil Ernest Harris, "Organized Labor in Politics, 1906–1932" (Ph.D. diss., State University of Iowa, 1936), 172–85. Only AFL proposals for a postal savings bank and a women's suffrage amendment were omitted. The platform contained a lengthy discussion of the injunction and contempts (of court) issues and the necessity of legally affirming labor's rights. Johnson, *National Party Platforms*, 147–48.

244. Gompers, *Seventy Years of Life and Labor* 2:263–65.

245. David Sarasohn, *The Party of Reform* (Jackson: University of Mississippi Press, 1989), 44–45.

246. The *American Federationist* printed the letter in its October 1908 issue, 869–70.

247. Ibid., 892–94 (quotation at 892).

248. Ibid., 894. As for an electoral alliance, Gompers emphasized, in traditional AFL fashion, its *negative* aspects. The worker and farmer organizations would join in "'knifing' candidates not favorable to our legislative demands." Ibid, 893.

249. Greene, "Strike at the Ballot Box," 183, 187–88; *American Federationist*, November 1908, 957. See also Greenberg, *Theodore Roosevelt and Labor*, 357–65. In the fall of 1908 rumors circulated in the press that President Roosevelt had offered AFL vice-president Daniel J. Keefe of Detroit, who was president of

the Longshoremen's Union, the post of Commissioner of Immigration in return for his support of Taft. Indeed, Keefe was appointed to the position. Harris, "Organized Labor in Politics," 191–96; Karson, *American Labor Unions and Politics,* 63–64.

250. Greene, "Strike at the Ballot Box," 184–87; Harris, "Organized Labor in Politics," 188–206.

251. "Official Circular," *American Federationist,* November 1908, 957.

252. Greene, "Strike at the Ballot Box," 183–86; Karson, *American Labor Unions and Politics,* 61. According to Greene, half of the AFL's organizers probably received paychecks from the Democratic Party in 1908.

253. Greene, "Strike at the Ballot Box," 185; Karson, *American Labor Unions and Politics,* 62. For the flavor of the consultation, see Bryan to Gompers, March 11, June 30, and August 1, and Gompers to Bryan, June 27, July 24, and August 15, in Harold L. Miller, ed., *American Federation of Labor Records: The Gompers Era* (Madison: State Historical Society of Wisconsin, 1981), pt. 2, reels 65–66.

254. *American Federationist,* November 1908, 957.

255. Quoted in Bonnett, *Employers Associations in the United States,* 327.

256. Karson, *American Labor Unions and Politics,* 64–66 (quotation at 66).

257. Robert F. Hoxie, "President Gompers and the Labor Vote," *Journal of Political Economy* 16 (December 1908): 693–700.

258. Sarasohn, *Party of Reform,* 53–54.

259. Karson, *American Labor Unions and Politics,* 67–68. Julia Marie Greene, "The Strike at the Ballot Box" (Ph.D. diss., Yale University, 1990), 542–45. It is interesting to compare the small amounts raised by the AFL for political campaigns (about $3,000 in 1910) with the $236,000 it collected for the defense of the McNamara brothers (trade unionists accused of the bombing of the *Los Angeles Times* building in the same year). Foner describes the AFL's advice to workers for the 1910 elections as "innocuous and meaningless." See *The AFL in the Progressive Era, 1910–1915,* vol. 5 of Foner, *History of the Labor Movement,* 96–97.

Chapter Four

1. Fred A. Shannon, *The Farmer's Last Frontier: Agriculture, 1860–1897* (1945; reprint, White Plains, N.Y.: M. E. Sharpe, 1973), 351 (chart).

2. Chester M. Destler, *American Radicalism, 1865–1901* (New York: Octagon Books, 1963), 50.

3. Shannon, *Farmer's Last Frontier,* 51, 353 (table).

4. Douglas C. North, *Growth and Welfare in the American Past* (Englewood Cliffs, N.J.: Prentice-Hall, 1966), 138–43. One must make temporal distinctions as well as regional ones. The midwestern states that were most agitated by the Granger movement of the early 1870s were relatively cool to populism in the 1890s. Twenty years of economic change and the development of their own urban and industrial economies took Illinois, Indiana, Iowa, and Wisconsin from the frontier to relatively comfortable "diverse" economies.

5. C. W. Thompson, "Interest Rates Paid by American Farmers," in Edwin G. Nourse, *Agricultural Economics* (Chicago: University of Chicago Press, 1916), 705.

6. Kenneth A. Snowden, "Mortgage Rates and American Capital Market Development in the Late Nineteenth Century," *Journal of Economic History* 47 (September 1987): 675, table 1. His results confirm the conclusions (about capital-market segmentation) of Lance E. Davis, "Capital Mobility and American Growth," in *The Reinterpretation of American Economic History,* ed. Robert W. Fogel and Stanley L. Engerman (New York: Harper and Row, 1971), 285–300. Regional interest-rate differentials tended to narrow over time (most dramatically between the east-north-central region and New England), but interest rates in the southern, west-north-central, and far-western states remained far in excess of the core states in 1910. John A. James, *Money and Capital Markets in Postbellum America* (Princeton: Princeton University Press, 1978), 19 (chart), 86–87, 236–43.

7. D. M. Frederiksen, "Mortgage Banking in America," *Journal of Political Economy* 2 (March 1894): 203–34. See also Allan G. Bogue, *Money at Interest: The Farm Mortgage on the Middle Border* (Lincoln: University of Nebraska Press, 1955), 272.

8. James H. Stock, "Real Estate Mortgages, Foreclosures, and Midwestern Agrarian Unrest, 1865–1920," *Journal of Economic History* 44 (March 1983): 89–105.

9. Carl C. Taylor, *The Farmers' Movement, 1670–1920* (Westport, Conn.: Greenwood Press, 1953), 115–31; Solon J. Buck, *The Granger Movement* (Cambridge: Harvard University Press, 1913), 40–47. The Grange was, according to Buck, "the first secret order to admit women to full and equal membership" (281). On the importance of women in the Grange, see also D. Sven Nordin, *Rich Harvest* (Jackson: University of Mississippi Press, 1974), 193.

10. Buck, *Granger Movement*, 53–57; Taylor, *Farmers' Movement*, 156–59.

11. The denominator was computed by averaging 1870 and 1880 census figures for the agricultural workforce (1875 est. 6,796,482).

12. Buck, *Granger Movement*, table after 88. On the later (1880–1900) expansion of a more conservative Grange in the Northeast, see Nordin, *Rich Harvest*.

13. Buck, *Granger Movement*, 59.

14. Ibid., 76–82.

15. George H. Miller, *Railroads and the Granger Laws* (Madison: University of Wisconsin Press, 1971), 87–160; Taylor, *Farmers' Movement*, 163–64. Miller argues, in contradistinction to Buck, that except in Wisconsin, farmers were not responsible for the first postwar midwestern railroad laws (1868–71); rather, according to Miller, leadership in those campaigns was provided by mercantile interests in towns threatened with loss of commercial importance by the new East-West railroad grids (river towns in Iowa, for example). Since one had to *have* a railroad to propose regulating it, the more remote farmers in areas not yet tracked were not a part of the early antirailroad agitation. In Miller's account, they often joined with the railroads in opposing any regulatory system that might discourage railroad building in their sections. However, the situation in the Midwest had changed by 1873–74, when rail lines were denser and agricultural depression had set in. Miller's conclusion that "the awakening of the farmer to the need for political action undoubtedly broadened the base of support for railroad regulation in the Granger states" seems rather an understatement. Miller often confuses the drafters of the laws (who were usually not themselves farmers) with the laws' supporters, and he draws unwarranted conclusions from the evidence he cites—for example, that the large and radical Illinois Farmers' Association could only have had a negative influence on regulatory legislation. Like Lee Benson (*Merchants, Farmers, and Railroads: Railroad Regulation and New York Politics* [Cambridge: Harvard University Press, 1955]) and Sven Nordin (*Rich Harvest*), Miller goes to great lengths to debunk older arguments about agrarian sponsorship and sectional differences and to build a case for mercantile leadership of the antirailroad movement.

16. Buck, *Granger Movement*, 87–88.

17. Ibid., 89–95; Taylor, *Farmers' Movement*, 172–83.

18. Buck, *Granger Movement*, 102–237; see also chapter 6.

19. Buck, *Granger Movement*, 302–8; Robert C. McMath Jr., *The Populist Vanguard* (Chapel Hill: University of North Carolina Press, 1975), 4, 18–21.

20. Taylor, *Farmers' Movement*, 183–84.

21. Milton Friedman and Anna J. Schwartz, *A Monetary History of the United States, 1867–1960* (Princeton: Princeton University Press, 1963), 18–23; James, *Money and Capital Markets*, 77–78.

22. The regional imbalance can be seen in a comparison of the per capita value of national bank notes issued in 1869: to New York, Massachusetts, and Pennsylvania, $11.83; to southern and border states, $1.31. In 1877, the figures were $10.18 and $1.42. Richard F. Bensel, *Yankee Leviathan* (New York: Cambridge University Press, 1990), 271 (table 4.3). See also Robert H. Sharkey, *Money, Class, and Party* (Baltimore: Johns Hopkins University Press, 1959), 235, who puts the midwestern figure at about one-fifth that of New England and New York.

23. Friedman and Schwartz, *Monetary History of the United States*, 21–25; Irving Unger, *The Greenback Era* (Princeton: Princeton University Press, 1964), 264–65; Allen Weinstein, *Prelude to Populism* (New Haven, Conn.: Yale University Press, 1970), 8–32.

24. Computed from tables in *Statistical History of the United States* (New York: Horizon Press, 1965), 7, 647. Economic historians have pointed out that other forms of money, such as bank deposits on which

checks and drafts could be written, increased rapidly in the late nineteenth century and that the development of a commercial-paper market enhanced liquidity and national financial integration. See Friedman and Schwartz, *Monetary History of the United States,* 3–4 and chart 1. Why, then, asks John A. James, did monetary debates focus so exclusively on notes and currency, neglecting other components of the monetary stock? James, *Money and Capital Markets,* 22 n. The answer must be that these new developments affected some regions later and less completely than others and that they did little to overcome the periphery farmer's worsening relative position in the political economy. And unlike bank deposits and commercial paper, the volume of metallic and paper currency was directly reachable through the political system.

25. Friedman and Schwartz, *Monetary History of the United States,* 35–42.

26. Unger, *Greenback Era,* 55–59, 120–62; Sharkey, *Money, Class, and Party,* 84–86, 145–63, 285–86; Weinstein, *Prelude to Populism,* 125–27, 263–66.

27. Clarence D. Long, *Wages and Earnings in the United States, 1860–1890* (Princeton: Princeton University Press, 1960), 20, 65 (calculated from figures in tables 3 and 19).

28. Willford I. King, *The Wealth and Income of the People of the United States* (New York: Macmillan, 1915), 169–70.

29. Paul H. Douglas and Aaron Director, *The Problem of Unemployment* (New York: Macmillan, 1931), 25–30, 35, 48–54; Unger, *Greenback Era,* 265–66.

30. Sharkey, *Money, Class, and Party,* 85–86, 135–40. See also Unger, *Greenback Era,* 271–72. Weinstein, in *Prelude to Populism,* emphasizes the diversity of interests and individuals supporting greenbacks or silver in the 1870s and the significance of urban publicists in the campaign for bimetallism. However, it is clear from his vote tables that by 1878 the South, Midwest, and West were the bastions of bimetallism in Congress, against the New England and mid-Atlantic hard-money contingent.

31. Carl V. Harris, "Right Fork or Left Fork: The Section-Party Alignment of Southern Democrats in Congress, 1873–1897," *Journal of Southern History* 42 (November 1976): 471–506. See also John P. Maddex Jr., *The Virginia Conservatives* (Chapel Hill: University of North Carolina Press, 1970). Maddex notes that in national politics, "even the most orthodox fiscal thinkers in Virginia were inflationists by northern standards" (257).

32. On the operation of the tenancy system in the South, see Oscar Zeichner, "The Legal Status of the Agricultural Laborer in the South," *Political Science Quarterly* 55, 3 (1940): 412–28, and Shannon, *Farmer's Last Frontier,* 83–96.

33. Gavin Wright: *Old South, New South* (New York: Basic Books, 1986), 84–121, and *The Political Economy of the Cotton South* (New York: W. W. Norton, 1978), 160–65; Steven Hahn, *The Roots of Southern Populism* (New York: Oxford University Press, 1983), 152–203; Theodore Saloutos, *Farmer Movements in the South, 1865–1933* (Lincoln: University of Nebraska Press, 1960), 237; Gilbert C. Fite, *Cotton Fields No More* (Lexington: University Press of Kentucky, 1984), xii, 21–29.

34. Roger L. Ransom and Richard Sutch, "Debt Peonage in the South after the Civil War," *Journal of Economic History* 32 (September 1972): 651–65; Gilbert C. Fite, "The Agricultural Trap in the South," *Agricultural History* 60 (fall 1986): 41. Among cotton growers, at least 80 percent were "ensnared by the lien system" to greater or lesser extent by the late 1890s. Alex M. Arnett, *The Populist Movement in Georgia* (New York: Columbia University Press, 1922), 57.

35. Fite, "The Agricultural Trap in the South," 41–45; John A. James, "Financial Underdevelopment in the Postbellum South," *Journal of Interdisciplinary History* 11 (winter 1981): 443–54; Ransom and Sutch, "Debt Peonage in the South," 642–51. The scarcity of financial institutions put even large landowners at a disadvantage. Shannon points out, "The planter himself was usually in debt, directly or indirectly, to Northern banks or merchants." *Farmer's Last Frontier,* 93.

36. C. Vann Woodward, *Origins of the New South, 1877–1913* (Baton Rouge: Louisiana State University Press, 1951), 132–34; Wright, *Old South, New South,* 130–31; David L. Carlton, "Capital Mobilization and Southern Industry, 1880–1905," *Journal of Economic History* 49 (March 1989): 73–99.

37. Harris, "Right Fork or Left Fork," 478–83.

38. Hannah Grace Roach, "Sectionalism in Congress (1870 to 1890)," *American Political Science Review* 19 (August 1925): 504.

39. Harris, "Right Fork or Left Fork," 482 (table). On the late sixties to mid-seventies greenbackism of manufacturers and businessmen in the Midwest and Pennsylvania, see Unger, *Greenback Era*, 218–24; Ellis B. Usher, *The Greenback Movement of 1875–1884 and Wisconsin's Part in It* (Milwaukee: Meisenheimer Printing Co., 1911), 21–29; and Sharkey, *Money, Class, and Party*, 149–71.

40. Unger, *Greenback Era*, 278–85, 325–26.

41. Ibid., 361–62; Weinstein, *Prelude to Populism*, 305–41.

42. Woodward, *Origins of the New South*, 83–94.

43. Charles Chilton Pearson, *The Readjuster Movement in Virginia* (New Haven, Conn.: Yale University Press, 1927), 127–31, 144–47; Maddex, *Virginia Conservatives*, 224–29, 233–75.

44. Unger, *Greenback Era*, 293–321; Solon J. Buck, *The Agrarian Crusade* (New Haven, Conn.: Yale University Press, 1921), 79–89; Fred E. Haynes, *Third Party Movements since the Civil War* (Cedar Rapids: State Historical Society of Iowa, 1916), 105–19; Roscoe C. Martin, "The Greenback Party in Texas," *Southwestern Historical Quarterly* 30 (January 1927): 165–66; Stephen Cresswell, *Multiparty Politics in Mississippi, 1877–1902* (Jackson: University Press of Mississippi, 1995), esp. 22–57.

45. Nathan Fine, *Labor and Farmer Parties in the U.S.* (New York: Russell and Russell, 1961), 66–72; Haynes, *Third Party Movements*, 136.

46. This and subsequent quotations from the 1880 Greenback platform are found in Donald B. Johnson, ed., *National Party Platforms*, vol. 1 (Urbana: University of Illinois Press, 1978), 57–58.

47. The national bank system was to be abolished, with legal tender paper money, silver (in unlimited coinage), and gold to take the place of national bank notes.

48. Haynes, *Third Party Movements*, 140.

49. Buck, *Agrarian Crusade*, 95.

50. For a map of per capita bank deposits in 1877 that presents a rough mirror image of the 1880 Greenback vote, see Bensel, *Yankee Leviathan*, 270.

51. Orin G. Libby, "A Study of the Greenback Movement, 1876–84," *Transactions of the Wisconsin Academy of Sciences, Arts, and Letters* 12, pt. 2 (1899): 532–33.

52. Congressional Quarterly, *Guide to U.S. Elections* (Washington, D.C.: Congressional Quarterly, 1975), 276.

53. The above relies on McMath, *Populist Vanguard*, 3–12, and Taylor, *Farmers' Movement*, 194–97.

54. McMath, *Populist Vanguard*, 14–16, 44–53; Theodore R. Mitchell, *Political Education in the Southern Farmers' Alliance 1887–1900* (Madison: University of Wisconsin Press, 1987), 151–57.

55. McMath, *Populist Vanguard*, 12.

56. Lawrence Goodwyn, *The Democratic Promise* (New York: Oxford University Press, 1976), 36–40; McMath, *Populist Vanguard*, 17–21. On the early FA cooperative efforts, see also Michael Schwartz, *Radical Protest and Social Structure* (Chicago: University of Chicago Press, 1988), 201–15.

57. McMath, *Populist Vanguard*, 21–22.

58. Ibid., 23–24; Goodwyn, *Democratic Promise*, 51–76.

59. McMath, *Populist Vanguard*, 25–26.

60. "Demands of the Farmers' Alliance of Texas, 1886," reprinted in Vernon Carstensen, ed., *Farmer Discontent, 1865–1900* (New York: John Wiley and Sons, 1974), 73–75; see also Goodwyn, *Democratic Promise*, 79–81.

61. Goodwyn, *Democratic Promise*, 80.

62. Ibid., 83–85; McMath, *Populist Vanguard*, 28–30.

63. Taylor, *Farmers' Movement*, 199–214 (quotation at 205).

64. McMath, *Populist Vanguard*, 44–46; Goodwyn, *Democratic Promise*, 278–85; Gerald H. Gaither, *Blacks and the Populist Revolt* (University: University of Alabama Press, 1977), 2–25. Gaither estimates CFA membership at about 825,000 at its 1890 peak (ibid., 12).

65. John D. Hicks, *Populist Revolt* (Lincoln: University of Nebraska Press, 1961), 96–104.

66. Goodwyn, *Democratic Promise*, 154–64, 639 n.

67. McMath, *Populist Vanguard*, 87; Goodwyn, *Democratic Promise*, 162–64, 587–90. See also Scott McNall, *The Road to Rebellion* (Chicago: University of Chicago Press, 1988), 54.

68. Goodwyn, *Democratic Promise*, 590.

69. McMath, *Populist Vanguard*, 87.

70. The St. Louis platform can be found in George B. Tindall, *A Populist Reader* (New York: Harper Torchbooks, 1966), 76–77.

71. McMath, *Populist Vanguard*, 106.

72. Goodwyn, *Democratic Promise*, 589.

73. Michael Schwartz, "An Estimate of the Size of the Southern Farmers' Alliance and Cotton Tenancy, 1880–1890," *Agricultural History* 51 (1977): 768.

74. Julie R. Jeffrey, "Women in the Southern Farmers' Alliance," *Feminist Studies* 3 (fall 1975): 72–91.

75. Mitchell, *Political Education in the Southern Farmers' Alliance*, 112–18. For Alliance songs, see Leopold Vincent, comp., *The Alliance and Labor Songster* (Indianapolis: Vincent Bros. Publishing Co., 1891).

76. Goodwyn, *Democratic Promise*, 175.

77. Schwartz, *Radical Protest and Social Structure*, 217–18.

78. Ibid., 235–46, 262–65. See also Goodwyn, *Democratic Promise*, 127–29.

79. Schwartz, *Radical Protest and Social Structure*, 228–30. See also Goodwyn, *Democratic Promise*, 125–40.

80. Schwartz, *Radical Protest and Social Structure*, 210.

81. McMath, *Populist Vanguard*, 119, 154; Schwartz, *Radical Protest and Social Structure*, 232, 261. On the failure of the Alabama exchanges, see William W. Rogers, "The Farmers' Alliance in Alabama," in *From Civil War to Civil Rights: Alabama, 1860–1960*, ed. Sara W. Wiggins (Tuscaloosa: University of Alabama Press, 1987), 162–72.

82. Arnett, *Populist Movement in Georgia*, 81.

83. Goodwyn, *Democratic Promise*, 155–56; McMath, *Populist Vanguard*, 84–85, 119–23.

84. Goodwyn, *Democratic Promise*, 167–69, 565–71. Macune may have gotten the idea for the subtreasury from a system, improvised during the French revolution of 1848, for currency issuance on warehouse receipts. James C. Malin, "The Farmers' Alliance Subtreasury Plan and European Precedents," *Mississippi Valley Historical Review* 31 (June 1944): 256.

85. Donna A. Barnes, *Farmers in Rebellion* (Austin: University of Texas Press, 1984), 121–23.

86. Taylor, *Farmers' Movement*, 245–46. The Missouri and Virginia Alliances voted down the subtreasury plan, and there was significant opposition in Mississippi, Louisiana, Tennessee, and even Texas. McMath, *Populist Vanguard*, 95; Hicks, *Populist Revolt*, 201–2.

87. Hicks, *Populist Revolt*, 192–94. See also Bruce Palmer, *Man over Money* (Chapel Hill: University of North Carolina Press, 1980), 104–9.

88. Goodwyn, *Democratic Promise*, 169–75. Macune remained chairman of the executive committee and, in McMath's view, "retained effective control of the organization" (*Populist Vanguard*, 92).

89. Goodwyn, *Democratic Promise*, 189–94. Ralph Beaumont, instructed by Terence Powderly to cultivate the Alliancemen, backed the subtreasury in public but without conviction. McMath, *Populist Vanguard*, 94.

90. McMath, *Populist Vanguard*, 93–96.

91. Hicks, *Populist Revolt*, 178; McNall, *Road to Rebellion*, 243.

92. Hicks, *Populist Revolt*, 78.

93. Goodwyn, *Democratic Promise*, 211.

94. Ibid., 213–25. Hicks, *Populist Revolt*, 170–78. Sectional passions and their partisan manifestation were exacerbated by the introduction by Sen. Henry Cabot Lodge (R, Massachusetts) of a bill to provide federal protection for black voting rights in the South. A Mississippi delegate to the December 1890

convention sought Alliance condemnation of the "Force Bill." Southern members backed him 35–11 while northern and western delegates voted 18–13 in opposition. Goodwyn, *Democratic Promise*, 227.

95. Goodwyn, *Democratic Promise*, 214–35, 651–52 n; McMath, *Populist Vanguard*, 97–101, 117–18.

96. Goodwyn, *Democratic Promise*, 213–31 (quotation at 231).

97. Hicks, *Populist Revolt*, 211–17 (quotations at 211); Goodwyn, *Democratic Promise*, 244–48; McMath, *Populist Vanguard*, 128.

98. McMath, *Populist Vanguard*, 124–26.

99. Thomas E. Watson, "The Negro Question in the South," in Tindall, *Populist Reader*, 188–28.

100. McMath, *Populist Vanguard*, 125–26.

101. Goodwyn, *Democratic Promise*, 290–91.

102. Ibid., 283.

103. William F. Holmes, "The Arkansas Cotton Pickers Strike of 1891 and the Demise of the Colored Farmers' Alliance," *Arkansas Historical Quarterly* 23 (summer 1973): 107–19; Gaither, *Blacks and the Populist Revolt*, 14–16. In Arkansas, strikers killed two nonstriking cotton pickers and a plantation manager. The escaping strikers were hunted down, and fifteen were lynched in retaliation.

104. Goodwyn, *Democratic Promise*, 295–99, 324. On the Alabama contest, see also Hicks, *Populist Revolt*, 249–50.

105. Hicks, *Populist Revolt*, 222–27.

106. McMath, *Populist Vanguard*, 132.

107. Ibid., 137.

108. McNall, *Road to Rebellion*, 253–63. Stanley B. Parsons, Karen Tooms Parsons, Walter Killilae, and Beverly Borgers have argued, like McNall, that Goodwyn exaggerates the importance of cooperatives as the principal springboard of populism. With an interpretation akin to that of John Hicks, they emphasize that farmers did not require the socialization of a cooperative subculture to define their political interests. "The Role of Cooperation in the Development of the Movement Culture of Populism," *Journal of American History* 69 (March 1983): 866–85.

109. Schwartz, *Radical Protest and Social Structure*, 265–69 (quotation at 269).

110. Goodwyn, *Democratic Promise*, 209–10, 315, 430–32, 452–74. Palmer, *Man over Money*, 141–68, concurs in this condemnation.

111. McMath, *Populist Vanguard*, 132, 144.

112. On the achievements (and limitations) of state-level populism in the Midwest and West, see Peter H. Argersinger, *The Limits of Agrarian Radicalism* (Lawrence: University Press of Kansas, 1995); Daniel Kryder, "Insurgent Legislators: The People's Party in the Georgia House of Representatives, 1894–95" (master's thesis, New School for Social Research, 1988); McNall, *Road to Rebellion*, 258–61; and William J. Gaboury, *Dissension in the Rockies* (New York: Garland Publishing, 1988).

113. For a criticism of the argument that the FA destroyed itself by the shift into politics, see McMath, *Populist Vanguard*, 154. For a defense of the political fusionists, see Norman Pollack, *The Just Polity* (Urbana: University of Illinois Press, 1987), 56, 354n.

114. The Omaha platform is reprinted in Tindall, *Populist Reader*, 90–96.

115. Pollack, *Just Polity*, 4–10, 43–79; Palmer, *Man over Money*, esp. 111–37.

116. Pollack, *Just Polity*, 10, 203–9, 218–29, 288–93.

117. Ibid., 55ff.; Norman Pollack, *The Populist Response to Industrial America* (New York: W. W. Norton, 1962), 43–67; see also the two chapters on labor in W. Scott Morgan, *History of the Wheel and Alliance and the Impending Revolution* (St. Louis: C. B. Woodward Co., 1891). Evidence of the Populist commitment to labor in national politics is presented in Gene Clanton, "'Hayseed Socialism' on the Hill: Congressional Populism, 1891–1895," *Western Political Quarterly* 15 (April 1984): esp. 157–58.

118. Goodwyn, *Democratic Promise*, 190–99, 270–71, 366; Hicks, *Populist Revolt*, 238–45; H. Wayne Morgan, "The Election of 1892," in *History of American Presidential Elections*, vol. 5, ed. Arthur M. Schlesinger Jr. (New York: Chelsea House, 1985), 1727.

119. Quoted in Goodwyn, *Democratic Promise*, 271.

120. Quoted in Hicks, *Populist Revolt*, 248.

121. Buck, *Agrarian Crusade,* 148–50.

122. Hicks, *Populist Revolt,* 247–50; Roscoe C. Martin, *The People's Party in Texas: A Study in Third Party Politics* (Austin: University of Texas Press, 1970), 266–67; Barnes, *Farmers in Rebellion,* 143–44.

123. Goodwyn, *Democratic Promise,* 324–28; McMath, *Populist Vanguard,* 142.

124. Congressional Quarterly, *Guide to U.S. Elections,* 279, 667–71. Within the states most sympathetic to populism, relative poverty (value of production), debt burden, and interest rates show fairly high associations with populist voting, as does the percentage of people outside towns, the percentage of whites, and the distance from major urban centers. See Gaither, *Blacks and the Populist Revolt,* appendix, 140–56; Stanley B. Parsons, *The Populist Context* (Westport, Conn.: Greenwood Press, 1973), 126–27; Peter H. Argersinger, *Populism and Politics* (Lexington: University of Kentucky Press, 1974), 64–70; Hahn, *Roots of Southern Populism,* 278–82; and Sheldon Hackney, *Populism to Progressivism in Alabama* (Princeton: Princeton University Press, 1969), 336–37. Jeffrey Ostler has persuasively argued that differences in populist appeal *between* states had much to do with *political* factors—principally the degree of genuine party competition and the receptivity of one or both of the major parties to the agrarian reform program. Jeffrey Ostler, *Prairie Populism* (Lawrence: Kansas University Press, 1993).

125. Morgan, "Election of 1892," 1731.

126. Percentages calculated from Walter Dean Burnham, *Presidential Ballots, 1836–1892* (Baltimore: Johns Hopkins University Press, 1955), 705.

127. The Silver Purchase Act of 1890 had been passed at the insistence of southern Democrats and western Republicans, against lopsided northeastern opposition. It doubled silver purchases, in payment for which the government issued Treasury notes redeemable at the government's discretion in either gold or silver. Chester W. Wright, *Economic History of the U.S.* (New York: McGraw-Hill, 1941), 820–23.

128. Horace S. Merrill, *Bourbon Leader: Grover Cleveland and the Democratic Party* (Boston: Little, Brown, 1957), 192–95.

129. Hicks, *Populist Revolt,* 322–24.

130. William Warren Rogers, *The One-Gallused Rebellion* (Baton Rouge: Louisiana State University Press, 1970), 272–75 (quotation at 272); Robert D. Ward and William W. Rogers, *Labor Revolt in Alabama* (Tuscaloosa: University of Alabama Press, 1965), 120–25.

131. Argersinger, *Populism and Politics,* 197–98; Clanton, "'Hayseed Socialism' on the Hill," 157–58.

132. Pollack, *Populist Response to Industrial America,* 52–57.

133. Quoted in Lawrence Goodwyn, *The Populist Moment* (New York: Oxford University Press, 1978), 250.

134. Even Goodwyn makes this charge (*Democratic Promise,* 310) while also citing the absence of a movement culture in the ranks of labor. See also Mitchell, *Political Education in the Southern Farmers' Alliance,* 162–64, and McNall, *Road to Rebellion,* 158, 180–82.

135. Goodwyn, *Populist Moment,* 343.

136. Hicks, *Populist Revolt,* 333–38.

137. Ibid., 338–39.

138. Ibid., 340–52; Goodwyn, *Democratic Promise,* 387–401, 422–81.

139. Goodwyn, *Populist Moment,* 233. See also Argersinger, *Populism and Politics,* 167–68, 201–10.

140. Friedman and Schwartz, *Monetary History of the United States,* 134.

141. The labor petition is reprinted in William Jennings Bryan, *The First Battle* (Chicago: W. B. Conkey Co., 1896), 166–67. See also Robert F. Durden, *The Climax of Populism* (Westport, Conn.: Greenwood Press, 1965), 12, and Harvey Wish, "John Peter Altgeld and the Background of the Campaign of 1896," *Mississippi Valley Historical Review* 24 (1937–38): 505–10.

142. Hicks, *Populist Revolt,* 349–69.

143. S. K. Stevens, "The Election of 1896 in Pennsylvania," *Pennsylvania History* 4 (1937): 67.

144. Quoted in James Peterson, "The Trade Unions and the Populist Party," *Science and Society* 8 (1944): 152.

145. McAlister Coleman, *Eugene V. Debs* (New York: Greenberg, Publisher, 1930), 184. According

to Ray Ginger, "If Bryan had been elected President in 1896, Eugene Debs might never have become a socialist." Ray Ginger, *The Bending Cross* (New York: Russell and Russell, 1969), 190.

146. Gilbert C. Fite, "The Election of 1896," in Schlesinger, *History of American Presidential Elections,* 1798–99.

147. *New York Times:* August 27, 1896, 3, September 3, 1, September 13, 2, September 24, 1 et passim. See also Paul W. Glad, *McKinley, Bryan, and the People* (Philadelphia: J. B. Lippincott, 1964), 181–82, and Fite, "Election of 1896," 1815.

148. Louis W. Koenig, *Bryan* (New York: Capricorn Books, 1971), 234; Bryan, *The First Battle,* 564–65.

149. Koenig, *Bryan,* 232; J. Rogers Hollingsworth, *The Whirligig of Politics* (Chicago: University of Chicago Press, 1963), 87.

150. In Iowa, for example, a data bank collected names of farmers leaning toward free silver and "flood[ed] them with literature on the financial question." Fite, "Election of 1896," 1816–17. At the campaign's peak, Republican material reached five million homes per week. According to Matthew Josephson, the fund paid for 120 million copies of 275 million pamphlets in seven different languages, as well as subventions to academics to publish articles attacking Bryan's program. Matthew Josephson, *The Politicos* (New York: Harcourt Brace, 1938), 699. The Hanna quotation can be found in Koenig, *Bryan,* 225.

151. *New York Times,* August 5, 1896, 2. A column titled "Practical Talks about Silver," ostensibly written by a "wage earner," was the source of this particular quotation. The panic, wrote "Wage Earner," would fill New York with idle and starving men.

152. The San Francisco papers "depicted Bryan as a radical whose candidacy was backed by 'maddened demagogues' and 'social revolutionists.'" W. Hal Williams, *The Democratic Party and California Politics, 1880–1896* (Stanford: Stanford University Press, 1973), 246. See also Samuel T. McSeveney, *The Politics of Depression* (New York: Oxford University Press, 1972), 181; Fite, "Election of 1896," 1820–21; Hollingsworth, *Whirligig of Politics,* 88–90; *New York Times,* July–November 1896; and Paolo Coletta, *William Jennings Bryan,* 3 vols. (Lincoln: University of Nebraska Press, 1964–69), 1:70–72.

153. Koenig, *Bryan,* 240.

154. Ibid., 243. See also McSeveney, *Politics of Depression,* 181–82.

155. From excerpts quoted in Bryan, *The First Battle,* 463–64, and Koenig, *Bryan,* 243. See also the remarks of Rev. Cortlandt Myers of Brooklyn's Baptist Temple, reported in the *New York Times,* October 4, 1896, 5.

156. Alan F. Westin, "The Supreme Court, the Populist Movement, and the Campaign of 1896," *Journal of Politics* 15 (February 1953): 30–36.

157. McSeveney, *Politics of Depression,* 183–84; Koenig, *Bryan,* 243; Williams, *Democratic Party and California Politics,* 447–48; Harold E. Taggart, "The Party Realignment of 1896 in California," *Pacific Historical Review* 9 (December 1939): 443–48; Stevens, "Election of 1896 in Pennsylvania," 75–77, 84; Durden, *Climax of Populism,* 136–44 (quotation at 137). The 1896 election may constitute one of the clearest examples of the concept of "capital strike." With McKinley's election, the withheld investment came surging back as production plans and orders contingent on Republican victory were released. See, for example, *New York Times,* November 9, 1896, 4, and Durden, *Climax of Populism,* 141 n.

158. The following discussion of Bryan's campaign circuit relies on the following: *New York Times;* Bryan, *The First Battle;* Koenig, *Bryan,* 223–39; Glad, *McKinley, Bryan, and the People,* 147–77; Stanley L. Jones, *The Presidential Election of 1896* (Madison: University of Wisconsin Press, 1964), 316; and Hollingsworth, *Whirligig of Politics,* 87.

159. On the significance of the contrasting political economy of core and periphery agriculture in 1896, see McSeveney, *Politics of Depression,* 179–80.

160. From an August 8 speech in Bryan, *The First Battle,* 300.

161. Bryan, *The First Battle,* 604; *New York Times,* November 2, 1896, 1.

162. One of the most colorful demonstrations greeted the candidate during his brief foray into the South. In mid-September, Bryan's train arrived in Asheville, North Carolina, where "he was met by a great cavalcade, men and women, mounted on all kinds of horseflesh, from spirited thoroughbreds to

hard-worked mules. . . . The party proceeded under escort of 1,000 horsemen and horsewomen to a natural amphitheater near the Southern Railway station, where the candidate addressed an immense audience . . . [hundreds of which] had come in from the mountains on horse-back and in wagons." *New York Times,* September 17, 1896, 3. The presence of large numbers of women in his audiences was a striking feature of the Bryan campaign. Though they could not vote in national elections in any of the states he visited, women demonstrated great enthusiasm for the campaign, as the *Times* noted in its coverage of the visits to Niagara, several Michigan towns, Boston, Grand Rapids, Minneapolis, Duluth, and Chicago. At several stops in midwestern cities, the campaign made special arrangements for Bryan to speak to huge audiences of women who had demanded separate addresses. *New York Times,* 1896: September 4, 6, September 26, 1, October 13, 2, October 16, 6, October 29, 1.

163. Bryan produced an early formulation, and critique, of the theory in his "Cross of Gold" speech: "There are two ideas of government. There are those who believe that if you just legislate to make the well-to-do prosperous, that their prosperity will leak through on those below. The Democratic idea has been first if you legislate to make the masses prosperous their prosperity will find its way up and through every class." The speech is reprinted in Ignatius Donnelly, *The Bryan Campaign for the American People's Money* (Chicago: Laird and Lee Publishers, 1896), xiii–xxv.

164. The Chicago speech is printed in the *New York Times,* September 8, 1896, 2.

165. The speech is printed in Donnelly, *The Bryan Campaign,* xv. The Democratic campaign committee took up Bryan's "true businessman" argument and made up posters proclaiming that "the millions of farmers, producers and laborers of all classes are as much businessmen as the few who live, thrive and grow rich trading in the product of labor." *New York Times,* August 11, 1896, 5.

166. *New York Times,* September 8, 1896, 2.

167. Paul Kleppner, *The Cross of Culture* (New York: Free Press, 1970), 302–4, 340–41, 375. See also Williams, *Democratic Party and California Politics,* 252; McSeveney, *Politics of Depression,* 186; and Leon Fink, *Workingmen's Democracy* (Urbana: University of Illinois Press, 1983), 139–41.

168. Durden, *Climax of Populism,* 148–55; McSeveney, *Politics of Depression,* 180–82. To impugn Bryan among urban workers, the GOP disseminated rumors that he was in league with the anti-Catholic American Protective Association (APA). The APA itself, which had worked hard to defeat Bryan in previous Nebraska races, charged that "Bryan had sold out to the Catholics and would be under their control if elected." Durden, *Climax of Populism,* 154–55. See also Koenig, *Bryan,* 108, 153. The *New York Times* attacked Bryan for his *tolerance* of ethnic and cultural diversity. As a congressman, he had twice voted against the compulsory teaching of English in New Mexico territory schools. "It would seem from this," wrote the *Times,* "that Bryan considered that the Spanish 'greaser' was a likelier person to vote for free silver if left in his original and benighted condition." *New York Times,* September 18, 1896, 4.

169. Kleppner, *Cross of Culture,* 298–300 (emphasis added).

170. For a recent elaboration of such worker choices, see Adam Przeworski and Michael Wallerstein, "The Structure of Class Conflict in Capitalist Democracies," *American Political Science Review* 76 (June 1982): 215–38. For a discussion of the difficulty that the ethnocultural historians have had in dealing with the powerful economic issues of the 1896 campaign, see Richard L. McCormick, "Ethno-Cultural Interpretations of Nineteenth Century American Voting Behavior," *Political Science Quarterly* 89 (June 1974): 372–77.

171. Walter Dean Burnham, "The System of 1896: An Analysis," in *The Evolution of American Electoral Systems,* by Paul Kleppner et al. (Westport, Conn.: Greenwood Press, 1981), 161. Gold-standard defenders often repeated the argument that, based on the current value of the metal, a silver dollar would be worth, to the wage earner and everyone else, only fifty-three cents. To this, Bryan replied that the decline in the price of silver reflected its demonetization. On reinstatement of a bimetalic standard in the United States, with selection of payment mode in the hands of debtors or the government, other countries would be encouraged to adopt or maintain a silver or bimetalic standard, and increased demand would raise the price of the silver dollar, with gold and silver maintaining a rough, albeit fluctuating, parity (as the situation existed in France). *New York Times,* July 16, 1896, 4; W. J. Bryan, Madison Square Garden speech, reprinted in Bryan, *The First Battle,* 315–38.

172. McNall, *Road to Rebellion*, 158.

173. Bryan's reasoning bears striking similarities to two extremely different scholarly perspectives. His arguments for silver resonate with Friedman and Schwartz's contention, cited above, that early adoption of a silver standard would have moderated or eliminated deflation and encouraged price stability in the United States and the world at large. Friedman and Schwartz, *Monetary History of the United States*, 134, 472–74. The other echo can be found in Karl Polanyi:

> Social protection and interference with the currency were not merely analogous but often identical issues. . . . These [1920–31 European] examples show how crippling the effect of the sound currency postulate was on popular policies. The American experience taught the same lesson. . . . The New Deal could not have been launched without going off gold. . . . Under the gold standard the leaders of the financial market are entrusted, in the nature of things, with the safeguarding of stable exchanges and sound internal credit on which government finance largely depends. The banking organization is thus in the position to obstruct any domestic move in the economic sphere which it happens to dislike. . . . That social protectionism did not in this case result in a deadlock was due to the fact that the United States went off gold in time. (Karl Polanyi, *The Great Transformation* [Boston: Beacon Press, 1944], 227–29)

The United States went off gold, one might add, as a result of the raucous pressure of southern and western congresspeople from the old "Popocrat" regions.

174. McKinley received 51.0 percent of the total vote; Bryan received 46.7 percent. (The National [gold] Democrat John M. Palmer and the Prohibition candidate took most of the remaining 2.3 percent.) Bryan, *The First Battle*, 610 (table). Using the census division breakdown in William Diamond, "Urban and Rural Voting in 1896," *American Historical Review* 46 (January 1941): 281–305 (slightly modified by regrouping Delaware with New York, New Jersey, and Pennsylvania), yields a Bryan percentage of 33.7 in the core (New England plus mid-Atlantic plus Ohio and Michigan) and 55.9 percent in the southern, mountain, and west-north-central periphery. Diamond separately analyzed the vote in cities of 45,000 or more, finding that the Democrat received 40.6 percent in cities and 48.3 percent in nonurban areas. However, within the mountain and New England states, his urban percentage exceeded his nonurban vote (in the former, 87.1 versus 80.3, and in New England, 33.5 versus 24.4). Bryan's urban vote in the mid-Atlantic states was 37.5 percent. In Ohio and Michigan the city vote was higher, 43.6 and 42.3 percent. In the South (the census-Diamond grouping minus Delaware), Diamond's figures show that Bryan received 44.7 percent in cities of more than 45,000. However, according to the *World Almanac and Encyclopedia, 1896* (New York: Press Publishing, 1896), Bryan carried the counties containing Savannah, Dallas, Mobile, New Orleans, Richmond, and Norfolk while losing those containing Baltimore, Louisville, Chattanooga, Nashville, and Memphis (the latter two quite narrowly). By David Burner's count, McKinley won forty-five of the nation's fifty most-populous counties; four of the five Bryan counties were southern. The Democratic plurality in the eighty-five principal cities of the United States had been 162,000 in 1892; in 1896 the situation was reversed, for a 464,000 GOP plurality. David Burner, *The Politics of Provincialism* (New York: W. W. Norton, 1975), 7.

Chapter Five

1. E. E. Schattsneider, *The Semi-Sovereign People* (New York: Holt, Rinehart and Winston, 1960), 78–86; Walter Dean Burnham, "The System of 1896: An Analysis," in *The Evolution of American Electoral Systems*, by Paul Kleppner et al. (Westport, Conn.: Greenwood Press, 1981), 147–202.

2. J. Morgan Kousser, *The Shaping of Southern Politics* (New Haven, Conn.: Yale University Press, 1974), 139–223; V. O. Key, *Southern Politics* (New York: Random House, 1949), 533–50; C. Vann Woodward, *Origins of the New South* (Baton Rouge: Louisiana State University Press, 1951), 321–49.

3. Key, *Southern Politics*, 232–33, 263–71, 304–5.

4. Works attributing the progressive reform movements in the states to the new urban business and professional classes include Sheldon Hackney, *Populism to Progressivism in Alabama* (Princeton: Princeton University Press, 1969); Kousser, *Shaping of Southern Politics;* Dewey W. Grantham, *Southern Progressiv-*

ism (Knoxville: University of Tennessee Press, 1983); George E. Mowry, *The Era of Theodore Roosevelt* (New York: Harper and Row, 1958); Woodward, *Origins of the New South;* and William A. Link, *The Paradox of Southern Progressivism, 1880–1930* (Chapel Hill: University of North Carolina Press, 1992).

5. The most notable works in this genre are Gabriel Kolko, *The Triumph of Conservatism* (Chicago: Quadrangle Books, 1963); James Weinstein, *The Corporate Ideal in the Liberal State* (Boston: Beacon Press, 1968); and Martin J. Sklar, *The Corporate Reconstruction of American Capitalism, 1890–1916* (New York: Cambridge University Press, 1988).

6. Carl C. Taylor, *The Farmers' Movement, 1670–1920* (Westport, Conn.: Greenwood Press, 1953), 332–33; Solon J. Buck, *The Granger Movement* (Cambridge: Harvard University Press, 1913), 306.

7. Lowell K. Dyson, *Farmers' Organizations* (New York: Greenwood Press, 1986), 369.

8. Marilyn P. Watkins, *Rural Democracy: Community, Gender, and Politics in Western Washington, 1890–1925* (Ithaca, N.Y.: Cornell University Press, 1995), chap. 5.

9. Robert Lee Hunt, *A History of Farmers' Movements in the Southwest, 1873–1925* (College Station: Texas A&M University Press, 1935), 41–49.

10. Taylor, *Farmers' Movement,* 336–43; Hunt, *History of Farmers' Movements in the Southwest,* 52–53. The following were the first five (of thirteen) goals listed: "To establish justice. To secure equity. To apply the Golden Rule. To discourage the credit and mortgage system. To assist our members in buying and selling." Charles S. Barrett, *The Mission, History, and Times of the Farmers Union* (Lincoln: University of Nebraska Press, 1960), 107.

11. Woodward, *Origins of the New South,* 413; *Minutes of the National Farmers' Educational and Cooperative Union of America,* 1908 (Fort Worth, Texas), 14.

12. Taylor, *Farmers' Movement,* 349–50. According to Charles P. Loomis, of North Carolina locals that reported the gender of their members, 37 percent were female. "The Rise and Decline of the North Carolina Farmers' Union," *North Carolina Historical Review* 7 (July 1930): 314. As convention minutes (major speeches, committee service, etc.) make clear, women played an active role in the national organization. At the 1908 convention, for example, of the eight people delivering addresses to the assembled members (including President Barrett and Samuel Gompers), five were women. However, with the exception of the Committee on Education, which they dominated, women were not listed on the executive board or on committees concerned with cooperation and legislation. *Minutes,* 1908.

13. Taylor, *Farmers' Movement,* 346–48; Gilbert C. Fite, *Cotton Fields No More* (Lexington: University Press of Kentucky, 1984), 64. The Midwest also spawned other farm organizations in this period. For a description, see Dyson, *Farmers' Organizations,* entries under American Society of Equity, Nonpartisan League, and Farmers' National Congress. On the radical agrarian Nonpartisan League, founded in North Dakota in 1915, see Grant McConnell, *The Decline of Agrarian Democracy* (Berkeley: University of California Press, 1953), 41, and Richard M. Valelly, *Radicalism in the States* (Chicago: University of Chicago Press, 1989), 17–21.

14. The Texas and Oklahoma organizations, however, did conduct some collaborative activities across racial lines. On the race issue in the FU, see Theodore Saloutos, *Farmer Movements in the South, 1865–1933* (Lincoln: University of Nebraska Press, 1960), 192–94, 203. Some breach in the racial exclusiveness of membership was permitted for "Indians of industrious habits." Barrett, *Mission, History, and Times of the Farmers Union,* 107.

15. Fite, *Cotton Fields No More,* 63; Hunt, *History of Farmers' Movements in the Southwest,* 62 (quotation).

16. Taylor, *Farmers' Movement,* 350–55 (quotation at 355). See also Woodward, *Origins of the New South,* 414; Fite, *Cotton Fields No More,* 64; Saloutos, *Farmer Movements in the South,* 200–204.

17. Woodward, *Origins of the New South,* 413–15.

18. The FU's legislative demands of 1912 ran the gamut of economic, social, and political reforms. See *Minutes,* 1912 (Chattanooga, Tennessee), 31–33. One of the constituent committees of the organization was the Committee on Child and Animal Protection, whose reports declaimed against the evils of child labor and mental or physical child abuse, as well as the poor treatment of domestic animals in both the United States and abroad (in terms that call to mind 1990s animal rights organizations). See, for

example, *Minutes*, 1911 (Shawnee, Oklahoma), 86–91; *Minutes*, 1913 (Salina, Kansas), 68–71; and *Minutes*, 1914 (Fort Worth, Texas), 26, 38–40. The protection of both classes of "dependent" creatures was portrayed as a logical extension of the organization's humane moral philosophy. Child labor in mines and factories during the school year was condemned as a "curse to civilization" calling for national legislation (*Minutes*, 1913, 68). The 1911 *Minutes* proclaimed: "The proper protection of children and animals by law constitutes the highest state of civilization. No country nor state can claim to be civilized at this date that has not provided reasonable protection, not only for the child, but for . . . the lesser animals. A wilful injury to one of these dependent, helpless creatures not only injures the child or animal, but it also injures the one who does it and the community that carelessly or willingly permits it" (86–87).

19. Barrett, *Mission, History, and Times of the Farmers Union*, 31–32, 45–48. In the old producerist language, Barrett argued that when "the farmers and the laborers convince[d] the world that they know their strength and their rights, and are determined to use the one to secure the other," the political system would not dare to refuse their demands (415).

20. Taylor, *Farmers' Movement*, 358–59; *Minutes*, 1911, 65–67; *Minutes*, 1912, 31–33. See also Hunt, *History of Farmers' Movements in the Southwest*, 70, 76–80, 82–83, 131–32, and William C. Tucker, "Populism Up-to-Date: The Story of the Farmers' Union," *Agricultural History* 21 (October 1947): 200–202.

21. McConnell, *Decline of Agrarian Democracy*, 39; Samuel Gompers, *Seventy Years of Life and Labor*, 2 vols. (New York: E. P. Dutton, 1925), 2:271; Tucker, "Populism Up-to-Date," 200–201. In 1908, for example, the first (and only) "outsider" to address the FU convention was Samuel Gompers. *Minutes*, 1911, 1. The 1915 FU convention directed its national offices "to cooperate with the Federation of Labor in national legislation for the benefit of labor" and expressed appreciation to the AFL for "the help it has extended this organization in this past." *Minutes*, 1915 (Lincoln, Nebraaska), 53. Cooperation between labor and farm groups within the southern states was apparently stronger in Texas, Oklahoma, and North Carolina than elsewhere. Grantham, *Southern Progressivism*, 295–97.

22. Hunt, *History of Farmers' Movements in the Southwest*, 70, 76, 80. The condemnation of convict labor was not without loopholes. The Texas FU endorsed convict labor for road repair and for activities providing competition with monopolies—such as in the prison manufacture of cotton bagging and the development of iron resources. Ibid., 82, 91, 98; Jack Temple Kirby, *Darkness at the Dawning* (Philadelphia: J. B. Lippincott, 1972), 152–54.

23. James Aubrey Tinsley, "The Progressive Movement in Texas" (Ph.D. diss., University of Wisconsin, 1953), 67, 135–37.

24. Worth R. Miller, "Building a Progressive Coalition in Texas: The Populist-Reform Democrat Rapprochement, 1900–1907," *Journal of Southern History* 52 (May 1986): 176–77, 181–82.

25. Taylor, *Farmers' Movement*, 359. See also Grantham, *Southern Progressivism*, 330–31, and Saloutos, *Farmer Movements in the South*, 191–92. FU President Barrett was appointed to a variety of advisory groups by Presidents Roosevelt, Taft, and Wilson (Saloutos, *Farmer Movements in the South*).

26. On the tenant farmers' organization, see James Green, *Grass Roots Socialism* (Baton Rouge: Louisiana State University Press, 1978), 108–15, 224–25, 323–27, and Tinsley, "Progressive Movement in Texas," 170–72. In 1906–8, Kentucky, Tennessee, and Virginia tobacco growers, ranging from sharecroppers to planters, battled the "tobacco trust" (American Tobacco) in the "Black Patch War." Participants blew up factories, burned warehouses, and destroyed plant beds in a wave of violence that had to be curbed by military force. Cotton growers in Texas, Arkansas, Mississippi, and Georgia imitated their tactics in efforts to enforce a collective reduction of surplus cotton production after admonitions from the FU leadership failed to reduce planting. Woodward, *Origins of the New South*, 386–87; Fite, *Cotton Fields No More*, 66; Saloutos, *Farmer Movements in the South*, 198–99; George L. Robson Jr., "The Farmers' Union in Mississippi," *Journal of Mississippi History* 27 (November 1965): 381–83.

27. Woodward, *Origins of the New South*, 372–73; Paul Lewinson, *Race, Class, and Party* (New York: Russell and Russell, 1963), 111–20, 153–56; Kousser, *Shaping of Southern Politics*, 72–80. By 1903 a majority of southern states, and by 1913 all but North Carolina (which waited until 1915), had primaries. The absence of primary elections may account for some of the failures of the reform movement in the latter state (see Joseph F. Steelman, "The Progressive Era in North Carolina" [Ph.D. diss., University of

North Carolina, 1955]). In Alabama, Arkansas, Florida, Mississippi, and Texas, the institution of primary elections paved the way for progressive reforms. Woodward, *Origins of the New South,* 373.

28. Key, *Southern Politics,* 298–310; Lewinson, *Race, Class, and Party,* 190–91; Kousser, *Shaping of Southern Politics,* 80.

29. Albert D. Kirwan, *Revolt of the Rednecks* (New York: Harper Torchbooks, 1951), 314. Nevertheless, one might argue that reforms aimed at improving the position of periphery farmers in the national political economy had even more significance for black than white southerners. Blocked from most urban careers, blacks were even more bound to the land than whites and landownership was a potential escape route from poverty. On campaigns for black land purchase and their surprising successes, see Kirby, *Darkness at the Dawning,* 159–76.

30. Kirwan, *Revolt of the Rednecks,* 144, 163–77.

31. Kousser, *Shaping of Southern Politics,* 234.

32. Kirwan, *Revolt of the Rednecks,* 259–67.

33. Louis W. Koenig, *Bryan* (New York: Capricorn Books, 1971), 354–68.

34. Ibid., 333.

35. Paolo Coletta, *William Jennings Bryan,* 3 vols. (Lincoln: University of Nebraska Press, 1964–69), 1:252.

36. Koenig, *Bryan,* 305, 329–44; Coletta, *Bryan* 1:252–85. However, McKinley's plurality increased by only about 100,000 votes.

37. Coletta, *Bryan* 1:306–52; Koenig, *Bryan,* 368–98. The conservative faction, with critical support from New York City financiers, was led by David Bennett Hill, Grover Cleveland, Abram S. Hewitt, and Alton B. Parker of New York, John G. Carlisle of Kentucky, and Sen. Arthur Pue Gorman of Maryland.

38. Coletta, *Bryan* 1:353–73; Koenig, *Bryan,* 400–405; and see also David Sarasohn, *The Party of Reform* (Jackson: University of Mississippi Press, 1989), ix–xv, 22–23, 35–58.

39. Willard H. Smith, *The Social and Religious Thought of William Jennings Bryan* (Lawrence, Kans.: Coronado Press, 1975), 41–65. For some more positive evidence, see Koenig, *Bryan,* 334–35, 357–58, 449–50, and Kirby, *Darkness at the Dawning,* 125.

40. Koenig, *Bryan,* 358, 417; Smith, *Social and Religious Thought of William Jennings Bryan,* 13.

41. "Oklahoma's Radical Constitution," *Outlook* 87 (1907): 229–31. See also Charles A. Beard's more favorable description in "The Constitution of Oklahoma," *Political Science Quarterly* 24 (1909): 95–114.

42. Koenig, *Bryan,* 436–37.

43. On the Wilson-Bryan relationship and the 1912 platform, see Arthur S. Link, *Wilson,* vol. 1, *The Road to the White House* (Princeton: Princeton University Press, 1947), 316–27, 341, 452–65; Koenig, *Bryan,* 473–96; Coletta, *Bryan* 2:27–32, 54–78; and Sarasohn, *Party of Reform,* 119–44. For Bryan's influence on New Freedom legislation and the antiwar effort in Congress, see Coletta, *Bryan* 2:121–46, and Lawrence W. Levine, *Defender of the Faith, William Jennings Bryan: The Last Decade, 1915–1925* (New York: Oxford University Press, 1965), 39–90.

44. Quoted in David Burner, *The Politics of Provincialism* (New York: W. W. Norton, 1975), 13. Robert M. La Follette described Bryan as "a great moral teacher" who exerted "a powerful influence for good upon the political thought and standards of his time." *La Follette's Autobiography* (Madison: University of Wisconsin Press, 1960), 148–49.

45. Quoted in Smith, *Social and Religious Thought of William Jennings Bryan,* 191.

46. Ibid., 189–92. See also Levine, *Defender of the Faith,* 261–66, and Koenig, *Bryan,* 606–45.

47. Woodward, *Origins of the New South,* 371.

48. See, for example, Robert S. La Forte, *Leaders of Reform: Progressive Republicans in Kansas, 1900–1916* (Lawrence: University Press of Kansas, 1974), 6–7.

49. For a discussion of the South's colonial status in the early twentieth century, see Woodward, *Origins of the New South,* 291–320, 371–72. On income trends in agriculture, see Willford I. King, *The National Income and Its Purchasing Power* (New York: National Bureau of Economic Research, 1930), 152, 297, 304–14. King wrote that in nine of the seventeen years between 1909 and 1927, "the return on the farmer's investment was less than nothing" (314).

50. Rupert B. Vance, *All These People* (New York: Russell and Russell, 1945), 217, 224.

51. U.S. Department of Commerce, Bureau of the Census, *Statistical Abstract of the United States, 1933* (Washington, D.C.: GPO, 1933), 259 (table). Nonperiphery Delaware and the District of Columbia were subtracted from the South Atlantic totals; Delaware was added to the mid-Atlantic census region. Nevada (a diverse state due to its location in the San Francisco trade area) was subtracted from the mountain region for these comparisons.

52. Woodward, *Origins of the New South*, 318–19.

53. The 1910 census found 46.3 percent of all Americans living in towns or cities of 2,500 or more population. In the core industrial states, the range was from 47.5 percent in Vermont to over 92 percent in Rhode Island and Massachusetts. In the periphery, the southern state average was 19.8; the midwestern and plains states, 32.6; and the mountain states, 32.6. U.S. Department of Commerce, Bureau of the Census, *Statistical Abstract of the United States, 1913* (Washington, D.C.: GPO, 1914), 41.

54. Harold Hull McCarty, *The Geographic Basis of American Economic Life* (Port Washington, N.Y.: Kennikat Press, 1940), vol. 2, 331.

55. On the formation of these biregional alliances, see Richard F. Bensel, *Sectionalism and American Political Development* (Madison: University of Wisconsin Press, 1984), chap. 7.

56. The complexity is captured in Daniel T. Rodgers's summary description of the period as "an era of shifting, ideologically fluid, issue-focused coalitions, all competing for the reshaping of American society." Daniel T. Rodgers, "In Search of Progressivism," in *The Promise of American History: Progress and Prospects*, ed. Stanley I. Kutler and Stanley N. Katz (Baltimore: Johns Hopkins University Press, 1982), 114.

57. A. Bower Sagaser, *Joseph L. Bristow: Kansas Progressive* (Lawrence: University of Kansas Press, 1968), 99–100; David P. Thelen, *Robert M. La Follette and the Insurgent Spirit* (Boston: Little, Brown, 1976), 41–44; George E. Mowry, *Theodore Roosevelt and the Progressive Movement* (New York: Hill and Wang, 1946), 173; Sarasohn, *Party of Reform*, 85–86.

58. Thomas J. Bray, *Rebirth of Freedom* (Indianola, Iowa: Record and Tribune Press, 1957), 15–16. See also Mowry, *Theodore Roosevelt and the Progressive Movement*, 15–16, and Kenneth Hechler, *Insurgency* (New York: Columbia University Press, 1940), 18–19.

59. Richard Lowitt, *George Norris*, vol. 1, *The Making of a Progressive* (Syracuse, N.Y.: Syracuse University Press, 1963), 27–62; Howard W. Allen, *Poindexter of Washington* (Carbondale: Southern Illinois University Press, 1981), 10–31; Patrick F. Palermo, "Republicans in Revolt: The Sources of Insurgency" (Ph.D. diss., State University of New York, 1973), 119–83; Harlan Hahn, *Urban-Rural Conflict: The Politics of Change* (Beverly Hills, Calif.: Sage, 1971), 53–55; Claudius O. Johnson, *Borah of Idaho* (Seattle: Washington University Press, 1967), 31–97; Thelen, *Robert L. La Follette and the Insurgent Spirit*, 1–31; James Holt, *Congressional Insurgents and the Party System* (Cambridge: Harvard University Press, 1967), 4–5.

60. Borah was not "progressive" on the tariff or on most labor issues, and on roll-call votes he lagged behind the midwesterners in support for "reform" issues. He did, however, support antitrust laws, the income tax, financial decentralization, and railroad regulation.

61. Lowitt, *The Making of a Progressive*, 16–96; Palermo, "Republicans in Revolt," 148–90; Hahn, *Urban-Rural Conflict*, 53–56. Among the leading progressive Republicans, only Beveridge failed reelection in 1910, defeated by a progressive Democrat.

62. Sarasohn, *Party of Reform*, 30, 61–86, 240–42.

63. So reluctant was one historian to label southerners "progressive" that he adopted a dual standard. Republican senators who voted the "progressive" position at least 50 percent of the time were labeled progressive, whereas Democrats had to achieve at least a 90 percent score to win the label. Howard W. Allen, "Geography and Politics: Voting on Reform Issues in the U.S. Senate, 1911–1916," *Journal of Southern History* 27 (May 1961): 218–19. Allen goes on to derive a second, broader list of progressive-issue roll calls but unaccountably subtracts from the list all votes that were highly partisan. This procedure sharply reduces the "progressive" scores of southern Democrats. Another often-cited study employed selective and misleading roll-call descriptions to argue that southern congressional members were actually

opponents, rather than leaders (or even followers), of reform. Richard Abrams, "Woodrow Wilson and the Southern Congressmen," *Journal of Southern History* 22 (November 1956): 417–37. The latter contains numerous errors in the descriptions and omissions of essential context of roll calls (for criticism of the interpretation of particular roll calls, see chapter 8). The typical study of Republican insurgents seldom mentions the southern Democrats who provided the great bulk of supporting votes on most issues championed by the insurgents, or it takes note of their voting patterns only when they deviate from the norm.

64. John Wells Davidson, "The Response of the South to Woodrow Wilson's New Freedom, 1912–1914" (Ph.D. diss., Yale University, 1954), 95–96.

65. Historians who focus on the state political arena are prone to see agrarian radicalism as more symbol than substance (in Arsenault's view, as a "culturally confused" program serving mainly as a kind of psychological affirmation by increasingly marginalized farmers). The fact that local elites got off lightly as farmers directed their wrath at a national economic system is used as evidence of the farmers' confusion and their addiction to symbolic politics. But a national focus makes sense from a political-economy perspective. Local redistribution could not greatly improve the periphery farmers' position; a rearrangement of the national production, marketing, and monetary system could. Whether, as Arsenault argues, agrarians "wanted respect" above all else is impossible to prove. See Raymond Arsenault, *The Wild Ass of the Ozarks: Jeff Davis and the Social Bases of Southern Politics* (Knoxville: University of Tennessee Press, 1988), 14–15. But the national program of the periphery agrarians was about economics and was quite pragmatic.

66. Mowry, *Era of Theodore Roosevelt*, 198–223; John Braeman, *Albert J. Beveridge* (Chicago: University of Chicago Press, 1971), 98–121.

67. This count is based on the March 19, 1910, vote, specifically the Dalzell motion to table Norris's appeal from the Speaker's ruling (that it was not in order)—the first vote of the Norris rules change series. *Congressional Record* (*CR*), 61st Cong., 2d sess. (hereafter cited in the form 61–2), 3426–27. The first vote is probably a better gauge of "insurgency," since it avoids much of the "bandwagon" effect of later votes. As leaders of the House Republican insurgency, Hechler lists Norris (NE), Madison (KS), Nelson (WI), Murdock (KS), Poindexter (WA), and Lindbergh (MN). Gardner (MA), Fish (NY), and Fowler (NJ) opposed Cannon, mainly for personal reasons. Hechler, *Insurgency*, 34–42.

68. On identification of Senate "insurgents," see Holt, *Congressional Insurgents and the Party System*, 3–9; Edgar G. Robinson, *The Evolution of American Political Parties* (New York: Harcourt, Brace and World, 1924), 313; Hechler, *Insurgency*, 83–91; Mowry, *Era of Theodore Roosevelt*, 244; and Allen, *Poindexter of Washington*, 60–61. Perkins and Works of California, Dixon of Montana, Nelson of Minnesota, and Brown and Burkett of Nebraska are sometimes identified as Senate "progressives" or "insurgents" but clearly were not among the group's major activists. In Allen's study, the five senators voting most in opposition to their party on progressive issues were La Follette, Clapp, Gronna, Kenyon, and Poindexter. Of the fourteen senators listed in the text, eight represented periphery, five diverse, and one (Poindexter of Washington) core states.

69. On the rules fight, Hechler reports that Democratic leaders were miffed that the insurgent Republicans "monopolized the limelight." Clayton of Alabama branded it "a case of the tail wagging the dog" (quoted in Hechler, *Insurgency*, 74). However, as Sarasohn argues, it was good politics to let the insurgents lead the charge in the years when the Republicans held the majority (*Party of Reform*, 65), and the Democrats seemed much more gracious about sharing the limelight than did the insurgents, who "tended to treat the Democrats as political untouchables who happened to be voting the same way" (ibid., 63). The progressive Republicans were particularly ungracious and increasingly uncooperative when the tables were turned and Democrats led the Congress and the executive branch. As Sarasohn summarizes, the insurgents "played an important role in the politics of the Progressive Era. But they were rarely as radical and never as numerous as the Democrats whom they denounced, despised, and depended upon" (ibid., 86; see also 76, 80–81).

70. Computed from Jerome M. Clubb, "Congressional Opponents of Reform, 1901–1913 (Ph.D. diss., University of Washington, 1963), table 28, 209–10.

71. Ibid. Six of the ten rural "opponents of reform" were from the Pacific states. All were Republican.

Introduction to Part II

1. The attribution of this complex of state-expanding reform legislation to the post–Civil War farmers' movement and the farmer-labor alliance finds some support in older historical treatments like those of John D. Hicks and Solon J. Buck and resonates with the more recent work of Arthur S. Link, Ann Firor Scott, Jerome Clubb, Claude Barfield, and David Sarasohn. John D. Hicks, *The Populist Revolt* (Lincoln: University of Nebraska Press, 1961); Solon J. Buck, *The Agrarian Crusade* (New Haven, Conn.: Yale University Press, 1921); Arthur S. Link, *Wilson*, 5 vols. (Princeton: Princeton University Press, 1947–65), and "The Progressive Movement in the South, 1870–1914," *North Carolina Historical Review* 23 (1946): 172–95; Ann Firor Scott, "Progressives in Congress, 1900–1916" (Ph.D. diss., Radcliffe College, 1958), and "A Progressive Wind from the South, 1906–1913," *Journal of Southern History* 29 (February 1963): 53–70; Jerome M. Clubb, "Congressional Opponents of Reform, 1901–1913" (Ph.D. diss., University of Washington, 1963); Claude Barfield, "The Democratic Party in Congress 1909–1913" (Ph.D. diss., Northwestern University, 1965); David Sarasohn, *The Party of Reform* (Jackson: University of Mississippi Press, 1989).

2. Samual P. Hays, *Conservation and the Doctrine of Efficiency* (New York: Atheneum, 1969); James H. Young, *Pure Food* (Princeton: Princeton University Press, 1989).

3. Stephen Skowronek, *Building a New American State* (New York: Cambridge University Press, 1982).

4. Joel Silbey, *The American Political Nation, 1838–1893* (Stanford: Stanford University Press, 1991), 225–26.

Chapter Six

1. Solon J. Buck, *The Granger Movement* (Cambridge: Harvard University Press, 1913), 205. However, Buck noted the decline of the Grangers by the 1880s and, ignoring other agrarian sentiment for regulation, also gave credit to manufacturing and commercial interests for the 1887 Interstate Commerce Act (230).

2. Gerald D. Nash, "Origins of the Interstate Commerce Act of 1887," *Pennsylvania History* 24 (1957): 181–90.

3. Lee Benson, *Merchants, Farmers, and Railroads: Railroad Regulation and New York Politics* (Cambridge: Harvard University Press, 1955). Among Benson's more notable, and dubious, claims is that far in advance of their country cousins, New York and other northeastern big-city merchants became aware of the need to publicly control railroad practices and thenceforth "supplied the basic thinking" on the subject and persuaded agrarians to go along. Benson characteristically describes a meeting of New York merchant-reformers in a Manhattan restaurant in 1881 as "the first major counterattack against corporate power after the Civil War" (quotation at 150; see also 207, 227–30). Among the most obvious alternatives are the postwar labor uprisings (e.g., 1877) and the Granger and antimonopoly movements of the same decade.

4. George H. Miller, *Railroads and the Granger Laws* (Madison: University of Wisconsin Press, 1971). Miller did not distinguish between the home addresses of followers and leaders in legislative struggles (for example, an individual regulation advocate might come from Milwaukee—as it happened—but his ideas might, as Miller himself describes it, be supported by rural areas and opposed by Milwaukee business interests). It is unclear why, in an era of universal manhood suffrage and high voter turnout, legislators would be more deferential to a small number of merchants than to a very large number of aroused farmers. Gerald Berk agrees with Miller that merchants led the way to state regulation in the upper Midwest, though he acknowledges, "Not until the meteoric rise of the Grange . . . were merchants able to secure rules against rate discrimination." Gerald Berk, *Alternative Tracks* (Baltimore: Johns Hopkins University Press, 1994), 78. Farmers, in his view, turned the tide when they "united behind the merchants' demands."

5. Gabriel Kolko, *Railroads and Regulation, 1877–1916* (New York: W. W. Norton, 1965). The business-dominance interpretation has been readily accepted by both Marxists and economists of a libertarian

bent. Paul W. MacAvoy offers some support for Kolko's argument in the period before 1900 by showing that trunk-line railroads did achieve a beneficial stability of rates during the few years (1887–93) before the Supreme Court emasculated the 1887 act. Paul W. MacAvoy, *The Economic Effects of Regulation* (Boston: MIT Press, 1965). However, the connection between regulation and long-haul rate increases has been disputed by others. For a review, see Barry Weingast and Thomas G. Marshall. "Regulation and the Theory of Legislative Choice: The Interstate Commerce Act of 1887," *Journal of Law and Economics* 32 (April 1989): 38–39.

6. Albro Martin, *Enterprise Denied* (New York: Columbia University Press, 1971); see also Albro Martin, "The Troubled History of the Railroad Regulation in the Gilded Age," *Journal of American History* 61 (September 1974): 338–71, in which he explicitly refutes Kolko's interpretation.

7. Ari Hoogenboom and Olive Hoogenboom, *A History of the ICC* (New York: W. W. Norton, 1976), 12–17, 159–89.

8. Stephen Skowronek, *Building a New American State* (New York: Cambridge University Press, 1982), 31.

9. Martin J. Sklar, *The Corporate Reconstruction of American Capitalism, 1890–1916* (New York: Cambridge University Press, 1988).

10. Berk, *Alternative Tracks,* esp. 177–81. Berk's contention that a regionally decentralized, bureaucratically supervised railroad system was a realistic alternative in the late nineteenth century is not well supported (relying on a very small set of business, congressional, and bureaucratic advocates), but he offers a fascinating account of the critical assistance lent by the federal courts, as receivers of bankrupt railroads, to the construction of giant national railroad systems (chap. 3). For Berk, this is a victory of "ideology," with no specified grounding in class or institutional interests.

11. Lewis Henry Haney, *A Congressional History of Railways in the United States, 1850–1887,* bulletin #342 (Madison: University of Wisconsin, 1910), 157–58, 212, 230, 281–82.

12. Ben H. Proctor, *Not without Honor: The Life of John H. Reagan* (Austin: University of Texas Press, 1962), 132–37. Reagan coerced the railroads into compliance with his rate and service recommendations by threatening to deny them mail contracts.

13. Haney, *Congressional History of Railways,* 200–212.

14. Martin, *Enterprise Denied,* 33–34. Parcel post service, a 1912 victory for congressional progressives, was, in Martin's account, a substantial burden for the railroads and a financial disaster for the express companies that had handled business deliveries.

15. Haney, *Congressional History of Railways,* 212.

16. Ibid., 260–68.

17. U.S. Senate, Committee on Commerce, *National Transportation Policy,* 87th Cong., 1st sess., 1961, S. Rept. 445, 231–32; Julius Grodinsky, *The Iowa Pool: A Study in Railroad Competition, 1870–1884* (Chicago: University of Chicago Press, 1950), 3–7; William Z. Ripley, *Railroads: Rates and Regulation* (New York: Longmans, Green and Co., 1913), 411–13, 431–32.

18. Grodinsky, *The Iowa Pool.* The original members of the Iowa Pool were the managers of the Northwestern, Burlington, and Rock Island Railroads.

19. Buck, *Granger Movement,* 123–94; I. L. Sharfman, *The Interstate Commerce Commission,* vol. 1 (New York: Commonwealth Fund, 1931), 14–19; Miller, *Railroads and the Granger Laws.*

20. *Munn v. Illinois,* 94 U.S. 113 (1877).

21. Buck, *Granger Movement;* Miller *Railroads and the Granger Laws.* On the corrupting power of railroads in midwestern state governments, see Thomas J. Bray, *Rebirth of Freedom* (Indianola, Iowa: Record and Tribune Press, 1957), and Harlan Hahn, *Urban-Rural Conflict: The Politics of Change* (Beverly Hills, Calif.: Sage, 1971).

22. Haney, *Congressional History of Railways,* 283–85; Buck, *Granger Movement,* 222–26. An explanation of the McCrary bill, as well as the roll-call vote, can be found in the *Congressional Record* (*CR*), 43d Cong., 1st sess. (hereafter cited in the form 43–1), 2424, 2493. Representatives from Indiana, Illinois, and Iowa were the bill's principal backers in floor debate (2230–493).

23. The north-central states voted 65–25 for the bill. The southern vote was 30–41; New England

and the North Atlantic region voted 22–47. The Far West voted 4–2. Hannah Grace Roach, "Sectionalism in Congress (1870 to 1890)," *American Political Science Review* 19 (August 1925): 514 (table).

24. Terry L. Seip, *The South Returns to Congress* (Baton Rouge: Louisiana State University Press, 1983), 236–37. Northern Republicans, Seip reports, shortsightedly refused their southern copartisans an adequate share of developmental appropriations (thus hastening their replacement by Democrats) (233, 259–67).

25. C. Vann Woodward, *Origins of the New South* (Baton Rouge: Louisiana State University Press, 1951), 120–21.

26. William H. Joubert, *Southern Freight Rates in Transition* (Gainesville: University of Florida Press, 1949), 18–63; John F. Stover, *The Railroads of the South: A Study in Finance and Control* (Chapel Hill: University of North Carolina Press, 1955), 150–52, 233–36. The SRSA had twenty-seven member corporations by 1877. In Joubert's words: "The Southern Railway and Steamship Association had the power of life and death over individual communities, and it exercised that power. Instead of adopting a policy of aiding farmers and small communities by grading local rates into large centers so that they were reasonable, as was true in Official Territory [the Northeast and the Great Lakes], the association was interested in basing points and neglected the rural economy" (63).

27. On Senate corruption and conservative power structure in the years of industrial maturation and indirect elections, see J. Rogers Hollingsworth, *The Whirligig of Politics* (Chicago: University of Chicago Press, 1963); George H. Haynes, *The Elections of Senators* (New York: Henry Holt and Co., 1912), and *The Senate of the United States* (Boston: Houghton-Mifflin, 1938); and David Graham Phillips, *The Treason of the Senate* (Chicago: Quadrangle Books, 1964).

28. The New York Board of Trade, to which Benson's "merchant reformers" belonged, never endorsed the Reagan bill (which it considered far too radical), and the region's congressional representatives consistently opposed the bill. New York merchant agitation did lead to a state investigation in 1879, the outcome of which was the creation, in 1882, of the Board of Railroad Commissioners to collect information and exert a mild supervision over railroad affairs. The New York Board of Trade supported a similar kind of weak and discretionary commission regulation at the national level, and its legislative representative, Simon Sterne, is said to have helped draft the Cullom commission bill in 1886. Benson, *Merchants, Farmers, and Railroads*, 115–32, 204–22, 230–31, 246. Ignoring or misunderstanding regional political economy, Benson writes that it is unclear why Reagan carried on his ten-year battle for regulation; as for midwestern farmers, Benson asserts that the Reagan bill was not really in their interest, and he attributes their support (like Reagan's) to the persuasiveness of the New York merchants (214–16, 227–28).

29. Nash, "Origins of the Interstate Commerce Act of 1887," 182–86; Proctor, *Not without Honor*, 224–26; Haney, *Congressional History of Railways*, 286–88; Ida M. Tarbell, *The Nationalizing of Business, 1878–1898* (New York: Macmillan, 1936), 75–79.

30. Proctor, *Not without Honor*, 224–27; Ripley, *Railroads*, 446–47; Joubert, *Southern Freight Rates in Transition*, 31–48; Grodinsky, *The Iowa Pool*, 87, 110–12. Kolko states that all but the Southern Railway and Steamship Association "rapidly failed," without explaining his criteria for failure. It is true that the pools were frequently restructured after rate violations by member roads, but Kolko's assessment of their success in controlling competition while they were in operation appears overly negative. For example, his description of the weakness of the Iowa Pool gives a picture very different from that presented in the account by Grodinsky, Kolko's only cited source on the pool. Kolko, *Railroads and Regulation*, 8 (cf. Grodinsky, *The Iowa Pool*, 87–112). Kolko's argument, to which all such citations are bent, is that the railroads could not govern themselves and restrict competition without the help of national government; hence they desired federal regulation.

31. MacAvoy, *Economic Effects of Regulation*, 25–109.

32. Ripley, *Railroads*, 239–52, 391–92, 396; Joubert, *Southern Freight Rates in Transition*, 117–21. In 1882, for example, first-class freight rates into Columbia, South Carolina, were $.99 per hundredweight from New York and Philadelphia, as opposed to $1.85 from Chicago, $1.70 from St. Louis, and $1.35 from Cincinnati (Joubert, 77). For an eloquent statement of the midwestern interest in long/short-haul differentials, see the remarks of Sen. John Sherman of Ohio in *CR*, 49–1, 4405–6.

33. The 1878 Reagan bill is printed as an appendix in Haney, *Congressional History of Railways*, 293–99.

34. *CR*, 45–3, 101–2. Minnesota's vote was unanimous. In Iowa, representatives from the river towns of Burlington, Davenport, Iowa City, and Council Bluffs were among the yeas (supporting the thesis of Miller, *Railroads and the Granger Laws*); but the Chicago and northern Illinois areas that were said to have produced strong regulation backers in the early seventies were now solidly opposed, as was the Milwaukee district. Only the congressmen from Oshkosh and Wisconsin's far northern periphery backed the Reagan bill in that state. In Illinois, the ten representatives whose town residence had only one railroad voted 6–3 for the bill; the nine whose home base had two or more railroads voted against the bill by a 2-to-1 margin (using the *Congressional Directory* and a contemporary atlas for town and railroad location). Both parties were split. Although Indiana, Ohio, Michigan, Minnesota, and Iowa strongly supported the Reagan bill, many doubts were expressed in the Midwest about disturbing the region's favorable east-west long-haul rates.

35. *CR*, 45–3, 101–2. Within the Democratic Party, two-thirds of southern and western Democrats were opposed by a large majority of the northeastern wing. Carl V. Harris, "Right Fork or Left Fork: The Section-Party Alignment of Southern Democrats in Congress, 1873–1897," *Journal of Southern History* 42 (November 1976): 493.

36. *New York Times*, December 12, 1878, 1.

37. The Adams bill is printed in U.S. House, 47th Cong., 1st sess., 1882, H. Misc. Doc. 55.

38. The passage from Adams's book is quoted by Reagan in ibid., 249.

39. H. Misc. Doc. 55, 154. Fink's testimony was reprinted in *CR*, 48–2, 1084.

40. See, for example, Fink's views in H. Misc. Doc. 55, 187–89. Such positions are interpreted by Kolko as demonstrating that Fink "wanted the *object* of the Reagan bill [fair and reasonable rates] . . . carried out." Kolko, *Railroads and Regulation*, 27. See also Blanchard's testimony in U.S. Senate, *Report of the Senate Select Committee on Interstate Commerce*, 49th Cong., 1st sess., 1886, vol. 2, 162–66 (hereafter cited as Cullom Committee Report). Both railroad spokesmen and sympathetic northeastern intellectuals often favorably cited aspects of the government-railroad relationship in Great Britain, where construction of railroads in competition with existing lines was strictly controlled and railroads could set rates jointly under commission supervision. See, for example, Fink's testimony in Cullom Committee Report, vol. 2, 90, and the report of Simon Sterne, counsel to the New York Board of Trade, printed in U.S. Senate, 49th Cong., 2d sess., 1887, S. Misc. Doc. 66.

41. Good legislative histories of the Interstate Commerce Act can be found in Robert E. Cushman, *The Independent Regulatory Commissions* (New York: Octagon Books, 1972), 39–65; Skowronek, *Building a New American State*, 121–50; and Haney, *Congressional History of Railways*, 288–92.

42. H. Misc. Doc. 55, 236.

43. *CR*, 48–2, 25–29.

44. Ibid., 31.

45. Ibid., 41–42, 97, 116, 120–33 (remarks of Representatives Seymour of Connecticut, Long and Rice of Massachusetts, Davis of Illinois, and Horr of Michigan).

46. Ibid., 87, 295.

47. Ibid., 554–55. The final bill also contained a provision limiting passenger fares to three cents per mile. Opponents of the Reagan bill proposed another amendment to desegregate passenger coaches, but it did not survive.

48. James W. Neilson, *Shelby M. Cullom, Prairie State Republican* (Urbana: University of Illinois Press, 1962), v–vi, 29–87; Shelby M. Cullom, *Fifty Years of Public Service* (Chicago: A. C. McClurg and Co., 1911), 305–10.

49. Neilson, *Shelby M. Cullom*, 90–91; *CR*, 48–2, 1253–54. Only one Republican—Van Wyck of Nebraska—joined the disgruntled Democrats (who hoped for a stronger law) in opposition.

50. Cullom, *Fifty Years of Public Service*, 318.

51. "Cullom Committee Report," vol. 1, 208–15. Fink's testimony in favor of an investigatory, information-gathering, and mediating commission is found at vol. 2, 123. For other railroad testimony in favor

of such a commission, see that by Blanchard of the Erie and Ackerman of the Illinois Central, vol. 2, 162–66, 598.

52. The "unanimity" was also exaggerated. Though Cullom had stacked the testimony toward his own preference for a commission, the agrarian view was expressed in testimony to the committee by J. J. Woodman, head of the National Grange, who advocated specific prohibitions and statutory maximum rates, with enforcement through the courts. "The people," claimed Woodman, "want no board of railroad commissioners. They want just and wholesome laws, with well defined provisions for enforcing them." "Cullom Committee Report," vol. 1, appendix, 108–9.

53. *CR*, 49–1, 7280–84. The Reagan bill (H.R. 6657) is printed in U.S. Congress, House, *House Bills,* 49–1 (microfilm).

54. See Cullom's explanation of his bill in *CR*, 49–1, 3471–74. The bill (S. 5312) is printed in U.S. Congress, Senate, *Senate Bills,* 49–1 (microfilm). House and Senate bills as passed are printed in Edward McPherson, *A Hand-book of Politics for 1886* (Washington, D.C.: James J. Chapman, 1886), 138–45.

55. *CR*, 49–1, 4423. Included among the four voting opponents were two octogenarians (Morgan of Alabama and Ransom of North Carolina), who still doubted Congress' power to regulate railroads. Senator Morgan proposed a Cullom bill amendment, inspired by his disapproval of the recent railroad strikes, that would have punished "conspiracies" to impede the movement of interstate trains. The antilabor amendment was tabled on a decisive 49–3 vote. Ibid., 4240, 4357.

56. Ibid., 7752, 7755–56.

57. The Cleveland, Cincinnati, Columbus, Detroit, Omaha, and Indianapolis trade areas went 27–7 for the Reagan substitute, and the St. Louis trade area backed it 13–2. However, the major rail junctures of the Midwest—the Chicago, Milwaukee, and Kansas City trade areas—preferred the Cullom bill 14–10. In the South, Reagan's fortress, only a handful of votes could be found against his substitute bill. Using conventional geographic boundaries, the House party/regional breakdown was as follows: (GOP) Northeast, 1 yea–51 nay; South, 2–3; Midwest, 11–26; West, 0–6; (Dem.) Northeast 10–14; South 70–2; Midwest, 40–2; West 0–0. For an argument that is different from but not orthogonal to mine, stressing the role of party electoral competition on ICA votes, see Scott James, "A Party System Perspective on the Interstate Commerce Act of 1887," *Studies in American Political Development* 6 (spring 1992): 163–200; my response follows on pp. 201–5.

58. Nash, "Origins of the Interstate Commerce Act of 1887," 188; Tarbell, *Nationalizing of Business,* 76.

59. *Wabash, St. Louis & Pacific Ry. Co. v. Illinois,* 118 U.S. 557 (1886).

60. On the Supreme Court's recognition of the national character of business enterprise and its turn to judicial activism in service of a laissez-faire ideology, see Charles McCurdy, "Justice Field and the Jurisprudence of Government-Business Relations: Some Parameters of Laissez-Faire Constitutionalism," *Journal of American History* 61 (1975): 970–1005; Robert C. McClosky, *The American Supreme Court* (Chicago: University of Chicago Press, 1960), 118–35, and *American Conservatism in the Age of Enterprise* (Cambridge: Harvard University Press, 1951), 72–103; and the muckraking Progressive Era account of Gustavus Myers, *History of the Supreme Court of the United States* (Chicago: Charles H. Kerr and Co., 1912). Myers makes much of the fact that the late-nineteenth-century court weighed heavy with former railroad lawyers and protegés (like Field) of rail magnates (see 517, 499–502, 531, 557–61, 582–84). McCurdy emphasizes the forces of capitalist development that brought the court to recognize that not only railroads but a growing number of other businesses were truly national in scope—hence leading the Court to lose its tolerance for decentralizing restrictions on business freedom. The Court's awareness of the nationalization of markets grew, McCurdy contends, from the impressive arguments of the talented lawyers hired by the nation's leading corporations to challenge the barriers thrown up against them by state law.

61. It is clearly inaccurate to say, as Neilson does (*Shelby M. Cullom,* 113), that "Reagan gave way on everything but pooling." Certainly Cullom deserves credit for the innovation represented by the first federal regulatory commission, but Cullom's own bill had moved substantially in Reagan's direction since its first introduction, and as Schwartz and other careful legislative historians have concluded, what the conference did was to adopt "most of the substantive provisions of the Reagan bill and the administrative machinery of the Cullom bill." Bernard Schwartz, ed., *The Economic Regulation of Business and Industry,*

vol. 1 (New York: Chelsea House, 1973), 309. On the pros and cons of the compromise for shippers and railroads, see Weingast and Marshall, "Regulation and the Theory of Legislative Choice," 46–53.

62. In 1907, the Supreme Court would foreclose the judicial option altogether. The Court argued in *Texas and Pacific Railroad Co. v. Abilene Cotton Co.*, 204 U.S. 426 (1907), that the commission had been endowed "with plenary administrative power . . . to hear complaints concerning violations of the act" and that it would not be consonant with the purpose of the law to allow an individual shipper to secure for himself through suit a rate different from that in force for others.

63. On railroad opposition to the conference bill, see Hoogenboom and Hoogenboom, *History of the ICC*, 12–15.

64. *Commercial and Financial Chronicle*, September 4, 1886, 257. The significance of railroad investments for the nation's leading banking houses is clear in the pages of the *Chronicle*. Bankers had fostered the dramatic growth of railroads in the 1870s and 1880s and were, by 1886, heavily involved in reorganization plans to recoup losses from the mid-1880s recession and overbuilding generally—foretelling the undisputed banker dominance of the industry following the more severe economic crisis of the 1890s. Dolores Greenberg, *Financiers and Railroads, 1869–1889* (Newark, N.J.: University of Delaware Press, 1980), 137–218.

65. *Commercial and Financial Chronicle*, November 27, 1886, 618.

66. Ibid., December 18, 1886, 762, 731. After this hope was dashed, the paper hoped for a presidential veto (January 22, 1887, 100).

67. Ibid., January 29, 1887, 134. Somewhat mollified by Cleveland's appointments to the ICC in the following months, the *Chronicle* nevertheless feared the "very limited" discretionary powers lodged in the commission. In April, its attitude turned nearly hysterical again. If the act were enforced, it would "throw about one fourth of our railroad mileage into bankruptcy," benefit half, and leave the other quarter to "just scrub along" (April 9, 1887, 448). The *Chronicle* noted Cullom's attempt, during Senate debate on the conference bill, to reassure investors, but it had no confidence that the courts would follow his interpretation of the act's provisions, particularly the long/short-haul clause. Senator George of Mississippi and others who had long supported a strict long/short-haul provision had emphatically rejected Cullom's interpretation of the broad grounds for exception. "Senator George, too, represents the opinion of a large class of the advocates of the measure," the *Chronicle* warned, and a court in search of legislative intent might well follow his reasoning rather than Cullom's (January 15, 1887, 72).

68. On the penultimate Senate vote, 25 had attempted to recommit the bill, against 36 supporters. Neither of California's senators (one of whom was Leland Stanford) voted for the bill, but Oregon's two senators joined the South, Midwest, and Colorado in support. *CR*, 49–2, 664, 666, 881. Party designations are listed in Edward McPherson, *A Hand-book of Politics for 1888* (Washington, D.C.: James J. Chapman, 1888), 12–13.

69. Skowronek, *Building a New American State*, 141–42.

70. See, for example, the views expressed by Sen. John Sherman of Ohio in *CR*, 49–1, 4404.

71. Skowronek, *Building a New American State*, 150–54. In May 1887, the *Commercial and Financial Chronicle* noted, "Trade is gradually adjusting itself to the changes required by the Inter-State Commerce law." By November, the journal was expressing considerable relief at the commission's early interpretations of its mandate (May 21, 1887, 667, and November 19, 660).

72. Ripley reports that after five years of operation, the ICC received only thirty-nine formal complaints in 1892. *Railroads*, 457.

73. Ibid., 456–57. For good summaries of the commission's modus operandi under Cooley (1887–91), see Hoogenboom and Hoogenboom, *History of the ICC*, 25–32, and Skowronek, *Building a New American State*, 150–56.

74. Ripley, *Railroads*, 458–59; Frank Parsons, *The Heart of the Railroad Problem* (Boston: Little, Brown, 1906), 2–18, 43–54. It likewise took years of litigation to establish the ICC's power to subpoena written evidence. Sharfman, *Interstate Commerce Commission* 1:24.

75. Sharfman, *Interstate Commerce Commission* 1:24–25; Ripley, *Railroads*, 461–62.

76. *Chicago, Milwaukee, and St. Paul Ry. Co. v. Minnesota*, 134 U.S. 418 (1890); *Regan v. Farmers Loan and Trust Co.*, 154 U.S. 362 (1894).

77. *Interstate Commerce Commission v. Cincinnati, N.O. & Texas Pacific Ry. Co.*, 167 U.S. 479 (1897).

78. Hoogenboom and Hoogenboom, *History of the ICC*, 21–23; Sharfman, *Interstate Commerce Commission* 1:28–29; Henry J. Friendly, *The Federal Administrative Agencies* (Cambridge: Harvard University Press, 1962), 27–32.

79. *Interstate Commerce Commission v. Alabama Midland Ry. Co.*, 168 U.S. 144 (1897). The impact of the decision is discussed by Sharfman, *Interstate Commerce Commission* 1:30–32, and Ripley, *Railroads*, 474–84.

80. After the ICA's prohibition on the pooling of traffic or revenues, pools were reorganized into "traffic associations" in which member roads again attempted to fix rates, without the benefit of pooling. In 1897, going against the grain of its other antitrust and railroad regulation dicta, the Supreme Court found traffic association rate-fixing to be a violation of the 1890 Sherman Antitrust Act. *U.S. v. Trans-Missouri Freight Assn.*, 166 U.S. 290 (1897). This decision is generally held to have been an incentive to consolidation of railroad ownership, since collusion among independent roads was now outlawed. Sharfman, *Interstate Commerce Commission* 1:34.

81. See the complaints (about the interrelationship of railroads with other monopolies exploiting the farmer) made by spokesmen for the National Grain Growers Alliance and the National Farmers' Alliance and Industrial Union, in Civic Federation of Chicago, *Chicago Conference on Trusts* (Chicago: Civic Federation of Chicago, 1900), 202–18. The tendency of the railroads, especially after 1900, to build up a few favored enterprises at the expense of the others is described, with examples, in Ripley, *Railroads*, 185–92.

82. Sharfman, *Interstate Commerce Commission* 1:34–35; Harold V. Faulkner, *The Decline of Laissez Faire, 1897–1917* (New York: Rinehart and Co., 1951), 187–202; Emory R. Johnson, *American Railway Transportation*, 2d ed. (New York: D. Appleton and Co., 1908), 52–66, 250–56; Martin, *Enterprise Denied*, 17–21. For a graphic and statistical tabulation of railroad consolidation as of 1910, see the material inserted in *CR*, 61–2, 6886–87, by Senator La Follette.

83. One of the organizers of the Central Pacific and Southern Pacific Railroads spoke of "two or three—and one would be better—great carrying companies." Quoted in W. N. Leonard, "The Decline of Railroad Consolidation," *Journal of Economic History* 9 (May 1949): 3. Edward H. Harriman told the ICC in 1906 that he personally would buy up railroads coast to coast if the law permitted. Quoted in Ripley, *Railroads*, 491, who asks, "Was there ever a clearer case of megalomania?"

84. U.S. House, *Eleventh Annual Report of the Interstate Commerce Commission*, 55th Cong., 2d sess., 1897, H. Doc. 157, 18–19.

85. Hoogenboom and Hoogenboom, *History of the ICC*, 44–45; *Eighteenth Annual Report of the Interstate Commerce Commission* (Washington, D.C.: GPO, 1904), 8. The 1903 Elkins bill passed the Senate unanimously and drew only six opposing votes in the House. While sharply increasing fines, the amendments abolished the penalty of imprisonment, on the theory that witnesses would be less reluctant to testify in its absence. Ripley, *Railroads*, 493.

86. U.S. House, Committee on Interstate and Foreign Commerce, *Hearings before the Committee on Interstate and Foreign Commerce on Bills to Amend the Interstate Commerce Act*, 58th Cong., 3d sess., 1905, H. Doc. 422; U.S. Senate, Committee on Interstate Commerce, *Hearings before the Committee on Interstate Commerce on Bills to Amend the Interstate Commerce Act*, 59th Cong., 1st sess., 1906, S. Doc 243, 5 vols. A good summary of the grievances against railroads is Frank Parsons, *The Heart of the Railroad Problem* (Boston: Little, Brown, 1906).

87. Skowronek, *Building a New American State*, 254. Roosevelt's annual message to Congress in 1905 stressed the need for "temperate and cautious action" aimed at developing an "orderly system" and his emphatic opposition to any "improperly radical or hasty action" in dealing with the railroads. Quoted in John M. Blum, "Theodore Roosevelt and the Hepburn Act: Towards an Orderly System of Control," appendix II in *The Letters of Theodore Roosevelt*, vol. 2, ed. Elting E. Morison (Cambridge: Harvard University Press, 1952), 1558.

88. George E. Mowry, *The Era of Theodore Roosevelt* (New York: Harper and Row, 1958), 59–84; Woodward, *Origins of the New South*, 292–469; Hahn, *Urban-Rural Conflict*, 47–56; Dewey W. Grantham, *Southern Progressivism* (Knoxville: University of Tennessee Press, 1983), 111, 147–55.

89. Richard H. K. Vietor, "Businessmen and the Political Economy: The Railroad Rate Controversy of 1905," *Journal of American History* 64 (June 1977): 47–66. Analyzing the five volumes of testimony in Senate hearings, Vietor reports that (among those whose firm size could be determined) 93 percent of large shippers opposed regulatory expansion, compared with 40 percent of small shippers (52). Southern fruit, lumber, and livestock producers were prominent among supporters (56–57). Of the twenty-one major railroads represented, all but one were "forthrightly opposed" to expansion of ICC powers (50). In this position, railroad management and labor were in agreement. In late 1905, five railway unions sent a delegation to President Roosevelt to express their opposition to a strong rate-control bill, fearing that downward pressure on wages would result. *New York Times,* November 15, 1905, 5, 10.

90. The 1905 Townsend-Esch bill, unlike the later Roosevelt-backed Hepburn bill, provided that the new ICC-set maximum rate would go into effect immediately (in thirty days). House Democrats were delighted that the Republicans were suddenly willing to consider such a bill. However, they strongly objected to a Townsend bill provision that provided for a special "transportation court" to hear ICC appeals, predicting that it would produce interminable delays. The Democratic substitute, a stronger measure without such a court, was defeated on a partisan 151–187 vote; the bill (H.R. 18588) then passed, with four supporters of the Democratic substitute joining thirteen conservative Republicans in opposition. *CR,* 58–3, 2064–206. The bill expired in the Senate Commerce Committee.

91. Frank H. Dixon, "The Interstate Commerce Act as Amended," *Quarterly Journal of Economics* 21 (November 1906): 22–23; Ripley, *Railroads,* 496–98. In *Railroads and Regulation* (127–31), Kolko argues that this railroad opposition—which he discounts—was to the Townsend-Esch bill and not to the Hepburn bill considered in the next Congress, but the former was less threatening, since it contained a commerce court and no restriction on court review. Both Vietor and Martin have effectively refuted Kolko's revisionist claim that shippers were apathetic and railroads favorable to expanded ICC rate powers in 1905–6. See Martin, *Enterprise Denied,* 111–14, and Vietor, "Businessmen and the Political Economy."

92. Hoogenboom and Hoogenboom, *History of the ICC,* 50–51; Ann Firor Scott, "A Progressive Wind from the South, 1906–1913," *Journal of Southern History* 29 (February 1963): 56.

93. Blum, "Theodore Roosevelt and the Hepburn Act," 1561–1562.

94. Ibid., 1564–67; Mowry, *Era of Theodore Roosevelt,* 203–5; Sam H. Acheson, *Joe Bailey, the Last Democrat* (New York: Macmillan, 1932), 189–210. Nathanial W. Stephenson, *Nelson W. Aldrich* (New York: Charles Scribner's, 1930), 293–317. William E. Chandler of New Hampshire, an advocate of railroad regulation who had been defeated for reelection by the Republican-railroad machine in his state, was a mutual friend of Roosevelt's and Tillman's and served as go-between during negotiations over the bill. On his role, see Leon Burr Richardson, *William E. Chandler* (New York: Dodd, Mead and Co., 1940), 654–74.

95. The best accounts of the byzantine politics surrounding the construction of the Hepburn bill court review sections can be found in newspapers and in Richardson's biography of Chandler. Mowry inexplicably describes Bailey's position as one of "broad review" (*Era of Theodore Roosevelt,* 204), and both he and Blum ("Theodore Roosevelt and the Hepburn Act,") ascribe the failure of the compromise amendment to the Democrats. It seems clear, however, from newspaper accounts, *Congressional Record* debates, and floor votes, that Bailey and Tillman were the prime spokesmen for narrow review and that the periphery Democrats provided most of their troops. According to the *Atlanta Constitution,* about twenty-four Democrats (all but seven) were counted as supporters of Bailey's narrow-review amendment (April 17, 1906, 1, and April 19, 1906, 1). Tillman and Bailey hoped to deliver as many as twenty-six Democratic votes for narrow review and to add—with Roosevelt's support—about twenty Republicans to the Democratic contingent. This would permit passage of at least the legal-procedural restriction; then they would try for the anti-injunction limitation as well. In view of Roosevelt's opposition, however, only three Republicans were willing to join the Democrats (only twenty of whom materialized for the futile vote). The vote on the amendment, which lost 23–54, is reported in *CR,* 59–1, 6672. By region, only one core senator (Hale of Maine) and two diverse-area senators joined twenty periphery supporters of the amendment. A second Democratic amendment restricting judicial review but leaving the injunction power

failed 24–55 (ibid., 6695–96). See also the *New York Times* reports in 1906: April 7, 1; April 17, 1; April 18, 2; April 21, 13; April 24, 8; May 4, 1; and May 5, 1.

96. Ripley, *Railroads,* 506.

97. The final Senate vote on the Hepburn bill was 71–3.

98. Jerome M. Clubb, "Congressional Opponents of Reform, 1901–1913" (Ph.D. diss., University of Washington, 1963), 50–51.

99. The power of the circuit courts to set aside ICC orders pending appeal was somewhat hedged by the dissidents' insistence that the ICC have five days' notice of such suspensions and that a prior hearing take place before three federal judges rather than one.

100. Ripley, *Railroads,* 520–24.

101. *Interstate Commerce Commission v. Illinois Central Railroad Co.,* 215 U.S. 452 (1910). The case and its significance are discussed in Ripley, *Railroads,* 538–42.

102. Skowronek, *Building a New American State,* 260. One might say that in this instance it appears that the Court's institutional interest and that of the capital and regional interests with which it had previously sided came into conflict—and the institutional interest, which required some deference to the regulatory preferences of the legislative majority, won out.

103. George E. Mowry, *Theodore Roosevelt and the Progressive Movement* (New York: Hill and Wang, 1946), 94–97; Kenneth Hechler, *Insurgency* (New York: Columbia University Press, 1940), 164–65.

104. The Senate majority report on the administration bill (S. 6737) is printed in *CR,* 61–2, 2817–21, followed by two minority reports (one by Senators Cummins and Clapp and the other by Democratic Senator Newlands) at ibid., 2821–29.

105. Martin, *Enterprise Denied,* 184–85. For the reformers' perspective, see the speech by La Follette in *CR,* 61–2, 6899–908.

106. *CR,* 61–2, 5745–47. The vote was not recorded.

107. Ibid., 5840. The southern region had pioneered telephone company regulation early in the Progressive Era, followed by the West; though southern state regulation was less radical than municipal regulation in the region, the South and periphery states generally were more likely to exercise regulation that included rate control, as contrasted with weaker forms elsewhere. Twelve out of fifteen states with statewide rate regulation in 1910 were in the periphery, eight of them in the South. See Jeffrey E. Cohen, "The Telephone Problem and the Road to Telephone Regulation in the U.S., 1876–1917," *Journal of Policy History* 3 (1991): 57–63.

108. *CR,* 61–2, 5863, 5887–94. The vote on Adamson's motion was by division.

109. Ibid., 5901–6, 6956–72. Broad and diverse opposition to the stock-issue provisions caused the Senate committee to delete them. However, Senator Dolliver's proposal to reinstate federal control occasioned the Senate debate. Hughes of Colorado, for example, assailed the proposals both on grounds of constitutionality and destruction of vital state regulatory functions and because they would help to consolidate control by "few great systems of lines" and have "blighting effects" on "that portion of the country not yet adequately supplied with railroads." Ibid., 6970. Three Democrats, citing a platform pledge to address the issue of watered stock, voted with sixteen mostly progressive Republicans for the Dolliver amendment.

110. The bill passed the House 201–126, with the Republicans unanimously in favor. Ibid., 6031–33.

111. Hechler, *Insurgency,* 163–74.

112. For a summary of major Senate amendments, see *CR,* 61–2, 7273–84. A provision was also added to protect water carriers from destructive railroad competition. It specified that rates lowered to meet water competition could not be raised again unless, after a hearing, the railroad could convince the ICC that the proposed increase was necessitated by changed conditions.

113. In all, twenty-three roll calls on the Mann-Elkins Act were analyzed. The patterns present in tables 6.1–6.5 are typical of the sectional and party support patterns found in the larger analysis.

114. See, for example, Hechler, *Insurgency,* 171–73, and *New York Times,* May 14, 1910, 2.

115. Clubb's analysis of "opponents of reform" on thirty-one Mann-Elkins votes found forty-four

Senate Republicans who voted 58 percent or more of the time against reform. In my sectional categories, twenty-four represented states in the core, thirteen in the periphery, and seven in diverse economic regions. Of the periphery "opponents of reform," seven were senators from Utah, Wyoming, Colorado, Idaho, and Montana; the rest were from midwestern or border states. The bulk of the reform troops was composed of twenty-four Democrats: fourteen southerners, seven from mountain, plains, and border states, and three from far-western diverse states. Calculated from Table 20 in Clubb, "Congressional Opponents of Reform," 152–55.

116. Nine out of twelve Republicans voting for Cummins's indefinite suspension amendment had also bolted their party to oppose the Payne-Aldrich Tariff on Senate passage in 1909.

117. *CR,* 61–2, 6956–65. Mowry, citing "a confidential source," implies that Aldrich won the support of an unnamed group of Democrats by pledging his support for statehood for Arizona and New Mexico. Mowry, *Theodore Roosevelt and the Progressive Movement,* 101–2; see also Mowry, *Era of Theodore Roosevelt,* 260, in which Mowry speaks of a deal by which the Democrats would help Aldrich "pass the measure against progressive opposition"—an odd claim in view of the fact that the Democrats opposed the bill on final passage and the progressive Republicans supported it. Claude Barfield also suggests that some sort of bargain was made that entailed Arizona and New Mexico statehood, omission of the sections on stocks and bonds, and addition of an amendment restricting the raising of rates lowered to meet water competition. Claude Barfield, "The Democratic Party in Congress, 1909–1913" (Ph.D. diss., Northwestern University, 1965), 175–84. This would have been a good bargain for the Democrats, since they opposed the stock sections anyway (for the reasons given above) and since admission of Arizona and New Mexico appeared to promise four more Democratic senators and votes for periphery positions.

118. Hoogenboom and Hoogenboom, *History of the ICC,* 60; Martin, *Enterprise Denied,* 186–89; *CR,* 61–2, 5845.

119. The Senate vote on the conference bill was 50–11. All eleven opponents were Democrats, but seven Democrats did vote for the bill, citing its strong positive aspects. The insurgent Republicans, who also had grave doubts about the court, closed ranks to carry the bill as a party measure. A number of conservative Republicans—Aldrich, Briggs, Bulkeley, Dillingham, Guggenheim, Kean, Lodge, Lorimer, Penrose, Root, and Warren—abstained on the conference vote, apparently finding the Commerce Court insufficient compensation for the bill's many "dangerous" provisions. *CR,* 61–2, 8391. There was no roll call on the House conference vote.

120. Ripley, *Railroads,* 581.

121. Sharfman, *Interstate Commerce Commission* 1:65.

122. See Hoogenboom and Hoogenboom, *History of the ICC,* 62–66, and Martin's disparaging account in *Enterprise Denied,* 194–230.

123. Martin, *Enterprise Denied,* 243–49, 263–97. K. Austin Kerr also notes support for the railroads by merchants and manufacturers in big cities, in contrast with the position of agricultural shippers. For urban shippers, especially in cities with large railroad terminals, it was vital to the commerce of the cities to maintain such facilities—for which the railroads' capital needs must be met. Thus the Massachusetts Board of Trade, the New York Merchants' Association, and the Milwaukee and Chicago Chambers of Commerce sided with the railroads on regulatory issues. K. Austin Kerr, *American Railroad Politics, 1914–1920* (Pittsburgh: University of Pittsburgh Press, 1968), 30–31.

124. *History of the ICC,* 66, 73–80; see also Martin, *Enterprise Denied,* 307–9, 331–49, 377–79; Frank Dixon, *Railroads and Government: Their Relations in the United States, 1910–1921* (New York: Scribner's, 1922), 103.

125. Arthur S. Link, *Wilson,* vol. 2, *The New Freedom* (Princeton: Princeton University Press, 1956), 449–50; *La Follette's Weekly,* April 18, 1914, 1; Kerr, *American Railroad Politics,* 26. Wilson's later appointments were far less objectionable to the reformers.

126. Antitrust prosecution dissolved the Northern Securities project and an attempt at merger by the Union Pacific and Southern Pacific. Jay Gould's rail empire collapsed in the Panic of 1907, and financial problems drove ninety-four railroads into receivership by mid-1916. By 1920, there was a widespread perception that the railroads suffered from too *little,* rather than the public from too much, consolidation.

But the form of consolidation now urged on the railroads by government—which entailed strong roads absorbing weak ones in order to maintain service—proved unpopular and largely unsuccessful. Leonard, "Decline of Railroad Consolidation."

127. *Speeches of William Jennings Bryan*, vol. 2 (New York: Funk and Wagnall, 1913), 92.

128. Quoted in Lawrence W. Levine, *Defender of the Faith, William Jennings Bryan: The Last Decade, 1915–1925* (New York: Oxford University Press, 1965), 150.

129. Dixon, *Railroads and Government*, 19–32; Hoogenboom and Hoogenboom, *History of the ICC*, 84–88; Sharfman, *Interstate Commerce Commission* 1:153–64; Skowronek, *Building a New American State*, 272–79.

130. Dixon, *Railroads and Government*, 182–89.

131. Wilson secured passage of the Federal Control Act through appeals to party loyalty and the exigencies of war. The act was in operation from March 21, 1918, until March 1, 1920. The first attempt to return to progressive-style regulation came with the passage, in the fall of 1919, of an amendment to restore ICC rate powers and prohibit intrastate increases. Opposed by the Railroad Administration, the railroads, financial interests, and organized labor, it was vetoed by President Wilson. Kerr, *American Railroad Politics*, 126–27.

132. H.R. 10453, text printed in Rogers MacVeagh, *The Transportation Act of 1920* (New York: Henry Holt and Co., 1923), 597–627; remarks of Rep. John Esch in *CR*, 66–1, 8309–17.

133. *CR*, 66–1, 8318–24, followed by an explanation of the Plumb Plan at 8325–28.

134. Ibid., 8328–34 (Barkely), 8337–40 (Sanders), 8382–83, 8402–3 (Huddleston), 8453–56 (Connally). On a contrary note, Representative Rayburn supported most sections of the committee bill and condemned the nationalization alternative (8375–76).

135. Ibid., 66–1, 8691–92. The Anderson labor amendment passed in Committee of the Whole and was sustained subsequently on a 254–111 roll call (8689–90). The Democratic vote was as follows: core, 40–3; diverse, 10–0; periphery, 76–41. The Republican vote was: core, 49–39; diverse, 36–15; periphery, 43–13. Thus, although periphery Democrats still furnished the largest bloc of supporters, their willingness to back the labor position in the sensitive transportation arena showed considerable slippage since 1916. Given the new rate-making rule in the Republican bill, sharp wage increases were likely to bring increased freight rates for farmers.

136. MacVeagh, *Transportation Act of 1920*, chart ("Proposed Plans for Railroad Legislation") and S. 3288, printed on 565–97. An amendment to strike the labor sections failed on a 25–46 vote that also revealed declining labor support among periphery Democrats (who split 16–11). Core Republicans voted 0–17; periphery Republicans voted 3–11. In all, five Republicans joined twenty Democrats in support of the amendment to strike. *CR*, 66–2, 811.

137. MacVeagh, *Transportation Act of 1920*, chart between pp. 8 and 9; Kerr, *American Railroad Politics*, 149–56. Most railroad executives strongly objected to mandatory consolidation and to the recapture and redistribution of "excess" earnings.

138. The Cummins bill passed the Senate 46–30. Twenty-three of the thirty opponents represented southern, plains, and mountain periphery states; two other opponents were from Oregon, one from Nevada, two from Wisconsin (including La Follette, who had backed nationalization), and two from New England. *CR*, 66–2, 952.

139. John J. Esch, an ICC commissioner himself in 1926, is so quoted in Sharfman, *Interstate Commerce Commission* 1:177.

140. Kerr, *American Railroad Politics*, 218–21; *CR*, 66–2, 3286, 3315–16.

141. Skowronek, *Building a New American State*, 283.

142. Regarding labor, the ICC had now become, in effect, a secondary guarantor of worker gains. For example, after the Railroad Labor Board granted wage increases worth $618 million in 1920, the commission increased passenger and freight rates from 20 to 40 percent. Hoogenboom and Hoogenboom, *History of the ICC*, 101. On the evolution of labor relations under the Interstate Commerce Act, from stabilization to overt protection of labor, see Karen Orren, *Belated Feudalism* (New York: Cambridge University Press, 1991), 182–204.

143. James Landis, *Report on the Regulatory Agencies to the President-Elect*, U.S. Senate, Committee on the Judiciary, 86th Cong., 2d sess., 1960.

144. Elizabeth Sanders, "The Regulatory Surge of the 1970's in Historical Perspective," in *Public Regulation*, ed. Elizabeth Bailey (Cambridge: MIT Press, 1986), 141–42. In 1995 the ICC was abolished, its few remaining functions transferred to the Department of Transportation. The granting, as railroad executives had long urged, of merger and other authority to a friendly executive agency set the stage for federal approval of a gigantic merger of the Union Pacific and Southern Pacific Railroads. With a virtual monopoly over a 37,000-mile, twenty-five-state network, the new behemoth soon confirmed the fears of the farmers and agricultural shippers who had protested the 1995 law and merger.

Chapter Seven

1. F. W. Taussig, *The Tariff History of the United States*, 8th ed. (New York: Capricorn Books, 1964), 8–115.

2. Howard K. Beale argues that the tariff was the central concern of Reconstruction policy. Radical Republicans were leading protectionists, "determined never to allow the South to re-enter the Union as long as New England tariff schemes might thereby be endangered." Howard K. Beale, "The Tariff and Reconstruction," in *The Economic Impact of the American Civil War*, ed. Ralph Andreano (Cambridge, Mass.: Schenkman Publishing Co., 1967), 128.

3. Taussig, *Tariff History of the United States*, 198–200; Beale, "The Tariff and Reconstruction," 132. Taussig is inclined throughout this work to view agricultural interests as instigators of protection (see, for example, 331–33), but it is clear from the record of congressional debate and votes, and from Taussig's own account of the wool bargain, that these tariff schemes were initiated by, and for the principal benefit of, manufacturing interests. It is true, however, that those agricultural representatives who were marginal members of the Republican coalition were often resigned to the success of the protection coalition and so attempted to get their own products included.

4. Wool production tripled between 1867 and 1900, with most of the increase in mountain and Pacific states. For a sample of western and Republican devotion to the wool tariff, see *Congressional Record* (*CR*), 53d Cong., 2d sess. (hereafter cited in the form 53–2), 7088, 7094.

5. The sugar tariff also attracted some Louisiana representatives to protection but was principally designed to benefit midwestern and western sugar-beet areas (Colorado, Michigan, Utah, Nebraska, California, Montana, Wyoming, and Idaho). Under a system of protective duties and bounties, sugar-beet production in the United States quintupled between 1899 and 1909. U.S. Department of Commerce, Bureau of the Census, *Statistical Abstract of the United States, 1930* (Washington, D.C.: GPO, 1930), 678, 711.

6. Richard F. Bensel, *Sectionalism and American Political Development* (Madison: University of Wisconsin Press, 1984), 62–73.

7. See, for an example of this argument, the remarks of Representative McCreary (D, Kentucky) in *CR*, 50–1, 3585. During the same debate, Representative McKinley introduced resolutions from "the representatives of at least a half million workingmen" in favor of the protective tariff. Ibid., 4406.

8. Taussig, *Tariff History of the United States*, chap. 7; U.S. Tariff Commission, *The Tariff and Its History* (Washington, D.C.: GPO, 1934), 73–74.

9. Marc Karson, *American Labor Unions and Politics, 1900–1918* (Boston: Beacon Press, 1958), 33.

10. Patrick F. Palermo, "Republicans in Revolt: The Sources of Insurgency" (Ph.D. diss., State University of New York, 1973), 232.

11. U.S. Department of Commerce, *Statistical Abstract* (1930) tables 547, 548 (1910–14 averages). Coal and copper were also important exports.

12. Further, as Rudolf Hilferding has argued, protection of domestic markets yielded extraordinary profits for large corporations, enhanced control of competition, and subsidized export penetration abroad. Rudolf Hilferding, *Finance Capital* (London: Routledge, 1981), 307–10.

13. For business divisions on the tariff issue in the Progressive Era and the 1920s, see Robert H. Wiebe, *Businessmen and Reform* (Chicago: Quadrangle Books, 1962), 90–97; Joan Hoff Wilson, *American Business and Foreign Policy, 1920–1933* (Boston: Beacon Press, 1971), 65–98; and Frank Burdick, "Woodrow Wilson and the Underwood Tariff," *Mid-America* 50 (October 1968): 277–84.

14. The sober voice of finance capital, the *Commercial and Financial Chronicle,* though sympathetic to cuts in tariffs on imported food and raw materials, found the industrial reductions in the 1913 Underwood Tariff "radical and drastic," "ruthless," and motivated by "political expediency . . . to placate farming interests." *Commercial and Financial Chronicle,* April 12, 1913, 1046.

15. Taussig, *Tariff History of the United States,* 363–65.

16. The votes on raw materials revealed the extensive localistic pressures generated by individual tariff schedules. Only 54 of 174 voting periphery representatives took a consistent free-trade position on lumber, barley, hides, and oil (the only schedules open to amendments). All were Democrats, 35 of whom came from the South. *CR,* 61–1, 1296, 1298–300. See also H. Parker Willis, "The Tariff of 1909: The Legislative History of the Act," *Journal of Political Economy* 18 (January 1910): 4–10. The 54 free-trade supporters, almost all of whom held seats in areas devoted to cotton, corn, or tobacco cultivation, composed the modest core of free traders in the House and set Democratic Party policy. Even though their prospects for forging a broad, tariff-cutting alliance with the corn- and wheat-belt Republicans to the north were dim (all the midwestern insurgents rallied to their party's standard on the final Payne Tariff vote in the House—see table 7.1), there *was* a range of tariff revisions on which southern and midwestern agrarians could ally.

17. Nathaniel W. Stephenson, *Nelson W. Aldrich* (New York: Charles Scribner's, 1930), 347.

18. Ibid., 345–60; Taussig, *Tariff History of the United States,* 373–76; Kenneth Hechler, *Insurgency* (New York: Columbia University Press, 1940), 99–104.

19. For a typical vote, see *CR,* 61–1, 4313.

20. *Pollack v. Farmers' Loan and Trust,* 157 U.S. 429 (1895); Sam H. Acheson, *Joe Bailey, the Last Democrat* (New York: Macmillan, 1932), 61–62, 262–70. The 1909 Democratic amendment provided for a 3 percent tax on individual and corporate incomes over $5,000 a year. Cummins's proposal started at 2 percent, increasing to 6 percent for incomes over $100,000. Hechler, *Insurgency,* 147.

21. Stephenson, *Nelson W. Aldrich,* 354.

22. Ibid., 353–56; Hechler, *Insurgency,* 146–48.

23. The income tax amendment was duly passed in 1909. Because of the circumstances, it drew no opposing votes in the Senate and only fourteen in the House. *CR,* 61–1, 4121, 4440. It was declared ratified by the states in February 1913.

24. Taussig, *Tariff History of the United States,* 382–408. Motions to lower the tariff on wool, iron and steel, and sugar drew over 60 percent of periphery votes but 0–4 percent in the core. *CR,* 61–1, 2442, 3881, 4313.

25. *CR,* 61–1, 4755, 4949; the final vote on House passage is on 1301.

26. Hechler, *Insurgency,* 178–86; *CR,* 62–1, 559, 3175. There were, in addition, attempts at selective tariff reductions by Democrats and insurgent Republicans in the 62nd Congress. These involved mainly tariffs on manufactured goods, with one of the largest majorities obtained for a "farmer's free list" of agricultural implements and supplies. All succumbed to Taft vetoes. See, for example, *CR,* 62–1, 1121, 2356, 3584, and Hechler, *Insurgency,* 186–93.

27. *CR,* 61–2, 1671–75, and 62–2, 9918.

28. U.S. Tariff Commission, *The Tariff and Its History,* 76–77. The Underwood bill substituted simple ad valorem duties for the complicated specific and compound duties of past laws. It abolished the extra discriminating duties of the Payne-Aldrich law and substituted a 5 percent rebate for goods carried in American ships, in lieu of the 10 percent additional penalty of the old law. (Even this provision was later dropped as a violation of commercial treaties.)

29. Arthur S. Link, *Wilson,* vol. 2, *The New Freedom* (Princeton: Princeton University Press, 1956), 194.

30. Ibid., 178–81; John Wells Davidson, "The Response of the South to Woodrow Wilson's New Freedom, 1912–1914" (Ph.D. diss., Yale University, 1954), 52, 121.

31. For Democratic caucus rules, see *CR,* 62–1, 3565, and James S. Fleming, "Reestablishing Leadership in the House of Representatives," *Mid-America* 54 (October 1972): 234–50.

32. Wilson deftly employed the traditional presidential persuasive strategies: frequent consultation and patronage. Link, *The New Freedom,* 153–54, 180–81.

33. U.S. Congress, *Congressional Directory,* 63d Cong., 1st sess. (Washington, D.C.: GPO, 1913), 140. Poindexter of Washington is included with the Republicans, though he called himself a Progressive in 1913. The final House and conference votes are in *CR,* 63–1, 1386–87 and 5274.

34. *CR,* 63–1, 3102–752, 4617. On amendment votes, protectionist sentiment in the diverse and peripheral regions was faint on manufactured goods—particularly those (such as automobiles) that hardly seemed to need protection but grew with the compound schedules combining western raw materials and eastern manufacturers; the sentiment reached its highest point, predictably, on schedules affecting wool and sugar. Western wool and sugar-beet states had sent to the Senate staunch protectionists such as Borah and Brady of Idaho, Clark and Warren of Wyoming, and Smoot and Sutherland of Utah. On the final vote and on amendments dealing with both agricultural and industrial schedules (those presented in table 7.3—*CR,* 63–1, 3112, 4471, 4353, 4617, 5347—along with other amendments on cattle, wheat, sugar, raw wool, and steel-engraving forms), these six were the only noncore senators who both voted at least half the time and had perfect "protectionist" scores. Core senators with perfect scores were Republicans Brandegee and McLean of Connecticut, Dillingham of Vermont, Colt and Gallinger of New Hampshire, Lippitt of Rhode Island, Root of New York, Penrose of Pennsylvania, and Lodge and Weeks of Massachusetts.

35. *CR,* 63–1, 4353. "It is simply protectionism reduced to a science," scoffed Williams of Mississippi. "I do not see how Democrats can support it." However, Thornton of Louisiana and Lewis of Illinois expressed support for a commission.

36. Less than 2 percent of the population had incomes over $2,000 in this period. Rufus Tucker, "The Distribution of Income among Income Taxpayers in the U.S., 1863–1935," *Quarterly Journal of Economics* 52 (August 1938): 568 (table). As late as 1929, only 28 percent of families had incomes of $4,000 or more; 65 percent made less than $2,000. U.S. Department of Commerce, Bureau of the Census, *Historical Statistics of the U.S.: Colonial Times to 1970,* pt. 1 (Washington, D.C.: GPO, 1975), G269–282, p. 299.

37. *CR,* 63–1, 3817–19, 3773–852, 4469; *Statutes at Large* 38, pt. 1 (1915): 66–68. It was estimated that only about 425,000 people would be subject to the income tax, making it, in effect, "a class tax on the rich." Ibid., 3817; Roy G. Blakey, "The New Income Tax," *American Economic Review* 4 (1914): 43, 35.

38. Link, *The New Freedom,* 192–93; *CR,* 63–1, 4379.

39. Link, *The New Freedom,* 192–93; *CR,* 63–1, 3840, 4379, 4418–19. Not only had congressional votes on the income tax always been sectional, but Supreme Court justices, in striking down the tax in 1895, voted along industrial-agricultural lines. Willard C. King, *Melville Weston Fuller* (Chicago: University of Chicago Press, 1967), 193–216.

40. From tables inserted by Representative Mann of Chicago in *CR,* 64–1, 10742–43.

41. During the debate on the 1894 Wilson-Gorman Tariff, Sen. David Hill, Democrat of New York, warned his southern colleagues that the inclusion of this "odious" income tax "imperils the possibility of a permanent Democratic success in any northern state for years to come." He added, "As between a Populistic income tax, on the one hand, and a Republican tariff on the other, I choose the latter as the lesser of two evils." *CR,* 53–2, 7134–36. In the House, where there were more core Democrats, the intraparty split had been much greater. When an income tax amendment was offered by Reps. Benton McMillin of Tennessee and William Jennings Bryan of Nebraska, the Democratic Party split 167 to 45. Forty votes were lost in New England and the Atlantic coast states. Outside these states, the Democratic vote for an income tax was 159 to 5. Ronald F. King, "From Redistributive to Hegemonic Logic: The Transformation of American Tax Politics, 1894–1963," *Politics and Society* 12 (winter 1983): 9. See also Sidney Ratner, *Political and Social History of Federal Taxation* (New York: W. W. Norton, 1942), 178–87.

42. Though none of the House core Democrats opposed the income tax on this 1912 vote, almost as many abstained as voted yea. Among periphery Democrats, on the other hand, 116 voted yea and only 25 abstained. In the Senate, Democrats from Maine, New Jersey, Ohio, and New York joined 23 periphery and 7 diverse-state senators for the tax. *CR,* 62–2, 3637, 9709. The bill died in conference.

43. Arthur S. Link, *Woodrow Wilson and the Progressive Era* (New York: Harper and Row, 1954), 192–95; *Statutes at Large* 39, pt. 1 (1917): 756–57. As Link points out, even after passage of the 1913 income tax law, federal revenues were largely derived from customs receipts (though these declined after

1913) and from taxes on tobacco and alcohol. In 1915, corporate and individual income taxes supplied only 11 percent of ordinary federal receipts. As a result of the 1916 law, that percentage rose to 32 percent of ordinary revenues in 1917, with inheritance and munitions taxes adding another 3 percent. U.S. Department of Commerce, Bureau of the Census, *Statistical Abstract of the United States, 1921* (Washington, D.C.: GPO, 1922), 750–54.

44. *CR*, 64–1, 10731–65.

45. Arthur S. Link, *Wilson*, vol. 4, *Confusions and Crises* (Princeton: Princeton University Press, 1964), 343.

46. Three core Democrats—Hughes and Martine of New Jersey and Pomerene of Ohio—voted for the bill on Senate passage; four others abstained (O'Gorman of New York, Hollis of New Hampshire, Johnson of Maine, and Saulsbury of Delaware). *CR*, 64–1, 13873. The final House vote is on 10768.

47. Lewis L. Lorwin, *The American Federation of Labor* (Clifton, N.J.: Augustus M. Kelley Publishing, 1972), 46, 89. The proposal was first incorporated in the Union Labor Party platform in 1888 and was endorsed by the Populists in 1892. Donald B. Johnson, ed., *National Party Platforms*, vol. 1 (Urbana: University of Illinois Press, 1978), 83, 91.

48. E. W. Kemmerer, "The United States Postal Savings Bank," *Political Science Quarterly* 61 (September 1911): 462–63. Quotation from Henry F. Pringle, *The Life and Times of William Howard Taft*, vol. 1 (New York: Farrar and Rinhart, 1939), 517–18.

49. Quoted in Hechler, *Insurgency*, 158–59.

50. Pringle, *Life and Times of William Howard Taft*, 516–18. See also Richard Lowitt, *George Norris*, vol. 1, *The Making of a Progressive* (Syracuse, N.Y.: Syracuse University Press, 1963), 122–23.

51. Hechler, *Insurgency*, 159; Stephenson, *Nelson W. Aldrich*, chap. 23; John Braeman, *Albert J. Beveridge* (Chicago: University of Chicago Press, 1971), 175–76; Pringle, *Life and Times of William Howard Taft*, 494; James Livingston, *Origins of the Federal Reserve System* (Ithaca, N.Y.: Cornell University Press, 1986), 147, 181–212.

52. Hechler, *Insurgency*, 160–62; Kemmerer, "United States Postal Savings Bank," 489; *CR*, 61–2, 1433; *New York Times*, June 23, 1910, 3.

53. *CR*, 61–2, 8633, 8634, 8741.

54. E. W. Kemmerer, "Six Years of Postal Savings in the United States," *American Economic Review* 7 (March 1917): 49–63. Of all depositors, 60 percent were foreign-born, accounting for almost 72 percent of deposits. Eight states (New York, Pennsylvania, Illinois, Ohio, Massachusetts, California, Michigan, and New Jersey) had 70 percent of all deposits in 1916.

55. Midwestern Republicans, again demonstrating the greater nationalism that so distinguished them from the southern agrarians, argued in debate that the postal savings system would both inculcate thrift in the foreign-born and bind them to the United States (a function underlined by the provision to let the president tap into the postal savings funds whenever, in his judgment, the national interest required it). *CR*, 61–2, 7728–42. After 1934, most postal savings funds were invested in U.S. government securities. The number of depositors peaked in 1947 (at four million, with deposits of $3.4 billion) and then rapidly declined. The postal savings system was abolished in 1966. U.S. House, *Discontinuance of the Postal Savings System*, 89th Cong., 1st sess., 1965, H. Rept. 483.

56. *CR*, 63–2, 835.

57. Ibid., 1442.

58. Ibid., 1443.

59. See, for example, William Greider, *Secrets of the Temple: How the Federal Reserve Runs the Country* (New York: Simon and Schuster, 1987).

60. Livingston, *Origins of the Federal Reserve System*, 226. However, Livingston's account of the actual crafting, revising, and passing of the Federal Reserve Act is curiously truncated. The book is much more useful as a description of the early banking-reform movement than of the politics of the actual FRA in 1913.

61. As Paul Warburg demonstrated in *The Federal Reserve System*, vol. 1 (New York: Macmillan, 1930), 178–406.

62. Livingston, *Origins of the Federal Reserve System,* 226.

63. Richard H. Timberlake, *Origins of Central Banking in the United States* (Cambridge: Harvard University Press, 1978), 42–89; Robert Craig West, *Banking Reform and the Federal Reserve, 1863–1923* (Ithaca, N.Y.: Cornell University Press, 1977), 15–25.

64. John A. James, *Money and Capital Markets in Postbellum America* (Princeton: Princeton University Press, 1978), 102–7.

65. George Macesich, *Commercial Banking and Regional Development in the United States* (Tallahassee: Florida State University Press, 1965), 20–21; Timberlake, *Origins of Central Banking,* 93–96.

66. See the tables and summaries in James, *Money and Capital Markets,* 8–21, and table 4.2 above. Lenders' discounts, bonuses, commissions, and other loan fees increased the regional spread, despite the "marked decline" in interest rate differentials noted by scholars for the 1870–1914 period. On the latter, see Lance E. Davis, "Capital Mobility and American Growth," in *The Reinterpretation of American Economic History,* ed. Robert W. Fogel and Stanley L. Engerman (New York: Harper and Row, 1971), 288–93.

67. David M. Kotz, *Bank Control of Large Corporations in the United States* (Berkeley: University of California Press, 1978), 31–36.

68. On the Aldrich plan and its genesis, see West, *Banking Reform and the Federal Reserve;* Stephenson, *Nelson W. Aldrich;* Link, *The New Freedom,* 200–201; and Livingston, *Origins of the Federal Reserve System,* 159–212. Warburg was with Kuhn, Loeb; Vanderlip was president of National City Bank of New York; Davison was a partner with J. P. Morgan.

69. West, *Banking Reform and the Federal Reserve;* 67–79; Warburg, *Federal Reserve System,* 220–29, 274–75, 287–91, 317, 342–49. Since the ceiling on total notes would include the existing national bank notes (about seven hundred million dollars in bank notes were already in circulation), the NMC plan would have limited the paper money supply to an additional $200 million to accommodate fall crop-moving demands. U.S. Senate, *Report of the National Monetary Commission,* 62d Cong., 2d sess., 1912, S. Doc. 243, 36. By comparison, the Federal Reserve System added 275 million notes after only two years of operation, the quantity held down by the plentiful supply of Aldrich-Vreeland Act "emergency currency" issued in response to conditions growing out of the European war, and by the influx of European gold. H. Parker Willis, *The Federal Reserve System* (New York: Ronald Press Co., 1923), 862–63.

70. West, *Banking Reform and the Federal Reserve,* 51–82; J. Laurance Laughlin, *The Federal Reserve Act: Its Origins and Problems* (New York: Macmillan, 1933), 141; Warburg, *Federal Reserve System,* 414. See also Wiebe, *Businessmen and Reform,* 76–79, and Livingston, *Origins of the Federal Reserve System,* 208–12.

71. West, *Banking Reform and the Federal Reserve,* 138–53; Livingston, *Origins of the Federal Reserve System,* 144–54, 169, 192, 196–97, 200–201.

72. On the structural implications of the "real bills" theory, see West, *Banking Reform and the Federal Reserve,* 152–53, 206–8. Though Livingston implies that Laughlin had admitted "the error of his ways" and been "welcomed back into the fold" of central bank advocates in 1910 (*Origins of the Federal Reserve System,* 204), Wiebe portrays the Chicago economist as a dissenter who "bridled at Wall Street dictates" and who, by late 1912, was sponsoring speeches in opposition to the Aldrich plan (*Businessmen and Reform,* 78–79). Laughlin himself saw irony in the fact that Glass was hesitant to be seen with him in public because of his connections with the NMC while the New York group was attempting to "dispose" of him for his heresy (Laughlin, *Federal Reserve Act,* 125). Willis, for his part, seems to have embraced the "extreme" (decentralist) real-bills doctrine even more strongly after going to work for the Glass Committee. The Democratic victory of 1912 had significantly changed the calculus of reform possibilities and made it necessary to forgo earlier visions of banking reform.

73. Willis had also served as an expert advisor to Representative Underwood on the tariff. Laughlin, *Federal Reserve Act,* 105.

74. *CR,* 62–2, 7042–47.

75. Willis, *Federal Reserve System,* 90–115. The Pujo Committee report, along with a skeptical summary of the investigation and its results, can be found in Richard N. Sheldon, "The Pujo Committee

1912," in *Congress Investigates: A Documentary History, 1792–1974*, vol. 3, ed. Arthur M. Schlesinger Jr. and Roger Bruns (New York: Chelsea House, 1983), 287–350.

76. The *Commercial and Financial Chronicle*, April 5, 1913, 975, held the Pujo investigations indirectly responsible for Morgan's death a few months thereafter.

77. Democratic National Committee, *The Democratic Textbook, 1912* (New York, 1912), 309–10; Kirk H. Porter, *National Party Platforms* (New York: Macmillan, 1924), 326–27, 342, 356.

78. Glass, an opponent of the Martin machine in Virginia, has sometimes been labeled a "moderate progressive" during this period (Davidson, "Response of the South to Woodrow Wilson's New Freedom," 97–98). He was a fairly representative politician of the upper South, with its budding industrial base, larger business class, and mildly protectionist inclinations. Though positioned at the center-right of his party's spectrum, his public positions on reform legislation placed Glass to the progressive "left" of the national politics of his time.

79. Willis, *Federal Reserve System*, 155–57; U.S. Congress, House of Representatives, *Hearings before the Subcommittee on Banking and Currency, January 28, 1913* (Washington, D.C.: GPO, 1913), 493–526; see also West, *Banking Reform and the Federal Reserve*, 97–100.

80. Willis, *Federal Reserve System*, 140–49, 170–77; Laughlin, *Federal Reserve Act*, 122–24, 128; Carter Glass, *An Adventure in Constructive Finance* (Garden City, N.Y.: Doubleday, Page and Co., 1927), 83–84. Men prominent in the banking-reform movement, particularly Victor Morawetz and Laurence Laughlin, had earlier proposed that a small number of stockholder-controlled regional reserve banks be yoked together by a central board elected by the banks to control note issue. However, the large majority of elite banking reformers continued to advocate a single central bank with branches. Morawetz was simply acknowledging political reality in moving toward decentralization. West, *Banking Reform and the Federal Reserve*, 61–62, 95–96; Warburg, *Federal Reserve System*, 587–91. Warburg, one of the leading advocates of a central bank, attempted to dissuade Glass and Willis by arguing that the extreme and artificial decentralization proposed in their bill, by creating so many weakly capitalized reserve banks, actually would *enhance* New York's dominance. Warburg, *Federal Reserve System*, 121–22.

81. Davidson, "Response of the South to Woodrow Wilson's New Freedom," 147–50; Link, *The New Freedom*, 202–6.

82. Link, *The New Freedom*, 203–5; Willis, *Federal Reserve System*, 146–47.

83. *New York Times*, January 9, 1927, 18. In a bitter speech to the New York Academy of Political Science a month after House passage of the FRA, Aldrich laid the blame for the bill's "populistic doctrine" and "greenbackism" at Bryan's door. With the enactment of the bill, Aldrich claimed, "Mr. Bryan will achieve the purpose for which he has been contending for a decade." Ibid., October 16, 1913, 13.

84. Link, *The New Freedom*, 206–8; Robert L. Owen, *The Federal Reserve Act* (N.p.: Published by the author, 1919), 72–79.

85. Owen, *Federal Reserve Act*, 75.

86. Ibid., 78–82.

87. Link, *The New Freedom*, 208.

88. Ibid., 114–15.

89. William Gibbs McAdoo, *Crowded Years* (Boston: Houghton Mifflin, 1931), 232–43; Willis, *Federal Reserve System*, 201–9; Link, *The New Freedom*, 209–10; Glass *Adventure in Constructive Finance*, 100–104.

90. McAdoo, *Crowded Years*, 242–44; on the bankers' opposition, see 226–27.

91. Link, *The New Freedom*, 209.

92. Warburg, *Federal Reserve System*, 99, 109.

93. Link, *The New Freedom*, 214–15.

94. Ibid., 215–16.

95. Ibid., 226–27, 229; *New York Times*, October 9, 1913, 1, 7. See also Willis, *Federal Reserve System*, 402–6, 427–36.

96. McAdoo, *Crowded Years*, 248–49 (Hadley quotation at 248); *New York Times*, October 16, 1913, 13. For the Vanderlip and Hill remarks, see *New York Times*, October 31, 1.

97. *New York Times*, November 16, 1913, 6.

98. Both the *Journal* and the *Sun* are quoted in Link, *The New Freedom*, 216.

99. Wiebe defines three broad groups of bankers on the FRA: the "financial magnates of New York," to whom most other big businessmen were allied in preference for a banker-controlled central bank; "lesser city bankers, predominantly from the midwest," who were concerned mostly about the structure of control; and "country bankers," concerned about big-banker domination as much as or more than about government control and intent on the inclusion of long-term agricultural paper in the discount mix. Almost all of the prominent New York financial community "flatly rejected" the Glass bill, while a majority of the country bankers "liked the general outline of the bill." In between there were city bankers outside the core, such as Festus Wade of St. Louis, Sol Wexler of New Orleans, and George Reynolds of Chicago, who were inclined to be "conciliationists" and maintain a dialogue with the bill's proponents, salvaging what they could from an unpropitious situation. Wiebe, *Businessmen and Reform*, 129–36.

100. Link, *The New Freedom*, 217; Willis, *Federal Reserve System*, 394–95. One northeastern "conciliationist," Irving Bush, an officer of the New York Merchants' Association, wrote Warburg on August 7 to express his approval of the concessions and of the earlier reduction of the number of reserve banks to twelve. He recognized, as did other astute conservatives, that Glass had fended off much more radical proposals, including Bryan's desire for at least fifty regional banks and the inflation measures currently agitating the wild-eyed radicals of the Democratic caucus (see below). Letter reprinted in Warburg, *Federal Reserve System*, 678–81. However, Glass was exasperated that some bankers at the meeting continued to hold out for more concessions. Glass, *Adventure in Constructive Finance*, 116–21.

101. Link, *The New Freedom*, 220.

102. On September 16, Representative Murray of Oklahoma specifically listed twenty-five members of the House, twenty-one of whom represented periphery districts, who supported some or all of the amendments. The other supporters were unnamed. *CR*, 63–1, 5020–21.

103. The *Times* described the proposals, drafted as amendments to the Glass bill, as "fished out of the Ocala platform." The paper editorialized: "These Wingo-Ragsdale-Henry-Pujo notions about currency are quite beyond the pale of discussion. . . . But it is just as well that these uncouth ideas should come to the surface. They are like impurities in the blood—the cutaneous eruption may be unsightly but the patient is the better for getting rid of his peccant humors." *New York Times*, July 25, 1913, 6.

104. Link, *The New Freedom*, 220; *New York Times*, August 18, 1913, 6.

105. Link, *The New Freedom*, 221–22; Davidson, "Response of the South to Woodrow Wilson's New Freedom," 158–66.

106. Link, *The New Freedom*, 222; *CR*, 63–1, 4864–68 (quotation at 4868).

107. Ibid., 5127–28.

108. The vote split among diverse and periphery Republicans was 13–20 and 11–22, respectively. Core Republicans divided 6–38. From the list of 1909–10 insurgents in table 5.2, eleven remained and voted on House passage of the FRA, five for and six against. *CR*, 63–1, 5128–29.

109. Hitchcock, a wealthy conservative at odds with the Bryan faction in Nebraska, resented Bryan's control of patronage in the state. O'Gorman was associated with the Tammany organization currently opposed by Wilson in New York politics; Reed, a fiery radical on economic question, also had patronage-based grievances with the administration. *New York Times Magazine*, November 16, 1913, 1. Reed is described by Link as a "congenital maverick and cunning demagogue." Link, *The New Freedom*, 228.

110. *New York Times*, July 26, 1913, 8.

111. Ibid., October 4, 1913, 1. The "public ownership" feature was much touted by midwestern progressives but made little impression on southerners. It is likely that the stock-owning "public" would have been regionally concentrated, as were stockholders generally, in the manufacturing belt (particularly in its urban centers).

112. Wiebe, *Businessmen and Reform*, 11, 65, 71.

113. Wiebe, noting that Vanderlip "was simultaneously preparing a bitter denunciation of the Glass-Owen bill's political controls for the New York Clearing House," believed that the New Yorker aimed by this tactic "to block all financial legislation" (ibid., 136). A pamphlet published by Vanderlip described

political control as a "fundamental weakness" in the Democratic bill and argued that it was better to have "no federal reserve system at all than one that put bank management and the credit system under separate controls." *New York Times,* July 26, 1913, 8. Vanderlip had more than just ideological motives, however. He had testified in Senate committee hearings that City Bank stood to lose more than any other bank, perhaps $50 million, if the Glass-Owen bill were passed. *New York Times,* October 9, 1913, 7. In his autobiography, McAdoo dismisses the Vanderlip proposals as "the last expiring effort of our adversaries." McAdoo, *Crowded Years,* 253.

114. The provisions of the Vanderlip plan are described in the *New York Times,* October 24, 1913, 1.

115. The House-passed and Owen-Senate bills are compared in a table printed in *CR,* 63–2, 175–78. The Hitchcock-Vanderlip proposals are described in the *New York Times* articles previously cited and in Senate debate as reported in *CR,* 63–2, 20–1488. Both plans are summarized in Link, *The New Freedom,* 232–38, and Davidson, "Response of the South to Woodrow Wilson's New Freedom," 170–76.

116. *CR,* 63–2, 175–78. The *Commercial and Financial Chronicle* expressed the core financial community's appreciation for the more favorable treatment of the 2 percent bonds (via a more generous and complete refunding) and the lower capital subscription requirements. The *Chronicle* had been extremely apprehensive that the terms of compulsory national bank membership in the Federal Reserve System were so onerous that they would cause many banks to forgo their national charters, causing great financial disruption. See December 13, 1913, 1684–85. For the *Chronicle's* assessment of other proposed changes, see November 29, 1913, 1542–44.

117. Link, *The New Freedom,* 235. Amendments added in caucus included the deposit insurance provisions and an increase in gold backing from 33.3 to 40 percent, the two provisions aimed at opposite poles of opinion.

118. *CR,* 63–2, 337, 1225.

119. Ibid., 828–35 (quotation at 831).

120. Ibid., 899–903.

121. Ibid., 1149.

122. Ibid., 1230. The Republicans were Jones of Washington, Perkins of California, Norris of Nebraska, Sterling of South Dakota, and Weeks of Massachusetts. Miles Poindexter of Washington, a Republican in 1912 but wearing the Progressive label in the 63rd Congress, also voted yea. Jones, Norris, Poindexter, and Weeks subsequently backed the conference bill.

123. *CR,* 63–2, 1305–7, 1463–64, 1488. The deposit insurance program, strongly backed in the agricultural areas of the South and West but just as strongly resisted in the manufacturing belt, was finally enacted as a part of the Glass-Steagall Banking Act in 1933. Glass's cosponsor then was an Alabama Democrat.

124. *Statutes at Large* 38, pt. 1 (1915): 251–75. A simple description of the rediscounting process as it functioned under the 1913 act can be found in McAdoo, *Crowded Years,* 230–31.

125. According to Livingston, capitalists rejoiced that the treasury secretary (always suspect, as McAdoo's actions illustrated) was placed in a "clearly subordinate role" (*Origins of the Federal Reserve System,* 223), but the secretary's influence on the board was quite substantial in the early period. See, for example, Milton Friedman and Anna J. Schwartz, *A Monetary History of the United States, 1867–1960* (Princeton: Princeton University Press, 1963), 229–31, 445–46; Warburg, *Federal Reserve System,* 445–46; and Donald F. Kettl, *Leadership at the Fed* (New Haven, Conn.: Yale University Press, 1986), 24–29.

126. Davidson, "Response of the South to Woodrow Wilson's New Freedom," 180.

127. Livingston, *Origins of the Federal Reserve System,* 226–34.

128. On the increase, see Friedman and Schwartz, *Monetary History of the United States,* 193–98; Harold L. Reed, *The Development of Federal Reserve Policy* (Boston: Houghton-Mifflin, 1922), 5–6, 135–40. After World War I, however, the board's deflationary policies elicited angry protests from the farmers (see below).

129. *Commercial and Financial Chronicle,* December 13, 1913, 1685.

130. *New York Times,* July 28, 1913, 2.

131. This term, used for the farmers' later experience with the Department of Agriculture, is bor-

rowed from Theda Skocpol and Kenneth Finegold, "State Capacity and Economic Intervention in the Early New Deal," *Political Science Quarterly* 97 (summer 1982): 74.

132. *CR*, 63–1, 4863–64. Callaway argued, "The people of this country are entitled to . . . legislation that will . . . answer *automatically* [emphasis added] to the demands of commerce . . . not subject to the control of any individual or board, safe from the domination of any coterie of financiers." Ibid., 4862. His remarks were greeted with "Loud Applause." (To be fair to the Democrats' mixed emotions, Representative Hardy's subsequent defense of the Glass bill, quoted above, was also met by applause—though the *Congressional Record* does not say it was "loud.")

133. Link, *The New Freedom*, 261–62; Link, *Confusions and Crises*, 345–46; Murray R. Benedict, *Farm Policies of the United States, 1790–1950* (New York: Twentieth Century Fund, 1953), 146–47; Willis, *Federal Reserve System*, 1459–66. On the farm organizations' position (for a government-capitalized bank), see the *Minutes of the National Farmers' Educational and Cooperative Union of America* annual conventions: 1912 (Chattanooga, Tennessee), 44–50; 1913 (Salina, Kansas), 26–47; 1914 (Fort Worth, Texas), 54–56; and 1915 (Lincoln, Nebraska), 10–11, 48; and see *Journal of the Proceedings of the National Grange of the Patrons of Husbandry, 47th Annual Session* (1913), 15–16. On the business press campaign for a private system, see Stuart Shulman, "The Origins of the Federal Farm Loan Act: Agenda Setting in the Progressive Era Print Press" (Ph.D. diss., University of Oregon, 1999).

134. Link, *The New Freedom*, 263–64; *CR*, 63–3, 4593–97, 5054. The eighty-nine supporters of Wingo's amendment (direct federal support for the land banks) were a bipartisan group of periphery and diverse agrarians, overlapping extensively with the group that backed rural credit amendments to the Federal Reserve Act in 1913.

135. "Washington Notes," *Journal of Political Economy* 22 (May 1914): 582.

136. Link, *Confusions and Crises*, 346–47.

137. Willis, *Federal Reserve System*, 1466.

138. The rural credits bill (Federal Farm Loan Act) passed the House 295 to 10 (125 not voting). The conference report passed the House 311 to 12, with only core Republicans in opposition. *CR*, 64–1, 8017, 10114.

139. Ibid., 7411–12.

140. Ibid., 10093–104 (text of conference bill and conferees' explanation).

141. Link, *Confusions and Crises*, 350.

142. Harold V. Faulkner, *The Decline of Laissez Faire, 1897–1917* (New York: Rinehart and Co., 1951), 364. Legislation passed in 1923, during the peak of agitation against the Federal Reserve's deflation policies, greatly liberalized the initial farm-credit system with a new network of "intermediate credit" banks directly capitalized by the federal government. Benedict, *Farm Policies of the United States*, 184–85; Willis, *Federal Reserve System*, 1481–83.

143. Faulkner, *Decline of Laissez Faire*, 364.

144. Timberlake, *Origins of Central Banking*, 204–5.

145. McAdoo, *Crowded Years*, 285–86; Kettl, *Leadership at the Fed*, 24–25.

146. Lester V. Chandler, *Benjamin Strong, Central Banker* (Washington, D.C.: Brookings Institution, 1958), 149–55; Friedman and Schwartz, *Monetary History of the United States*, 221–28.

147. Chandler, *Benjamin Strong*, 124–27, 153–64; Friedman and Schwartz, *Monetary History of the United States*, 226, 254.

148. Chandler, *Benjamin Strong*, 161–73; Friedman and Schwartz, *Monetary History of the United States*, 221–35.

149. Chandler, *Benjamin Strong*, 149, 184–89.

150. Ibid., 31–39.

151. Ibid., 208–16; A. Jerome Clifford, *The Independence of the Federal Reserve System* (Philadelphia: University of Pennsylvania Press, 1965), 93–111; Kettl, *Leadership at the Fed*, 30–31.

152. Clifford, *Independence of the Federal Reserve System*, 120–21.

153. Friedman and Schwartz, *Monetary History of the United States*, 228–69.

154. Chandler, *Benjamin Strong*, 177. For the former comptroller's charges, see his testimony in

Agricultural Inquiry: Hearings before the Joint Commission of Agricultural Inquiry, July 11–August 24, November 16, 1921, 67th Cong., 1st sess., 1921, 3 vols. (Washington, D.C.: GPO, 1922), 1:20–48.

155. Clifford, *Independence of the Federal Reserve System,* 118; Chandler, *Benjamin Strong,* 174. On the agricultural outcry, see also Willis, *Federal Reserve System,* 1478–83.

156. Chandler, *Benjamin Strong,* 174–75.

157. Ibid.

158. *Agricultural Inquiry.* The final report, while condemning the inflationary-deflationary excesses of 1919–21, supported the Fed's independence. However, the inquiry itself "provided concrete evidence of the likelihood of political retaliation when the Federal Reserve officials took actions which rightly or wrongly restricted the flow of credit." Clifford, *Independence of the Federal Reserve System,* 118. The committee's recommendations on monetary and credit policy were published as *House Reports,* 67th Cong., 1st sess., 1921 (Washington, D.C.: GPO, 1922), vol. 3, pt. 2.

159. Willis, *Federal Reserve System,* 1481–83, 1493.

160. Chandler, *Benjamin Strong,* 201.

161. Bill counts were taken from the *CR* indices for each of the six sessions; bill content was taken from the Index description, *Congressional Record* debates, and House and Senate reports. See, for example, S. 4560 (66–3) introduced by Senator Harris of Georgia, H.R. 15324 and 15875 (66–3) by Representative McLaughlin of Nebraska, H.R. 5941 (67–1) by Representative Brand of Georgia, H.R. 5825 (67–1) by Representative Hudspeth of Texas, and S. 3639 (67–2) by Senator Capper of Kansas. The percentage of Federal Reserve bills introduced by periphery representatives in the House was lowered by the extraordinary number (twenty-one) introduced by one member, Representative McFadden of Pennsylvania, who chaired the House Banking Committee. If he is taken out of the count, the periphery percentage of bill sponsors rises to 78. The periphery held 58 percent of Senate seats and 47 percent of House seats.

162. *Statutes at Large* 42, pt. 1 (1922): 620–21.

163. Warburg, *Federal Reserve System,* 446–47. The member involved was W. P. G. Harding. According to Warburg, "There was opposition to the governor's reappointment on the part of senators representing agricultural sections, whose unreasonable demands the governor had found himself duty bound to oppose; and there was resentment on account of the deflation period." Warburg, who had himself been denied reappointment in 1918, lamented that "there did not remain, under President Harding, a single banking expert among the appointive members of the Board" at a "juncture when America, now the gold pivot of the world, was called upon to play a leading role."

164. Chandler, *Benjamin Strong,* 201–2. In 1922 Strong anticipated that leaders in the consumer-goods industry, in particular Henry Ford and Thomas A. Edison, would join William Jennings Bryan in a cheap-money campaign. Virginian John Skelton Williams, "the colorful and pugnacious" former comptroller who had made the explosive accusations against Fed actions in 1920–21, was also expected to play a prominent role in the movement. Ibid., 81, 201–2.

165. Ibid., 199. Open-market operations had before been used for the reserve banks' purposes (to build their earning portfolios in order to meet expenses and pay the required dividends), rather than with an eye to their effects on the national economy. A third goal, most strongly promoted by the New York governor, was "assistance to monetary reconstruction and stability abroad." Ibid., 199, 208–10.

166. Chandler, *Benjamin Strong,* 181, 238–46; Friedman and Schwartz, *Monetary History of the United States,* 240–41.

167. Chandler, *Benjamin Strong,* 188–246.

168. Clifford, *Independence of the Federal Reserve System,* 120.

169. Chandler, *Benjamin Strong,* 423–70; Friedman and Schwartz, *Monetary History of the United States,* 254–63, 288–315, 414–16; Clifford, *Independence of the Federal Reserve System,* 32–36.

170. Friedman and Schwartz, *Monetary History of the United States,* 446–50; Clifford, *Independence of the Federal Reserve System,* 126–41. Eccles argued that centralization was necessary to combat the extraordinary and improper influence of New York money-center banks acting through the New York Reserve Bank. Clifford, *Independence of the Federal Reserve System,* 128–29. On House passage of the 1935 Banking Act, 87 percent of periphery representatives voted yea, supplying the largest block of supporters

(the core percentage was 58 percent). *CR,* 74–1, 7270–71 (there was no final Senate roll call). However, the agrarians did not put all their eggs in the Federal Reserve basket. Two years earlier, on their own initiative through an amendment to the Agricultural Adjustment Act, the agrarians had provided the president and the treasury secretary with specific money and banking powers not involving the Fed. These included setting the price of gold and silver and issuance of paper money by the U.S. Treasury rather than the reserve banks. A year later they passed a law directing the secretary to purchase silver (Clifford, *Independence of the Federal Reserve System,* 144; and see the roll-call votes in *CR,* 73–1, 2551, and 73–2, 11060). The president's budget director, Lewis Douglas, might have been speaking for all the Benjamin Strongs, Frank Vanderlips, and J. P. Morgans of American history when he commented on the first of these populist bills, "Well, this is the end of Western Civilization." Raymond Moley, *After Seven Years* (New York: Harper and Brothers, 1939), 160.

171. Edward Tufte, *Political Control of the Economy* (Princeton: Princeton University Press, 1978).

172. The last representative of the tendency was probably Wright Patman, an East Texas populist Democrat deposed as chair of the House Banking Committee in 1975. For a brief account of Patman's long struggle to increase the democratic accountability of the Fed, see Kettl, *Leadership at the Fed,* 75–78, 141–43, 152–57. One of Patman's last projects was "Federal Reserve Directors: A Study of Corporate and Banking Influence," *Staff Report for the Committee on Banking and Currency, House of Representatives,* 94th Cong., 2d sess. (Washington, D.C.: GPO, 1976).

Chapter Eight

1. Yale Brozen, *Concentration, Mergers, and Public Policy* (New York: Macmillan, 1982), 371–75; John D. Clark, *The Federal Trust Policy* (Baltimore: Johns Hopkins University Press, 1931), 3–5.

2. In the "trust," stockholders of separate companies turned their stock over to a group of trustees, who managed the combined companies and paid the stockholders dividends. In the later "holding company" variant, a new corporation was formed to take the shares or assets of individual companies and issue new stock in the holding company to the original stockholders and to the public.

3. Alfred D. Chandler Jr., *The Visible Hand* (Cambridge, Mass.: Belknap Press, 1977), chaps. 9–10; William Letwin, *Law and Economic Policy in America* (Chicago: University of Chicago Press, 1965), 69–70. See also Frederick L. Allen, *The Lords of Creation* (New York: Harper and Bros., 1935), 5–21; Henry R. Seager and Charles A. Gulick Jr., *Trust and Corporation Problems* (New York: Harper and Bros., 1929), 49–61; and Thorelli, *Federal Antitrust Policy,* 256–58.

4. Dewey W. Grantham, *Southern Progressivism* (Knoxville: University of Tennessee Press, 1983), 149–59; C. Vann Woodward, *Origins of the New South* (Baton Rouge: Louisiana State University Press, 1951), 291–320.

5. The 1888 Union Labor Party stated in the conclusion of its platform: "The paramount issues to be solved in the interests of humanity are the abolition of usury, monopoly and trusts, and we denounce the Democrat and Republican parties for creating and perpetuating these monstrous evils." Donald B. Johnson, ed., *National Party Platforms,* vol. 1 (Urbana: University of Illinois Press, 1978), 84.

6. For antitrust bills introduced before 1890, see U.S. House of Representatives, Committee on the Judiciary, *Bills and Debates in Congress Relating to Trusts* (Washington, D.C.: GPO, 1914), vol. 1, and Thorelli, *Federal Antitrust Policy,* 169–76. On the agrarian origins of antitrust, see Thorelli, *Federal Antitrust Policy,* 143–47, and A. D. Neale and D. G. Goyder, *The Antitrust Laws of the United States of America,* 3d ed. (Cambridge: Cambridge University Press, 1980), 14–19. Fourteen states, mostly in the periphery, had constitutional provisions against monopoly, and six of these (Kentucky, North Carolina, North Dakota, South Dakota, Tennessee, and Texas) also had antitrust statutes that predated the Sherman Act. Seager and Gulick, *Trust and Corporation Problems,* 341–49. Northeastern states generally did not pass such laws until after 1890.

7. Thorelli, *Federal Antitrust Policy,* 108–23. Thorelli notes, "It is indeed remarkable that of the several university-affiliated economists and political scientists setting forth their views on the trust problem in writings published before 1890 apparently no one favored the enactment of general antitrust legislation of the specific preventative-prohibitory type represented by the Sherman Act." The lack of intellectual

support did not, of course, deter Congress, which "considered one antimonopoly bill after another without ever, insofar as is known, calling on the advice of professional economists." Ibid., 120–21.

8. Ibid., 156–59.

9. Ibid., 170–76; Letwin, *Law and Economic Policy*, 85–90. Sherman's first bill (S. 3445, 1888) made all "arrangements, contracts, agreements," and so forth, "with a view, or which tend, to prevent full and free competition" or "to advance the cost to the consumer" of goods produced or imported into the United States, "to be against public policy, unlawful and void." Errant corporations were subject to loss of their "corporate franchise" and could be sued for double damages in the federal courts. Reagan's first bill (S. 3440, 1888) contained a four-part definition of a "trust" and made its perpetrators subject to personal penalties (up to $10,000 and one to five years in jail). The bills are printed in U.S. House of Representatives, *Bills and Debates in Congress Relating to Trusts*. Reagan's definition grew even more detailed and his penalties more severe. See *Congressional Record* (*CR*), 51st Cong., 1st sess. (hereafter cited in the form 51–1), 2469.

10. See Harold G. Vatter, *The Drive to Industrial Maturity* (Westport, Conn.: Greenwood Press, 1975), 201. The same sort of trade was presumably implicated in core Republican support for the moderate silver-purchase bill enacted in 1890. The Fifty-first Congress was a profligate one, marked by expensive pension bills and naval appropriations, as well as the highly protectionist McKinley Tariff. The Antitrust Act was a prudent gesture in the Republican record but was not enough to save the party from the voters' wrath in the 1890 election, in which the GOP lost its control of the House.

11. *CR*, 51–1, 1772, 2611.

12. Ibid., 2463, 2612, 2613.

13. Ibid., 2608–9, 2611.

14. Ibid., 2615–16.

15. Ibid., 2639–55. Sherman charged that the intent of these latter amendments (which included amendments by hostile Senators Stewart of Nevada and Aldrich of Rhode Island) was "to destroy and defeat this bill" (ibid., 2655). Although Sherman apparently did not oppose the Reagan and Ingalls amendments, they probably awakened the fears of Aldrich and the conservative Republicans, who had been quiet during floor debate (only Hiscock of New York and Stewart of Nevada had openly opposed the antitrust bill). The conservatives then attempted to kill the bill by amendment. Aldrich's amendment, for example, would have exempted combinations whose proponents claimed to be motivated by a desire to achieve efficiencies that would lead to price reduction (ibid., 2655).

16. Ibid., 2731. Twenty-two Democrats and nine Republicans voted for Judiciary Committee referral; twenty-two Republicans and six Democrats opposed it.

17. Thorelli, *Federal Antitrust Policy*, 212–13; Letwin, *Law and Economic Policy*, 94.

18. Thorelli, *Federal Antitrust Policy*, 197–216. In contrast to Edmunds and the large majority of core Republicans, Sherman seems genuinely to have desired an antitrust law—although whether out of personal conviction or the desire to accommodate periphery Republicans, it is impossible to say. Ibid., 166–69.

19. George spoke for Reagan's (dual-court jurisdiction) amendment, saying it would benefit the "small men" by making action against corporate giants more convenient for them. George also hoped to add a provision allowing plaintiffs to combine their suits (a position that he had argued in committee and that Edmunds opposed), but this was rejected by voice vote. *CR*, 51–1, 3147–53.

20. Ibid., 5983, 6314; Thorelli, *Federal Antitrust Policy*, 202–10. The House voted 106–98 to recede from the Bland amendment. Only one-seventh of the amendment's backers represented northeastern industrial states; these were Democrats supporting the (periphery-defined) party position.

21. Letwin, *Law and Economic Policy*, 95–96.

22. Thorelli, *Federal Antitrust Policy*, 585–94; Letwin, *Law and Economic Policy*, 106–21.

23. Richard A. Posner, "A Statistical History of Antitrust Enforcement," *Journal of Law and Economics* 13 (1970): 336.

24. Letwin, *Law and Economic Policy*, 103–22; *U.S. v. E. C. Knight*, 156 U.S. 1 (1895).

25. John Moody, *The Truth about the Trusts* (New York: Moody Publishing Co., 1904), 133–204; Woodward, *Origins of the New South*, 315–16; *CR*, 57–2, 1788; G. Warren Nutter, *The Extent of Enterprise*

Monopoly in the United States, 1899–1939 (Chicago: University of Chicago Press, 1951), appendix B, table 37. Letwin and Ralph K. Nelson see the expanding market for industrial securities as a contributing factor in the 1897–1903 merger wave. Letwin, *Law and Economic Policy*, 139; Ralph K. Nelson, *Merger Movements in American Industry, 1895–1956* (Princeton: Princeton University Press, 1959), 89–100.

26. Thorelli, *Federal Antitrust Policy*, 500–518, lists almost ninety strengthening bills introduced by forty-seven House members, at least thirty of whom represented districts in the southern, plains, and mountain nonindustrial regions (nineteen were southern Democrats).

27. State antimonopoly penalties were often much more severe than those incorporated in the Sherman Act. North Carolina had the highest absolute fines and longest prison terms. In Iowa, however, the penalty for conviction under the state's antitrust law was 20 percent of capital investment. Texas probably had the strictest enforcement and was successful in its drive to keep Standard Oil from dominating the state's petroleum industry. Joseph A. Pratt, "The Petroleum Industry in Transition: Antitrust and the Decline of Monopoly Control in Oil," *Journal of Economic History* 40 (December 1980): 815–37; Thorelli, *Federal Antitrust Policy*, 155.

28. Thorelli, *Federal Antitrust Policy*, 157; George E. Mowry, *The Era of Theodore Roosevelt* (New York: Harper and Row, 1958), 78. On the AFL, see also chapter 3 above.

29. *New York Times*, 1899: August 28, 3; September 14, 1–2; September 15, 3; September 16, 3; September 17, 3 (the Wooten quotation is from September 14). William Jennings Bryan drew "tumultuous applause" at the closing session of the conference when he described the trust movement as a "curse" for which he proposed drastic legislative remedies.

30. Johnson, *National Party Platforms*, 122–23.

31. Thorelli, *Federal Antitrust Policy*, 517–24, 538–49. House votes on previous strengthening amendments, which reveal the sectional and partisan differences on antitrust, can be found in *CR*, 56–1, 6494–501. The 1903 bill (which incorporated new penalties but only for trusts thereafter organized) passed with no dissents after Democratic strengthening amendments were defeated on voice votes. The February 28, 1903, Senate vote against consideration of the Littlefield bill is found in *CR*, 57–2, 2792. Twenty-six of the thirty senators voting to take up the bill represented states of the southern-plains-mountain periphery. One Populist and four Republicans joined the Democrats in voting to consider the bill.

32. Posner, "Statistical History of Antitrust Enforcement," 366. Two other initiatives marked the institutionalization of antitrust policy in 1903: passage of the Expediting Act, which gave antitrust cases a fast track in the circuit courts; and a $500,000 appropriation devoted to Justice Department antitrust prosecutions—the first instance of an earmarked antitrust appropriation and the first step toward the creation of an antitrust division in the department. The legislative proposal for the appropriation was put forward by Representative Bartlett (D, Georgia). Thorelli, *Federal Antitrust Policy*, 534–38.

33. Letwin, *Law and Economic Policy*, 244–45.

34. Ibid., 240–47; Thorelli, *Federal Antitrust Policy*, 552–54; *CR*, 57–2, 927–29.

35. Divestitures ordered as a result of Sherman Act prosecutions included (through 1920) Standard Oil, American Tobacco, DuPont (explosives), International Harvester, Corn Products, and Eastman Kodak. Richard A. Posner, *Antitrust Law* (Chicago: University of Chicago Press, 1976), 85–86. Most economists (Posner included) do not believe that antitrust law has had much effect on industrial structure. Chandler, *Visible Hand*, 375, concedes only that the law discouraged monopoly in markets where concentration was already well advanced and that it encouraged the transformation of monopoly into oligopoly. Arguing for the primacy of technological and organizational developments, he contends that American firms simply accomplished by merger what, in absence of strong antitrust laws, European firms achieved by cartel. This argument overlooks the demonstrably higher level of antitrust prosecutions and private suits authorized by American law, as well as the differences in competition that resulted in the United States (even before the merger loophole in the Clayton Act was closed) and Europe. In the latter, particularly in Germany, cartels might legally incorporate all major producers, and cartel sanctions were enforceable at law (and might even be imposed by the government itself). See William R. Cornish, "Legal Control over Cartels and Monopolization, 1880–1914: A Comparison," in *Law and the Formation of the Big Enterprises in the 19th and Early 20th Centuries*, ed. Norbert Horn and Jürgen Kocka (Gottingen: Vandenhoeck

and Ruprecht, 1979), 287–303. For a more sanguine view of the impact of antitrust and a comparison of more recent European policy, see Neale and Goyder, *Antitrust Laws of the United States of America*.

36. Arthur M. Johnson, "Antitrust Policy in Transition, 1908: Ideal and Reality," *Mississippi Valley Historical Review* 48 (December 1961): 420–31.

37. An example of the intellectual-big business consensus can be seen in the proceedings of a 1908 symposium on trusts sponsored by the American Academy of Political and Social Science, which heard speakers denounce the Sherman Act as "absurd and mischievous" and endorse the Hepburn bill. Clark, *Federal Trust Policy*, 136. On leading economists' contempt for the kind of antitrust legislation that was supported by congressional agrarians, see also Mary O. Furner, "The Republican Tradition and the New Liberalism," in *The State and Social Investigation in Britain and the United States*, ed. Michael J. Lacey and Mary O. Furner (Cambridge: Cambridge University Press, 1993), 223–33. On the rise and demise of the Hepburn approach, see Martin J. Sklar, *The Corporate Reconstruction of American Capitalism, 1890–1916* (New York: Cambridge University Press, 1988), 228–85. Sklar rather incongruously maintains, toward the end of his account, that a consensus on antitrust policy had now formed, encompassing "a cross section of capital, union labor, and farm groups" (282).

38. Louis W. Koenig, *Bryan* (New York: Capricorn Books, 1971), 436–39; Johnson, *National Party Platforms*, 146–48.

39. See the votes on amendments offered by Representatives Thomas of Kentucky and Garrett of Tennessee, *CR*, 61–2, 4226, and 61–3, 1070. On the Thomas amendment, for example, 76 percent of periphery representatives supported a higher threshold of removal to federal courts, compared with only 22 percent of representatives from core industrial districts. The 106 mostly periphery Democrats were joined by 17 Republicans. The major concern voiced by supporters of the Thomas and Garrett amendments during floor debate was for injured people of modest income who found it almost impossible to proceed with a suit for damages once the corporation secured removal to a distant (and probably less sympathetic) federal court. It was felt that corporations used petitions for removal to delay cases and exhaust the plaintiff. Representative Douglas of Pennsylvania attempted to alter the Garrett amendment so that it applied *only* to personal injury suits, but his amendment was defeated on a voice vote. *CR*, 61–3, 1060–74.

40. With northern success in the 1910 elections, the periphery wing of the Democratic Party dropped to 60 percent of party seats, but periphery dominance of the party's legislative agenda was undisputed.

41. *U.S. v. American Tobacco*, 221 U.S. 179 (1911).

42. For a good discussion of the important post-Knight cases, see Letwin, *Law and Economic Policy*, 131–78. The *Joint Traffic* and *Trans Missouri* cases involved railroad pooling; the *Addyston Pipe* case concerned pooling and price fixing by six cast-iron pipe manufacturers. In upholding the government against Addyston Pipe, the *Knight* ruling (manufacturers' exemption) was narrowed. The Court's decision, authored by Taft, held that "reasonable" restraints in contracts among manufacturers were permitted only when they were ancillary to some other, legitimate purpose and did not directly affect interstate commerce. The pipe manufacturers' contracts, which involved interstate sales, failed this test and were thus struck down.

43. Bill numbers are listed in Letwin, *Law and Economic Policy*, 267 n. 7. Bill sponsors and identifications are taken from *CR*, 62–1, index, and Kenneth C. Martis, *The Historical Atlas of United States Congressional Districts, 1789–1983* (New York: Free Press, 1982).

44. U.S. Senate, *Control of Corporations, Persons, and Firms Engaged in Interstate Commerce: Report of the Committee on Interstate Commerce, U.S. Senate, Pursuant to Senate Resolution 98*, vol. 3 (Washington, D.C.: GPO, 1912), 524–57, 971–1024, 1089–145. The testimony of Gary and other big business spokesmen indicates that at this point the fear of competition and of antitrust proceedings by the government rendered at least some business leaders willing to accept even government price setting in return for official toleration of consolidation and a policy of business-government "cooperation."

45. U.S. Senate, *Control of Corporations*, 2503–24, 2916; David Sarasohn, *The Party of Reform* (Jackson: University of Mississippi Press, 1989), 164–65. The issue of federal licensing has repeatedly arisen in antitrust debates. A bill to establish federal licensing (with statutory standards) was introduced by

periphery Senators Borah and O'Mahoney in the late 1930s, and in the 1970s a new generation of antitrust advocates again promoted federal licensing. See Morton Mintz and Jerry S. Cohen, *Power, Inc.* (New York: Viking Press, 1976), 99–100, and Ralph Nader, *Taming the Giant Corporation* (New York: W. W. Norton, 1976), 69–70. From the divergent uses anticipated by licensing advocates, it is clear that a federal charter mechanism could be made to serve a variety of interests. Thus, despite the broad appeal of the charter, disagreement over the component procedures and standards has kept corporate chartering in the hands of the fifty states.

46. The three other prominent examples discussed above (in chapters 6 and 7) are the Interstate Commerce Commission, sponsored by Sen. Shelby Cullom of Illinois, the Tariff Commission, promoted by midwestern and Pacific progressive Republicans, and the Federal Reserve Board, the most centralized and autonomous version of which was sponsored by Senator Hitchcock of Nebraska, with strong support from progressive Republicans. The congressmen who played the most important roles in designing and promoting the new Federal Trade Commission were Senators Cummins of Iowa, Newlands of Nevada, Kern of Indiana (all states within "diverse" midwestern and Pacific trade areas) and Representative Stevens and Senator Hollis of New Hampshire (a "core" state in the Boston trade area). Core Democrats, facing Republican charges that their party's program threatened regional business prosperity, had their own incentives to back a bureaucratic softening of corporate regulation. The difference is that the midwestern and Pacific congressmen came to bureaucratic regulation as an original, preferred position, whereas core representatives tended to back it defensively, preferring the status quo (no federal regulation).

47. Brandeis's defense of an intermediate approach, embodied in a bill he had drafted with Senator La Follette and Representative Lenroot in 1911, can be found in U.S. Congress, House of Representatives, *Hearings before the Committee on the Judiciary on Trust Legislation, January-February 1912* (Washington, D.C.: GPO, 1912), 13–47, and in "The Solution of the Trusts: A Program," *Harper's Weekly* 58 (November 8, 1913): 18–19. See also Phillippa Strum, *Louis D. Brandeis* (Cambridge: Harvard University Press, 1984), 145–53. The legislative product was H.R. 15926 (*CR*, 62–2) and S. 3276 (*CR*, 62–1). In testimony before the House Judiciary Committee in 1912, Brandeis staked out a "middle ground" between the polar alternatives of (1) declaring the Sherman Act obsolete and repealing it, or (2) amending the act to eliminate the "reasonableness" loophole. Brandeis's principal contribution at this point was in the legal specification of offenses that should be prohibited because in the past they had helped to build monopolies. He particularly opposed discrimination between potential customers and contracts compelling the acquisition of other products from firms selling or leasing an original (often patented) item—methods used by the Boston-based United Shoe Co. to gain control of the shoe machine business. Brandeis was sympathetic to the idea of a trade commission and did not object to giving the commission the discretionary power to approve trade agreements, though the burden of proving "reasonableness" should be on the corporation. He opposed national incorporation and licensing and generally remained much more ideologically committed to economic decentralization—both political and economic—than were Roosevelt and the New Nationalists.

48. Melvin I. Urofsky, *A Mind of One Piece: Brandeis and American Reform* (New York: Scribner's, 1971), 85.

49. Ibid., 73–81. On the Brandeis-Wilson relationship, see also Sarasohn, *Party of Reform*, 161–64; Strum, *Louis D. Brandeis*, 196–223; Louis J. Paper, *Brandeis* (Seacaucus, N.J.: Citadel Press, 1983), 182–93; and note 71 below.

50. A recent addition is Gerald Berk, "Neither Markets nor Administration: Brandeis and the Antitrust Reforms of 1914," *Studies in American Political Development* 8 (spring 1994): 24–60. There is almost nothing of the legislative process in this account.

51. Wilson's evolution from economic conservatism began after 1908 as his presidential ambitions developed. Though he had formerly disdained "Bryanism," Wilson embraced almost the whole of the periphery party's philosophy in order to win its nomination. Only after Roosevelt taunted him during the campaign with his failure to make any effort toward reforming New Jersey's corporate regulation did Governor Wilson belatedly submit antitrust legislation to the state legislature. Arthur S. Link: *Wilson,* vol. 2, *The New Freedom* (Princeton: Princeton University Press, 1956), 34–35, and *Wilson,* vol. 1, *The Road to the White House* (Princeton: Princeton University Press, 1947), chap. 10. On Wilson's native

conservatism and politically induced transformation, see also William Diamond, *The Economic Thought of Woodrow Wilson* (Baltimore: Johns Hopkins University Press, 1943), 38–91.

52. Johnson, *National Party Platforms*, 169. On Bryan's authorship, see Paolo Coletta, *William Jennings Bryan*, 3 vols. (Lincoln: University of Nebraska Press, 1964–69), 2:62, and Koenig, *Bryan*, 487, 496. The northeastern wing of the party had virtually no influence on the content of the platform, except, through Bryan, on the labor plank. Bryan made a crusade of excluding the northeastern "corporation element" from the convention, a crusade for which he got the ambitious Wilson's endorsement. Coletta, *Bryan* 2:69–70; Koenig, *Bryan*, 484–95.

53. John Wells Davidson: *A Crossroads of Freedom: The 1912 Campaign Speeches of Woodrow Wilson* (New Haven, Conn.: Yale University Press, 1956), and "Wilson in the Campaign of 1912," in *The Philosophy and Policies of Woodrow Wilson*, ed. Earl Latham (Chicago: University of Chicago Press, 1958), 85–99 (Roosevelt quotation at 89); Strum, *Louis D. Brandeis*, 198–200. Unlike the surprisingly harmonious Democrats, the Republican Party in 1912 was split into three camps on the issue of trust regulation. La Follette, Taft, and Roosevelt held distinct views on the Sherman Act. La Follette, representing the diverse and agrarian regions, proposed amendments to specify anticompetitive abuses and encourage private suits; Taft, representing traditional business opinion, preferred the status quo to any likely alternatives; Roosevelt, representing "enlightened" big business and intellectual opinion, opposed Taft's antitrust enforcement, condemned the Sherman Act as totally unsuited to the modern industrial economy, and favored its repeal. In lieu of a prosecutorial strategy, Roosevelt would substitute cooperation and, where necessary, guidance by the executive branch.

54. *CR*, 63–2, 1962–64.

55. Williams to Wilson, January 13, 1914, in Wilson Papers, Library of Congress; Wilson to Williams, January 26, 1914, in *The Papers of Woodrow Wilson*, ed. Arthur S. Link et al., 69 vols. (Princeton: Princeton University Press, 1966–94), 29:184.

56. First drafted in four separate bills, the original provisions were somewhat softened (in response to strong business opposition) before being merged into the omnibus Clayton bill. The major omission was a definitions section opposed by the attorney general and President Wilson. Brandeis was influential in persuading the House Judiciary Committee to limit the interlocking directorates prohibition to corporations and banks above a certain size, and he drafted the commission section for the president. Allyn A. Young, "The Sherman Act and the New Antitrust Legislation II," *Journal of Political Economy* 23 (April 1915): 308–19; Gerard C. Henderson, *The Federal Trade Commission* (New Haven, Conn.: Yale University Press, 1925), 24–26; Link, *The New Freedom*, 425–26; Paper, *Brandeis*, 190–91. The text of the House-passed bill was printed as H. Rept. 6, 63d Cong., 2d sess., 1914. A fifth bill provided for an auxiliary investigatory and advisory body (see below). Two other measures, attributed to Representative Rayburn of Texas and Senator Owen of Oklahoma, would have established federal regulation of railroad securities and stock exchanges. The former passed the House but died in the Senate. The latter was not included in the package of antitrust bills, due to opposition from President Wilson. The Rayburn bill was finally enacted in 1920.

57. *American Federationist*, January 1913, 53. The principal labor spokesmen in the Clayton Act negotiations were Representatives Casey of Pennsylvania, Keating of Colorado, Lewis of Maryland, and Sherwood of Ohio. Casey had ties to a plumbers' union, Lewis to the mineworkers. The other two had been journalists with labor sympathies.

58. See chapter 3. Gompers had little confidence in Wilson's willingness to support labor's legislative goals and had not supported him for the Democratic nomination.

59. Link, *The New Freedom*, 267–68, 428–29. For votes on the 1910, 1912, and 1913 labor measures, see chapter 10.

60. The following account of the drafting of the labor provisions relies on Dallas L. Jones, "The Enigma of the Clayton Act," *Industrial and Labor Relations Review* 10 (January 1957): 206–11; Link, *The New Freedom*, 427–30; Young, "Sherman Act and the New Antitrust Legislation," 321–22; John Wells Davidson, "The Response of the South to Woodrow Wilson's New Freedom, 1912–1914" (Ph.D. diss., Yale University, 1954), 228–33; and *New York Times*, May 2, 1914, 8, and May 27, 1914, 1.

61. The breadth of organizational coverage reflected pressure, largely from the midwestern and Pacific agricultural regions, to protect the growing farmers' cooperative movement from "restraint of trade" suits. Young errs in describing this paragraph as "well-nigh meaningless" ("Sherman Act and the New Antitrust Legislation," 321–22). "What was really wanted," he argues, "was the legalizing of the secondary boycott." Whether or not that was the case—and the Danbury hatters' case (see chapter 3) *did* involve a highly organized and effective boycott—other union activities were also at risk.

62. Davidson, "Response of the South to Wilson's New Freedom," 231.

63. Quoted in "Labor's Influence over Congress," *Literary Digest,* June 13, 1914, 1423. See also George Harvey, "Equality before the Law," *North American Review,* June 1914, 814–26.

64. Jones, "Enigma of the Clayton Act," 211, 220. The 1912 platform had declared, "Such labor organizations and their members should not be regarded as illegal combinations in restrain of trade."

65. Link, *The New Freedom,* 431.

66. *CR,* 63–2, 9540–41.

67. See the explanation by Representative Henry, interspersed with Democratic applause, in ibid., 9540–42. In Henry's words, "This executes the meritorious and just contract the Democratic Party has made with labor" (9541).

68. George Rublee, "The Original Plan and Early History of the Federal Trade Commission," *Proceedings of the American Academy of Political Science* 11 (January 1926): 116. Rublee was later nominated by Wilson to serve on the FTC, but Senate opposition by both conservative Republicans and agrarian radicals prevented his confirmation. The Senate vote is found in *CR,* 64–1, 7962.

69. *New York Times,* May 2, 1914, 8. The labor exemption had intensified business opposition. The U.S. Chamber of Commerce informed the Senate Judiciary Committee that its members had voted 669–9 against this "class legislation," and the United Engraving and Foundry Co. of Pittsburgh warned that unless the committee retracted its support for the "manifestly unfair" labor sections, "the excesses they are sure to produce will put the blood on your head." Senate Committee on the Judiciary, Correspondence file 63A-E5, National Archives, Washington, D.C. To the Antiboycott Association, the Clayton bill was "revolutionary and destructive." *New York Times,* June 17, 1914, 20. "The consensus of the businessmen of this country," wrote the Philadelphia Board of Trade, "is against the passage of this or any other so-called antitrust bill" directed against "some more or less mythical embodiment of evil called a trust." Reprinted in *CR,* 63–2, 9412–13. Ohio and Illinois Manufacturers' Associations still hoped for "an interstate trade commission properly regulated," but it urged that "all other business legislation be deferred." *CR,* 63–2, 9417, 13917, see also 12736–43.

70. *CR,* 63–2, 9081–82.

71. Rublee, "Original Plan and Early History," 668–69; Davidson, "Response of the South to Wilson's New Freedom," 204–12; 63d Cong., 2d sess., 1914, S. Rept. 597; Strum, *Louis D. Brandeis,* 214–15. Brandeis, who, at Wilson's request, had drafted the original (adjuvant) commission bill, had at first opposed the extensive discretionary power of the Rublee measure. However, to the surprise of Rublee and Stevens, he enthusiastically recommended their approach to the president.

72. The principal defenders of administrative regulation during Senate debate—Cummins, Newlands, and majority leader Kern of Indiana—argued that administrative regulation by expert and thoughtful men chosen especially for the task and subject to congressional scrutiny would be far preferable to the present reality of judicial regulation. They had a powerful faith in the wisdom and ability of the future administrators and objected to any attempt (such as that made repeatedly by Senator Reed) to define the unfair competition that the commission was to restrain. Cummins insisted that the commissioners would not simply implement their own personal philosophies. Rather, it would "be the duty of the board to consult the decisions of the courts, the learning of the time, the custom of merchants, the habits of trade, the writings of studious and thoughtful men, all of which go to make up our understanding of the words 'unfair competition.'" *CR,* 63–2, 1794. The commissioners would be, in short, intellectuals, distilling and implementing the best of current scholarship and business practice in their guidance of economic processes. Neither core capitalists nor periphery representatives shared this faith in the intellectual guidance of business by a public agency. The mood of periphery senators during the transformation of the trade commission

bill was sullen and uneasy. They clearly resisted the standardless grant of regulatory authority to the new administrative body. Senators Clapp of Minnesota, Borah of Idaho, Reed of Missouri, Shields of Tennessee, Thomas of Colorado, Sterling of South Dakota, and Fletcher of Florida all expressed strong opposition to the bureaucratization of antitrust policy during the FTC debate in the Senate.

73. Young, "Sherman Act and the New Antitrust Legislation," 315. See also Davidson, "Response of the South to Wilson's New Freedom," 213–15.

74. 63d Cong., 2d sess., 1914, S. Rept. 698. The chairman of the Senate Judiciary Committee was Charles Culberson of Texas, a loyal, moderately progressive Democrat. Culberson, who was in bad health, apparently played no significant role in the revisions, other than as a conduit for the new administration line. Senator Cummins, a member of both the Judiciary and the Commerce Committees and linked to the northern progressives now in Wilson's favor, probably played the pivotal role in revising the Clayton bill to accommodate the new commission emphasis. The committee's rationale for weakening the government's evidence section, striking criminal penalties or omitting specific prohibitions altogether, and hedging the labor sections was more frequently defended on the floor by Cummins than by Chairman Culberson. Cummins was also probably responsible for inserting the restraining terms "lawful" and "lawfully" into the labor protections. He was intent on proscribing the secondary boycott, which, he believed, the House bill legalized. See, for example, *CR*, 63–2, 13855, 13981–83, 14225, 14229, 14314, and the tenor of Cummins's substitute amendment on 12726, 14546, and 14585.

75. On the cotton crisis, see James L. McCorckle Jr., "Cotton, War, and Mississippi," *Journal of Mississippi History* 45 (May 1983): 90–113; George C. Osborn, *John Sharp Williams* (Gloucester, Mass.: Peter Smith, 1964), 248–49; and Arthur S. Link, "The Cotton Crisis, the South, and Anglo-American Diplomacy," in *Studies in Southern History*, ed. J. Carlyle Sitterson (Chapel Hill: University of North Carolina Press, 1957), 122–38. Williams did, however, attempt to prevent weakening of the labor guarantees by Cummins and others. *CR*, 63–2, 13982–83, 14588.

76. I have separately analyzed thirty proposed Senate Clayton Act amendments, which fall naturally into three categories: committee-administration weakening amendments; noncommittee weakening amendments; and strengthening amendments (the bulk of which were offered by Senators Reed and Poindexter). Those in the first category were passed by large majorities, with little regional variation; the second (noncommittee weakening amendments) lost by large majorities, meeting greatest opposition among southern-Plains-western senators; the third group (strengthening amendments) generated unusual patterns, winning support from a small group of Pacific, southern, and northeastern Democrats, a few core Republicans probably casting strategic votes, and dissident midwestern and western Republicans. The major amendments are found in *CR*, 63–2, 13907–14602.

77. *CR*, 63–2, 14464, 14591 (emphases added); Samuel Gompers, *Seventy Years of Life and Labor*, 2 vols. (New York: E. P. Dutton, 1925), 2:296–97. Gompers praised Senator Cummins for using such language in an amendment he offered unsuccessfully on the floor. Gompers was apparently unaware that the primary purpose of the Iowa senator's amendment was to outlaw secondary boycotts. After the Cummins amendment was defeated, the Democrats lifted the attractive phrase and added it to the language of the committee bill. On Culberson's role, see James W. Madden, *Charles Allen Culberson* (Austin, Tex.: Gammels Bookstore, 1929), 154, 178–79. Subsequent historians also failed to recognize Cummins's maneuver to outlaw the secondary boycott. Richard Abrams, "Woodrow Wilson and the Southern Congressmen," *Journal of Southern History* 22 (November 1956): 427–28, interprets Cummins's amendment as an attempt to *strengthen* the labor provisions of the Clayton Act. Similarly, he misconstrues (428) Senator Borah's amendment to extend the right of trial by jury in contempt proceedings to businessmen (who would be targets of FTC cease-and-desist orders), describing it as an effort to strengthen the *labor* trial guarantees of the Clayton Act. For Borah's forthright acknowledgment of his desire to scuttle the FTC, see *CR*, 63–2, 14377, 14413–14. Cummins's anti-labor sentiments were more clearly revealed in 1919 when he sponsored punitive antistrike proposals in the bill that became the 1920 Transportation Act.

78. In the Progressive Era, it will be recalled, Washington was classified as "core" because the majority of the state's population resided in the artificially truncated Seattle trade area (see chapter 2).

79. Contemporary legal and economic critiques of the Clayton Act, and later scholars who rely on

them, have interpreted the conference bill as even weaker than the Senate bill. Such was not the case. Contemporary critics tended to prefer the New Nationalist antitrust program and saw the Clayton bill as wrongheaded populism. The FTC bill was viewed in a much more favorable light by both scholarly and journalistic commentators.

80. This meant, for example, that section 6 now said, "Nothing contained in the antitrust laws shall be construed to forbid or restrain individual members of such organizations from *lawfully* carrying out their legitimate objects" (emphasis added). This was another invitation to judicial interpretation and emasculation.

81. Rublee, "Original Plan and Early History," 669–70; Douglas W. Jaenicke, "Herbert Croly, Progressive Ideology, and the FTC Act," *Political Science Quarterly* 93 (fall 1978): 447–80, 485–86.

82. *CR,* 63–2, 15987, 16280–85, 16329.

83. So argued Representative Nelson of Wisconsin, ibid., 16322.

84. Ibid., 14802, 16170, 16344. Senate Democrats voted unanimously for the FTC conference bill.

85. Gabriel Kolko, *The Triumph of Conservatism* (Chicago: Quadrangle Books, 1963), chap. 10.

86. G. Cullom Davis, "The Transformation of the Federal Trade Commission, 1914–1929," *Mississippi Valley Historical Review* 44 (December 1962): 441; Murray R. Benedict, *Farm Policies of the United States, 1790–1950* (New York: Twentieth Century Fund, 1953), 149–50.

87. On the FTC and the basing point case, see Earl Latham, *The Group Basis of Politics* (New York: Octagon Books, 1965), 54–58.

88. Davis, "The Transformation of the Federal Trade Commission," 441–42; Thomas C. Blaisdell Jr., *The Federal Trade Commission* (New York: Columbia University Press, 1932), 37–83; Marc A. Eisner, *Antitrust and the Triumph of Economics* (Chapel Hill: University of North Carolina Press, 1991), 62–69.

89. Paper, *Brandeis,* 193–94, citing the decision in *F.T.C. v. Gratz,* 253 U.S. 421, 427 (1920).

90. *Swift and Co. v. FTC,* 272 U.S. 554 (1926); *Duplex Printing Press Co. v. Deering et al.,* 254 U.S. 443 (1921). On the *Duplex* case, see Edward Berman, *Labor and the Sherman Act* (1930; reprint, New York: Russell and Russell, 1969), 103–10, and Stanley I. Kutler, "Labor, the Clayton Act, and the Supreme Court," *Labor History* 3 (winter 1962): 19–38. Subsequent legislation (the Celler-Kefauver Act of 1950 and the Norris-LaGuardia Act of 1932) repaired the damage caused to the Clayton Act by these decisions. Though conservatives like William Howard Taft and the head of the Antiboycott Association had been delighted with the changes introduced by the Senate, Taft's former attorney general believed that the Clayton Act *did* reverse the Danbury hatters decision and legalize the secondary boycott. Judge Parker had assured Gompers that the act freed labor from antitrust prosecutions, and Wilson's new attorney general concurred that it rendered labor unions "absolutely immune from prosecution." Nevertheless, the Court focused on the act's ambiguous language and the interpretation by Representative Webb to overturn the intent of the labor and agrarian representatives in Congress. See Jones, "Enigma of the Clayton Act," 218–20. The major blame for the fateful ambiguity, according to Jones, rests with President Wilson, whose opposition prevented a more explicit exemption.

91. *Munn v. Illinois,* 94 U.S. 113 (1877).

92. See the reports of the committees on warehouses in the *Minutes of the National Farmers' Educational and Cooperative Union of America,* 1908 (Fort Worth, Texas), 59–60; and Theodore Saloutos, *Farmer Movements in the South, 1865–1933* (Lincoln: University of Nebraska Press, 1960), 194–96, 200–204.

93. On the evils of the extant warehousing system (as of 1914–16), see *CR,* 63–2, 5793, and 64–1, 6985, 10849–50, 12044; Oscar Refsell, "The Farmers' Elevator Movement," *Journal of Political Economy* 22 (November 1914): 872–88; and H. A. Haring, *Warehousing* (New York: Ronald Press, 1929), chaps. 12, 20. As to why there was so little warehouse regulation in the South before 1916, there are few hints in the secondary literature or congressional debates. These were poor states, with minimal governmental apparatus, and local farm organizations put more emphasis on the building of public and cooperative warehouses than on state regulation. Whatever the reason, as Haring puts it, "the states seemed helpless to aid their growers until the [Federal] Warehouse act of 1916" (535).

94. *CR,* 64–1, 7073.

95. Link, "Cotton Crisis," 125–28; McCorckle, "Cotton, War, and Mississippi," 90–91; Saloutos,

Farmer Movements in the South, 238–40; Dewey W. Grantham Jr., *Hoke Smith* (Baton Rouge: Louisiana State University Press, 1967), 277–79.

96. Link, "Cotton Crisis," 123–30 (quotation of Treasury Secretary McAdoo at 123); Grantham, *Hoke Smith*, 277.

97. *CR:* 63–2, 13905, 14128; 63–3, 463; 64–1, 10780–82.

98. *CR*, 63–2, 16209.

99. Ibid., and 64–1, 6982.

100. *CR*, 64–1, 6984.

101. The 1916 House bill passed on a separate vote, 292–42. Most opponents were core Republicans, and core abstention rates were high. Ibid., 7271. The Senate vote is in ibid., 10852.

102. *CR*, 63–3, 475. An exception to the southern preference for a unitary national system was presented by Texas congressmen. Texas had recently enacted a strong state regulatory law, and its representatives were reluctant to jeopardize the state system for a less certain federal solution.

103. John H. Frederick, *Public Warehousing* (New York: Ronald Press, 1940), chap. 18; Haring, *Warehousing*, chap. 12.

104. Haring, *Warehousing*, 338. Haring remarks that within a few years after passage, bankers' "preference for the federal receipt had the effect of disqualifying all other receipts" (337).

105. Theodore Saloutos and John D. Hicks, *Agricultural Discontent in the Middle West, 1900–1939* (Madison: University of Wisconsin Press, 1951), 132–33; Refsell, "Farmers' Elevator Movement," 876. See also the remarks of Senator Sterling of South Dakota, *CR*, 63–2, 5793.

106. In pursuit of a cross-party agrarian alliance sufficient to enact their policy agenda, the southern Democrats who controlled the House and Senate agriculture committees more or less granted the grain state representatives a free hand to reach a consensus among themselves and write their own grain-regulation statutes. The grain state congressmen, mostly Republicans, often acknowledged this deference during the floor debate. See, for example, *CR*, 64–1, 10781–83.

107. *CR*, 63–2, 7253–58, and 64–1, 7077, 10780 (remarks of Representative Madden of Illinois and Senators Nelson of Minnesota and Smith of Michigan).

108. The issue of whether the United States should employ its own grain inspectors or license state and local personnel had been a stumbling block in the 63rd Congress. A grain-grading bill was defeated in the Senate after both opponents of any federal regulation and supporters of direct federal control (via federally employed graders) voted against a licensing amendment offered by Senator Gore (see *CR*, 63–2, 7557). By 1916, advocates of federal regulation recognized that only a federal licensing system could win passage. *CR*, 64–1, 10632.

109. *Statutes at Large* 39, pt. 1 (1917): 482–85. Final passage of the Grain Standards Act in 1916 was accomplished without a separate roll-call vote. An amendment by Senator Cummins to strike all of the act's provisions beyond the simple promulgation of USDA standards was defeated without a record vote. *CR*, 64–1, 10782–83.

110. A "bucket shop," according to Robert Lee Hunt, "was an establishment nominally conducted for dealing in cotton futures, grain, etc. but in fact used for the registration of wagers on the rise or fall of the prices bet on. . . . No actual transfer of goods was ever made. The proprietor received a commission on each transaction. The patron put up a margin when he bet prices would go one way or the other, and these margins would be appropriated by the proprietor of the business if the market went against the customer. The customer, however, won his bet if he guessed the price movement correctly. The margins were small in order to catch more suckers." Robert Lee Hunt, *A History of Farmers' Movements in the Southwest, 1873–1925* (College Station: Texas A&M University Press, 1935), 134.

111. Elizabeth Sanders, "Business, Bureaucracy, and the Bourgeoisie: The New Deal Legacy," in *The Political Economy of Public Policy*, ed. Alan Stone and Edward Harpham (Beverly Hills, Calif.: Sage, 1982), 115–40.

112. Cedric B. Cowing, *Populists, Plungers, and Progressives* (Princeton: Princeton University Press, 1965), 5.

113. Ibid., 6–23, vote table, 22. In the House, the South (minus Texas) cast 88.5 percent of its vote

for the Hatch bill, but most of the region's senators, indirectly elected and still resistant to the populist tide, opposed it. On the Hatch bill, see also Henry Crosby Emery, *Speculation on the Stock and Produce Exchanges of the United States* (1896; reprint, New York: Greenwood Press, 1969), 219–33.

114. Cowing, *Populists, Plungers, and Progressives,* 7–9; *CR,* 63–2, 5079–80, 5523–24 (remarks of Senators Smith and Williams); Saloutos, *Farmer Movements in the South,* 199–200.

115. Newton Hoffman, "The Cotton Futures Act," *Journal of Political Economy* 23 (April 1915): 469.

116. New York Cotton Exchange, *Charter, Bylaws, and Rules of the New York Cotton Exchange,* 6th ed. (New York: Charles H. Jones and Co., 1872), and 25th ed. (New York: N.p., 1930); Kenneth J. Lipartito, "The New York Cotton Exchange and the Development of the Cotton Futures Market," *Business History Review* 57 (spring 1983): 50–72.

117. Lipartito, "New York Cotton Exchange," 64–68; Hoffman, "Cotton Futures Act," 468–74; *Report of the Commissioner of Corporations on Cotton Exchanges,* pts. 2 and 3 (Washington, D.C.: GPO, 1908), 1–12. For congressional opinion condemning exchange practices, see *CR,* 63–2, 5079–80, 5523–25 (remarks of Senators Smith and Williams) and U.S. Senate, *Trading in Cotton Futures,* 63d Cong., 2d sess., 1914, S. Rept. 289, 1–3. The New Orleans and New York Cotton Exchanges were the only exchanges dealing in futures in the early 1900s. The New Orleans Exchange, however, merely allowed buyers and sellers of the delivered cotton to use the exchange arbitrators and facilities to settle classifications (which could be appealed to a group of arbitrators). Furthermore, the New Orleans Exchange forbade delivery of the inferior grades of cotton that were used to settle futures contracts in New York.

118. Quoted in Saloutos, *Farmer Movements in the South,* 200. See also the remarks of Herbert Knox Smith in *Report of the Commissioner of Corporations on Cotton Exchanges,* pt. 1, quoted in Hoffman, "Cotton Futures Act," 472; and *Minutes of the National Farmers' Educational and Cooperative Union of America,* 1913 (Salina, Kansas), 93.

119. Eleven farm states plus New Hampshire, Rhode Island, and New York banned bucket shops in the early 1900s. In the last case, the New York Stock Exchange supported the move in order to limit competition. Cowing, *Populists, Plungers, and Progressives,* 27–30.

120. *CR,* 61–1, 4244. Ninety-two percent of core votes opposed Bacon's amendment, compared with 38 percent of periphery senators' votes.

121. Cowing, *Populists, Plungers, and Progressives,* 43–44.

122. *CR,* 62–2, 9147–53.

123. Cowing, *Populists, Plungers, and Progressives,* 44–45. Among the published goals of the Farmers' Union was "to eliminate gambling in farm products by Board of Trade, Cotton Exchanges and other speculators." Saloutos, *Farmer Movements in the South,* 185–91.

124. "Raking the Cotton Futures Tax," *Literary Digest,* July 19, 1913, 83–84, quoting the *New York Evening Post,* the *New York Herald,* and the *New York Times.*

125. Emery, *Speculation on the Stock and Produce Exchanges,* 226. See also Cowing, *Populists, Plungers, and Progressives,* 47–52.

126. Henry C. Emery, "Speculation on the Stock Exchanges and Public Regulation of the Exchanges," *American Economic Review* 5 (March 1915): supplement, 69–86, 94.

127. The Owen bill was similar in content and objective, if not in method, to the Securities Act finally passed in 1933. Samuel Untermeyer, "Speculation on the Stock Exchanges and Public Regulation of the Exchanges," *American Economic Review* 5 (March 1915): 24–68; Young, "Sherman Act and the New Antitrust Legislation," 309; Link, *The New Freedom,* 426.

128. *CR,* 63–1, 5277–81.

129. Ibid., 5275–78.

130. Ibid., 5280. For an example of the negative reaction to the Clarke amendment in the press, see *Literary Digest,* July 19, 1913, 83–84.

131. *CR,* 63–1, 5288.

132. Ibid.

133. *CR,* 70–2, 3214, 3433; Cowing, *Populists, Plungers, and Progressives,* 128–32.

134. *CR,* 63–2, 12851. For two such interpretations, see Lipartito, "New York Cotton Exchange,"

69–71; and Robert H. Wiebe, *Businessmen and Reform* (Chicago: Quadrangle Books, 1962), 144. Only two core Republicans voted for the conference bill in the House. Eight of the fourteen Republican votes for the bill came from the periphery. The majority of core representatives—of both parties—simply abstained (a frequent pattern when bills enjoying overwhelming periphery support seemed certain of passage). Eleven Massachusetts representatives of textile districts had voted 2-to-1 against the Clarke amendment; on the 1914 conference report, the voting majority was negative, but most abstained.

135. Wiebe, *Businessmen and Reform*, 144. Wiebe acknowledges that by 1914 there was no significant support for regulation among nonsouthern manufacturers. See also "Spinners Denounce Cotton Exchange," *New York Times*, April 29, 1914, 12, for southern textile manufacturers' complaints against the NYCE.

136. *New York Times*, June 30, 1914, 12. See also ibid., March 28, 1914, 15, and March 29, 1914, 4. On NYCE internal reforms, see ibid., November 26, 1913, and December 5, 1913, 16, and Hoffman, "Cotton Futures Act," 479–81.

137. *New York Times*, June 30, 1914, 12.

138. In 1865 the federal government had effectively abolished state bank notes by taxing them, an event that still rankled the agrarians. Taxation was also used (at the urging of northern lard and butter producers) to reduce consumption of oleomargarine made with cottonseed oil.

139. Cowing, *Populists, Plungers, and Progressives*, 19.

140. *New York Times*, March 28, 1914, 15.

141. Untermeyer, "Speculation on the Stock Exchanges," 50.

142. Albert Atwood charged that Burleson had no real knowledge of business but was an instinctive regulator who would paralyze business and bring great losses to many in order to realize his "grotesque theory" of regulation. Albert Atwood, "Papers on Speculation on Stock Exchanges and the Public Regulation of Exchanges," *American Economic Review* 5 (supplement, March 1915): 91–96. Burleson, a Texas Democrat, had a plan for nationalization of the country's telephone and telegraph facilities. As a member of the cabinet, he worked for nationalization in 1913–14 but ultimately had to abandon the idea because of business antagonism and Wilson's lack of enthusiasm. Link, *The New Freedom*, 136–37.

143. 63d Cong., 2d sess., 1914, S. Rept. 289, 3.

144. *CR*, 63–2, 5524.

145. Ibid., 5526; Cowing, *Populists, Plungers, and Progressives*, 15, 43, 150.

146. *Hill v. Wallace*, 259 U.S. 68, 69 (1922); *Chicago Board of Trade v. Olsen*, 262 U.S. 1 (1923); *Statutes at Large* 42, pt. 1 (1923): 998–1003. On the Packers and Stockyards and Grain Futures Acts, see G. O. Virtue, "Legislation for the Farmers: Packers and Grain Exchanges," *Quarterly Journal of Economics* 37 (August 1923): 687–704; Saloutos and Hicks, *Agricultural Discontent in the Middle West*, 323–27; and Harry R. Mayers, "Federal Regulatory Legislation: The Federal Grain Futures Act," *George Washington Law Review* 2 (May 1934): 457–62. The Grain Futures Act required the exchanges to admit agricultural cooperatives to membership and prohibited the dissemination of false or misleading crop reports or market information, price manipulation, and attempts to corner a grain market; it also mandated record keeping and report filing and weighing, trading, and inspection by licensed officials.

147. The Packers and Stockyards Act was upheld in *Stafford v. Wallace*, 258 U.S. 495 (1922). Passage of the act came after five large meatpackers were unsuccessfully prosecuted for conspiracy to violate the antitrust laws and President Wilson directed the FTC to investigate the industry with an eye to corrective legislation. The act prohibited unreasonable, deceptive, or discriminatory prices and attempts to manipulate prices and restrain competition among packers. Charges had to be publicly posted and records open to government inspection.

Chapter Nine

1. Larry Cuban, "Enduring Resiliency: Enacting and Implementing Federal Vocational Education Legislation," in *Work, Youth, and Schooling*, ed. Harvey Kantor and David B. Tyack (Stanford: Stanford University Press, 1982), 48; Roy V. Scott, *The Reluctant Farmer: The Rise of Agricultural Extension to 1914* (Urbana: University of Illinois Press, 1970); David B. Danbom, *The Resisted Revolution* (Ames: Iowa

State University Press, 1979); Melvin L. Barlow, *The Unconquerable Senator Page* (Washington, D.C.: American Vocational Association, 1976); John Gadell, "Charles Allen Prosser" (Ph.D. diss., Washington University, 1972). Efforts by the National Association of Manufacturers (NAM) to use vocational education against the trade-union movement are detailed in Sarah L. Watts, *Order against Chaos: Business Culture and Ideology in America, 1880–1915* (New York: Greenwood Press, 1991), 147–51. In Robert Wiebe's account of business organizations in the Progressive Era, federal aid for vocational education is cited as a consensual interest of business groups and an implicitly business-dominated NSPIE. Robert H. Wiebe, *Businessmen and Reform* (Chicago: Quadrangle Books, 1962), 198. A more balanced, pluralist account that nevertheless concentrates on the role of the NSPIE and critical business backing (scarcely mentioning agrarian support) is Elizabeth Fones-Wolf, "The Politics of Vocationalism: Coalitions and Industrial Education in the Progressive Era," *Historian* 46 (November 1983): 39–55. For a critique of business-centered interpretations of education policy expansion, see Ira Katznelson and Margaret Weir, *Schooling for All* (New York: Basic Books, 1985).

2. As Lawrence A. Cremin writes: "Historians of education have long tended to portray the vocational education movement as essentially urban in character. . . . The difficulty with that view is that it virtually ignores the telling support that derived from a half-century of agrarian protest and innovation." *The Transformation of the School* (New York: Random House, 1961), 41–42.

3. Alfred Charles True, *A History of Agricultural Education in the United States, 1785–1925* (New York: Arno Press, 1969), 95–111; Mary Summers, "Conflicting Visions: Farmers' Movements and the Making of the United States Department of Agriculture" (Ph.D. diss., Yale University, 1999), chap. 4. Among the early agitators for practical education were the following: Horace Greeley and his populist agricultural editor on the *Chicago Tribune;* an 1840s "People's College" movement in upstate New York spearheaded by the Mechanics' Mutual Protection Association founded by a machinist during the depression of 1843; the Illinois Industrial League, organized by a convention of farmers in that state; and agricultural societies in Iowa, Michigan, Maryland, Pennsylvania, and Massachusetts. Summers, "Conflicting Visions," chap. 4.

4. True, *History of Agricultural Education*, 102–6; Arthur F. McClure, James R. Christman, and Perry Mock, *Education for Work* (Rutherford, N.J.: Fairleigh Dickinson University Press, 1985), 42–43.

5. Conceived by northern Republicans as a way to disperse the accumulating treasury surplus and thus reduce opposition to the tariff, the Blair bill drew its most significant additional support from southerners who desperately needed funding help for their impoverished schools and the postwar mandate to educate black children. It also had the endorsement of the Knights of Labor. The bill passed the Senate in 1884, 1886, and 1888 but failed in 1890, never to emerge again. Northern Democrats opposed it as an unnecessary program legitimating high tariffs. Southern majorities backed it by 71–82 percent in 1884, 1886, and 1888, dividing narrowly against it (7–8) only in 1890 (even as northeastern and midwestern Democrats unanimously opposed it). Blair bill votes by party are listed in various editions of Edward McPherson, *A Hand-book of Politics* (Washington, D.C.: James J. Chapman, 1872–94): (1884), 147; (1886), 160–66; (1888), 122–25; and (1890), 194–95.

6. Murray R. Benedict, *Farm Policies of the United States, 1790–1950* (New York: Twentieth Century Fund, 1953), 84.

7. McClure, Christman, and Mock, *Education for Work*, 46–47; Scott, *The Reluctant Farmer*, 33–59.

8. True, *History of Agricultural Education*, 200. The increased federal expenditures under the second (1890) Morrill Act were to be used to support the teaching of "agriculture, the mechanic arts, the English language and the various branches of mathematical, physical, natural and economic science, with special reference to their application in the industries of life." According to McClure, Christman, and Mock, in *Education for Work*, "This Act was the first federal grant that allowed a federal official to withhold funds if he felt the requirements were not being met" (43–44).

9. Scott, *The Reluctant Farmer*, 42–46; Robert Lee Hunt, *A History of Farmers' Movements in the Southwest, 1873–1925* (College Station: Texas A&M University Press, 1935), 130–32; Robert Smith, "The Contribution of the Grangers to Education in Texas," *Southwestern Social Science Quarterly* 21 (March 1941): 317; Theodore Saloutos, *Farmer Movements in the South, 1865–1933* (Lincoln: University of Ne-

braska Press, 1960), 40–41; Rush Welter, *Popular Education and Democratic Thought in America* (New York: Columbia University Press, 1962), 160–76; Theodore R. Mitchell, *Political Education in the Southern Farmers' Alliance, 1887–1900* (Madison: University of Wisconsin Press, 1987), 124–29, 140–47, 182; D. Sven Nordin, *Rich Harvest* (Jackson: University Press of Mississippi, 1974), 45–108.

10. Summers, "Conflicting Visions," chap. 4, 21.

11. Ibid., 18–27; Smith, "Contribution of the Grangers to Education in Texas," 320–22.

12. Summers, "Conflicting Visions," chap. 4, 19–20; Scott, *The Reluctant Farmer*, 52–57; H. Leon Prather, *Resurgent Politics and Educational Progressivism in the New South* (Rutherford, N.J.: Fairleigh Dickinson University Press, 1979), 89, 119–24.

13. The second Morrill Act (1890) provided grants to the states rising over ten years to $25,000 per year. States were required either to make no racial distinctions in admission to the subsidized college or to support a separate college for blacks with a "just and equitable" distribution of the funds. This requirement led to the creation of seventeen new land-grant colleges. Scott, *The Reluctant Farmer*, 27. The much more ambitious proposal of Senator Blair for federal aid to public "common schools" (see note 5) was ultimately displaced by the narrower Morrill bill for increased aid to the land-grant colleges. On the congressional struggles, see Welter, *Popular Education and Democratic Thought*, 152–56, and True, *History of Agricultural Education*, 196–200.

14. Lloyd E. Blauch, *Federal Cooperation in Agricultural Extension Work, Vocational Education, and Vocational Rehabilitation*, U.S. Department of the Interior, bulletin no. 15, 1933 (Washington, D.C.: GPO, 1935), 10, 52–53.

15. Robert W. Cherny, *Populism, Progressivism, and the Transformation of Nebraska Politics* (Lincoln: University of Nebraska Press, 1981), 75, 87–111.

16. Blauch, *Federal Cooperation in Agricultural Extension Work*, 47–48.

17. Ibid., 49–50; *Congressional Record* (*CR*), 59th Cong., 2d sess. (hereafter cited in the form 59–2), 3546.

18. *CR*, 59–2, 3547. Bacon of Georgia remarked that the amounts envisaged were barely adequate, given the importance of the goal; Nelson implied that a larger appropriation was politically impossible at the time.

19. Ibid., 4490–93.

20. Ibid., 4491.

21. Ibid.

22. Ibid., 4494.

23. Blauch, *Federal Cooperation in Agricultural Extension Work*, 53–54; U.S. House of Representatives, Committee on Agriculture, *Hearings on House Bills Relating to Granting Federal Aid to Agricultural Education and Also on Bills Having for Their Object Amendments to the Oleomargarine Law*, 60th Cong., 1st. sess. (Washington, D.C.: GPO, 1908), 3–10.

24. Alfred C. True, *A History of Agricultural Extension Work* (Washington, D.C.: GPO, 1928), 14–42; Fred A. Shannon, *The Farmer's Last Frontier* (New York: Farrar and Rinehart, 1945), 277–79; Scott, *The Reluctant Farmer*, 45–122, 166–68. In some states there were farmers' institutes especially for women, although women were active participants in all phases of the institute movement. In the South, the institutes drew increasing numbers of black farmers. Some institutes were distinct activities organized by the black land-grant colleges, but there was some degree of integrated participation as well. Scott, *The Reluctant Farmer*, 115, 120.

25. Joseph C. Bailey, *Seaman A. Knapp, Schoolmaster of American Agriculture* (New York: Columbia University Press, 1945), 109–214; Scott, *The Reluctant Farmer*, 208–9.

26. Bailey, *Seaman A. Knapp*, 109–214; Scott, *The Reluctant Farmer*, 209–16.

27. Scott, *The Reluctant Farmer*, 212, 298; *CR*, 58–2, 568–75.

28. Scott, *The Reluctant Farmer*, 208–34; Bailey, *Seaman A. Knapp*, 219–233; Allen W. Jones, "The South's First Black Farm Agents," *Agricultural History* 50 (October 1976): 636–44. Historians inclined to see the president as the prime mover of American politics have drawn attention to President Roosevelt's appointment of a Country Life Commission in 1908 as a seminal moment in the drive for farmer education.

But as the president himself acknowledged, Knapp's extension network had already reached 30,000 farmers by then. Russell Lord, *The Agrarian Revival* (New York: American Association for Adult Education, 1939), 51–53, 70. And serious bills to promote agricultural education had been introduced in Congress in 1906–7 (see above).

29. Bailey, *Seaman A. Knapp*, 230–36 (quotation at 235); Cremin, *Transformation of the School*, 81. The estimate of women agents is based on figures reported by True, *History of Agricultural Education*, 290.

30. Bailey, *Seaman A. Knapp*, 215–27, 277; Raymond B. Fosdick, *Adventure in Giving* (New York: Harper and Row, 1962), 8–50; U.S. Senate, *Rockefeller Foundation*, 63d Cong., 2d sess., 1914, S. Doc. 538. For a thoughtful appraisal of the ease with which "Farmer Alliance members were . . . recruited into the educational crusade that followed closely on the heels of the 1896 election," despite the key roles played by professional educators and philanthropists linked to great corporate wealth, see Mitchell, *Political Education in the Southern Farmers' Alliance*, 148–95.

31. Scott, *The Reluctant Farmer*, 254–71; Clarence B. Smith and Meredith C. Wilson, *The Agricultural Extension System of the United States* (New York: John Wiley and Sons, 1930), 39–40. The involvement of women was also more extensive in the southern FCDW. Scott, *The Reluctant Farmer*, 249.

32. Scott, *The Reluctant Farmer*, 218–20; Lord, *Agrarian Revival*, 71; Bailey, *Seaman A. Knapp*, 223–24, 232–41, 250–54, 265, 273. The first quotation is from Lord; the last two are from Bailey, *Seaman A. Knapp*, 241, 250.

33. On the McLaughlin bill, see True, *History of Agricultural Extension Work*, 100–103.

34. Welter, *Popular Education and Democratic Thought*, 186–87. "Oriented to immediate gains and eschewing ultimate ends, the AFL had little or no use for the kinds of organization and education that appealed to the Farmers' Alliances and the Knights of Labor" (187). See also Katznelson and Weir, *Schooling for All*, 24–26, 61–73, 107.

35. Cremin, *Transformation of the School*, 21–34 (quotation at 34).

36. Samuel Gompers, *Seventy Years of Life and Labor*, 2 vols. (New York: E. P. Dutton, 1925), 1: 436–37; Philip R. V. Curoe, *Educational Attitudes and Policies of Organized Labor in the U.S.* (New York: Columbia University Teachers College, 1926), 163–64. If such courses were to be taught, the AFL argued, they should be given only by teachers with practical experience in manual trades and only by *men*.

37. Cremin, *Transformation of the School*, 34–38 (quotation at 38). See also Charles Alpheus Bennett, *History of Manual and Industrial Education 1870–1917* (Peoria, Ill.: Manual Arts Press, 1937), 317–464, 507–16; Watts, *Order against Chaos*, 147–50; and Richard T. Auchmuty, "An American Apprentice System," *Century Magazine*, n.s., 15 (1888–89): 401–5.

38. Bennett, *History of Manual and Industrial Education*, 507–24; Katznelson and Weir, *Schooling for All*, 150–77.

39. Bennett, *History of Manual and Industrial Education*, 507–20; Fones-Wolf, "Politics of Vocationalism," 39–45; Curoe, *Educational Attitudes and Policies of Organized Labor*, 134–36; Mollie Ray Carroll, *Labor and Politics* (Boston: Houghton Mifflin, 1923), 125–26; Gadell, "Charles Allen Prosser," 176–80, 183. On the AFL's concern, see also AFL, "Reports of the Committee on Industrial Education (1910) and Commission on Industrial Relations (1915)" in *American Education and Vocationalism: A Documentary History*, ed. Marvin Lazarson and W. Norton Grubb (New York: Teachers College Press, 1974), 20–21, 101–32; and Lazarson and Grubb, *American Education and Vocationalism*, introduction (20–21).

40. Gadell, "Charles Allen Prosser," 114–66. See also Arthur G. Wirth, *Education in the Technological Society* (Scranton, N.Y.: Intext Educational Publishers, 1972), 162–66.

41. Sol Cohen, "The Industrial Education Movement, 1906–17," *American Quarterly* 20 (spring 1968): 95–110; Lazarson and Grubb, *American Education and Vocationalism*, 22–27.

42. Fones-Wolf, "Politics of Vocationalism," 45.

43. Ibid., 44–46.

44. Fones-Wolf, "Politics of Vocationalism," 46–48; Curoe, *Educational Attitudes and Policies of Organized Labor*, 163; Cremin, *Transformation of the School*, 38–40.

45. Fones-Wolf, "Politics of Vocationalism," 47–48; Blauch, *Federal Cooperation in Agricultural Extension Work*, 55–60; Cremin, *Transformation of the School*, 40.

46. Compare drafts of the Davis bill printed in U.S. House of Representatives, Committee on Agriculture, *Hearings on House Bills Relating to Granting Federal Aid to Agricultural Education,* and the AFL-endorsed bill (the Davis-Dolliver bill) printed in the *American Federationist,* February 1910, 140–41. On "continuation schools," see Bennett, *History of Manual and Industrial Education,* 532–33. The centralization of administrative responsibility in the Bureau of Education of the Interior Department reflected the AFL's concern for maintaining the new vocational education program within a unitary general-education system—as contrasted with the separate, technical system preferred by the NAM and NSPIE.

47. Lazarson and Grubb, *American Education and Vocationalism,* 20–21, 33–38; Curoe, *Educational Attitudes and Policies of Organized Labor,* 107–11, 134–36, 163–64.

48. Cohen, "The Industrial Education Movement," 103–6; Curoe, *Educational Attitudes and Policies of Organized Labor,* 164.

49. U.S. Senate, Committee on Agriculture and Forestry, *Vocational Education, Hearings, April 12, 13, 1910* (Washington, D.C.: GPO, 1911), 47. See also *American Federationist,* April 1911, 302. Which "Farmers' Organization" is not specified; most likely it was the Grange.

50. U.S. Senate, Committee on Agriculture and Forestry, *Vocational Education,* 3ff.

51. Holder's first witness was Herbert Myrick, editor-in-chief of a syndicate of farm publications including the *Orange Judd Farmer* and the *American Agriculturalist,* which had broad coverage in the West and South. Myrick had been named president of the National League for Industrial Education, formed to promote the Davis bill at the grass roots. U.S. Senate, Committee on Agriculture and Forestry, *Vocational Education,* 3–4. On the second day of the hearings, Holder's lead witness was Mrs. H. J. Patterson, representing the national Grange. Ibid., 22–27.

52. Fones-Wolf, "Politics of Vocationalism," 48; Blauch, *Federal Cooperation in Agricultural Extension Work,* 60–61; Gadell, "Charles Allen Prosser," 170–71; Barlow, *The Unconquerable Senator Page,* 22–23.

53. Blauch, *Federal Cooperation in Agricultural Extension Work,* 58–59.

54. True, *History of Agricultural Extension Work,* 103–5; Blauch, *Federal Cooperation in Agricultural Extension Work,* 62–65; *Cooperation with the States in Providing Vocational Education,* 61st Cong., 2d sess., 1910, S. Rept. 902; Scott, *The Reluctant Farmer,* 294–95.

55. Gadell, "Charles Allen Prosser," 170–77 (quotation at 177).

56. Blauch, *Federal Cooperation in Agricultural Extension Work,* 65–66; True, *History of Agricultural Extension Work,* 105–6; Scott, *The Reluctant Farmer,* 293–97; Gladys Baker, *The County Agent* (Chicago: University of Chicago Press, 1939), 103–4.

57. Bailey, *Seaman A. Knapp,* 225–26, 272–74; Scott, *The Reluctant Farmer,* 298–99.

58. Bailey, *Seaman A. Knapp,* 273–75; True, *History of Agricultural Extension Work,* 109. In the final statute, the 75 percent requirement was dropped in favor of a definition of "cooperative agricultural extension work" and a prohibition on certain types of traditional extension work. *Statutes at Large* 38, pt. 1 (1914): 373–74.

59. Prominent college officials who held out against the new federal extension program included Liberty Hyde Bailey and Eugene Davenport, deans of agriculture at Cornell and the University of Illinois, respectively. Bailey, *Seaman A. Knapp,* 251–52, 265; Lord, *Agrarian Revival,* 46–47. Davenport was even more opposed to the omnibus measure, however, and finally endorsed the narrower Lever bill in 1912. Barlow, *The Unconquerable Senator Page,* 37.

60. Barlow, *The Unconquerable Senator Page,* 23–27.

61. Although the NSPIE and the NAM now supported a revised Page bill, there was an as yet unacknowledged conflict between the two organizations over administration. The NSPIE favored a highly centralized system in order to implement the "correct" form of vocational education. The NAM, however, urged "the widest latitude given" to the states and localities, with very limited federal control. It hoped that employers would be able to influence the content of vocational education through membership on independent state and local boards. See the NAM statement submitted by Senator Page in U.S. Senate, Committee on Agriculture and Forestry, *Hearing: To Establish Agricultural Extension Departments* 62d Cong., 2d sess., 1912 (Washington, D.C.: GPO, 1912), 76–77, and Albert K. Steigerwalt, *The National*

Association of Manufacturers, 1895–1914 (Grand Rapids: University of Michigan Bureau of Business Research, 1964), 159.

62. Barlow, *The Unconquerable Senator Page,* 23–30; Gadell, "Charles Allen Prosser," 172–82; Blauch, *Federal Cooperation in Agricultural Extension Work,* 72–75; Fones-Wolf, "Politics of Vocationalism," 49–50.

63. Fones-Wolf, "Politics of Vocationalism," 50. Attention to the vocational education bill in the *American Federationist* fell off sharply after 1911, even as the legislative battle was heating up. The AFL's behavior after 1911 follows the pattern noted by Katznelson and Weir in their urban case studies: once overt challenges by capitalists had receded, labor's attention to education issues flagged. Katznelson and Weir, *Schooling for All,* 160.

64. Representative Wilson introduced the NSPIE's redrafted bill in early 1912. Blauch, *Federal Cooperation in Agricultural Extension Work,* 77.

65. Senators Lodge, Root, and Smoot were unenthusiastic about the bill, and the GOP (in contrast to the Democrats) refused to endorse vocational education or extension in its 1912 platform. Barlow, *The Unconquerable Senator Page,* 30–31; Donald B. Johnson, ed., *National Party Platforms,* vol. 1 (Urbana: University of Illinois Press, 1978), 171, 183–88.

66. See the testimony of the female Grange representative cited in note 51. The teaching of home economics, though it emphasized traditional female domestic roles, also promised to keep more girls in high school, to provide a socially legitimate way to introduce girls to chemistry, nutrition, and other scientific subjects, and of course, to increase the number of women teachers. Its inclusion in the agricultural extension program also resulted in the gender integration of southern land-grant colleges that had not previously admitted women.

67. U.S. Senate, Committee on Agriculture and Forestry, *Hearing,* 38–40.

68. *Minutes of the National Farmers' Educational and Cooperative Union of America,* 1912 (Chattanooga, Tennessee), 32. The Georgia FU, however, was apparently persuaded by Senator Smith, the Lever bill's cosponsor, to endorse passage of the extension bill first. U.S. Senate, Committee on Agriculture and Forestry, *Hearing,* 42–43.

69. U.S. Senate, Committee on Agriculture and Forestry, *Hearing,* 80–81.

70. See remarks by Representatives Haugan, Sloan, and Towner of Iowa, Cline of Indiana, Morgan of Oklahoma, Sloan of Nebraska, and Davis of Minnesota in *CR,* 62–2, 11613, 11617, 11621, 11623, 11626–29, 11732.

71. Ibid., 11710–12, 11720, 11727, 11733.

72. Ibid., 11743.

73. *CR,* 62–3, 1664–67, 1958, 1962–63, 2094–95, 2216; Barlow, *The Unconquerable Senator Page,* 32–41, 51–57. Senators Cummins of Iowa, Gronna of North Dakota, Hitchcock of Nebraska, Crawford of South Dakota, and Sanders of Tennessee applauded the combination, and efforts by Smith to narrow the scope of the substitute were voted down overwhelmingly. *CR,* 62–3, 2106–8, 2214–16.

74. *CR,* 62–3, 2216–28; Blauch, *Federal Cooperation in Agricultural Extension Work,* 83–84; Barlow, *The Unconquerable Senator Page,* 58–59. The original Page bill lacked specific protection for the FCDW and required that all (rather than a portion of) federal expenditures be matched by the states—a burden for the hard-pressed southern state governments. It also provided equal amounts to the white and black colleges. The Lever bill authorized lower appropriations but left the racial distribution to the state legislatures. The two senators who were probably organized labor's most reliable friends and spokesmen in the upper chamber (Kern and La Follette) both joined the southern Democrats in opposition to the Page substitute. Thus, it seems unlikely that the AFL had lobbied strongly for the Page bill. See also Barlow, *The Unconquerable Senator Page,* 30, 49, on labor's weak support.

75. Barlow, *The Unconquerable Senator Page,* 65–85. Debate on the resolution revealed, once more, the broad support for vocational education among both rural and urban congressional members. See, e.g., the remarks of Representatives Abercrombie of Alabama and Murray of Oklahoma and labor representatives Buchanan of Illinois and Sherwood of Ohio. *CR,* 63–1, 5352, and 63–2, 714, 726–30, 1611.

76. Barlow, *The Unconquerable Senator Page*, 90–100; Blauch, *Federal Cooperation in Agricultural Extension Work*, 95–98; Gadell, "Charles Allen Prosser," 185–90.

77. U.S. House, Committee on Agriculture, *Cooperative Agricultural Extension Work*, 63d Cong., 2d sess., 1914, H. Rept. 110, 7. Arthur Holder, the AFL official who had once conducted a hearing on the Davis-Dolliver bill, was brought into the House committee hearing to testify to the AFL's acquiescence in the "extension first" bargain. House of Representatives, Committee on Agriculture, *Agricultural Extension*, 63d Cong., 1st sess., 1913 (Washington, D.C.: GPO, 1913), 46–47.

78. *CR*, 63–2, 1944. The Lever bill passed the House on an unrecorded 177–9 vote. Ibid., 1947.

79. Ibid., 2574–75.

80. Ibid., 2650–51, 2929, 2937, 2946–47, 3035, 3123–25, 3129, 7493–94. Angry at Smith's high-handed tactics, four Democratic senators (Hitchcock, Hollis, Lane, and Shafroth) joined the Republicans in an unsuccessful attempt to delay approval of the conference report. *CR*, 63–2, 7416–18. See also John W. Davis, "The Negro Land Grant College," *Journal of Negro Education* 2 (July 1933): 314–17.

81. Fosdick, *Adventure in Giving*, 59. The "Ludlow massacre" of about thirty people—coal miners, women, and children camped out in tents during a strike and shot or burned to death—took place in April 1914. See Philip S. Foner, *History of the Labor Movement in the United States*, 7 vols. (New York: International Publishers, 1975–), 5:196–213. To compensate for the loss of the GEB funds, Congress authorized an additional $300,000 for the southern FCDW. True, *History of Agricultural Extension Work*, 121. See also *CR*, 63–2, 7675–82.

82. True, *History of Agricultural Extension Work*, 69, 129, 189, 197. On the work of, and limitation imposed on, black extension agents after the Smith-Lever Act, see Baker, *The County Agent*, 75–76, 191–206. As Davis has pointed out, the number of black agents should have been much larger if allocated on the basis of black rural population. Davis, "Negro Land Grant College," 121.

83. Problems of racism, favoritism, political influence, and domination of agents and their work by local elites are catalogued by Baker, *The County Agent*. The extension service also promoted the development of the Farm Bureau, an organization with origins and impetus quite distinct from those of grass-roots farmers' movements. The first "farm bureau" was organized by the Binghamton, New York, Chamber of Commerce in about 1910 to spur the weak local agricultural economy and support the work of extension agents. Other cities and business organizations followed suit. Since local groups—including, in particular, businesses—were expected to contribute toward the expense of hiring and maintaining county agents, farm bureaus became enmeshed in extension work, first in the North and West and then in the South. It was in the interest of the demonstration agents to encourage membership in the organizations that supported them. This even extended to helping the farm bureaus collect dues and involving them in the agent's educational work. The bureaus formed state and national federations and became, ultimately, conservative rivals of other farmers' organizations such as the Farmers' Union and the Grange. The Farm Bureau Federation, with a membership of about 200,000 in 1932, underwent a "spectacular revival" as a result of the integration of the organization into New Deal farm programs. Baker, *The County Agent*, 14–24; Lord, *Agrarian Revival*, 103–110, 136–37; Grant McConnell, *The Decline of Agrarian Democracy* (Berkeley: University of California Press, 1953), 44–54; William J. Block, *The Separation of the Farm Bureau and the Extension Service* (Urbana: University of Illinois Press, 1960), 1–21.

84. U.S. House, *Report of the Commission on National Aid to Vocational Education*, 63d Cong., 2d sess., 1914, H. Doc. 1004.

85. Compare the draft bill in ibid., 82–87, with the draft in the February 1910 *American Federationist*, 140–41. See also Blauch, *Federal Cooperation in Agricultural Extension Work*, 99–100, 116–18, 122–23.

86. "Industrial Education and Progress," *American Federationist*, January 1913, 48–52. See also Curoe, *Educational Attitudes and Policies of Organized Labor*, 130–35; Blauch, *Federal Cooperation in Agricultural Extension Work*, 31–32; and *American Federationist*, January 1916, 36–37.

87. The quoted passages are from U.S. House, *Report of the Commission on National Aid to Vocational Education*, 12. On the distinctive earmarks of the NSPIE in the final Smith-Hughes Act, see Gadell, "Charles Allen Prosser," 191–97.

88. Barlow, *The Unconquerable Senator Page*, 125–26, citing remarks by Representatives Huddleston of Alabama and Dallinger of Massachusetts.

89. The principal modifications in Congress were the addition of home economics (omitted in the commission's draft but restored by the House on the urging of the General Federation of Women's Clubs) and changes in the composition of the federal board. As ultimately passed, the board consisted of the secretaries of labor, commerce, and agriculture, the commissioner of education, and three members appointed by the president to represent labor, business, and agriculture. Both labor and business favored the concept of a representative board. See Barlow, *The Unconquerable Senator Page*, 129–30, and *CR*, 64–2, 777.

90. Passage came by voice vote after a brief debate. *CR*, 64–1, 11878. On Gompers's efforts, see Fones-Wolf, "Politics of Vocationalism," 53. Gompers's relationship with Smith is difficult to characterize and, indeed, must have been marked by the same uneasy and incomplete collaboration seen elsewhere between labor and the southern Democrats. In his own state, Smith was considered a friend of labor. However, in national politics, the Georgia senator clearly put agrarian interests first. He opposed the convict labor, seamen's, and child-labor acts and delayed the vocational bill in favor of the extension measure (even though, as governor of Georgia, he had promoted both industrial education and a child-labor law and had ended the state's convict-lease system). Because of his textile state's position in the national political economy, Smith was not a reliable friend of labor in Congress; on the other hand, he was sometimes indispensable. See Grantham, *Hoke Smith*, 118–19, 127, 173–74, 212–13, 225–28, 270–72, 282, 332, and *American Federationist*, August 1914, 647.

91. Blauch, *Federal Cooperation in Agricultural Extension Work*, 104–5. Rep. Dudley Hughes of Georgia, who now chaired the House Education Committee, was an enthusiastic supporter of vocational education, but like the rest of the House, he was compelled to spend much time during the summer of 1916 campaigning in his district, in a close race that he ultimately lost. One author has suggested that both Hughes and Page were, in fact, content to delay matters until after the election, since both stressed passage of the bill as a reason for their constituents to return them. Barlow, *The Unconquerable Senator Page*, 119, 123–28.

92. Blauch, *Federal Cooperation in Agricultural Extension Work*, 103–4.

93. McClure, Christman, and Mock, *Education for Work*, 63; Blauch, *Federal Cooperation in Agricultural Extension Work*, 105–8. Amendments sponsored by the NSPIE were introduced in the House by Representative Lenroot, a progressive Republican from Wisconsin.

94. *CR*, 64–2, 716–24, 761–68; the Huddleston speech is at 723–24. There is, of course, a great irony in the fact that the man touting the virtues of democratic education himself represented a region that enforced rigid racial segregation in schools.

95. It was the AFL's Arthur Holder who nominated Prosser to direct the board. Gadell, "Charles Allen Prosser," 197. On the board's policy-making under Prosser, see ibid., 197–201, and Wirth, *Education in the Technological Society*, 166.

96. In addition to the Morrill-Hatch Acts, which congressional vocational education supporters referred to, an agrarian statute passed between the Smith-Lever and Smith-Hughes Acts also served as a precedent for the vocational measure. The Federal Aid Roads Act (also referred to as the Bankhead-Shackleford Highway or "Good Roads" Act) passed in 1916 created an unprecedented federal involvement in a previously locally controlled activity. Like the two practical education laws, the Roads Act created a large-scale federal-state "cooperative" program in which states matched the federal expenditures and shared administration. The act was cited several times during congressional debate as a legitimating precedent for the vocational bill. See, e.g., *CR*, 64–2, 3428.

Chapter Ten

1. In addition to resistance to child-labor measures, important examples of such southern opposition include the following: Bailey's hostility to the federal eight-hour workday (Sam H. Acheson, *Joe Bailey, the Last Democrat* [New York: Macmillan, 1932], 288, 379); an unsuccessful attempt by Representative Heflin of Alabama (joined by seventeen other, mostly southern Democrats) to block debate on the 1912

eight-hour bill because labor legislation had been "crowding out" matters such as tariff revision (*Congressional Record* [*CR*], 62d Cong., 2d sess. [hereafter cited in the form 62–2], 9208); opposition by Representatives Bartlett, Underwood, and twenty-two other southern Democrats to a widely supported bill levying a punitive tax on phosphorus-tipped matches (Evans C. Johnson, *Oscar W. Underwood* [Baton Rouge: Louisiana State University Press, 1980], 159–60; *CR*, 62–2, 3967–79); and an unsuccessful attempt by Senator Bacon and others to amend a section of a 1913 Senate resolution to investigate abuses against workers after (state) martial law was imposed in the West Virginia coalfields (*CR*, 63–1, 1778; Virginia Haughton, "John W. Kern and Labor Legislation," *Mid-America* 57 [July 1975]: 185–99). The last two examples are particularly striking because they involve the principal sponsors (Bacon and Bartlett) of bills to require jury trials in contempt-of-court cases arising from labor disputes, important labor reforms that were incorporated in the 1914 Clayton Act. Hoke Smith's delay of vocational education, convict labor, and workmen's compensation bills is discussed below and in chapter 9.

2. David Sarasohn, *The Party of Reform* (Jackson: University of Mississippi Press, 1989), 83.

3. On the example of Senator Cummins, see chapter 8, note 77.

4. See chapter 3, and Sarasohn, *Party of Reform*, 89. Gompers did publish an editorial entitled "Labor's Political Opportunity" in the October 1910 *American Federationist*. Without mentioning either party, he predicted that wage earners would "divest themselves of loyalty to a political party [the Republicans, presumably] once they [had] come to understand that the party [had] ceased its loyalty to them," and he urged that workers elect candidates from their own ranks to office (899–900). The *American Federationist* was strangely silent on the remarkable turn in national politics occasioned by the November elections. Not until November 1911 was there an elliptical reference to "militant labor's" satisfaction with the results of its nonpartisan political strategy (467).

5. Counted from Congressional Quarterly, *Guide to U.S. Elections* (Washington, D.C.: Congressional Quarterly, 1975), 707–16.

6. *American Federationist*, January 1912, 33.

7. In addition to Wilson, three other "union-card" representatives became labor committee members in 1911 (Maher of New York, Lewis of Maryland, and Buchanan of Illinois).

8. *CR*, 61–2, 7654, 8656, 8852; Samuel Gompers, *Seventy Years of Life and Labor*, 2 vols. (New York: E. P. Dutton, 1925), 2:290–93. See also Sarasohn, *Party of Reform*, 83–84. The Hughes amendment provided, in Gompers's words, "a clear-cut issue" on which to distinguish labor's friends and enemies. The AFL distributed hundreds of thousands of pamphlets in 1910 describing the amendment and listing those who had voted pro and con. Gompers, *Seventy Years of Life and Labor* 2:291; Arvil Ernest Harris, "Organized Labor in Politics, 1906–1932" (Ph.D. diss., State University of Iowa, 1936), 239.

9. Gompers, *Seventy Years of Life and Labor* 2:250, 290.

10. From Sarasohn's title; on the 1911–12 "trying on of power," see his chapter 4.

11. For a list of labor bills passed by the House in the 62nd Congress, see *American Federationist*, October 1912, 812–13.

12. See chapter 3; Gompers, *Seventy Years of Life and Labor* 2:229–30; and John R. Commons and John B. Andrews, *Principles of Labor Legislation* (New York: Harper Bros., 1916), 44–45.

13. Felix Frankfurter and Nathan Greene, *The Labor Injunction* (New York: Macmillan, 1930), 155.

14. Ibid., 157–59.

15. *CR*, 62–2, 6470–71, 8902–3. For Republican arguments against the injunction bill (emphasizing violations of employer property rights and the rights to work and privacy of nonunion, nonstriking employees), see ibid., 6465–69. Among voting core Republicans, there was more support, on both bills, in the less industrial districts than in the more urban-industrial areas within the core. Periphery Republicans as a group voted 28–4 for the anti-injunction bill; core Republicans voted 19–18.

16. The 1896 bill passed on a voice vote (*CR*, 54–1, 6381) (Bacon quotation at 6378). Amendments offered by senators from North Carolina and Utah made jury trial a *right* not contingent on the judge's discretion. See also Frankfurter and Greene, *Labor Injunction*, 182–93, and William H. Harbaugh, *Lawyer's Lawyer: The Life of John W. Davis* (New York: Oxford University Press, 1973), 70–72.

17. Harbaugh, *Lawyer's Lawyer*, 72.

18. Philip G. Wright, "The Contest in Congress between Organized Labor and Organized Business," *Quarterly Journal of Economics* 29 (1915): 257; Harbaugh, *Lawyer's Lawyer*, 72.

19. Claude Barfield, "The Democratic Party in Congress 1909–1913" (Ph.D. diss., Northwestern University, 1965), 387; *American Federationist*, April 1913, 289. According to the latter, Senators Martin of Virginia, Owen of Oklahoma, Culberson of Texas, Martine of New Jersey, "and others [including Borah of Idaho] made a vigorous protest against the action of the Committee on Judiciary in withholding the Clayton bill."

20. *American Federationist*, April 1913, 279, and January 1916, 35.

21. *CR*, 62–2, 10790–93 (quotation at 10791); the Jones amendment vote is at 10792.

22. Ibid., 10795.

23. Ibid., 10796, 10799, 10802.

24. *American Federationist*, April 1913, 279 (attributing passage to the "persistent work" of the AFL).

25. Ibid., January 1916, 35. The dredgeworkers had accidentally been omitted from coverage of the general eight-hour bill; nevertheless, according to Anne Firor Scott, there was "prolonged objection" to the bill in the Senate, where it passed 37–27. Thirteen of the favorable votes came from southern Democrats; only three were counted among the twenty-seven opponents. Anne Firor Scott, "A Progressive Wind from the South, 1906–1913," *Journal of Southern History* 29 (February 1963): 67.

26. *CR*, 62–2, 7455. Before final passage, Senator Lodge attempted to substitute a forty-eight-hour week. His amendment failed on a 14–35 vote (6941). Two Florida Democrats joined the (mostly northeastern) Republicans in the minority. Bailey of Texas spoke against the bill but did not join the voting opposition. The overwhelming majority of southern Democrats voted to uphold the eight-hour day on both Senate votes. House passage was by voice vote (396).

27. John Lombardi, *Labor's Voice in the Cabinet* (New York: Columbia University Press, 1942), 15–27 (quotation at 26).

28. Ibid., 30–45.

29. Ibid., 52–54; *CR*, 57–2, 929–30.

30. Lombardi, *Labor's Voice in the Cabinet*, 63–69, 96–100. The AFL had long opposed compulsory arbitration, and Department of Labor mediation efforts relied on voluntary acceptance of proposed solutions. Employers were highly skeptical, and appropriations for the service were modest, rising from \$5,000 in the fall of 1913 to \$50,000 in 1915 and \$75,000 the next year. Ibid., 97–98, 101–2.

31. See the statement of Dr. John B. Andrews, secretary of the American Association for Labor Legislation, in U.S. House of Representatives, Committee on Ways and Means, *White Phosphorous Matches*, 61st Cong., 3d sess., 1910–11 (Washington, D.C.: GPO, 1911), 279–86.

32. Johnson, *Oscar W. Underwood*, 160.

33. *CR*, 62–2, 3967–78.

34. Over 95 percent of core and diverse votes backed the bill, compared with 68 percent in the periphery. Ibid., 3979. The southern objections led to a bitter exchange with labor representative William Hughes of New Jersey (3974–75). See also Barfield, "Democratic Party in Congress," 399–400.

35. Elizabeth H. Davidson, *Child Labor Legislation in the Southern Textile States* (Chapel Hill: University of North Carolina Press, 1939); John Braeman, "Albert J. Beveridge and the First National Child Labor Bill," *Indiana Magazine of History* 60 (1964): 1–34; Dewey W. Grantham, *Southern Progressivism* (Knoxville: University of Tennessee Press, 1983), 178–200; Elizabeth Sands Johnson, "Child Labor Legislation," in Elizabeth Brandeis, *Labor Legislation*, vols. 3 and 4 of John R. Commons et al., *History of Labor in the United States* (New York: Macmillan, 1935), 409–37. In the South, the pioneer state for the child-labor movement was Alabama, where a campaign led by an Episcopal minister prodded by the AFL and the Federation of Women's Clubs produced a twelve-year threshold law (with loopholes and weak enforcement) in 1903. It was strengthened somewhat in 1909 and 1911 (and more substantially in 1913). Davidson, *Child Labor Legislation*, 46–51, 215–33. On the legislative campaigns of women's organizations, see also Theda Skocpol et al., "Women's Associations and the Enactment of Mothers' Pensions in the United States," *American Political Science Review* 87 (September 1993): 686–701.

36. Note, for example, the opposition of Georgia's Hoke Smith to the national child-labor law of

1916. Smith had been a strong advocate of *state* child-labor restriction. Dewey W. Grantham Jr., *Hoke Smith* (Baton Rouge: Louisiana State University Press, 1967), 127, 300. The National Child Labor Committee was founded in 1904 to work for state legislation. After a decade, its activists (which included Florence Kelly and Jane Addams) recognized the need for a uniform national standard to overcome the "unwholesome competitive advantage" that accrued to the laggard states. Robert H. Bremner, *From the Depths* (New York: New York University Press, 1956), 219–25. See also Walter I. Trattner, *Crusade for the Children* (Chicago: Quadrangle Books, 1970), and Davidson, *Child Labor Legislation,* 262.

37. The National Association of Manufacturers opposed a federal child-labor law as a dangerous precedent for other national regulatory interventions. Arthur S. Link, *Woodrow Wilson and the Progressive Era* (New York: Harper and Row, 1954), 227 n. The AFL, likewise, saw a national law as "a dangerous precedent for federal interference in labor questions." Braeman, "Albert J. Beveridge and the First National Child Labor Bill," 22. See also Roger W. Walker, "The AFL and Child Labor Legislation: An Exercise in Frustration," *Labor History* 11 (summer 1970): 323–40.

38. Barfield, "Democratic Party in Congress," 394–96; Robert H. Wiebe, *Businessmen and Reform* (Chicago: Quadrangle Books, 1962), 198–99; Susan Tiffin, *In Whose Best Interest? Child Welfare Reform in the Progressive Era* (Westport, Conn.: Greenwood Press, 1982), 232–36; Josephine Goldmark, *Impatient Crusader* (Urbana: University of Illinois Press, 1953), 98–101.

39. David Carlton, *Mill and Town in South Carolina, 1880–1920* (Baton Rouge: Louisiana State University Press, 1982), 199–212, 235. According to Carlton, South Carolina orphanages "reported a tremendous rush of applications from mill villages following successive child labor enactments, forcing [the orphanages] to stop taking the children of living mothers" (203).

40. *CR,* 62–2, 1579. Southern opponents offered various limiting amendments; one of these, a largely symbolic amendment by Culberson affirming "the right of the people to be secure in their persons, papers and effects against unreasonable search and seizure" (by the bureau's investigators), passed 39–34. Ibid., 1578.

41. *Minutes of the National Farmers' Educational and Cooperative Union of America,* 1913, (Salina, Kansas), 69.

42. The National Child Labor Committee and the National Association for Labor Legislation were the principal advocates. U.S. House of Representatives, Committee on Ways and Means, *White Phosphorus Matches,* 61st Congress, 3rd session, 279–91. However, Gompers did write to members of the Ways and Means Committee, urging passage of the bill. *American Federationist,* April 1911, 316–17. See also Walker, "The AFL and Child Labor Legislation," 329.

43. Gwendolyn Mink, *Old Labor and New Immigrants in American Political Development* (Ithaca, N.Y.: Cornell University Press, 1986); A. T. Lane, "American Trade Unions, Mass Immigration, and the Literacy Test: 1900–1917," *Labor History* 25 (winter 1984): 5–26. Lane contends that most labor organizations did not accept the "racist ideas then current in certain intellectual and genteel circles," relying instead, mostly, on cultural and individual explanations for unassimilability.

44. Mink, *Old Labor and New Immigrants,* 64–66; Link, *Woodrow Wilson and the Progressive Era,* 60–61.

45. Richard Lowitt, *George Norris,* vol. 2, *The Persistence of a Progressive* (Urbana: University of Illinois Press, 1971), 38, 325–27.

46. Immigration restriction composed both the second and the last items in the AFL's 1906 "Bill of Grievances" (see chapter 3) and remained in the highest ranks thereafter.

47. *CR,* 62–2, 4974.

48. Southerners had an additional reason to support this bill, one suspects. Its method was the requirement that prospective immigrants pass a literacy test, the method used for denial of black suffrage. For the complete, reinforcing array of southern arguments, see Johnson, *Oscar W. Underwood,* 73–75. Williams offered an amendment to exclude immigrants of African descent, just as the law already excluded the Chinese. *CR,* 62–2, 5029. Senator Root of New York responded that although he agreed "fully with the many things the Senator from Mississippi has said," there were important diplomatic reasons to avoid such exclusion (ibid., 5030). The Williams amendment failed on a 25–28 vote (ibid., 5032).

49. The commission was unanimous on the need to restrict immigration, and it arrived at the conclu-

sion (though not unanimously) that the literacy test was the most practical way to exclude the least desirable class of (unskilled) immigrants. See the letter from Jeremiah Jenks printed in *CR*, 62–3, 3316.

50. *Minutes*, 1911 (Shawnee, Oklahoma), 36–42. The FU's Committee on Immigration lamented that "of last year's million and a fifth, three-fourths were adult males, coming alone and single handed, with the intention of saving every possible cent and carrying their parsimonious savings back to their native land. Nearly one-half were penniless, and forced to settle down in the slums and sweatshops at any work and any wage. One-third of the adults were unable to read or write a single line in any language or dialect. . . . Less than fifteen thousand were 'farmers'!" Ibid., 39.

51. *Official Proceedings of the 32nd Annual Session of the Farmers' National Congress*, 1912 (New Orleans), 170.

52. The president's brief veto message expressed regret, in view of the large support, but stated that he could not countenance the literacy test. He referred to a letter from his secretary of commerce and labor; the letter, after alluding to administrative difficulties, argued for consideration of "industrial conditions." "We need labor in this country and the natives are unwilling to do it." *CR*, 62–3, 3417, 3427.

53. Ibid., 3307–18.

54. House passage is in *CR*, 62–3, 864; the votes to override are in *CR*, 62–3, 3318, 3429.

55. Contrast the opposing speeches in the House by Reps. Adolf J. Sabath of Illinois and James L. Slayden of Texas before the override vote. Ibid., 3424–28. Among the "union-card" contingent, Democrats Buchanan and Lewis supported the AFL position, voting to override; but five other Democrats and one Republican voted to uphold the veto.

56. Link quotes a letter from Wilson to Senator Williams in which the president refers to explicit commitments made to "groups of our fellow citizens of foreign extraction." Link, *Woodrow Wilson and the Progressive Era*, 61 n.

57. Ibid., 62–63. The 1898 act discussed in chapter 3 abolished the penalty of imprisonment for desertion from American ships in American ports; it did not apply to foreign ships in U.S. ports.

58. Jerold S. Auerbach, "Progressives at Sea: The La Follette Act of 1915," *Labor History* 2 (fall 1961): 348.

59. Ibid. See also Hyman Weintraub, *Andrew Furuseth: Emancipator of the Seamen* (Berkeley: University of California Press, 1959), 113–17.

60. Belle Case La Follette and Fola La Follette, *Robert M. La Follette*, vol. 1 (New York: Macmillan, 1953), 521–23. Furuseth was Norwegian, which may also have enhanced his standing with the Wisconsin senator.

61. *CR*, 62–2, 9249.

62. See, for example, the remarks of Representatives Hardy (D, Texas) in ibid. at 9259, Post (D, Ohio) at 9432, and Wilson (D, Pennsylvania) at 9434; and Auerbach, "Progressives at Sea," 354–55.

63. Auerbach, "Progressives at Sea," 352–53; La Follette and La Follette, *Robert M. La Follette*, 530.

64. See, for example, the arguments of Representatives Gallagher and Buchanan of Illinois, *CR*, 62–2, 9493, 9497.

65. *CR*, 62–3, 4585–88.

66. Weintraub, *Andrew Furuseth*, 117–19; Auerbach, "Progressives at Sea," 348–49.

67. Weintraub, *Andrew Furuseth*, 120; *CR*, 62–2, 10689. There was no roll call.

68. *CR*, 62–3, 4584–87. The Wisconsin senator succeeded, however, in several strengthening amendments.

69. Ibid., 4585–86. On the three losing roll calls, southern Democrats opposed strengthening the bill's provisions by votes of 4–8, 6–8 (this was the labor amendment), and 6–8. For Williams's arguments *against* the anti-labor section, see *CR*, 62–3, 4573.

70. The two other opponents were an Ohio Democrat (John J. Whitacre) and, surprisingly, Wisconsin Socialist Victor Berger. *CR*, 62–3, 4853.

71. *American Federationist*, October 1912, 812–13.

72. Jerome M. Clubb, "Congressional Opponents of Reform, 1901–1913" (Ph.D. diss., University of Washington, 1963), 270–71. Three of the six oppositional southern Democrats (Bailey, Percy, and

Foster) were lame ducks and would be replaced in 1913 by senators (Sheppard, Vardaman, and Ransdell) more favorable to labor.

73. Harris, "Organized Labor in Politics," 251–60.

74. Donald B. Johnson, ed., *National Party Platforms*, vol. 1 (Urbana: University of Illinois Press, 1978), 172, 177. See also Mink, *Old Labor and New Immigrants*, 215.

75. Harris, "Organized Labor in Politics," 249–50, 257.

76. William Diamond, *The Economic Thought of Woodrow Wilson* (Baltimore: Johns Hopkins University Press, 1943), 55, 70–71.

77. Sarasohn, *Party of Reform*, 61, 128–38; Gompers, *Seventy Years of Life and Labor* 2:280–82 (quotation at 282). On the convention maneuvers, see also Arthur S. Link, *Wilson*, vol. 1, *The Road to the White House* (Princeton: Princeton University Press, 1947), 431–45, and Louis W. Koenig, *Bryan* (New York: Capricorn Books, 1971), 482–96.

78. *American Federationist*, October 1912, 801–13.

79. Mink, *Old Labor and New Immigrants*, 222–27.

80. Although he won 435 electoral votes, Wilson received a popular majority in only twelve states: the former Confederacy plus Arizona. His vote was significantly less than Bryan's in the core and diverse states of Pennsylvania, Ohio, Michigan, Indiana, and Illinois. He did better than Bryan in New England and the Pacific coast and had the support of the San Francisco labor movement, but middle-class women voters also contributed to the increase here. Edgar E. Robinson, *The Presidential Vote, 1896–1932* (Stanford: Stanford University Press, 1934), 14–17. On Bay-area labor support, see Alexander Saxton, "San Francisco Labor and the Populist and Progressive Insurgencies," *Pacific Historical Review* 34 (November 1965): 432–33. In California, Wilson's nativist image was an advantage in labor circles.

81. Calculated from Congressional Quarterly, *Guide to U.S. Elections*, 717–23.

82. Marc Karson, *American Labor Unions and Politics, 1900–1918* (Boston: Beacon Press, 1958), 74; Arthur S. Link, *Wilson*, vol. 2, *The New Freedom* (Princeton: Princeton University Press, 1956), 19, 139–40. See Lombardi, *Labor's Voice in the Cabinet*, 75–132, on William Wilson's contributions to labor legislation.

83. *CR*, 63–1, 319. A recommittal motion failed 47–198. Passage was by voice vote.

84. The two Democrats voting to strike the proviso were Pomerene of Ohio and Thomas of Colorado.

85. Link, *The New Freedom*, 266–68 (quotations 267–68); Dallas Lee Jones, "The Wilson Administration and Organized Labor 1912–1919" (Ph.D. diss., Cornell University, 1954), 115–31; Ray Stanndard Baker, *Woodrow Wilson: Life and Letters*, vol. 4 (Garden City, N.Y., Doubleday, Page and Co., 1931), 360–63.

86. *American Federationist*, January 1914, 35–46.

87. Ibid., October 1914, 860, and November 1914, 957, 971–74.

88. *Statutes at Large* 38, pt. 1 (1913–15): 103–8, 291–92; Lombardi, *Labor's Voice in the Cabinet*, 116–18. On the Paint Creek, West Virginia, investigation, see note 1 of this chapter, and *American Federationist*, October 1913, 825–35, and February 1915, 118–19.

89. There was little opposition to the safety and health bill, and it passed by voice vote. *CR*, 63–2, 4706. Its progress was stalled in the Senate, where Senators Dillingham and Overman objected to its consideration. *American Federationist* 22 (April 1915): 289. In the 64th Congress, a labor-safety-bureau bill would again pass the House and die in the Senate after being recommitted on a motion by Hoke Smith. One suspects that a few senators concerned to protect their states' textile industries were the principal agents in the bill's defeat in the Wilson era. It also suffered, as is clear from perfunctory Senate debate, because it had no strong labor advocates in the Senate. *CR*, 64–1, 1268, 12164, 12315, 12411. In 1915, Congress *did* consent, with very little opposition, to a labor-backed bill to expand the safety functions of the Bureau of Mines. *American Federationist* 22 (April 1915): 284; *CR*, 63–3, 2814–15, 4950. The convict labor bill, H.R. 1933, was sponsored by Representative Lewis of Maryland, one of the "union-card" group and chair of the House Labor Committee. It was modeled after the Webb (liquor) prohibition bill and passed the House with only two dissenting votes on March 4, 1914. *CR*, 63–2, 4302–3. See also *American Federationist* 21 (May 1914): 403–5.

90. *CR*, 63–2, 4292.

91. For a grim portrait of the southern convict-lease system and its successors, see John Dittmer, *Black Georgia in the Progressive Era* (Urbana: University of Illinois Press, 1977), 72–89. On the prison reform movement led by then-governor Vardaman in Mississippi, see Albert D. Kirwan, *Revolt of the Rednecks* (New York: Harper Torchbooks, 1951), 167–77. Of the convict-lease system (replaced in 1906 by state farm work), Kirwan writes, "Compared to the treatment accorded these convicts [by those who leased them from the government] . . . slavery was a mild and humane institution" (168).

92. See the remarks of Senator Williams in *CR*, 63–2, 5652. The argument that "open-air" work on prison farms was a humane reform was not confined to the South. New York prison reformers also saw prison farms as a significant improvement over the leasing of convict labor and argued that it served "the moral and physical betterment of the convicts" while defraying the state's costs. *New York Times*, February 1, 1914, 11. See also "Reformatory Boys Going on a Farm . . . Youthful Offenders Will Reform Themselves by Open-Air Work, It Is Hoped," *New York Times*, February 8, 1914, 9, and, more generally, Sidney Wilmot, "Use of Convict Labor for Highway Construction in the North," *Proceedings of the Academy of Political Science* 4 (January 1914): 246–309. Calling the convict-goods bill a "mischievous measure," the *New York Times* opined, "There can be no good argument against putting convicts to work" (May 28, 1914, 12). From organized labor's point of view, road work was the least objectionable use of convict labor.

93. The vote to take up the bill was 33–19. Only five southerners voted yea. No sooner was it made the order of business than Senator Works of California interrupted with a speech on another matter. The bill did not come to the floor again. *CR*, 63–3, 966. The convict-labor bill long championed by the AFL (and passed three times by the House) would finally become law in 1928. See Lorwin, *American Federation of Labor*, 404, and *American Federationist*, March 1929, 278. In the Senate, four southerners' arguments against passage echoed the earlier debates; however, eighteen southern Democrats joined supporters to pass the bill 65–11. *CR*, 70–2, 733–876.

94. H.R. 14330 (the import ban) had also passed the House in 1914, only to be passed over in the Senate on the objection of Senator Smith of Georgia. *CR*, 63–3, 4947. The Underwood Tariff Act had carried a prohibition on importation of convict-made goods, but the new bill extended the ban to "pauper"-made goods (that is, produced by people in public eleemosynary institutions) and imposed heavier penalties. *New York Times*, March 10, 1914, 8.

95. Karson, *American Labor Unions and Politics*, 79–80.

96. *New York Times*, November 4, 1914, 1, 4, and November 8, 1, 2. The Progressive vote, of course, had almost faded away, mostly returning to the GOP, from whence it had come.

97. *New York Times*, November 4, 1914, 1, and November 5, 1914, 1, 4; Congressional Quarterly, *Guide to U.S. Elections*, 724–29.

98. *CR*, 63–3, 616, 1483–84.

99. Arthur S. Link, *Wilson*, vol. 3, *The Struggle for Neutrality* (Princeton: Princeton University Press, 1960), 137–38.

100. Wayne Flynt, *Duncan Upshaw Fletcher: Dixie's Reluctant Progressive* (Tallahassee: Florida State University Press, 1971), 96–97; Link, *The Struggle for Neutrality*, 81–90; Jeffrey J. Safford, *Wilsonian Maritime Diplomacy* (New Brunswick, N.J.: Rutgers University Press, 1978), 35–41.

101. Safford, *Wilsonian Maritime Diplomacy*, 43–47; Link, *The Struggle for Neutrality*, 94–100, 143–61; Flynt, *Duncan Upshaw Fletcher*, 99–104; Paul M. Zeis, *American Shipping Policy* (Princeton: Princeton University Press, 1938), 83–89; *New York Times*, January 22, 1915, 5, and January 23, 1915, 5; *CR*, 63–3, 3905–23. On the final House roll call (*CR*, 63–3, 3923), the core voted 55–47 (most voting core Democrats backed the shipping bill, but a third abstained); the diverse districts voted 32–31 and the periphery, 127–40. On final passage of the measure in 1916, see chapter 11.

102. Link, *The New Freedom*, 274–76; *American Federationist*, March 1915, 186–90.

103. *CR*, 63–3, 3077–78 (vote). Forty-one percent of core representatives voted to override, versus 66 percent in diverse and 82 percent in periphery districts. For the Democratic Party, the more- and less-industrialized regions *within* each region were again split along the same lines: the more urban and industrial districts were more likely to sustain the veto than the more rural, less industrial. The small minor-

party vote favored override by 12–2. The "union-card" contingent split 7–6 (the Democrats divided 4 to 6). With similar voting patterns but higher support in each region, a subsequent presidential veto was successfully overridden in February 1917.

104. See text above, and Link, *The New Freedom*, 255.

105. Brandeis, *Labor Legislation*, 413–19, 437–40; Davidson, *Child Labor Legislation*, 251–57.

106. Davidson, *Child Labor Legislation*, 257. Davidson describes the House vote: "The vote was sectional, however, not in the sense of the whole South against the whole North, but rather of the manufacturing South against the rest of the country."

107. Link, *The New Freedom*, 257.

108. The *Brooklyn Eagle* described the seamen's bill as "a measure to kill the coastwise and passenger steamship interests . . . [and] to turn over to vessels under the British flag the business on the Great Lakes," and it urged defeat of the bill "to prevent the Labor Trust from making competitive running of ships under our flag wholly impossible." The Association of Passenger Steamboat Lines described the bill to the *New York Sun* as a "revolutionary and anarchistic bill" that would be "the hardest blow that our merchant marine has ever received." Quoted in "Finding Flaws in the Seamen's Bill," *Literary Digest*, November 8, 1913, 860.

109. Link, *The New Freedom*, 270–71.

110. Ibid., 271–72; La Follette and La Follette, *Robert M. La Follette*, 521–32; Weintraub, *Andrew Furuseth*, 122–28; *CR*, 63–3, 14362. In the Senate, weakening amendments supported by Republicans and a handful of Democrats (three from the South, one from Kansas, one from New York) were easily defeated. *CR*, 63–2, 5790–91. There were no roll calls on House or Senate passage.

111. Richard Abrams, in his attempt to demonstrate the conservatism of southern congressmen in the Wilson years, writes, "Although the [seamen's] bill passed with heavy majorities, the only important opposition was from the South." Richard Abrams, "Woodrow Wilson and the Southern Congressmen," *Journal of Southern History* 22 (November 1956): 429. However, on Senate amendment votes, no more than four southern senators joined the Republican and New York Democrat opponents, and on the final critical and highly contested vote reported in table 10.10, southern senators composed only seven of the bill's thirty-three opponents, two-thirds of whom were Republicans (mainly from core states). *CR*, 63–3, 4817.

112. *CR*, 63–3, 4807–8, 4813–14. See also Grantham, *Hoke Smith*, 280–82.

113. Link, *The New Freedom*, 272–73.

114. *American Federationist*, April 1915, 284.

115. For a detailed discussion of the feudal origins and character of nineteenth- and early-twentieth-century labor relations in the United States, see Karen Orren, *Belated Feudalism* (New York: Cambridge University Press, 1991).

116. See chapter 3 and the text above.

117. Link, *Woodrow Wilson and the Progressive Era*, 223–30.

118. Arthur S. Link, *Wilson*, vol. 4, *Confusions and Crises* (Princeton: Princeton University Press, 1964), 325–27. As the *New York Times* archly stated, "It need never be said, and cannot rightly be said, that the court needs among its members some advocate of 'social justice.'" Quoted in ibid., 325.

119. Alpheus Thomas Mason, *Brandeis: A Free Man's Life* (New York: Viking Press, 1946), 141–52, 248–53, 300–332, 431–32.

120. Labor union support for the Brandeis nomination included endorsements from New York, Houston, and San Francisco city labor councils, the International Ladies' Garment Workers' Union, and the United Mine Workers. Link, *Confusions and Crises*, 327 n. Georgia labor unions helped to persuade Hoke Smith to work actively for the nomination. Grantham, *Hoke Smith*, 298.

121. Mason, *Brandeis*, 470–71. Cummins and Borah opposed the nomination in the Senate. Borah also worried about Brandeis's defense of retail price maintenance as a way of maintaining small business competition. Ibid., 424–28, 501.

122. Link, *Confusions and Crises*, 323–24. Gregory had consulted Brandeis on Justice Department appointments and on early Clayton Act prosecutions. Mason, *Brandeis*, 405–8.

123. Letter of January 29, 1916, in *The Papers of Woodrow Wilson,* ed. Arthur S. Link et al., 69 vols. (Princeton: Princeton University Press, 1966–94), 36:51.

124. Link, *Confusions and Crises,* 356; Mason, *Brandeis,* 469–70, 472–78, 489–90.

125. The Republicans in favor were La Follette, Poindexter, and Norris. Senator O'Gorman of New York and several periphery Democrats had to be pressured by the president, McAdoo, Gregory, and Postmaster General Burleson to fall in line. The periphery contingent's reservations stemmed mainly from wounded pride at not being initially consulted (as in Hoke Smith's case), objection to Brandeis's role in the Federal Trade Commission affair (which had angered Senator Reed), and some sentiment that the seat should be filled by a southerner (which the previous occupant had been). In the end, only Senator Newlands of Nevada—ironically, a strong commission supporter—deserted the Democrats. Mason, *Brandeis,* 465–505. *CR,* 64–1, 9032.

126. The vote was 337–46, and the regional pattern largely coincided with that of the 1915 (63rd Congress) vote shown in table 10.9. The large majority of representatives from North and South Carolina and Georgia opposed the bill; outside these three states, the large majority of southern votes supported the child-labor bill. *CR,* 64–1, 2035; Davidson, *Child Labor Legislation,* 257.

127. Ibid., 258.

128. Ibid., 111, 126–29, 258; A. J. McKelway to Wilson, May 17 and July 17, 1916, in Link et al., *Papers of Woodrow Wilson* 37:65, 429; Arthur S. Link, *Wilson,* vol. 5, *Campaigns for Progressivism and Peace, 1916–1917* (Princeton: Princeton University Press, 1965), 58.

129. J. Daniels to Wilson, July 17, 1916, in Link et al., *Papers of Woodrow Wilson* 37:429.

130. R. L. Owen to Wilson, June 2, 1916, in ibid., 151.

131. Ibid., 161–62.

132. Wilson to R. L. Owen, June 5, 1916, in ibid., 162.

133. R. L. Owen to Wilson, June 8, 1916, in ibid., 175. I have not seen, in such correspondence or in secondary accounts of the policy direction urged on Wilson in 1916, specific reference to the need to attract the labor vote. Rather, emphasis is placed on the need to attract those who, in 1912–14, voted for the Progressive Party. Owen, for example, wrote of the need to "attract the progressive elements in the country who ought to be with us, and not dividing their forces as an independent party." However, labor was undoubtedly important. Daniels, who had targeted the labor vote as the Democratic National Committee's publicity chairman in the 1912 campaign, had stated then: "If we get our share of [the labor vote] there is nothing in the world that can defeat us. It is the crux of the situation." Quoted in Julia Marie Greene, "The Strike at the Ballot Box" (Ph.D. diss., Yale University, 1990), 576.

134. Johnson, *National Party Platforms,* 198–99.

135. Link, *Campaigns for Progressivism and Peace,* 59; *CR* 64–1, 12313.

136. Orren, *Belated Feudalism.*

137. Harry Weiss, "Employers' Liability and Workmen's Compensation," in Brandeis, *Labor Legislation,* 564–68.

138. Robert Asher, "Failure and Fulfillment: Agitation for Employers' Liability Legislation and the Origins of Workmen's Compensation in New York State," *Labor History* 24 (spring 1983): 201; Weiss, "Employers' Liability and Workmen's Compensation," 568–69.

139. *Howard v. Illinois Central Railway Co.* 207 U.S. 463 (1908). Where the employee's *own* negligence (as opposed to that of a "fellow servant") was established, the employee might still collect, but the amount would be reduced proportionately. Thus the "contributory negligence" doctrine was only partly modified in the 1906–8 federal liability laws.

140. James Weinstein, "Big Business and the Origins of Workmen's Compensation," *Labor History* 8 (spring 1967): 157–61.

141. Robert Asher, "The Ignored Precedent: Samuel Gompers and Workmen's Compensation," *New Labor Review* 4 (fall 1982): 51–77; *American Federationist:* August 1910, 697; November 1910, 971; April 1911, 299.

142. *Federal Employees' Compensation,* 63d Cong., 2d sess., 1914, H. Rept. 561, 25–31.

143. *Literary Digest,* March 2, 1912, 414; *New York Times,* February 21, 1912, 6; *CR,* 62–2, 5926–27.

144. *Literary Digest,* May 18, 1912, 1026; *Survey,* July 6, 1912, 492–93.

145. *New York Times,* February 21, 1912, 6; *Literary Digest,* May 18, 1912, 1027; *CR,* 62–3, 4483, 4543–47.

146. *Literary Digest,* May 18, 1912, 1027.

147. Grantham, *Hoke Smith,* 225–27; *CR,* 62–2, 5944, 5949.

148. Grantham, *Hoke Smith,* 226. Other examples include Jeff Davis of Arkansas (*CR,* 62–2, 5935) and, later, Huey Long of Louisiana. See T. Harry Williams, *Huey Long* (New York: Knopf, 1969), 85–109.

149. *CR,* 62–2, 5950–58; Grantham, *Hoke Smith,* 227–28.

150. Such was the reasoning of Senator Newlands, who joined the Republicans in favor of the compensation system. *CR,* 62–2, 5938–39. As Newlands and other supporters noted, the bill was "carefully balanced" or "nicely adjusted" to win the support of both employers and employees.

151. *CR,* 62–2, 5954.

152. Representative Hardwick of Georgia defended "the sacred right of the Anglo-Saxon to have a jury of the vicinage assess the amount of the damages." *CR,* 62–3, 4543. Aside from the other issues at stake, the agrarians opposed transferring the costs of worker compensation from railroad profits (as in the employer liability system) to those (such as farmers) who used railroad services. Under the compensation bill, railroads could have these expenses incorporated into the rate base and thus passed on to those whose freight they hauled. Ibid., 4483.

153. *CR,* 62–2, 5959. Kern and Shively, both of Indiana, were the diverse-state senators.

154. *CR,* 62–3, 4547.

155. Grantham, *Hoke Smith,* 228.

156. See ibid., and *CR,* 62–2, 5923–24, 5939, 5940, 5942–43, for labor objections from Arkansas, Georgia, Missouri, Montana, and Tennessee.

157. Weiss, "Employers' Liability and Workmen's Compensation," 594.

158. A "Joint Commission" of the AFL and the National Civic Federation issued a report in 1914, published as *Workmen's Compensation* and printed as S. Doc. 419, 63d Cong., 2d sess., 1914, which "found the sentiment among employers and employees almost universally for "comprehensive workmen's compensation laws."

159. H.R. 15222, sponsored by Representative McGillicuddy of Maine, was reported from the Judiciary Committee in April. During a brief debate, two southern congressmen (Quin and Sisson) petulantly complained of its cost to the government and the fact that injured farmers had no such recourse. Representative Bryan of Washington asked whether Sisson realized that "the farmers' associations and organizations in this country are all in favor of this legislation and are continually passing resolutions in regard to it." Sisson (D, Mississippi) said that he was not aware of such support and proceeded to object to the bill's consideration under unanimous consent. It was not brought up again in this Congress. *CR,* 63–2, 10482–87.

160. *CR,* 64–1, 10886. The speaker was Representative Adair, now running for governor of Indiana.

161. *Compensation of Federal Employees Suffering Injuries while on Duty,* 64th Cong., 1st sess., 1916, H. Rept. 678. This 1916 report was silent on whether the bill covered disability from occupational disease as well as accidents. The 1914 bill sponsored by Representative McGillicuddy had contained the explicit phrase "and [compensation] for the disability, death or suspension from work of an employee resulting from an occupational disease contracted in the course of his employment." *Federal Employees' Compensation,* H. Rept. 561, 3. This sentence was stricken from the 1916 bill due to some wariness on the part of sponsors (or fear of provoking conservative opposition?). One of the bill's supporters on the Judiciary Committee, Representative Volstead, stated during House debate that it had proved difficult to define "occupational diseases" but that he was hopeful the courts would interpret "personal injury" to include occupational disease, as they had in fact already been inclined to do. *CR,* 64–1, 10899–10900, 10913–14.

162. *CR,* 64–1, 10916. Five other Democrats—four from the South and one from Indiana—voted "present."

163. Ibid., 12898, 12902; Grantham, *Hoke Smith,* 299. Smith had offered a similar amendment in 1912.

164. *CR,* 64–1, 10886–88.

165. Ibid., 12902–4, 12912–15.

166. *CR*, 55–2, 5046–57; *Statutes at Large* 30 (1897–99): 424–28. Employees were also given rights to present their claims in receivership proceedings, and injunctions to compel employees to work were prohibited.

167. Mary O. Furner, "The Republican Tradition and the New Liberalism," in *The State and Social Investigation in Britain and the United States,* ed. Michael J. Lacey and Mary O. Furner (Cambridge: Cambridge University Press, 1993), 218. Unfortunately for labor, the Supreme Court declared this prohibition unconstitutional in 1908. Congress reinserted it in the 1926 Railway Labor Act.

168. David A. McCabe, "Federal Intervention in Labor Disputes under the Erdman, Newlands, and Adamson Act," *Proceedings of the Academy of Political Science* 7 (January 1917): 98.

169. Ibid., 99–102; Leifur Magnusson and Marguerite A. Gadsby, "Federal Intervention in Railroad Disputes," *Monthly Labor Review* 11 (July 1920): 38.

170. McCabe, "Federal Intervention in Labor Disputes," 99–100; I. Leo Sharfman, *The American Railroad Problem* (New York: Century Co., 1921), 326–28; Harold V. Faulkner, *The Decline of Laissez Faire, 1897–1917* (New York: Rinehart and Co., 1951), 288.

171. Sharfman, *American Railroad Problem,* 328–29; Link, *Campaigns for Progressivism and Peace,* 83–87.

172. *CR*, 64–1, 13335–36; Link, *Campaigns for Progressivism and Peace,* 88–90.

173. *CR*, 64–1, 13643. Underwood's amendment, supported by eleven Democrats and three Republicans, including Senator Norris, was defeated on a 14–57 vote (ibid., 13649).

174. The Norris proposal, rejected by voice vote, is found at ibid., 13635; see also Senator Owen's similar sentiments at 13630–31.

175. Ibid., 13647.

176. Ibid., 13583.

177. On La Follette's attempts to amend the 1906 rate bill, see La Follette and La Follette, *Robert M. La Follette,* 208–9, 581. During consideration of the Mann-Elkins bill in 1910, La Follette offered an amendment reducing the hours of train-operating workers to fourteen and requiring ten-hour rest periods between working days. It lost 24–31. The regional pattern was as follows: core, zero percent in favor; diverse, 64 percent; periphery 61 percent. The periphery supplied 71 percent of the supporting votes. Whereas core Republicans were unanimously opposed, periphery Republicans split almost evenly. *CR*, 61–2, 7355.

178. *CR*, 64–1, 13396, 13481, 13571, 13580, 13588, 13592–94 (remarks of Senators Borah and Oliver and Representatives Bennet, Greene, Browning, Gray, and Platt).

179. See, for example, the remarks of Representative Parker of New Jersey and Senator Brandegee of Connecticut. *Cr*, 64–1, 13585, 13632–33.

180. Ibid., 13581–82, 13585, 13587, 13600–601, 13633 (remarks of Representatives Russell, Caldwell, Boland, Cullop, Britt, Heflin, and Hulbert and Senator Johnson).

181. Ibid., 13592, 13600, 13581, 13630–31 (remarks of Representatives Adamson, Small, Heflin, and Buchanan and Senator Owen). Senator Reed also argued that U.S. freight trains were run very slowly (ten to twelve miles per hour) and could easily be sped up for greater efficiency (ibid., 13575). For his part, William Jennings Bryan insisted that "the question of hours is not a matter for arbitration. Congress can fix the length of a working day." Quoted in Sarasohn, *Party of Reform,* 203.

182. *CR*, 64–1, 13600–601.

183. Brandeis, *Labor Legislation,* 554–57.

184. Lorwin, *American Federation of Labor,* 57 n; Gompers, *Seventy Years of Life and Labor* 2:131–37.

185. Gompers, 144. Gompers notes that he found himself "substantially in agreement" with conservative Republican Sen. Boies Penrose, who opposed the Adamson law and most other labor legislation. Ibid., 145.

186. *CR*, 64–1, 13589.

187. Ibid., 13591, 13580. Senator Cummins, also an opponent (though for different reasons, as would become obvious later: he supported anti-strike and compulsory arbitration laws), gave another AFL-type argument against the legislation. Ibid., 13575.

188. U.S. House of Representatives, Committee on Labor, *Hearings on House Joint Resolution 159, 64th Cong.,* 1st sess., 1916 (Washington, D.C.: GPO, 1916), 123–37. Once again, Gompers's preference

for private, contractual, and union pension plans was echoed by conservative Republican opponents. See, e.g., the remarks of Representative Moore, *CR,* 64–2, 2651.

189. *CR,* 64–2, 2654. Even Representative Buchanan abandoned the AFL on this vote. Representative Johnson (R, Washington) was the only member of the labor group to vote against the bill. Periphery Democrats were as strongly supportive as their core copartisans; 80 percent voted yea (compared with 76 percent among core Democrats). Periphery Republicans gave 49 percent of their votes to the bill, whereas only 24 percent of core Republicans backed it. Despite the substantial majority, the bill had been called up by London under suspension of the rules, which required a two-thirds vote for passage. With only 58 percent voting aye, it failed.

190. In February 1916, Rep. Jeff McLemore of Texas had introduced a resolution asking the president to warn Americans not to travel on armed merchant ships lest German attacks lead to a loss of life that would propel the country toward war. Wilson, determined not to let Congress impinge on his foreign policy power, adamantly opposed the resolution, arguing that by provoking further combatant infringement of America's neutral rights on the seas, the United States would actually make war more likely. The McLemore resolution was ultimately tabled 276–142, with midwestern Republicans and thirty-three mostly periphery Democrats in opposition. However, as Bryan and McLemore subsequently observed, the resolution had served its purpose in conveying to the president the powerful antiwar sentiment in his own party and almost everywhere in the country outside the Northeast. Link, *Confusions and Crises,* 167–94. Wilson was able to suppress the resolution only by promising to do all in his power to avoid war with Germany (ibid., 194). If that was not sufficient indication, the message was dramatically brought home in the June Democratic convention when the delegates spontaneously and enthusiastically took up a raucous chant reminding the president and their fellow citizens that many times in the past, the country had suffered challenges and indignities but nevertheless had held its patience and "we didn't go to war." This chant from the floor punctuated the address of Martin H. Glynn. *Official Report of the Proceedings of the Democratic National Convention,* June 14, 1916 (St. Louis, Missouri), 28–45. In view of the public's powerful pacifism, the Republicans too retreated from an earlier intention to make Wilson's "weak" foreign policy stance the major campaign issue. Link, *Woodrow Wilson and the Progressive Era,* 230–32.

191. Link, *Campaigns for Progressivism and Peace,* 91–103, 140 (quotation); Sarasohn, *Party of Reform,* 200–236; Arthur S. Link and William M. Leary Jr., "The Election of 1916, in *The Coming to Power,* ed. Arthur M. Schlesinger Jr. et al. (New York: Chelsea House, 1971), 312–17.

192. Link, *Campaigns for Progressivism and Peace,* 103–10 (quotation at 109).

193. Sarasohn, *Party of Reform,* 217. On GOP use of the tariff issue, see ibid., 212–13, and *Literary Digest,* October 7, 1916, 871–72.

194. Link, *Campaigns for Progressivism and Peace,* 126–27; Sarasohn, *Party of Reform,* 206; Mink, *Old Labor and New Immigrants,* 256; Karson, *American Labor Unions and Politics,* 85–86.

195. Link, *Campaigns for Progressivism and Peace,* 126–27; *American Federationist,* November 1916, 1067–68. Political cues in the *American Federationist* in the months before the election are scant and indirect. Though the November statement contrasted Hughes ("the reactionary candidate of predatory wealth") with Wilson and his "clear vision and courageous heart," the July editorial was decidedly low-key (see *American Federationist,* July 1916, 537–42), and there were no political endorsements in the August-October issues.

196. *Literary Digest,* October 7, 1916, 871–74; Link, *Campaigns for Progressivism and Peace,* 126–27.

197. Greene, "Strike at the Ballot Box," 599–600. On Ohio and California labor, see also Sarasohn, *Party of Reform,* 206, and S. D. Lovell, *The Presidential Election of 1916* (Carbondale: Southern Illinois University Press, 1980), 81–88, 165–66.

198. Elizabeth McKillen, *Chicago Labor and the Quest for a Democratic Diplomacy, 1914–1924* (Ithaca, N.Y.: Cornell University Press, 1995), 34–35. One of the defeated Chicago Democrats was "union-card" member Frank Buchanan.

199. Computed from county table #8 in Robinson, *The Presidential Vote.* The remaining counties (eight of the eighty-eight) continued in the Republican column.

200. Congressional Quarterly, *Guide to U.S. Elections,* 485–509. The *New York Times* (November 12, 1916, 6) did credit the union labor vote with the defeat of Senator Lippitt in Rhode Island and with

the expansion of the Democratic vote in Vermont (where railroad workers were a factor), though both states went Republican in the presidential and in four of five House races.

201. For 1916 election results, see Robinson, *The Presidential Vote*, 16–19 and tables; *New York Times*, November 9, 1916, 1, 4, and November 12, 1916, 1, 6, 7; and Link, *Campaigns for Progressivism and Peace*, 160–63. Link (162) cites figures showing that Wilson's 1912–16 gains reached 30–109 percent of the 1912 Progressive vote in the following states (ranked from lowest to highest percent gain): Kansas, Ohio, Nebraska, New Mexico, North Dakota, New Hampshire, Washington, Colorado, Montana, Idaho, Wyoming, and Utah. As for the urban labor vote, it (along with women and progressives) helped to carry Cleveland, Toledo, Milwaukee, San Francisco, and Seattle for Wilson. In downstate New York, the normally Democratic vote, bolstered by Jewish Republican defections, held New York (Manhattan) and Kings (Brooklyn) Counties, though by lower-than-expected margins. Working-class and former progressive votes also held Boston for Wilson. He lost Philadelphia, Queens, northern New Jersey, Buffalo, Pittsburgh, Chicago, Indianapolis, Detroit, St. Louis, and Los Angeles. See Robinson, *The Presidential Vote*, county map, 18, and table 19; the *New York Times* issues and pages cited above; and Sarasohn, *Party of Reform*, 209–33.

202. Link, *Campaigns for Progressivism and Peace*, 163.

203. *New York Times*, November 10, 1916, 12. The *Baltimore Sun* remarked, "If anyone had said two days ago that a Democratic presidential candidate could lose New York, New Jersey, Connecticut, Illinois, Indiana, and Wisconsin and still be elected, he would have been accounted a first-class idiot." Quoted in Sarasohn, *Party of Reform*, 219.

Chapter Eleven

1. See, for example, Isaac Kramnick, *Republicanism and Bourgeois Radicalism* (Ithaca, N.Y.: Cornell University Press, 1991); Joyce O. Appleby, *Liberalism and Republicanism in the Historical Imagination* (Cambridge: Harvard University Press, 1992); and Samuel P. Huntington, *American Politics: The Promise of Disharmony* (Cambridge: Harvard University Press, 1981).

2. See, for example, Robert H. Wiebe, *The Search for Order, 1877–1920* (New York: Hill and Wang, 1967), 148–67.

3. Eldon Eisenach, *The Lost Promise of Progressivism* (Lawrence: University Press of Kansas, 1994), esp. 21 n, 72–73, 128–37. Eisenach's categorization of Wilson as wedded to a reactionary, laissez-faire perspective relies on his *prepolitical* ideology, which was, indeed, quite traditional and conservative. However, once Wilson became ambitious for a prominent role in politics (after 1908), he was compelled to become, in effect, a Bryanite. Subsequent electoral insecurity propelled him further in a progressive direction, as described above.

4. Harold V. Faulkner, *The Decline of Laissez Faire, 1897–1917* (New York: Rinehart and Co., 1951), 350–51; John M. Gaus and Leon O. Wolcott, *Public Administration and the United States Department of Agriculture* (Chicago: Public Administration Service, 1940), 19–26.

5. Edward Wiest, *Agricultural Organization in the United States* (Lexington: University of Kentucky Press, 1923), 34–35; U.S. Department of Commerce, Bureau of the Census: *Statistical Abstract of the United States, 1905* (Washington, D.C.: GPO, 1906) and *Statistical Abstract of the United States, 1915* (Washington, D.C.: GPO, 1916).

6. U.S. Department of Commerce, Bureau of the Census, *Statistical Abstract of the United States, 1901* (Washington, D.C.: GPO, 1901), 27, and *Statistical Abstract* (1915), 617. D.C. employment is from U.S. Civil Service Commission, *34th Annual Report* (Washington, D.C.: GPO, 1917), 213.

7. David F. Houston, *Eight Years with Wilson's Cabinet*, vol. 1 (Garden City, N.Y.: Doubleday, 1926), 37–38, 80–111, 206–7; Arthur S. Link, *Wilson*, vol. 2, *The New Freedom* (Princeton: Princeton University Press, 1956), 137–39; chapters 7 and 8 above.

8. Alfred C. True, *A History of Agricultural Extension Work* (Washington, D.C.: GPO, 1928), 111–12.

9. The term "cooperation" was again employed in the Smith-Hughes Act to legitimate the new federal role in what had been entirely a state and local function.

10. For the House debate, see *Congressional Record* (*CR*), 64th Cong., 1st sess. (hereafter cited in the form 64–1), 1269–537. Core Republicans opposed the bill, but their diverse and periphery colleagues backed it with large majorities. Periphery Democrats backed it 135–3; core Democrats supported it 18–11, with almost as many abstentions as yeas. The chamber's one (core) Socialist voted for passage. Ibid., 1536–37. Some urban opponents were willing to put federal money into great interstate highways, and in a later period, supported by the expanded automobile and tourism lobbies, Congress would move in that direction. However, the 1916 law was a farmers' measure. On the background of the bill, see Wayne E. Fuller, "Good Roads and Rural Free Delivery of Mail," *Mississippi Valley Historical Review* 42 (June 1955): 67–83.

11. *Statutes at Large* 39, pt. 1 (1917): 357–59; Houston, *Eight Years with Wilson's Cabinet*, 207–10.

12. G. O. Virtue, "Legislation for the Farmers: Packers and Grain Exchanges," *Quarterly Journal of Economics* 37 (August 1923): 693–94; Theodore Saloutos and John D. Hicks, *Agricultural Discontent in the Middle West, 1900–1939* (Madison: University of Wisconsin Press, 1951), 326.

13. Wiest, *Agricultural Organization in the United States*, 34; Van L. Perkins, *Crisis in Agriculture: The Agricultural Adjustment Administration and the New Deal* (Berkeley: University of California Press, 1969), 97; Gaus and Wolcott, *Public Administration and the United States Department of Agriculture*, 47–48, 64–65.

14. Daniel P. Carpenter, "The Corporate Metaphor and Executive Department Centralization in the U.S., 1880–1928," *Studies in American Political Development* 12 (spring 1998): 101–46.

15. Theda Skocpol and Kenneth Finegold, "State Capacity and Economic Intervention in the Early New Deal," *Political Science Quarterly* 97 (summer 1982): 274.

16. Cedrick B. Cowing, *Populists, Plungers, and Progressives* (Princeton: Princeton University Press, 1965), 47–50, 57–58, 108.

17. Theda Skocpol and Kenneth Finegold, *State and Party in America's New Deal* (Madison: University of Wisconsin Press, 1995), 57–59.

18. On Wilson's earlier philosophy of government, his opposition to Bryanism, and his record on labor and trusts, see Arthur S. Link, *Wilson*, vol. 1, *The Road to the White House* (Princeton: Princeton University Press, 1947), esp. 25–32, 127, 158–59, 381, and Link, *The New Freedom*, 34–36.

19. Link, *The New Freedom*, 446–47.

20. Political scientists often argue that Congress writes discretionary laws in order to "pass the buck" to the bureaucracy and thus avoid making difficult political choices. I believe it is much more accurate to see bureaucratic outcomes as a result of necessary legislative compromises in which some members of Congress, typically those initiating the proposal, have quite specific preferences but are opposed by those who want no legislation. At this point, strategically placed actors who prefer bureaucratic solutions (the president and the existing bureaucracy, perhaps joined by representatives of mixed political economies or strong middle-class constituencies) are able to win acceptance of discretionary bureaucracy as a compromise between radical legislative specificity and the status quo.

21. Link, *The New Freedom*, 451–57; *New York Times*, July 15, 1914, 3.

22. This statement is scarcely arguable, but support for the localism, electoral sensitivity, and party dominance of the legislature can be found in, among others, Stephen Skowronek, *Building a New American State* (New York: Cambridge University Press, 1982); David R. Mayhew, *Congress: The Electoral Connection* (New Haven, Conn.: Yale University Press, 1974); and Richard F. Fenno, *Home Style* (Boston: Little, Brown, 1978).

23. In 1888, the Wisconsin Union Labor Party included the following plank in its platform, a nice example of the farmers' movement commitment to codified democracy: "All laws should be simplified so that there is but one law on the subject, and that worded in plain language, which will enable the people to understand the law without paying enormous fees to lawyers." *Appleton's Annual Cyclopaedia for 1888* (New York: D. Appleton, 1889), 846.

24. See, for example, Edward Tufte, *Political Control of the Economy* (Princeton: Princeton University Press, 1978), and Alberto Alesina and Howard Rosenthal, *Partisan Politics, Divided Government, and the Economy* (New York: Cambridge University Press, 1995).

25. There are numerous studies supporting an electoral connection to presidential instigation of military involvement abroad. A good summary can be found in Bruce M. Russett, *Controlling the Sword* (Cambridge: Harvard University Press, 1990). Solid empirical evidence for an electoral use-of-force cycle for the U.S. president from 1946 to 1992 can be found in Mark Kesselman, "Rally 'round the Calendar: Election Cycles and Presidential Use of Force" (honors thesis, Cornell University, Department of Government, 1993). On foreign investment and U.S. military intervention, see Faulkner, *Decline of Laissez Faire*, chap. 4, and Walter Lafeber, *The American Age*, 2d ed. (New York: W. W. Norton, 1994).

26. Before World War I, the debate on Philippine independence in 1914–16 provides an example. Rep. William A. Jones of Virginia had sponsored a bill granting immediate self-government for the islands, to be followed in a few years by full independence. The president opposed the bill and supported, in its place, only a limited amount of self-government. However, an amendment by Senator Clarke of Arkansas proposed to reinstate the provision for full independence (Arthur S. Link, *Woodrow Wilson and the Progressive Era* [New York: Harper and Row, 1954], 227–28; *New York Times*, January 18, 1916, 5). The Clarke amendment passed the Senate on a tie vote, broken in favor by Vice-President Marshall. The periphery supported the amendment by 60.4 percent; the core opposed it by 86.4 percent. In the House a motion to strike the amendment for full independence was passed by a unanimous Republican Party and thirty-one Democrats. Twenty-five of the latter represented core industrial districts; four represented industrial sections of the diverse regions. The core vote to strike was 120–15; the periphery voted 41–135. The roll-call votes are in *CR*, 64–1, 1998, 7210–11. For further support of the argument on imperialism and preparedness, see Richard F. Bensel, *Sectionalism and American Political Development* (Madison: University of Wisconsin Press, 1984), 88–103.

27. Some would undoubtedly bestow this accolade on Theodore Roosevelt, but I would simply point out that his break from the GOP and creation of an independent party came *after* he was president; and TR, to his disappointment, since he felt that his destiny was to be a great war leader, missed World War I (which was, he seemed to feel, wasted on Wilson's presidency). On Roosevelt's bitter jealousy of Wilson during the war, see Milton Cooper Jr., *The Warrior and the Priest* (Cambridge: Harvard University Press, 1983), 282–87.

28. In its "Reconstruction Program" drawn up toward the end of World War I, the AFL, while still avoiding any significant endorsement of social legislation, did declare for government regulation or ownership of "public and semipublic utilities," continued government control of the merchant marine, and public development of water power. Reprinted in John R. Commons, ed., *Trade Unionism and Labor Problems*, 2d series (Boston: Ginn and Co., 1921), 569–70. The (non-AFL) railroad brotherhoods supported government ownership of railroads in 1919–20 (see chapter 6 above).

29. *CR*, 64–1, 8374. On the battle for the Shipping Act, from 1914 to 1916, see Arthur S. Link, *Wilson*, vol. 3, *The Struggle for Neutrality* (Princeton: Princeton University Press, 1960), 137–61, and *Wilson*, vol. 4, *Confusions and Crises* (Princeton: Princeton University Press, 1964), 339–41 (quotation at 340); William Gibbs McAdoo, *Crowded Years* (Boston: Houghton Mifflin, 1931), 305–15; Jeffrey J. Stafford, *Wilsonian Maritime Diplomacy* (New Brunswick, N.J.: Rutgers University Press, 1978), 41–72, 90–93; Paul M. Zeis, *American Shipping Policy* (Princeton: Princeton University Press, 1938), 74–97; and chapter 10 above. The Shipping Act passed the Senate on a straight party division; periphery Democrats provided thirty of thirty-eight votes for passage. *CR*, 64–1, 12825. After the government shipping corporation was first proposed by the administration in the late summer of 1914, seven Senate Democrats (four southerners, two other periphery senators, and O'Gorman of New York) had opposed it, whereas three progressive Republicans (La Follette, Norris, and Kenyon) had indicated support. The resisters were ultimately brought around with amendments that proposed (1) to phase out direct government operation after the war, (2) to lessen the danger of war involvement by forbidding the purchase of belligerent ships, and (3) to add to the shipping corporation bill a permanent regulatory apparatus for ocean shipping rates and services, an apparatus that would function much like the ICC did for railroads. The last proposal had been developed in the House Merchant Marine Committee over several years, and the composite bill had the support of southern and western farm organizations (particularly the Grange and the Farmers' Union), who saw it as a measure to control the shipping oligopoly and hold down freight rates. It was also endorsed by the AFL (see 64th Cong., 1st sess., 1916, H. Rept. 659, 74). Congressional agrarians

had long pressed to allow the few remaining U.S. shipping companies to purchase cheaper foreign-built ships, in order to hold down their costs, and to apply the Sherman Act to domestic and foreign shipping monopolies. A bill to accomplish the latter was passed by the House in 1912. *CR*, 62–2, 7561–63. The Republican policy preference was to provide government subsidies and coastal monopoly franchises to the companies operating expensive U.S.-built ships. The "free ships versus subsidies" issue was a major fault line dividing the Democratic agricultural export areas from the ship-building Republican Northeast. The Democratic dissenters of 1915–16 found the government shipping corporation proposal too great a departure from earlier party doctrine and far too expensive. At least one of them (Vardaman of Mississippi) agreed with the three progressive Republicans that the government corporation would be a good idea if it was *permanent* but that making it temporary guaranteed that it would only serve, in the end, as a gigantic subsidy for private shipping interests. *CR*, 63–3, 3098–100. In that prediction, Vardaman proved correct. As is so often the case, the business interests that fiercely opposed the 1916 bill ended up drawing great profit from it, via the construction and leasing of government ships and the cut-rate purchase of U.S.-owned ships after the mandated postwar sell-off. See Zeis, *American Shipping Policy*, 109–14.

30. *Minutes of the National Farmers' Educational and Cooperative Union*, 1915 (Lincoln, Nebraska), 52. On workers' support, see Philip Foner, *History of the Labor Movement in the United States*, 7 vols. (New York: International Publishers, 1975–), 7:50.

31. *CR*, 64–1, 4516–53 (vote, 4553), and 11306–10; Melvin I. Urofsky, *Big Steel and the Wilson Administration* (Columbus: Ohio State University Press, 1969), chap. 4; Link, *Confusions and Crises*, 335–36; Francis B. Simkins, *Pitchfork Ben Tillman* (Baton Rouge: Louisiana State University Press, 1944), 512–13; E. David Cronon, ed., *The Cabinet Diaries of Josephus Daniels* (Lincoln: University of Nebraska Press, 1963), 126 n. Though Wilson delayed construction, the armor-plate factory was finally established in Charleston, West Virginia, and produced some steel and shells, although the armor facilities were still unfinished when the war ended. The Republicans, on their return to power, abandoned the project. For the flavor of the debate between core opponents and periphery defenders of a government factory, see *CR*, 64–1, 4525, 4530–32, 4552–53.

32. *CR*, 64–1, 7598. Among the legislative demands adopted at the 1912 Farmers' Union convention was a proposal that "natural resources such as iron ore, coal, petroleum, phosphate beds, and water powers, should be reclaimed by the government and held for the benefit of the people." *Minutes*, 1912 (Chattanooga, Tennessee), 32.

33. *CR*, 64–1, 6031. It must be noted, however, that like the progressive Republicans, southern agrarians picked their socialism to regional advantage. Though they strongly backed the armor and nitrate plants and the final Shipping Act of 1916, many in the House opposed government construction of the Alaska railroad in 1914. Periphery- and diverse-area Republicans, on the other hand, opposed the nitrate plant and the Shipping Act (they had less export exposure) but backed the Alaska railroad because of its promise to deliver cheap coal to the Pacific and midwestern states. Final House and Senate votes on the administration's Alaska railroad bill are found in *CR*, 63–2, 2250, 3646–47. Southern Democrats in the Senate backed the bill 7–4, though less enthusiastically than core and diverse Democrats (who went 10–0 for it) or diverse-area Republicans (4–1). The periphery supplied the majority of favorable votes in the Senate but not in the House (due to a roughly even split in the South).

34. *CR*, 64–1, 4730. See also Link, *Confusions and Crises*, 331.

35. *CR*, 64–1, 7612.

36. The combination of the weak army bill and the government nitrate plant left leaders of the preparedness movement—mostly Republicans—"sick at heart," notes Link, *Confusions and Crises*, 329–32.

37. *American Federationist*, October 1914, 875.

38. Ibid., March 1916, 198–99. See also the disparaging commentary on the projects of the American Association for Labor Legislation in the April 1916 issue, 268–74.

39. Ibid., February 1915, 113.

40. Graham Adams Jr., *Age of Industrial Violence* (New York: Columbia University Press, 1966), 33–49. Taft agreed to appoint to the Industrial Commission the three labor leaders proposed by the AFL and the railroad brotherhoods, along with three conservative business representatives approved by the National Association of Manufacturers (NAM). For the three "public" representatives, he disappointed

the intellectuals by refusing to turn to their ranks. One of the three named was Charles Barrett, head of the Farmers' Union. The intellectuals strongly objected to Taft's slate, and the NAM counsel "suspected that Barrett really belonged with the labor commissioners and expected him to side with the A.F.L." Gompers defended the slate at the time, but the Democratic Senate hesitated to confirm Taft's appointees after the November election. Wilson kept the three labor nominees but made his own substitutions for the business and public representatives (replacing Barrett with John R. Commons). Ibid., 44–57. James Weinstein, who heavily relies on but in this instance misconstrues Adams, describes Barrett as a conservative who was active in the National Civic Federation (NCF). James Weinstein, *The Corporate Ideal in the Liberal State* (Boston: Beacon Press, 1968), 184. Weinstein may have confused Barrett with New Hampshire ex-governor and Grange Master Nahum Bachelder, who was a vice-president, along with Gompers, on the NCF. See Martin J. Sklar, *The Corporate Reconstruction of American Capitalism, 1890–1916* (New York: Cambridge University Press, 1988), 205 n. 35, 219–21, 254–55. At any rate, Barrett would not accurately be described, then or now, as "conservative"; nor was Bachelder a reliable supporter of the NCF's major legislative projects.

41. A man of strong social ideals, Walsh overrode "both the representatives of business and the self-styled impartial social scientists . . . to make the commission the tribune for the oppressed worker." David Montgomery, *The Fall of the House of Labor* (New York: Cambridge University Press, 1987), 361. The commission's final report generally attributed the era's violent labor conflicts to the injustices perpetuated by employers. The report was published as S. Doc. 415: 64th Cong., 1st sess., 1916—see esp. 265–66.

42. Melvin Dubovsky, *The State and Labor in Modern America* (Chapel Hill: University of North Carolina Press, 1994), 249 n. 83; Link, *The New Freedom*, 458–59.

43. Marc Karson, *American Labor Unions and Politics, 1900–1918* (Boston: Beacon Press, 1958), 90–92; Samuel Gompers, *Seventy Years of Life and Labor*, 2 vols. (New York: E. P. Dutton, 1925), 2:322–31.

44. Simeon Larson, *Labor and Foreign Policy* (Rutherford, N.J.: Fairleigh Dickinson University Press, 1975), 47–55; Elizabeth McKillen, *Chicago Labor and the Quest for a Democratic Diplomacy, 1914–1924* (Ithaca, N.Y.: Cornell University Press, 1995), 26–55; Foner, *History of the Labor Movement* 7:46–54.

45. *Minutes*, 1915, 52. The FU went so far as to urge all who favored peace to transfer their deposits out of Federal Reserve banks in order to deny credit to the warring nations for prosecution of the war. Ibid., 51–52.

46. See the list of war opponents in Link, *Confusions and Crises*, 27 n.

47. Gompers, *Seventy Years of Life and Labor* 2:331.

48. Larson, *Labor and Foreign Policy*, 92–94. Gompers also unofficially worked for the Industrial Preparedness Committee organized by the Navy Department, having been brought into contact with the group by NCF Director Ralph Easley, an early supporter of U.S. war preparations.

49. Gompers, *Seventy Years of Life and Labor* 2:339–42.

50. Larson, *Labor and Foreign Policy*, 43–46, 87.

51. Ibid., 83–85; McKillen, *Chicago Labor and the Quest for a Democratic Diplomacy*, 57, 67–68. The conference, on March 12, 1917, was called on the suggestion of the Council of National Defense. Larson, *Labor and Foreign Policy*, 83.

52. Gompers, *Seventy Years of Life and Labor* 2:334–49; Larson, *Labor and Foreign Policy*, 44–45, 56–58; *New York Times*, May 4, 1917, 20, and May 21, 1917, 1. Buchanan, along with six others affiliated with Labor's National Peace Council, was indicted by a federal grand jury in New York City in 1915 for interfering (through strike activity) with the shipment of munitions to the Allies. See Foner, *History of the Labor Movement* 7:41–54, 55–61. Buchanan, defeated for reelection in 1916, was acquitted in 1917.

53. See Link, *Confusions and Crises*, 173–92, on the pressures exerted by Wilson on congressional Democrats to dissuade them from supporting the McLemore resolution in 1915. On congressional opposition to preparedness, see Bensel, *Sectionalism and American Political Development*, 105–28.

54. Gompers, *Seventy Years of Life and Labor* 2:333–36, 346–64; McKillen, *Chicago Labor and the Quest for a Democratic Diplomacy*, 72–73, 97–98.

55. Gompers, *Seventy Years of Life and Labor* 2:359, 393; McKillen, *Chicago Labor and the Quest for a Democratic Diplomacy*, 72–73, 97–98.

56. Arthur S. Link, *Wilson*, vol. 5, *Campaigns for Progressivism and Peace, 1916–1917* (Princeton: Princeton University Press, 1965), 317–18, 414–15.

57. Lewis L. Lorwin, *The American Federation of Labor* (Clifton, N.J.: Augustus M. Kelley Publishing, 1972), 137–38. On NCF influence, see also Gompers, *Seventy Years of Life and Labor* 2:350–51, and Larson, *Labor and Foreign Policy,* 57.

58. Lorwin, *American Federation of Labor,* 138.

59. Larson, *Labor and Foreign Policy,* 149, 41–46, 142–58; Lorwin, *American Federation of Labor,* 147–52; Foner, *History of the Labor Movement* 7:117–24.

60. Foner, *History of the Labor Movement* 7:124.

61. Lorwin, *American Federation of Labor,* 139, 155, notes the "dazzling" nature of such experiences and Gompers's "growing conviction that he was destined to play a leading part in the settlement of the war."

62. Gompers, *Seventy Years of Life and Labor* 2:362.

63. Foner, *History of the Labor Movement* 7:159, 172–76; Gompers, *Seventy Years of Life and Labor* 2:366–76, 408–72; Lorwin, *American Federation of Labor,* 153–65.

64. McKillen, *Chicago Labor and the Quest for a Democratic Diplomacy,* 69–84.

65. Lorwin, *American Federation of Labor,* 155–72; Foner, *History of the Labor Movement* 7:168–76, 234–38.

66. Leo Wolman, *Ebb and Flow in Trade Unionism* (New York: National Bureau of Economic Research, 1936), 138.

67. Foner, *History of the Labor Movement* 7:264–314.

68. McKillen, *Chicago Labor and the Quest for a Democratic Diplomacy,* 98–99, 111–13.

69. Lorwin, *American Federation of Labor,* 201–13, 226–29; Wolman, *Ebb and Flow in Trade Unionism,* 139.

70. See also Valerie Jean Connor, *The National War Labor Board* (Chapel Hill: University of North Carolina Press, 1983), esp. chaps. 10–11.

71. McKillen, *Chicago Labor and the Quest for a Democratic Diplomacy,* 158. See also Gregg Andrews, *Shoulder to Shoulder: The American Federation of Labor, the United States, and the Mexican Revolution* (Berkeley: University of California Press, 1991). Samuel Gompers died on a train returning from one of his missions to Mexico in 1924.

Chapter Twelve

1. The term is from Doug McAdam, *Political Process and the Development of Black Insurgency, 1930–1970* (Chicago: University of Chicago Press, 1982), 34–35.

2. Theda Skocpol and Kenneth Finegold, "State Capacity and Economic Intervention in the Early New Deal," *Political Science Quarterly* 97 (summer 1982): 260–75; Christopher L. Tomlins, *The State and the Unions* (New York: Cambridge University Press, 1985).

3. Nathan Fine, *Labor and Farmer Parties in the U.S.* (New York: Russell and Russell, 1961), 363–77; Carl C. Taylor, *The Farmers' Movement, 1670–1920* (Westport, Conn.: Greenwood Press, 1953), 421–69; Stuart A. Rice, *Farmers and Workers in American Politics* (New York: Columbia University Press, 1924), 152–77; Richard M. Valelly, *Radicalism in the States* (Chicago: University of Chicago Press, 1989). Nationally, the NPL had about 300,000 members in 1918, the bulk of them in Minnesota, North and South Dakota, and Montana, followed by Washington and Idaho. Fine, *Labor and Farmer Parties,* 373.

4. Kenneth C. McKay, *The Progressive Movement of 1924* (New York: Octagon Books, 1966), 28–32, 39–46. A trade-union-dominated Farmer-Labor Party was on the ballot in 1920, its presidential and vice-presidential nominees a Utah labor lawyer, Parley Parker Christensen, and a socialist, Max Hayes. The ticket received about 250,000 votes, running strongest, proportionately, in Washington (19.4 percent), South Dakota (19.0), Illinois (9.3), and Montana (6.8). Washington, Illinois, and South Dakota registered the highest absolute tallies. Fine, *Labor and Farmer Parties,* 395.

5. Fine, *Labor and Farmer Parties,* 398–408; McKay, *Progressive Movement of 1924,* 28–68. "Candidates endorsed by the CPPA . . . won in Oklahoma, Iowa, Nebraska, Kansas, Colorado and Arizona.

Ninety-three undesirable members of the 67th Congress [including several 'staunch supporters' of the 1920 Transportation Act] had been defeated" (McKay, *Progressive Movement of 1924,* 67–68). Two Farmer-Labor candidates won Senate seats in Minnesota in 1922–23, and the two western agricultural districts sent Farmer-Labor representatives to Congress. In Wisconsin, La Follette won reelection by a large margin.

6. McKay, *Progressive Movement of 1924,* 143–96.

7. Ibid., 221. The Progressive ran second in the counties containing the cities of San Francisco, Minneapolis, Cleveland, Pittsburgh, Cincinnati, and Detroit. David P. Thelen, *Robert L. La Follette and the Insurgent Spirit* (Boston: Little, Brown, 1976), 190. However, the author of a statistical analysis of the 1924 results concludes that ethnic influences (specifically, percentage Scandinavian, German, or Catholic) "had the greatest influence" on support for the Progressive, and found "no evidence that urban workers contributed significantly to the La Follette vote." David L. Waterhouse, *The Progressive Movement of 1924 and the Development of Interest Group Liberalism* (New York: Garland Publishing, 1991), 83–88. David Burner nevertheless sees La Follette's urban support as important in the weaning of the immigrant working class from Republican and Socialist political tendencies. David Burner, *The Politics of Provincialism* (New York: W. W. Norton, 1975), 137.

8. McKay, *Progressive Movement of 1924,* 188–204.

9. Thelen, *Robert L. La Follette and the Insurgent Spirit,* 186.

10. The sectional breach in agrarian ranks was in part a legacy of World War I price-control politics, which were strongly perceived as biased against wheat and in favor of cotton. Burner, *The Politics of Provincialism,* 34–40.

11. Trade-union membership reached a peak of just over 5 million in 1920 but fell back to 3.4 million by 1929. Leo Wolman, *Ebb and Flow in Trade Unionism* (New York: National Bureau of Economic Research, 1936), 16. Grange membership dropped a bit after 1917 but was roughly stable between 1921 and 1933, at about 300,000. The Farmers' Union declined from 154,000 in 1917 to 91,000 by 1930, the loss particularly evident in the South. Their competition, the American Farm Bureau Federation, nurtured by business and government support (and thus not properly a grass-roots agrarian organization), fell from 466,000 in 1921 to 163,000 by 1933, after which it was revived by its connection to the Department of Agriculture and New Deal production-control programs. For membership figures, see Lowell K. Dyson, *Farmers' Organizations* (New York: Greenwood Press, 1986), appendix 3. The North Dakota Nonpartisan League held control of state government for a few years before succumbing to severe financial problems (especially a boycott of state bonds in national capital markets), factionalism, and a recall election in 1921. The national NPL it spawned also declined rapidly during the post–World War I depression. Valelly, *Radicalism in the States,* 32.

12. See, for example, Charles P. Loomis, "The Rise and Decline of the North Carolina Farmers' Union," *North Carolina Historical Review* 7 (July 1930): 319–25. Loomis also highlights the Farmers' Union leaders' opposition to the war as a cause of factionalism and social opprobrium contributing to decline.

13. See chapter 9, and William J. Block, *The Separation of the Farm Bureau and the Extension Service* (Urbana: University of Illinois Press, 1960), 5–21, 48–53.

14. Elizabeth Sanders, "Business, Bureaucracy, and the Bourgeoisie: The New Deal Legacy," in *The Political Economy of Public Policy,* ed. Alan Stone and Edward Harpham (Beverly Hills, Calif.: Sage, 1982), 115–40.

15. Theodore J. Lowi, who led the critique of pluralism as process, norm, and analytical method, has been the leading contemporary exponent of specific, rule-bound statutes and party/legislature-centered policy-making. The central argument is contained in Theodore J. Lowi, *The End of Liberalism,* 2d ed. (New York: W. W. Norton, 1978).

16. Jack Kemp, secretary of housing and urban development under Reagan, was the leading exponent of the voucher-based welfare state. James Pinkerton, a deputy assistant for policy planning in the Bush administration, was another advocate. The Family Assistance Plan debated in the Nixon administration represented a serious attempt to implement the concept.

Index